Cambridge Studies in Early Modern British History

CIVIL WAR AND RESTORATION IN THE THREE STUART KINGDOMS

This is a biography of Randal MacDonnell, first marquis of Antrim (1609–83), an important Irish statesman of Scottish extraction who was a Caroline loyalist, Catholic confederate, Cromwellian collaborator and Restoration pragmatist. It focuses on Antrim's political career between his marriage to the duchess of Buckingham in 1635 and his restoration to his County Antrim estates in 1665.

Antrim's extraordinary career highlights three important truths about early modern Britain. It illustrates the elastic nature of the concept of 'patriotism' in the turbulent years of the mid-seventeenth century; it demonstrates that Ireland was and must be viewed as part of the triple monarchy of the Stuart kings; and, finally, it shows that Ireland – at least in the 1640s – was seen, for the first and last time before 1922, as part of the European state system. This is the only book which examines these crucial issues of the period 1635–65 from a primarily Irish stance.

Cambridge Studies in Early Modern British History

Series editors

ANTHONY FLETCHER
Professor of Modern History, University of Durham

JOHN GUY
Professor of Modern History, University of St Andrews

and JOHN MORRILL
Lecturer in History, University of Cambridge, and Fellow and Tutor of Selwyn College

This is a series of monographs and studies covering many aspects of the history of the British Isles between the late fifteenth century and the early eighteenth century. It includes the work of established scholars and pioneering work by a new generation of scholars. It includes both reviews and revision of major topics and books which open up new historical terrain or which reveal startling new perspectives on familiar subjects. All the volumes set detailed research into broader perspectives and the books are intended for the use of students as well as of their teachers.

For a list of titles in the series, see end of book.

Randal MacDonnell, second earl and first marquis of Antrim (1609–83). The only extant portrait of the marquis, painted during the Restoration by Michael Wright. As a young man the earl of Clarendon described him as being 'a tall, clean-limbed, handsome man with red hair'. (Reproduced by permission of Viscount Dunluce.)

CIVIL WAR AND RESTORATION IN THE THREE STUART KINGDOMS

*The career of Randal MacDonnell,
marquis of Antrim, 1609–1683*

JANE H. OHLMEYER

Published by the Press Syndicate of the University of Cambridge
The Pitt Building, Trumpington Street, Cambridge CB2 1RP
40 West 20th Street, New York, NY 10011–4211, USA
10 Stamford Road, Oakleigh, Victoria 3166, Australia

© Cambridge University Press 1993

First published 1993

Printed in Great Britain by Redwood Press Limited, Melksham, Wiltshire

A catalogue record for this book is available from the British Library

Library of Congress cataloguing in publication data
Ohlmeyer, Jane H.
Civil War and Restoration in the three Stuart kingdoms: the career of Randal MacDonnell, marquis of Antrim, 1609–1683 / Jane H. Ohlmeyer.
 p. cm. – (Cambridge studies in early modern British history)
Includes bibliographical references.
ISBN 0 521 41978 6
1. Antrim, Randal MacDonnell, Earl of, 1609–1683. 2. Ireland – History – 17th century – Biography. 3. Great Britain – History – Civil War, 1642–1649. 4. Great Britain – History – Restoration, 1660–1688. 5. Antrim (Northern Ireland: County) – Biography. 6. Statesmen – Ireland – Biography. I. Title. II. Series.
DA940.5.A58034 1992
941.506 – dc20   92-8873 CIP

ISBN 0 521 41978 6 hardback

For Shirley Ohlmeyer

CONTENTS

List of illustrations	*page* xi
List of tables	xii
Acknowledgments	xiii
Notes on dates, currencies and spelling	xv
Chronology	xvi
List of abbreviations	xix

	Introduction: Antrim and the history of the 'three kingdoms'	1
	Antrim and the historians	1
	Antrim: a patriot for whom?	6
	Antrim: a man of the 'three kingdoms'	10
	Antrim: a man of the 'five kingdoms'	14
1	A man of the 'three kingdoms' (1609–1637)	18
2	Caroline courtier (1637–1640)	49
3	Antrim and the 'Scottish business' (1638–1641)	77
4	Popish plotting in Caroline Ireland and Britain (1641–1643)	100
5	The 'War of the Three Kingdoms' (November 1643–December 1644)	127
6	The 'War of the Five Kingdoms' (January 1645–June 1646)	152
7	Gaelic warlord and Irish politician (June 1646–June 1647)	174
	War in Scotland, Ireland and Flánders	174
	Antrim and the supreme council	188

8	In search of new patrons (November 1647–August 1649)	201
	Antrim and Henrietta Maria	201
	Antrim and Ormond	210
	Antrim and the Independents	217
9	Cromwellian conquest and occupation (August 1649–May 1660)	230
	Compromise and collaboration (1649–51)	230
	Surviving the storm	240
10	Antrim after the Restoration (1660–1683)	258
	Conclusion: A seventeenth-century survivor	278
	Bibliography	290
	Index	340

ILLUSTRATIONS

PLATES

Frontispiece: Randal MacDonnell, second earl and
                 first marquis of Antrim (1609–83)   *page* iii
1   Dunluce castle   52
2   York House   53

MAPS

1   Antrim's world   9
2   The MacDonnell archipelago   20
3   Ireland on the eve of the cessation of arms, September 1643   118

GENEALOGICAL TABLES

1   The MacDonnells of Antrim   34
2   The extended family   44

TABLES

1	1637 leases: type of lease granted	page 36
2	1637 leases: occupation of lessee	38
3	Occupations of Antrim's creditors and amounts borrowed during the 1630s	63

ACKNOWLEDGMENTS

This book, based on my doctoral thesis, was made possible by the help of many people and I would like to take this opportunity to express my gratitude to them. First, I would like to acknowledge the help of the staff in the following institutions: the Archives Générales du Royaume in Brussels; Cambridge University Library; the King's Inn Library, Marsh's Library, the Public Library, Pearse St, the Public Record Office, the Representative Church Body, the Royal Irish Academy, the Royal Society of Antiquaries and Trinity College in Dublin; the National Library of Scotland and the Scottish Record Office in Edinburgh; the Cambridgeshire Record Office in Huntingdon; the British Library, the House of Lords Record Office, the Institute of Historical Research, Lambeth Palace, the Public Records Office (Chancery Lane), the University of London Library and the Westminster Record Office in London; the Archivo Histórico Nacional in Madrid; St Patrick's College in Maynooth; the Bodleian Library and Christ Church Library (the Evelyn Trustees) in Oxford; the Bibliothèque Nationale and the Ministère des Affaires Etrangères in Paris; the Huntington Library in San Marino, California; the Archivo General in Simancas; Sheffield City Library; the University of Illinois Library at Urbana-Champaign; and St Peter's College in Wexford.

    I would like to add a special word of thanks to the staff of the National Library of Ireland and the Public Record Office of Northern Ireland in general, for their cheerful assistance, and to Dr Anthony Malcomson in particular. I would also like to thank the following individuals for permission to cite from their family papers housed in PRONI: the late Major-General Sir Allan Adair, Mr H. A. Boyd, Mr David Good, Messrs Greer, Hamilton and Gailey, the late Lord Lurgan, the Honourable Randal McDonnell, the late T. H. Maginniss, the Viscount Massereen and Ferrard DL, the late S. Shannon Millin, Dr I. A. P. Smythe-Wood, the late C. J. Robb, the late Mrs Waring. I am also deeply grateful to his Grace the duke of Argyll for permission to consult his family papers and to Archibald Campbell of Inverary Castle for his assistance; to Sir Lionel Tollemache for allowing me to consult the Tollemache papers at Buckminster; and to Viscount Dunluce for allowing me to reproduce the portrait of the marquis of Antrim in his possession. The Public Record Office, Westminster City Archives and the Trustees of the British Museum have also kindly allowed me to reproduce material in their keeping.

Second, I would like to thank the following people who have allowed me to draw on their expert knowledge and have offered support and encouragement throughout: Professor Nicholas Canny, Dr Jerrold Casway, Dr Kathleen Colquhoun, Tom Connors, Father Donal Cregan, Dr Jane Dawson, Dr Peter Donald, Professor Caroline Hibbard, Robert Hunter, Billy Kelly, Dr Phil Kilroy, Dr Peter Le Fevre, Professor John Lynn, Bríd McGrath, Trevor Parkhill, Professor Michael Perceval-Maxwell, Professor Peter Roebuck, Professor Conrad Russell, John Scally, Dr Kevin Sharpe, Dr Victor Treadwell and Dr Kevin Whelan. In addition, I am greatly indebted to Dr Raymond Gillespie for suggesting this topic to me and for his constant support and enthusiasm. I would also like to thank Dr John Adamson, the Honourable Hector McDonnell, Dr John Morrill, Professor Geoffrey Parker and Dr David Stevenson for kindly reading earlier drafts of this manuscript and for making numerous helpful and incisive comments. I am indebted to Professor John Kenyon who generously read the entire typescript in its final form and made a number of invaluable suggestions for improvement. My thanks also to Julie Fawcett, Geoffrey Parker, Claudine Rose and Bruce Swann for helping me to translate some Latin, Spanish and Italian items.

Finally, I am deeply grateful to Professor Aidan Clarke who as my thesis supervisor gave me his time, advice and support with unlimited generosity. My greatest debt, however, is to my family – especially my husband, Geoffrey, my son, Richard, and my mother, Shirley – who, from the outset, have unstintingly supported my research and without whose encouragement, enthusiasm and tolerance this book would never have been possible. And it is to my mother, Shirley Ohlmeyer, that I would like to dedicate this book in appreciation for everything she has done for me.

NOTE ON DATES, CURRENCIES AND SPELLING

Dates throughout are given according to the Old (Julian) Calendar, which was used in Britain but not in most of continental Europe. The beginning of each year is taken, however, as 1 January rather than 25 March. It has been assumed, unless specifically stated otherwise, that foreign Catholics writing from Britain in the seventeenth century and that British persons writing from Catholic Europe dated their correspondence according to the New (Gregorian) Style, which was ten days ahead of the Julian calendar.

As far as possible, all foreign currencies have been given with a rough conversion into pounds sterling at the exchange rates prevailing at the time, as follows:

$$13 \text{ Brabant florins} = £1$$
$$4.5 \text{ Spanish escudos} = £1$$
$$12 \text{ livres tournois} = £1$$
$$12 \text{ pounds Scots} = £1$$

Spellings from contemporary sources have been modernized and with proper names the modern spellings have been preferred. Quotes from Spanish, French, Italian and Latin sources have all been translated in the interests of consistency and comprehensibility.

The use of the term 'Britain' in this study includes England, Scotland and Wales, but not Ireland. Though English and Scottish Protestant settlers in Ireland referred to themselves as being 'British', James I and Charles II were in fact kings of Great Britain, France and *Ireland* (Charles I was crowned king of Scotland, England, France and Ireland). Thus while Ireland can be viewed as one of the Stuart kingdoms it was never part of Britain and technically speaking 'British' history excludes Ireland.

A CHRONOLOGY OF THE CAREER OF RANDAL MACDONNELL, FIRST MARQUIS AND SECOND EARL OF ANTRIM (1609–1683)

1609	Born at Dunluce castle, County Antrim
1620	Created Viscount Dunluce
1625–7	Lived in France
1627	Returned to live at court
1635	Married Katherine Villiers, duchess of Buckingham (died 1649)
1636	Succeeded his father as second earl of Antrim
1639	*May–June:* offered to rally his Irish and Scottish kin against the covenanters during the first Bishops' War
1640	*April–May:* Short Parliament in England
	August–October: second Bishops' War
	November: meeting of the Long Parliament
1641	*spring–late summer:* instructed by Charles I to remuster the 'New Irish army' against the English parliament (the 'Antrim plot')
	May: Strafford executed
	October: outbreak of the Ulster rebellion
1642	*February:* Antrim's estate confiscated by the English parliament
	April: a Scottish army under Monro landed in East Ulster and Antrim offered to raise his Irish and Scottish kin for the royalist cause
	May: Antrim imprisoned in Carrickfergus castle
	August: outbreak of first English Civil War
	October: formation of Catholic confederacy in Ireland and Antrim's escape from Carrickfergus castle
1643	*spring:* Antrim offered to raise his Irish and Scottish kin for the royalist cause
	May: Antrim imprisoned in Carrickfergus castle for the second time
	September 15: ceasefire concluded between the royalists and confederates in Ireland

A chronology of the career of Randal MacDonnell

	September 25: 'Solemn League and Covenant' between the English parliament and the Scots
	November: Antrim escaped from Carrickfergus for the second time
1644	*June:* Antrim raised and sent *c.* 2,000 Irish troops to fight in Scotland with Montrose
	July: English royalists defeated at Marston Moor
1645	*January:* Antrim created a marquis
	c. May: Antrim approached the governor-general in Brussels, Flanders, for military assistance
	July: Charles I defeated at Naseby
	October: Rinuccini, the papal nuncio, arrived in Ireland
	September: Montrose defeated at Philiphaugh
	December: 'Glamorgan treaty'
1646	*spring:* Antrim abandoned the king's cause
	May: Charles I surrendered to Scots
	June: confederate victory over the Scots at Benburb
	July–August: proclamation of the 'first Ormond peace'
	summer: Antrim offered a further 1,200 veterans to the administration in Flanders
	September: Rinuccini's coup d'état
	winter: confederate offensive against Dublin
1647	*March–November:* Antrim joined the Old Irish Faction within the confederation of Kilkenny and became president of the supreme council
	June: Ormond surrendered Dublin to a parliamentary army
	August: confederate defeat at Dungans Hill
	November: confederate defeat at Knockanauss
	November: Antrim ceases to be president of the supreme council
1648	*February:* Antrim sent as an envoy to the royal court-in-exile in France
	May: declaration of the 'Inchiquin truce'
	May–August: beginning of the second Civil War in England
	October: Peace of Westphalia ended the war in Germany
	December: using Crelly as his agent Antrim began to negotiate with the English Independent party
	December: Colonel Pride's purge of parliament
1649	*January:* execution of Charles I and declaration of the 'second Ormond peace'
	August: Cromwellian invasion of Ireland

	September: fall of Drogheda
	October: fall of Wexford and New Ross
1650	*March:* Antrim openly sided with the Cromwellians
	June: beginning of the third Civil War in Britain
	December: Antrim visited London
	July: Antrim threatened to invade Western Scotland on behalf of the Cromwellians
1651	*September:* defeat of Charles II at Worcester and the end of the 'War of the Three Kingdoms'; Antrim awarded a Cromwellian pension
1653	*April:* Cromwellian conquest of Ireland completed
1660	*May:* Charles II restored
	July: Antrim imprisoned in the Tower
1661	*May:* Antrim sent back to Dublin for trial: Argyll executed for treason
1662	*October:* Antrim cleared of all charges
1663	*August:* Antrim declared an 'innocent papist' by the court of claims
	October: Charles II reversed the commissioners' verdict
1665	*December:* Antrim restored to his estates in Ulster
1683	*February:* Antrim died without issue and was succeeded by his brother Alexander (from whom the present earls are descended).

ABBREVIATIONS

AGR	Archives Générales du Royaume, Brussels
SEG	Secrétairerie d'Etat et de Guerre
AGS	Archivo General, Simancas
CMC	Contaduría Mayor de Cuentas
Eo.	Secretaría de Estado
GA	Guerra Antigua
TMC	Tribunal Mayor de Cuentas
AHN	Archivo Histórico Nacional, Madrid
Eo. Libro	Sección de Estado, Libro
Aiazza, *Embassy*	Giuseppe Aiazza, *The embassy in Ireland of Monsignor G. B. Rinuccinni, archbishop of Fermo, in the years 1645–1649 ...*, translated by Annie Hutton (Dublin, 1873)
AMAE	Archives du Ministère des Affaires Etrangères, Paris
Anal. Hib.	*Analecta Hibernica, Including the Reports of the Irish Manuscripts Commission* (Dublin, 1930–)
Archiv. Hib.	*Archivium Hibernicum: or Irish Historical Record* (Catholic Record Society of Ireland, Maynooth, 1912–)
Bibl. Apost. Vat.	Biblioteca Apostolica Vaticana, Rome
BIHR	*Bulletin of the Institute of Historical Research*
BL	British Library, London
Add. MSS	Additional Manuscripts
Eg. MSS	Egerton Manuscripts
Harl. MSS	Harleian Manuscripts
Lansd. MSS	Lansdowne Manuscripts
BN	Bibliothèque Nationale, Paris
Bodl.	Bodleian Library, Oxford
Cal. SP Dom., 1635–6 [etc.]	*Calendar of state papers, domestic series, 1635–6* [etc.] (London, 1866–)

Cal. SP Ire. 1608–10 [etc.]	*Calendar of state papers relating to Ireland, 1608–10* [etc.] (London, 1874–)
Cal. SP Ven., 1636–9 [etc.]	*Calendar of state papers and manuscripts, relating to English affairs, existing in the archives and collections of Venice 1636–9* [etc.] (London, 1923–)
Carte, *Ormond*	Thomas Carte, *History of the life of James, first duke of Ormond* (2nd edn, 6 vols., Oxford, 1851)
Civil survey	R. C. Simington (ed.), *The civil survey, A.D. 1654–56* (IMC, 10 vols., Dublin, 1931–61)
Clan Donald	Angus J. MacDonald and Archibald MacDonald, *The Clan Donald* (3 vols., Inverness, 1896–1904)
Clanricarde letter-book	John Lowe (ed.), *Letter-book of the earl of Clanricarde 1643–47* (IMC, Dublin, 1983)
Clarendon, *Rebellion*	Edward Hyde, earl of Clarendon, *The history of the rebellion and civil wars in England*, ed. W. D. Macray (6 vols., Oxford, 1888)
Clarendon SP	*Calendar of the Clarendon state papers preserved in the Bodleian Library*, ed. O. Ogle, W. H. Bliss and W. D. Macray (3 vols., Oxford, 1869–76), vol. IV, ed. F. J. Routledge (Oxford, 1932)
Collect. Hib.	*Collectanea Hibernica: Sources for Irish History* (Dublin, 1958–)
Comment. Rinucc.	Richard O'Ferrall and Robert O'Connell, *Commentarius Rinuccinianus, de sedis apostolicae legatione ad foederatos Hiberniae catholicos per annos 1645–9* ed. Rev. Stanislaus Kavanagh (6 vols., IMC, Dublin, 1932–49)
CUL	Cambridge University Library
Add.	Additional Manuscripts
Desid. cur. Hib.	[John Lodge (ed.)], *Desiderata curiosa Hibernica, or a select collection of state papers* (2 vols., Dublin, 1732)
Diplomatic correspondence	J. G. Fotheringham (ed.), *The diplomatic correspondence of Jean de Montereul and the brothers Bellièvre, French ambassadors in England and Scotland, 1645–8* (2 vols., Scottish History Society, vols. XXIX and XXX, Edinburgh, 1898)
DNB	*Dictionary of national biography*, ed. Sir Leslie Stephen and Sir Sidney Lee (66 vols., London, 1885–1901; reprinted with corrections, 22 vols., London, 1908–9)

Econ. Hist. Rev.	Economic History Review (London, 1927–)
Egmont MSS	Report on the manuscripts of the earl of Egmont, vol. I, part I (HMC, London, 1905)
EHR	English Historical Review (London, 1886–)
Franciscan MSS	Report on Franciscan manuscripts preserved at the convent, Merchants' Quay, Dublin (HMC, Dublin, 1906)
Gardiner, Commonwealth and protectorate	S. R. Gardiner, History of the commonwealth and protectorate 1649–56 (new edn, 4 vols., London, 1903; reprint, 1988)
Gardiner, Eng.	S. R. Gardiner, History of England from the accession of James I to the outbreak of the civil war, 1603–1642 (new edn, 10 vols., 1883–4)
Gilbert, Contemp. hist. 1641–52	J. T. Gilbert (ed.), A contemporary history of affairs in Ireland, from A.D. 1641 to 1652 … (3 vols. Irish Archaeological Society, Dublin, 1879)
Gilbert, Ir. confed.	J. T. Gilbert (ed.), History of the Irish confederation and the war in Ireland, 1641–3 … (7 vols., Dublin, 1882–91)
The Glynns	The Glynns: Journal of the Glens of Antrim Historical Society (Coleraine and Ballycastle, 1973–)
Historical Research	Historical Research: Bulletin of the Institute of Historical Research
HLRO	House of Lords Record Office, London
HMC rep. 2 [etc.]	Historical Manuscripts Commission Second report [etc.] (London, 1874–)
Hunt. HA MSS	Huntington Library, San Marino, California Hastings Manuscripts
IHS	Irish Historical Studies: The Joint Journal of the Irish Historical Society and the Ulster Society for Irish Historical Studies (Dublin, 1938–)
IMC	Irish Manuscripts Commission
Innes Review	Innes Review: Journal of the Scottish Catholic Historical Association (Glasgow, 1950–)
Ir. Econ. &. Soc. Hist.	Irish Economic and Social History: The Journal of the Economic and Social History Society of Ireland (Dublin and Belfast, 1974–)
Ir. Sword	The Irish Sword: The Journal of the Military History Society of Ireland (Dublin, 1949–)

Knowler, *Letters*	William Knowler (ed.), *The earl of Strafforde's letters and despatches with an essay towards his life by Sir George Radcliffe* ... (2 vols., London, 1739)
Laing, *Letters*	David Laing (ed.), *The letters and journals of Robert Baillie, principal of the University of Glasgow, 1637–1662* (3 vols., Bannatyne Club, vol. LXXIII, 3 parts, Edinburgh, 1841–2)
Laud works	W. Scott and J. Bliss (eds.), *The works of ... William Laud ... Archbishop of Canterbury* (7 vols., Oxford, 1847–60)
Montagu MSS	*Report on the manuscripts of Lord Montagu of Beaulieu* (HMC, London, 1900)
NHI	T. W. Moody, F. X. Martin and F. J. Byrne (eds.), *A new history of Ireland, III, Early modern Ireland 1534–1691* (Oxford, 1978)
NLI	National Library of Ireland, Dublin
NLS	National Library of Scotland, Edinburgh
Adv. MSS	Advocates Manuscripts
Wod. MSS	Wodrow Manuscripts
NS	New series; or, in dating, New Style
Ormonde MSS	*Report on the manuscripts of the duke of Ormonde*, NS (HMC, 8 vols., London, 1902–20)
PRO	Public Record Office of England, London
HCA	High Court of Admiralty
LC	Lord Chamberlain's Department
SP	State Papers
PROI	Public Record Office of Ireland, Dublin
PRONI	Public Record Office of Northern Ireland, Belfast
RCB	Representative Church Body, Dublin
MS Libr.	Manuscript Library
Reg. privy council Scot., 1630–2 [etc.]	*Register of the privy council of Scotland*, 2nd series, II, *1630–2* [etc.] (Edinburgh, 1902–)
R. Hist. Soc. Trans.	*Transactions of the Royal Historical Society* (London, 1872–)
RIA	Royal Irish Academy
RIA Proc.	*Proceedings of the Royal Irish Academy* (Dublin, 1836–)
RSAI Jn.	*Journal of the Royal Society of Antiquaries of Ireland* (Dublin 1836–)
SCL	Sheffield City Library
Seanchas	*Seanchas Ardmhacha: Journal of the Armagh*

Ardmhacha	*Diocesan Historical Society* ([Armagh], 1954–)
SHR	*Scottish Historical Review* (Glasgow, 1903–)
SRO	Scottish Record Office, Edinburgh
GD	Gifts and Deposits
Studia Hib.	*Studia Hibernica* (Dublin, 1961–)
TCD	Trinity College, Dublin
UJA	*Ulster Journal of Archaeology* (Belfast, 3 series: 1853–62, 9 vols.; 1895–1911, 17 vols.; 1938–)
Wild Geese	Brendan Jennings (ed.), *Wild Geese in Spanish Flanders, 1582–1700. Documents relating chiefly to Irish regiments from the Archives Générales du Royaume, Brussels, and other sources* (IMC, Dublin, 1964)

INTRODUCTION: ANTRIM AND THE HISTORY OF THE 'THREE KINGDOMS'

ANTRIM AND THE HISTORIANS

Arrogant, condescending, crafty, calculating, childish, fickle, greedy, headstrong, haughty, indiscreet, impatient, importuning, interfering, loud-mouthed, manipulative, myopic, perfidious, pretentious, self-centred, uncooperative and whining: these are merely a selection of the adjectives used by his contemporaries and by later historians to describe the personality of Randal MacDonnell, second earl and first marquis of Antrim.

And the criticisms started at the top. Lords lieutenant Thomas Wentworth, earl of Strafford, and James Butler, duke of Ormond, were his most vocal and malevolent critics. The former, who disliked his character and religion and questioned his competence and loyalty, denigrated and ridiculed Antrim at every opportunity. In a letter to the king on the eve of the first Bishops' War, he noted 'I neither hope much of his Parts, of his Powers, or of his Affections.'[1] Wentworth later added 'That lord hath much of the Irish in him. Whatsoever they desire must be done; and in their own time forsooth, or else they presently fall out with you ... [He is] all for ostentation, no moderate thing will suffice, as if land and sea and all were to minister to [his] glory.'[2] As Strafford's protégé, Ormond imbibed the lord deputy's antipathy towards Antrim. The language Ormond later used to describe him – 'so shallow an engine as my Lord Antrim' – was typical of Wentworth's caustic scorn.[3]

Many members of the Old English, the New English, the Presbyterian and even the native Irish communities clearly shared this contempt for Antrim. For instance, his disloyalty to the Stuart cause during the 1640s particularly rankled with the powerful grandee, Ulick Burke, earl of Clanricard, who alleged spitefully that Antrim had 'gained the reputation of pulling down the side he is on'.[4] His 'differing tempers' (read: temper tantrums) infuriated

[1] Wentworth to Charles I, 28 July 1638 (Knowler, *Letters*, II, 187).
[2] Wentworth to Laud, [September] 1638 (SCL, Strafford MSS 7, fo. 131v).
[3] Ormond to Charles II, 15 December 1649 (Bodl., Carte MSS 26, fos. 381–3v). I am grateful to Billy Kelly for sharing his views on Ormond with me.
[4] Clanricard to Fanshawe, 27 August 1651 (*Ormonde MSS*, I, 194).

everyone.⁵ Ormond suggested that one particular outburst in 1644 'proceeded rather from some present passion or resentment, than from any settled solution';⁶ while his Catholic colleagues in the confederation of Kilkenny attributed his unpredictable behaviour 'to his own inclination, his youth and want of experience'.⁷ But it was Antrim's 'vanity' and 'boastfulness' which attracted most adverse comment. According to one observer, he might 'promise very largely: but I presume your e :cellency [Ormond] guesses whereabout the balance of the account will be';⁸ while another waspishly suggested that 'a good piece of battery is much more powerful to take in a castle than is his lordship's oratory'.⁹

Contemporary historians shared – and thereby perpetuated – this unflattering image. Sir Richard Bellings, a much respected politician and author of *Fragmentum historicum: or, the second and third books of the war in Ireland*, portrayed him as bombastic, pompous, two-faced, conniving and untrustworthy.¹⁰ In another near-contemporary history of the Irish Civil War, Antrim's stupidity, vanity and self-interest were vigorously condemned – for, according to the author, he only deluded 'his maggot paled brains with a dream of being great'.¹¹ The English statesman and historian Edward Hyde, earl of Clarendon, openly admitted that he was never 'fond' of the marquis and found him vain, presumptuous, undiscerning and of limited intelligence.¹²

To quote further condemnations of Antrim, which are extremely numerous, would be both boring and pointless. Suffice it to say that the opinions and writings of these men – the majority of whom were either political opponents or jealous rivals – have left a permanent blemish on the marquis's historical reputation which has influenced the writings of later historians.

---

⁵ Wentworth to Laud, 10 May 1639 (Knowler, *Letters*, II, 334–7).
⁶ Ormond to Antrim, 1 June 1644 (Carte, *Ormond*, VI, 139).
⁷ Supreme council to Ormond, 30 May 1644 (Bodl., Carte MSS 11, fo. 67r–v).
⁸ Arthur Trevor to Ormond, 9 March 1644 (Carte, *Ormond*, VI, 57). Trevor appears to have been an 'Ormondist'.
⁹ Barry to Ormond, 18 April 1644 (Gilbert, *Ir. confed.*, III, 150). Barry was allegedly involved in the 'O'More–Maguire plot' to capture Dublin castle in 1641. He later joined the confederates but remained a loyal supporter of Ormond, Gilbert, *Contemp. hist., 1641–52*, I, 181–3, 190, 282, 611.
¹⁰ For examples see *Desid. cur. Hib.*, pp. 241–5, 249–51.
¹¹ NLI MS 345, pp. 942–3, 946.
¹² Edward Hyde, earl of Clarendon, *The life of Edward, earl of Clarendon. Being a continuation of the history of the great rebellion from the restoration to his banishment in 1667* (3 vols., Oxford, 1827), II, 77–8. Clarendon to Ormond, 18 July 1663 (Bodl., Carte MSS 32, fo. 719). Clarendon, *Rebellion*, III, 510 described him as 'a man of excessive pride and vanity, and of a marvelous weak and narrow understanding'. Even the French ambassador commented on his 'vanity', see Séneterre to Bouthillier, 4/14 November 1635 (PRO, PRO 31/3/68, fo. 137v).

Thus in his eighteenth-century life of the duke of Ormond, Thomas Carte clearly followed the bias of his hero: Antrim, he wrote, 'fancied himself equal to the most difficult and important charges, though really unfit to be employed in any'.[13] The nineteenth-century historian, Sir John Gilbert, dismissed him as 'well meaning but unstable';[14] as did S. R. Gardiner who, in his influential *History of England*, dubbed Antrim 'a weak and inefficient catholic peer'.[15] Richard Bagwell, author of the only comprehensive narrative account of Stuart Ireland to date, described Antrim as 'a man of much ambition and some cunning, but his practical abilities were small, and neither Strafford, Ormonde nor Clarendon rated him highly'.[16] Hardly surprisingly, then, such recent scholarly attention as the marquis has attracted is largely unfavourable: C. V. Wedgwood thought he was 'ridiculous';[17] Jerrold Casway in his biography of General Owen Roe O'Neill described Antrim as 'vain and impulsive';[18] while a biographer of Montrose dismissed him as 'a stage Irishman ... with no money, no brains, and a limitless supply of charm and vain promises ... [who] had married the blowsy, aging widow of the duke of Buckingham'.[19] More recently he was damned as a 'flamboyant adventurer' and as 'selfish, vain and ambitious'.[20]

This study will attempt to establish the degree to which Antrim deserved his dismal reputation. Did he, for instance, like his contemporary Sir Piers Crosby, suffer 'the dual misfortune of crossing Wentworth's path and being remembered only by what Wentworth wrote of him'?[21] Certainly this was

---

[13] Carte, *Ormond*, III, 438. Despite this Carte claimed that 'I have been very particular in my account of the marquis of Antrim ... I am sure I have been very impartial', *ibid.*, I, xii.
[14] Gilbert, *Contemp. hist. 1641–52*, I, xxv.
[15] Gardiner, *Eng.*, X, 7. Also see L. Aikin, *Memoirs of the court of Charles the first* (2 vols., London, 1833), I, 535–6.
[16] Richard Bagwell, *Ireland under the Stuarts* (3 vols., London, 1909–16; reprint, 1963), II, 285.
[17] C. V. Wedgwood, *The king's peace 1637–1641. The great rebellion* (London, 1955), p. 425.
[18] Jerrold I. Casway, *Owen Roe O'Neill and the struggle for Catholic Ireland* (Philadelphia, 1984), p. 265.
[19] M. Hastings, *Montrose. The king's champion* (London, 1977), p. 71. See also Dorothea Townsend, *George Digby, second earl of Bristol* (London, 1924), pp. 98–9.
[20] William Neely, *Kilkenny. An urban history 1391–1843* (Belfast, 1989), pp. 90, 96.
[21] Aidan Clarke, 'Sir Piers Crosby, 1590–1646: Wentworth's "tawney ribbon"', *IHS*, 26, no. 102 (Nov. 1988), p. 142. The same fate has befallen King James VI and I. See for example Maurice Lee, *Great Britain's Solomon. James VI and I in this three kingdoms* (Urbana and Chicago, 1990), who aims to offer 'a coherent and persuasive picture of a king whose reputation is finally emerging from the cloud under which circumstance and historical fashion formerly combined to shadow it' (p. xv).

also true of Richard Boyle, first earl of Cork, for as Nicholas Canny has noted: 'Despite the several acknowledgements of his importance, historians have viewed Boyle from a distance, and would appear to have been repelled by the aura of suspicion which surrounded him in his own lifetime. Consequently, what is known of Boyle comes from official records, or the frequently hostile correspondence of his contemporaries.'[22]

A further objective is simply to provide a more balanced account of the life of an important Irish statesman who (as the MacDonnell family historian quite rightly observed) was 'destined to take a prominent place in the affairs of Ulster, and indeed of Ireland, during the greater part of the seventeenth century'.[23] For as yet there is no critical biography – witness a recent call by Strafford's biographer, Hugh Kearney, for a fresh analysis of the role played by the MacDonnells of Antrim in the events of the later 1630s and 1640s.[24] The only serious account of his career was written over a century ago by George Hill who, in his history of the MacDonnells, of Antrim, devoted a long chapter to the marquis and published many of the seminal documents relating to his life.[25] But, for all its merits, his narrative is chaotically arranged and often inaccurate; moreover, though he used every source available to him in the nineteenth century, he did not gain access to many important collections of papers (such as the Hamilton manuscripts) which were then in private hands, or to documents in European and North American archives. Apart from Hill, Antrim's career seems to have been noted by recent historians only when it impinged upon Scottish history: his role in the first Bishops' War of 1638–9 and his contribution to the Scottish war effort in 1644–5.[26]

---

[22] Nicholas P. Canny, *The upstart earl. A study of the social and mental world of Richard Boyle first earl of Cork, 1566–1643* (Cambridge, 1982), pp. 1 and 9–18.
[23] George Hill, *An historical account of the MacDonnells of Antrim: including notices of some other septs, Irish and Scottish* (Belfast, 1873; reprint Ballycastle, 1978), p. 252. Yet even Hill, in *The Stewarts of Ballintoy: with notices of other families of the district in the seventeenth century* (Coleraine, 1865; reprint, Ballycastle, 1976), p. 8, described him as 'imprudent, ambitious and unprincipled'.
[24] Hugh F. Kearney, *Strafford in Ireland 1633–41. A study in absolutism* (Manchester, 1959; 2nd edn, Cambridge, 1989), p. xx.
[25] Hill, *MacDonnells*, chapter 5.
[26] Aidan Clarke, 'The earl of Antrim and the first Bishops' War', *Ir. Sword*, 6, no. 23 (1963), pp. 108–15; John Lowe, 'The earl of Antrim and Irish aid to Montrose in 1644', *Ir. Sword*, 4, no. 16 (Summer 1960), pp. 191–8; Caóimhin Ó Danachair, 'Montrose's Irish Regiments', *Ir. Sword*, 4, no. 14 (1959), pp. 61–7; Lucy Duggan, 'The Irish brigade with Montrose', *Irish Ecclesiastical Record*, 5th series, 89 (Jan.–June 1958), pp. 171–84, 246–58. Summary references to his activities have also been made by David Stevenson, *Alasdair MacColla and the Highland problem in the seventeenth century* (Edinburgh, 1980); *idem, Scottish Covenanters and Irish Confederates. Scottish–Irish Relations in the mid-seventeenth century* (Belfast, 1981); and Casway, *Owen Roe O'Neill.*

Introduction

This dearth of scholarship is perhaps explained by the fact that historians – blinded by 'that bitch goddess, success' – have found it distasteful to write about 'losers' and 'failures' such as Antrim. In a collection of essays entitled *Worsted in the game. Losers in Irish history* the careers of a number of prominent early modern Irish 'failures', whose aims and actions have been consistently misrepresented by generations of commentators, have been critically reassessed.[27] It was found that these 'losers' all played an important role in Irish history 'because they embodied and gave voice to the most profound tensions of their times in a manner in which their less sensitive contemporaries, and subsequent historians, blinded by what came after, could not match'.[28] In fact the absence of secondary literature is not limited to the marquis. Apart from the Boyle family – particularly Nicholas Canny's refreshing, thematic study of Richard Boyle, first earl of Cork – very few seventeenth-century Irish figures, even when successful, have commanded serious, recent scholarly attention.[29]

Unlike Canny's biography of *The upstart earl* this study takes a traditional chronological approach. It focuses on Antrim's political career between his marriage to the duchess of Buckingham in 1635 and his restoration to his County Antrim estates in 1665; and on how he managed to survive the great political, social and economic upheavals of the mid-seventeenth century. Chapters 1 and 2 discuss the physical and mental world in which he operated: the impact of the physical environment on his actions, ambitions and behaviour; his resources – both human and territorial – and his ability to manage them; the role of indebtedness in his life; his position at the Stuart court, and his skill in manipulating factional groupings to his own advantage. The remainder of the study addresses Antrim's role in, and his contribution to, the great political and military events of the mid-seventeenth century: his part in the unsuccessful royalist attempts to suppress the Scottish covenanters during the Bishops' Wars and in the 'War of the Three Kingdoms' (chapters 3, 5 and 6); his role in the various 'popish plots' of the early 1640s, especially the 'Antrim plot' of spring 1641 (chapter 4); his relationship with the Irish insurgents after the outbreak of rebellion in 1641 and his position in the

---

[27] Ciaran Brady (ed.), *Worsted in the game. Losers in Irish history* (Dublin, 1989), pp. 1, 4. They include Thomas Butler, earl of Ormond, Bishop William Bedell, the earl of Tyrconnell and Archbishop William King.
[28] Brady (ed.), *Worsted in the game*, p. 6.
[29] On the Boyle family, see Canny, *The upstart earl*; Terence Ranger,'Richard Boyle and the making of an Irish fortune, 1588–1614', *IHS*, 10, no. 39 (Mar. 1957); and K. M. Lynch's superficial study of Richard's son, Roger Boyle, Lord Broghill – *Roger Boyle, first earl of Orrery* (Knoxville, 1965). Though a racy read, and a useful summary of Carte's lengthy biography, J. C. Beckett, *The cavalier duke. A life of James Butler first duke of Ormond 1610–88* (Belfast, 1990), is disappointing.

Catholic confederacy (chapters 4 to 8); his role as a Cromwellian collaborator during the 1650s and his relationship with the Restoration government in the 1660s (chapters 9 and 10).

In addition to being a biography of Antrim, this study highlights three important truths about early modern Britain and Ireland. First, it illustrates the elastic nature of the concept of 'patriotism' in the turbulent years of the mid-seventeenth century; second, it demonstrates that Ireland was and must be viewed as a part of the triple monarchy of the Stuart kings; and, finally, it shows that Ireland – at least in the 1640s – was seen, for the first and last time before 1922, as part of the European state system.

ANTRIM: A PATRIOT FOR WHOM?

However, for all its advantages, a chronological framework gives rise to an obvious limitation: it tends to underplay the continuities and constants which shaped and influenced Antrim's career, and thus prevents him from being seen in the context of his own times. It obscures the salient themes which appeared and reappeared throughout his complex life.

Thus Antrim's own 'personal agenda' would probably have stressed three pertinent facts: physical and cultural geography and inherited values. In the first place, the geographical setting of Antrim's world was of paramount importance in his life. In the early modern period distance was 'public enemy number one' and the marquis's territorial and political base was far from the centre of power: his traditional world stretched from the Hebridean islands of Uist, Skye, Rhum and Canna in the north to Kintyre and Jura in the east and to County Antrim in the west, encompassing some of the most remote and inaccessible regions of Stuart Scotland and Ireland. For instance, in 1609 (the year of Antrim's birth) Sir John Davies confessed that Ulster was 'heretofore as unknown to the English here as the most inland part of Virginia is yet unknown to our English Colony there'.[30]

Antrim's world was indeed almost totally inaccessible by land. Though there were 'several high ways' linking Glenarm with the more northerly towns of the county, overland travel was almost impossible without a guide since 'the lower ways are deep clay, and the upper ways great and steep hills'.[31] But one could travel easily between the outposts of Antrim's world by sea. Thus the North Channel between Torr Head and Kintyre was only twelve miles wide and on a fine day could be crossed in a matter of hours (while, by contrast, the journey to London – via Dublin – could take between seven and ten days even in good weather). For example in July 1635 it took Sir

[30] Davies to Salisbury, 24 August 1609, (HMC, *Salisbury MSS*, XXI, 121).
[31] Hill, *MacDonnells*, p. 386.

William Brereton a few hours to reach East Ulster from Portpatrick in Galloway but it was a further four days of arduous travel through 'wild country ... stony, craggy, hilly and uneven' before he finally arrived in Dublin.[32] It was the sea, not the land, which united the Clan Donald archipelago.[33]

This physical proximity between Ulster and Western Scotland also facilitated social interaction at every level. Indeed, to all intents and purposes, Gaelic Ireland and Gaelic Scotland 'were parts of the same ethos' and had formed a single cultural, linguistic and even political entity since earliest times.[34] Certainly King James VI and I regarded the Highlands and Ireland in this light and believed that the natives of these outlying areas were 'utterly barbarous, without any sort or show of civility'.[35] The fact that a peculiar dialect, known as 'Highland Irish', was spoken in County Antrim well into the eighteenth century reflected this close relationship; as did Charles I's preference during the mid-1640s for sending troops from Ulster to fight in Scotland 'as agreeing perfectly with the highlanders in their manners and language'.[36] The location of Antrim's power base on the periphery of Britain,

---

[32] Sir William Brereton, *Travels in Holland, the United Provinces, England, Scotland and Ireland, 1634–1635*, ed. Edward Haskins (Chetham Society, vol. I, [London], 1844), pp. 132–3.

[33] For a detailed discussion of the close links between MacDonalds and MacDonnells see Stevenson, *Scottish Covenanters*, pp. 1–14, and Andrew McKerral, *Kintyre in the seventeenth century* (Edinburgh, 1948), p. 1. For a recent study of Irish influences on Kintyre, see Angus Martin, *Kintyre. The hidden past* (Edinburgh, 1984), chapter 5.

[34] Aidan Clarke, 'The plantations of Ulster', in Liam de Paor (ed.), *Milestones in Irish History* (Cork and Dublin, 1986), p. 62. On the close relationship between the two countries see Jane E. A. Dawson, 'Two kingdoms or three?: Ireland in Anglo-Scottish relations in the middle of the sixteenth century', in Roger Mason (ed.), *Scotland and England 1286–1815* (Edinburgh, 1987), pp. 113–14, 117; Steven Ellis, ' "Not mere English". The British perspective, 1400–1650', *History Today*, 38, no. 12 (Dec. 1988), p. 43; Hugh Trevor-Roper, 'The invention of tradition: the Highland tradition of Scotland', in E. Hobsbawn and T. Ranger (eds.), *The invention of tradition* (Cambridge, 1983), pp. 15–16; R. A. Dodgshon, *Land and society in early Scotland* (Oxford, 981), pp. 40–8; R. S. Tompson, *The Atlantic archipelago. A political history of the British Isles* (New York, 1986), pp. 1–3; L. M. Cullen, 'Scotland and Ireland 1600–1800: their role in the evolution of British society', in R. A. Houston and I. D. Whyte (eds.), *Scottish society 1500–1800* (Cambridge, 1989), p. 226. See also the articles by Thomas Hudson and A. T. Q. Stewart in Jack W. Weaver (ed.), *Selected proceedings of the Scotch–Irish heritage festival, II, at Winthrop College* (Baton Rouge, 1984), and J. A. Stewart, 'Peoples of the Clan Ranald: a traditional gaelic kindred in decline 1644–1851' (unpublished PhD thesis, University of Edinburgh, 1982), p. 5.

[35] Lee, *Great Britain's Solomon*, p. 197.

[36] *Cal. SP Ire.*, 1660–2, p. 457; Hugh Alexander Boyd (ed.), 'Dean William Henry's topographical description of the coast of County Antrim and North Down c.1740', *The Glynns*, 2 (1974), p. 7; Carte, *Ormond*, III, 52.

which was a particularly 'high risk' area during the early modern period, and the cultural homogeneity of his followers, made him a particularly valuable asset to all other political figures.

The final, overriding constant in Antrim's 'personal agenda' was his 'tribal' ambition to use every artifice available to him in order to preserve intact (and, where possible, to extend) his inheritance. He was determined to consolidate further the MacDonnell foothold in East Ulster; to regain the forfeited Scottish lands of Clan Donald (Kintyre and Jura) which were controlled by the earls of Argyll; and, in addition, to keep his corner of Stuart Britain and Ireland Catholic. But Antrim's Scottish ancestry, his Irish upbringing and his determination to uphold these Gaelic values created a personal dilemma for him. Throughout the marquis's life one is forced to ask time and again where, or with whom, did his loyalty lie? On the one hand, he wished to preserve Catholic Ireland, to see Clan Donald rise again in both Ireland and Scotland with him at its head, and to protect the great families of Catholic Ulster; while, on the other, he hoped to secure political power in Protestant England and favour at the Caroline court. In short, he sincerely wanted to succeed in, and to be accepted by, two very different worlds; to be both lauded by Gaelic bards and painted by Van Dyck. Strafford captured his ambiguous situation exactly in a letter to Laud written after a meeting with Antrim in the spring of 1639: 'His lordship was in [as] differing tempers as ever I saw; sometimes the grand-child of great Tyrone ... and sometimes again he descended and became more merciful and gracious, indeed, even to make himself like one of ourselves, such was his gentleness and civility.'[37] The outbreak of the Irish rebellion in 1641 exacerbated Antrim's dilemma. While he wanted to see 'the free exercise of the Roman religion, which I am devoted to and am engaged to maintain in duty to God and respect of my future happiness and salvation',[38] he, nevertheless, was – for the time being at least – 'quite overborne by the interest of his majesty's honour and power'.[39]

His divided loyalties, occasionally amounting almost to an identity crisis, help to explain his inconsistent and chameleon-like behaviour, particularly during the 1640s. Up until 1645 the marquis, a conservative with great respect for the monarchy and the established hierarchy, reconciled himself to the acceptance of the *status quo*. His pragmatic willingness 'to entertain dual allegiances to church and state', and his belief that loyalty to Catholicism and

---

[37] Wentworth to Laud, 10 May 1639 (Knowler, *Letters*, II, 335–6).
[38] *A copie of a letter from the Lord Intrim [sic] in Ireland to the right honourable earle of Rutland, bearing date the 25 day of February anno dom. 1642 [sic]* ... (London, 1642), pp. 3–4.
[39] Digby to Ormond, 14 March 1644 (Carte, *Ormond*, VI, 62).

Map 1 Antrim's world

the English crown were compatible, was indeed more typical of the Old English mentalité than that of the native Irish.[40] Yet the counter-reformation attitude traditionally associated with the Old Irish, which allowed no obligation to heretical rulers and even promoted resistance to English rule in Ireland, was something to which Antrim was driven by force of circumstances after 1645.[41] Any study of Antrim thus calls into question what concepts such as 'patriotism' or 'treason' actually meant to Irish and British Catholics amid the warfare and political instability of the mid-seventeenth century.

ANTRIM: A MAN OF THE 'THREE KINGDOMS'

Ormond was reminded early in 1643 that Antrim's career 'is an index to the history of Ireland'.[42] This, as we will see, was certainly true; but his career was also an index to the history of Britain.[43] Until recently the 'cloven hoof of anglocentricity' (the phrase is Conrad Russell's) has permeated the study of events in all three of the Stuart kingdoms during the mid-seventeenth century.[44] Apart from S. R. Gardiner, writing in the mid-nineteenth century, and C. V. Wedgwood, writing nearly a century later, the collective history of seventeenth-century Ireland and Britain received little scholarly attention.[45] Then in 1975 J. G. A. Pocock wrote an article provocatively entitled 'British history: a plea for a new subject' in which he attempted to define the field and set an agenda for its study.[46] Yet it was still over a decade before Scottish, English and, to a lesser, extent Irish historians paid heed to Pocock's plea.[47]

---

[40] Aidan Clarke, 'Colonial identity in early seventeenth century Ireland' in T. W. Moody (ed.), *Nationality and the pursuit of national independence* (Historical Studies, vol. XI, Belfast, 1978), pp. 60–1.
[41] For further details, see Nicholas P. Canny, 'The formation of the Irish mind: religion, politics and Gaelic Irish literature', *Past and Present*, 95 (May, 1982), pp. 91–116.
[42] Arthur Trevor to Ormond, 19 January 1643 (Carte, *Ormond*, VI, 15).
[43] J. G. A. Pocock, 'The limits and divisions of British history: in search of an unknown subject', *American Historical Review*, 87, no. 2 (Apr. 1982), p. 318, and *idem*, 'British history: a plea for a new subject', *Journal of Modern History*, 47, no. 4 (Dec. 1975), pp. 601–3, 620, 622–8. For a discussion of the use of the term 'Britain' in this work, see p. xvii above.
[44] Conrad Russell, *The fall of the British monarchies 1637–1642* (Oxford, 1991), p. vii.
[45] Wedgwood, *The king's peace*, was intended to be 'a narrative history of the British Isles' (p. 13).
[46] Pocock, 'British history', pp. 602–28, and *idem*, 'The limits and divisions of British history', pp. 311–36.
[47] For Scottish and English examples, see nn. 48, 49, 50, 52, 53, 55 below. Increasingly Irish historians are setting early modern Irish history in its three kingdoms context. See J. C. Beckett, *The making of modern Ireland 1603–1923* (London, 1966), especially chapter 4; *idem*, *The Anglo-Irish tradition* (Belfast, 1976); Ellis, '"Not mere English". The British

Even then as a recent avalanche of monographs and articles admirably illustrates,[48] scholarly attention has concentrated on the years 1634 to 1642, which according to John Morrill are the 'most-studied of all conundrums of English and of British history'.[49] In particular the work of Conrad Russell, which includes four illuminating articles and two books on the 'British theme' and the problems of running a 'multiple kingdom' in this period, has transformed the historiography of the field.[50] However, the 'British problem' did not end with the outbreak of the English Civil War in 1642 for, as another proponent of British history has recently noted, 'the struggle for the Covenant led inexorably on to the War of the Three Kingdoms, in which the affairs of each became inextricably bound up with the affairs of the others'.[51] Though the British context of the Irish and British Civil Wars still needs to be fully unravelled, historians such as David Stevenson have been particularly sensitive to the study of the 'British experience' and to the importance of Ireland for Scottish history and for Anglo-Scottish relations.[52] Ivan Roots and Ronald Hutton have also recognized the significance of British history in their studies of the British Isles during the mid-seventeenth century,[53] when, according to S. R. Gardiner,

perspective', pp. 41, 43, 46–8; Michael Perceval-Maxwell, 'Ireland and the monarchy in the early Stuart multiple kingdom', *Historical Journal*, 34, no. 2 (1991), pp. 279–95, and *idem*. 'Ireland and Scotland 1638–1648', in John S. Morrill (ed.), *The Scottish national covenant in its British context 1638–51* (Edinburgh, 1990), pp. 193–211.

[48] Special attention has been devoted to the British perspective in Morrill (ed.), *The Scottish National Covenant*; Peter Donald, *An uncounselled king. Charles I and the Scottish troubles 1637–1641* (Cambridge, 1990), especially chapters 1 and 5; and, to a lesser extent, Allan I. Macinnes, *Charles I and the making of the covenanting movement 1625–1641* (Edinburgh, 1991). On Anglo-Scottish relations see Brian Levack, *The formation of the British state: England, Scotland and the union 1603–1707* (Oxford, 1987).

[49] John S. Morrill (ed.), *The impact of the English civil war* (London, 1991), p. 10.

[50] His articles 'The British problem and the English civil war', 'Why did Charles I call the Long Parliament?', 'The British background to the Irish rebellion of 1641' and 'The first army plot of 1641' have been conveniently reprinted in Conrad Russell, *Unrevolutionary England, 1603–42* (London, 1990), part IV. His two monographs on the subject are *Fall* and *The causes of the English Civil War* (Oxford, 1990). In the preface to *Fall* Russell noted how in the course of his research he became 'convinced that it is impossible to tell the English story by itself, and this book has been slowly transformed into an attempt at genuinely British history' (p. vii).

[51] Morrill (ed.), *The Scottish national covenant*, p. 20.

[52] See in particular Stevenson, *Scottish Covenanters*. See also *idem*, 'The century of the Three Kingdoms', *History Today*, 35, no. 3 (Mar. 1985), pp. 28–33.

[53] Ivan Roots, 'Union and disunion in the British Isles 1637–60', in I. Roots (ed.), *'Into another mould'. Aspects of the Interregnum* (London, 1981), pp. 5–23, and Ronald Hutton, *The British republic 1649–1660* (London, 1990).

the conflict between King and Parliament for the supremacy at Westminster was widening out into a conflict for the supremacy of England in the British Isles. That it was so was owing to the eagerness of Royalists to enlist the forces of Scotland and Ireland in their own behoof, and it is no wonder that Cromwell and his officers had made up their minds that rather than Scotland or Ireland should interfere in the political development of England, an English army should interfere in the political development of Scotland and Ireland.[54]

Moreover, in his recent biography of Charles II Hutton assessed the consequences of the Restoration in England, Scotland and Ireland and effectively demonstrated how closely events in the three Stuart kingdoms continued to be intertwined during the later decades of the seventeenth century.[55] Sadly, however, despite advances 'against the consuming insularity, and even introspection, of English, Scottish and Irish historiography',[56] historians of the 'three kingdoms' continue to be the exception rather than the rule.

Contemporaries, by contrast, were all acutely sensitive to the interrelations between the Caroline kingdoms. After 1638 Charles I himself treated his problem in Scotland as a 'British one' and mobilized Irish and English armies to quell his rebellious subjects there; in fact, according to Peter Donald, 'the triple sovereignty was central to the king's strategy of attack'.[57] Likewise throughout the 1640s foreign observers carefully monitored the intricate war dance of all three kingdoms.[58] Antrim too was keenly aware of the progress of political events in Scotland and in England for, as his determination to preserve Clan Donald influence and reduce that of Clan Campbell in Western Scotland admirably illustrates, Antrim was not 'merely Irish' but rather a Gaelic lord of Highland extraction with a vested interest in Scottish and (after his marriage to the duchess of Buckingham in 1635) in English affairs.[59] Contemporary observers were quick to note Antrim's extensive Irish and British connections. 'Antrim is of Scottish extraction, descended of the noble and ancient family of the MacDonalds', wrote one pamphleteer in 1652; he continued that the marquis was 'a man of great estate and power in Ireland,

---

[54] Gardiner, *Commonwealth and protectorate*, I, 27.
[55] Ronald Hutton, *Charles II, King of England, Scotland and Ireland* (Oxford, 1989).
[56] Dawson, 'Two kingdoms or three?', p. 113.
[57] Peter Donald, 'The Scottish national covenant and British politics 1638–40' in Morrill (ed.), *The Scottish national covenant*, p. 99, also see pp. 17, 93.
[58] For instance early in 1647 the Madrid government feared that their recruiting grounds in Ireland might be cut off as a result of 'the union of the parliament of England and of Scotland and of the capture of the King of Great Britain', consulta of the council of state, 20/30 March 1647(AGS, Eo. 2068 unfol.).
[59] It is no coincidence that Antrim's principal Irish residence, Dunluce castle, is on the cover of a recent work on the British Isles; for, according to Hugh Kearney, 'this castle ... illustrates the close connections between various parts of the British Isles during the early modern period', Hugh F. Kearney, *The British Isles. A history of four nations* (Cambridge, 1989).

and allied to the prime nobility of England, by matching with the duchess of Buckingham'.[60] Antrim's cosmopolitan heritage thus offered him *three* potential theatres of action, and this was particularly pertinent during the 1640s. For the conflict between Charles I and his various groups of subjects created both opportunities and openings – as well as endless problems and headaches – for the enterprising marquis which would otherwise have been denied him: thwarted in Ireland, he could always try his luck in Scotland or even in England. 'Public commotions' had become (as one covenanter bitterly pointed out) Antrim's 'private subsistence'.[61]

What light, then, does Antrim's career shed on the 'British problem'? From the outset the marquis operated within the sphere of British politics. He was involved in Charles's plans to subdue the Scots and in 1638 he offered to rally the MacDonnells on both sides of the North Channel as bulwarks against the rebellious covenanters in Western Scotland. In the event, Antrim's army never left Ireland; yet the abortive expedition was not without its significance and had an immediate domino-like impact. In Scotland, Argyll, one of the most powerful Scottish nobles, openly sided with the covenanters. In England, the king's willingness to conspire with an 'Irish papist' did little to dispel the rumours of his being involved in popish plots. While in Ireland, the divisions and animosities aroused by Antrim's proposed invasion served to divide the country's meagre resources at a time when a united and concerted effort might have produced very dramatic results in all three kingdoms.[62]

When, three years later, Ireland itself had risen in rebellion, Antrim once again tried to solve his master's British problems. Between the spring of 1642 and the spring of 1644 he hatched at least three separate plots with the king and queen which involved raising and sending an Irish army against the Scottish rebels. The first ended in disaster after Antrim's design was made public following his capture in 1643. It was even suggested that this was 'one of the worst plots against this kingdom [Ireland] and Scotland, and so by consequence against England that hath yet been discovered except the plot of the rebellion which hath already almost consumed us'.[63] The political and military ramifications ran deep and, once again, 'the billiard-ball effect of each of the kingdoms on the affairs of the others' quickly became apparent.[64] In Scotland news that the royal couple had been conspiring against the

[60] *Montrose redivivus, or the portraiture of James late marquis of Montrose...* (London, [July], 1652), p. 18.
[61] Baillie to Spang, 26 July 1643 (Laing, *Letters*, II, 74).
[62] See pp. 92–3 below.
[63] 'T.N.' to Robert Reynolds, 7 June 1643 (HMC *rep. 5*, app., p. 89; HLRO, main papers, 7/6/1643).
[64] Russell, *Causes*, p. 27.

covenanters was decisive in convincing the more moderate party to ally with parliament and to sign the 'Solemn League and Covenant' (September 1643). Moreover, the covenanters now agreed to send an army of 21,000 men into England to fight for parliament against the king.[65]

In the event, only one of Antrim's conspiracies reached fruition. In 1644 Antrim sent nearly 2,000 Irish veterans to serve in Scotland under the marquis of Montrose. Their arrival there had an immediate and dramatic impact on British politics. The Scots were obliged to send an army of 6,000 covenanters to counter the Irish invasion; but this force met with little success, for 1644–5 was the royalists' *annus mirabilis* in Scotland and Antrim's troops played an important role in Montrose's victories at Tippermuir, Aberdeen, Inverlochy, Auldearn, Alford and Kilsyth. The invasion also impinged significantly on English affairs, for Montrose's continued victories in the north resulted in the removal of regiment after regiment of the covenanting army from English soil and also prevented a second Scottish army of invasion from crossing the border.[66] Finally Antrim's refusal in June 1646 to surrender at the end of the first English Civil War, together with his determination to raise an army of 30,000 men with which he hoped first to reduce Scotland and then to march into England and free Charles I, seriously threatened any chance of securing a peace between the king and the English and Scottish parliaments.[67]

Antrim's career thus provides a welcome opportunity to see the crisis of the mid-seventeenth century as an equilateral triangle viewed from a primarily Irish stance. For there can be little doubt that events looked very different when viewed from Kintyre, Dunluce or Kilkenny than they did to those sitting in London, Edinburgh or Dublin.

ANTRIM: A MAN OF THE 'FIVE KINGDOMS'

In his 1975 inaugural lecture H. G. Koenigsberger drew attention to the fact that the 'dramatic events' of the 1640s could not 'be understood in a purely English context. Like most European monarchies, the Stuart monarchy was a composite monarchy ... Moreover Great Britain [and Ireland] was part of the European state system and subject to foreign intervention.'[68] More recently another prominent historian of early modern Europe, while praising the efforts of English historians to write 'British history', also condemned them

---

[65] See. pp. 122–4 below.   [66] See pp. 146–7 below.
[67] See pp. 176–8 below.
[68] H. G. Koenigsberger, 'Dominium regale or dominium politicum et regale', reprinted in *Politicians and virtuosi. Essays in early modern history* (London, 1986), p. 21.

for the 'unwarranted and entrenched practice of viewing English history apart from continental Europe'.[69] Though there has been a recent drive to set Ireland in its 'Atlantic context',[70] a similar charge could be raised against historians of seventeenth-century Ireland.[71]

And yet, thanks to the constant passage of priests and scholars, traders and mercenaries, links between Ireland and the continent were always strong.[72] This was particularly true during the early modern period when the Catholic princes of Europe carefully monitored, and occasionally directly interfered in, Irish affairs. In 1579 a papal force of Italians and Spaniards landed at Smerwick in order to help Irish insurgents; in 1601 King Philip III of Spain, eager to divert English attention and resources from the Netherlands, sent

---

[69] Jonathan I. Israel (ed.), *The Anglo-Dutch moment* (Cambridge, 1991), p. 11. There are, of course, exceptions to this. See for instance, Ian Roy, 'Les puissances européenes et la chute de Charles I', *Revue d'Histoire Diplomatique*, 92 (1978), pp. 92–109.

[70] See D. B. Quinn, 'Ireland and sixteenth century European expansion', in T. Desmond Williams (ed.), *Historical studies* (London, 1958), pp. 20–32; K. R. Andrews, N. P. Canny and P. E. H. Hair (eds.), *The Westward enterprise. English activities in Ireland, the Atlantic and America 1480–1650* (Liverpool, 1978); Nicholas P. Canny, *Kingdom and colony. Ireland in the Atlantic world 1560–1800* (Baltimore, 1988); and Nicholas P. Canny and Anthony Pagden (eds.), *Colonial identity in the Atlantic world 1500–1800* (Princeton, 1987), especially chapter 6.

[71] There are once again a number of notable exceptions. See for instance Michael J. Hynes, 'The Irish republic in the seventeenth century', *The Catholic Historical Review*, 23, no. 3 (Oct. 1937), pp. 293–4; Sir Charles Petrie, 'Ireland in Spanish and French strategy 1558–1815', *Ir. Sword*, 6, no. 24 (Summer 1964), pp. 154–65; W. A. Maguire (ed.), *Kings in conflict. The revolutionary war in Ireland and its aftermath 1689–1750* (Belfast, 1990), especially chapter 1 by G. C. Gibbs.

[72] For examples see Cathaldus Giblin, 'The Irish colleges on the continent', in Liam Swords (ed.), *The Irish French connection, 1578–1978* (Paris, 1978), pp. 9–20; Thomas Morrissey, *James Archer of Kilkenny ...* (Dublin, 1979); Donal F. Cregan, 'The social and cultural background of a counter-reformation episcopate 1618–60', in Art Cosgrove and Donal McCartney (eds.), *Studies in Irish history presented to R. Dudley Edwards* (Dublin, 1979), pp. 85–117, especially pp. 107ff; the introduction in Brendan Jennings (ed.), *Louvain papers 1606–1827* (IMC, Dublin, 1968); and Tomás O Fíaich, *The Irish colleges in France* (Dublin, 1990), especially pp. 7–10. On trade with the continent see the chapters by John De Courcy Ireland, Timothy O'Neill and D. M. Woodward in Michael McCaughan and John Appleby (eds.), *The Irish sea. Aspects of maritime history* (Belfast and Cultra, 1989), and Rolf Loeber, 'English and Irish sources for the history of Dutch economic activity in Ireland 1600–89', *Ir. Econ. & Co. Hist.*, 8 (1981), pp. 70–85. On the passage of troops, see *Wild Geese*; Mark G. McLaughlin, *The Wild Geese. The Irish brigades of France and Spain* (London, 1980); Pierre Carles, 'Troupes Irlandaises au service de la France, 1635–1815', *Etudes Irlandaises*, new series, 8 (Dec. 1983), pp. 193–212; Pierre Gouhier, 'Mercenaires Irlandais au service de la France (1635–1664)', *Ir. Sword*, 7 (1965), pp. 58–75; R. D. FitzSimon, 'Irish swordsmen in Imperial service in the Thirty Years' War', *Ir. Sword*, 9 (1969), pp. 22–31; John Hennig, 'Irish soldiers in the Thirty Years' War', *RSAI Jn.*, 82 (1952), pp. 28–38.

another Spanish expeditionary force to Kinsale to aid the rebels led by Hugh O'Neill; and early in 1690 Louis XIV of France sent a substantial army to Ireland.[73] Though no army of invasion was sent from Europe during the 1640s there were, according to a leading historian of the confederate era, 'few periods in which Irish politics have been so much a part of the main stream of European history'.[74]

European history during the first half of the seventeenth century was dominated by the struggle between the Bourbons and the Habsburgs (particularly the Spanish branch) to dominate the continent. The Spanish Habsburgs were not only deeply involved in a protracted and bitter struggle in the Netherlands, which became particularly acute in 1645 as the French amplified their assault on Dunkirk, but were also totally committed to the Imperial cause in Germany.[75] Their already tenuous hegemony in western Europe was further undermined by the revolt of a large portion of the Iberian peninsula – namely Catalonia and Portugal – thereby distracting Spain's attention, and meagre resources, from the all-important theatres of war abroad. To top it all, the demographic decline of Castile – Spain's traditional recruiting ground – further reduced the number of available soldiers.[76] France, just like Spain, after 1636 dispatched armies to fight in Germany and, in addition, was committed to sending troops to Italy, to the Netherlands and (after 1640) to Spain itself to aid the Catalan and Portuguese rebels.

In the 1630s England, Scotland and Ireland were able to isolate themselves effectively from these bitter struggles. However, the outbreak of the Bishops' Wars in Scotland, of rebellion in Ireland and of the first Civil War in England

---

[73] John J. Silke, *Ireland and Europe, 1559–1607* (Dundalk, 1966), and Hiram Morgan, 'The end of Gaelic Ulster: a thematic interpretation of events between 1534 and 1610', *IHS*, 26, no. 101 (May 1988), pp. 30–2.

[74] Donal F. Cregan, 'The confederation of Kilkenny', in Brian Farrell (ed.), *The Irish parliamentary tradition* (Dublin, 1973), p. 102.

[75] For an account of why Spain lost the Eighty Years' War in the Netherlands, see Geoffrey Parker, *The Army of Flanders and the Spanish Road 1567–1659. The logistics of Spanish victory and defeat in the Low Countries' wars* (Cambridge, 1972; 3rd edn, 1990). And for a penetrating narrative analysing why the Dutch won the war, see Jonathan I. Israel, *The Dutch Republic and the Hispanic world 1606–1661* (Oxford, 1982). The best recent account of the Thirty Years' War is Geoffrey Parker, *The Thirty Years' War* (London, 1984), and for a brief account of Spain's role in the war, see pp. 103–9.

[76] The best guide to Spanish 'over-stretch' is John H. Elliott, *The Count-Duke of Olivares. The statesman in an age of decline* (New Haven and London, 1986). For further details on the origins of the revolt in Catalonia, see John H. Elliott, *The revolt of the Catalans. A study in the decline of Spain 1598–1640* (Cambridge, 1963); a good brief account of the rebellion, in English, is John H. Elliott, *Imperial Spain 1469–1716* (London, 1963), pp. 341–9; the Portuguese revolt has been sadly neglected by English-speaking historians.

ensured that all the three Stuart kingdoms were drawn into the European conflict in the 1640s. In the words of C. V. Wedgwood: 'European governments, aware of the strategic importance of the British Isles, intervened with open or secret help. The French, the Dutch and the Danes offered to mediate between King Charles and his subjects. The pope sent his nuncio, and the kings of France and Spain sent their ambassadors to the Irish at Kilkenny.'[77]

For Antrim at least this continental dimension, especially the Bourbon–Habsburg struggle for western European hegemony, transformed the 'War of the Three Kingdoms' into a 'War of Five Kingdoms', since his willingness to serve as a diplomat to the courts of France and the Spanish Netherlands, as a military entrepreneur or as a privateer, inevitably drew him into the European theatre of war. Moreover, the 'War of the Five Kingdoms' provided him with an opportunity, as chief of the MacDonnells, to flex his military muscles, for the ability to muster and lead a substantial number of his kinsmen and followers – whether in Ireland, England, Scotland, France or Flanders – played an important part in determining his standing in the eyes of both Irish and British contemporaries. Therefore this study, using Antrim as the guide, aims, on the one hand, to explore mid-seventeenth-century Ireland's international status during its brief period of independence and, on the other, the role played by Catholic Irish diplomats and profiteers (such as the marquis himself) in the wars then raging on the continent.

[77] Wedgwood, *The king's peace*, p. 13.

1

A man of the 'three kingdoms' (1609–1637)

Randal MacDonnell was born in 1609 and 'bred the highland way' wearing 'neither hat, cap, nor shoe, nor stocking' until he was seven or eight years old.[1] He was the eldest legitimate son of Sir Randal MacDonnell, first earl of Antrim, and Ellis (Alice) O'Neill, daughter of Hugh, third earl of Tyrone.[2]

He enjoyed an illustrious pedigree. In brief, he was descended from Somerled, first Lord of the Isles, through his son Domhnall (the eponymous ancestor of Clan Donald) whose descendant John Mor (the second son of John of Islay and Princess Margaret of Scotland) married Margaret, daughter and heiress of the MacEoin Bisset, Lord of the Glynns of Antrim. They ruled the Glynns jointly with the MacEoin Bissets throughout the fifteenth century, the MacDonnells being primarily based in Scotland, though John Mor's son temporarily resided in the Glynns and married a daughter of O'Donnell, chief of Tirconnell.[3] Their great-grandson, Alexander, fifth of Dunyveg (who died in 1538), was the first MacDonnell to reside permanently in County Antrim and from this point onwards the family began to extend its sphere of influence from the original Bisset inheritance of the Glynns to include the lands to the

---

[1] Quoted in Hill, *MacDonnells*, p. 252. Gaelic was his mother tongue, *Clan Donald*, II, 719.
[2] For histories of the MacDonnells of Antrim see Hill, *MacDonnells*, and Archibald MacDonald (ed.), 'A fragment of an Irish MSS: history of the MacDonalds of Antrim', *Transactions of the Gaelic Society of Inverness*, 37 (1934–6), pp. 262–84 (a manuscript copy of this is in PRONI, D358). For their early history, see W. D. Lamont, 'Alexander of Islay, son of Angus Mor', *SHR*, 60, no. 170 (Oct. 1981), pp. 160–8; Hector MacLean, 'The MacDonnells of Antrim', *Transactions of the Gaelic Society of Inverness*, 17 (1890–1), pp. 85–101; George Hill, 'Chiefs of the Antrim MacDonnells prior to Sorley Boy', *UJA*, 1st series, 7 (1859), pp. 247–59; *idem*, 'Notices of the Clan Ian Vor or Clan-Donnell Scots, especially of the branch settled in Ireland', *UJA*, 1st series, 9 (1861), pp. 301–17; *idem*, 'Shane O'Neill's expedition against the Antrim Scots, 1565', *ibid.*, pp. 122–42.
[3] Chris Lynn and Hector McDonnell, 'Glenarm friary and the Bissets' (privately printed, 1987), pp. 2, 4–13.

north-west, known as the Route. However, continued settlement in Ireland had an important destabilizing effect on the already volatile political balance of power in sixteenth-century Ulster because the MacDonnells, territorially ambitious and loyal to the Scottish rather than the English crown, not only prevented the ruling house of O'Neill from uniting Ulster under its leadership but also weakened native Irish resistance to Tudor reform.[4]

Despite repeated attempts during the mid-sixteenth century by both the English administration and the O'Neills of Tyrone to curb MacDonnell hegemony in County Antrim (which was won at the expense of the native ruling families of MacQuillan and Savage), Elizabeth I finally decided to recognize them, rather than the O'Neills of Clandeboy, as the real power in north-east Ulster.[5] In 1561 the queen granted Sir James, sixth of Dunyveg (Alexander's son) the 'captainship' of the Route for twenty-one years; and a more lasting settlement between the Tudor regime and the troublesome MacDonnells was made in 1586 when Sorley Boy (the youngest son of Alexander, fifth of Dunyveg) became an English subject and in return was granted part of the Route and the constableship of Dunluce castle.[6] Thus, by the end of the sixteenth century, Sorley Boy managed to establish the MacDonnells 'as one of the more important east Ulster families'.[7] Sorley Boy was succeeded by his son, James, who continued a policy of territorial expansion by seizing any remaining MacQuillan lands in the Route and in 1596 he annexed lands belonging to his Scottish cousins in the Glynns.[8]

From an English perspective, governed by the practice of primogeniture, the succession became confused after Sir James died (1601) and his eldest son and natural heir Alexander was passed over in favour of his younger brother (and Antrim's father) Randal Arranach. In fact in the context of the Irish and

---

[4] T. E. McNeill, 'Lordships and Invasions: Ulster 1177–1500', pp. 73–5, and Ciaran Brady, 'Sixteenth century Ulster and the failure of Tudor reform', in C. Brady, M. O'Dowd and B. Walker (eds.), *Ulster an illustrated history* (London, 1989)', pp. 91–2; Dawson, 'Two kingdoms or three?', pp. 116–17.
[5] Morgan, 'The end of Gaelic Ulster', pp. 13–16.
[6] *Ibid.*, p. 15; Constantia Maxwell, *Irish history from contemporary sources (1509–1610)* (London, 1923), pp. 299–300.
[7] Raymond Gillespie, *Colonial Ulster. The settlement of East Ulster 1600–1641* (Cork, 1985), p. 4.
[8] For details on the MacQuillans, see Edmund Curtis, 'The MacQuillan or Mandeville lords of the Route', *RIA Proc.*, section C, 44 (1937–8), pp. 99–113, and George Hill, 'The MacQuillans of the Route,' *UJA*, 1st series, 9 (1861), pp. 57–70, 241; M. Webb, 'The clan of MacQuillins of Antrim', *UJA*, 1st series, 8 (1860), pp. 251–60. For an interesting discussion of the history of Dunluce, see F. J. Bigger, 'Some historical notes about Dunluce and its builders', *UJA*, 2nd series, 11, no. 4 (Oct. 1905), pp. 154–62, and 2, no. 1 (Jan. 1906), pp. 22–35.

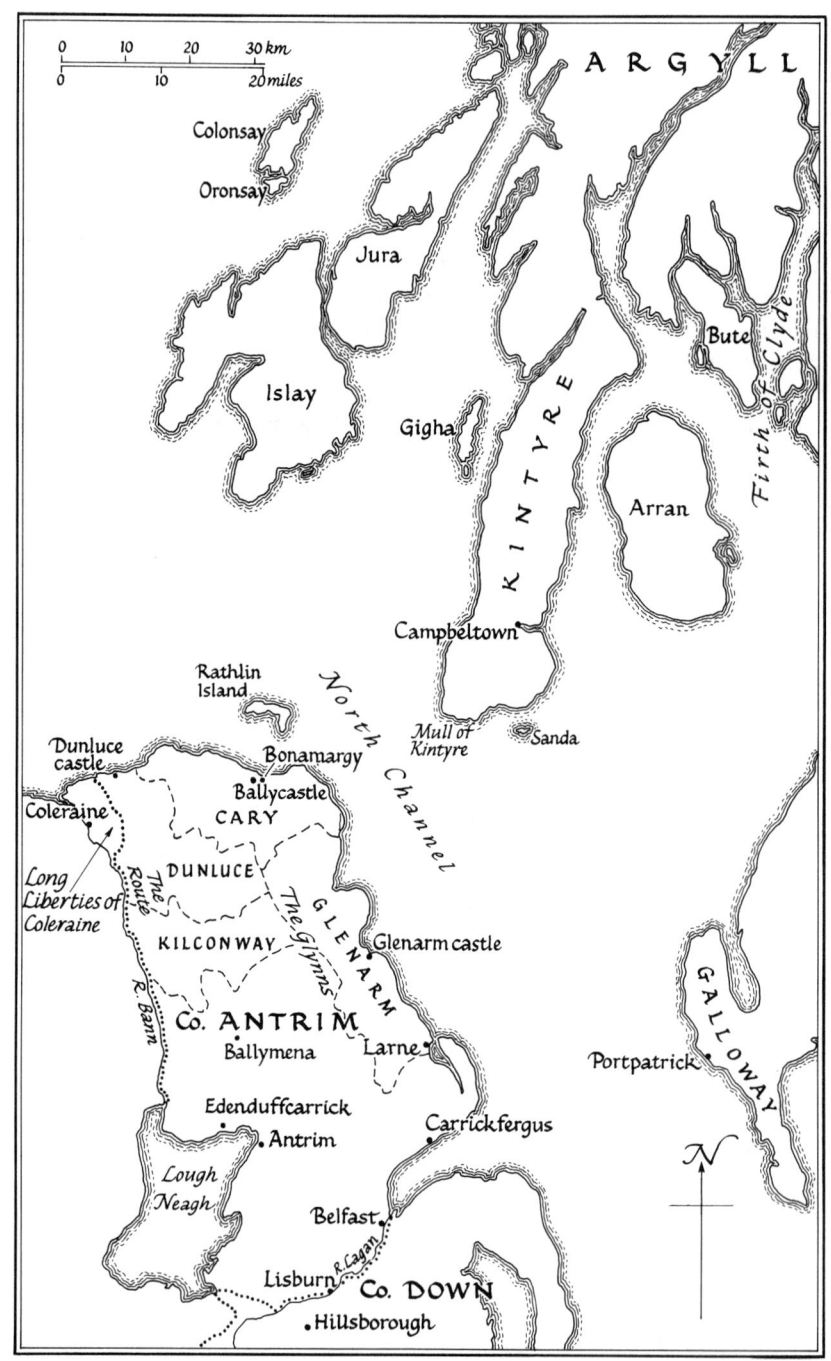

Map 2 The MacDonnell archipelago

Scottish Gaelic worlds, where 'the man with the strongest following in the lordship' was usually nominated as leader, this was by no means unusual; nevertheless, keenly aware of the changing world in which he was operating, Randal was quick to secure legal recognition from England for his new found position.[9] By skilfully demonstrating his loyalty to the crown (he not only dissociated himself from his rebellious father-in-law, the earl of Tyrone, after his defeat at Kinsale in 1601 but also supported James VI's expedition against his cousin Angus who had also risen in rebellion), Randal was able to secure in 1603 a legal title to the 333,907 acres in the Route and Glynns which he had, at least in English eyes, usurped.[10] Despite this, his claim to fishing rights on the River Bann was disputed by Sir Arthur Chichester;[11] while his title to much of the County Antrim estate was later challenged by his nephew, Alexander, who in 1614–15 conspired with his Irish and Scottish kinsmen to recover by force the inheritance which might otherwise have been his.[12] By and large the king sided with Randal. In addition to confirming by Act of Parliament his legal title to the County Antrim estate, James VI and I rewarded Randal with a knighthood in 1603, then in 1618 he created him Viscount Dunluce.[13] Finally, on 12 December 1620, the king elevated him to the dignity of earl of Antrim, much to the disgust of Chichester who regarded him as a 'cankered and malicious person ... who from a beggar is made great and yet rests unthankful'.[14]

The rise of Clan Donald in Ireland was mirrored by its decline in Scotland.

---

[9] Mary O'Dowd, 'Gaelic economy and society', in Ciaran Brady and Raymond Gillespie (eds.), *Natives and newcomers. Essays on the making of Irish colonial society 1534–1641* (Dublin, 1986), p. 123, and Michelle O Riordan, *The Gaelic mind and the collapse of the Gaelic world* (Cork, 1990), pp. 10–11.

[10] Maxwell, *Irish history*, pp. 300–1; Michael Perceval-Maxwell, *Scottish migration to Ulster in the reign of James I* (London, 1973), pp. 3–10, 47–8, 60–4.

[11] T. M. Healey, *Stolen waters. A page in the conquest of Ulster* (London, 1913), pp. 108, 113, 120–30, 180–7 and 194–9.

[12] Lord Deputy Arthur Chichester also (unsuccessfully) challenged his title, Chichester to Argyll, 12 April 1608 (NLS, MS 3368, fo. 26); *Cal. SP Dom., 1629–31*, p. 39; Bigger, 'Some historical notes', pp. 25–34; Stevenson, *Alasdair MacColla*, pp. 39–41; Raymond Gillespie, *Conspiracy. Ulster plots and plotters in 1615* (Belfast, 1987); idem, *Colonial Ulster*, pp. 85, 87–8, 109, 130. For a transcript of the trial, see Thomas Gogarty, 'The Ulster roll of gaol delivery, 1615', *Archiv. Hib.*, 6 (1917), pp. 83–93.

[13] For this honour he paid the duke of Buckingham £5,000, C. R. Mayes, 'The early Stuarts and the Irish peerage', *EHR*, 73, no. 287 (Apr. 1958), p. 240.

[14] Cited in Healey, *Stolen waters*, p. 126. Also see James I to Chichester, 3 May 1613 (BL, Add. MSS 4794, fo. 233); *Cal. SP Ire., 1615–25*, p. 307. His rapid rise to power excited much jealousy and every effort was made by his Protestant peers to discredit him. For instance, he was accused of harbouring popish priests, *ibid.*, pp. 324–5, 337.

As Lords of the Isles, the MacDonalds had ruled the Western Highlands and Islands from the late fourteenth century until the forfeiture of the lordship in 1493 wreaked havoc among the already feuding clans. The death in 1546 of Donald Dubh, 'the last chief of the MacDonalds to be recognized by the entire clan', enabled Clan Campbell, which had long been established in mainland Argyll, to emerge, by the late sixteenth century, as the most powerful sept in the Western Highlands.[15] Campbell power was further enhanced after a series of feuds – instigated by Clan Donald South – which had so destabilized the west of Scotland that King James VI was forced in 1607 to declare forfeit their hereditary lands of Kintyre and Jura. The king then promptly assigned them to Archibald Campbell, seventh earl of Argyll, on the condition that the land was not leased to any MacDonald.[16]

Despite this royal injunction Randal (and later his son) endeavoured time and again to recover these forfeited estates.[17] In 1627 he offered to purchase lands in Islay from Sir John Campbell of Calder for £5,170; early in 1633 he attempted (again without success) to acquire Kintyre and Jura.[18] Then in January 1635 Randal finally managed to buy Kintyre and Jura for which he paid Lord Kintyre (Argyll's younger son) £1,500 'earnest money' plus £250 for legal expenses.[19] However, just as the transaction was being finalized Kintyre's elder brother Lord Lorne (who succeeded his father as the eighth earl of Argyll in October 1638) discovered who the true purchaser of his brother's estates was and with 'a great number of friends', hurried to Edinburgh to frustrate the deal. Lorne petitioned the Scottish privy council to intervene on the grounds that 'there were many of the name of McDonnell dwelling there and if they got one of the McDonnells to dwell there and to be their master that they would prove rebels'.[20] In addition to destabilizing the political *status quo* in the Isles, Lorne claimed that Antrim 'would bring in a number of priests and so make the people turn papists'. Finally he threatened that if the transaction went through he would not be able to 'quiet his own

---

[15] Dawson, 'Two kingdoms or three?', p. 120.
[16] Stevenson, *Alasdair MacColla*, pp. 20–8; Stewart, 'Peoples of the Clan Ranald', pp. 37, 57. Islay was forfeited a decade later.
[17] The MacDonalds, with Irish support, had tried to regain these lands in 1614–15, Bagwell, *Stuarts*, I, 142–3.
[18] *Clan Donald*, II, 714–17. He briefly leased lands in Islay in 1613, Lee, *Great Britain's Solomon*, pp. 217–18.
[19] PRONI, D2977/Kintyre papers; Lord Lorne to Morton, January [1635] (NLS, MS 79, fo. 34).
[20] PRONI, D2977/Kintyre papers and privy council to Charles I, 15 January 1635 (Inverary castle, Argyll muniments, bundle 3/66).

name but that they and the MacDonnells would be still in blood'.[21] Convinced by his plea, the council ordered (on 14 January) the clerk of the register of seisins 'to discharge ... any enfeoffment or seisin' taken out by the first earl, Lord Dunluce or anyone else in Kintyre.[22] To make sure his case was also won with the king Lorne complained to the earl of Morton, a privy councillor in England and Scotland, of his brother's 'ignorant carriage in all his business' and begged Morton to inform the king of this 'and to secure myself again of His Majesty's favour'.[23]

It was almost too late, for back in Kintyre an extract of seisin (dated 16 January) had already been issued to Archibald Stewart, Randal's representative and factor, for the lands.[24] Nevertheless, early in February 1635, the privy council (with the king's full backing) issued a further order forbidding any member of Clan Donald or their representatives from taking possession of land in Jura or Kintyre and ordered Stewart to destroy the original extract of seisin.[25] Randal made no further effort to regain his Scottish patrimony, but his son resolved that, even though the Campbells had won the first round, the fight was far from finished.

MacDonnell failure in Scotland was compensated by spectacular successes in Ireland. Randal's meteoric rise within the Irish peerage was largely due to his enthusiastic support for James I's schemes for the plantation of Ulster; and on numerous occasions the king thanked him for 'his services in improving those barren and uncultivated parts of the country, and planting a colony there'.[26] As it was, the concept of plantation was familiar to Randal who had been fostered on the Scottish island of Arran (hence his name Randal Arranach) and thus exposed to James's (unsuccessful) attempts to 'plant' the troublesome Highlands with Scottish Lowlanders during the later sixteenth century. In fact one recent scholar has suggested that the charter issued to Randal after 1603, which enabled him to divide his estate into four manors with a stipulation that a castle be built on each, represented 'in embryo ... the

---

[21] *Ibid.*
[22] *Reg. privy council Scot., 1633–35*, pp. 463–4.
[23] Lord Lorne to Morton, 25 January [1635] (NLS, MS 79, fo. 34). Also see Sir James Balfour, *The historical works of Sir James Balfour* (3 vols., Edinburgh, 1824), III 70. The first earl also had recourse to powerful friends at court. He begged the marquis of Hamilton to support his case on the grounds that Lorne was simply unwilling that anyone 'should come there but those that should be at his command' and he promised to treat these lands as he had his own in Ulster; see first earl of Antrim to Hamilton, 10 February 1635 (SRO, GD 406/1/283).
[24] PRONI, D2977/Kintyre papers.
[25] *Reg. privy council Scot., 1633–35*, pp. 479–80, 493–4.
[26] Maxwell, *Irish history*, p. 301.

pattern of the Ulster plantation' and that Randal himself formed an important human link between the Irish and Scottish plantations.[27] Then in 1610 Randal surrendered nine townlands (or roughly 2,000 acres) near Coleraine for the 'official' plantation of Ulster.[28]

However, whether informally (as was the case in Counties Antrim and Down) or officially (as in the six escheated counties where the confiscated lands of Irish lords were granted to Protestant English and Scots settlers), the introduction of 'civility, order and government amongst a barbarous and unsubdued people' (as James I termed it) was central to the whole concept of plantation.[29] James's distaste for the native Irish was clearly apparent and it was shared by many other British statesmen and politicians. Thus Lord Deputy Sir Arthur Chichester described them as 'a proud, obstinate, and disobedient people', as 'a barbarous, irreligious, and headstrong people, inured to crimes and spoils'; while Ireland was, in his opinion, 'that barbarous land where the people know not God, nor care not for man'.[30] But, unlike the Amerindians (whom the Spaniards regarded as a lower order of humanity), the native Irish, though they may have been barbarous, licentious pagans, were, according to their English masters, capable of being civilized.[31] Stuart policy in Ireland was founded upon this premise.

If they were to survive and succeed in this 'civilizing' English world and be considered 'worthy subjects', the MacDonnells therefore had no alternative but to adopt English customs and habits. Randal was merely one of the first Gaelic lords to adopt British ways and to recognize the economic advantages of the English system of landlord–tenant relations and of a commercial economy – both of which were introduced with the plantation.[32]

---

[27] Lee, *Great Britain's Solomon*, p. 212. See also pp. 199, 213 on the plantation in Scotland.
[28] George Hill, *An historical account of the plantation in Ulster in the seventeenth century: 1608–1620* (Belfast, 1877; reprint, Shannon, 1980), pp. 395–7. In return the king reduced by half the rent for the remainder of his estates and ensured that the title to his property received parliamentary approval.
[29] James I to Chichester, 21 December 1612 (*Cal. SP Ire., 1611–14*, p. 310).
[30] Cited in Lee, *Great Britain's Solomon*, pp. 203–4.
[31] Nicholas P. Canny, *The Elizabethan conquest of Ireland. A pattern established 1565–76* (New York, 1976), pp. 119, 125–7, 133–5, 160–1.
[32] The first earl's qualities as a landlord and local magnate have received recent scholarly attention from Michael Perceval-Maxwell in his study of Scottish migration to Ulster and from Raymond Gillespie in his monograph on East Ulster: Perceval-Maxwell, *Scottish migration*, pp. 60–7, 229–34, and Gillespie, *Colonial Ulster*, pp. 16, 70, 75, 90–101, 106, 118–20, 130–8, 145–9, 155–8, 230–2. See also MacDonald, 'A fragment of an Irish MSS', p. 276.

For instance between 1609 and 1626 he leased considerable amounts of land to Lowland Scots and within a relatively short period of time there was a thriving colony of Scottish Protestants living in the baronies of Dunluce and Glenarm.[33] Certainly the town of Dunluce consisted 'of many tenements, after the fashion of the Pale, peopled for the most part with Scotsmen'.[34] Randal's far-sighted policies soon paid off, for by 1629 the earl of Clanricard noted that he 'hath good tenants and is very well paid his rents';[35] whereas, in stark contrast, many of his native Irish neighbours, unable to adapt to the changing economic environment, were forced into debt and bankruptcy.[36]

In addition to progressive economic and agrarian policies, Randal improved his property by building castles at Kilwaughter, Ballygally, Glenarm and Ballycastle.[37] Though the outer buildings at Dunluce were defensive in character the inner great house – 'a good house of stone with many lodgings and other rooms'[38] – built by Randal was more like an English manor house with three mullioned, two-storeyed bay windows and leaded, diamond-shaped panes of glass. Likewise his 'pleasant house' at Glenarm was built to impress both the natives and his peers and to demonstrate his 'Englishness'.[39] Without doubt Randal's principal residences rivalled any of the other planter castles at Belfast, Carrickfergus, Mountjoy or Donegal and were 'very richly

---

[33] Perceval-Maxwell, *Scottish migration*, pp. 231–2. Also see pp. 39–40 below.

[34] 'A report of the voluntary works done by servitors ... within the counties of Downe, Antryme, and Monahan' (PRONI, T811/3, fo. 13). A study of settlement patterns during this period by an historical geographer confirms that the unofficial plantation, spearhead in County Antrim by Randal, had been tremendously successful in attracting British immigrants, William J. Smyth, 'Society and settlement in seventeenth century Ireland: the evidence of the "1659 census"' in William J. Smyth and Kevin Whelan (eds.), *Common ground. Essays on the historical geography of Ireland presented to T. Jones Hughes* (Cork, 1988), pp. 73–5.

[35] Earl of Clanricard to earl of Essex, 14 November 1629 (BL, Add. MSS 46188, fo. 120). I am grateful to Tom Connors for bringing this document to my attention.

[36] O Riordan, *The Gaelic mind*, pp. 12–13.

[37] The first earl probably built his castle at Glenarm during the 1630s. A map dating from *c.* 1580 shows an extensive two-storey building near the site of the present castle with a cross on it, but this was probably either a church or a priory, PRO, MPF 88. Richard Bartlett's map of 1602–3 also shows a church-like structure, *ibid.*, 35. I am grateful to Hector McDonnell for discussing this source with me.

[38] 'A report of the voluntary works done by servitors ... within the counties of Downe, Antryme, and Monahan' (PRONI, T811/3, fo. 13).

[39] Monro to [Argyll], 11 June 1642 (NLS, MS 3368, fos. 1–3). I am grateful to Hector McDonnell for providing me with this information.

furnished' – presumably according to the latest London fashions.⁴⁰ He also promoted the Protestant religion and rebuilt or refurbished churches for his Protestant tenants.⁴¹ In addition Randal tried to streamline his military establishment in accordance with the English example and in 1625, as the Spaniards threatened to invade Ireland once again, he asked that his men be suitably attired with his colours (crimson and yellow tafetta) and properly equipped with the latest weapons since he was loath to let them 'go to the field like kernes'.⁴² Small wonder, then, that the first earl was *persona grata* with James I, and in a letter to the lord deputy the king drew attention to 'his dutiful behaviour to the state and the example of his civil and orderly life endeavour very much of the reformation and civilizing of those rude parts ... where he dwells'.⁴³

Randal's son, Viscount Dunluce, was a particularly valuable asset in this quest for 'civility' and survival. For instance in 1613 in return for an assurance that the Antrim estate would pass to his legitimate heirs by Ellis O'Neill, Randal affianced his four-year-old son to the daughter of James Hamilton, first earl of Abercorn.⁴⁴ Of Scottish descent, Abercorn was a leading, wealthy planter in County Tyrone with Catholic sympathies; more important, he was a great favourite of James VI and I and related to the marquis of Hamilton.⁴⁵ To consolidate further the alliance between the planter and the Gael, Randal also requested that, in the event of his early death, Abercorn be awarded the wardship of his young son who was to be raised in Abercorn's household 'for the better education of his said son and heir'. James I, eager to have the youth reared 'religiously and civilly', readily agreed.⁴⁶ Thus Randal secured in one fell swoop the MacDonnell claim to his Ulster estate, the succession of his

---

⁴⁰ Earl of Clanricard to earl of Essex, 14 November 1629 (BL, Add. MSS 46188, fo. 120).
⁴¹ MacDonald, 'A fragment of an Irish MSS', pp. 278, 280. During the 1630s, as Randal tried to lay claim to some of his patrimonial lands in the Isles, he promised to treat these estates as he had his own in Ulster; to rebuild the ruined churches and populate the countryside with 'land Scots men' or Lowlanders, first earl of Antrim to Hamilton, 10 February 1635 (SRO, GD 406/1/283).
⁴² Antrim to Lord Deputy [Falkland], 5 December 1625 (*Cal. SP Ire., 1625–32*, p. 64).
⁴³ James I to Chichester, 3 May 1613 (BL, Add. MSS 4794, fo. 233).
⁴⁴ James I to Chichester, 5 February and 3 May 1613 (BL, Add. MSS 4794, fos. 223, 233); *Cal. SP Ire., 1625–32*, p. 325.
⁴⁵ Perceval-Maxwell, *Scottish migration*, pp. 232, 272, 325–7.
⁴⁶ James I to Chichester, 5 February 1613 (BL, Add. MSS 4794, fo. 223). Also see *Clan Donald*, II, 711, 714–15; D. J. MacDonald, *Clan Donald* (Loanhead, 1978), pp. 261–74. On the importance of fostering in the Gaelic world see Kenneth Nicholls, *Gaelic and gaelicized Ireland in the middle ages* (Dublin, 1972), p. 79.

heir, a firm alliance with the powerful house of Hamilton and easy access to the royal ear.[47]

Yet despite furthering the plantation in East Ulster with enthusiasm and courting the king, Randal upheld – and exposed his children to – traditional Gaelic values, the Gaelic language and, above all, the Catholic religion.[48] For Randal (as for many of his contemporaries) 'religion was a public duty, not a private opinion or a voluntary profession';[49] and he publicly demonstrated his devotion by building a religious house at St Patrick's Purgatory at Lough Derg and by giving a yearly pension to the prior there.[50] In 1625 Randal also built a well and chapel in honour of St Bridget near the town of Athlone in County Roscommon. Closer to home he also encouraged the Franciscans to maintain a friary at Bonamargy near Ballycastle which became the headquarters from which they ministered to his tenants and set out on missions to the Western Isles.[51] Furthermore between 1625 and 1627 Randal sent his eldest son for eighteen months to France, allegedly to complete his education and to master the language; but presumably he was also eager (as his enemies suggested) to expose the youth to continental Catholicism.[52]

However, by sending his son to Europe the earl was also grooming him for a career at court for, as Caroline Hibbard has recently noted, 'Foreign travel had come to be regarded as almost a prerequisite of entry into the upper ranks

---

[47] As late as 1636 he promised the marquis of Hamilton that if his son failed to attend him as instructed 'Your lordship shall see what punishment I will inflict upon him for his neglect', first earl of Antrim to Hamilton, 22 April 1636 (SRO, GD 406/1/333).
[48] *Clan Donald*, II, 719.
[49] Patrick Collinson, *The Elizabethan puritan movement* (London, 1967), p. 25.
[50] MacDonald, 'A fragment of an Irish MSS', p. 280.
[51] *The miscellany of the Irish Archaeological Society* (Irish Archaeological Society, vol. 1, Dublin, 1846), pp. 176–7. I am grateful to Tom Connors for bringing this reference to my attention. On Bonamargy, see Gillespie, *Colonial Ulster*, p. 92; Cathaldus Giblin (ed.), *The Irish Franciscan mission to Scotland 1619–1646. Documents from Roman archives* (Dublin, 1964), pp. xi, 32–3, 101–2, 105–6, 175, 180–1; *idem*, 'Francis MacDonnell O.F.M., son of the first earl of Antrim (d. 1636)', *Seanchas Ardmhacha*, 8, no. 1 (1976–7), pp. 51–2; MacDonald, 'A fragment of an Irish MSS', pp. 278, 280; Ronald Black, 'Coll Ciotach', *Transactions of the Gaelic Society of Inverness*, 48 (1972–4), pp. 221–3.
[52] Antrim to Wentworth, 19 September 1632 (SCL, Strafford MSS 22, fo. 101), and *Cal. SP Ire., 1625–32*, pp. 81, 186, 689. How exactly Dunluce spent his time in France is unclear: presumably he did indeed master the French language; certainly he enjoyed the company of other Irish, Catholic youths (such as Lord Roscommon's son, George Talbot, Lord Louth's son and Father Robert Netterville), *ibid.*, p. 168.

of royal service for the nobility and aspiring gentry.'[53] In the spring of 1627 Viscount Dunluce returned from France and was presented at the English court of King Charles I and his French queen, Henrietta Maria.[54] He was to remain there for the next ten years and Charles I, anxious to keep the powerful earl of Antrim in line, insisted that all Dunluce's visits to Ireland were brief.[55] The young viscount was allegedly 'a tall, clean-limbed, handsome man with red hair';[56] and certainly he made a favourable impression in London and was later described as 'one of the best courtiers in the three kingdoms'.[57] One privy councillor even predicted that 'it is not to be doubted, but that his good p[ar]tes and virtuous qualities will soon improve him within that favour and good opinion His Majesty is pleased to conceive of him'.[58]

Few details on Dunluce's career as a young bachelor at court appear to have survived, except that he was eager to become a military entrepreneur like many of his contemporaries. Over the summer of 1635 the French ambassador, desperate to secure Catholic troops for the continental wars, approached Dunluce – whom he described as 'a person of quality' – and persuaded him to raise two regiments of Irish troops for service in France. Dunluce readily agreed; but his profiteering venture was stillborn because the king refused to give him permission for the levy.[59]

No doubt Dunluce's other preoccupation was to find a suitable spouse.[60] As it was, in 1613 the first earl had betrothed his four-year-old son to Lady Lucy Hamilton, Abercorn's daughter, and had promised to pay a 'bride price' of £3,000; however, fifteen years later Lady Lucy was jilted in favour of one of James Stewart duke of Lennox's daughters.[61] Ultimately nothing came of this match either. Yet it is noteworthy that the first earl, who spent

---

[53] Caroline M. Hibbard, 'The role of a queen consort. The household and court of Henrietta Maria, 1625–1642', in Ronald G. Asch and Adolf M. Birke (eds.), *Princes, patronage, and the nobility* (Oxford, 1991), pp. 396–7, also see p. 411.
[54] Dunluce travelled back to London with the English ambassador, *Cal. SP Ire., 1625–32*, p. 203.
[55] *Cal. SP Dom., 1627–8*, p. 175; *Cal. SP Ire., 1625–32*, pp. 248, 428; *Cal. SP Dom., 1628–9*, p. 377.
[56] *DNB* 'Randal MacDonnell'; Clarendon, *Rebellion*, III, 509. The only surviving portrait of Dunluce dates from the Restoration period: see frontispiece.
[57] MacDonald, 'A fragment of an Irish MSS', pp. 280, 282.
[58] [Conway] to Antrim, 31 May 1627 (*Cal. SP Ire., 1625–32*, p. 239/PRO, SP 63/244, fo. 691).
[59] Séneterre to Bouthillier, 15/25 July 1635 (PRO, PRO31/3/68, fo. 88v). Also see *ibid.*, fos. 95, 102v, 137v, and 31/3/69, fo. 12r–v.
[60] On the importance of securing a 'good match', see Lawrence Stone, *The family, sex and marriage in England 1500–1800* (London, 1977), pp. 42, 60–1.
[61] *Cal. SP Ire., 1625–32*, pp. 325, 480, and *Clan Donald*, II, 714–15, 779.

considerable amounts of time in London during these years, perceived his rank and resources to be on a par with those of Lennox, who was the king's cousin.[62]

Having failed to wed his son to a Stewart, the first earl turned to Honora Burke, a half-sister of the earl of Essex and the daughter of Frances Walsingham and the fourth earl of Clanricard and St Albans, the most powerful Old English grandee in Connaught. Between 1629 and 1630 a possible union was seriously considered by both families and, for his part, the first earl offered to purchase the couple an English estate and to pay a 'bride price' of £5,000.[63] Finally the match was dismissed by the countess of St Albans as 'most inconvenient and dangerous'. Not only was Viscount Dunluce 'Tirons grandchild' but, to make matters even worse, his seat was 'so far remote for my daughter from all her friends and acquaintance[s], the uttermost north part of Ireland, and a country so different in condition and breeding'.[64]

This prejudice against suitors from the Celtic fringe was not, however, shared by Katherine Villiers, widowed duchess of Buckingham since the murder of her husband, Charles I's favourite, in 1628; for early in April 1635, following intense speculation and cruel gossip, the couple were married.[65] The duchess was without doubt the most eligible widow at court. Her father, Francis Manners, sixth earl of Rutland, was the leading noble of the Midlands while her mother was the daughter and heiress of a rich Wiltshire gentleman, Sir Francis Knyvet. In 1620, at the tender age of seventeen, she had married George Villiers, marquis (and later duke) of Buckingham; she bore him four children (Charles, George, Francis and Mary) and remained a loyal and devoted wife to him until his assassination. Together with her sons she inherited an enormous fortune from Buckingham which included his London mansions – Wallingford House, Walsingham House and York House – regarded by contemporaries as amongst the finest places in Europe. These were all near Whitehall. There were nineteen more modest properties on the Strand, a mansion in Chelsea and another, New Hall, north of

---

[62] While in London he appears to have stayed in Sir William Smith's house, *Cal. SP Dom., 1625–6*, p. 64. For further details on Lennox, see pp. 50–1 below.
[63] Earl of Clanricard to earl of Essex, 14 November 1629 (BL, Add. MSS 46188, fo. 120).
[64] Countess of St Albans and Clanricard to earl of Essex, *c.* January 1630 (*ibid.*, fos. 124, 126); Lawrence Stone, *The crisis of the aristocracy 1558–1641* (Oxford, 1965), p. 626.
[65] Knowler, *Letters*, I, 413. 'This which she hath done' Archbishop Laud waspishly noted 'being but a piece of women's frailty', Laud to Wentworth, 21 April 1635 (*Laud works*, VII, 124). The marriage was consummated and the duchess conceived almost at once but miscarried in the autumn of 1635, see Garrard to [Conway], 18 September 1635 (*Cal. SP Dom., 1635*, p. 385) and Garrard to Wentworth, 3 October 1635 (SCL, Strafford MSS 15, fo. 232).

Chelmsford in Essex. The duchess was extremely wealthy in her own right. She received an annual income of roughly £4,550 from the Irish customs and a state pension of £6,000; she was sole heir both to her mother's fortune and to extensive, unentailed portions of the Manners estates in Northamptonshire and Yorkshire; and also owned estates near Winslow and Bletchley in Buckinghamshire and others in Leicestershire.[66] In addition to being rich Katherine had, after Buckingham's assassination, reverted to Catholicism which made her an even more attractive catch for the devoutly Catholic MacDonalds.

Of her personality little is known, though Clarendon described her as a woman of 'very great wit and spirit'.[67] Buckingham's most recent biographer suggested that 'Katherine was no doormat. She had a temper to match her husband's ... [and] could be jealous ... Yet she could also be remarkably generous and understanding.'[68] An examination of her household accounts between 1629 and 1634, which she carefully annotated in her rather childish hand, provide a fascinating insight into the style and quality of her life. As one would expect she lived at the height of luxury with attendants at every turn. She had a delicate palate for wine and exotic food; her wine bill (white wine, canary wine, muscadet, port and claret) over six months amounted to £73-15-04 and a small fortune was spent on buying exotic delicacies such as pistachio nuts, almonds, orange chips, damsons, apricots, cherries, amber and raspberries, sweet fennel seeds, marshmallow roots, red sugar aloes, tartar oil and shavings of ivory.[69] Despite their repetitive monotony these

---

[66] Roger Lockyer, *Buckingham. The life and political career of George Villiers, first duke of Buckingham 1592–1628* (London, 1981), pp. 26, 56–8, 60, 119–20, 212–16, 286, 412–13, 419, 460–2; E. B. Chancellor, *The private palaces of London, past and present* (London, 1908), pp. 27, 40–6, 161–5; Edgar Shephard, *The old royal palace of Whitehall* (London, 1902), pp. 176–7. For details of the duchess's indenture for Irish customs, see SCL, Strafford MSS 12, fo. 289, and Lawrence Stone, *Family and fortune. Studies in aristocratic finance in the sixteenth and seventeenth centuries* (Oxford, 1973), pp. 197–200; and on her pension, *Montagu MSS*, p. 147. In June 1634 it was reported from court that the duchess of Buckingham and the earl of Rutland (her uncle) had divided the Rutland estate between them: the earl was to receive an annual income of £7,000; his heir – Mr John Manners – Belvoir and £2,000 per annum; 'all the rest falls upon the duchess and her children', Garrard to Wentworth, 3 June 1634 (Knowler, *Letters*, I, 261). See also *Victoria history of the countries of England. Buckinghamshire*, ed. William Page (4 vols., London, 1905–28), III, 466, and IV, 277.

[67] Clarendon, *Rebellion*, III, 509.

[68] Lockyer, *Buckingham*, p. 60.

[69] Accounts of the household of the duchess of Buckingham, 1629–34 (Bodl., Eng. Misc.C.208, fos. 56–7, 74–81, 109–19, 122–32). I am grateful to Dr John Adamson for bringing this item to my attention. Though Katherine's household accounts for the years after her marriage are sadly lacking, the couple's subsequent expenditure suggests that her husband shared her expensive tastes and habits, see pp. 61–3 below.

accounts suggest that she was pampered and extravagant, yet fastidious, resilient and an extremely shrewd business woman. Extant letters (roughly thirty in all) which she either wrote or received between her marriage in 1635 and her death in 1649 confirm this impression and illustrate her loyalty and devotion to her second husband – to whom she also appears to have been temperamentally well matched. She was his closest confidante and adviser, acting as his deputy, secretary and watchdog, and was prepared to abandon her friends, her royal mentors and even her children for his sake.

The duchess was forced to pay a high price for marrying a Catholic from Ireland seven years her junior. Every measure was taken to ensure that Dunluce, who was obviously regarded by many at court as something of a 'gold digger', should have no jurisdiction over her children's inheritance.[70] Moreover, shortly after their marriage, the couple had to agree that the contents of York House, including the first duke's renowned art collection, the Chelsea house, and various manors and lands in Herefordshire, Derbyshire, Yorkshire, Rutland, Essex and Buckinghamshire would pass intact to the young duke of Buckingham.[71] In addition, the duchess was snubbed by her contemporaries. Her friends were all 'ill-satisfied with her marriage' which had lost her much ground 'with the king himself as well as all others of quality'.[72] Even Wentworth in Dublin 'conceived some displeasure against the young lord'[73] and only after much coaxing agreed to treat him 'with all outward civility possible'.[74] However, within a relatively short period of time, the court – led by the king – became reconciled to the match, and the duchess was restored to her former position of favour.[75] By the summer of

---

[70] All jurisdiction over her daughter, Lady Mary, was handed over to her father-in-law Philip, earl of Pembroke, and Montgomery, lord chamberlain; while the well-being of her sons became the responsibility of William Laud, archbishop of Canterbury. Pembroke, Sir Robert Pye, William, earl of Newcastle, and George, earl of Rutland, were appointed legal guardians of the children and trustees of the estate of the young duke (a ward of the king), Knowler, *Letters*, I, 413.

[71] The collection included paintings by Michelangelo, Breugel, Correggio, Dürer, Holbein, Rubens, Raphael, Van Dyke and Titian: see indenture between Lord Dunluce, Katherine duchess of Buckingham and the earl of Pembroke and Sir Robert Pye, 11 May 1635 (BL, Add. MS 18,914 fos. 2–15); *Cal. SP Dom.*, 1635–6, p. 342; Knowler, *Letters*, I, 427. Other courtiers were concerned how the interests of the first duke's children would be affected if the couple had their own offspring, *ibid.*, 518.

[72] Laud to Wentworth, 26 and 12 May 1635 (*Laud works*, VII, 137 and 135).

[73] Laud to Wentworth, 12 May 1635 (*Laud works*, VII, 133).

[74] Wentworth to Laud, 18 May 1635 (SCL, Strafford MSS 6, fo. 185). Laud thanked Wentworth for supporting Dunluce: 'I shall still be your debtor, and pay as I am able', Laud to Wentworth, 12 June 1635 (*Laud works*, VII, 146), and Laud to Wentworth, 14 July 1635 (*ibid.*, 151). Also see Gardiner, *Eng.*, VIII, 146.

[75] Knowler, *Letters*, I, 427.

1635 even Wentworth, who now referred to Dunluce as 'my creature', had been temporarily won over.[76]

However, it would seem that the first earl never fully accepted his son's marriage. Though he had been initially delighted with the match, and had promised to settle his estate upon his son at once in order to pay off his debts (which on the eve of the marriage were £3,000)[77] and to allow the couple an annual allowance of £2,000, he quickly took umbrage with the duchess and refused to honour his word despite pressure from Wentworth and Laud to do so.[78] His dishonourable behaviour made little difference in the end, for within eighteen months of their wedding the first earl was dead.

The twenty-seven-year-old Dunluce now became the second earl of Antrim and left England for Ireland towards the end of January 1637 amid rumours that he had been disinherited by his father who 'had an older son now living'.[79] The story was untrue: although he did have elder illegitimate brothers the second earl of Antrim was his father's legal heir and primary beneficiary. He was bequeathed the baronies of Dunluce and Kilconway, together with Dunluce castle, which had been described in the late sixteenth century as 'the strongest piece of this realm'.[80] His legitimate younger brother, Alexander, inherited the barony and castle of Glenarm; while his mother – Countess Ellis – received lands in the barony of Cary worth £1,500 per annum and a house at Ballycastle as her jointure. To each of his six daughters the first earl left £2,800; to his illegitimate son Maurice he left an annual allowance of £100.[81] Though the will divided the estate between the first earl's legitimate sons (as was often the practice in Gaelic Ireland), Alexander – in return for 'a certain sum of money yearly for his maintenance'

---

[76] Wentworth to Wandesford, 25 July 1636 (Knowler, *Letters*, II, 22). On Antrim's relations with Wentworth see, *Laud works*, VII, 156; Wentworth to Laud, 14 July 1635 (SCL, Strafford MSS 6, fo. 202); Dunluce to Wentworth, 25 [October?] 1635 (*ibid.*, 15, fos. 303 + 1).

[77] Wentworth to Antrim, 30 July 1636 (SCL, Strafford MSS 21, fo. 149).

[78] *Laud works*, VII, 133; Wentworth to Antrim, 30 July 1636 (SCL, Strafford MSS 21, fo. 149). As Laud was quick to note, 'now my lady duchess is married to his son he [the earl] proves not overkind, or overfull of performance', Laud to Wentworth, 30 November 1635 (*Laud works*, VII, 213–14) and Laud to Wentworth, 8 April 1636 (*ibid.*, 247).

[79] Wentworth to Laud, 28 February 1637 (SCL, Strafford MSS 7, fo. 21). Also see *Laud works*, VII, 312, 330–1.

[80] Bigger, 'Some historical notes', p. 23.

[81] Gillespie, *Colonial Ulster*, p. 148; Hill, *MacDonnells*, pp. 246–7, for further details on the will see pp. 430–7; F. J. Bigger, 'The Bally Castle, County Antrim', *UJA*, 2nd series, 8, no. 1 (Jan. 1902), pp. 7–9. For details on Maurice, see pp. 47–8, 84, 94, 157 below.

– handed over his inheritance to his brother, who also controlled his mother's jointure.⁸²

The new earl's empire – 'thirty miles of territory and vast estates with several castles' – measured nearly 340,000 acres and was divided untidily by the seven Glens of Antrim.⁸³ It was bounded by the River Bann in the west, the Giant's Causeway and the coastal towns of Coleraine and Ballycastle in the north and the ports of Cushendall, Glenarm and Larne in the east,⁸⁴ It comprised four baronies (Dunluce, Cary, Kilconway and Glenarm) in County Antrim, 2,200 acres in the Long Liberties of Coleraine in neighbouring County Londonderry and thirty parishes in the diocese of Down and Connor: the earl ruled in all over 600 townlands.⁸⁵

The estate's topography was varied. All four baronies were littered with patches of bogland and were in places barren, mountainous, wooded or inaccessible, but this was offset by fertile coastal plains suitable for tillage, especially along the north-east coast.⁸⁶ The Glynns was described in 1598 as being 'full of rockie and woodie dales; it stretcheth in length xxiv miles on the one side, being backed with a very steep boggy mountain, and on the other part with the sea, on which side there are many creeks'; while the Route 'is a pleasant and fertile country, being between the Glynns and the River of the Bann'.⁸⁷ Of the 2,200 acres he owned in County Londonderry 2,030 acres were described in 'Civil survey' (of 1654) as 'profitable' and fit for both arable and pastoral farming while only the remaining 170 acres of 'red bog' were described as 'unprofitable and waste'.⁸⁸ Despite the first earl's attempts to improve the roads and build bridges, internal communications remained

---

82 Petition from Alexander MacDonnell, [4 February 1641] (*HMC rep. 5*, app., p. 6/HLRO, main papers, 4/2/1642). Alexander continued to enjoy an interest in the barony of Glenarm and co-signed all deeds concerning the leasing of land in it.
83 Plunkett to [Airoldi], 17/27 September 1671 (John Hanly (ed.), *The letters of Saint Oliver Plunkett, 1625–81, archbishop of Armagh and primate of all Ireland* (Dublin, 1979), p. 247).
84 *Civil survey*, III, 155–7; Hill, *MacDonnells*, pp. 451–67; Webb, 'The clan of the MacQuillins', pp. 258–9.
85 The number of townlands in each parish varied enormously: for example, the parish of Culfeightrin in Cary was the largest parish in the barony with seventy-two townlands, Cahal Dallat, 'Place names in the parish of Culfeightrin', *The Glynns*, 9 (1981), p. 33. For a detailed topographical description, see R. A. Hume, 'Origin and characteristics of the population in the counties of Antrim and Down with notices by M. N. and R. P. Killinchy', *UJA*, 1st series, 1 (1853), pp. 9–26.
86 Gillespie, *Colonial Ulster*, pp. 11–13; *Civil survey*, x, 56–7, 60–1.
87 Edmund Hogan (ed.), *The description of Ireland, and the state thereof as it is at this present in anno 1598* (Dublin, 1878), p. 15.
88 *Civil survey*, III, pp. 155–7.

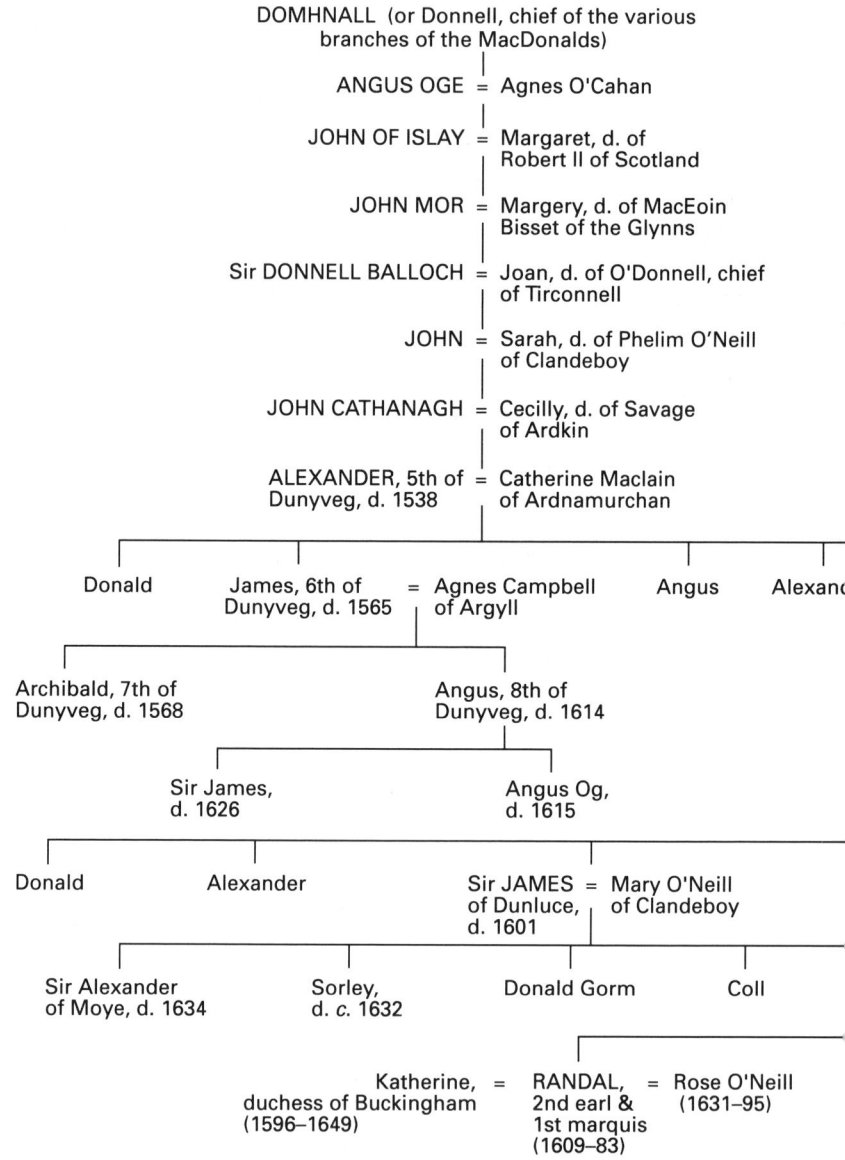

Genealogical table 1 The MacDonnells of Antrim

A man of the 'three kingdoms'

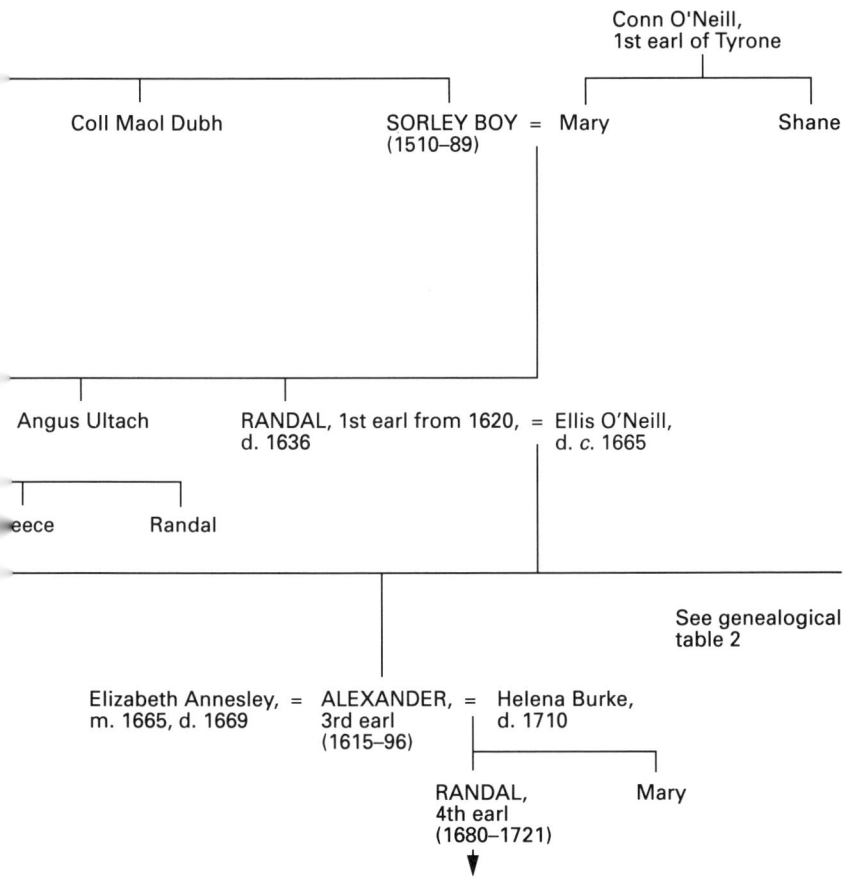

Table 1 *1637 leases: type of lease granted*

	Glenarm	Dunluce	Kilconway	Cary	Total
Fee farm	6	2	1	3	12 [9.75%]
21 years	8	14	17	—	39 [31.70%]
41 years	16	35	14	5	70 [56.91%]
Other	1*	—	1†	—	2 [1.63%]
Total	31	51	33	8	123

* The length of this lease was not stated.
† This lease was for 31 years.
Source: PRONI, D2977, D265.

poor and only two roads, one of which was impassable in winter, linked the Antrim estate with the outside world.[89] Nevertheless, this sprawling, isolated territorial base on the periphery of Stuart Britain made its owner by far the largest landowner in Ulster and one of the greatest in Ireland.[90]

Moreover, the Antrim estate was reputed to be 'very improvable, and shortly like to be [worth] much more than now it is'.[91] Hardly surprisingly, then, the foremost question in the second earl's mind was how best to manage and to exploit his vast inheritance. He discussed the matter at some length with Lord Deputy Wentworth and Archbishop Laud, as well as with his wife, over the spring of 1637. In June he returned to County Antrim with Patrick Darcy, one of Ireland's most able Catholic lawyers, in order to draw up new leases that would put his estates on a nice stable footing.[92] The 123 surviving

---

[89] MacDonald, 'A fragment of an Irish MSS', p. 281; Hill, *MacDonnells*, pp. 377–89; and Jimmy Irvine, 'Richard Dobb's notes for his description of County Antrim, written in 1683', *The Glynns*, 7 (1979), pp. 43–4.

[90] The Antrim estate was sizably larger than the Ormond estate in Counties Tipperary and Kilkenny, which during the seventeenth century was c. 190,000 acres, see William Smyth, 'Territorial, social and settlement heirarchies in seventeenth century Kilkenny', in William Nolan and Kevin Whelan (eds.), *Kilkenny: history and society. Interdisciplinary essays on the history of an Irish county* (Dublin, 1990), p. 156.

[91] Earl of Clanricard to earl of Essex, 14 November 1629 (BL, Add. MSS 46188, fo. 120).

[92] Wentworth to Laud, 28 February 1637 (SCL, Strafford MSS 7, fo. 21); Antrim to Wentworth, 30 April [1637] (*ibid.*, 17, fo. 49). Darcy also represented the earls of Ormond and Cork, Liam O'Malley, 'Patrick Darcy, Galway lawyer and politician, 1598–1668', in Diarmuid Ó Cearbhaill (ed.), *Galway. Town and gown 1484–1984* (Dublin, 1984), pp. 91–9.

estate deeds from 1637, besides painting a vivid picture of life on the Antrim estate during the early seventeenth century, provide a fascinating insight into the earl's ability to husband his resources.[93] The provisions in each lease were remarkably consistent. First came the name of the townland (or quarter of land) being let, together with the amount of rent to be paid biannually in cash to the earl, the amount due to the king and to the receiver who executed the transaction, followed by a provision for distraint if the rent was not paid or if the terms of the lease were not upheld.[94] The earl retained his rights to the estate's assets which included all mills, waterways, mines or quarries, together with all fishing, hawking and gaming privileges. He insisted that the lessee should grind grain at his mill and seek justice at the manor courts of Glenarm, Dunluce, Oldstone or Ballycastle.[95] The tenant was also obliged to offer his best beast or a fine in lieu as heriot, and to improve the land either by fencing or digging ditches and by planting trees (although no fine was levied for failing to do so). Some – but by no means all – of the leases included a

[93] The leases in PRONI, D2977 and D265, are particularly abundant (123 out of 152) for the 1637 re-leasing which the earl set in motion on his return from London. The Glenarm deeds (thirty-one) were made between 4 and 17 August; the Dunluce ones (fifty-one) were completed between 20 June and 17 August with most of the re-leasing taking place in late June and late July; the Kilconway leases (thirty-three) were made between 21 July and 17 August; and the Cary leases (eight) dated from 8 to 27 July. Unfortunately, these deeds are sadly incomplete: later leases often recite a deed dating from 1637 which does not appear to have survived; while a careful comparison of names with the 1641 rental for the barony of Dunluce indicates that for a sizeable number of tenants who leased their property directly from the earl no deed is known at all. See BL, Harl. MS 2138, fos. 111–16.
[94] There was no common agreement on land measurement in seventeenth-century Ulster. There were 40 square perches to a rood and 4 roods to an acre but an English perch was 16.5 feet; while an Irish one varied between 21, 24 and 29 feet! A plantation acre was equivalent to an Irish acre and they were larger than a statute (or English) acre by a ratio of 1.62 to 1. See J. S. Carroll, 'Cromwell's plantation measure', *Decies, Old Waterford Society*, no. 3 (Oct. 1976), p. 25, and Michael MacCarthy-Morrogh, *The Munster plantation. English migration to southern Ireland 1583–1641* (Oxford, 1986), pp. 287–9. By and large all acres given in the 1637 leases were Irish ones of 21 feet to the perch.
[95] Both of these stipulations made good economic sense; moreover, the manor courts provided a point of contact between the tenants and the landlord, or his factors, and an important forum for settling disputes. The first earl made extensive use of his manorial courts and resented any interference with the way he dispensed justice on his territory, Gillespie, *Colonial Ulster*, pp. 90–2, 135–5, 153–5; idem (ed.), *Settlement and survival on an Ulster estate. The Brownlow leasebook 1667–1711* (Belfast, 1988), pp. lvii-lix; I. D. Whyte, *Agriculture and society in seventeenth century Scotland* (Edinburgh, 1979), pp. 44–7. Peter Roebuck, 'The economic situation and functions of substantial landowners 1690–1815: Ulster and lowland Scotland compared', in Rosalind Mitchison and Peter Roebuck (eds.), *Economy and society in Scotland and Ireland, 1500–1939* (Edinburgh, 1988), p. 86, suggests that by the later seventeenth century these manor courts had become redundant.

Table 2 *1637 leases: occupation of lessee*

	Glenarm	Dunluce	Kilconway	Cary	Total
Yeoman	11	13	5	—	29 [23.57%]
Gentleman	15	25	20	6	66 [53.65%]
Esquire	—	—	2	—	2 [1.62%]
Clerk	1	—	1	—	2 [1.62%]
Not stated	4	13	5	2	24 [19.51%]
Total	31	51	33	8	123

Source: PRONI, D2977, D265; BL, Harl. MS 2138, fos. 111–16.

clause obliging the tenant to contribute to 'all risings and general hostings and other public services that will require to be done in or by the inhabitants of the said County of Antrim'.[96]

Leases were, however, mutual contracts. The *quid pro quo* was that the landlord agreed to provide his tenant with land for a fixed period of time and to protect and safeguard his legal, physical and financial interests.[97] The duration of these 1637 leases, as table 1 illustrates, were varied: thirty-nine (or 31.70 per cent) of those which survive ran for twenty-one years (expiring in 1658) and seventy (or 56.91 per cent) ran for forty-one years (expiring in 1678).[98] On the one hand, the notable absence of short leases (under ten years) suggests that there was stability and continuity of tenantry on the Antrim estate while, on the other, it indicates that the earl was prepared to forego any immediate financial reward in return 'for capital investment by the tenants in improving their properties'.[99] Moreover, the surviving 1637 leases indicate that Antrim leased the bulk of his property – at least 80 per cent – either to 'gentlemen' or to substantial 'yeoman' farmers who were presumably better

[96] See, for example, lease between Antrim and Daniel Og McCollin, 24 July [16]37(PRONI D2977/3A/3/24/1).
[97] Antrim's leases were typical of early seventeenth-century leases in Ulster, W. H. Crawford, 'Landlord–tenant relations in Ulster 1609–1820', in *Ir. Econ. & Soc. Hist.*, 2 (1975), p. 7; Gillespie, *Colonial Ulster*, pp. 70–1.
[98] Interestingly, there is no apparent correlation between the length of lease issued and the status or occupation of the lessee in any of the four baronies.
[99] Crawford, 'Landlord–tenant relations', p. 8.

able to husband it (see table 2). For in a society where land was abundant and where good tenants were in constant demand, long improving leases to well-established individuals were a means of retaining better tenants and of preventing neighbours from poaching them.[100] Antrim also encouraged a select handful of tenants, almost 10 per cent according to the surviving leases, to participate in developing his property by leasing land in 'fee farm' (that is in perpetuity) at fixed rents.[101]

The prudent way in which the young earl reorganized his inheritance indicates that he was a sensible, astute individual who was willing to listen to his advisers in London and Dublin and to his factors in Ulster. In the eyes of his contemporaries (and subsequent historians) he qualified, as his father had done, as an 'improving' landlord.[102] First, he encouraged English and Scottish Protestant tenants to settle on his estate – thus Simon Hillman, an alderman from Coleraine who took out a lease of some property in the barony of Dunluce, was obliged to introduce ten English families to Oldstone within three years.[103] The Antrim estate could by now boast well over 300 'British' (or Protestant) families (particularly Lowland Scots), the majority of whom had settled in the baronies of Dunluce and Glenarm.[104] While these Protestant immigrants increased the competition for land and resources, they do not appear to have displaced the established Catholic tenants.[105] At least half of Antrim's known chief tenants (including one of his factors) were Catholic and the incomplete 1641 rental for the barony of Dunluce clearly demonstrates that these men – James MacDonnell, James MacHenry,

---

[100] *Ibid.*, p. 11; I. D. Whyte and K.A. Whyte 'Some aspects of the structure of rural society in seventeenth century lowland Scotland', in T. M. Devine and David Dickson (eds.), *Ireland and Scotland 1600–1850. Parallels and contrasts in economic and social development* (Edinburgh, 1983), p. 40; and Whyte, *Agriculture and society*, pp. 159–62.

[101] David Dickson, 'Property and social structure in eighteenth century south Munster', in L. M. Cullen and F. Furet (eds.), *Ireland and France, seventeenth–twentieth centuries. Towards a comparative study of rural history* (Paris, 1980), p. 130; Roebuck, 'The economic situation', pp. 83–6; and *idem*, 'The making of an Ulster great estate: the Chichesters, barons of Belfast and viscounts of Carrickfergus', *RIA Proc.*, section C, 79 (1979), pp. 16–19, 24–5.

[102] Dickson, 'Property and social structure', pp. 131–3; Gillespie (ed.), *Settlement and survival*, pp. xxvii-xxviii; *idem, Colonial Ulster*, pp. 77, 133; Whyte, *Agriculture and society*, chapter 8; Canny, *Kingdom and colony*, pp. 53–6. For further details on the first earl, see pp. 23–6 above.

[103] PRONI, D265/80.

[104] BL, Add. MS 4770, fo. 280v; Gillespie, *Colonial Ulster*, pp. 55, 59; S. Alexander Blair, 'Presbyterianism in Glenarm', *The Glynns*, 9 (1981), p. 37.

[105] Brady, 'Sixteenth century Ulster', pp. 93–5.

Alexander, Daniel and John MacNaughten, Donnell and William O'Sheyll – acted as landlords to the Protestant immigrants.[106]

The second aspect which earned Antrim the accolade of an 'improving' landlord was the way in which he carved his estate into manageable units of around one or more townlands which were then handed over to men of substance who were prepared to invest time and capital in improving the property and in attracting good farmers. The size of the units leased to the chief tenants varied considerably: at one end of the tenurial spectrum were the Agnews, Stewarts, MacNaughtens and Shaws, who leased very large estates of up to six townlands; at the other were the Dunlops, Hamiltons, MacAuleys and O'Cahans, whose holdings of one townland (while still substantial) were by comparison more modest.[107] These individuals (described in the leases as 'gentlemen' or occasionally as 'yeomen') were made responsible for finding suitable subtenants to farm and improve the land. As has already been noted, the leading Catholic families and their Protestant neighbours in the barony of Dunluce attracted both 'British' and native subtenants and so at a local level there was a high degree of mutual interdependence between Catholics and Protestants. In the barony of Glenarm the Agnew estate was doled out in a similar fashion to around 125 individuals.[108] These subtenants presumably repeated the process by subletting holdings to a silent and undocumented rural peasantry which was undoubtedly as diverse and stratified as the hierarchy above it.[109]

Third, and finally, came other ways in which Antrim sought to 'improve' his estate. Beside the prevalence of long leases, the earl insisted that his rents be paid in cash rather than in kind, as had been the custom, thus stimulating – in theory at least – the development of a market economy. He was also eager to encourage his tenants to enclose poor land, to mark boundaries, to build stone houses and to plant trees.[110] The skilful way he husbanded the land's

---

[106] The religion of many of Antrim's tenants are given in the TCD, MS 838, depositions for County Antrim. For further details, see Jane H. Ohlmeyer, 'A seventeenth century survivor: the political career of Randal MacDonnell, first marquis and second earl of Antrim (1609–83)' (unpublished PhD thesis, Trinity College, Dublin, 1990), appendix 1.2.

[107] The size of a townland varied from 120–600 Irish acres. For further details, see Ohlmeyer, 'A seventeenth century survivor', appendix 1.3.

[108] PRONI, D265/3; SRO, GD 154/512/7 and /515; also see 154/505, /509/1–4, /514; Gillespie, *Colonial Ulster*, p. 228; Ohlmeyer, 'A seventeenth century survivor', appendix 1.2. For further details on the Agnews, see Andrew Agnew, *The Agnews of Lochnaw. A history of the hereditary sheriff of Galloway 1330–1747 ...* (Edinburgh, 1864), pp. 316–25, and John M. Dickson, 'The Agnews in County Antrim', *UJA*, 2nd series, 7, no. 4 (Oct. 1901), pp. 166–71.

[109] Gillespie, *Colonial Ulster*, pp. 116–17; Whyte, *Agriculture and society*, pp. 5, 31–41, 70–9.

[110] See, for example, PRONI, D265/80.

natural resources is also revealing. Fishing rights (especially salmon) were parsimoniously handed out to a select coterie of favoured tenants, while liberty to cut wood and turf was carefully monitored.[111] All rights to coal and mineral deposits were jealously guarded and leased out separately: thus the salt pans and coal mines at Bonamargy were granted for twenty-one years at an annual rent of £80 to Archibald Stewart and Henry Maxwell, chancellor of Connor.

Naturally the earl was well aware of his own achievement and it was with some pride that he reported to Dublin in August 1637 that 'I have compounded my affairs here with my tenants wherein I was not so inward to my [own] profit as to the general good and settlement by binding them to plant [trees] and husband their holdings so near as may be to the manner of England.'[112] Nevertheless, the massive re-leasing raises a number of intriguing questions. First, on what basis – legal or otherwise – was Antrim able to call in, and then reissue, all the unexpired leases made by his father? Second, why did his tenants offer virtually no opposition to such an arbitrary move by a landlord who had spent most of his life in England?

There seems to have been no historical or legal precedent for this unilateral re-leasing in either Ireland or Scotland. It is possible that until this point a number of the tenants were tenants-at-will (that is, they held their farms without a written deed) and therefore had no recourse to legal redress for breach of contract.[113] But there may have been more at stake. A casual remark by Wentworth – that Antrim 'hath improved his estate very much, having absolutely overthrown all his father's leases' – not only suggests that he both knew about and approved of this, but may also have encouraged it in an attempt to further anglicize, civilize and discipline one of the darkest corners of Ireland.[114] Equally significant was the apparent support of the king – no doubt for similar reasons – for the reorganization of the estate. And, as it was, only Cahill O'Hara, who had been involved in endless disputes with the first earl, 'refused to compound and agree with me for he is the only man of my tenants that hath refused to submit, though he is come by what he holds of me'. Significantly Antrim dealt with his recalcitrance by asking Wentworth

---

[111] The MacNaughtens of Benvarden, for instance, enjoyed salmon fishing rights, *ibid.*, D2977.
[112] Antrim to Ormond[?], 2 August 1637 (SCL, Strafford MSS 17, fo. 151).
[113] This was the case in Lowland Scotland where written leases only really appeared in the 1620s and 1630s, Whyte, *Agriculture and society*, pp. 153–4.
[114] Wentworth to Laud, 18 October 1637 (Knowler, *Letters*, II, 120). Certainly Antrim's agent was instructed 'to acquaint you with the abuse and grievances of the country from time to time', Antrim to Wentworth, 21 November 1637 (SCL, Strafford MSS 17, fo. 234).

to discipline him 'more for example, and credit, than any benefit'.[115] When this did not suffice, the king himself intervened on Antrim's behalf.[116] Small wonder that any opposition from the tenants soon crumbled.

But owning, and successfully managing, a vast estate was merely one of the pivots about which Antrim's power and influence turned. Equally important was the way in which he controlled and nurtured his human resources, since his was after all still a patriarchal society, greatly influenced by Gaelic practices, where the ability to call out one's family and followers was as important in determining a man's status as the amount of property he owned. An historian of the Yorkshire gentry of this period has noted that, even in England, 'kinship was not simply a matter of genealogical interest. Contemporary opinion held that ties of blood, however tenuous, involved special obligations and loyalties.'[117] The cultural homogeneity and physical isolation of Antrim's estates accentuated these tendencies, since virtually all members of this Gaelic society enjoyed 'kinship status'.[118] English observers were particularly conscious of these powerful ties. One who feared a Gaelic revival under Antrim's leadership during the 1640s inadvertently paid tribute to the earl's human power base when he warned Ormond to watch the earl carefully 'lest Antrim's friends and dependents in Ulster should under the pretense of serving the king ... carry along designs of reestablishing themselves of their ancient territories and their ancient septs'.[119]

But who exactly were Antrim's 'friends and dependents'? First, he was able to command the loyalty and support of many of his County Antrim tenants (especially the native Irish and Highland Scottish ones) and they formed the backbone of the armies he recruited during the 1640s.[120] Secondly, the second earl, as head of the Irish MacDonnells, was able to call upon the services of families such as the MacDonnells of Tenekilly in Queen's County or those in Counties Mayo and Tyrone and other MacDonnell kinsmen who were scattered throughout the four provinces. The majority of these clansmen

---

[115] Antrim to Wentworth, 21 November 1637 (SCL, Strafford MSS 17, fo. 234).
[116] The king ruled in favour of Antrim and against O'Hara, Charles I to Wentworth, 6 November 1637 (SCL, Strafford MSS 4, fos. 304–5). For details on the first earl's dispute with O'Hara, see Wentworth to Coke, 8 November 1633 (*ibid.*, 5, fo. 26); Antrim to Wentworth, 21 January 1634 (*ibid.*, 22, fo. 103). *Cal. SP Ire., 1615–25*, p. 491; Gillespie, *Colonial Ulster*, p. 119; Hill, *Stewarts of Ballintoy*, p. 16.
[117] J. T. Cliffe, *The Yorkshire gentry from the reformation to the civil war* (London, 1969), p. 11.
[118] R. A. Dodgshon, '"Pretense of blude" and "place of thair dueling": clans, 1500–1745', in Houston and Whyte (eds.), *Scottish society*, pp. 179–98, especially p. 185.
[119] Digby to Ormond, 29 March 1644 (Carte, *Ormond*, VI, 80).
[120] See pp. 113–14, 138–9, 168 below.

had originally come to Ireland, from the thirteenth century onwards, as 'gallowglasses' and had served, among others, the earls of O'Neill, Kildare and Desmond.[121] According to one account these MacDonnell mercenaries 'were soldiers by tradition, by force of circumstance, by choice' and, to top it all, they were 'highly efficient fighters'.[122] Shakespeare's well-known passage in *Macbeth*, written in 1605–6, captured the military prowess of these mercenaries; and these descendants of 'the merciless Macdonwald' owed their allegiance to Antrim:

> The merciless Macdonwald
> (Worthy to be a rebel, for to that
> The multiplying villanies of nature
> Do swarm upon him) from the Western Isles
> Of kerns and gallowglasses is supplied.[123]

Thirdly, the MacDonnells of Antrim, the MacDonalds of Dunyveg and the Glens, of Clanranald, of Glengarry, of Keppoch and of Sleat all shared a common heritage and outlook.[124] Above all they were united by an overriding ambition to rid the Western Isles of their arch-rivals, Clan Campbell. In return for the support of his Scottish kin, Antrim offered them protection from Campbell aggression. 'I have a natural affection to these [islanders] allied to me both by name and blood' he later wrote, and added that 'their safety I shall seek as much as my own'.[125] The feeling was mutual and Antrim was 'beloved by divers of his name'[126] who saw him as the 'helping warrior of the fair plain of the chieftains and unique protecting hand of our churches'.[127] The earl was

---

[121] Gerald A. Hayes-McCoy, *Scots mercenary forces in Ireland (1565–1603)* ... (Dublin, 1937); 'The army of Ulster, 1593–1601', *Ir. Sword*, 1, no. 2 (1905–1), pp. 106–7; Andrew McKerral, 'West highland mercenaries in Ireland', *The Kintyre Antiquarian and Natural History Society Magazine*, 9 (June 1981), p. 10; Erasmus D. Borrowes 'Tennekille castle, Portarlington, and glimpses of the MacDonnells', *UJA*, 1st series, 2 (1854), pp. 34–43; Donald M. Schlegel, 'The MacDonnells of Tyrone and Armagh. A genealogical study', *Seanchas Ardmhacha*, 10, no. 1 (1980–1), pp. 193–219.
[122] Duggan, 'The Irish brigade', p. 174.
[123] *Macbeth*, act one, scene II, lines 10–14.
[124] The most comprehensive is *Clan Donald*; also see for their early history J. R. N. MacPhail (ed.), *Highland papers* (4 vols., Scottish History Society, 2nd series, vols. V, XII and XX, and 3rd series, vol. XXII, Edinburgh, 1914–34); I, 2–101; Ronald Williams, *The lords of the Isles. The Clan Donald and the early kingdom of the Scots* (London, 1984). Stewart, 'Peoples of the Clan Ranald', takes a more anthropological approach. For a useful overview, see MacDonald, *Clan Donald*, and Alexander MacKenzie, *History of the MacDonalds and lords of the Isles with genealogies of the principal families of the name* (Inverness, 1881).
[125] Antrim to Wentworth, 11 April 1639 (Knowler, *Letters*, II, 321).
[126] Hamilton to Charles I, 15 June 1638 (SRO, GD 406/1/10488).
[127] Brian Ó Cuív, 'A poem on the second earl of Antrim', *Scottish Gaelic Studies*, 13, no. 2 (1981), p. 303.

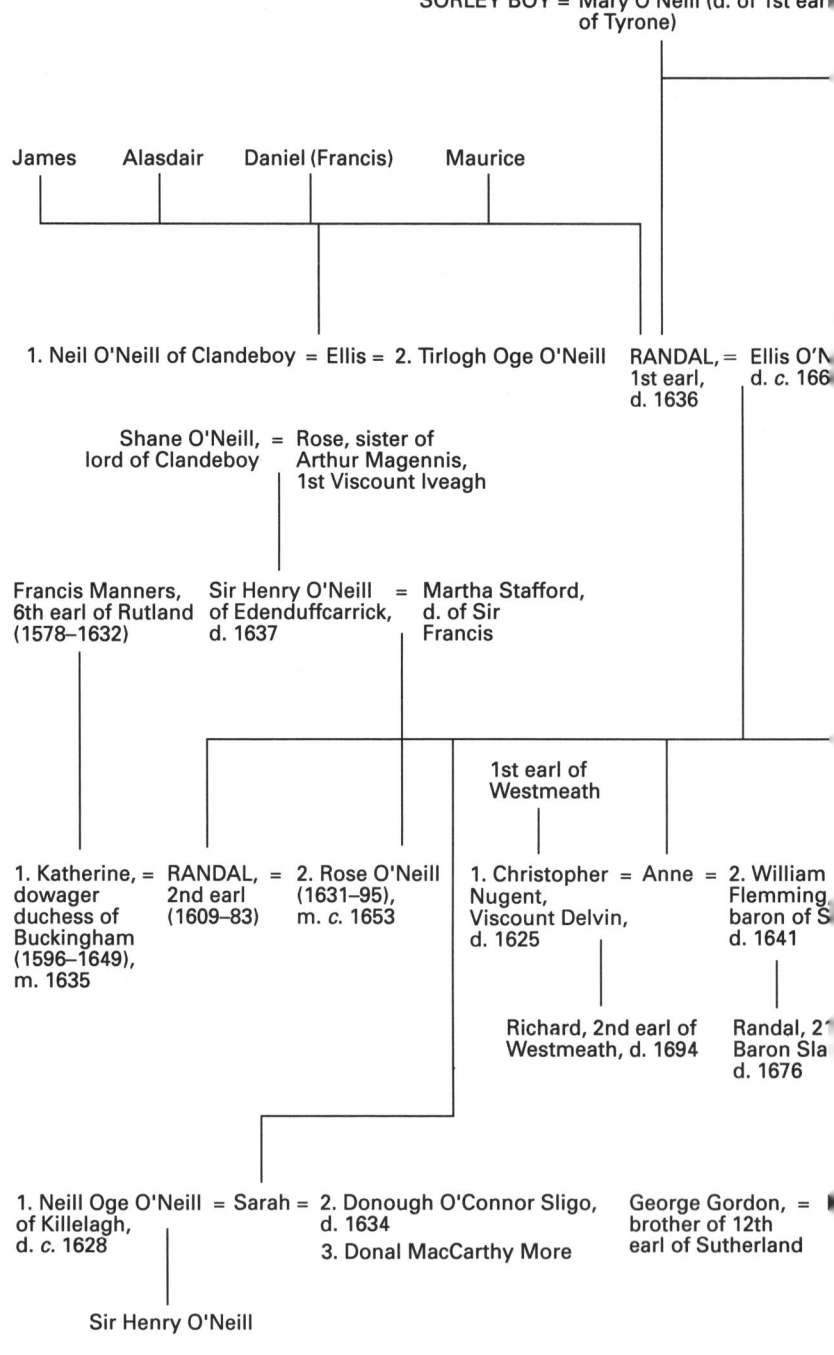

Genealogical table 2 The extended family

A man of the 'three kingdoms'

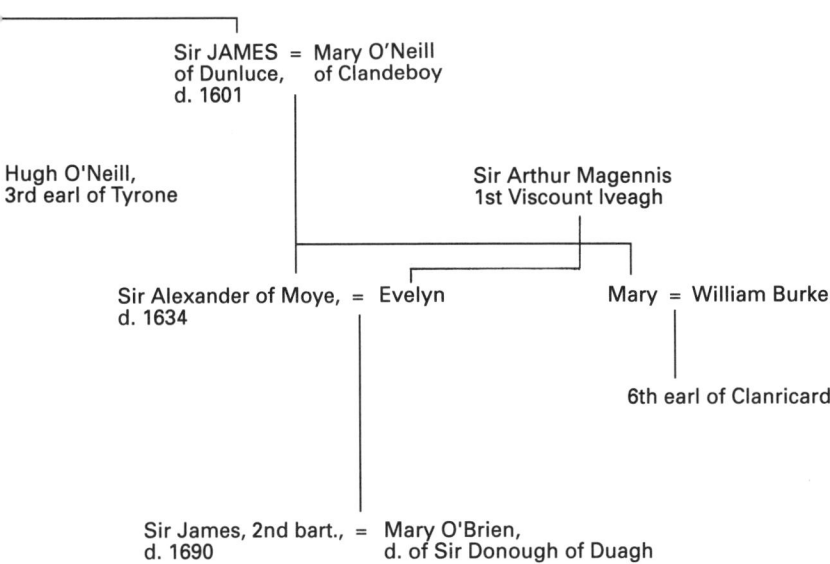

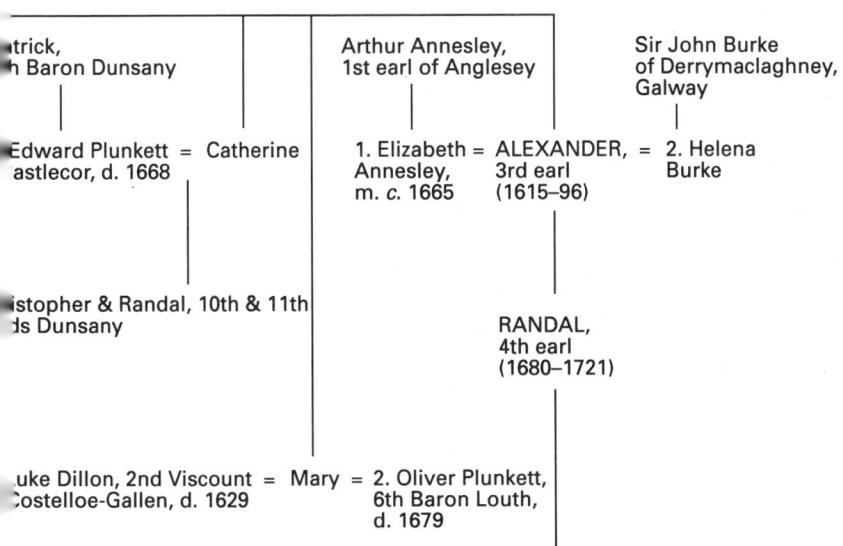

also closely allied to the great Catholic, Scottish house of Gordon and, as an opponent of Campbell hegemony, was supported by the Ogilvies, the Hamiltons and the lesser clans of Macleods of Lewis, MacNeils of Gigha, MacAllasters of Loup and MacFies of Colonsay.[128]

These ties of blood and animosity were supplemented by bonds of marriage. The first earl of Antrim's daughters were sought as spouses by some of Ireland's leading Catholic noblemen. The eldest girl, Lady Anne, was married first to Christopher Nugent, Viscount Delvin and heir to the first earl of Westmeath; and second to William Flemming, baron of Slane. Lady Mary's first husband was Luke, second Viscount Dillon of Costelloe-Gallen, and her second was Oliver Plunkett, sixth Baron Louth. Lady Sarah was married three times: first to Neal Oge O'Neill of Killelagh, County Antrim; second to Donough O'Connor of Sligo; and third to Donal MacCarthy More. Lady Catherine wed Edward Plunkett, son of Patrick ninth Baron Dunsany, and Lady Rose married (in 1642) the Scotsman George Gordon, a younger brother of the twelfth earl of Sutherland. Finally his 'natural daughter', Lady Ellis, married first Neil O'Neill of Clandeboy and then Tirlogh Oge O'Neill (brother of Sir Phelim O'Neill of Kinard).[129] The first earl also secured good matches for his extended family. For example his nephew Sir Alexander of Moye (the son or Sir James MacDonnell and Mary O'Neill of Clandeboy) married the daughter of Arthur Magennis, first Viscount Iveagh, while Sir Alexander's sister Mary married Sir William Burke (brother of the fifth earl of Clanricard).

Thanks to these and other carefully calculated marriages, the MacDonnells of Antrim were allied with leading Old English families in the Pale (the Westmeaths, Slanes, Dillons and Louths), native Irish ones in Munster (MacCarthy More) and in Connaught (the O'Connors).[130] But, as one might expect, their strongest connections were in Ulster, where they had

---

[128] McKerral, *Kintyre*, p. 15. For further details on the MacDonald–Campbell feud and Campbell aggrandizement in the Isles, see Edward J. Cowan, 'Clanship, Kinship and the Campbell acquisition of Islay', *SHR*, 58, no. 166 (Oct. 1979), pp. 132–57; *idem*, 'The Angus Campbells and the origin of the Campbell–Ogilvie feud', *Scottish Studies*, 25 (1981), pp. 25–38; William Gillies, 'Some aspects of Campbell history', *Transactions of the Gaelic Society of Inverness*, 50 (1976–8), pp. 256–8. For details on the Hamiltons, see pp. 51, 78–9 below.

[129] Hill, *MacDonnells*, pp. 247–50; Donald Jackson, *Intermarriage in Ireland 1550–1650* (Montreal, 1970), pp. 75–6; MacDonald, 'A fragment of an Irish MSS', pp. 278–80; John J. Marshall, 'Sir Phelim O'Neill, 1604–1652 [-3]', *UJA*, 2nd series, 10, no. 4 (Oct. 1904), p. 146.

[130] The authorities in London were particularly alarmed by the matches with Westmeath and the O'Connors, *Cal. SP Ire.*, 1615–25, pp. 476, 484, 491, 553, and *ibid.*, 1625–32, pp. 201, 206, 459. Also see MacDonald, 'A fragment of an Irish MSS', p. 271.

intermarried with most of the leading Gaelic families (the O'Haras, O'Cahans, MacQuillans, O'Donnells and Savages) and even with English Protestant settlers such as Sir Moses Hill. The links between the MacDonnells and the 'Great O'Neills', hereditary overlords of Ulster, were particularly strong. The second earl's grandfather (Sorley Boy) had married Catherine O'Neill, daughter of the first earl of Tyrone; and his mother was a daughter of Hugh, third earl of Tyrone; while other family members had intermarried with the O'Neills of Killelagh, of Kinard and of Clandeboy.[131] These close MacDonnell–O'Neill ties alarmed many English administrators. Wentworth, for one, was later convinced that Antrim – 'of the race of O'Neale, and upon my own knowledge the great admirer of his grandfather Tyrone' – would one day rally the native Irish in rebellion as his grandfather had done less than fifty years before.[132]

Wentworth found equally alarming the fact that the two families had remained in close contact after the O'Neills had fled from Ireland to the continent during the early years of the century.[133] MacDonnell ties with the continent were further strengthened by the presence there of Antrim's four natural half-brothers. Two of them, James and Alasdair, died in Spain (possibly during the 1630s); another (described by the first earl as 'onlie a bastard') – Maurice – served as an infantry captain in Flanders; while the fourth – Daniel (or Francis as he was later known) – was a Franciscan friar who, after being trained at St Anthony's College in Louvain, returned to County Antrim and, using Bonamargy friary as his base, served in the Scottish mission in the Western Isles.[134] Antrim, like his father, was eager to maintain these intimate links with Catholic Europe and he remained in close contact

---

[131] Jackson *Intermarriage*, pp. 72–5; Gillespie, *Conspiracy*, p. 40; Gerald A. Hayes-McCoy, 'The making of an O'Neill: a view of the ceremony at Tullaghoge, Co. Tyrone', *UJA*, 3rd series, 33 (1970), p. 89.

[132] Wentworth to Laud, 11 August 1638 (SCL, Strafford MSS 7, fo. 124v).

[133] Dunluce's sojourn on the continent (1625–7) would also have given him the opportunity to make contact with his exiled cousins and he may even have visited them, *Cal. SP Ire., 1625–32*, p. 398; Micheline Walsh, 'O'Neills in exile', *Seanchas Ardmhacha*, 8, no. 1 (1976–7), pp. 55–60.

[134] First earl of Antrim to Conway, 21 January 1626 (PRO, SP 63/242/204; *Cal. SP Ire., 1625–32*, p. 81); MacDonald, 'A fragment of an Irish MSS', p. 278. It seems that James and Alasdair predeceased their father since they were not mentioned in his will. It is not clear whether Francis died in 1636 as indicated in Giblin, 'Francis MacDonnell'; *idem, The Irish Franciscan mission*, pp. 111, 114, 127. Certainly a 'Francis MacDonnell' still served in the Franciscan mission in the Isles until 1684, Cathaldus Giblin 'St. Oliver Plunkett, Francis MacDonnell O.F.M. and the mission to the Hebrides', *Collect. Hib.*, 17 (1974–5), pp. 73–7, 81–2. I am grateful to Hector McDonnell for bringing this ambiguity to my attention.

with his two surviving half-brothers.[135] In addition, according to Wentworth, he formalized his relationship with his exiled kinsmen by becoming patron of Tyrone's regiment, which was then serving in Flanders.[136]

The heterogeneous, human pool from which the earl was able to draw supporters (and later sailors and soldiers too) over the course of the next half-century thus stretched from the Hebrides in the north-west to Flanders in the south-east and was, without a doubt, one of his most valuable assets. Clearly his power and influence were not limited to the Celtic fringe as his father's had been. Yet it was the first earl who, in less than thirty years, had turned the family's fortunes around: in addition to making the MacDonnells a force to be reckoned with in Ireland, he had brought home to his son the need to regain Clan Donald's Scottish patrimony and to cultivate a power base at court. In so doing the first earl had also laid down the parameters within which his son would henceforth operate for, despite the fact that the second earl of Antrim was principally an 'Irish Scot' of Gaelic extraction, he had also – thanks to his marriage to an influential heiress – a strong foothold in Britain's other kingdom, England. Antrim thus enjoyed the rare privilege of truly being a man of the 'three kingdoms'.

[135] For details on Maurice, see pp. 32 above, and 84, 94, 157 below.
[136] Knowler, *Letters*, II, 225–6. For details on the services performed by later MacDonnells in the armies of the king of Spain, see Micheline Walsh, *The MacDonnells of Antrim on the continent* (O'Donnell lecture, Dublin, 1960).

2

Caroline courtier (1637–1640)

Having settled his affairs in Ulster, Antrim now handed over the day-to-day running of his rationalized estate to his factors and, in September 1637, hurried back to London.[1] At court (according to Edward Hyde, later earl of Clarendon) he was 'very well received by both their majesties, and was frequently in their presence'.[2] His marriage to the duchess had transformed his status from that of a peripheral bystander to a courtier with 'permanent influence' who was now in a position to advance the interests of his family and friends and to hinder those of his opponents.[3] That influence, however, stemmed not from any office he held – for he held none – but from his privileged access to the royal couple.[4]

There were a number of reasons for this close contact. The physical proximity of Antrim's London residences (Wallingford – and later York – Houses) to Whitehall facilitated close and easy communications with the royal court.[5] At the same time his wife was cultivating the king and queen on his behalf. Next to Henrietta Maria, the duchess of Buckingham, as

---

[1] His factors, Archibald Stewart and Daniel MacNaughten, were now responsible for maintaining good relations with, and among, the tenants and for collecting the rents. The importance of a good agent cannot be overstated, Whyte, *Agriculture and society*, pp. 41–5; Gillespie (ed.), *Settlement and survival*, pp. lvii–lix; *idem, Colonial Ulster*, pp. 133–5; HMC, *Report on the manuscripts of the Right Honourable Viscount De L'Isle, V.C., preserved at Penshurst Palace, Kent*, VI, 122-3.

[2] Clarendon, *Life*, II, 77; Aikin, *Memoirs of the court*, I, 536. Whether he was 'bred in his [Charles I's] own bosom, his fellow gamster and comrade' (as the anonymous author of the *Aphorismical discovery* claimed) is another matter, Gilbert, *Contemp. hist. 1641–52*, I, 80.

[3] Hill, *MacDonnells*, p. 253; Clarendon, *Rebellion*, III, 509.

[4] The typed index PRO, LC 3/1 suggested that Antrim was a gentleman of Charles's bedchamber after 1641; in fact the entry (fo. 1) should read the earl of ANCRAM. For further details on the workings and paths of patronage within the court, see the articles by David Starkey and Kevin Sharpe in David Starkey (ed.), *The English court from the Wars of the Roses to the civil war* (London, 1987), especially pp. 5–15, 229–31, 246–50.

[5] Antrim paid £5-4-0 in rates for his 'waterside' property in 1636 and 1637 (Westminster Record Office, F363, fo. 5, and F364, fo. 5, ratebooks, 1636–7) and 52 shillings in 1638 and 1639 (*ibid.*, F365, fo. 4, and F366, fo. 4, ratebooks, 1638–9).

one of Charles I's favourites, was probably the most important and influential woman at the Caroline court and, together with her sister-in-law Lady Denbigh, the duchess of Richmond and the Catholic countess of Roxburgh, she held a position of honour in the queen's household.[6]

Closely related to this were Katherine's extensive contacts at court, which in turn provided her husband with a large pool of allies and benefactors who were prepared to keep his interests under the king's nose. Thanks to her Villiers connections, she was related to the earls of Desmond, Arundel, Suffolk, Northampton, Nithsdale and Pembroke. Loyalty to the late duke's memory also brought the patronage of numerous old Buckingham clients including Endymion Porter, Sir Robert Pye, Sir Edward Conway and Secretary Windebank.[7] However, the most important and influential was William Laud, archbishop of Canterbury.[8] Though Laud was primarily concerned 'that nothing may be done to the prejudice of my lord duke's memory, or the young duke's fortune', he nevertheless intervened on many occasions with Lord Deputy Wentworth, and even with the King himself, on Antrim's behalf.[9]

The earl's connections with the most high-ranking Scots at court were especially strong. The marriage of Katherine's daughter – Lady Mary Herbert – to James Stewart, fourth duke of Lennox (and, after 1641, of Richmond), in the summer of 1637 brought the earl another ally who had the king's ear.[10] For Lennox was not only a Knight of the Garter, lord chamberlain and lord

---

[6] Even after her husband's death she continued to entertain diplomats and dignitaries, see Albert J. Loomie (ed.), *Ceremonies of Charles I. The note books of John Finet master of ceremonies, 1628–1641* (New York, 1987), pp. 156, 170; Michael Van Cleave Alexander, *Charles I's lord treasurer. Sir Richard Weston, earl of Portland (1577–1635)* (London, 1975), pp. 191–2; Thomas Birch (ed.), *The court and times of Charles the first* ... (2 vols., London, 1848), II, 401; Quentin Bone, *Henrietta Maria* (Urbana, 1972), p. 56; Rosalind K. Marshall, *Henrietta Maria. The intrepid queen* (London, 1990). For details on access to the queen's court, see Kevin Sharpe, 'The image of virtue: the court and household of Charles I, 1625–1642', in Starkey (ed.), *The English court*, pp. 247, 250, 256–7, and Hibbard, 'Queen consort', pp. 409–11. Interestingly, Katherine held no formal office in the queen's household, I am grateful to Caroline Hibbard for this information.

[7] *Laud works*, VII, 133, 169–71. For details on the Buckingham clients within the queen's household, see Hibbard, 'Queen consort', pp. 407–11.

[8] Laud had been devoted to the first duke of Buckingham, upon whose patronage his career was founded, and had served him both as an intimate friend and religious adviser, see Lockyer, *Buckingham*, pp. 115, 372, and Hugh R. Trevor-Roper, *Archbishop Laud 1573–1645* (London, 1940; 3rd edn, London, 1988), pp. 59–60, 184.

[9] Laud to Wentworth, 14 May 1638 (Knowler, *Letters*, II, 169). I am grateful to John Scally for sharing his views with me on this point.

[10] Lady Mary's first husband was Charles Herbert who had died of smallpox shortly after their marriage. She was betrothed to Lennox in January 1637. Hamilton, Dorset, Holland, Portland, Russell, Goring, and Ladies Carlisle, Denbigh, Holland, Portland, Blanch Arundel and Mme Vantelet were all guests at her wedding that summer; and Lady Mary was sworn in as a member of the queen's household the following day, see Knowler, *Letters*, II,

admiral in Scotland, a gentleman of the bedchamber and a privy councillor in both England and Scotland; he was also Charles's closest blood relative and one of his most intimate friends, who 'used to discourse with his majesty in his bedchamber rather than at the council board'.[11] The duke's sympathetic attitude towards Catholicism (the D'Aubigny–Lennox branch of the Stewarts, of which he was head, was almost entirely Catholic) further endeared the earl to him.[12] Antrim's other great Scottish patron at court during this period – James, third marquis of Hamilton – was next in line to the Scottish throne after the royal Stuarts and had replaced Buckingham as Charles's favourite and trusted adviser.[13] He had succeeded to Buckingham's office as master of the horse and gentlemen of the bedchamber, was a Knight of the Garter and in 1633 became a privy councillor for England and Scotland.[14] Hamilton's marriage to Lady Mary Fielding (the duke of Buckingham's niece) brought him into close contact with her Catholic relatives; and his leasing of Wallingford House (until 1640) and a common fear of Campbell hegemony in Scotland cemented a firm alliance between him and Antrim.[15] In addition, the staunchly Catholic Robert Maxwell, earl of Nithsdale, who had married one of Buckingham's cousins, was another useful ally at court since he was a close confidant of the king and a privy councillor.[16] The same was true of Sir Patrick Maule of Panmure, a groom of the bedchamber and a former client of

---

45, 47–8, 114–18; *Cal. SP Dom., 1637*, pp. 355–6; Birch, *The court and times*, II, 407; Clarendon, *Rebellion*, I, 160–1, 207, 361. See also Brian Manning, 'The aristocracy and the downfall of Charles I', in Brian Manning (ed.), *Politics, religion and the English civil war* (London, 1973), pp. 69–70.

[11] Clarendon, *Rebellion*, I, 207, also see 160–1 and 361. For further details on Lennox, see Keith Brown, 'Courtiers and cavaliers. Service, anglicisation and loyalty amongst the royalist nobility', in Morrill (ed.), *The Scottish national covenant*, pp. 159–60.

[12] Caroline M. Hibbard, *Charles I and the popish plot* (Chapel Hill, 1983), pp. 23, 55, 143; L. J. Reeve, *Charles I and the road to personal rule* (Cambridge, 1989), p. 196.

[13] I am grateful to John Scally for bringing this to my attention.

[14] Brown, 'Courtiers and cavaliers', pp. 160–1.

[15] Hilary L. Rubinstein, *Captain luckless. The life of James first duke of Hamilton* (Edinburgh, 1975), pp. 43, 56, 60, 144; Rosalind K. Marshall, *The days of duchess Anne. Life in the household of the duchess of Hamilton 1656–1716* (London, 1973), pp. 14–24; Hibbard, *Popish plot*, p. 95; Manning 'The aristocracy and the downfall of Charles I', pp. 48–9; David Stevenson, *The Scottish revolution 1637–1644. The triumph of the covenanters* (Newton Abbot, 1973), pp. 94–5. Hamilton, however, was reluctant to move out of Wallingford House which caused Antrim much anxiety, Antrim to Hamilton, 2 December 1639 (SRO, GD 406/1/1167), Antrim to Hamilton, 10 January 1640 (*ibid.*, 406/1/1158), Antrim to Hamilton, 11 March 1640 (*ibid.*, 406/1/1160).

[16] Maurice Lee, 'Charles I and the end of conciliar government in Scotland', *Albion*, 12 (1980), p. 318; Brown, 'Courtiers and cavaliers', pp. 175–6. See pp. 78, 119, 121 below for details of their exploits together.

Antrim's residences

Plate 1 Dunluce castle
This majestic castle perched above the rugged County Antrim coastline and overlooking the Western Isles was described in the late sixteenth century as 'the strongest piece of this realm'. Though the outer buildings were defensive in character, the inner stone house built by the first earl, with its three mullioned, two-storeyed bay windows was more like an English manor house and was so designed in order to demonstrate the MacDonnells' 'civility' and 'Englishness'.

Buckingham's; and Patrick Murray, earl of Tullibardine, who later lent the earl considerable sums of money.[17]

Access to such an extensive network of patrons and such close proximity to the king was a luxury few Irish nobles – never mind a Catholic one – enjoyed, and Antrim undoubtedly used his advantage to maximum effect.[18] Unfortunately the earl's career as a Caroline courtier during the late 1630s is so poorly documented that we cannot be sure of his affiliations. Katherine's friendship with the wife of the Spanish envoy (she was a member of Katherine's household), and traditional MacDonnell ties to the house of

---

[17] Brown, 'Courtiers and cavaliers', pp. 165–6, 169; bond dated 25 March 1644 between Antrim, Tullibardine and James Cunningham (NLS, MS Ch. 2473).

[18] He had more extensive contacts than many of the other Irish nobles – such as the earl of Ormond, Kildare, Desmond and Clanricard – at court. There was a distinct absence of Irishmen in king's household, Nicholas Carlisle, *An inquiry into the place and quality of the*

Plate 2 York House
Antrim lived in York House, London, here drawn by Hollar, briefly between 1635 and 1638. The physical proximity of the house to Whitehall gave him easy access to the court. Originally the old London residence of the archbishops of York, it was rebuilt by the first duke of Buckingham in about 1625 to house his art collection and was deemed to be one of the finest palaces in Europe. It was dismantled during the 1670s and only the old stairs to the river, designed by Inigo Jones, survive. (Reproduced with the permission of the Westminster City Archive.)

Habsburg, suggests that the couple could well have been members of the 'Spanish faction' at court.[19] But Antrim also had a strong French connection: he had spent eighteen months in Paris as a teenager, had been willing (in 1635) to levy two Irish regiments for service in France, and was a confidant of the French ambassador in London.[20] Whether pro-Spanish or pro-French, however, the couple were devoted to the Catholic faith, which they openly flaunted as members of the queen's court.[21] The duchess was particularly

---

gentlemen of his majesty's most honourable privy chamber (London, 1829), pp. 105, 125–44. I am grateful to Dr Kevin Sharpe for bringing this reference to my attention.
[19] Albert J. Loomie, 'The Spanish faction at the court of Charles I, 1630–8', *BIHR*, 59, no. 139 (May 1986), pp. 37–49; *idem*, 'Alonso de Cárdenas and the Long Parliament, 1640–1648', *EHR*, 97, no. 383 (Apr. 1982), p. 289; Hibbard, *Popish plot*, pp. 30–7, 83–9.
[20] See pp. 27–8 above and Séneterre to Bouthillier, 15/25 July 1635 (PRO, PRO 31/3/68, fo. 88v).
[21] Keith Lindley, 'The lay catholics of England in the reign of Charles I', *Journal of Ecclesiastical History*, 22, no. 3 (July 1971), pp. 204–6, 209, describes the Catholic community in London and the favoured position it enjoyed thanks to the patronage of the queen and the

devout and later vowed that she 'would pour out my life in defence of it [Catholicism]... nothing can frighten me from my faith'.²² An intimate of the papal agent George Con (who addressed her as 'fond Kate'), she was instrumental in converting 'women of quality' (including Endymion Porter's wife and Lady Newport) to Catholicism, while her husband harboured Irish Catholics and entertained foreign priests in his London homes.²³

In addition to this influence in the capital, Antrim was able to exploit his position of favour at the royal court to further the causes of his Catholic friends, kin and dependants – as well as his own interests – in Ireland.²⁴ Thus in 1637–8 he (together with Laud, Lennox and the duchess) begged Wentworth that his elderly and impoverished cousin 'germain', Lord Magennis of Iveagh, 'be admitted to composition [before the commission of grace] as other men are' and requested that 'no part of that which he now possesses be diminished or taken from him'.²⁵ On Iveagh's death the earl immediately pleaded with the king and with Hamilton that the wardship of Iveagh's eldest teenage son (by one of Tyrone's daughters) be granted either to him or to his Protestant second cousin, Arthur Hill.²⁶ Wentworth was resolutely opposed to this and referred the matter to the court of wards with the recommendation that the youth be educated under the king's supervision so that 'he might easily be set straight in his religion, and civilized in his education... for I do

Catholic ambassadors. Also see Hibbard, 'Queen consort', pp. 404–6; Albert J. Loomie, 'London's Spanish chapel before and after the civil war', *Recusant History*, 18 (1987), pp. 402–8, and Gordon Albion, *Charles I and the court of Rome* (London, 1935), p. 366.

²² Duchess of Buckingham to Rinuccinni, 10/20 February 1647 (*Comment. Rinucc.*, II, 757).
²³ Albion, *Charles I*, p. 230. Garrard to Wentworth, 9 November 1637 (Knowler, *Letters*, II, 128–30); Birch, *The court and times*, II, 412–13; *HMC. rep. 12, app. 2*, p. 80; Gervas Huxley, *Endymion Porter* (London, 1959), p. 44. Hibbard, *Popish plot*, pp. 39–40, 51–7; Reeve, *Charles I*, p. 201.
²⁴ Mary O'Dowd, 'Land and lordship in sixteenth and seventeenth century Ireland', in Mitchison and Roebuck (eds.), *Economy and society*, pp. 20–2 and Raymond Gillespie, 'The trials of Bishop Spottiswood 1620–40' *Clogher Record*, 12, no. 3 (1987), emphasize the importance of having powerful friends at court who could act as brokers with the English administration.
²⁵ Laud to Wentworth, 26 January 1637 (*Laud works*, VII, 407). Also see Antrim to Wentworth, 25 November 1637 (SCL, Strafford, MSS 17, fo. 236); Antrim to Wentworth, 28 January 1638 (*ibid.*, fo. 279); duchess of Buckingham to Wentworth, 29 January 1638 (*ibid.*, fo. 280); Lennox to Wentworth, 30 January 1638 (*ibid.*, fo. 281); Antrim to Wentworth, 25 June 1638 (*ibid.*, 18, fo. 69); and Gillespie, *Colonial Ulster*, pp. 109–10.
²⁶ Antrim to Hamilton, 6 January [1639] (SRO, GD 406/1/1171); Hugh Magneil [Magennis] to Antrim, 6 February 1639 (*ibid.*, 406/1/1145); Antrim to Wentworth, 9 January [1639] (SCL, Strafford MSS 18, fo. 168). Hill was the youngest son of Moses Hill, a lawyer and high sheriff of County Antrim in 1634.

not take the earl of Antrim to be so good at breeding up of children'.²⁷ But the king ruled in Antrim's favour on the rather unpromising grounds that 'the youth had but little time to be in wardship and was soured already'.²⁸ The earl also interceded on behalf of another cousin, Hugh MacMahon, who (he argued) had been 'oppressed by his elder and illegitimate brothers in his minority'.²⁹ In 1639 he persuaded Wentworth to knight his Catholic kinsman (and the future leader of the Irish rebellion) Phelim O'Neill of Kinard.³⁰ He further supported his Protestant cousin Daniel O'Neill, son and heir to Con O'Neill of Clandeboy, by backing his suit for the return of his hereditary estates in County Down and by providing him with an annual pension of £400.³¹ In addition to protecting his own family and power base among the native Irish families in East Ulster, Antrim also promoted the causes of his Irish friends. He worked hard, for instance, to have two outlawed Catholic lawyers from Galway – Patrick Darcy and Richard Martin (Darcy's brother-in-law) – restored to the bar.³² Though Wentworth eventually agreed to all these requests he was clearly irritated by Antrim's interference and particularly by his support for Darcy.³³

Nor was Antrim's interest in Ireland confined to personalities. Despite spending most of the time in London the earl was eager to speculate in the Irish property market in order to maintain, reinforce and enhance his

---

[27] Wentworth to Laud, 10 April 1639 (SCL, Strafford MSS 7, fo. 178). Also see Wentworth to Laud, 12 February 1639 (*ibid.*, fo. 169).

[28] Laud to Wentworth, 27 February 1639 (*Laud works*, VII, 528). There was some confusion over the youth's age: Wentworth claimed that he was only thirteen while Antrim assured the king that he was sixteen and therefore beyond redemption, see for details Antrim to [Hamilton], 17 March 1639 (SRO, GD 406/1/1154); *Laud works*, VII, 562, 571–2; Wentworth to Antrim, 3 June 1639 (SCL, Strafford MSS 10A, fos. 335–7). The king's letter in favour of Antrim was delivered to the court of wards in July and at that point the earl confessed 'if the young lord be not ruined I am indifferent how it is disposed', Antrim to [Hamilton], 13 July 1639 (SRO, GD 406/1/1164). Since the Iveagh estates in County Down (worth only £1,300) were heavily encumbered with jointures and the family was in debt to the tune of £4,500 it is unlikely that the earl was motivated by financial gain, see Antrim to [Hamilton], 6 January [1639] (*ibid.*, 406/1/1171), and Antrim to Wentworth, 9 January [1639] (SCL, Strafford MSS 18, fo. 168).

[29] Antrim to Wentworth, 13 November [1638] (SCL, Strafford MSS 18, fo. 114).

[30] Knowler, *Letters*, II, 334–7. Phelim's brother, Tirlogh Oge, was married to Antrim's half sister, Ellis.

[31] Donal F. Cregan, 'An Irish cavalier: Daniel O'Neill', *Studia Hib.*, 3 (1963), pp. 77–8, 82.

[32] Wentworth to Laud, 26 April 1638 (SCL, Strafford MSS 7, fo. 96). Laud drew the line with Darcy and, after muttering a few words in his favour, abandoned his cause, Laud to Wentworth, 8 October 1638 (*Laud works*, VII, 492).

[33] Wentworth to Laud, [September] 1638 (SCL, Strafford MSS 7, fo. 131v).

traditional authority there.³⁴ In July 1637 Antrim's sister, Lady Sarah, allowed him £2,000 from her inheritance on condition that he buy a certain 'manor and ... land in the County of Meath'.³⁵ In August he purchased 866 acres in the barony of Glenarm and paid £440 for a number of tenements and 120 acres of land in the 'newtowne of Inver [Larne]'.³⁶ After discovering that the king had in effect put the city of London's Irish lands on the market he also offered to buy 3,000 acres around Coleraine (2,000 of which his father had sold to the plantation).³⁷ However, this straightforward attempt to regain part of his hereditary lands in County Londonderry soon led to a much more ambitious venture involving not just 3,000 acres in the Long Liberties but all the lands belonging to the city of London in the county.

The subsequent struggles over the 'Londonderry business' illustrate more clearly than anything else that Antrim's power at court revolved around his ability to manipulate the machinery of patronage to his own advantage. After his offer for the 3,000 acres had been rejected by Wentworth he promptly appealed to Hamilton for assistance. This time he found a more sympathetic ear.³⁸ Whether or not the marquis actually broached the matter with the king is unclear, for there is no further mention of Antrim's petition for the lands about Coleraine in the records. The surviving evidence in Hamilton's archive indicates, however, that he probably advised Antrim against pursuing the matter further since it was unlikely that the Londoners' lands would be handed over to an Irish Catholic, however loyal to the crown. Instead, during the autumn of 1637, the two noblemen hammered out the details of a combined offer for all of the city of London's lands in County Londonderry

---

³⁴ On the importance of the acquisition of land, see O'Dowd, 'Gaelic economy', p. 125.

³⁵ PRONI, D2977/3A/Various Old Nos ... Upper Dunluce Barony. Whether he actually bought land in Meath is unclear since the surviving sources contain no further mention of the transaction.

³⁶ *Ibid.*, D2977/1/Title Deeds, Glenarm Old No. 11 and D2977/3A/Old No. 72, Leases Larne. Antrim may have bought other property in County Antrim. Certainly he had contemplated doing so, '[He] speaks of great purchases of [a] house there for himself and of lands here for his brother', Wentworth to Laud, 10 July 1637 (SCL, Strafford MSS 7, fos. 35v–6v).

³⁷ See p. 24 above. The city of London and the Irish society were tried early in 1635 in the court of Star Chamber for mismanagement and neglect of the Londonderry plantations. They were fined £70,000. For a discussion of the various offers made, see pp. 59, 60 below. Interestingly, Hamilton was one of the judges at the trial in Star Chamber. For a full discussion of the bungled plantation and subsequent trial, see T. W. Moody, *The Londonderry plantation 1609–1641. The city of London and the plantation in Ulster* (Belfast, 1939).

³⁸ Antrim to Wentworth, 19 September 1637 (SCL, Strafford MSS 17, fo. 191). Antrim to Hamilton, [c. September 1637?] (SRO, GD 406/1/1502); reasons why the king should consider Antrim's petition, [c. September 1637] (*ibid.*, 406/M 1/277).

with Antrim acting as a 'silent' partner.³⁹ Despite being the smallest county in Ireland with few natural assets and 'not much arable [land]' one estimate prepared for them claimed that the annual income from the city of London's lands was about £10,200.⁴⁰ Another suggested that if the lands and waterways were well managed they would yield an annual income in excess of £19,500.⁴¹ While Archibald Stewart (the earl's factor) provided Hamilton with facts and figures, Antrim offered advice on how his patent should be drawn up, in the event that the king accepted his offer.⁴² According to the earl, Hamilton should request the rights to all ferries on the River Bann and Lough Foyle; to salmon and eel fishing on the Bann, Lough Foyle, and Lough Neagh; to elect all local officials in Derry and Coleraine; to keep courts, fairs and markets; to make wine and whiskey; and to hold two annual quarter sessions. Antrim also advised him on what was worth bargaining for and urged him to double the rent to be offered for the town of Coleraine (which the earl desperately coveted) 'rather than go without it'.⁴³

Initially Hamilton, confident that 'the deputy nor none for him will give so much', thought in terms of proposing an annual rent of £9,200.⁴⁴ However, in December 1637 he offered £12,000 for the Londoners' lands – payable to the English Exchequer in instalments every May and November – together with an entry fine of £10,000 on condition that he received the lands by May 1638, that he be exempt from paying rent for the first six months 'for the settling and disposing of the estate', that he should have liberty to cut timber

---

39 He had already made tentative enquires about acquiring lands in Connaught and in County Down, Hamilton to 'Lord Deputy Sibolds', 7 October 1635 (SRO, GD 406/1/246); Hamilton to Wentworth, [1636] (*ibid.*, 406/1/8381); Hamilton to Thomas Lord Cromwell, [1636] (*ibid.*, 406/1/8377).
40 List of revenues available from lands in Londonderry (probably drawn up late in 1637), *ibid.*, 406/1/501. According to Bishop Bramhall the customs, fishing and rents of Derry and Coleraine were worth (at most) £4,000, *Cal. SP Ire., 1633–47*, pp. 181–3; Moody, *Londonderry plantation*, p. 395. Under the Londoners' control the fisheries of Derry and Coleraine were worth, by 1635, £1,000 per annum and the customs (by 1614) were worth £700, Moody, *Londonderry plantation*, pp. 271–2.
41 The customs alone were said to be worth £3,000, Archibald Stewart to Hamilton, 1 February 1637[-8] (SRO, GD 406/1/359). Wentworth valued the lands at £8,000 per annum, Wentworth to Laud, 11 August 1638 (SCL, Strafford MSS 7, fos. 124–5).
42 Memorandum (presumably prepared by Antrim late in 1637) for Hamilton of what was to be asked of the king regarding his patent for County Londonderry (SRO, GD 406/M 1/37).
43 Antrim's advice on what was worth bargaining for (probably drawn up late in 1637) (*ibid.*, 406/M 1/324). Stewart repeated this advice, Archibald Stewart to Hamilton, 1 February 1637[-8] (*ibid.*, 406/1/359).
44 For further details, see Ohlmeyer, 'A seventeenth century survivor', appendix 1.4/D.

from the king's wood for building and firewood, and that fish worth under 100 marks should be exported without charge.⁴⁵ Wentworth nevertheless rejected this offer on three grounds.⁴⁶ First, including the customs in the agreement would deprive the king of many thousands of pounds.⁴⁷ Secondly, the offer made no provision for the future security of the present tenants; on the contrary the 'main drift' was 'to turn out all the now occupants without any consideration', which would ruin the English plantation in Ulster so that the province would become 'totally possessed by the Scottish'.⁴⁸ Finally, he objected to selling the county to an individual and argued that the state should control it.⁴⁹ Laud enthusiastically endorsed Wentworth's objections but for slightly different reasons:

First, that they [Hamilton and Antrim] which make the offer can never make it good. Secondly, if they could, it will be a very ill operation and full of disheartening to the English in relation to the plantation now in hand. And thirdly, you have all the reason in the world to fear, if the Scottishmen should multiply too much in those parts, they may break into the same distempers there, which now trouble their own country.⁵⁰

The anxious archbishop even feared that if Hamilton were granted the lands and they ceased to be 'independent upon the state ... that example will go on

---

⁴⁵ Valuation of several propositions made to the king for the lands and customs belonging to the Londoners sent to Laud, 30 October 1638 (BL, Add. MSS 21,125, fos. 1–4v). Also see details of an offer for Londonderry made to the king, December 1637 (SCL, Strafford MSS 3, fo. 309). Moody, *Londonderry plantation*, pp. 394–6, discusses this offer but misleadingly suggests that it 'must have come from a group of Scottish projectors' (p. 394).
⁴⁶ Charles I to Wentworth, 29 January 1638 (SCL, Strafford MSS 40, fos. 28 + 1, and MSS 3, fos. 308–9). Laud was apparently not privy to Antrim's intrigues with the marquis and was only aware that these two noblemen 'are grown into some nearness', Laud to Wentworth, [10 September] 1638 (*Laud works*, VII, 483–5).
⁴⁷ The customs of Derry and Coleraine between 1632 and 1636 brought in £6,829-13-10 (an annual average of £1,365-18-09), (SCL, Strafford MSS 3, fo. 321).
⁴⁸ Wentworth to Charles I, 27 February 1638 (*ibid.*, fo. 310). This was clearly only Wentworth's opinion; in fact the only surviving mention of the existing tenants clearly suggests that Hamilton was more sympathetic to them than Wentworth argued, see p. 60 below.
⁴⁹ Wentworth to Charles I, 7 May 1638 (*ibid.*, fos. 319–20). Laud agreed that Londonderry should not be 'under the command of any one great man', Laud to Wentworth, 13 November 1638 (*Laud works*, VII, 504). As time passed, Wentworth's resolution was strengthened: '198 [Hamilton] must not , will not have' the Londonderry lands, Wentworth to Laud, 11 August 1638 (SCL, Strafford MSS 7, fos. 124–5). Wentworth also urged the king to assign the lands to the duke of York for in twenty-one years the value of the lands would have doubled, Wentworth to Charles I, 3 April 1637 (*ibid.*, MSS 3, fos. 275–6).
⁵⁰ Laud to Wentworth, 30 May 1638 (*Laud works*, VII, 439).

like a canker and that government be lost ... and perhaps that kingdom too'.⁵¹

Due to Hamilton's lengthy absences from court in Scotland after the spring of 1638, Antrim feared that the marquis had lost interest in the venture and made a further, very similar offer on his own behalf in August 1638.⁵² Hardly surprisingly the lord deputy scornfully rejected this also: 'I am believing that his lordship will fail there too ... [and] will loose much by it, having offered more than the lands are worth.'⁵³ In the final analysis this proposition was not even seriously considered when, in October 1638, the merits of all the offers made for the city of London's lands – including ones from Wentworth and Sir John Clotworthy – were assessed.⁵⁴ Renewed hostilities in Scotland, however, delayed a firm decision over Londonderry and only during the winter of 1639 was Hamilton's offer, made precisely two years previously, finally rejected. The king instead 'resolved the conflict of interest by appointing a commission to manage the property directly'.⁵⁵

The tussle between Antrim and Wentworth over the 'Londonderry business' highlights the extent to which attitudes towards Irish Catholics had altered. Unlike his son, who was happy to defer to the lord deputy, James I had taken a keen personal interest in Irish matters – especially the Ulster plantation – and had been particularly eager to use the first earl as an instrument with which he could 'civilize' the barbarous Irish. Yet only a generation later the London and Dublin administrations were determined to exclude his son, who was much more 'English' in his behaviour and orientation than the first earl had ever been and who had already demonstrated his willingness to promote English agricultural methods on his estate, from meddling in County Londonderry. There were three reasons for this. First, circumstances in north-east Ulster had changed dramatically in a very short period of time. The first earl had been involved in the plantation during its

---

51 Laud to Wentworth, [10 September] 1638 (*ibid.*, 484).
52 Antrim to Hamilton, 11 June 1638 (SRO, GD 406/1/1156). Antrim was not named specifically but other evidence suggests that it was the earl who offered an entry fine of £10,000 and £11,500 annual rent to the king for the Londonderry lands and the customs, Wentworth to Laud, 11 August 1638 (SCL, Strafford MSS 7, fos. 124–5).
53 Wentworth to Conway, 31 August 1638 (*ibid.*, 10A, fo. 172).
54 See Ohlmeyer, 'A seventeenth century survivor', appendix 1.4/E, where the offers are discussed in detail.
55 Aidan Clarke, 'The government of Wentworth, 1632–40', in *NHI*, p. 266. As far as the earl was concerned this loss was offset by the grant (in September 1639) of a lease, for twenty-one years, to 300 acres in the Long Liberties of Coleraine near Mountsandle 'to build him a house on'; Wentworth also opposed this but, on this occasion, was outwitted by Hamilton, Antrim to [Hamilton], 13 July 1639 (SRO, GD 406/1/1164), Knowler, *Letters*, II, 422–4, order by

60   Civil War and Restoration in the three Stuart kingdoms

earliest, embryonic stage and well before the 'official' plantation, which was essentially a Protestant affair, began after the 'Flight of the earls' in 1607. Thus by the later 1630s the crown had a surplus of Protestant planters upon whom it preferred to call for assistance in times of crisis. Second, in this particular instance, Wentworth had his own designs on the lease for the Londoners' lands and, in an effort to further his own claim, asserted that Antrim (and his partner Hamilton) would overthrow the existing settlement and restore the former, native proprietors to their old farms.[56] In fact this was not the case. For example, in one offer made for the lease Hamilton and Antrim had been loath to increase Derry's rent to over £800 (from £450) because the present inhabitants 'will clamour much if their rent be doubled they being so ancient inhabitants and having built some of the houses with their own stock'.[57] No doubt if Antrim had acquired the lease for the Londonderry lands he would have husbanded them as carefully and progressively as he had his own County Antrim estates.[58] Third, and less equivocal, came the issue of religion and the 'need for an effective common front against catholicism'.[59] Antrim openly flaunted his Catholicism at a time when one of the primary objects of Stuart policy was to alter fundamentally the political hierarchy in favour of the 'New English'. This consideration alone would have probably sabotaged his bid for the lands of the ill-fated London Company.

Yet in the unlikely event that the king had accepted his offer the earl could not have afforded to buy the Londoners' lands. For, besides his speculations in Ireland, he was also investing heavily in English property. Thus late in 1637 he purchased for £12,000 a magnificent mansion at Bramshill in Hampshire, together with neighbouring lands which were worth £400 per year, because his wife disliked 'the air at Newhall [in Essex]'.[60] Almost everyone regarded

[Charles I] to the Irish treasury commissioners, Edinburgh castle, [13] July 1639 (SRO, GD 406/1/1163) – this copy is in Antrim's hand. Also see Antrim to Hamilton, 26 September 1639 (ibid., 406/1/1166).
[56] Clarke, 'The government of Wentworth', p. 266.
[57] Details of the offer made by Hamilton for County Londonderry including customs and fishing rights, [c. mid-1637-c. spring 1638] (SRO, GD 406/M 1/33).
[58] See pp. 39–41 above.
[59] Clarke, 'The government of Wentworth', p. 257.
[60] Laud to Wentworth, 11 November 1637 (Knowler, Letters, II, 131–2); ibid., 100. It was claimed that Antrim had in fact paid £14,000 for Bramshill, ibid., 85–7. The original medieval manor of Bramshill, formerly owned by Henry VIII, Edward VI and the Winchesters, was demolished by Edward Lord Zouch of Haringworth during the first decade of the seventeenth century. In its place he built a vast, beautiful and highly ornate mansion. For a detailed description see Victoria county history of Hampshire and the Isle of Wight, ed. William Page (5 vols., London, 1900–14), IV, 37–9.

the purchase as 'an excellent bargain',[61] but Wentworth was furious that Antrim had ignored his advice to economize and claimed that he 'did not exchange Newhall with Bramsell [sic] for unhealthfulness so much, as because he conceived it in diminution to himself to live in his wife's house forth of his own. This I assure you was the magnificat which fell forth of his own mouth.'[62]

That Antrim wanted an impressive English estate is, given his position at court, understandable but, whatever the reason, he had well and truly overstretched himself.[63] Contemporary estimates of his debts vary enormously, but all figures were large. On the eve of his marriage in 1635, according to Wentworth, he had contracted debts in excess of £3,000.[64] Three years later the lord deputy suggested that Antrim was £30,000 in debt and increased his estimate to £50,000 the following spring – which was the total sale value of the Antrim estate (according to Wentworth).[65] The lord deputy was, as usual, well informed: although data is hard to come by, the surviving figures suggest that Antrim's debts probably hovered between £40,000 and £42,000 during the late 1630s.[66]

On the one hand, Antrim's enormous debts highlight the magnificence in which he lived and reflect his political and social ambitions and his view of his rightful status within society. On the other, they were chronic and one wonders how the earl had managed to accumulate such vast debts in such a relatively short period of time. To begin with, £15,000 was spent buying

---

[61] 'A great pennyworth' was how the archbishop described Bramshill, Laud to Wentworth, 28 August 1637 (Knowler, *Letters*, II, 100).
[62] Wentworth to Laud, 18 October 1637 (Knowler, *Letters*, II, 120). Antrim, anticipating Wentworth's fury, apologized for seeming 'fickle in any weighty matter that ever I promised your lordship'; but his wife had persuaded him to purchase the house, Antrim to Wentworth, [c. May] 1637 (SCL, Strafford MSS 22, fo. 141).
[63] Wentworth to Laud, 11 August 1638 (SCL, Strafford MSS 7, fos. 124–5).
[64] Wentworth to Antrim, 30 July 1636 (*ibid.*, 21, fo. 149).
[65] Knowler, *Letters*, II, 278, 289, 296–7; Wentworth to Laud, [April?] 1639 (SCL, Strafford MSS 7, fo. 181v).
[66] *Cal. SP Ire., 1660–2*, p. 70. Gillespie, *Colonial Ulster*, p. 138, estimated Antrim's debts to be £39,377 by 1640; while Bagwell, *Stuarts*, I, 285, misleadingly suggested that he was £80,000 in debt! Calculating precisely how much the earl spent between the death of his father in December 1636 and the outbreak of the Irish rebellion is frustrated by the fragmentary nature of the sources. For instance, the list of Antrim's debts and creditors in 1638 reproduced by George Hill (*MacDonnells*, pp. 473–7) is misleading, incomplete and inaccurately transcribed from the original in PRONI, D2977/Kintyre papers. Hill not only transcribed names and figures incorrectly but also failed to indicate whether the debt had been paid or was being paid. This list in any case does not include any debts contracted before 1638; nor those of his wife, who unbeknown to the trustees of her son's estate, also borrowed considerable sums from other courtiers, *Cal. SP Dom., 1635*, pp. 449, 512; *ibid., 1635–6*, pp. 372, 429, 467, 535; *ibid., 1636–7*, p. 217.

property in Ireland and in England, and a further £22,000 in furnishing his houses (especially Bramshill and Dunluce) in a style appropriate to the couple's station.[67] In addition, the earl, although mainly resident in England, was heavily taxed in Ireland.[68] He was charged £3,200 in parliamentary subsidies (which he claimed was four times as much as any English nobleman 'that had double my fortune') and a further £3,500 in extraordinary taxation.[69] To some extent extravagance was also to blame.[70] Gambling was one of Antrim's vices. According to one account he lost 'at the Wells at Tunbridge almost £2,000 at ninepins, most of it to Sir John Sutlin [Suckling?].[71] Living lavishly was another: Antrim, according to Hyde, 'lived in the court in great expense and some lustre'.[72] By the end of 1638 it appears that there was hardly a leading merchant or tradesman in London and Dublin to whom Antrim did not owe money. His creditors included three individual goldsmiths, five jewellers, three merchants, four widows, the court painter (Anthony Van Dyck), two physicians, one haberdasher, one linen draper, eight mercers, two milliners, one seamstress, one steamster, one shoemaker, one stocking seller, one tailor, two upholsterers and three woollen drapers. All had supplied goods to Antrim on credit; many waited in vain for repayment.[73] In addition, the couple entertained in York House, attended court masques and pageants and gave generous gifts to their family, friends and benefactors: for example, the earl sent Wentworth a suit of rare Indian armour and presented Hamilton with a 'bag [of money] ... found upon my land, which I believe has been long coined'.[74] He obviously worked (as his predecessor the duke of Buckingham had done) 'on the assumption that means would somehow be found to pay for his expenditure – an attitude ... widely shared at the Stuart ... Court'.[75]

---

[67] See Ohlmeyer, 'A seventeenth century survivor', appendix 1.5, and Hill, *MacDonnells*, pp. 475–6.
[68] Crown office docket book, 1629–43 (PRO, C231/5, fo. 306).
[69] Antrim to Charles I, 4 June 1641 (SRO, GD 406/1/1356).
[70] Keith Brown, 'Aristocratic finances and the origins of the Scottish revolution', *EHR*, 104, no. 410 (Jan. 1989), pp. 60, 62, 64, 71, suggests that extravagance was seen as a means of protecting a nobleman's honour.
[71] Garrard to [Conway], 18 September 1635 (*Cal. SP Dom., 1635*, p. 385). For a further example, see PROI, MS 2448A, p. 148, where Antrim bet £151 with William Owny and Tibbett McPhillibin that Ormond would win a suit over land. On this occasion he won the wager but the debt was never paid and so he sued his debtors in 1638.
[72] Clarendon, *Rebellion*, III, 509, 522.
[73] Ohlmeyer, 'A seventeenth century survivor', appendix 1.6.
[74] Antrim to Hamilton, 15 April 1640 (SRO, GD 406/1/1161). Also see Antrim to Wentworth, 23 May 1637 (SCL, Wentworth MSS 22, fo. 133); Charles Dalton, *Life and times of Sir Edward Cecil, Viscount Wimbledon* ... (2 vols., London, 1885), II, 333.
[75] Lockyer, *Buckingham*, p. 213.

Table 3 *Occupations of Antrim's creditors and amounts borrowed during the 1630s*

Amounts	Number of Debts	Occupation of Creditors	Number
Under £10	—	Alderman	1
£10–50	12	Chandler	1
£50–100	24	Esquire	2
£100–150	29	Gentleman	11
£150–200	11	Goldsmith	3
£200–250	22	Haberdasher	1
£250–300	6	Jeweller	5
£300–350	15	Knight	10
£350–400	6	Lady	3
£400–450	7	Lawyer	1
£450–500	2	Linen draper	1
£500–600	17	Mercer	8
£600–700	4	Merchant	3
£700–800	2	Milliner	2
£800–900	4	Painter	1
£900–1,000	4	Peer	5
£1,000–1,500	20	Picture Maker	1
£1,500–2,000	5	Physician	2
£2,000–2,500	2	Saddler	1
£2,500–3,000	1	Seamstress	1
£3,000–3,500	1	Seamster	1
£3,500–4,000	1	Servant	3
£4,000–5,000	1	Shoemaker	1
£5,000–6,000	—	Skinner	1
£6,000–7,000	1	Spinster	1
Not given	4	Stocking seller	1
		Tailor	1
		Tenant	8
		Upholsterer	2
		Widow	4
		Woollen draper	3
		Not given	69
		Total	158

Source: Ohlmeyer, 'A seventeenth century survivor', appendix 1.6.

But the scale of indebtedness is always relative to income. Antrim's Ulster estate should in theory have been a major source of revenue. His annual income in 1637 (calculated from the 123 surviving leases) amounted to only £2,424-14-08, which seems pitifully low for a man whose annual expenditure was so high.[76] However, more realistic estimates are provided by contemporary valuations, which suggest that he received an approximate annual rental from his Irish lands of between £6,000 and £8,300.[77] This was supplemented by £400 from Bramshill and by the revenues accruing from estates the duchess owned in her own right. Her Buckinghamshire manors yielded a yearly rental of just under £2,000, while her property in Leicestershire brought in a further £1,400.[78] Their combined income from land was therefore in the region of £10,000 to £12,000 – which was double that of Arthur Chichester, the other great landowner in Ulster – and it was supplemented by an annual pension of £6,000 and the £4,450 which the duchess

---

[76] Based on surviving leases in PRONI, D2977 and D265, his income was calculated as follows:

Barony	£	s	d
Glenarm	595 –	13 –	10
Dunluce	1123 –	09 –	00
Kilconway	578 –	16 –	10
Cary	126 –	15 –	00
Total	£2,424 –	14 –	08

[77] BL, Harl. MS 2138, fos. 111–16; Knowler, *Letters*, II, 296–7. The French ambassador estimated in 1635 that Antrim received in rents 100,000 livres which is roughly equivalent to £8,333, Séneterre to Bouthillier, 15/25 July 1635 (PRO, PRO 31/3/68, fo. 88v). Certainly within less than a century the annual rental from the Antrim estate was £15,219, see PRONI, T904. The annual rental on the earl of Thomond's estate in County Limerick during these years was c. £7,000, J. Hogan (ed.), *Letters and papers relating to the Irish rebellion between 1642–46* (IMC, Dublin, 1935), pp. 200–3.

[78] It is unlikely that Antrim was able to cream off any of the profit produced by the second duke's estates. Estimating accurately the value of the estate held by the duchess is, in the absence of further sources, impossible; but crude (and very probably undervalued) estimates of their pre-Civil War income are given in *Calendar of the proceedings of the committee for compounding, 1643–1660*, ed. Mary Anne Everett Green (5 vols., London, 1889–92), I, 66–7/PRO, SP 23/246/631 (fo. 112), *ibid.*, 23/96/619. For a discussion on the problems involved in using these sources, see C. B. Phillips, 'The royalist composition papers and the landed income of the gentry: a note of warning from Cumbria', *Northern History*, 13 (1977), pp. 161–70, and J. T. Cliffe, 'The royalist composition papers and the landed income of the gentry: a rejoinder', *Northern History*, 14 (1978), pp. 164–8.

received each year from Irish customs.[79] The total annual receipts for the couple were therefore in excess of £20,000.

But all this income, which made Antrim the richest man in Ulster and one of the most affluent in Ireland, was clearly not enough.[80] Hence he mortgaged many of his own – and his wife's – properties and other assets in order to raise money.[81] In July 1638, using Bramshill as collateral, Antrim borrowed £10,000 from the estate of his stepson, the second duke of Buckingham.[82] At much the same time the rental of York House was used as security for various bonds amounting to £2,000, and nineteen older and more modest properties on the Strand were mortgaged for £800. In East Ulster any available land (and there does not appear to have been much) was leased out at ridiculously low rents in return for the payment of substantial entry fines. Finally, in November 1637, he had to mortgage the barony of Cary, the lordship of Ballycastle and Rathlin Island for ninety-nine years in trust for payment of select debts.[83]

---

[79] *Montagu MSS*, p. 147. Chichester's Irish and English property yielded £6,100 per annum, Roebuck, 'The making of an Ulster great estate', pp. 21–3; while Sir Charles Coote's annual revenue was estimated in 1642 at £4,000 (*Ormonde MSS*, II, 125). Prior to the reorganization in 1632 the duchess had kept up her husband's interest in the customs farm, see C. V. Wedgwood, *Thomas Wentworth, first earl of Strafford 1593–1641. A Revaluation* (London, 1935; revised edn, 1962), pp. 196–7; Kearney, *Strafford*, pp. 37, 159–68, 181; idem, 'Mercantilism and Ireland 1620–40', in T. Desmond Williams (ed.), *Historical studies*, I (London, 1958), pp. 59–60, 63–8; Lockyer, *Buckingham*, pp. 48, 116. *Laud works*, VII, 409–11, Knowler, *Letters*, II, 91; Charles I to Wentworth, 9 January 1637 (SCL, Strafford MSS 4, fos. 238–40).

[80] Daniel O'Neill claimed that his father's estate had been worth £12,000 per annum, which was probably an exaggeration, Cregan, 'An Irish cavalier', pp. 74, 77. In 1624 Conway's estate was valued at £2,000 per annum and in 1632 Arthur Hill received an income of £1,000 from his, Gillespie, *Colonial Ulster*, pp. 129, 136, 232; SCL, Strafford MSS 24/25 (121).

[81] The ease with which land could be mortgaged in Ulster during the 1630s is discussed in Gillespie, *Colonial Ulster*, pp. 124–26, 140–1, 200, 203–4. For Scotland, see Keith Brown, 'Noble indebtedness in Scotland between the reformation and the revolution', *Historical Research*, 62, no. 149 (Oct. 1989), pp. 260–75.

[82] Sir Robert Pye believed that, even if the duchess died, the debt would be honoured or would be secured in the court of wards, *Cal. SP Dom., 1637–8*, p. 574. In fact the debt had been repaid by 1640 but only after legal action against the earl had been taken, see Hill, *MacDonnells*, p. 475, and PRO, LC4/217.

[83] Hill, *MacDonnells*, p. 476. Petition to the committee for compounding with delinquents, 19 January 1652 (PRO, SP 23/79/ pp. 759–63 and 23/135/ pp. 267–8). It is possible that the earl mortgaged other property (for £900) to John Green, Hill, *MacDonnells*, p. 474. The mortgaging of Cary was intended to protect his principal guarantors – Archibald Stewart, Alexander MacDonnell, John Traylman and Dr Moore. However, it did not prevent Antrim's guarantors from being hounded by his creditors. In the autumn of 1639 Hamilton was obliged to protect Stewart from them during his trip to England. Antrim's brother Alexander was harassed by a number of creditors when he visited England late in 1641 while others petitioned parliament that Alexander not be jailed in the hope that they would finally be repaid, Antrim to Hamilton, 26 September 1639 (SRO, GD 406/1/1166); *HMC, rep. 4*, p. 108; *HMC, rep. 5*, p. 6.

The earl even pawned for £900 'the two pendant pearles given my lady by the Queen, and hangings of [the story of] Alexander'.[84]

When even this did not suffice, Antrim simply borrowed money from anyone who would lend it. A close analysis of surviving material dealing with his debts (see table 3 on p. 63 above) indicates that, apart from the mortgages, he tended to borrow relatively small amounts of money – ranging between £100 and £1,500 – from a wide group of individuals (nearly 160 in all).[85] Family members, friends, fellow courtiers and royal servants all lent him cash during the late 1630s. He borrowed from his stepson-in-law the duke of Lennox, from Lord and Lady Dunsany (his sister's in-laws), from Viscount Purbeck (his wife's brother-in-law by her first marriage), from Lord Deputy Wentworth, from the Catholic lawyer Patrick Darcy, from Arthur Hill (his second cousin), from Lord Justice Sir William Parsons (Hill's father-in-law), from James Maxwell (a groom of the bedchamber and Derbyshire iron manufacturer), from the merchant-adventurers Sir Paul Pindar and Sir John Wolstenhome, from Lady FitzGerald, from Viscount Wimbledon, from the king's jewellers, James Duart and Alexander Harriott, and from his saddler Thomas Smithsby. Between 1637 and 1640 these sixteen individuals alone lent the earl in excess of £24,000 (the equivalent of roughly two to three years' rental from his Ulster estate) of which almost half (£10,700) was still outstanding in October 1641.[86] The earl also borrowed substantial sums from his English servants and Irish tenants. For instance, Edmund Cooper and Matthew Dalby (servants at Newhall), and John Glasse, James Hamilton, Robert Harper, Walter Kennedy, John Oge McCollum, Mrs MacNaughten, Edward Muddreman and John Ross (all tenants from County Antrim) between them lent their lord in only two years some £5,000.[87]

Borrowing, however, was one thing, repaying overdue loans and outstanding debts was quite another. Antrim was rarely able to repay his

---

[84] The pawnbroker was found to have resold these treasures by the time he went to redeem them, Hill, *MacDonnells*, p. 474.
[85] For further details, see Ohlmeyer, 'A seventeenth century survivor', appendix 1.5, and Hill, *MacDonnells*, pp. 473–7.
[86] How much money he borrowed from Lennox and Wentworth is unclear. Laud merely thanked Wentworth for lending Antrim 'so much money', Laud to Wentworth, 28 August 1637 (Knowler, *Letters*, II, 100). See Ohlmeyer, 'A seventeenth century survivor', appendix 1.5, for further details.
[87] Only half of this sum was repaid before the outbreak of rebellion. These calculations are based on Ohlmeyer, 'A seventeenth century survivor', appendix 1.5. Borrowing from servants and tenants was not uncommon in Lowland Scotland, L. D. Whyte and K. A. Whyte, 'Debt and credit, poverty and prosperity in a seventeenth century rural community', in Mitchison and Roebuck (eds.), *Economy and society*, pp. 72–3, 76–8.

creditors on time and was occasionally taken to court for this failure.[88] Early in January 1639 Wentworth took considerable delight in letting it be known that the earl was unable to scrape £300 together in Dublin 'to stay a seisure which in default was ready to issue against his land'.[89]

Antrim was not the only Stuart nobleman to be reputed a 'poor risk'. The majority of his Ulster neighbours, Catholic and Protestant alike – the Magennises of Iveagh, Sir Phelim O'Neill, Antrim's future in-laws the O'Neills of Edenduffcarrick, Sir William Brownlow and Lords Chichester, Cromwell and Conway – were in a similar predicament.[90] Other prominent Irish figures such as Sir Charles Coote,[91] together with many leading Scottish nobles, namely the earl of Nithsdale (whose debts in 1627 amounted to roughly £10,500), the earls of Stirling and Ancram, were also deeply in debt, while it was rumoured that Robert Ker, earl of Lothian, had committed suicide rather than pay off his enormous debt.[92] In fact indebtedness plagued leading figures throughout early modern Europe: consider the extreme example of a Castilian nobleman, the duke of Infantado, whose rents did not even cover the interest due on his debts, while his compatriot – the duke of Béjar – spent 50 per cent of his income merely on servicing his debts![93]

---

[88] If the earl paid his debt by the date stated in the bond no interest appears to have been charged. Working out interest rates is in this instance frustrated by the fact that the rate was not stated in the bond. Creditors could, and did, take legal action against Antrim. The 'Index of bad debtors' in 1638 (PRO, LC 4/185) lists Antrim, Alexander MacDonnell, John Moore and Archibald Stewart. Unfortunately, the reference given in the index is incompatible with the corresponding recognizance rolls (*ibid*., 4/66, 67). The same is true for the main working registers – the entry book – of the clerk of the recognizance (*ibid*., 4/202): though the index (*ibid*., 4/216) lists Antrim, Alexander, Moore and Stewart, no corresponding reference in the original was found.

[89] Wentworth to Windebank, 15 February 1639 (Knowler, *Letters*, II, 289). Also see *ibid*., 278, Wentworth to Cottington, 10 February 1639 (SCL, Strafford MSS 10B, fo. 35).

[90] Gillespie, *Colonial Ulster*, pp. 138, 195; *idem* (ed.), *Settlement and survival*, p. li; Roebuck, 'The making of an Ulster great estate', pp. 13–15, 19–25; Jerrold I. Casway, 'Two Phelim O'Neills', *Seanchas Ardmhacha*, 11, no. 2 (1985), p. 340; Canny, *Kingdom and colony*, p. 59.

[91] *Ormonde MSS*, II, 125.

[92] Macinnes, *Charles I*, pp. 78, 97; Brown 'Courtiers and cavaliers', pp. 163–5; *idem*, 'Noble indebtedness', p. 260. Also see Gillespie, *Colonial Ulster*, pp. 200–2; Brown, 'Aristocratic finances', pp. 52–3; Allan Macinnes, 'The impact of the civil wars and Interregnum: political disruption and social changes within Scottish Gaeldom', in Mitchison and Roebuck (eds.), *Economy and Society*, pp. 62, 67; and Stone, *Crisis of the aristocracy*.

[93] Charles Jago, 'The influence of debt on the relations between the crown and aristocracy in seventeenth century Castile', *Econ. Hist. Rev.*, 2nd series, 26, no. 2 (May 1973), pp. 218–36 at p. 227, and *idem*, 'The "crisis of the aristocracy" in seventeenth century Castile', *Past and Present*, 84 (1979), pp. 60–90.

Ironically, however, indebtedness also had a positive side, and in Antrim's case his indebtedness – particularly to leading landowners in Ulster and to members of the London business community – helped to ensure his political survival. At the Restoration his creditors formed a powerful pressure group which lobbied for the earl's restoration principally to ensure that the money he owed them from the late 1630s might at last be repaid.[94] In the long term, therefore, Antrim's debts bought him political and tenurial security, while in the middle term (1640s and 1650s) his indebtedness was relative since the majority of his class were similarly embarrassed.

However, his debts had their dangers in the short term (the late 1630s) because they put him in severely straitened circumstances. Frequently, he could neither meet his current expenses nor raise further capital. This brought him social and political embarrassment, and Wentworth for one was aghast both at the scale of Antrim's debts and at the dubious methods used to alleviate them.[95] The lord deputy was, for instance, determined to prevent Antrim exploiting the young duke of Buckingham's inheritance to his own advantage. In England there was little Wentworth could do to curb Antrim's manipulation of the Buckingham estate, but Ireland was another matter. When in the summer of 1637 the couple demanded that the lord president of Munster – William St Leger – pay the duchess 'her dower' (an annual allowance of £200) out of a manor and estate in Queen's County demised to him by the late duke for twenty-one years, Wentworth immediately took St Leger's part on the grounds that he was a loyal and faithful servant to the crown.[96] After much wrangling Antrim secured a ruling in his favour whereby St Leger was to pay him £200 per annum for the twelve remaining years of his lease plus £1,800 in arrears.[97] Determined not to suffer any slight either to his own authority or to that of his representative, however, Wentworth refused to accept the settlement and, early in 1638, insisted that the matter be referred to the court of wards.[98] The battle between Antrim and the

---

[94] For details, see chapter 10 below.
[95] Knowler, *Letters*, II, 131–2; Wentworth to Laud, 10 July 1637 (SCL, Strafford MSS 7, fos 35v–6v).
[96] Petition from St Leger to Charles I, [*c*. October 1637] (SCL, Strafford MSS 4, fos. 300–1).
[97] The second duke also received an annual sum of £100, Coke to Wentworth, 5 October 1637 (*ibid*., 11, fo. 325), and Coke to Wentworth, 7 November 1637 (*ibid*, fo. 331).
[98] Before the matter was referred to the court of wards Laud tried (unsuccessfully) to persuade the duchess to acquiesce to Wentworth's demands, Laud to Wentworth, 11 November 1637 (Knowler, *Letters*, II, 131–2), and Laud to Wentworth, 23 November 1637 (*Laud works*, VII, 391–2). Laud to Wentworth, 27 March 1638 (*ibid*., 418–19); Wentworth to Laud, 10 April 1638 (Knowler, *Letters*, II, 157); Laud to Wentworth, 14 May 1638 (*ibid*., 169, 171).

lord president of Munster therefore raged on for a further eight months until the king, largely to placate his lord deputy, intervened and ruled against Antrim.[99]

The St Leger affair was merely one source of friction between Antrim and Wentworth. Relations between the two had deteriorated steadily since the earl's visit to Ireland in the spring of 1637 during which – according to Wentworth – he passed 'his judgment upon me privately that he liked me not, and that I was proud'.[100] Antrim's patronage of St Patrick's Purgatory on Lough Derg (County Donegal) forced the rift even wider.[101] The devoutly Catholic queen – unaware that it had already been destroyed – instructed Antrim to discuss the preservation of St Patrick's Purgatory with Wentworth on her behalf.[102] Wentworth penned a polite reply to the queen explaining that since the site had been destroyed for over six years it was impossible to restore it, especially since it was situated 'in the midst of the great Scottish plantations'; and so he begged her 'to let this devotion rest a while, till there may be a fitter opportunity'.[103] There was no need, however, for such respect towards the queen's Catholic agent and so Antrim became the target of Wentworth's waspish pen. Lord Conway was sarcastically informed how Antrim 'desires St Patrick may have his purgatory here on earth again where I thought he had been sure enough in heaven'.[104] Laud, who agreed that St Patricks was 'a Babel indeed', received similar outbursts.[105] Seen in the context of Antrim's ambitions towards the plantation lands in Londonderry and the volatile political situation in Scotland, Wentworth's outrage was understandable. At times he must have seriously wondered if the earl – whom both he and the archbishop of Canterbury had supported – was trying to recreate the old, Gaelic world into which he had been born. In any case, Antrim's active Catholicism did not endear him to Wentworth, who hoped to transform the Church of Ireland into Ireland's national church.

---

[99] Knowler, *Letters*, II, 205–8, 207.
[100] Wentworth to Laud, 10 July 1637 (SCL, Strafford MSS 7, fo. 35v).
[101] For details see William Pinkerton, 'Saint Patrick's purgatory, part IV', *UJA*, 1st series, 5 (1857), pp. 61–81, especially pp. 74–5.
[102] Antrim to Wentworth, 25 June 1638 (SCL, Strafford MSS 18, fo. 69); Knowler, *Letters*, II, 221; Cathaldus Giblin (ed.), 'Vatican Library: MSS Barberini Latini. A guide to the material of Irish interest on microfilm in the National Library, Dublin', *Archiv. Hib.*, 18 (1955), p. 127; Bagwell, *Stuarts*, I, 188–9; Hibbard, *Popish plot*, p. 60. His father had been active in preserving St Patrick's Purgatory, see p. 27 above.
[103] Wentworth to Henrietta Maria, 10 October 1638 (Knowler, *Letters*, II, 221–2).
[104] Wentworth to Conway, 31 August 1638 (SCL, Strafford MSS 10A, fo. 172).
[105] Laud to Wentworth, 29 December 1638 (*Laud works*, VII, 508). Also see *ibid.*, 483–5, 508.

Antrim also fell foul of the lord deputy's attempts to make Ireland financially self-sufficient by developing and revitalizing instruments of royal government such as the commission for defective titles, created to overhaul security of tenure, and the court of wards, which was responsible for collecting alienation fines, livery and wardship dues.[106] The trouble began in 1637. Upon his father's death, the new earl of Antrim was eager to secure a fresh title to his inheritance in the form of a new patent. He naively hoped this would include the 2,000 acres in the Long Liberties of Coleraine which his father had given for the plantation.[107] The Dublin administration insisted, however, that he should in turn relinquish some of his lucrative fishing rights and pay a number of hefty fines.[108] He was charged £2,200 in livery and alienation fines, and a further £1,300 in extraordinary fines.[109] By the spring of 1639 he still owed £700 to the court of wards, 'being the last payment of all my fines of alienation and liveries' and £1,200 to the Dublin Exchequer.[110] This was noted by the lord deputy: 'As for my Lord of Antrim, all is quiet and still there; all so fast asleep, as his lordship neither pays licenses of alienation, subsidies or rent.' He went on to wonder whether the king wished him to be awakened, 'lest otherwise he fall into the cave of those seven sleepers we read of in the legend?'.[111] Wentworth was determined to make the earl pay, in case 'others by his example will immediately pretend like reasons' thereby creating

---

[106] Raymond Gillespie, 'The end of an era: Ulster and the outbreak of the 1641 rising', in Brady and Gillespie (eds.), *Natives and newcomers*, pp. 194–5; Aidan Clarke, *The Graces, 1625–41* (Irish Historical Series, vol. VIII, Dundalk, 1968), pp. 27–9; Terence Ranger, 'Strafford in Ireland: a revaluation', in Trevor Aston (ed.), *Crisis in Europe 1560–1660* (London, 1970), pp. 282–91; Jonathan Watts, 'Thomas Wentworth, earl of Strafford' in Timothy Eustace (ed.), *Statesmen and politicians of the Stuart age* (London, 1985), pp. 100–3.

[107] Gillespie, *Colonial Ulster*, p. 97. Reason's why the king should consider Antrim's petition, [c. September 1637] (SRO, GD 406/M 1/277); *Laud works*, VII, 391–2, 438–9, 444–5, 448; Knowler, *Letters*, II, 157; Wentworth to Laud, 8 June 1638 (SCL, Strafford MSS 7, fo. 104r-v).

[108] Antrim to Wentworth, 6 April 1638 (SCL, Strafford MSS 18, fo. 12); Antrim to Wentworth, 25 June 1638 (*ibid.*, 18, fo. 69); *Laud works*, VII, 438–9, 444–5; Knowler, *Letters*, II, 426–8. Note that Chichester also was only granted a new patent after he surrendered his Lough Neagh fishing rights and paid a composition fine of £500, Roebuck, 'The making of an Ulster great estate', p. 20.

[109] Antrim to Charles I, 4 June 1641 (SRO, GD 406/1/1356); Knowler, *Letters*, II, 157, 169, 171; Wentworth to Laud, 8 June 1638 (SCL, Strafford MSS 7, fo. 104r–v); Gillespie, *Colonial Ulster*, pp. 98, 101.

[110] Antrim to Wentworth, 29 May 1639 (SCL, Strafford MSS 19, fo. 63). Also see Antrim to Wentworth, 10 November 1637 (*ibid.*, 22, fo. 139), and Antrim to Wentworth, 17 April 1639 (*ibid.*, 19, fo. 22).

[111] Wentworth to Vane, 24 July 1639 (Knowler, *Letters*, II, 426).

'very great disorder and confusion to his majesty's receipts here'.[112] However, no cash was forthcoming.[113]

What light do Antrim's clashes with Wentworth over the Ulster plantation, religion, crown finances and royal prerogatives shed on the nature of early Stuart policies in Ireland?[114] Aidan Clarke noted that James I aimed 'to gain full freedom of government action and to create a Protestant establishment upon a firm legal basis', but in order to do so it was first necessary 'to overcome the political and constitutional power of Catholics'. James adopted two strategies. On the one hand, civilizing, English influences were introduced into Ireland through schemes such as 'plantation' or the creation of a Protestant peerage which was designed to act as a bulwark against its Irish, Catholic counterpart. On the other, the Catholic interest was undermined by 'stricter enforcement of the statutes requiring religious conformity, and to the setting up of a Commission, and later a Court of Wards and Liveries, to organize this enforcement in the most effective and lucrative manner possible'.[115] In practice, of course, James's anti-Catholic policy was tempered. As his relationship with the first earl of Antrim clearly illustrates he was prepared, on a personal level, to tolerate Catholicism: neither the first earl's patronage of the Franciscan mission and Lough Derg nor his efforts to win the wardship of his kin had been issues of contention; and even after receiving complaints that the first earl was harbouring popish priests the king preferred to reason with, rather than punish, him.[116] Given his father's relationship with James I and the fact that he and his wife were allowed to worship freely at court, the second earl could only have been affronted and surprised by Wentworth's determination not only to frustrate his efforts to rebuild St Patrick's Purgatory but also to prevent him from being granted the wardship of his nephew or leasing the Londoners' lands.

Clearly attitudes towards Irish Catholic aristocrats had changed and hardened significantly by the 1630s. For as Sir William Parsons, master of the

---

[112] Wentworth and council to Vane, 4 June 1639 (Knowler, *Letters*, II, 358).
[113] Finally, the earl asked Hamilton to arrange for him to pay the money off in instalments, Antrim to Hamilton, 15 April 1640 (SRO, GD 406/1/1161). But on the eve of the rebellion the debt to the Exchequer had still not been repaid, Antrim to Hamilton, 19 July 1641 (SRO, GD 406/1/1389). Interestingly, his father had been equally tardy in paying his fines, *Laud works*, VII, 169–71, 236.
[114] I am grateful to Dr John Adamson and to Billy Kelly for their views on these issues.
[115] Aidan Clarke, *The Old English in Ireland 1625–1642* (Cornell, 1966), p. 20. Also see Mayes, 'The early Stuarts', p. 227, of eighty new Irish peers created between 1603 and 1641, nearly fifty or two-thirds were English and Protestant (p. 247).
[116] *Cal. SP Ire., 1615–25*, pp. 324–5, 337. For example, Antrim was granted the wardship of Lord Slane in 1629, *ibid., 1625–32*, p. 487.

court of wards, noted 'We must change their course of government, apparel, manner of holding land, language and habit of life. It will otherwise be impossible to set up in them obedience to the laws and [to] the English empire.'[117] Yet Wentworth's administration did not mark a radical departure; for his 'thorough' policies, which turned out to be extremely successful, were designed to implement effectively the policies laid down by James – namely the extension of royal control and the promotion of a Protestant establishment.[118] In fact this signified a return to Sir Henry Sidney's lord deputyship of the 1570s; or even to the 1540s when the crown attempted to 'impose policies for reform on all the island's communities in hope of creating a politically and culturally homogeneous kingdom'.[119] Thus in every respect Antrim was cutting against the grain of Stuart government in Ireland. A clash was almost inevitable.

Antrim's refusal to compromise over these key issues totally alienated the lord deputy who, in retaliation, ignored the earl.[120] Laud once again came to the rescue and ordered Wentworth to restore his patronage: 'The truth is I will not be denied this kindness from you but that you shall be heartily reconciled to my Lord Antrim and do him and his estate there all the real and just kindness that you can.'[121] Shortly afterwards the archbishop issued a further warning claiming that if his request was denied Wentworth would 'utterly discredit me, and make the world think I have no interest in you'.[122]

So it was with Laud's full support and Wentworth's grudging approval that in 1638 the couple prepared to move to Ireland in order to economize and

---

[117] Parsons to Conway [December 1625] (ibid., p. 58).
[118] During the 1630s the first and second earls both tried not to pay their dues to the crown (usually by appealing directly to Laud or the king) and Wentworth pursued them without mercy. For instance in November 1635 the lord deputy refused to be intimidated by 'the pardon petitioned for by my lord of Antrim for alienations made without our license' and referred this 'business of great consequence' to the court of wards, Wentworth to Laud, 2 November 1635 (SCL, Strafford MSS 6, fo. 274).
[119] Kearney, *Strafford*, p. xvii; Brady and Gillespie (eds.), *Natives and newcomers*, p. 20.
[120] Antrim was genuinely peeved by this and claimed only to want Wentworth's affection, Antrim to Wentworth, 25 April 1638 (SCL, Strafford MSS 18, fo. 23). This then upset Laud who was distressed that '192 [Antrim] is much fallen from your favour ... and I am heartily sorry for it'. He begged to know what the earl had done now so that he could straighten matters out between them, Laud to Wentworth, 30 May 1638 (*Laud works*, VII, 438–9, 444–5).
[121] Laud to Wentworth, [June?] 1638 (*Laud works*, VII, 455). The duchess reinforced Laud's message, duchess of Buckingham to Wentworth, [June 1638?] (SCL, Strafford MSS 22, fo. 42).
[122] Laud to Wentworth, 31 August 1638 (*Laud works*, VII, 479). Also see [Laud] to Wentworth, July 1638 (SCL, Strafford MSS 7, fo. 128).

Caroline courtier 73

thus reduce their debts.[123] To facilitate the move the king agreed that they should use one of his own ships for the passage and in July 1638 Antrim asked Wentworth to send a substantial vessel with a 'large sweet cabin' for the duchess to meet them near Liverpool during the last week in August.[124] After a series of minor delays they were finally met by a pinnace at Chester which transferred them to Captain Kettleby's 'great ship' at Beaumaris.[125] This journey cost the crown nearly £500, and Wentworth was furious: 'we are all for ostentation, no moderate thing will suffice, as is land, sea and all were to minister to [his] glory' he fumed.[126] In another letter to Lord High Admiral Northumberland he complained of the navy being 'led up and down in the masques or pageants' of one man's vanity.[127] But the journey was eventually completed: on 29 September 1638, Sir James Ware recorded in his diary that 'Randal earl of Antrim and his wife Katherine duchess of Buckingham landed at Bloick [Bullock] in the County of Dublin and went that night to Powerscourt. From whence the next day they took their journey towards the north.'[128]

The couple settled down to life in East Ulster remarkably swiftly. They made Dunluce castle their primary residence and, after September 1639 (when the king leased them 300 acres in the Long Liberties), they also spent time in a house near Coleraine.[129] As an inventory of furnishings removed from these properties in 1642 illustrates, the duchess maintained her Irish homes as lavishly as her English ones.[130] Items in the living quarters included twelve armchairs, sixty-three stools, thirty-seven cushions and sixty-six pairs of curtains, all of which were either upholstered in or made out of the most exquisite, expensive fabrics (scarlet and blue silk, crimson and black velvet,

---

[123] Knowler, *Letters*, II, 217. Impoverished Scottish nobles also retreated to their estates to economize, Brown 'Aristocratic finances', p. 76.
[124] Antrim to Wentworth, 17 July 1638 (Knowler, *Letters*, II, 184). Once again Laud backed up his request, Laud to Wentworth, 30 July 1638 (*Laud works*, VII, 467, 471). Also see Antrim to Wentworth, 6 August 1638 (SCL, Strafford MSS 18, fo. 99).
[125] Wentworth to Laud, [September] 1638 (SCL, Strafford MSS 7, fo. 131v); Laud to Wentworth, 8 October 1638 (*ibid.*, fo. 140); *Cal. SP Dom., 1638–9*, p. 4. No record of their voyage or what they brought with them to Ireland appears to have survived.
[126] Wentworth to Laud, [September] 1638 (SCL, Strafford MSS 7, fo. 131v). Also see Knowler, *Letters*, II, 300–5.
[127] Wentworth to Northumberland, 18 September 1638 (SCL, Strafford MSS 10B, fo. 19).
[128] Sir James Ware's diary of occurrences (Dublin City Library, MS 169, p. 218). Their reception (much to Laud's chagrin) was not, however, a particularly warm one, Knowler, *Letters*, II, 248, 262–3.
[129] Where exactly they lived is a mystery; certainly Antrim intended building a house on this land but whether it was ever completed, or even started, is another matter.
[130] The need to keep up appearances was crucial, Brown 'Aristocratic finances', pp. 63–4.

gold and silver lace, white silver damask, and green satin were the most common). These handsomely upholstered items were complemented by over thirty Turkish or Persian carpets of varying sizes, ornate and exotic cabinets of ebony and ivory, delicately crafted folding screens, gilt framed pictures, exquisite wall hangings and sumptuous tapestries and fifty-nine damask tablecloths with matching napkins to adorn the earl's table. The sleeping quarters – containing at least seventeen beds – were equally well equipped with over 100 damask towels and astonishing amounts of bedlinen (pillows, bolsters, counterpanes, blankets, quilts, valances and so on). There was also a library of over fifty books (in octavo, quarto and folio), and an opulent collection of miscellaneous items such as mirrors, maps, abacuses, a telescope, a celestial and terrestrial globe; while the altars and pulpits in Antrim's chapel were adorned with 'sixteen pieces of rich embroidered green satin vestments'.[131] Nearly every item listed in this inventory is exceptionally regal and splendid and it is interesting to note that the earl of Kildare's castle at Maynooth, the earl of Cork's various residences and Ormond's houses (after the Restoration) were furnished in similar fashion.[132] Details of Antrim's wardrobe also survive; he wore elaborate suits of green satin or black velvet lined with silk cloth interwoven with silver and gold thread, 'cassocks' and 'dubletts'.

A magnificent house richly furnished and expensive clothes cut in the latest London fashion impressed social equals and superiors; testified to Antrim's 'Englishness' and to his importance as an influential Caroline courtier;[133] and also proclaimed his standing as a Gaelic, Catholic overlord.[134] Yet Antrim ensured that, despite these luxurious appearances, Dunluce remained an Irish

---

[131] PRO, SP 23/237/25, fos. 62–9. Presumably this inventory is incomplete and comprises only the couple's more valuable and easily portable possessions. Large items such as long dining tables, benches and wardrobes were no doubt left behind. For a discussion of how the Commonwealth sequestered and then disposed of goods, see Ian Roy, 'The libraries of Edward, second Viscount Conway and others: an inventory and valuation of 1643', *BIHR*, 41 (1968), pp. 35–40. The duchess continued to import goods. For instance, in June 1639 one trunk and six boxes of Dutch cloth were dispatched from Chester to Dublin for her, Chester port book, 1639 (PRO, E190/1336/3, fo. 8v). I am grateful to Robert Hunter for bringing this reference to my attention.

[132] Knight of Glin, *Irish furniture* (Dublin, 1978), pp. 3–4; William Neely, 'The Ormond Butlers of County Kilkenny 1515–1715', in Nolan and Whelan (eds.), *Kilkenny*, pp. 120–1; Jane Fenlon, 'Some houses in England owned by the dukes of Ormond and their families', *Butler Society Journal*, 3 (1987), pp. 58–60.

[133] Peter Thornton, *Seventeenth century interior decoration in England, France and Holland* (Yale, 1978), p. 2.

[134] The same was true of other native lords such as Lords Maguire or Sir Phelim O'Neill, Russell, *Fall*, p. 374.

castle. The men wore native Irish clothing, and an Irish harper formed part of an extensive Gaelic retinue which included bards, poets, musicians and priests.[135] The bardic family of Ó Gnímh had traditionally associated itself with the MacDonnells; Fear Flatha Ó Gnímh had readily composed genealogies legitimizing the position of the first earl and no doubt other Gaelic poets continued to exalt the second earl and his Ulster lordship.[136] Moreover, Antrim continued to support the Franciscan mission at Bonamargy until the Superior of the mission – Patrick Hegarty – was arrested late in 1641.[137] Between 1632 and 1640 an annual average of 500 people came from Scotland alone to be reconciled with Catholicism at Bonamargy, where daily masses and the sacraments were celebrated, and as late as 1639 the bishop of Down and Connor, Bonaventure Magennis, accepted on a single occasion 700 Scots into the Catholic church.[138]

The couple had moved to Ireland in order to economize, however, and this they began to do with a vengeance.[139] In the spring of 1639 Wentworth updated Laud on their progress: 'It is reported the duchess expresseth much satisfaction in her present condition, and that they contract themselves into a narrow room, put away many of their servants, especially such, if not all of them, that were Protestant.'[140] But reducing the size of their Irish household and cutting back on the amount spent educating the duchess's sons did relatively little to pay off their 'great debt in England'; and so they decided, in the autumn of 1639, to sell Bramshill and the family jewels.[141] At last, by the

---

[135] PRO, SP 23/237/25, fos. 62–9; Canny, *Kingdom and colony*, p. 56. For further details on Irish dress, customs and eating habits, see T. Crofton Croker (ed.), *The tour of the French traveller M. de Boullaye le Gouz in Ireland, A.D. 1644* (London, 1837), pp. 39, 44–6, and Dionysius Massari, 'My Irish campaign', *The Catholic Bulletin*, (1917), p. 179.

[136] Bernadette Cunningham, 'Native culture and political change in Ireland, 1580–1640', in Brady and Gillespie (eds.), *Natives and newcomers*, pp. 149–50; Bernadette Cunningham and Raymond Gillespie, 'The East Ulster bardic family of Ó Gnímh' *Egise*, 20 (1984), pp. 108, 112–13.

[137] Black, 'Coll Ciotach', pp. 221–3.

[138] P. F. Anson, *Underground catholicism in Scotland, 1622–1878* (Montrose, 1970), pp. 39ff.

[139] Knowler, *Letters*, II, 262–3.

[140] Wentworth to Laud, 11 February 1639 (SCL, Strafford MSS 7, fo. 160v). Also see *Laud works*, VII, 531.

[141] Antrim and the duchess of Buckingham to Cottington, 20 February 1640 (*Cal. SP Dom., Addenda 1625–49*, p. 747). In September Archibald Stewart and the duchess travelled to England to carry out the business, duchess of Buckingham to Windebank, 9 September 1639 (*ibid., 1639*, p. 492), Antrim to Hamilton, 26 September 1639 (SRO, GD 406/1/1166), the duchess of Buckingham to Hamilton, 14 October [1639] (*ibid.*, 406/1/8175). Antrim to Hamilton, 29 April 1640 (*ibid.*, 406/1/1172).

early summer of 1640 matters were looking up; Bramshill was sold, and some (at least) of the creditors had received satisfaction.[142]

As the financial picture brightened in some areas, however, it darkened in others. Continued prosperity on the Antrim estates was threatened by a run of poor harvests between 1636 and 1639 and in the spring of 1639 the earl complained about the 'great want of money we have in these parts; and for my part I am sorry I find it true: for I am not like to receive the half of my rents in money'.[143] Worse still, the economic crisis was exacerbated by the gathering political storm. The Scottish wars (see chapter 3) caused considerable disruption on the Antrim estates. On the one hand, Wentworth's tyrannical measures against the Ulster Presbyterians forced hordes of Scotsmen, including many of the earl's own 'puritan' tenants, back across the Dalriadic sea, thereby depleting his pool of labour and his income.[144] On the other, Argyll's 'threatenings' forced the earl's Catholic tenants on Rathlin Island to flee to the mainland ('and by that means I loose my rent there').[145] They were soon joined by hundreds of MacDonald refugees from the Isles whom he was then obliged to support out of his own pocket.[146] For Antrim, as for his royal master, the outbreak of a rebellion in Scotland which could only be defeated by military action could scarcely have come at a worse time.

[142] Bramshill was sold to Robert Henley some time after April, Antrim to Hamilton, 29 April 1640 (SRO, GD 406/1/1172). *Victoria county history of Hampshire*, ed. Page, IV, 36; *Cal. SP Dom., 1639–40*, p. 339.

[143] Antrim to Wentworth, 16 May 1639 (Knowler, *Letters*, II, 339–40). For details on the harvest crises which plagued the 1630s, see Gillespie, 'End of an era', pp. 195, 205; *idem*, 'Harvest crises in early seventeenth century Ireland', *Ir. Econ. & Soc. Hist.*, 11 (1984), pp. 5–18; *idem*, 'Meal and money: the harvest crisis of 1621–4 and the Irish economy' in M. E. Crawford (ed.), *Famine. The Irish experience, 900–1900* (Edinburgh, 1989), pp. 75–95.

[144] Antrim to Hamilton, 14 January [1639] (SRO, GD 406/1/652); J. McLene [MacClean] to Sir Colin Campbell, 26 July 1639 (*ibid.*, 112/39/778); Patrick Adair, *True narrative of the rise and progress of the Presbyterian church in Ireland (1628–70)*, ed. W. D. Killen (Belfast, 1866), pp. 52, 59, 60; Gillespie, *Colonial Ulster*, pp. 52–3, 57, 82–3; M. Perceval-Maxwell, 'Strafford, the Ulster Scots and the covenanters', *IHS*, 8, no. 72 (Sept. 1973), pp. 524–51.

[145] Antrim to Hamilton, 13 October 1638 (SRO, GD 406/1/653). Also see duchess of Buckingham to Hamilton, 14 October [1639] (*ibid.*, 406/1/8175); Knowler, *Letters*, II, 339–40.

[146] Wentworth, hardly surprisingly, forbade him to billet them on the countryside 'for that would amount to a public scandal, and affright the whole kingdom', Wentworth to [Vane?], 21 May 1639 (SCL, Strafford MSS 10B, fos. 87–8), and Wentworth to Antrim, 23 May 1639 (Knowler, *Letters*, II, 353–4); Antrim to Hamilton, 23 December 1639 (SRO, GD 406/1/1168). Considerable numbers of these refugees were still in Ulster the following summer, Antrim to Hamilton, 3 June 1641 (*ibid.*, 406/1/1355).

3

Antrim and the 'Scottish business' (1638–1641)

'The Scottish business is extream ill indeed, and what will become of it God knows, but certainly no good' predicted Archbishop Laud in July 1638.¹ The 'Scottish business' had reached a head the previous year with riots in St Giles's church, Edinburgh, against the introduction of Laud's new English service book, and over the course of the next six months the king's opponents in Scotland had organized their resistance.² In March 1638 a national covenant binding these dissenters 'to defend both true religion and the king's authority' was signed, and with this control over Scottish affairs passed into the hands of the covenanters.³ Shortly afterwards the marquis of Hamilton was dispatched north to solve Scotland's problems. He failed. His uncompromising master, determined 'to stick to my grounds', now decided to use force to 'reduce that people [the Scots] to their obedience ... [since] not only now my crown but my reputation, forever, lies at stake'. He added ominously that 'I will rather die, than yield to those impertinent and damnable demands.'⁴ The English ambassador in Brussels supported his king's decision to use force against the Scots: 'Tis a thousand pities the Scots are possessed with a rebellious humour on pretense of religion, which hath ever been the worst pretense in all states and proved almost a[n] incurable fire, except the member infected [be] cut off at first instant.'⁵

As the revolt in Scotland gathered momentum the need to cut off the

---

¹ Laud to Wentworth, 20 July 1638 (Knowler, *Letters*, II, 185).
² For background on the troubles in Scotland, see Maurice Lee, *The road to revolution. Scotland under Charles I, 1625–37* (Urbana and Chicago, 1985), chapters 6 and 7; Stevenson, *The Scottish revolution*, chapters 1 and 2; Donald, *An uncounselled king*; and Macinnes, *Charles I*. Russell, *Fall*, chapter 3, explains why England lost the Bishops' Wars while Caroline M. Hibbard, 'Episcopal warriors in the British wars of religion', in Mark Charles Fissel (ed.), *War and government in Britain 1598–1650* (Manchester, 1991), pp. 164–92, provides a fascinating account on the contribution of the English clergy to the conflict.
³ Stevenson, *The Scottish revolution*, p. 85.
⁴ Charles I to Hamilton, 11 June 1638 (SRO, GD 406/1/10484).
⁵ [Gerbier] to Windebank, 1/11 June 1639 (PRO, SP 105/16, fo. 203).

infected 'member' became increasingly urgent. Early in 1638, the Catholic earl of Nithsdale (who had been urging the king to use force since October 1637) suggested sending an army of Irish and Scottish troops against the covenanters. The cooperation of all the leading Scottish Catholic nobles (Huntly, Douglas, Hamilton of Abercorn and Seton of Winton) reinforced by Lennox, Dumfries, Galloway and Herries was seen as vital if his plan was to succeed; equally important was support from the leading Irish nobles.

Whether Nithsdale had actually selected Antrim as a potential ally at this stage is unclear, but their subsequent relationship suggests that the earl was somehow privy to their plans.[6] Furthermore, Antrim was certainly involved in other plots at this time hatched by Hamilton. Over the summer of 1638 covenanting spies in London (particularly the earl's Ulster neighbour, Sir John Clotworthy) were convinced that he was up to no good. 'Antrim was recommended by the marquis [of Hamilton] to the king, as a man that might contribute largely to his service in this business' it was reported back to Edinburgh. Even the earl's intention to move back to Ireland over the summer of 1638 was made to seem sinister: 'I am certified he takes with your employment, and as a vizor to cover his intent this way he very shortly carries his duchess into Ireland with him and there resolves to live. Now I suppose his main design is to make what party he can there and in the highlands of Argyll.'[7] Antrim's letters to the marquis of Hamilton reveal that Clotworthy was extraordinarily well informed. Prior to his departure to Edinburgh in May, Hamilton – who was eager to foster an anti-Campbell alliance – had indeed recommended Antrim to the king and suggested using the MacDonnells on both sides of the North Channel as bulwarks against the covenanters in Western Scotland; and on 11 June 1638 Antrim reminded the king that 'the small remnant of my name in Scotland have refused to sign the covenant' and offered his own men for royal service.[8]

---

[6] Donald, *An uncounselled king*, pp. 55–6, 71; Stewart, 'Peoples of the Clan Ranald', pp. 63–4; Hibbard, *Popish plot*, pp. 97–8. Nithsdale was related by her first marriage to Katherine.

[7] [Clotworthy?] to John Flemming, 21 June 1638 (*Cal. SP Dom., 1637–8*, pp. 524–5). Also see [Clotworthy] to John Flemming, 26 June 1638 (NLS, Wod. Fo. 66, fos. 92–3); [Clotworthy] to 'my worthy friends', 11 July 1638 (NLS, Wod. Fo. 66, fos. 109–10), printed in David Dalrymple, *Memorials and letters relating to the history of Britain in the reign of Charles I* (Glasgow, 1766), pp. 42–3. It was rumoured in Scotland that Antrim 'has hired a Scottish ship, laden and furnished with powder and munition of war for Ireland', *News from England*, 15 July [1638] (reprinted in Laing, *Letters*, I, 72). For details on Clotworthy's mission to London, see Donald, *An uncounselled king*, pp. 191–6, and Stevenson, *Scottish Covenanters*, pp. 15–16.

[8] Antrim to Hamilton, 11 June 1638 (SRO, GD 406/1/1156). Also see Edward J. Cowan, *Montrose for covenant and king* (London, 1977), pp. 50–3; Stevenson, *Alasdair MacColla*, p. 65.

His offer came at an opportune moment, for it was precisely in the middle of June that Hamilton recognized that all hope of concluding a peaceful settlement with the covenanters had vanished and recommended the use of force to the king as the only realistic solution. From Edinburgh he urged Charles to use the earl:

I can not neglect the representing to your majesty that the earl of Antrim may be of use to you in this business, for [he] is beloved by divers of his name, and hath some pretensions to lands in Kintyre, [the] isles and highlands and will no doubt repair to Ireland and bring such forces with him as will put those covenanters in that disorder; and chiefly if the deputy can spare any of the army then to join with him, as I hope, that part of the country will do us little hurt.[9]

In short Hamilton suggested that an army levied and paid for by Antrim, and supplemented where possible by Wentworth, should be the first line of royalist offence in the west of Scotland.[10]

From Antrim's perspective Charles I's refusal to 'yield to the demands of those traitors the covenanters'[11] gave him a legitimate excuse to stir up the old MacDonnell–Campbell feud and to make a fresh bid for Clan Donald's patrimonial lands in the Western Isles.[12] The earl was at this point promised by Charles I 'whatsoever land he can conquer from them, he, having pretense of right, he shall have the same'.[13] And so over the summer of 1638, while still in London, the earl began mobilizing his support groups on both sides of the North Channel. In June, using Archibald Stewart as his intermediary, he contacted the leading Scottish MacDonalds – Archibald MacDonald of Sanda, Coll Ciotach MacDonald, the captain of Clan Ranald, the laird of

---

[9] Hamilton to Charles I, 15 June 1638 (SRO, GD 406/1/10488 and /10775. Also see S. R. Gardiner (ed.), *The Hamilton papers: being selections from original letters in the possession of his Grace the duke of Hamilton and Brandon, relating to the years 1638–1650* (Camden Society, London, 1880), pp. 12–13); Stevenson, *The Scottish revolution*, pp. 98–9; Gardiner, *Eng.*, VIII, 344, 353; Donald, *An uncounselled king*, pp. 71–5.

[10] Antrim later mentioned 'directions and authority by his majesty given at his last being in England, concerning his lordship's going upon the Isles of Scotland', Wentworth to Windebank, 20 March 1639 (Knowler, *Letters*, II, 300).

[11] Charles I to Hamilton, 20 June 1638 (Gilbert Burnet, *Memoirs of the lives and actions of James and William, dukes of Hamilton* ... (London, 1677), p. 59).

[12] See pp. 22–3 above.

[13] Vane to Wentworth, 11 April 1639 (Knowler, *Letters*, II, 319). Nearly a year later (April 1639) Wentworth discovered the truth: 'It would seem to me, for I was not of the council, my lord marquis of Hamilton and my lord of Antrim, had to his majesty undertaken the business before the earl's coming forth of England, consequently before Argyll was declared covenanter; my lord of Antrim was for his reward to have a share of his estate. What other shares there were, any, or none, in truth I know not', Wentworth to Vane, 16 April 1639 (Knowler, *Letters*, II, 325). Also see Wentworth to Charles I, 17 October 1638 (*ibid.*, 225–6); McKerral, *Kintyre*, p. 38; PRONI, D2977/Kintyre papers.

Glengarry and Sir Donald MacDonald of Sleat – who were only too willing to serve the Stuart king.[14] 'The earl of Antrim and the Clandonald in Ireland would come to Scotland with an army of men' Lord Lorne later learned; while his informant added 'that all the Clandonald in Scotland would join with them to take up arms against the earl of Argyll and his friends for recovering their old patrimonies'.[15]

The earl's eagerness to serve the king in Scotland bought him instant favour at court and Laud noted (without knowing the precise details) that 'he hath done the king lately very good service in Scotland. And I believe there will be further use of him and his kindred there'.[16] The king's willingness to make use of the earl can be explained by Hamilton's persistent and timely interventions on Antrim's behalf, by his own desperation and exasperation with the covenanters and by the need to find a speedy and, above all, a cheap solution to his Scottish problems. For, as Conrad Russell has noted, by the early seventeenth century the English crown was effectively demilitarized and was therefore dependent on military contractors (or foreign powers) to raise the royal army.[17] However, since entrepreneurs, capable of levying a large body of men, were entirely lacking in England, the king had no alternative but to look for support in Ireland in order to create a military power capable both of counteracting the covenanting forces and of guaranteeing an English political settlement. In this the king was fully justified for (in theory at least) 'as king of three kingdoms, Charles was as entitled to use the Irish as to use the English to repress his rebellious subjects of Scotland'.[18]

While this plan made sound economic and military sense, it was disastrous politically for it alienated from the king's cause Lord Lorne, one of the most

---

[14] Stevenson, *Alasdair MacColla*, pp. 65–6; *idem, Scottish Covenanters*, pp. 22–3; Stewart, 'Peoples of the Clan Ranald', p. 65; Huntly to [Hamilton], 18 January 1638 (SRO, GD 406/1/412); Sir Donald MacDonald of Sleat to Hamilton, 24 August 1638 (*ibid.*, 406/1/533; HMC, *Supplementary report*, p. 50); Sir Donald MacDonald of Sleat to Huntly, 25 July 1638 (SRO, GD 406/1/427); Antrim to Hamilton, 11 June 1638 (*ibid.*, 406/1/1156).
[15] Testimony of Duncan Omey of Kintyre, 21 July 1638 (SRO, GD 14/9, p. 135).
[16] Laud to Wentworth, [June?] 1638 (*Laud works*, VII, 455). Laud subsequently claimed that if Antrim had been 'led into any undertaking by 198 [Hamilton]' he would have confided this to the archbishop, Laud to Wentworth, 1 May 1639 (*ibid.*, 571–2). Wentworth later asserted that Antrim had actually admitted that 'his intent only was thereby to gain favour and honour from his majesty, without either hazard or expense to himself', Wentworth to Laud, 10 May 1639 (Knowler, *Letters*, II, 336).
[17] Conrad Russell, 'The Scottish party in English parliaments 1640–1642 or the myth of the English revolution' (Inaugural lecture, Department of History, King's College, London, 1991), pp. 3–8; Russell, *Fall*, pp. 79–81.
[18] Russell, *Fall*, p. 127.

important Scottish noblemen.[19] Thanks to well-informed covenanting leaks at court and in the Isles Lorne had quickly learnt of Antrim's plans and, fearing a Catholic crusade on his own doorstep, allied with the covenanting movement.[20] He argued that this was an attempt by 'the rebellious race of Clandonald' to take 'advantage of troublesome times to execute their rebellions' and believed that they were not only conspiring with the exiled Irish O'Donnells and O'Neills but also with the MacDonnells under Antrim's command.[21] And so, on the grounds 'that some of the Clandonalds had a design upon his country' he began to fortify the Western Isles and Kintyre (including Lochhead fort), to construct long boats, and to mobilize his men in preparation for war.[22] Having goaded Argyll into taking an offensive stance Antrim now claimed to be the 'injured' party and begged Wentworth – who was unaware of the minutiae of his clandestine negotiations with the king – for help. He asserted that his Campbell rival was preparing to attack his Ulster estates and insisted that his men should be armed by the crown, promising that 'these arms may alway[s] be kept in a store house in Coleraine, because it would be too far for me and my tenants to send to Carrickfergus, if there were any sudden invasion'.[23] Wentworth not only resented arming a Catholic 'of the race of O'Neale, and upon my own knowledge the great admirer of his grandfather Tyrone', but feared that the arms could be used against the crown by either the Irish, 'ill affected to the English', or the Ulster Scots, '[who are] ready to burn the hierarchy of the church to ashes, nay to sew and scatter them through the four corners of the world'.[24] So Wentworth not only refused to arm Antrim's tenants but also insisted that the earl

---

[19] It also meant that the Scots gave more support to Argyll's ambitions in Ireland, Russell, *Causes*, p. 125.
[20] Stevenson, *Scottish Covenanters*, pp. 23–4. Lorne believed 'That the earl came to take it [Kintyre] by strong hand; to which purpose three of your majesty's ships full of arms were appointed to bring and furnish him for the attempt', Wentworth to Charles I, 17 October 1638 (Knowler, *Letters*, II, 225–6). Also see *ibid.*, 325.
[21] Lorne to Wentworth, 25 July 1638 (Knowler, *Letters*, II, 187). Wentworth encouraged Lorne's outbursts against Clan Donald by reciting how a clan member – after being rejected as a suitable suitor for a County Down lass – murdered her father and then raped and abducted the girl, see Wentworth to [Coke], 8 May 1638 (SCL, Strafford MSS 11, fo. 77); Knowler, *Letters*, II, 210, 220–1.
[22] Wentworth to Charles I, 17 October 1638 (Knowler, *Letters*, II, 225–6). Also see *ibid.*, 235; Huntly to Hamilton, 10 November [1638] (SRO, GD 406/1/462).
[23] Antrim to Wentworth, 17 July 1638 (Knowler, *Letters*, II, 184). Also see Wentworth to Laud, 11 August 1638 (SCL, Strafford MSS 7, fos. 124–5).
[24] Wentworth to Laud, 11 August 1638 (SCL, Strafford MSS 7, fos. 124–5). Also see Knowler, *Letters*, II, 187–8, 211. Laud, while empathizing with Wentworth's fears (if Antrim was furnished with arms 'the world will have cause to wonder, and I to despair'), also believed that he was not a threat, Laud to Wentworth, [10 September] 1638 (*Laud works*, VII, 483–5).

should have no part in the army which he hoped to send against the covenanters:

> His religion, nor yet his descent (being the grandchild and son of your majesty knows whom) sort not well with it. And I am upon very probable reason for believing that in the way of pretending service, but doing nothing for your majesty, he attentively watcheth to do something for his own fortune and power, for which hereafter to thank himself far more than your majesty.[25]

At first it seemed as if Wentworth would have his way, for on his return to Ireland in September 1638 Antrim made no apparent effort to mobilize his own army or to intervene in Wentworth's levy.[26] But in fact the nine months between August 1638 and May 1639 represented a period of 'phoney war' which fell neatly into two phases. The first stage (August to December 1638) was a war of nerves during which Antrim (based primarily at Carrickfergus) vigilantly monitored the Campbells' preparations, fretted about the fate of his Scottish allies and worried about the future of his own tenants.[27] The five months between December 1638 and the actual outbreak of the first Bishops' War in May 1639 marked the second phase, which was characterized by preparations for war in all three kingdoms.

The move towards outright hostility around Christmas 1638 was precipitated by the covenanters' refusal either to obey or to sign the proclamation dissolving the general assembly of the church convened by Hamilton. At this point Argyll, though he resisted signing the covenant for several more months, openly joined the covenanters to ensure that 'no MacDonnell shall be allowed to enjoy a foot of land in Scotland'.[28] This was interpreted as a formal declaration by Argyll in favour of the king's enemies and gave Antrim the 'green light' to set in motion the plans which had been discussed the previous summer. The royalist grand strategy envisaged a four-fold attack: Charles I and the main English army were to invade Scotland from the borders; Hamilton and the the Royal Navy were to land 5,000 troops at Aberdeen to rendezvous with those prepared in the north-east by Huntly; Wentworth was to send an Irish expeditionary force to Dumbarton; and finally, Antrim was to invade the Western Isles and join forces with the men mobilized by Sir Donald MacDonald, who was also in close contact with

---

[25] Wentworth to Charles I, 11 August 1638 (Knowler, *Letters*, II, 203–4). There was considerable opposition to using Irish troops at all in Scotland, George Gage to Windebank, 2/12 March 1639 (Bodl., Clarendon MSS 15, fo. 173); Donald, *An uncounselled king*, pp. 133–5.

[26] This may also be attributed to the king's (temporary) decision not to use Irish troops, Knowler, *Letters*, II, 228.

[27] See, for instance, Antrim to Hamilton, 13 October 1638 (SRO, GD 406/1/653).

[28] Antrim to Wentworth, 31 December 1638 (Knowler, *Letters*, II, 266). See also Derek Hirst, *Authority and conflict. England 1603–1658* (London, 1986), p. 184.

Huntly. The king's supporters hoped that this 'may drain them [the covenanters] out of the world, for rebels are monsters not to be suffered amongst reasonable creatures'.[29]

Early in January 1639 Antrim renewed his requests for government arms and munition.[30] The king immediately instructed Wentworth to provide them: 'I should be glad if you could find some way to furnish the earl of Antrim with arms, though he be a Roman Catholic; for he may be of much use to me at this time, to shake loose upon the earl of Argyle'.[31] Though totally against arming 'so great a body of Irish together', Wentworth reluctantly agreed to do so, although even at this stage he attached little importance to Antrim's contribution to his master's grand strategy:[32] 'There is some opinion there may be some heats break forth betwixt the two great earls of Antrim and Argyle, but the sea is so happily set betwixt them, as perchance may so allay their warmth, as they will not give any great hurt one to the other, nor much trouble to other men.'[33]

In spite of the lord deputy's characteristic pessimism, Antrim began levying his army of 5,000 foot and 200 horse. In the absence of a formal commission from the king this was difficult.[34] Nevertheless, he exploited his position as a Gaelic lord in both Ulster and the Western Isles and summoned, as his ancestors had done, the men of his own lordship and of neighbouring sublordships to mobilize for war.[35] His Scottish allies, who could muster up to 4,000 Catholic MacDonalds, willingly agreed 'to recover me Kintyre and my ancient right to the Isles', while his Irish kin, friends and tenants also rallied to his call.[36] By March 1639 Antrim had written to 'all my chief kindred and tenants acquainting them with the king's pleasure, and [asking them] to prepare a list of such number of men they were able to raise and to have them in readiness upon a week's warning'.[37] These men were drawn

---

[29] [Gerbier] to Mr Walker, 10/20 April 1639 (PRO, SP 105/16, fos. 120–1).
[30] Antrim to Hamilton, 14 January [1639] (SRO, GD 406/1/652).
[31] Charles I to Wentworth, 25 January 1639 (Knowler, *Letters*, II, 275).
[32] Wentworth to Windebank, 20 March 1639 (*ibid*., 301). Also see *ibid*., 278.
[33] Wentworth to Newcastle, 10 February 1639 (*ibid*., 281). Wentworth did suggest that of the two Argyll was more likely to act aggressively, *ibid*., 289. Antrim's later demands for 1,200 barrels of powder were, however, denied since there were only 528 barrels in the whole kingdom! Wentworth and council to Vane, 4 June 1639 (*ibid*., 357–9).
[34] *Ibid*., 300–5. At the turn of the century his grandfather had mustered a force of 4,000 men, Morgan, 'The end of Gaelic Ulster', p. 19.
[35] Gillespie, 'End of an era', p. 209, argues that the plantation had not destroyed, but rather rationalized, the basic structure of Gaelic society, see also O'Dowd, 'Land and lordship', pp. 18–22.
[36] Antrim to Hamilton, 14 January [1639] (SRO, GD 406/1/652). See also Giblin, 'St. Oliver Plunkett', pp. 78–80.
[37] Antrim to [Hamilton], 17 March 1639 (SRO, GD 406/1/1154).

from the leading Irish families in Ulster: the O'Neills, O'Haras, O'Lurgans, Magennisess, MacGuires, MacMahons, MacDonnells, MacHenrys; or, as the lord deputy charmingly phrased it, 'as many Oe's and Macs's as would startle a whole council board' and 'in a great part the sons of habituated traitors'.[38] Antrim's personal army was to be supplemented by other units. For example, Lord Dillon from Athlone – 'a noble gallant gentleman, and a special friend ... and very ambitious to serve the king in this public action' – offered to serve with 2,000 men 'upon such conditions as others have'.[39]

Rallying an army 'of naked and inexperienced Irishmen' (as Wentworth dubbed it) on paper was one thing; preparing it for war, however, was more difficult.[40] Antrim needed experienced officers not only to train and discipline his motley bunch, but also to lead them, 'for there are no principal commanders in these parts' and he himself had 'no experience in war'.[41] In the absence of veteran officers in Ulster, Antrim's first instinct was to import from the continent men – such as his cousins Owen Roe O'Neill and Daniel O'Neill, or his half-brother Captain Maurice MacDonnell – well versed in the ways of modern warfare.[42] The very idea horrified Wentworth and so the earl was forced to make do with 100 relatively inexperienced drill sergeants from the king's army with 'one or two able old soldiers to be commanders'.[43]

Though inexperienced, Antrim had a surprisingly clear idea of how this army should be organized. The three regiments of foot were to consist of two

[38] Wentworth to Windebank, 20 March 1639 (Knowler, *Letters*, II, 300); Wentworth and council to Vane, 4 June 1639 (*ibid.*, 358).
[39] Dillon to Antrim, 8 March 1639 (SRO, GD 406/1/1152). Also see Antrim to [Hamilton], 17 March 1639 (*ibid.*, 406/1/1155). The earl of Kildare suggested that Crosby raise a regiment to serve in Scotland, Clarke 'Sir Piers Crosby', p. 147.
[40] Wentworth to Charles I, 13 May 1639 (Knowler, *Letters*, II, 338).
[41] Antrim to [Hamilton], 17 March 1639 (SRO, GD 406/1/1154).
[42] Antrim to Wentworth, 26 February 1639 (SCL, Strafford MSS 10A, fos. 257–8); Antrim to Wentworth [copy], 22 February 1639 (SRO, GD 406/1/1150). Antrim was only interested in bringing back carefully selected Irish officers and even warned the king of the dangers of allowing Tyrone and his regiment to return, Antrim to Hamilton, 14 January [1639] (*ibid.*, 406/1/652), and Knowler, *Letters*, II, 357–9. For his part, in May 1639, Tyrone suggested that Spain should send a force of 5,000 men to 'liberate' Ireland from British rule, see J. Alcalá-Zamora y Queipo de Llano, *España, Flandes y el mar del norte 1618–1639* (Barcelona, 1975), p. 410. Despite being warned not to, Antrim asked his half-brother Maurice to return, which he did in mid-1639, Cardinal Infante to Charles I, 17/27 June 1639 (Bodl., Clarendon MSS 17, fo. 17).
[43] Antrim's propositions [March] 1639 (Knowler, *Letters*, II, 305). Also see *ibid.*, 296–7. Henry Spottiswood who was later killed at Drogheda, Sir Henry Bruce – 'a very fair conditioned gentleman, and knowing in his profession' – and his nephew Captain (later Colonel) [John] Read were seconded 'to conduct Antrim's design', Charles I to Wentworth, 27 April 1639 (SCL, Strafford MSS 40, fo. 33); Wentworth to Vane, 21 April 1639 (*ibid.*, 10B, fo. 73); Wentworth to Charles I, 30 May 1639 (Knowler, *Letters*, II, 355–6).

parts 'shot' (musketeers), and one third pike ('with head-pieces and corslets, and small targents for defense against arrows'). The 200 horse were to be supplied with carbines, pistols, swords and buffcoats; the 3,200 musketeers were to be issued with 2 pounds of powder per man per week and appropriate amounts of lead; and the army as a unit was to be equipped with 12 field pieces, 2,000 spades, shovels and pickaxes, 200 sledges (to ferry victuals and munitions from the ships) and 1,000 sand baskets.[44] If this 'shopping list' was indeed drawn up without professional advice (as the earl claimed) it indicates that he had a very sound understanding of the latest developments in the ways of early modern warfare and that Wentworth's suggestion that he was an ignorant, incompetent amateur were unfounded.[45]

The earl had also worked out a very precise invasion plan. His men were to land first on Islay, which he intended to make 'my magazine' so that 'all my friends in the Isles may have free access to me'. Then, joined by his Highland allies, whom he intended to arm with long bows, he hoped to advance on the west side of Kintyre and to send about 500 men 'about the mule [sic] of Kintyre' to meet with Hamilton's forces in Arran.[46] The logistics of transporting and feeding 5,000 hungry men was a further formidable problem, but Antrim proposed to ship the soldiers in thirty Clan Donnell galleys 'of the burden to carry 100, or 200 men and their arms' which were to be built at his expense with wood cut from the king's forests in County Londonderry.[47] For victuals he intended shipping 'ten thousand live cows to furnish them with milk, which he affirmed had been his grandfather's [Tyrone's] play'; if the cattle were captured the soldiers would 'feed their horses with leaves of trees, and themselves with shamrocks'.[48] Here the lord deputy's scorn was more

---

[44] Antrim's propositions [March] 1639 (Knowler, *Letters*, II, 305).
[45] Knowler, *Letters*, II, 305, 303–4. For details on the latest continental military technology, see Parker, *The Army of Flanders*, p. 274; idem, *The Military Revolution. Military innovation and the rise of the west, 1500–1800* (Cambridge, 1988; 2nd edn, 1989), p. 60. Wentworth's verdict on Antrim's military inexperience is well known: 'few men are born generals, they have not that from their mothers but gain it by time and practice', Wentworth to Vane, 14 May 1639 (SCL, Strafford MSS 10B, fo. 76).
[46] Antrim to [Hamilton], 17 March 1639 (SRO, GD 406/1/1154).
[47] *Ibid.* His initial estimate had been for fifty to sixty longboats, Antrim to Hamilton, 14 January [1639] (*ibid.*, 406/1/652); Knowler, *Letters*, II, 300–5. Antrim claimed the longboats had cost £4,000 to build which Wentworth found hard to believe and estimated their cost to have been only £720, *ibid.*, 422–4; Antrim to Hamilton, 23 December 1639 (SRO, GD 406/1/1169). Ultimately, construction was delayed by the absence of skilled ship builders: 'carpenters (especially Scots) are very hard to be found; unless they are prepaid they will not work for this occasion', Antrim to Wentworth, 17 April 1639 (SCL, Strafford MSS 19, fo. 22).
[48] Wentworth to Windebank, 20 March 1639 (Knowler, *Letters*, II, 301–2). He was probably referring to 'trifoil' which resembled a shamrock and was eaten with bread and butter and

justified. He concluded that a shamrock-fed army would operate poorly, and warned that no support could be expected from Dublin.[49]

Since Antrim's role in, and contribution to, the first Bishops' War has been thoroughly documented by Aidan Clarke, David Stevenson and, more recently, Brendan FitzPatrick, it is unnecessary to reexamine the minutiae here.[50] However, in the light of previously unavailable archival material, a summary review of the chronology and an explanation of why Antrim's plans failed so miserably seem justified. Until recently, historians of the episode were forced to rely almost exclusively on Wentworth's papers for information; the animosity felt by him towards the earl has therefore inevitably seeped into subsequent accounts. As Clarke has recently noted: 'one of Wentworth's major achievements was to impose his version of the events of his deputyship upon generations of historians ... His influence similarly colours historical impressions of the people with whom he dealt.'[51] This bias must be balanced by a thorough examination of the papers of Antrim's dearest and closest ally during these months of tortuous negotiation, the marquis of Hamilton; for Antrim's uncharacteristically long, rambling and often intimate letters to the marquis provide a unique insight into his own motives, ambitions and feelings.[52] Moreover, they illustrate very clearly that it was not incompetence on the earl's part, nor lack of support for the enterprise in the Isles, which frustrated the mission, but rather a breakdown of communications between Antrim and the king and a total lack of support, financial or otherwise, from the administration in Dublin.

From the outset preparations for the expedition were severely hindered by Charles I's inconsistent attitude towards it. After endorsing Antrim's plan in August 1638 Charles appears to have had cold feet about executing it until early in 1639; and, even then, the earl's ability to set the venture in motion was further compromised by a lack of royal orders or 'particular directions'.[53] Then, suddenly, towards the end of February 1639, Antrim was given the impossible task of preparing his army, which he still had not been

appears to have been a staple part of the diet in Ulster, see Massari, 'My Irish campaign', *The Catholic Bulletin*, 7 (1917), pp. 179, 249.

[49] Wentworth to Antrim, 3 June 1639 (SCL, Strafford MSS 10A, fos. 335–7).
[50] Clarke, 'The earl of Antrim', pp. 109–15; Stevenson, *Scottish Covenanters*, pp. 22–32; Brendan FitzPatrick, *Seventeenth-century Ireland. The war of religions* (Dublin, 1988), chapter 4.
[51] Clarke, 'Sir Piers Crosby', p. 142.
[52] Twenty-five letters from Antrim to Hamilton between October 1638 and October 1641 have survived. They were usually delivered by Antrim's most trusted servants (Traylman, Babington and Stewart), Antrim to Hamilton, 14 January [1639] (SRO, GD 406/1/652). Despite the worsening situation in Scotland channels of communication between the two were maintained, Knowler, *Letters*, II, 266.
[53] Antrim to Hamilton, 14 January [1639] (SRO, GD 406/1/652).

formally commissioned to muster, for the invasion of Western Scotland by the beginning of April.⁵⁴ Somewhat alarmed, Antrim hurried to Dublin to inform the lord deputy of the 'honour and charge the king did impose on me and to demand his lordship's assistance and instructions' for he had been warned not to levy men without a warrant or a commission under the great seal. The ever-paranoid Wentworth feared that Antrim was intent on making a laughing-stock of him and claimed that he knew nothing of the venture. He then asked for his demands in writing, but the earl was reluctant to comply 'having taken no advise from experienced soldiers'.⁵⁵ According to Antrim's own account of the interview, Wentworth was totally uncooperative. He was loath to give advice, and claimed that there were no arms to spare nor was there shipping available to support Antrim's invasion force.⁵⁶ The lord deputy's reasons for opposing the venture, which he articulated loudly, were endless. In order to avoid having to take any action he suggested the campaign be delayed until the following spring.⁵⁷ However, Antrim was insistent. He was angered by the recent capture of his kinsman Archibald MacDonald of Sanda and his sons by Argyll, and so begged Wentworth for immediate leave to 'revenge my friends, and especially the king's quarrel, and you shall shortly see or hear a great alteration'.⁵⁸

Early in April the king ordered Wentworth to stop hindering the design and to ensure that 'Antrim be set upon Argyll' as soon as possible.⁵⁹ Now at last, precisely ten months after the matter had been first discussed and three months after Antrim had been given permission to begin preparations, Charles declared that 'the time to be proper now to pass his lordship a commission under the Great Seal of Ireland for the raising of forces, with

---

54 Wentworth to Antrim [copy], 22 February 1639 (*ibid.*, 406/1/1149); Antrim to Wentworth, 26 February 1639 (SCL, Strafford MSS 10A, fos. 257–8); Antrim to Wentworth [copy], 22 February 1639 (SRO, GD 406/1/1150); Wentworth to Northumberland, 15 April 1639 (SCL, Strafford MSS 10B, fos. 65–6).
55 Antrim to [Hamilton], 17 March 1639 (SRO, GD 406/1/1154). Also see Knowler, *Letters*, II, 296–7, 300–5; Antrim to Wentworth, 12 March 1639 (SRO, GD 406/1/1153).
56 Antrim to [Hamilton], 17 March 1639 (SRO, GD 406/1/1154); Wentworth to Laud, [April?] 1639 (SCL, Strafford MSS 7, fo. 181v).
57 Knowler, *Letters*, II, 300–5. Wentworth complained about Antrim to the king, Laud, Northumberland and the royal secretaries. As the time passed his account of the interview became increasingly polished, for instance: 'But his lordship had not been twelve hours in town, but the crack of his bolt was heard all over the town, that my lord of Antrim was forthwith in an expedition against the Isles of Scotland', Wentworth to Northumberland, 15 April 1639 (SCL, Strafford MSS 10B, fos. 65–6).
58 Antrim to Wentworth, 12 April 1639 (Knowler, *Letters*, II, 321). Also see Antrim to [Hamilton], 17 March 1639 (SRO, GD 406/1/1154).
59 Charles I to Wentworth, 10 April 1639 (SCL, Strafford MSS 40, fo. 32).

power to transport them to Scotland'.⁶⁰ This letter of 11 April sent from York was, however, contradicted by one sent two days later from the king's secretary of state in London. This second missive, dated 13 April, suggested that the expedition be delayed until the following spring, since 'the fire in Scotland is not likely to be so soon extinguished'.⁶¹ This would give the earl (encouraged and supported this time by Wentworth) sufficient time to prepare his forces.⁶² These conflicting orders naturally created crisis and chaos in Dublin and a brief period of utter confusion followed. Initially Wentworth and the council decided to follow the orders from York on the grounds that they had been received eight days before those from London. Antrim, however, now changed his tune and favoured delaying the invasion as the letter of 13 April from London had directed.⁶³ This prevarication was a great tactical error on the earl's part, for Wentworth seized the opportunity to place all blame for the delays squarely on his shoulders. He also suggested abandoning the campaign altogether due to the lateness of the season and to Antrim's ill preparedness.⁶⁴

In any case it was by now apparent that the king's grand strategy for the recovery of Scotland was in a shambles. Charles had experienced enormous difficulties in raising – never mind training – an English army; Huntly's resistance in north-east Scotland had been quickly overwhelmed, so that there was no army with which Hamilton, who was sailing aimlessly up and down the east coast of Scotland, might rendezvous; Wentworth's own offensive had been frustrated by the covenanters' capture of Dumbarton castle, while Antrim's contribution had collapsed.⁶⁵ Despite these setbacks, however, an alternative was cobbled together. Hamilton's force was to be redirected to the Forth, where it was to meet up with an English army of invasion under the command of the king, who had arrived at York on 31 March 1639. In order to maintain the threat (for it could be nothing more than this) from Ireland, Antrim was urged to 'make show of having purpose to invade Kintyre, and the other western parts of Scotland belonging to the earl of Argyll'.⁶⁶

---

60 Vane to Wentworth, 11 April 1639 (Knowler, *Letters*, II, 318–19). Also see *ibid.*, 334.
61 Windebank to Wentworth, 13 April 1639 (Knowler, *Letters*, II, 322).
62 *Ibid.*, 322–3, 336.
63 Antrim to Wentworth, 17 April 1639 (SCL, Strafford MSS 19, fo. 22); Knowler, *Letters*, II, 334–7, 419–21, 357–9; Wentworth to Vane, 14 May 1639 (SCL, Strafford MSS 10B, fo. 76, and SRO, GD 406/1/1162).
64 Wentworth to Charles I, [end April] 1639 (SCL, Strafford MSS 3, fo. 71).
65 Stevenson, *The Scottish revolution*, p. 141.
66 Windebank to Antrim, 23 March 1639 (Knowler, *Letters*, II, 323). Also see *ibid.*, 336, 357–9, 419–21. To keep his spirits up the king sent the earl £300 and Sir Henry Bruce, Vane to Hamilton, 8 May 1639 (SRO, GD 406/1/1199/2).

While Wentworth realized the importance of having 'a party in the north [and west] of Scotland which, hanging over the covenanters as a dark cloud, might give them the apprehension to have their coats soundly washed in case they went too far from home', he was not convinced that this strategy would prevent Argyll from joining up with the main covenanting army on the borders.[67] He remarked, with typically bluff Yorkshire humour, 'How this physick will work with Argyll I know not, who looks upon things with other eyes (for I am told they are squint ones) perchance then our earl doth.'[68]

Towards the end of May this plan too was modified. Sir Donald MacDonald of Sleat and Archibald Stewart were sent to the borders, with Hamilton's approbation but without Wentworth's, on the pretext of securing royal shipping and aid for those persecuted by Argyll in the Isles. In fact Antrim had sent them to discuss with the king the possibility of a renewed MacDonnell–MacDonald offensive and to secure a commission 'to seize upon all covenanters goods that we can [acquire] of the Isles, and Highlands of Scotland'.[69] Charles met with Sir Donald and Stewart near Berwick on 5 June (just before negotiations with the covenanters began) and agreed to supply them with a ship and arms for over 1,000 men. The following week, after negotiations had begun, he appointed Antrim and Sir Donald to be his joint lieutenants and commissioners in the Highlands and Islands. Therefore at the very last minute Charles gave Antrim the commission for which he had been waiting so long and promised to confer on him his ancestral lands in Kintyre and Islay. Sir Donald was to be rewarded with Argyll's holdings in Ardnamurchan and Strathordale.[70]

Meanwhile, back in Ireland, Antrim (who had anticipated a favourable response from the king) had already begun to badger Wentworth for naval support for his invasion force.[71] Once again the lord deputy refused. As always his excuses were cogent and comprehensive. He was unable to issue a warrant without the king's express order; any money for the expedition must come from the English treasury; the campaigning season was virtually over; 'the earl of Antrim's party [in the Isles] is not so powerful as his lordship

---

[67] Wentworth to [Vane?], 21 May 1639 (SCL, Strafford MSS 10B, fos. 87–8).
[68] Wentworth to Northumberland, 15 April 1639 (*ibid.*, fo. 66).
[69] Antrim to Wentworth, 29 May 1639 (*ibid.*, 19, fo. 63). Also see Antrim to [Hamilton], 13 July 1639 (SRO, GD 406/1/1164); Knowler, *Letters*, II, 353–4, 386, 387; Wentworth to Sir Donald MacDonald, 23 May 1639 (SCL, Strafford MSS 10A, fo. 317).
[70] Hill, *MacDonnells*, pp. 253–4, 444–6; Stevenson, *Scottish Covenanters*, pp. 30–1; *idem*, *Alasdair MacColla*, pp. 68, 71; Cowan, *Montrose*, p. 53.
[71] Antrim to Wentworth, 29 May 1639 (SCL, Strafford MSS 19, fo. 63).

pretends';[72] the treacherous waters around the Isles were unnavigable; and finally, Antrim was only reviving the matter in an attempt to shift responsibility for failure on to the king and to undermine his representative in Ireland.[73] Privately, however, Wentworth wondered whether the king had lost his senses altogether and concluded that his dependence on Antrim's promises clearly indicated that 'His majesty is too close to himself, too scant to his ministers in his councels'.[74]

While Antrim and the lord deputy were still squabbling in Ireland the king made his peace with the covenanters at Berwick on 18 June.[75] As far as Antrim was concerned, the first Bishops' War was over before it had begun, but the debate over who was really to blame for the failure of his expedition continued to rage well into July when the king finally accepted (as subsequent historians have done) Wentworth's version of events.[76] Even then Antrim, eager to relate his side of the fiasco and to prevent Argyll's recent title to Kintyre being confirmed by parliament, begged Hamilton's permission to join the king at Berwick 'since he is so near me and I have much to say to your lordship which I cannot trust to paper'.[77] In the event he was unable to do so and no record of his 'defence' has survived; but, judging by his correspondence with Hamilton, he would have claimed that it was lack of direction from London and Dublin, together with Wentworth's animosity, which had thwarted the venture. Would he have been right; or was Wentworth justified in asserting that the earl's plans were doomed to failure from the outset?

A number of Scottish covenanters certainly took the expedition extremely seriously and felt that only Argyll's vigilance (combined, of course, with divine intervention) prevented the anti-Campbell alliance in Ireland and the Highlands, united by 'the king's money and authority', from recovering 'their ancestor's patrimony'.[78] The most convincing argument in Antrim's defence

---

[72] Wentworth and council to Vane, 4 June 1639 (Knowler, *Letters*, II, 357–9).
[73] Wentworth to Antrim, 30 May 1639 (SCL, Strafford MSS 10A, fo. 329); Wentworth to Vane, 30 May 1639 (*ibid.*, 10B, fo. 96); Wentworth to Antrim, 3 June 1639 (*ibid.*, 10A, fos. 335–7); Knowler, *Letters*, II, 359. Wentworth later added that as for 'the Isle of Skye, I had rather seek it forth in the map, than be bound to go thither for it, and for that and those mentioned by my lord of Antrim ... they are neither worth the taking nor the keeping', Wentworth to Vane, 7 July 1639 (*ibid.*, 422–4).
[74] Wentworth to Northumberland, 15 April 1639 (SCL, Strafford MSS 10B, fos. 65–6).
[75] On 16 June Antrim actually went to Dublin to repeat his request for arms and shipping, Wentworth to Vane, 19 June 1639 (*ibid.*, fos. 109–11). Stevenson, *The Scottish revolution*, pp. 151–6.
[76] Knowler, *Letters*, II, 363, 422–4; FitzPatrick, *Seventeenth-century Ireland*, pp. 108–12.
[77] Antrim to [Hamilton], 13 July 1639 (SRO, GD 406/1/1164).
[78] Baillie to Spang, 28 September 1639 (Laing, *Letters*, I, 193). Stewart, 'Peoples of the Clan Ranald', p. 88, stresses that 'divided, the clans were merely anachronistic and troublesome; united, they were a very real threat'.

is that only five years later (in 1644) he succeeded in executing a plan similar to the one mooted in 1638–9, under even more stressful and difficult conditions.[79] There were, however, two key differences between the situation in 1639 and 1644. Above all, in 1639 Antrim suffered from a chronic shortage of money which, in turn, increased his dependence on the Dublin administration. Though the earl had resolved to 'set my whole fortune' on the successful execution of the expedition, his enormous debts and his inability to secure further credit prevented him from doing so.[80] He was therefore forced to ask the king for a loan of £20,000 in order to maintain his army for three months and to beg Wentworth to delay the payment of £1,200 owed to the Irish Exchequer and a further £700 owed to the court of wards, so that some money would be available for victuals 'for I must lay out all my own rents in provision'.[81] The virtually empty Irish and English Treasuries were unable to meet these demands, still less to pay out the £29,751 requested to cover Antrim's purchase of arms, munitions, shipping and equipment.[82] By contrast, in 1644, though the confederate Catholics and the marquis of Ormond were also practically bankrupt, their determination to send Irish troops to Scotland inspired them to find the necessary resources.

The second factor which ultimately torpedoed Antrim's plan stemmed from the earl's poor relationship with Ireland's lord deputy. Though Ormond had his own misgivings about Antrim and his expedition in 1644 he supported him to the hilt.[83] Wentworth in 1639, by contrast, did everything possible to obstruct, misrepresent and undermine the earl.[84] In many ways conflict between the two was inevitable. On the one hand, Wentworth was a colonizing, Protestant Englishman determined to bring the Elizabethan conquest of Ireland to a happy conclusion; on the other, Antrim – despite his marriage and his other English connections – was born and bred a Catholic in Ireland.[85] While there is no surviving evidence to justify Wentworth's fears

---

[79] See chapter 5 for details.
[80] Antrim to Wentworth, 29 May 1639 (SCL, Strafford MSS 19, fo. 63). Also see Knowler, *Letters*, II, 334–7, and pp. 61–8 above for details on Antrim's debts.
[81] Antrim to Wentworth, 17 April 1639 (SCL, Strafford MSS 19, fo. 22). Also see Antrim to Wentworth, 29 May 1639 (*ibid.*, fo. 63); Antrim to [Hamilton], 17 March 1639 (SRO, GD 406/1/1154); Knowler, *Letters*, II, 305, 303–4.
[82] Knowler, *Letters*, II, 419–21, 357–9. In addition to the expenses generated by Antrim's expedition, a further £50,000 was needed to pay for the 8,000 men to be levied by Wentworth, Wentworth to Hamilton, 24 March 1639 (SRO, GD 406/1/803).
[83] See chapter 5 below.
[84] Stevenson, *Scottish Covenanters*, pp. 25–31; Gardiner, *Eng.*, IX, 8. Their relationship is discussed at some length in FitzPatrick, *Seventeenth-century Ireland*, pp. 80–5, 92–9, 102.
[85] Hugh F. Kearney, 'Strafford in Ireland, 1633–40', *History Today*, 39, no. 7 (July 1989), pp. 23–5. For further details, see pp. 71–2 above.

that Antrim was a traitor to the English cause, they were entirely understandable and were indeed exacerbated by the earl's own insensitivity.[86] For there can be little doubt that Antrim regarded Wentworth as a jumped up gentleman who had been raised by administrative service to the king far beyond his social status and who had little right to interfere with the prerogatives of a great aristocrat.[87]

Wentworth exactly captured the dichotomy of Antrim's position and personality in a perceptive description of their disastrous interview in March 1639: 'His lordship was in [as] differing tempers as ever I saw: sometimes the grand-child of great Tyrone... and sometimes again he descended... even to make himself like one of ourselves.'[88] Jealousy of any credit which the venture could win for Antrim exacerbated these cultural differences. As it was, he had already antagonized the lord deputy over a number of issues (discussed in chapter 2) and his undiplomatic, even clumsy, handling of the Scottish expedition did nothing to improve matters. Several specific incidents excited the lord deputy's sense of paranoia: the conception and orchestration of the invasion of the Isles without his knowledge; the earl's continued willingness to plot and conspire behind his back (exemplified in Sir Donald's trip to see the king at Berwick in June 1639); and his tactless insistence that Phelim O'Neill (later a leading insurgent in 1641) be knighted at the height of the Scottish crisis.[89] Finally Antrim's private correspondence with Hamilton and Charles was a constant irritant: 'I know full well what I think of these kinds of traps laid to take me by the fingers', Wentworth wrote, and continued '[I intend] to catch the earl in his own snares.'[90] It was in reality Wentworth's obsession with trapping Antrim 'in his own snares' that sabotaged Irish aid for the king against the Scottish covenanters.

The abortive expedition was not without its significance, however. First and foremost it further destablized affairs in Scotland by alienating support for the king and forcing Argyll and his followers into the covenanting camp. In Ireland the divisions and animosities aroused by Antrim's plans only served to generate negative and hostile feelings at all levels of society and, more practically, to divide the country's meagre resources at a time when a united and concerted effort might have produced very dramatic results in all

---

[86] *Laud works*, VII, 508.
[87] See, for example, Wentworth to Laud, 10 July 1637 (SCL, Strafford MSS 7, fo. 35v). I am grateful to Dr David Stevenson for this observation.
[88] Wentworth to Laud, 10 May 1639 (Knowler, *Letters*, II, 336).
[89] Wentworth to Laud, [April?] 1638 (SCL, Strafford MSS 7, fo. 181v). See pp. 55, 89 above.
[90] Wentworth to Laud, 10 May 1639 (Knowler, *Letters*, II, 334–7).

three kingdoms.[91] As for England, the king's willingness to conspire with an Irish papist – never mind with English and Scottish ones – against his Protestant subjects (albeit Scottish ones) did little either to dispel the rumours of popish plots which were circulating around London or to inspire confidence in a monarch reputed to have been brainwashed by a Catholic coterie at court.[92]

Moreover, the peace signed at Berwick was an uneasy one. For, as the king was reminded; 'There is a Scottish proverb, that bids you put two locks on your door, when you have made friends with a foe.'[93] As far as Antrim was concerned the peace settled nothing and a 'cold war' raged with Argyll, who retained a force of 200 troops and continued to build ships.[94] There were reports among the Campbells of MacDonnell atrocities, and the Campbells were quick to retaliate.[95] Argyll, for instance, molested many of Antrim's kin when they returned to the Isles to claim their land and goods under the terms of the peace, and he later raided the island of Colonsay, stripping and raping the women, 'which barbarity was never practiced by the Turks and all this cruelty is for my sake'.[96] In August 1640 Argyll's men did 'most cruelly and barbarously burn the principal dwelling house' at Keppoch, while furniture, outhouses, barns, crops and livestock belonging to other MacDonalds were either pillaged or destroyed.[97] In order to antagonize Antrim further, Argyll not only continued to seize MacDonnell property and possessions but also arrested his principal supporters – including Coll Ciotach and two of his sons – in the Isles.[98] The earl was powerless to offer his allies practical help apart

---

[91] Stevenson, *Scottish Covenanters*, pp. 31–2; FitzPatrick, *Seventeenth-century Ireland*, pp. 112–14.
[92] Hibbard, *Popish plot*, pp. 124–7, 157–62.
[93] Wentworth to Charles I, 22 June 1639 (Knowler, *Letters*, II, 361).
[94] J. McLene [MacClean] to Sir Colin Campbell, 4 July 1639 (SRO, GD 112/39/777); Knowler, *Letters*, II, 374.
[95] For example, MacDonnell seamen supposedly killed fifty Campbells in Jura in June, J. McLene [MacClean] to Sir Colin Campbell, 25 June 1639 (SRO, GD 112/39/776). A few months later a raiding party of eighty Irishmen, led by Coll McGillespik's sons, attempted to take Campbell hostages, George Campbell to Sir Colin Campbell, 18 November 1639 (*ibid.*, 112/39/823). There was nothing novel in this. For instance, the previous spring, suspected 'MacDonnell spies' in Kintyre were arrested, while MacDonalds, loyal to the king, living in Campbell territories were persecuted, Archibald Campbell of Glencarradale to Sir Colin Campbell, 5 April 1639 (*ibid.*, 112/39/757); Knowler, *Letters*, II, 321. Antrim was greatly disturbed by this, Antrim to Wentworth, 11 April 1639 (*ibid.*, 321).
[96] Antrim to [Hamilton], 14 July 1639 (SRO, GD 406/1/1165). Also see Knowler, *Letters*, II, 374; Stevenson, *Scottish Covenanters*, pp. 34–5.
[97] Suit by Aenas Lord MacDonald and other MacDonalds against Argyll for losses sustained in 1640, 1645 and 1654, 20 March 1661 (Inverary castle, Argyll muniments, bundle 801).
[98] Antrim to Hamilton, 23 December 1639 (SRO, GD 406/1/1168); Stevenson, *Alasdair MacColla*, pp. 69–71; Black, 'Colla Ciotach', pp. 225–6.

from begging Wentworth to discipline Argyll for violating the articles of the peace treaty and pleading with Hamilton to 'save them [his kinsmen] from this great covenanters oppressions'.[99] He also supported the anti-Campbell alliance orchestrated by Sir Donald in the weeks after Berwick.[100]

Seen from the perspective of Antrim in East Ulster and his kinsmen in Western Scotland the treaty of Berwick, which had brought a temporary, uneasy peace to the rest of Stuart Britain, was worthless. There was persistent violence in the Isles and this formed a bridge between the end of the first Bishops' War in June 1639 and the beginning of the second in August of the following year. Indeed from the spring of 1640 frenzied preparations were undertaken by the Dublin government to levy a fresh army of 8,000 foot and 1,000 horse.[101] Despite the fact that this 'new Irish army' was largely composed of Catholics, with Carrickfergus as its headquarters, Lord Deputy Wentworth (or Lord Lieutenant Strafford as he was now styled) excluded Antrim from all preparations.[102] He did, however, requisition the long boats built the previous year as troop carriers, and three or four of these, 'each of about fifteen tons, with twelve men a piece', were earmarked for the invasion of Dumbarton in August 1640.[103] However, by interfering with the appointment of the army's chaplains, through the Franciscan Father Hegarty, the earl did attempt to gain some influence over the Catholic rank and file, while the return from Flanders of his half-brother Maurice, who joined Charles's English army in September 1640, provided a link with developments in England.[104]

The general situation for the king and his supporters remained depressing, however. The mobilization of Strafford's army had caused much anxiety in

---

[99] Antrim to [Hamilton], 14 July 1639 (SRO, GD 406/1/1165). Also see Knowler, *Letters*, II, 374.

[100] Hamilton intervened repeatedly on their behalf, Antrim to Hamilton, 11 March 1640 (SRO, GD 406/1/1160); Antrim to Hamilton, 3 June 1641 (*ibid.*, 406/1/1355). Also see Stevenson, *Scottish Covenanters*, pp. 35, 38; *idem*, *Alasdair MacColla*, pp. 71–3; *idem*, 'The desertion of the Irish by Coll Keitach's sons, 1642', *IHS*, 21, no. 81 (Mar. 1978), pp. 75–6.

[101] Knowler, *Letters*, II, 399, 400. The cost of levying, arming and paying 8,000 foot and 1,000 horse between April and September 1640 amounted to £50,000, PRO, E405/285, fo. 143.

[102] Antrim to Hamilton, 24 January 1640 (SRO, GD 406/1/1159).

[103] Strafford to Ormond, 17 August 1640 (Bodl., Carte MSS 1, fo. 229r–v). Also see demands of Captain Taverner [governor of Dumbarton castle?], [August] 1640 (*ibid.*, fo. 335); Strafford to the governor of Dumbarton castle, 24 August 1640 (*ibid.*, fo. 237).

[104] Undated petition of Captain Maurice McDonnell [1640], (PRO, SP 77/22, fo. 383v); Giblin (ed.), *Irish Franciscan mission*, p. 181; David Stevenson, 'The Irish Franciscan mission to Scotland and the Irish rebellion of 1641', *Innes Review*, 30 (1979), p. 55; *Cal. SP Dom.*, *1640–1*, p. 52.

Scotland, and Argyll was appointed to defend the west coast from an Irish attack. Moreover, just as Antrim's plans had been fraught with delay the previous year, so too were Strafford's, and his army was not even assembled until July 1640. Meanwhile, centres of royalist resistance in Scotland (Nithsdale in the south-west; Dumbarton and Edinburgh castles; the Ogilvies in the central Highlands; the Gordons in the north-east) were quickly overcome by the covenanters.[105] On 20 August the main covenanting army invaded England and eight days later defeated the king's army at Newburn near Newcastle-upon-Tyne. Two days later the negotiations which culminated in the treaty of Ripon on 21 October began.

The Bishops' Wars were both military and political catastrophes for Charles. The Short Parliament (13 April–5 May 1640) had been summoned in England to finance the king's army against the Scots. It had refused to do so until its grievances were redressed and so was dissolved. Military defeat in 1640 forced the king to call yet another English parliament (the Long Parliament) which met on 3 November and, rather than supporting the continuation of the war effort as Charles had naively hoped, instead resolved to impeach his Irish lord lieutenant.[106] The Irish parliament, which had been summoned in March 1640 to pay for the 'new army', supported its English counterpart by adopting a petition of remonstrance which condemned every aspect of Strafford's government in Ireland. It also provided evidence against the lord lieutenant at Westminster in the lengthy trial which followed.[107]

Unable to participate directly in the 'Scottish business', Antrim buried himself in domestic affairs, hoping to 'make satisfaction for my follies in my youth'.[108] His precise movements between the spring of 1640 and the autumn of 1641, however, are something of a mystery.[109] He remained in Ulster, at Dunluce and Coleraine, at least until the end of April 1640 and in June 1640 he took his seat in the Irish House of Lords. In between, for the month of May, he could well have 'resided for a time' with the king at Oxford

---

[105] Stevenson, *The Scottish revolution*, chapter 6; Donald, *An uncounselled king*, p. 239.
[106] Conrad Russell, 'Why did Charles I call the Long Parliament?', *History*, 69 (1984), pp. 375–83; Russell, *Fall*, chapters 3–7.
[107] Aidan Clarke, 'The breakdown of authority, 1640–41', in *NHI*, pp. 270–88; Conrad Russell, 'The British background to the Irish rebellion of 1641', *Historical Research*, 61, no. 145 (June 1988), pp. 169–70; Hugh F. Kearney, 'The Irish parliament in the early seventeenth century', in Farrell (ed.), *The Irish parliamentary tradition*, pp. 89, 96, 98–101.
[108] Antrim to Hamilton, 26 September 1639 (SRO, GD 406/1/1166). See also Antrim to Hamilton, 24 January 1640 (*ibid.*, 406/1/1159).
[109] No letter either to or from Antrim between 29 April 1640 and 3 June 1641 appears to have survived: Antrim to Hamilton, 29 April 1640 (*ibid.*, 406/1/1172) and Antrim to Hamilton, 3 June 1641 (*ibid.*, 406/1/1355).

96   *Civil War and Restoration in the three Stuart kingdoms*

as one source suggested.¹¹⁰ From the summer of 1640 until the outbreak of the Irish rebellion he appears to have lived principally in Dublin where Sir Adam Loftus, a senior government official, leased the couple his house.¹¹¹

What role, if any, the earl played in the great parliamentary issues of the day is unclear, for the only mention of him in the journals of the Lords was in February 1641 when the House heard his petition against Ralph Gee, one of his creditors, 'for uttering many scandalous speeches of the said earl'.¹¹² Presumably Antrim joined the Protestant and Old English peers in condemning Strafford and was delighted by the king's decision in April 1641, in the midst of Strafford's trial, to implement the 'Graces' (the religious, tenurial and other concessions granted by the king in 1628 to his Catholic subjects in return for subsidies, but never confirmed by parliament).¹¹³ Whether he rejoiced over Strafford's execution on Tower Hill on 12 May is likewise unknown.

While the earl may not have made any novel contribution to the parliamentary debates raging in Ireland during these tumultuous months he certainly did not abandon political intrigue.¹¹⁴ Instead, if Antrim's own highly detailed 'declaration' made in May 1650 is to be believed, he began to deal with the king directly.¹¹⁵ According to this account, some time early in May 1641 Charles I sent Antrim and Ormond a messenger, one Thomas

---

[110] Hill, *MacDonnells*, p. 255, but he offered no evidence to support this assertion.

[111] *Ibid.*, pp. 257, 270, 305. Antrim later enquired whether any of the king's houses in the Pale – such as the one near Naas (which may well have been the Jiggenstown mansion built for the king by Strafford) – were vacant, Antrim to Hamilton, 3 June 1641 (SRO, GD 406/1/1355).

[112] *Journals of the House of Lords [of Ireland] (1634–1800)* (8 vols., Dublin, 1779–1800), I, 148–9. Antrim's father had also been uninterested in national politics and while he took his seat in the Irish House of Lords in July 1634 he quickly returned to Dunluce after appointing Westmeath as his proxy, Knowler, *Letters*, I, 285; *Journals of the House of Lords [of Ireland]*, I, 13.

[113] Clarke, *The Graces*, pp. 30–3; idem, *Old English*, pp. 136–52; Gillespie, 'End of an era', pp. 199–201.

[114] Antrim does not appear to have attended the House of Lords on a regular basis, see journal of the Irish House of Lords, 16 March 1639–2 May 1646 (TCD, MS 615).

[115] This was typical of the Gaelic Irish, O Riordan, *The Gaelic mind*, p. 14. These declarations are printed in Richard Cox, *Hibernia Anglicana, or the history of Ireland from the conquest thereof by the English to this present time* (2nd edn, 2 vols., London, 1692), II, 206–9, and Hill, *MacDonnells*, pp. 448–51. Cox printed Antrim's 'information' without indicating his source (Hill simply reprints Cox's version of the 'Antrim plot'); however, manuscript versions of it have been found in the PRO (*Cal. SP Ire., 1660–2*, p. 208/ PRO, SP 63/306/47 (fo. 92)) and the Bodl. (Carte MSS 28, fos. 365–6v; Carte MSS 65, fos. 508–9 and Clarendon MSS 40, fos. 151–2). For further details, see Jane H. Ohlmeyer, 'The "Antrim plot" of 1641 – a myth?', *Historical Journal* (forthcoming). Some historians have argued that Antrim's own account cannot be trusted and that the 'Antrim plot' never existed. For instance, Russell, *Fall*, believed that 'Charles I was guilty of many plots, but this appears not

Bourke,[116] with instructions that: 'those eight thousand men, raised by the earl of Strafford in Ireland, should be continued without disbanding, and that they should be made up to twenty thousand, and that they should be armed out of the store of Dublin, and employed against the parliament.'[117] Upon receipt of 'the king's pleasure', as he dubbed it nearly ten years later, Antrim and Ormond 'endeavoured a meeting with each other for ordering affairs accordingly; but there being (as they supposed) jealous eyes over them, they could not for a time encompass it conveniently'. Despite this the pair finally managed to discuss the matter further 'in the inner room within the parliament house' and at the bowling alley on College Green. According to Antrim these meetings took place while 'the parliament, [was] then sitting in Dublin'; in other word some time after 11 May.[118] 'After some debates' they agreed to send Lords Maguire and Muskerry to brief Charles I on the progress of their plans.[119] A few days later Antrim suggested that, in order to plot in greater privacy, they should retreat from Dublin and meet up again at Kilka in County Kildare on the pretext of hawking.[120] Just before they were to meet,

---

to have been one of them' (pp. 394–5). Also see Russell, 'The British background', pp. 166–82, and Perceval-Maxwell, 'Ireland and Scotland', p. 199.

[116] Bourke was a nephew of the earl of Clanricard and served on the delegation sent to London by the Irish House of Commons in November 1640, Clarke, *Old English*, pp. 127–8, 135, 159. Bourke and the other member of the Catholic party, Plunkett, 'were believed to have private access to the king' according to Russell, 'The British background', p. 172. Even after the outbreak of the rebellion Charles definitely continued to use Bourke as a messenger, Gilbert, *Ir. confed.*, II, iii–v.

[117] This and the rest of the account of the plot comes from 'Information of the marquis of Antrim' in Hill, *MacDonnells*, pp. 448–51. Neither Antrim nor Charles I could afford either to pay or to arm these troops. However, this had not deterred the impractical pair in 1638–9, see pp. 79–80, 83–91 above.

[118] He appears to have taken his seat in the Lords on 21 May, journal of the Irish House of Lords, 16 March 1639–2 May 1646 (TCD, MS 615).

[119] Related by marriage to Antrim, Conor Maguire, Lord Enniskillen, plotted the Ulster rebellion of 1641 together with O'More, Gilbert, *Contemp. hist. 1641–52*, I, xx–xxii. Donough MacCarthy, Viscount Muskerry, was Ormond's brother-in-law and (like Thomas Bourke) served on the delegation sent to London by the Irish House of Commons in November 1640, Clarke, *Old English*, pp. 127–8, 135, 159. During the 1640s he was a leading confederate (serving as president of the supreme council) and an 'Ormondist', Gilbert, *Ir. confed.*, IV, xlvii–lxv.

[120] By now it was probably early June for, according to a letter from Antrim to Hamilton, he left Dublin in the middle of June to spend a month 'at a friend's house', Antrim to Hamilton, 19 July 1641 (SRO, GD 406/1/1389). As luck would have it the earl did not state where his anonymous friend's house was. It was later claimed that he met Ormond at Lord Castlehaven's house at Maddenstown, County Kildare, see 'Viscount Montgomery's account of how he obtained a copy of Antrim's declaration', *c.* September 1650 (Bodl., Clarendon MSS 40, fo. 152).

however, using John Barry as his messenger,[121] Ormond suggested that, instead of Maguire and Muskerry, 'one of them should repair to the king immediately, rather than so great an affair should be trusted by any other' and he urged Antrim to visit the king at court in person for 'having been long a courtier [he] might go without suspicion'.[122] The earl refused to go alone, but in order to secure fresh instructions he agreed to send Captain Thomas Digby, constable of Dunluce castle, instead.[123] Digby (no doubt after travelling first to London in search of Charles) finally 'did overtake the king at York, he being then on his way to Scotland' in mid-August.

Somewhat later, according to Antrim (and given the poor communications between Ireland and England it was probably the end of August or early September) William Hamerton, one of Antrim's English servants (who had presumably accompanied Digby to York), returned to Ireland with fresh royal orders 'that all possible endeavours should be used for getting together again those 8,000 men so disbanded; and that an army should immediately be raised in Ireland, that should declare for him [the king] against the parliament in England'.[124]

However, Antrim asserted, these instructions were qualified with the important proviso that this Irish army should only be used against the parliament '*if occasion should be for so doing*'.[125] That occasion never arose. The political climate in England and Scotland appeared to shift in the king's favour so that by the early autumn, having secured the benevolent neutrality of the Scots, it was no longer in Charles's interest to use Irish troops against his parliamentary opponents.[126]

Nevertheless Antrim – who from this point on appears to have acted without Ormond's approbation or complicity – claimed to have set about rallying his fellow peers, friends and followers for the king's cause.[127]

---

[121] It was later claimed (by Sir Phelim O'Neill) that Barry was involved in plotting the Ulster rebellion, Gilbert, *Contempt. hist. 1641–52*, III, 367. Certainly he later joined the Catholic confederates. However, throughout the 1640s Barry remained a loyal supporter of Ormond and often acted as his messenger (*ibid.*, I, 181–3, 190, 282, 611).

[122] For further details on Antrim's career at court, see pp. 49–55 above.

[123] Digby was certainly a trusted servant of Antrim: shortly after the outbreak of rebellion the earl instructed Digby to take charge of Dunluce castle, TCD, MS 383, fo. 25.

[124] Hamerton, too, was another of Antrim's servants, for in 1650 he petitioned the committee for compounding for the 'allowance of a lease' granted to him by Antrim, *Calendar of the proceedings of the committee for compounding*, III, 2188, and PRO, SP 23/10/p. 228.

[125] Italics are mine.

[126] Russell, 'The British background', p. 179, and Robert Dunlop, 'The forged commission of 1641', *EHR*, 2, no. 7 (July 1887), p. 529.

[127] Interestingly, Ormond seriously contemplated visiting the king in Edinburgh during the autumn of 1641, Temple to Ormond, 2 September 1641 (Bodl., Carte MSS 1, fo. 444); Sir Patrick Wemys to Ormond, 25 September 1641 (*ibid.*, fo. 457); Sir Patrick Wemys to Ormond, [October] 1641 (*ibid.*, fo. 465).

According to his own subsequent account he ' imparted the design to the lord of Gormanstown, and to the lord of Slane, and after to many others in Leinster, and after going into Ulster, he communicated the same to many there'. Ultimately, he intended to secure the approval of the lords justices for the royal 'design' and, if they opposed him, to persuade the Irish parliament to declare 'for the king against the parliament of England'.[128] However, the earl's grand strategy to solve his royal master's British problems was frustrated by the outbreak of the Ulster rebellion in October 1641.[129]

[128] NLI, MS 476, 'A light to the blind', p. 61, the anonymous author (writing in *c.* 1720) suggested that Ormond and Antrim had set 16 November 1641 as the date for their rising.
[129] Patrick J. Corish, 'The rising of 1641 and the catholic confederacy, 1641–5', in *NHI*, 289–1; Beckett, *The cavalier duke*, p. 19. Antrim, despite later accusations, was not involved in the Ulster rebellion of October 1641, for further details, see pp. 101–4 below.

4

Popish plotting in Caroline Ireland and Britain (1641–1643)

The 1641 rebellion was a central military event in Irish history and played an important role in shaping the course of British history during the mid-seventeenth century. The main outlines of the conspiracy which resulted in the rising are reasonably well defined though the details remain obscure, but the origins are the subject of historical debate. Aidan Clarke has argued that particular circumstances in 1641 forced the Irish to rebel and that their objectives were limited: rebellion 'represented the only convenient means of restoring the relationship which had existed between the Old English and the king before the onset of those revolutionary changes which had begun with Wentworth's arrival in Ireland and been consummated by the assertion of parliamentary authority in England'.[1] Raymond Gillespie has modified Clarke's argument and suggested that the rebellion had more complex origins which involved the 'interrelationship of social, economic and political factors at specific points in time'.[2] More recently Conrad Russell and Michael Perceval-Maxwell have both stressed its British context. 'The Irish Rebellion,' Russell argued, 'like the Scottish National Covenant and the English Civil War, cannot be explained in terms of the history of a single kingdom.'[3] He suggested that three facts all contributed towards the rising: Anglo-Scottish rapprochement 'whose key term was an increased hostility to popery';[4] 'the tendency, encouraged by the trial of Strafford, for the English parliament to claim authority over Ireland'; and the future of the policy of plantation 'brought to the fore by renewed Irish demands to confirm the Graces'.[5] Finally the Scottish example of successful rebellion also had a

---

[1] Clarke, *Old English*, pp. 230–4.
[2] Gillespie, 'End of an era', pp. 19 and 193–204. Like Gillespie, Nicholas Canny has stressed the social and economic roots of the insurrection. See Canny, *Kingdom and colony*, pp. 60–1; idem, 'In defence of the constitution? The nature of Irish revolt in the seventeenth century', in *Culture et pratiques politiques en France et en Irlande XVIe-XVIIIe siècle* (Paris, 1991), pp. 22–40.
[3] Russell, *Causes*, p. 19.
[4] Russell, *Fall*, pp. 379–80.
[5] Russell, *Causes*, pp. 18–19, 129–30.

Graces'.⁵ Finally the Scottish example of successful rebellion also had a profound impact on Ireland 'since it suggested the possibility of a relationship of equality with England, without breaking the links which bound them together'.⁶ So by rising in insurrection in 1641 the Irish were (in the words of Perceval-Maxwell) 'both reacting to the Scottish challenge to royal authority and copying it'.⁷

Whatever its origins, it is clear that it was the 'O'More–Maguire plot', and not the 'Antrim plot', which gave rise to the insurrection.⁸ From February 1641, various designs were hatched – by Rory O'More, Lord Maguire, Colonel Hugh MacMahon, Sir Phelim O'Neill and others – which planned to overthrow the Ulster plantation by capturing key strongholds in the north.⁹ Some time late in the summer of 1641 the northern conspirators learnt from Antrim of the king's wishes to use – 'if occasion be for so doing' – an Irish army against his recalcitrant English parliament. This delighted them for it threw a cloak of quasi-legality over their own plot; but 'the Fools', Antrim later related, 'well liking the business, would not expect [sc. await] our time or manner for ordering the work, but fell upon it without us, and sooner, and otherwise than we should have done, taking to themselves, and in their own way, the managing of the work, and so spoiled it'.¹⁰

Nevertheless, the rising, which began on 22 October 1641, plunged Ulster, and within a short time all of Ireland, into a decade of total war. Sir Phelim O'Neill and his co-conspirators succeeded in taking the key strongholds of Charlemount, Mountjoy castle, Tandragee and Newry; only Londonderry, Coleraine, Enniskillen, Lisburn and Carrickfergus escaped capture. Inevitably the rising was accompanied by bloodshed and unnecessary cruelty but the extent of the 'massacre' of Protestants was exaggerated, especially in England where the wildest rumours were readily believed.

Reverberations from the uprising were quickly felt throughout Stuart Britain. Secretary Vane was not alone in wondering how 'those accidents in Ireland' would affect England.¹¹ He did not have long to wait for an answer,

---

⁵ Russell, *Causes*, pp. 18–19, 129–30.
⁶ Russell, *Fall*, p. 375.
⁷ Perceval-Maxwell, 'Ireland and Scotland', p. 198.
⁸ In a chapter entitled '1641: the plot that never was', FitzPatrick convincingly argues that parts of the 'O'More–Maguire plot' – namely that it included a conspiracy to seize Dublin castle – were in fact fabricated by the lords justices in order 'to secure their position with arms and money' (p. 133). For further details see *Seventeenth-century Ireland*, chapter 6.
⁹ For details, see Aidan Clarke, 'The genesis of the Ulster rising in 1641', in Peter Roebuck (ed.), *Plantation to partition. Essays in Ulster history in honour of J. L. McCracken* (Belfast, 1981), pp. 29–45, and Russell, *Fall*, pp. 392–4. On the 'Antrim plot', see pp. 96–9 above and Ohlmeyer, 'The "Antrim plot" of 1641'. Some historians have confused and conflated the two; see, for instance, Dunlop, 'The forged commission', pp. 528–9.
¹⁰ Hill, *MacDonnells*, p. 450, quoting Antrim's declaration made in May 1650.
¹¹ Vane to [Hamilton], 27 October 1641 (SRO, SD 406/1/1447).

for the struggle between the king and his English parliament over who should control the army to be raised to quell the Irish insurrection began almost at once, and ultimately resulted in parliament taking up arms against its monarch.

News of the Irish rebellion reached London on 1 November and, according to Conrad Russell, made it impossible for Charles to dissolve his parliament 'without sacrificing one of his three kingdoms, or with branding himself for ever as the ally of the papists. The Irish rebellion, as it were, caged the king and the parliament together, and so eliminated the possibility that they avoid fighting by separation.'[12] Despite the king's efforts to salvage his reputation rumours that Charles (and his queen) had somehow been involved in the Irish rebellion were rife and these both confirmed and inflamed fears of a great Catholic conspiracy.[13] The parliamentary leaders – especially John Pym – exploited this ruthlessly, claiming that England was on the verge of being reduced to popery.[14] An alarmed papal agent in London reported back to Rome in November how effective the anti-Catholic campaign was: 'the uprising in Ireland has greatly increased the malice of the Puritans ... it has also universally disposed people to believe anything evil about the Catholics'.[15]

Fortunately for their personal safety, the earl of Antrim and his wife were in Dublin, not London, in late October 1641; but this led to accusations that Antrim had somehow been involved in planning the seizure of Dublin castle.[16] According to one deposition, made by Dr Robert Maxwell in August 1642, Ellis O'Neill – 'a most bloody woman and natural daughter to the earl

---

[12] Russell, *Causes*, p. 18.
[13] While Charles was not involved in the 'O'More–Maguire' plot, his willingness to consider other conspiracies (such as the 'Antrim plot') meant that the majority of his Protestant subjects believed that 'morally he stood convicted of it', John Lowe, 'The negotiations between Charles I and the confederation of Kilkenny, 1642–9' (unpublished PhD thesis, University of London, 1960), p. 13.
[14] Stevenson, *Scottish Covenanters*, pp. 43–50, 55–60; Hibbard, *Popish plot*, pp. 214–16; idem, 'The contribution of 1639: court and country catholicism', *Recusant History*, 16 (May 1982), pp. 53–6; J. H. Hexter, *The reign of king Pym* (Cambridge, Mass., 1941; reprint, 1975), pp. 20, 29, 161–2; Keith Lindley, 'The impact of the 1641 rebellion upon England and Wales, 1641–5', *IHS*, 18, no. 70 (Sept. 1972), pp. 143–67; John S. Morrill, 'The religious context of the English civil war', *R. Hist. Soc. Trans.*, 5th series, 34 (1984), pp. 171–4; Peter Lake, 'Anti-popery: the structure of a prejudice', in Richard Cust and Ann Hughes (eds.), *Conflict in early Stuart England. Studies in religion and politics 1603–1642* (London, 1989), pp. 73, 82.
[15] Dispatch from London, 19/29 November 1641 (Bibl. Apost. Vat., Barberini Latini MSS 5253, fo. 110).
[16] Petition of adventurers and soldiers to king, [August 1663] (Bodl., Carte MSS 44, fos. 376–7); information against the marquis of Antrim, [August] 1663 (Bodl., Clarendon MSS 80, fo. 328); *Cal. SP Ire.*, 1663–5, p. 214; Hill, *MacDonnells*, pp. 310–11. For propaganda,

of Antrim' – told him shortly after the outbreak of the rising that 'my brother the earl of Antrim hath taken the castle and city of Dublin ... and my brother Alexander MacDonnell ... hath taken the town and castle of Carrickfergus'.[17] This was clearly wishful thinking on Ellis's part, and while accusations such as this were understandable, considering that Antrim was either related to, or intimate with, nearly all the leading insurgents, they were certainly false. Equally unfounded were the rumours, circulating in the months immediately following the rebellion, that he was the leader of the insurgents in the Pale.[18] Secretary Nicholas, for one, praised the earls of Antrim and Clanricard ('albeit they are Catholics')[19] for their loyalty to the crown, and as late as April 1642, Sir William Parsons – one of the lords justices in Dublin and a staunch Protestant – reassured his English counterparts that, despite rumours to the contrary, Antrim was still loyal to the king.[20] The earl's refusal to involve himself in the rebellion was, however, severely criticized by foreign Catholic powers and also by the rebels themselves. At the Spanish court in Madrid, for example, he was later condemned for having remained neutral, for it was generally believed that if Antrim and Clanricard had supported the insurgents from the outset the rebellion would have succeeded.[21] Antrim's neutrality particularly infuriated one Irish priest in Flanders who unleashed his scathing condemnation in a letter to Rome: 'among Ireland's ungrateful sons there will perchance be found a brood of vipers ... infamous by the name of neutrals, who know no other way to their own glory than through the destruction of their dear country'.[22] It was even rumoured in rebel quarters that Sir Phelim 'would never have undertaken the province of Ulster, if he had

and financial, purposes it later suited Scottish and parliamentary opponents to accuse Antrim of instigating the rising and to label him a rebel, *New treason plotted in France* ...; *likewise a letter sent from the councell of Scotland, to the house of commons* ... (London, 1642), and *A continuation of certain speciall and remarkable passages from both houses of parliament* ... From Wednesday 5 to 8 October 1642, no. 13 (London, 1642), pp. 1, 5.

[17] Deposition of Dr Robert Maxwell, 22 August 1642 (Mary Hickson, *Ireland in the seventeenth century* (2 vols., London, 1884), I, 328).
[18] Examination of Charles Campbell, 15 January 1642 (TCD, MS 834, fo. 57). T. L. Coonan, *The Irish catholic confederacy and the puritan revolution* (Dublin, 1954), p. 93; Thomas Carte, *The Irish massacre set in a clear light wherein Mr Baxter's account ... are fully considered* (London, 1714), pp. 14, 22, 24–5.
[19] Nicholas to Sir Thomas Roe, 17 December 1641 (*Cal. SP Dom., 1641–3*, p. 204; PRO, SP 16/486/fo. 66).
[20] *A letter written from Sir William Parsons ... to Sir Robert Pye* ... (London, 1642), p. 3.
[21] Relación del estado del reyno de Irlanda desde Diciembre 1644 (AGS, Eo. 2253, unfol.); *A declaration sent to the king of France and Spayne, from the catholiques or rebells in Ireland* ... (Paris, [14/] 24 April 1642; reprinted London, 1642), p. 3; *Franciscan MSS*, p. 135.
[22] Hugh Bourke to Luke Wadding, 7 November 1642 NS (*Franciscan MSS*, p. 217).

not been persuaded that the said earl [of Antrim] would have taken up arms as soon as himself'.[23] As for Antrim, after being rebuked in March 1642 for failing to join the rising, he allegedly replied that 'the business was already spoiled, especially in Ulster, by bloodshed and robbery, and that he would not declare himself one way or another, until after Mayday following'.[24]

Antrim's neutrality did place him in an unusual and potentially compromising position. He was loath to leave Dublin and the Pale, fearing that this would be interpreted as a sign that he had joined, or at least sympathized with, the insurrection, yet his failure to return home and organize resistance to the rebellion forced many to query his loyalty.[25] He later articulated his predicament to Hamilton: 'I should not strive to excuse myself if my knowledge could inform me to be plotter, or actor in the Irish rebellion. It was my misfortune to be absent out of my own country at the beginning of the troubles, which was much against my desires.'[26] While he remained in very close contact with his tenants and family in County Antrim he initially stayed in Dublin and 'did make several applications to the lords justices and council ... desiring them that they would give him their directions and assistance' to suppress the rebellion in Ulster.[27] He also resumed his seat in the predominantly Protestant House of Lords and, his opponents later asserted, 'urged (with unusual vehemence) that the Irish rebels should not be so termed rebels, but rather discontented gentlemen'.[28]

Antrim's potential as an intermediary with these 'discontented gentlemen' was indeed quickly recognized, and before the Irish parliament was prorogued in November he was one of those selected as a person fit to treat with the rebels, to hear their grievances and to persuade them to lay down their arms.[29] To execute his orders more effectively he moved to County Meath to stay with his brother-in-law, Lord Slane, but Slane's adherence to an alliance between the Old Irish insurgents and the Old English, forged early in December, forced the earl – who could not afford to be seen to live with 'rebels' – to

---

[23] Deposition of Dr Robert Maxwell, 22 August 1642 (Hickson, *Ireland*, I, 332).
[24] *Ibid.*
[25] The messengers sent by the earl from Dublin aroused much suspicion since in order to reach his estates they managed to pass safely through territory held by the enemy, memorandum by Colonel Arthur Chichester (CUL, Add. 4352, fos. 22v–3).
[26] Antrim to [Hamilton], 16 July 1642 (SRO, GD 406/1/1674).
[27] Hill, *MacDonnells*, p. 305.
[28] Petition of adventurers and soldiers, [26 July] 1663 (*Cal. SP Ire.*, 1663–5, p. 214).
[29] Gilbert, *Contemp. hist. 1641–52*, I, 370–1; *Late and lamentable news from Ireland ...* (London, 1641), p. 6; *Franciscan MSS*, p. 111; Clarke, *Old English*, pp. 172–3.

seek lodgings elsewhere.³⁰ Nevertheless, using the earl of Castlehaven's house at Maddenstown in County Kildare as his base, Antrim continued to liaise with local insurgents.³¹ He could well have visited (as was claimed twenty years later) 'rebel' quarters at Tenekilly in Queen's County (commanded by his kinsman James MacDonnell) or at Tullamore in King's County; but later assertions that he supplied them with money and ammunition and warned them of imminent attacks from Dublin seem unlikely.³² On the contrary, early in April 1642 he warmly welcomed an expeditionary force under Sir Charles Coote sent from Dublin to relieve Athy and other key locations in Queen's County, and he entertained Ormond after the battle of Kilrush (15 April 1642).³³ While the earl was not present at the battle, he was involved in other skirmishes against the insurgents; for instance, the headlines of one pamphlet revealed how 'Lord Dunluce obtained a wreath of fame, which shall never wither, for he with two bare troops of horse attempted to recover a drove of cattle that the rebels had taken from the inhabitants' and in the process captured his brother-in-law, Lord Dunsany, after engaging him in 'a hot combat'.³⁴

By and large, though, the earl and his wife lived a much more peaceful life at Maddenstown where they first harboured 'a great number of English Protestants that had been robbed by the rebels' and then helped them find

---

30 *DNB*, 'Randal MacDonnell'; some observations of adventurers and soldiers on the estate claimed by Antrim, [1661] (Bodl., Carte MSS 44, fos. 328–31) – a version of this, dated 28 June 1665, is printed in Hill, *MacDonnells*, pp. 326–39; Clarke, *Old English*, pp. 178–92.

31 He also spent some time at Leixlip, County Kildare, Account of transactions during the rebellion and 1642 (BL, Eg. MSS 80, fo. 46).

32 Hill, *MacDonnells*, pp. 304, 311; petition of adventurers and soldiers to king, [August, 1663] (Bodl., Carte MSS 44, fos. 376–7); some observations of adventurers and soldiers on the estate claimed by Antrim, [1661?] (*ibid.*, fos. 328–31).

33 *The earl of Castlehaven's review; or his memoirs* ... (London, 1684; reprinted New York, 1974), pp. 42–3; *A full relation, not only of our good successe in generall, but how, and in what manner God hath fought his own cause* (London, 1642), p. 1. There are similar accounts in *A true and perfect diurnall: of the most remarkable passages in Ireland* ... (London, 3 May 1642), p. 1; *A new declaration of the last affairs in Ireland shewing the great overthrow given the Irish rebels* ... (London, 2 May 1642), pp. 3–4; *A remonstrance of the right honourable James earl of Castlehaven* ... (Waterford, 1643), p. 9; *A continuation of very good newes from Ireland* ... From 8 to 19 April (London, 1642), p. 5. Apparently the duchess was less impressed, for she insulted Coote by calling him 'a poor mechanical fellow, raised by blind fortune, as informer and promoter, against all that is just and godly', Gilbert, *Contemp. hist. 1641–52*, I, 31.

34 *A renowned victory obtained against the rebels on the first day of June, neere Burros* ... (London, 9 June 1642).

their way to safety.³⁵ Nevertheless, Antrim's prolonged residence in County Kildare, 'where at the first this business was begun' and his failure to return to either Dublin or Dunluce, was not viewed favourably by Protestants and many felt that, while he maintained a neutral facade, his heart was in fact with the 'rebels'.³⁶ These reports genuinely distressed him. 'It is a great sorrow to me, [that] my name and my honour should be so much defamed and scandalized by false and slanderous reports, nay permitted to be published in print, that I have revolted from my king and turned rebel, the very name wounds me sore', he confided to his wife's uncle early in 1642, and added that 'I will rather perish at his majesty's feet, and suffer any punishment ... than live stained with such a horrid denomination as traitor.'³⁷ But in the same missive the earl also articulated his devotion to the Catholic faith and his ambition to see 'the free exercise of the Roman religion, which I am devoted to and am engaged to maintain in duty to God and respect of my future happiness and salvation'.³⁸ This letter, which was subsequently intercepted and published by parliament, highlights the impossible position in which the rebellion placed Antrim. On the one hand, he was a loyal and ardent servant of the crown; on the other, he was bonded by ties of kinship and friendship to many of the leading rebels and dedicated to preserving Catholicism in Ireland. His tragic dilemma was further exacerbated when members of his own family and most of his Catholic tenants in County Antrim joined the rebellion early in 1642.³⁹

After the outbreak of the October rising the earl had instructed Captain Digby to take charge of Dunluce castle and had remained in constant communication with his trusted, Protestant factor, Archibald Stewart, and with his younger brother, Alexander.⁴⁰ Early intelligence of the rising enabled Stewart to organize a rudimentary system of local defence. Within days he had mustered and armed Antrim's Protestant tenants; and once it was clear

---

35 Examination of William Collis, 4 May 1643 (TCD, MS 813, fo. 258r–v). For instance, a Kildare saddler – William Collis – and his family were sheltered, fed and clothed by Antrim for two months and then smuggled to the relative safety of Dublin. Interestingly, it was claimed that these Protestant refugees joined Antrim and Castlehaven in celebrating the mass, ibid., fo. 360v; *The earl of Castlehaven's review*, pp. 45–6.
36 *Articles of impeachment against George Lord Digby* ... (London, 28 February 1642); *Egmont MSS*, p. 163. These rumours delighted Catholic powers, see, for example, *Franciscan MSS*, pp. 116, 126, 134.
37 *A copie of a letter from the Lord Intrim* [sic] ..., pp. 3–4.
38 Ibid.
39 Stevenson, *Scottish Covenanters*, pp. 99–100; Hill, *Stewarts of Ballintoy*, pp. 11–28.
40 Hickson, *Ireland*, I, 252; *Cal. SP Ire. 1633–47* p. 344; memorandum by Colonel Arthur Chichester (CUL, Add. 4352, fos. 33v, 36v–7); Hill, *Stewarts of Ballintoy*, pp. 11–28.

that 'the natives' in Antrim's 'half county' did not intend to join their neighbours in insurrection he organized them too into units under the command of Alasdair MacColla and Tirlough Oge O'Cahan.[41] In all a force of between 700 and 1,500 troops were maintained to protect the earl's estates, armed either with their own swords or with weapons which had been stored in Dunluce since 1638.[42] While Stewart took charge at home, Alexander MacDonnell hurried first to Edinburgh and later to London in search of further instructions.[43]

This Indian summer of cooperation was, however, shortlived. Early in January 1642 Antrim's native Irish tenants, under the leadership of his cousin Sir James MacDonnell, O'Cahan and MacColla (of whom Stewart noted 'I trusted too much for my lord of Antrim his sake') joined the rebellion on the pretext that Stewart's 'cowboys' had daily provoked 'our tenants of purpose to pick quarrels, which no flesh was able to endure'.[44] Why Antrim's tenants had failed to join the insurrection even earlier is unclear. Perhaps they feared that without the earl's active support any attempt to raise an army in his county was doomed to fail. More likely they hoped that in time Antrim would join them and feared 'alienating him by undertaking a rising in the area he dominated without his co-operation'.[45] However, in January 1642 they were prepared to risk this in order 'to have their religion settled and everyone his ancient inheritance'.[46] Their attempt to win freedom for Catholicism and to

---

[41] *Cal. SP Ire., 1633–47* p. 344; memorandum by Colonel Arthur Chichester (CUL, Add. 4352, fos. 33v, 36v–7). Phelim O'Neill tried – unsuccessfully – to persuade the Scottish Mac-Donalds to join the insurgents, Stevenson, *Alasdair MacColla*, pp. 75–6; idem, *Scottish Covenanters*; idem, 'The Irish Franciscan mission', pp. 54–61.

[42] These soldiers were maintained at Antrim's expense since 'the tenants think while they serve the king upon their own charges they owe us no rent', petition from Alexander MacDonnell, 16 December 1641 (HMC *rep. 4*, p. 108; HLRO, main papers, 16/12/1641). As the 1630 muster illustrates, only half of Antrim's Protestant tenants were even armed with swords, BL, Add. MSS 4770, fo. 280v.

[43] Argyll to Hamilton, 22 November 1641 (SRO, GD 406/1/875). Despite claims to the contrary Alexander remained loyal to the crown until after the 1643 'cessation', *Cal. SP Ire., 1669–70*, p. 421, and *Franciscan MSS*, p. 111. When the king refused to give Alexander a commission to raise troops on the grounds he was a Catholic he begged for one for Stewart, HMC *rep. 4*, p. 108; HLRO, main papers, 16/12/1641.

[44] James McDonnell to Archibald Stewart, 10 January 1641 (Hogan (ed.), *Letters and papers*, pp. 6–7). Also see Sir John Vaughan to the lords justices, 10 January 1642 (*ibid.*, pp. 7–8); Hill, *MacDonnells*, pp. 64–8. It is not clear whether 'James MacDonnell' was Sir James or James MacColl MacDonnell, Stevenson, *Scottish Covenanters*, pp. 100–2; idem, *Alasdair MacColla*, pp. 76–80.

[45] Stevenson, *Scottish Covenanters*, p. 99.

[46] James McDonnell to Archibald Stewart, 10 January 1642 (Hogan (ed.), *Letters and papers*, pp. 6–7).

overthrow the plantation in County Antrim began when MacColla and O'Cahan led their companies in an attack on Protestant companies guarding the crossing of the River Bann at Portnaw, killing between sixty and ninety Protestant soldiers, before joining forces with the 'rebels' in County Londonderry.[47] They then moved against Ballintoy and Dunluce castles which held firm (although the town of Dunluce was burnt to the ground). Oldstone castle quickly surrendered, as did Ballycastle; however, Coleraine refused to submit and was besieged by MacColla.[48]

Stewart and the other Protestant settlers, eager to attract outside assistance, claimed that the rebels' cruelty was 'never used by the Turks to Christians ... no quarter is given, no faith kept, all houses burnt and demolished, man, wife and child put to the sword'.[49] Whether the character of the war in County Antrim actually lived up to Stewart's vivid imagery is debatable. Certainly there were violent deaths on both sides during the various military encounters of 1642 and there were casualties at Portnaw, Coleraine, Ballycastle, Ballintoy and Dunluce; while at the battle of the Laney (February 1642) nearly 600 men were said to have been killed.[50] Determining how many people actually died in these various encounters and skirmishes is impossible since the historian is forced to rely for information almost exclusively on the controversial depositions which in the case of County Antrim all date from the 1650s.[51] It seems clear though that there was regional variation within the county. The baronies of Cary and Dunluce, where the bulk of the

---

[47] Hill, *Stewarts of Ballintoy*, pp. 11–12; TCD, MS 838, fos. 25, 59v, 72v.

[48] TCD, MS 838, fo. 26. Oldstone was surrendered by Walter Kennedy to James McColl MacDonnell and it was later asserted that at least twenty women and children were slaughtered 'under the castle wall' and a further sixty (who had been given quarter) were murdered en route to Larne or Carrickfergus by MacDonnell's troops, examination of Donnell Graham McDonnell, 11 March 1653 (*ibid.*, fo. 30v) and examination of John Blaire, 8 March 1653 (*ibid.*, fo. 69); Hill, *MacDonnells*, p. 311. There was supposedly a further massacre of Protestants at Ballycastle and in the surrounding countryside, Hill, *Stewarts of Ballintoy*, pp. 17–23.

[49] Archibald Stewart to Charles I, 11 January 1642 (Hill, *Stewarts of Ballintoy*, pp. 14–15).

[50] *Ibid.*, pp. 17–23; Stevenson, *Alasdair MacColla*, pp. 82–4; and [Edmund Hogan (ed.)], *The history of the warr in Ireland from 1641 to 1653 by a British officer of the regiment of Sir John Clotworthy* (Dublin, 1873), pp. 22–3; and for a good account of the war in County Antrim see Hugh Hazlett, 'A history of the military forces operating in Ireland, 1641–9' (unpublished PhD thesis, Queen's University, Belfast, 1938), pp. 69–71.

[51] Many of the County Antrim depositions are reproduced in Hickson, *Ireland*, I, 234ff. Their historical value is assessed by Aidan Clarke, 'The 1641 depositions', in P. Fox (ed.), *Treasures of the library, Trinity College Dublin* (Dublin, 1986), pp. 111–21, especially at pp. 116–18. Raymond Gillespie, 'Migration and opportunity: a comment', *Ir. Econ. & Soc. Hist.*, 13 (1986), pp. 91–2, also highlights the problems involved in using them. See also Michael

fighting was concentrated, appear to have been the worst affected, while Kilconway was the least affected. Atrocities in the barony of Glenarm were limited to isolated encounters rather than 'massacres'.[52] By and large, then, horror stories of massacres were gross exaggerations and more people seem to have perished in the famine and pestilence – 'Colonel Hunger and Major Sickness' – which accompanied the disruption than by the sword.[53] At Ballycastle, for instance, witnesses (albeit ones of Irish extraction) consistently deposed that only one or two individuals, rather than hundreds of Protestants, were murdered.[54] Stories of kindness also pepper most of these testimonials. Donnell Magee, for instance, hurried to Oldstone when he heard of the Irish advance in order 'to save some British [Protestant] acquaintance of his'.[55]

The pattern of warfare on the Antrim estates reflected the national picture. Massacres were the exception; much more common was the plundering and pillaging of Protestant property and the theft of their livestock.[56] According to one recent scholar 'These attacks were usually associated with the economic tensions that had developed between the two communities in the years

Perceval-Maxwell, 'The Ulster rising of 1641 and the depositions', *IHS*, 21, no. 82 (Sept. 1978), pp. 144–9.

[52] Donnell O'Cahan 'a gentleman', for instance, claimed that well over 1,000 Protestants were murdered throughout the barony of Cary; while Shane McVickar McCormack a husbandman from the barony of Kilconway 'did not see any dead body at all', examination of Donnell O'Cahan, 14 March 1653 (TCD, MS 838, fo. 33v) and examination of Shane McVickar McCormack, 14 March 1653 (*ibid.*, fo. 34). It was later claimed that 954 people were murdered in one morning in County Antrim; and a further 1,100–1,200 supposedly killed, *A remonstrance of the barbarous cruelties and bloody murders committed by the Irish rebels...* (London, 12 June 1644), p. 7.

[53] Claims such as the one made by a soldier in Sir John Borlase's company that he saw 'divers houses and towns wherein were very great numbers of the persons of murdered British Protestants thrown upon heaps and stripped naked both men, women and children, and saw the very dogs feed upon some of their carcasses' should be written off as mere fabrication, examination of Anthony Stephens, 25 June 1646 (TCD, MS 830, fo. 41v). Also see [Anonymous], *Historical collections relative to the town of Belfast: from the earliest period to the union with Great Britain* (Belfast, 1817), p. 11.

[54] TCD, MS 838, fos. 31v, 38, 62.

[55] *Ibid.*, fos. 34v, 50. Other 'rebels' saved the lives of Isabell Kerr and her husband after the Portnaw massacre, *ibid.*, fo. 51. Various Protestants were taken in by the countess of Antrim: Jennett and John Hunter, John Murghlar, a blacksmith, were merely three of the Ballycastle residents who found refuge there, *ibid.*, fo. 47v.

[56] [Lords justices] to [Scottish privy council], [autumn] 1641 (SRO, GD 406/1/8335); *No pamphlet but a detestation against all such pamphlets as are printed concerning the Irish rebellion...* (London, 1642). For a similar critique, see CUL, Add. 4353; Clarke, 'The 1641 depositions', p. 113. In neighbouring County Fermanagh 'the reproach of the insurrection

before 1641.'⁵⁷ The major towns and cities – Dublin, Cork, Waterford, Youghal, Limerick, Galway, Kilkenny, Wexford, Ross, Clonmel, Londonderry, Carrickfergus and Belfast, where most of the Protestants resided – were not plundered; and when a town was attacked, most of the inhabitants were saved by their Irish neighbours.⁵⁸

True or false, however, these rumours of murder and pillage, and the news that 'his country' had risen in rebellion, depressed the earl greatly. Particularly alarming was the request by his Protestant tenants for aid from his arch-enemy, the marquis of Argyll, and a decision by the English House of Commons (in February 1642) to invite Argyll to occupy the earl's Ulster estates and to meddle again in the affairs of Ulster as Clan Campbell had done throughout the late sixteenth century.⁵⁹ On 18 March 1642 Argyll was issued with a royal commission to be colonel of a regiment which he was to levy for service in Ulster. In addition he was specifically granted Rathlin Island as a base for these men and given permission to remove or expel all rebels living there. As a result the bitter MacDonnell–Campbell feud was quickly sucked into the War of the Three Kingdoms.⁶⁰

But rather than hurrying to Ulster, Antrim remained in Leinster and planned 'how he might order his affairs to keep his country in peace that he

---

of 1641 is pillage and not massacre or deliberate murder', Thomas FitzPatrick, 'The Ulster civil war, 1641. "The king's commission" in the County Fermanagh', *UJA*, 2nd series, 13, no. 3 (Aug. 1907), p. 156. This was also true in England, see, for instance, Donald Pennington, 'The war and the people', in John Morrill (ed.), *Reactions to the English civil war 1642–1649* (London, 1982), pp. 115–22.

⁵⁷ Canny, *Kingdom and colony*, p. 61.

⁵⁸ Even Ormond later calculated that since the total Protestant population of Ireland could not have exceeded 125,000 it was impossible that 250,000 could have been murdered (or even 154,000 as the lords justices claimed) 'and it is certain that the half of them that were plundered and stripped were not killed', an account [by Ormond] of the Irish that preserved English Protestants, [1660s] (Bodl., Carte MSS 2, fo. 238r–v). See also Clarke, 'The 1641 depositions', p. 111.

⁵⁹ Hogan (ed.), *Letters and papers*, pp. 9–11; Archibald Stewart to Argyll, 28 January 1642 (Bodl., Carte MSS 2, fo. 321); *Journals of the House of Commons of the kingdom of Ireland ... (1613–1791)* (28 vols., Dublin, 1753–91), II, 417. On Argyll's pretensions in Ulster, see Dawson, 'Two kingdoms or three?', pp. 120–2, 128–9; commission to pursue Archibald als Gillespick McDonald and others for the murder of John Donaldson, Glenarrie, County Antrim, 11 November 1634 (Inverary Castle, Argyll muniments, bundle 823).

⁶⁰ Stevenson, *Alasdair MacColla*, pp. 80–1. For as one Scottish historian has recently noted 'the regiment's first loyalty was to Clan Campbell, which meant in practical terms opposing the Clan Ian Mor and its allies (in Ulster the MacDonnells ...) and extending the territory of the Campbells', Edward M. Furgol, *A regimental history of the covenanting armies 1639–1651* (Edinburgh, 1990), p. 80

might receive his rents'.⁶¹ It seems that in return for a formal military command (Clotworthy later suggested he was to be made 'General of the Catholic army in Ulster'), and a guarantee that his property would not be tampered with, Antrim offered to negotiate a peace in the north and to win Major-General Robert Monro (who had arrived from Scotland with three regiments on 3 April), and his Scottish allies in Ulster, over to the royalist camp.⁶² Some time in the late spring of 1642 Charles I approved his proposal and towards the end of April Antrim began his journey north.⁶³ As he travelled he was careful to spend the nights only with those of his kin loyal to the crown – refusing, for instance, to stay with his natural sister Ellis in Newry because of her rebel connections. He also promised to protect the persons and property of leading Protestant landowners (such as William Brownlow of Lurgan) and chastised the insurgents for their 'execrable cruelty, for which God's wrath and the king's just revenge hung over their heads, and would very speedily overtake them'.⁶⁴ En route he did, however, meet – as his plan necessitated – with Sir Phelim O'Neill at Charlemount and other leading rebels and upon his arrival in County Antrim he summoned those of his kin and tenants who were in revolt for a parley.⁶⁵

The carefully calculated talks were immediately productive, for the ensuing truce enabled the earl to send provisions, 100 fat cattle and 60 loads of corn bought at his own expense, into the besieged town of Coleraine, and to relieve Ballintoy.⁶⁶ Having skilfully demonstrated a willingness among the Irish

---

61 Conway to Ormond, 5 June 1642 (Bodl., Carte MSS 3, fo. 239v).
62 HMC, *Supplementary report*, pp. 68–9. Rumour had it that Antrim and the king and queen were regular correspondents, TCD, MS 815, fo. 103; *Franciscan MSS*, pp. 151, 154; Stevenson, *Scottish Covenanters*, pp. 62, 103.
63 When he was subsequently arrested by Monro the duchess assured Hamilton that he 'was not inclined to rebellion' and added cryptically that he had been 'sent to Monro to meet for the king's service', duchess of Buckingham to Hamilton, 17 July 1642 (SRO, GD 406/1/3110). Account of several transactions during the rebellion and 1642 (BL, Eg. MSS 80, fo. 46) suggests that he left Kildare early in June, which is clearly not the case.
64 Deposition of Dr Robert Maxwell, 22 August 1642 (Hickson, *Ireland*, I, 333). For his full itinerary see Hill, *MacDonnells*, pp. 258–60.
65 His political opponents later interpreted his progress simply as an opportunity to plot with Sir Phelim and Tirlough O'Neill, who (they claimed) 'attended [him] with all demonstrations of joy and affection', some observations of adventurers and soldiers on the estate claimed by Antrim, [1661] (Bodl., Carte MSS 44, fos. 328–31). He also sent regular intelligence reports back to the lords justices in Dublin, Conway to Ormond, 5 June 1642 (*ibid.*, MSS 3, fos. 239–40v).
66 TCD, MS 839, fo. 97; Hill, *MacDonnells*, pp. 270–5; *Comment. Rinucc.*, I, 328, 453–4. A contemporary estimated that 2,000 (out of 6,000) inhabitants died in Coleraine, TCD, MS 866, fo. 235. The anonymous author of the *Aphorismical discovery* dubbed 'that oversighted, seeming mercy of Coleraine', as 'Antrim's mistake', Gilbert, *Contemp. hist. 1641–52*, I, 33.

rebels to compromise, the earl focused his attention on winning over Monro and his supporters.[67] He wrote to welcome the major-general and his army to Ireland, apologized 'that in my absence my people were so unfortunate as to do any hostile act' and, finally, requested a meeting at Glenarm.[68] Similar letters were dispatched to the other parliamentary sympathizers in the province; General Leslie, Sir John Clotworthy and Colonel Arthur Hill were all invited to a meeting 'not in a soldierly manner but like friends'.[69]

Antrim's peace-making initiatives puzzled them all and their initial response was to ignore his request.[70] Only his move from Dunluce to Glenarm precipitated a response from Monro, who finally agreed to a rendezvous at Dunluce.[71] To celebrate the occasion Antrim set about preparing a 'mighty feast'.[72] But towards the end of May 1642 Monro, who believed that the earl was 'joined strong with the rebels, making a pretext of laying down of arms, in the meantime doth what he can to cut our throats', marched to Dunluce (according to a London pamphlet) with 1,000 foot and 'sent a trumpet to the gate to summon him, having all things in a readiness to assault the castle, if he refused upon summons'.[73] Antrim duly surrendered his house and person to the Scottish commander, who took 'an inventory of all that he had', left a heavy guard on the castle, and dispatched his prisoner to Carrickfergus.[74]

Monro had probably been planning Antrim's arrest ever since he received his letter. For, having captured him, the major-general put himself at the head of three regiments of Scottish foot and – together with five companies of foot

---

[67] One anonymous commentator claimed that he only did so 'to show his good service to the king and to expiate those jealousies [which] were conceived of him', Account of several transactions during the rebellion and 1642 (BL, Eg. MSS 80, fo. 46).

[68] *A true relation of the proceedings of the Scottish armie now in Ireland* ... (London, 1642), p. 9.

[69] Conway to Ormond, 25 May 1642 (Bodl., Carte MSS 3, fo. 214v). Also see Gilbert, *Contemp. hist. 1641–52*, I, 422–3.

[70] *A true relation of the proceedings of the Scottish armie* ... , p. 5. Antrim's behaviour also puzzled Conway, Conway to Ormond, 25 May 1642 (Bodl., Carte MSS 3, fo. 214r–v).

[71] Hill, *MacDonnells*, pp. 304–5, 312; *A true relation of the proceedings of the Scots and English forces in the North of Ireland* ... (London, 8 June 1642), p. 7; reprinted by William Pinkerton, 'Proceedings of the Scottish and English forces in the north of Ireland, A.D. 1642', *UJA*, 1st series, 8 (1860), pp. 77–87.

[72] Conway to Ormond, 5 June 1642 (Bodl., Carte MSS 3, fo. 239v).

[73] Monro to Leslie, 13 May 1642 (Gilbert, *Contemp. hist. 1641–52*, I, 423). See also *A true and exact relation of divers principall actions of a late expedition, undertaken in the North of Ireland* ... (London, 13 July 1642).

[74] *A true and exact relation of divers principall actions* ... ; Hill, *MacDonnells*, pp. 265–6. News of Antrim's capture spread fast and by the end of July had even reached Rome, *Cal. SP Dom., 1641–3*, p. 341; *Montagu MSS*, pp. 154–5; *Franciscan MSS*, pp. 164, 160; *Comment. Rinucc.*, I, 454.

and four troops of horse, raised by the local Protestant, or 'British', settlers – set about cleansing County Antrim of 'the rebels being O'Neills, O'Haras, MacDonnells, and the MacHenrys'.[75] Clotworthy and his men chased Alasdair MacColla's band of 700 Highlanders into the Glynns, killing a number and capturing 3,000 head of cattle. They then took a fort built by the MacNaughtens and executed 100 of the 'rebels' hiding in it.[76] For his part Monro took Ballycastle, though not before the dowager duchess, with Antrim's 'bastard brother and sisters', had escaped across the Bann.[77] This offensive took a mere three days, but it freed County Antrim of insurgents; and the strategic placing of Protestant garrisons throughout the four baronies (Dunluce, Coleraine, Ballycastle, Clough, Glenarm and 'some other of the earl of Antrim's houses') precluded any concerted attempt to regain the county.[78] The bulk of these soldiers were loyal to and supported by Clan Campbell.[79] After Argyll's men had taken Rathlin Island (where they murdered the local population), Sir Duncan Campbell of Auchinbreck, lieutenant colonel of the regiment, stationed his soldiers at Ballycastle, Ballintoy, Ballymoney and Dunluce.[80]

The consequences of Monro's actions were profound. First, at one fell swoop, a substantial proportion of the county's population was forced into exile. Thus Donnell Groome McDonnell, after fleeing across the Bann, first joined Phelim O'Neill's army and then lived by his 'husbandry' before signing up, in 1649, with Alexander MacDonnell's regiment of foot.[81] The tale of Brian Modder MacHenry O'Cahan was similar. After the Route had been cleared he 'and all the Irish fled over the Bann and ... he went into Ossory in the Queen's County' where Antrim had given him a piece of land; he lived

---

[75] Conway to Ormond, 5 June 1642 (Bodl., Carte MSS 3, fo. 240).
[76] An enquiry, in which Alexander MacNaughten laid the blame on Clotworthy, was made into this massacre at the Restoration. Clotworthy justified his behaviour on two grounds: first, many of his troops were Campbells who were eager to vent their fury on MacDonnell dependants 'for such hath been their practice, as is notoriously known'; and secondly, his men were enraged to discover English colours in the fort, *Cal. SP Ire.*, 1660–2, pp. 455–8.
[77] Henry Manners to [Lord Montagu], 22 June 1642 (*Montagu MSS*, pp. 154–5).
[78] *A true and exact relation of divers principall actions* ... Also see George Morchant to Francis Gutherie, 13 June 1642 (SRO, RH 1/2/452/12). 'The pleasant house' of Glenarm was burned, Monro to [Argyll], 11 June 1642 (NLS, MS 3368, fos. 1–3). Clotworthy pursued 500 or so surviving insurgents from County Antrim under James MacDonnell's command throughout County Tyrone, *A true relation of the taking of Mountjoy* ... (London, 1642), p. 5. See also Stevenson, *Scottish Covenanters*, pp. 111–15; idem, *Alasdair MacColla*, pp. 85–6.
[79] Between 1642 and 1643 Argyll advanced £6,675 (sterling) worth of provisions to his men serving in County Antrim (Inverary castle, Argyll muniments, bundle 7/138).
[80] Furgol, *A regimental history*, p. 80.
[81] TCD, MS 838, fo. 31. O'Neill's army numbered around 6,000 foot and 500 horse, Hogan (ed.), *Letters and papers*, pp. 49–50.

there for five years until 1647 when he joined the confederate army.[82] These dislocated tenants were to be a major source of recruits for the various regiments raised by Antrim during the 1640s. Secondly, there was great disruption and upheaval among Antrim's Protestant tenants. Some, like their Catholic neighbours, simply abandoned their homes. Thomas Dixon later claimed that he fled with 120 other families from County Antrim to a place near Armagh; and Hugh Cunningham, after the insurgents had pillaged and burned his farm, crossed the border into County Down.[83] As many English families fled inland, their Scottish counterparts retreated (albeit often temporarily) across the North Channel to Scotland; while those who remained now faced life with a greatly reduced pool of labour and without a patron to protect them from the demands of an army of occupation.

Inevitably these events brought chaos to the earl's affairs. Though her annual pension of £6,000 was stopped, the duchess, for the time being, retained control of her English property;[84] however, the Scottish occupation of his County Antrim estates deprived the earl of his only source of Irish income. Though Stewart and Alexander had encountered tremendous problems in collecting rents in the months after the outbreak of the rebellion there still remained the hope that cash would again be forthcoming soon.[85] The need to recover his confiscated estates therefore remained a permanent priority in the earl's mind for the next twenty years, and he was prepared to do almost anything in order to secure their return. As a leading covenanter astutely pointed out, now that Antrim and his royalist associates 'are ruined in their estates, public commotions are their private subsistence'.[86]

In June 1642, however, financial worries were eclipsed by the more pressing matter of Antrim's captivity. Lord Conway was uncertain about his ultimate fate but felt that 'the appearances are not very handsome'. He had not only spent the previous winter living in territory effectively controlled by the insurgents but had also journeyed north 'through all the country of the rebels free and untouched' which would be interpreted by his enemies as 'signs that they bear him not any ill will' and that in fact he was their accomplice.[87] Truth to tell Monro was in a quandary about what to do next and begged Argyll 'for any order concerning the earl of Antrim, his house,

---

[82] Examination of Brian Modder MacHenry O'Cahan, 11 March 1653 (TCD, MS 838, fo. 29r–v).
[83] Ibid., MS 838, fo. 87; ibid., MS 836, fo. 80r-v.
[84] Montagu MSS, p. 147.
[85] A letter written from Sir William Parsons ... p. 3; duchess of Buckingham to [Hamilton], 5 October [1642] (SRO, GD 406/1/3113).
[86] Baillie to Spang, 26 July 1643 (Laing, Letters, II, 74).
[87] Conway to Ormond, 5 June 1642 (Bodl., Carte MSS 3, fo. 240).

person and goods – how to carry myself therein without prejudice to my credit'.[88] Hardly surprisingly Argyll urged Monro, the Scottish commissioners, Hamilton and the king to try Antrim as a traitor.[89] But in the end it was the English parliament which decided his fate and, late in June, the House of Commons ordered that he should continue to be held in 'the castle of Carrickfergus or ... some such other place of strength' until he could be transferred to London for trial.[90]

Literally within days of his arrest the duchess of Buckingham, who had recently arrived from Dublin at Charles I's court in York, heard rumours of his capture and begged to be allowed to see her husband or, at least, to send him a messenger and money.[91] Throughout the summer and autumn of 1642 she pestered Hamilton for similar favours. She asked that her furniture from their residences in Dunluce and Coleraine be shipped to England, that messengers be sent to her husband and that every measure possible be taken to secure his release either to England or, failing that, to Dublin.[92] But the marquis, though acquiescing to each request, was unwilling to side openly with the earl.[93] Hamilton's coolness upset Antrim who felt confident that once he had heard the truth he would 'not be ashamed to appear my friend, for no man better knows my heart, and the loyalty of it than yourself'.[94] Hamilton nevertheless remained aloof. By the beginning of September

---

[88] Monro to [Argyll], 11 June 1642 (NLS, MS 3368, fos. 1–3).
[89] Argyll to Hamilton, 11 June [1642] (SRO, GD 406/1/1761); Stevenson, *Scottish Covenanters*, p. 116.
[90] Order for Antrim's imprisonment, [18 June 1642] (HMC *rep. 5*, app., p. 30; HLRO, main papers, 18/6/1642). Also see *Journals of the House of Commons ... Ireland*, II, 631, 665, III, 127, 137. It was not until October that the House of Commons ordered Captain Ashley in the *Imployment* to transport Antrim from Carrickfergus to London, HMC *rep. 5*, app., p. 52; *Journals of the House of Commons ... Ireland*, II, 797; and SRO, PA 7/23/18.
[91] Early in May Castlehaven escorted the duchess and her servants to Dublin, *More good newes from Ireland, in two letters from Dublin* (London, 16 May 1642), p. 3; Castlehaven to Sir Arthur Loftus, 9 May 1642 (Bodl., Carte MSS 3, fo. 126); duchess of Buckingham to [Hamilton], 1 June [1642] (SRO, GD 406/1/2410). The duchess spent ten days with the king before travelling on to her Leicestershire estates, Nicholas to Ormond, 11 July 1642 (Bodl., Carte MSS 3, fo. 314).
[92] Duchess of Buckingham to Hamilton, 21 June 1642 (SRO, GD 406/1/3109); duchess of Buckingham to Hamilton, 17 July 1642 (*ibid.*, 406/1/3110).
[93] Hamilton frequently met the duchess at York, duchess of Buckingham to Hamilton, 17 July 1642 (*ibid.*, 406/1/3110); duchess of Buckingham to [Hamilton], 5 October [1642] (*ibid.*, 406/1/3113). Shortly before Antrim finally escaped in October the more valuable items of their household were shipped to England and stored at Chester until 1651 when they were auctioned for roughly £1,850 by the Commonwealth, see Hill, *MacDonnells*, pp. 265–6; PRO, SP 23/237/25, fos. 62–79.
[94] Antrim to [Hamilton], 16 July 1642 (SRO, GD 406/1/1674).

Antrim had become depressed by his continued confinement and only the king's efforts to have him released cheered him.[95] However, the commander of the Scottish army in Ulster claimed to be bound by parliament's orders and refused to hand him over;[96] so that escape now seemed the only solution to Antrim's predicament. This was precisely what he did towards the end of October.[97] A relative of Archibald Stewart procured a passport for an invalid to leave Carrickfergus castle and Antrim, disguised as a cripple, escaped to a waiting ship bound for Carlisle and from there journeyed on to York, where he joined his wife some time in November 1642.[98]

During the six months he had been in prison the political situation in the three kingdoms had changed considerably. England had plunged into civil war: Edgehill had been fought; London had not been taken. Both king and parliament had appealed to Scotland for assistance. This had divided the covenanting movement between the moderates, who were unwilling to join parliament, and the hardliners, who allied with parliament fearing that if it were subdued the king would turn once more against Scotland.[99] The outbreak of war in England also put pressure on the uneasy Protestant alliance in Ireland – which, up until this point, had been loosely obedient to the king (see map 3). These 'Irish royalists' controlled Dublin, much of the Pale, County Louth and parts of Counties Down and Cork together with numerous small enclaves in and around Londonderry, Dungannon, Enniskillen, Boyle, Loughrea, Portumna and Carlow, while their Scottish allies were entrenched principally in County Antrim. By contrast the Catholic insurgents, who

---

[95] 'I suffer greatly by my long stay in this place', Antrim to [Hamilton], 3 September 1642 (*ibid.*, 406/1/1778). Also see Hill, *MacDonnells*, pp. 265–6; 'A narrative of the marquis of Antrim's deportment' (PRONI, D2977/5/1/2); *Journals of the House of Commons ... Ireland*, II, 763.

[96] Leven wrote to Archibald Stewart informing him of the king's demands for Antrim's release and requesting his presence to discuss 'moneys towards his [Antrim's] transportation'. Hill suggested that Leven was in fact extracting money under false pretences, Leven to Stewart, [15 September] 1642 (PRONI, D2977/5/1/1, and Hill, *MacDonnells*, p. 262); Lesley to lords justices, [early] November 1642 (SRO, GD 406/1/1790). Whether Alasdair MacColla and his brother defected to the Scottish side in September 1642 in the hope of securing Antrim's release is debatable; and if this had been their intention it failed. Orders for Randal and Alexander MacDonald, [10 November] 1642 (Bodl., Carte MSS 4, fo. 32); Stevenson, *Scottish Covenanters*, pp. 125–6; *idem, Alasdair MacColla*, pp. 88–90; *idem*, 'The desertion of the Irish', pp. 78–81; T. W. Moody and J. G. Simms (eds.), *The bishopric of Derry and the Irish society of London, 1602–1705*, I, *1602–70* (IMC, Dublin, 1968), p. 245.

[97] Conway reported to Ormond that 'I do now hear from Knockfergus that the earl of Antrim did the last night make an escape, and is gone but which way either by land or sea I know not', Conway to Ormond, 22 October 1642 (Bodl., Carte MSS 3, fo. 579).

[98] Hill, *Stewarts of Ballintoy*, p. 29; Laing, *Letters*, II, 73.

[99] Stevenson, *Alasdair MacColla*, p. 95.

controlled the rest of the country and were now bonded by an oath of association, went from strength to strength and in the spring of 1642 organized themselves into a formal confederation.[100] On 24 October the confederate Catholics held their first general assembly at Kilkenny and elected the supreme council which was a committee of twenty-four members (six representatives from each province), twelve of whom were supposed to sit permanently and run the confederation. But as Aidan Clarke has noted: 'extensive as the powers of the supreme council were, it was strictly subordinate to the assembly, a unicameral legislature composed partly of members elected on the normal parliamentary basis, and partly of temporal and spiritual peers who ... were differentiated from commoners only by certain ceremonial marks of precedence.'[101] Political homogeneity at Kilkenny was reinforced by military cohesion on the battlefield: four armies (one for each province) which were supposed to consist of 6,000 foot and 400 horse together with a 'running army' of 2,000 foot and 200 horse were set up. In August 1642 Antrim's cousin Owen Roe O'Neill – 'an old experienced commander' from the Spanish Army of Flanders – had been welcomed to Ireland by Sir James MacDonnell, the Catholic leader of the rebellion on the Antrim estates. The following month Colonel Thomas Preston, also fresh from a command in Spanish Flanders, landed at Wexford.[102] Within a relatively short period of time these and a flood of other continental veterans had 'reduced many of the natives to a more civil deportment, and to a pretty good understanding of military discipline'.[103]

Into 'these turbulent and murkey waters the earl of Antrim set out to fish'.[104] Between his escape in October 1642 and his return to Ireland the following April he spent most of his time at York where, according to Charles I, 'he so behaved himself, as became the duty of a good and loyal subject'.[105] But much depends on one's definition of 'good and loyal', for subsequent

---

[100] Clarke, *Old English*, pp. 214–15.
[101] *Ibid.*, p. 218. Also see Cregan, 'The confederation of Kilkenny', pp. 102–15, who describes the origins, structure and composition of the confederation. In addition to the supreme council there were councils for justice and finance and a chancery. The financial council had the least power, despite the fact that the army was (at least initially) very regularly paid, 'relación del estado del reyno de Irlanda desde Diciembre 1644' (AGS, Eo. 2253, unfol.).
[102] Leven to Hamilton, 8 August 1641 (SRO, GD 406/1/1777); Jerrold I. Casway, 'Owen Roe O'Neill's return to Ireland in 1642: the diplomatic background', *Studia Hib.*, 9 (1969), pp. 48–64.
[103] Sir James Turner, *Memoirs of his own life and times (1632–70)*, ed. T. Thomson (Bannatyne Club, vol. XXVIII, Edinburgh, 1829), p. 26.
[104] Stevenson, *Alasdair MacColla*, p. 95.
[105] Charles I to Leven, 11 June 1643 (Bodl., Carte MSS 5, fo. 45r–v).

Map 3 Ireland on the eve of the cessation of arms, September 1643

evidence clearly indicates that during these months Antrim furtively and frantically conspired to solve both the king's British problems and also his own economic and territorial ones. His masterplan was very similar to the projects of 1638–9 and 1644. First, a truce between the Irish royalists and confederate Catholics was to be negotiated, then their united armies were to move initially against the Scots in Ulster and subsequently into the Western Isles. Once in Scotland, the Irish troops were to join forces with an army raised by Antrim, Huntly, his son Aboyne, Montrose and Airlie in the Highlands; meanwhile a separate force would invade from England led by Nithsdale and Newcastle.[106] Finally, 'Hamilton and many others' were to rise in rebellion in the heart of Scotland so that, according to one horrified covenanter, 'in a trice we should become a field of blood'.[107] It was even hoped that this Irish army, after helping to subdue Scotland in the king's name, would then cross the border and invade England.[108]

Though John MacDonald, bard of Keppoch, identified Antrim as the 'leader of hosts' he did not conceive the plan alone: Nithsdale, Aboyne, Airlie and Newcastle were his leading accomplices.[109] But what of the king and queen: what royal support did this 'devilish plot' (as it was later called) have? The queen, who had arrived at York in March 1643, was certainly involved.[110] But it was not until 11 May 1643, in a cyphered letter, that she articulated her enthusiasm to her husband, informing him that she had instructed Antrim to proceed to Ireland 'to persuade the Irish to reach a reasonable compromise' and begging him to inform Ormond and no one else of his mission.[111] As it was the king was contemplating his own 'reasonable

---

[106] Examination of James Stewart, 12 June 1643 (HMC *rep. 13*, pp. 122–3; *ibid. rep. 5*, app., pp. 93–4; HLRO, main papers, 28/6/1643). Stevenson, *Alasdair MacColla*, pp. 95–9; *idem*, *The Scottish revolution*, pp. 270–2; Cowan, *Montrose*, pp. 139–41.
[107] Baillie to Spang, 26 July 1643 (Laing, *Letters*, II, 74).
[108] Proceedings of the council of war, 24 May 1643, and examination of Antrim, 12 June 1643 (HMC *rep. 13*, pp. 120–2; *ibid.*, *rep. 5*, app., pp. 93–4; HLRO, main papers, 28/6/43).
[109] Annie M. MacKenzie, *Orain Iain Luim. Songs of John MacDonald, bard of Keppoch* (Scottish Gaelic Texts Society, Edinburgh, 1964), pp. 15–19. Montrose was less enthusiastic and only agreed to support the venture if it were endorsed by the king, HMC *rep. 13*, pp. 121–2; *ibid. rep. 5*, app., pp. 93–4; HLRO, main papers, 28/6/1643.
[110] Antrim later suggested that the king's approval for the venture would only be sought after he had secured 'easy conditions' from the Irish. And so it was on Newcastle's warrant that Antrim and Aboyne were to raise their army in the Highlands, HMC *rep. 13*, pp. 121–2; *ibid.*, *rep. 5*, app., pp. 93–4; HLRO, main papers, 28/6/1643.
[111] Henrietta Maria to Charles I, 11 May 1643 (BL, Eg. MSS 2619, fos. 18v–19); Mary Anne Everett Green (ed.), *Letters of Queen Henrietta Maria* (London, 1857), pp. 198–9. From this letter it is clear that Antrim's masterplan had already been suggested to the king

compromise' with the Irish. Henrietta Maria had repeatedly reminded her husband that nothing was 'more necessary and essential to the support of your affairs, than the peace of that kingdom [Ireland]' and that 'all means possible' should be used to secure it.[112] Finally, on 23 April, in accordance with his wife's wishes, Charles, who regarded Ireland as no more than a 'strategic pawn', authorized Ormond to conclude a ceasefire with the Catholic party.[113] However, his willingness to treat with the enemy was kept secret because the king was loath to alienate the Scots and push them further into the parliamentary camp because if that happened, 'the two kingdoms will shatt upon him in despight of what his best servants can do'.[114] Though Antrim does not appear to have been directly involved in the delicate process of procuring a cessation of arms, it obviously suited his own plans. And so for a brief time Antrim and Ormond were both working on similar strategies aimed at winning Irish support for the king.

In order to prepare the ground for the successful implementation of his own design Antrim returned to Ireland in April 1643. His brother was immediately dispatched to Ulster to confer with Sir Phelim O'Neill while the earl liaised in person with Lords Taaffe, Dillon (confederates in favour of a ceasefire) and Ormond.[115] This preliminary reconnaissance trip appears to have been reasonably fruitful, although Monro refused to join the king's party in spite of the inducement of an offer of £5,000. By the middle of April, Antrim felt confident that Ormond would be willing 'to hasten the army into Ulster', ready for service in Scotland, and asked him to have ships ready at Carlingford or Greencastle by the end of the month 'where I shall have men ready and much more than I undertook which I considered would be no disadvantage to the service'.[116]

---

by the duchess of Buckingham. In an effort to disguise the queen's early involvement, Antrim later claimed that it was only early in May when ammunition, destined for the Western Isles, was held up at York that he had asked her to secure its redirection to Scarborough, HMC *rep. 13*, pp. 121–2; *ibid., rep. 5*, app., pp. 93–4; HLRO, main papers, 28/6/1643; Charles McNeill, *The Tanner letters. Documents of Irish affairs in the sixteenth and seventeenth centuries extracted from the Thomas Tanner collection in the Bodleian Library Oxford* (IMC, Dublin, 1943), p. 160.

[112] Henrietta Maria to Charles I, 20/30 January 1643 (Green (ed.), *Letters*, p. 156).

[113] John Lowe, 'Charles I and the confederation of Kilkenny, 1643–9', *IHS*, 14, no. 53 (Mar. 1964), pp. 13–14.

[114] Will Murray to Hamilton, September 1642, cited in Russell, *Causes*, p. 22.

[115] HMC *rep. 13*, pp. 121–2; *ibid., rep. 5*, app., pp. 93–4; HLRO, main papers, 28/6/1643; *Reg. privy council Scot., 1638–43*, pp. xxx, 648; Gilbert, *Ir. confed.*, II, xli–xlii and lxiii.

[116] Antrim to Ormond, 14 April 1643 (Bodl., Carte MSS 5, fo. 83). Also see Monro to Crafford, 25 May 1643 (*ibid.*, fos. 323–4v); HMC *rep. 13*, pp. 121–3; *ibid. rep. 5*, app., pp. 93–4; HLRO, main papers, 28/6/1643.

Back in England and Scotland, however, the complex plan was running awry. First, it was proving difficult to implement the grand royalist alliance, partly due to a breakdown of communications between the leading protagonists; a disconsolate Nithsdale even feared that Hamilton and Montrose had reneged on their promises. 'Matters are fallen out quite contrary to my expectation' he lamented to Antrim early in May and added 'how great folly it were to look for any assistance from Scotland'.[117] Second, the Scottish covenanters had caught wind of the plot and suspected that Antrim intended shipping Irish troops 'to take in this country'.[118] The advantage of surprise was thus now lost. Third, the ammunition so desperately needed to arm the Highland levies was embargoed and although it was subsequently redirected via Scarborough, this unexpected delay unnerved and unsettled the conspirators.[119] But the final, and fatal, blow to the venture came in the middle of May when the vessel commandeered to carry Antrim (who had briefly returned to York) and the arms to Ireland was captured by one of Monro's colonels off the coast of County Down.[120] Protesting that he was merely en route to collect some hangings and pictures belonging to his wife, and rents owed to his brother, Antrim was 'carried to his old lodging at Carrickfergus'.[121] In order to decide what should be done with the incorrigible earl, Monro summoned a council of war which interrogated him and his servants about the contents of letters he was carrying from his co-conspirators.[122] It was immediately apparent that they were resolved 'to do all mischief they could against the kingdom of Scotland' and that the earl should be held prisoner until a formal trial could be arranged.[123]

---

[117] Nithsdale to Antrim, 2 May 1643 (McNeill, *Tanner letters*, pp. 158–9).
[118] *Ibid.*
[119] *Ibid.*, pp. 158–60; HMC *rep. 13*, p. 133; *ibid., rep. 5*, app., p. 84; HLRO, main papers, 8/5/1643.
[120] *A letter of great consequence; sent by ... Monro ... to the committee for Irish affairs ...* (London, 8 July 1643), pp. 4–6; Monro to Crafford, 25 May 1643 (Bodl., Carte MSS 5, fos. 323–4v). It is unlikely that the ship was laden with arms for 6,000 as reported in *The kingdomes weekly intelligencer ... From Tuesday 13 to Tuesday 20 June 1643, no. 24* (London, 1643), p. 188; Stevenson, *Scottish Covenanters*, pp. 132–3. Antrim's pass from Newcastle was dated 4 May 1643 (SRO, PA 7/23/2/10).
[121] Baillie to Spang, 26 July 1643 (Laing, *Letters*, II, 73). Also see HMC *rep. 13*, pp. 122–3; *ibid., rep. 5*, app., pp. 93–4; HLRO, main papers, 28/6/1643; McNeill, *Tanner letters*, pp. 158–9; *Comment. Rinucc.*, I, 454. Apparently he was carrying £35 in gold and £12 in silver, *Clan Donald*, II, 724–5.
[122] Monro to Crafford, 25 May 1643 (Bodl., Carte MSS 5, fos. 323–4v).
[123] Proceedings of the council of war, 24 May 1643 (HMC *rep. 13*, pp. 120–1; *ibid., rep. 5*, app., pp. 93–4; HLRO, main papers, 28/6/1643). Also see *A letter of great consequence ...* pp. 4–6.

Monro now made it publicly known that Antrim – 'a prime man of the papist faction' – was being directed by the queen.[124] He notified the English House of Commons of the dangerous plot, advised the government in Edinburgh to 'spread the true report hereof to those you may trust unto, to guard the well-affected' and reminded men in Dublin loyal to the parliamentary cause to be on their guard.[125] Both the English and Scottish administrations condemned the 'treacherous plot of the Irish, English and Scottish papists' and ordered that the protagonists be punished.[126] In order to maximize the full value of the plot in propaganda terms parliament also had the conspirators' correspondence published.[127] All the leading London papers carried the story in varying degrees of accuracy and each one emphasized the traitorous character of 'popish Irish rebels' in general and of the earl of Antrim in particular.[128] One especially colourful pamphlet – *The character of an Oxford incendiary* – described the earl as 'a rebel not worth the naming, nor that precious piece of iron-work, his duchess; yet I must needs say, she was a lady rarely marked out for two eminent husbands, the beds of Buckingham and Antrim; this latter more pernicious than a bed of scorpions'.[129] More damaging still to the royalist case was the accusation that the queen had orchestrated 'this Horrid Plot' and the apparent proof that the Ulster massacres and the original 'monstrous rebellion of Ireland, was projected, incited, and assisted, by those councils now only prevalent with his majesty. That the queen with her romish priests, [and] the papists of all ... three

---

[124] Monro to Crafford, 25 May 1643 (Bodl., Carte MSS 5, fos. 323–324v).
[125] *A letter of great consequence* ..., pp. 4–6.
[126] *A declaration of the lords of his majesty's privie-councell in Scotland: and commissioners for conserving the articles of the treaty* ... (London, 27 June 1643), pp. 4–8; *Reg. privy council Scot., 1638–43*, pp. xxx, 442–4. Early in June Aboyne and Nithsdale were brought before the justice-general on charges arising from the letters; while the House of Commons ordered that Antrim be dispatched to England for further questioning, *Reg. privy council Scot., 1638–43*, pp. xxx, 436; English commissioners to Monro, 2 September 1643 (Bodl., Carte MSS 6, fo. 339v); *A declaration of the commons assembled in parliament; concerning the rise and progresse of the grand rebellion in Ireland ... with some letters and papers of great consequence of the earl of Antrim's* ... (London, 25 July 1643), pp. 17–22, 51–3; Stevenson, *The Scottish revolution*, pp. 270–4.
[127] Stevenson, *Scottish Covenanters*, p. 133; idem, *Alasdair MacColla*, pp. 98–9.
[128] See, for example, *The kingdomes weekly intelligencer ... From Tuesday 23 to Tuesday 30 May and Tuesday 27 June to Tuesday 4 July 1643*, nos. 21 and 24 (London, 1643), pp. 161, 3–4; *Mercurius civicus ... From Thursday 20 to Friday 28 July 1643*, no. 9 (London, 1643), p. 69.
[129] Printed in *The Harleian miscellany, or, a collection of scarce, curious and entertaining pamphlets and tracts* ... (12 vols., London, 1808–11), V, 345.

Popish plotting in Caroline Ireland and Britain   123

kingdoms, have been principal actors.'[130] The editor of the *Kingdomes weekly intelligencer* hoped that this would now convert any waverers to the parliamentary cause so that 'they may not still be seduced by the cunning connivers of the declarations ... from Oxford, that there is no intention to set up popery'.[131] A propaganda campaign directed against the queen was combined with a flood of literature over the summer of 1643 reminding the population at large of the atrocities supposedly committed by Irish papists against English and Scottish Protestants since the outbreak of the Irish rebellion.[132]

The Protestant population was duly alarmed. Edward Hyde later acknowledged the damage caused by 'the imputation raised by parliament upon the king, of an intention to bring in, or ... for conniving at and tolerating, Popery';[133] while 'The plot of Antrim', according to that discerning Scotsman Robert Baillie, 'had wakened in all a great fear of our own safety, and distrust of all the fair words that were or could be given us'.[134] A parliamentary sympathizer in Dublin even suggested that 'it is one of the worst plots against this kingdom and Scotland, and so by consequence against England that hath yet been discovered except the plot of the rebellion which hath already almost consumed us'.[135] The political and military ramifications ran even deeper. In Scotland news that the royal couple had been conspiring against the covenanters was decisive in convincing the more moderate party to ally with parliament and, accordingly, in August 1643 'a military, political and religious alliance based on the solemn league and covenant was agreed between a Scottish convention of estates and the English commissioners'.[136]

---

[130] *A declaration of the commons assembled in parliament* ... , pp. 17–22, 51–3. The parliament scout accused the queen of having 'countenanced and maintained that horrid and execrable rebellion now on foot in Ireland whereby many thousand Protestants have been barbarously murdered', *The parliament scout ... From Tuesday 20 to Tuesday 27 June 1643* (London, 1643), p. 4. See also *The kingdomes weekly intelligencer ... From Tuesday 4 to Tuesday 11 July 1643*, no. 25 (London, 1643), p. 193.

[131] *The kingdomes weekly intelligencer ... From Tuesday 27 June to Tuesday 4 July 1643*, no. 24 (London, 1643), pp. 3–4.

[132] R. Clifton, 'Fear of catholics in the English revolution 1640–60', *Past and Present*, 52 (1971), pp. 25–9, 39, 53; Robert E. Elkin, 'The interactions between the Irish rebellion and the English civil wars' (unpublished PhD thesis, University of Illinois at Urbana-Champaign, 1961), pp. 138–9; Hibbard, *Popish plot*, p. 225; Lindley, 'The impact of the 1641 rebellion', pp. 167–70.

[133] Clarendon, *Rebellion*, II, 276.

[134] Baillie to Spang, 26 July 1643 (Laing, *Letters*, II, 80). G. E. Aylmer, 'Presidential address: collective mentalities in mid-seventeenth century England: II. royalist attitudes', *R. Hist. Soc. Trans.*, 37 (1987), pp. 11–13.

[135] 'T. N.' to Robert Reynolds, 7 June 1643 (HMC *rep. 5*, app., p. 89; HLRO, main papers, 7/6/1643).

[136] Stevenson, *Alasdair MacColla*, pp. 98–9.

Above all the covenanters now agreed to send an army of 21,000 men into England to fight for parliament against the evidently perfidious king.[137]

Hardly surprisingly, both the king and queen denied all knowledge of 'any such business'.[138] Charles was very probably lying, and his wife definitely was. After the queen heard that Antrim had been 'taken by the Scots in Ireland', it was with evident relief that she reminded her husband that 'he has nothing of mine in writing'.[139] Their subsequent frenzied efforts to secure Antrim's release did little to inspire confidence in their denials. Thus Henrietta Maria, on hearing of his arrest on 30 May wrote to Hamilton of Antrim's 'misfortune'. She begged that he be 'not rudely treated' since he had only gone to take up outstanding rents and added significantly that 'if he were able to serve the king he would do so even against those of his own country and that he has none other intention'.[140] For his part, the king wrote similar letters to the Scottish commanders in Ulster insisting that the earl be dispatched to Dublin for trial and that his estates and possessions be 'saved harmless both from the spoil of the Irish rebels, and our own forces there'.[141] Charles also whipped up support for Antrim among the Irish royalists. Initially the Dublin government, afraid of a scandal involving the queen, prevaricated but then (at the king's insistence) dismissed Monro's reports as idle rumours; and both the lords justices and Ormond ordered him to send Antrim to Dublin. Monro refused.[142] So desperate were the king and queen to have Antrim released that they even sought French intervention. In September the duke of Orléans, the premier peer of France and Henrietta Maria's brother, made a personal plea on the earl's behalf to Hamilton; and early in November a French agent (disparagingly described by one covenanter as

---

[137] Stevenson, *The Scottish revolution*, pp. 273, 276–93; Donal F. Cregan, 'An Irish cavalier: Daniel O'Neill in the civil wars 1642–51', *Studia Hib.*, 4 (1965), pp. 107–8.
[138] The king even ordered an enquiry into those 'raisers and divulgers of such a false scandal', Charles I to the Scottish privy council, 31 June 1643 (SRO, GD 406/1/8303).
[139] Henrietta Maria to Charles I, 27 May 1643 (Green (ed.), *Letters*, pp. 212–13).
[140] Henrietta Maria to Hamilton, 30 May [1643] (SRO, GD 406/1/9602). The king also claimed that Antrim was in Ulster only 'to provide for the security of his estates', Charles I to Leven, 11 June 1643 (Bodl., Carte MSS 5, fo. 405r–v). The queen also badgered Ormond, Henrietta Maria to Ormond, 27 September 1643 (*ibid.*, 7, fo. 111).
[141] Charles I to Leven, 11 June 1643 (Bodl., Carte MSS 5, fo. 405r–v). Also see Charles I to Ormond, 12 June 1643 (*ibid.*, fo. 418).
[142] They only learnt of the plot early in June, lords justices to Nicholas, 10 June 1643 (*Ormonde MSS*, II, 288); Ormond to Monro, 11 August 1643 (Bodl., Carte MSS 65, fos. 61–2); lords justices to Monro, 11 August 1643 (*ibid.*, 6, fos. 194–5); Ormond to Monro, 16 August (*ibid.*, 65, fo. 220); Monro to Ormond, 9 September 1643 (*ibid.*, 6, fo. 440).

'A little Monsieur, some agent with letters from the Queen') was sent to Edinburgh to negotiate (among other things) for Antrim's release.[143] He arrived too late. On the very day the agent made his formal application to the Scottish council, news reached Edinburgh that Antrim had in fact escaped from Carrickfergus castle for the second time.[144]

On this occasion Captain George Gordon, the twelfth earl of Sutherland's brother 'had a cord sent into him amongst his linens, which a man carried to him by the friendship of an officer in the garrison'.[145] That night he managed to escape to a pre-arranged spot a mile from Carrickfergus where a man and horse were supposed to be waiting for him. When his accomplice, who was later caught and hanged, failed to appear he set off on foot towards Lisnagarvey, where the next morning an old man found and fed him and then guided him to Charlemount. From there he made his way to Mellifont and Kilkenny, where he arrived late in November 1643.[146]

Antrim's second escape from Carrickfergus marked the conclusion of the third attempt by Charles I, within a period of less than two and a half years, to use Irish Catholic soldiers against his Protestant English and Scottish subjects. Without question, the king was deeply involved in the plots hatched by the earl of Antrim in 1641, 1642 and 1643 and so the abundant rumours of 'popish plots' were entirely justified. Moreover, Charles's willingness to countenance Antrim's schemes drew Catholic Ireland even deeper into the

---

[143] Baillie to Spang, 17 November 1643 (Laing, *Letters*, II, 105). Also see Gaston, duke of Orléans to Hamilton, 18/28 September 1643 (SRO, GD 406/1/9614); HMC *rep. 13*, pp. 136–7.

[144] The French agent sent a detailed account of his embassy to Edinburgh back to Brienne: 'They had refused to me the release of the earl of Antrim and a quarter of an hour before my audience, I learned they had received the news of his escape from prison. I pretended not to know of it, and insisted strongly that they should gratify France by releasing this earl, which I learned afterwards they considered a very great mockery on my part, and as a reputation of this nature is not advantageous for those engaged in treating matters of importance, I called on the Chancellor and the principal members of [the] council, and showed that they had very badly interpreted what I had said at my audience relating to the earl of Antrim, and although I might have known of his escape or not, it was my duty to ask them that he be liberated, seeing I had received that order and that it was not for me to verify the exactitude of rumours circulating in the town.' Boisivon to Brienne, 10/20 November 1643 (*Diplomatic correspondence*, II, 543).

[145] [Hogan (ed.)], *History of the warr*, p. 24. Also see Stevenson, *Scottish Covenanters*, p. 136; A. S. Murdock and H. M. F. Simpson (eds.), *The memoirs of James, marquis of Montrose, 1639–50, written by his chaplain, George (later Bishop) Wishart* (London, 1893), p. 38; *Clan Donald*, II, 725.

[146] [Hogan (ed.)], *History of the warr*, pp. 24–6. The old man remained a servant; the washerwoman, who smuggled in his rope (Ann Orphin) was given an annual pension of £10, Hill, *MacDonnells*, pp. 265–6, 271. See also *Diplomatic correspondence*, II, 543; *The weekly account containing special and remarkable passages ... no. 16* (London, 20 December 1643), p. 8; *Comment, Rinucc.*, I, 455.

British political and military arena and ensured that it henceforth became an important dimension in the larger cross-channel struggle. This already 'highly untidy drama' was further complicated by the determination of both Antrim and Argyll to drag their personal feud into the wider conflict.[147] Antrim for one now planned to combine 'the linked but until now separate civil wars of England, Scotland and Ireland into a single war';[148] or, in the words of one contemporary, 'to embroil all three kingdoms... was the earl of Antrim's business'.[149]

[147] Russell, *Causes*, p. 109.
[148] Stevenson, *Alasdair MacColla*, p. 97.
[149] [Sir John Temple to Thomas Temple], 23 June 1643 (Gilbert, *Ir. confed.*, II, lxiii–lxiv).

5

The 'War of the Three Kingdoms' (November 1643–December 1644)

In September 1643 a ceasefire for one year – known as the 'cessation of arms' – was concluded between the Irish royalists, led by Ormond (who was soon to be appointed lord lieutenant), and the Catholic forces. In effect, official negotiations had begun the previous July, shortly after Galway fell into Catholic hands. After much haggling it was agreed that the confederates should pay the king £20,000 and provide him with troops and equipment for his English war-effort. In return the confederates were led to expect, but were not actually granted, the repeal of the penal laws and 'a large measure of political independence, permanent tenure of their lands, safeguards against reprisals, and a guarantee that the whole settlement would be enshrined in law'.[1] As things turned out the agreement was never ratified, so the 'cessation' proved a high price for the Irish Catholics to pay for little more than formal recognition of the confederate cause by the king at a time when its armies enjoyed a military and strategic advantage.[2]

Nevertheless, the ceasefire heralded a new departure in Anglo-Irish relations. Hardly surprisingly, it was not well received in Britain. One Scottish covenanter noted that it 'is much dislike[d] here, and particular exception taken against his majesty calling the Irish natives his Catholic subjects'.[3] As far as the English parliament was concerned, a 'united' Ireland – however tenuous the union – constituted a major strategic and military threat since the king now had access to previously unexploited resources in terms of men and money. The cessation also embarrassed English royalists, anxious to avoid being tarred as 'pro-papist', but considering the poor state of the king's affairs they either had to accept it reluctantly or shift their allegiance to parliament (as some indeed did).[4] In Ireland itself the ceasefire shattered the uneasy

---

[1] Lowe, 'Charles I and the confederation', p. 2. Also see Joyce Lee Malcolm, 'All the king's men: the impact of the crown's Irish soldiers on the English civil war', *IHS*, 21, no. 83 (Mar. 1979), pp. 246–7   [2] Lowe, 'Charles I and the confederation', pp. 1–2.
[3] [Lanerick] to Hamilton, 24 October 1643 (SRO, GD 406/1/1858).
[4] Lindley, 'The impact of the 1641 rebellion', pp. 168–70; Malcolm, 'All the king's men', pp. 247–9.

Protestant alliance and intensified the war in Ulster by driving the Scots into the parliamentary camp. The Protestant Irish royalists, whose power was essentially limited to Dublin and part of the Pale, were now allied with the Catholic confederates who controlled the rest of the country except for parts of Ulster (occupied by the Scots) and sundry strongholds along the south and west coast. The new allies were opposed only by the forces loyal to the English parliament, primarily represented by the Scottish covenanting army in Ulster, which did not adhere to the cessation.

It was in this much altered world that the earl of Antrim attempted to find his niche after escaping from Carrickfergus for the second time. This was not hard, for the cessation removed the dilemma into which the 1641 rebellion had plunged him. At last he could fraternize openly and legally with his 'rebel' friends and family without fear of retribution from the royalist party. It also created fresh opportunities to gain political power and prestige.

In order to exploit the new political configuration the earl hurried to Waterford, where the third general assembly had just convened in order to elect agents who were to be responsible for negotiating a permanent peace with the king and to discuss the progress of the war in Ulster. Antrim immediately used his influence as a traditional Ulster power-broker to ensure that the Gaelic lords in the north-east fulfilled their obligation under the terms of the cessation to provide the king's supporters with cattle.[5] He was also eager to secure a formal office in the confederation and to gain control over the force of 6,000 men the general assembly had decided to raise for service in Ulster against the Scots.[6] According to Richard Bellings, at this time the earl 'entertained thoughts of having himself declared lieutenant general of the confederate Catholics of Ireland, and having received encouragement therein from some friends of his that had a part in the government, the design was formed with much industry, and prosecuted with no little earnestness in his behalf at council'.[7] If offered this prestigious post, the earl promised to use his own and his wife's influence at court – about which, according to the same source, he boasted at great length – to further the confederate cause. He also

---

[5] Antrim to Ormond, [*c*. 7 November] 1643 (Bodl., Carte MSS 7, fo. 407); Henry O'Neill to Antrim, 8 November 1643 (*ibid.*, fo. 381); Phelim O'Neill to Antrim, 8 November 1643 (*ibid.*, fo. 381); Ormond to [Henry O'Neill], 17 November 1643 (*ibid.*, fo. 483); Stevenson, *Scottish Covenanters*, pp. 166–7.

[6] Anonymous author of the *Aphorismical discovery* (Gilbert, *Contemp. hist. 1641–52*, I, 79–80) suggested that there was a faction within the assembly which wanted Antrim declared lord lieutenant. This may well have been the case but Antrim's priorities at this point lay with retrieving his hereditary estates and not seriously vying 'for spectacular [political] reward' in the form of the lord lieutenancy, Lowe, 'The earl of Antrim', p. 191.

[7] *Desid. cur. Hib.*, p. 243. See also news from Waterford, 28 February/10 March 1644 (AMAE, Correspondence politique, Angleterre, Côte 51, fo. 22r–v).

argued that if he were made lieutenant-general of the confederate forces his followers in Scotland would join the struggle and 'consequently by diversion, free the confederates from some part of the harm they were to expect from the daily increasing power of the Scots in the north'.[8] The general assembly, eager to rid Ulster of the Scots, accepted the earl's proposals 'without debate' and, before its dissolution on 1 December, ordered the supreme council to inform him of their decision.[9] In addition the couple were awarded a generous pension to compensate them for the loss of revenue from their Irish and English estates.[10]

By making much of his own importance at court and in Scotland Antrim had secured – in theory at least – the position of lieutenant-general of the confederate army. He at once set off to the king's headquarters at Oxford to receive his master's approval. When he arrived there, sometime late in December 1643, he pursued a similar tactic, or rather, in the words of Richard Bellings, 'he made a double return, being magnified at court upon the account of the confederates, and at Waterford upon the score of his favour at court'.[11] By inflating his standing among the Catholic confederates (he claimed to be commander-in-chief of their armies) and by suggesting that he would be able to manipulate the Catholic party into filling all of Charles's needs, he was able to win the king's approval for new plans he had been hatching with leading courtiers and Scottish royalists.[12]

Antrim's plan had three components. First, he was to raise in the name of the confederates and at their expense 10,000 armed men, who were to be shipped to England 'to resist the Scotch invasion'. (A covenanting army crossed the Tweed on 19 January 1644.) In case the confederates 'insist upon such things as we cannot without great inconvenience and danger to the

---

[8] *Desid. cur. Hib.*, p. 242. See also Carte, *Ormond*, VI, 31–4; HMC *rep. 13*, pp. 172–3; Lowe, 'The earl of Antrim', p. 192.

[9] *Desid. cur. Hib.*, p. 243. See also Carte, *Ormond*, VI, 43–6; petition of adventurers and soldiers to king, [August, 1663] (Bodl., Carte MSS 44, fos. 376–7); Hill, *MacDonnells*, p. 313.

[10] The pension was never paid in full: Ormond to Fennell, 26 October 1644 (Bodl., Carte MSS 12, fo. 503); *Cal. SP Ire., 1633–47*, p. 396.

[11] *Desid. cur. Hib.*, pp. 244–5. See also *DNB*, 'Randal MacDonnell'; Bagwell, *Stuarts*, II, 61; Antrim to Ormond, [*c*. November] 1643 (Bodl., Carte MSS 7, fo. 411). Ormond financed the voyage, Antrim to Ormond, [*c*. 7 November] 1643 (*ibid.*, fo. 407).

[12] Carte, *Ormond*, VI, 31–4, 39; Stevenson, *Scottish Covenanters*, pp. 166–7; *idem, Alasdair MacColla*, pp. 102–3; Laing, *Letters*, II, 116; *The kingdomes weekly intelligencer ... From Tuesday 2 to Tuesday 9 January 1644*, no. 38 (London, 1644), pp. 289–90; Robert Blair, *The life of Mr Robert Blair, minister of St. Andrews, containing his autobiography, 1593 to 1636, with supplement...*, ed. T. M'Crie (Wodrow Society, Edinburgh, 1848), p. 173; Clarendon, *Life*, II, 78–9; Clarendon, *Rebellion*, III, 510–11.

whole frame of our affairs grant', Antrim was empowered to transport to Scotland as many men as he could muster in his own name.

The second component of his plan resembled the anti-Campbell alliances proposed in 1639, 1642 and 1643. Charles authorized Antrim to persuade the confederates to raise and transport 2,000–3,000 men to the Western Isles 'where you are to excite your party to rise with you to fall upon the marquis of Argyll's country'. Upon arrival in Scotland, he was first to join forces with troops levied by the earl of Seaforth and Sir Donald MacDonald and then to rendezvous with a new royal army in the Highlands under the command of the earl of Montrose. Towards the end of January 1644, Antrim signed a formal agreement with Montrose promising to have his troops in Scotland by 1 April, to liaise closely with the earl and to follow his orders.[13] As in 1639 and 1643, Antrim's invasion of Scotland was to coincide with uprisings there orchestrated in this instance by Montrose, named captain-general of the king's Scottish forces, by Huntly, 'lord lieutenant of all forces that may be raised in Scotland', and by other leading Scottish grandees (including his earlier co-conspirators Nithsdale and Aboyne) who had condemned the Solemn League and Covenant. In addition an invasion army was to be sent from England under the command of the marquis of Newcastle.[14]

Third, Antrim was instructed to try to win over, or failing that at least to neutralize, the covenanting army in Ulster by promising Monro, in the king's name, a Scottish title and an annual pension of £2,000. Finally, if the confederates refused to agree to any of the proposals, the earl was to do his utmost to sow dissension amongst their ranks so that they would prove no threat to the royalist cause.[15]

Antrim made several demands in return. First and foremost he asked for the immediate restitution of his estates in Ulster which were now occupied by Argyll's forces, and the governorship of nearby Derry and Coleraine.[16] The

---

[13] Hill, *MacDonnells*, pp. 266–7; *Comment, Rinucc.*, I, 456; Digby to Antrim, 14 March 1644 (*Cal. S.P. Ire.*, 1633–47, pp. 392–3/PRO, SP 63/260/120). Antrim secured liberty of worship for Catholics while the expedition lasted, William Forbes Leith (ed.), *Memoirs of Scottish catholics during the seventeenth and eighteenth centuries* (2 vols., London, 1909), I, 280, 282–3; Cowan, *Montrose*, pp. 144–5, 152.

[14] Commission to Huntly, 1 February 1644 (SRO, GD 44/unpublished HMC calendar to the Huntly MSS). Also see Cowan, *Montrose*, pp. 145–6.

[15] Instructions for Antrim, [*c.* January], 1644 (Bodl., Carte MSS 13, fo. 158r–v); instructions for Daniel O'Neill, early 1644 (*ibid.*, fos. 166–7v); Gilbert, *Ir. confed.*, III, 88–90; Bagwell, *Stuarts*, II, 61; HMC *rep. 13*, pp. 172–3; Stevenson, *Scottish Covenanters*, pp. 167–8.

[16] Gilbert, *Contemp. hist. 1641–52*, I, 572; Carte, *Ormond*, VI, 43–6, 79–82. Though he was promised the latter, a commission was never issued. For details on his earlier attempts to buy lands in County Londonderry, see pp. 56–60 above.

king agreed. In addition, he requested the return of his ancestral Scottish possessions and a formal command to take them by force. Almost immediately 'a commission of the lieutenant general of the Isles and Highlands, and a commission of justiciary' was drawn up in his name.[17] He also wanted the wardship of his young nephew, Baron Slane, but because he was a Catholic and 'the scandal would be so great', Ormond refused to grant him this.[18] Finally he was promised a marquisate.[19] According to Hyde, this was thanks to his importuning wife who was 'resolved he [Antrim] should carry with him [to Ireland] some testimony of the king's esteem'. Charles reluctantly agreed: 'Though his majesty was neither pleased with the matter nor the manner, he did not discern so great an inconvenience in gratifying him, as might weigh down the benefit he expected with reference to Scotland.'[20] However, instead of creating Antrim a marquis immediately (as Hyde misleadingly recorded in his *History of the rebellion*), the king prudently insisted that he complete his side of the bargain first.[21]

Overt royal favour did little to improve Antrim's relations with the Irish lord lieutenant. As it was, Ormond strongly disapproved of the king's use of interlopers and had already warned Digby not to pay attention 'to some [i.e. Antrim] that may pretend to be powerful with the Irish, and may promise to

---

[17] Hill, *MacDonnells*, pp. 266–7. Also see *Comment. Rinucc.*, I, 456; *Cal. SP Ire., 1633–47*, pp. 392–3.

[18] Ormond to Digby, 13 January 1644 (Carte, *Ormond*, VI, 9). For further details on Slane's wardship, see Sir James Ware's diary of occurrences (City Library, Dublin, MS 169, p. 227); Carte, *Ormond*, VI, 63.

[19] On the king's willingness to 'sell' titles in return for aid, see Paul H. Hardacre, *The royalists during the puritan revolution* (London, 1956), pp. 13–14.

[20] Clarendon, *Rebellion*, III, 522–3.

[21] The patent for Antrim's marquisate (PRONI, T473/1, pp. 43–5) was dated 1 January 1644[-5]. Though he had to wait one whole year before officially collecting his new title, some historians and many contemporaries referred to him as the 'marquis of Antrim' from January 1644. See, for example, Hill, *MacDonnells*, p. 268; A. Webb, *A compendium of Irish bibliography* (New York, 1970), p. 310; Brian Ó Cuív (ed.), 'Some Irish items relating to the MacDonnells of Antrim', *Celtica*, 16 (1984), p. 152; consulta of the junta on Irish levies, 29 January/8 February 1645 (AGS, Eo. 2523, unfol.); Contreras to Foissotte, 19 February/1 March 1645 (*ibid.*, 2525, unfol.). Apparently Antrim encouraged this, Gilbert, *Ir. confed.*, III, 149–50. Numerous London weeklies carried stories about 'the new created marquis of Antrim'. See, for examples, *A perfect diurnall... From Monday 22 to Monday 29 April 1644*, no. 39 (London, 1644), p. 311; *The true informer... From Saturday 3 to Saturday 10 August 1644*, no. 42 (London, 1644), p. 305; *The weekly account. Truly and faithfully communicating the choisest and most remarkable intelligence... From Wednesday 10 to Wednesday 17 April 1644*, no. 33 (London, 1644); *The spie, communicating intelligence from Oxford... From Tuesday 5 to 13 February 1644*, no. 12 (London, 1644), p. 96; *The kingdomes weekly intelligencer... From Wednesday 10 to Tuesday 16 April 1644*, no. 50 (London, 1644), p. 405, and *ibid.*, From Thursday 25 to 30 April 1644, no. 52 (London, 1644), p. 421.

work them to great matters for the king'.²² The king was, however, aware that Ormond, who had been totally excluded from the planning of the venture, would feel threatened by Antrim's commission, so he attached Daniel O'Neill to the mission.²³ O'Neill was Antrim's cousin and Digby reassured Ormond that he was 'the fittest person to steer my Lord Antrim by your directions'.²⁴ He was expected to mediate between Antrim and Ormond, to 'sway the said earl of Antrim according to the advice and direction of the marquis of Ormond' so that the two will cooperate, and to prevent 'all kind of jealousies that may arise not only in the marquis of Ormond but in any of our Protestant subjects of this employment'.²⁵ For, in the final analysis, the success or failure of the plan lay not in the hands of the confederates, but with Antrim's ability to cooperate with Ireland's lord lieutenant. As O'Neill despondently noted, the supreme council 'are so divided between these two great men, [the] marquis [of] Ormond and [the] earl [of] Antrim, that neither can serve the king eminently in this kind separate, but joined may do anything'. He added that if only Antrim and Ormond could agree they would be able to levy 'the old[est] and best soldiers in this kingdom' so that there would be no need to yield 'to any exorbitant demands of the agents, either of religion or anything else'.²⁶ As it turned out this is precisely what happened.

Early in February 1644, Antrim and O'Neill sailed for Ireland from Bristol in one of the king's ships.²⁷ Upon arrival they hurried directly to Kilkenny where the earl immediately requested the supreme council to provide Charles with 10,000 men for England and at least 2,000 for Scotland 'with arms and a sufficient proportion of ammunition and provisions', as well as with arms for

---

²² Ormond to Digby, 13 January 1644 (Carte, *Ormond*, VI, 7).
²³ Clarendon, *Rebellion*, III, 515–21. As his reward Daniel O'Neill was created a groom of the bedchamber, Cregan, 'An Irish cavalier ... 1642–51', pp. 108–12. Pressure was put on Ormond to cooperate with Antrim, see minute on O'Neill and Antrim's instructions, 1644 (Bodl., Carte MSS 13, fo. 152r–v); Charles I to Ormond, 20 January 1644 (*ibid.*, MSS 9, fo. 9); Carte, *Ormond*, VI, 20–2, 62–3.
²⁴ Digby to Ormond, 8 February 1644 (Carte, *Ormond*, VI, 32). According to Clarendon, *Life*, II, 79, O'Neill enjoyed 'great power over him [Antrim], and very much credit with the marquis of Ormond'. Also see Clarendon, *Rebellion*, III, 515, and Donal F. Cregan, 'Daniel O'Neill, a royalist agent in Ireland, 1644–50', *IHS*, 2, no. 8 (Sept. 1941), p. 399.
²⁵ Instructions for Daniel O'Neill, early 1644 (Bodl., Carte MSS 13, fo. 166). See also Lowe, 'The earl of Antrim', pp. 193–4.
²⁶ O'Neill to Digby, 2 March 1644 (Carte, *Ormond*, VI, 45). See also Cregan, 'Daniel O'Neill', pp. 401–3.
²⁷ News from Waterford, 28 February/10 March 1644 (AMAE, Correspondence politique, Angleterre, Côte 51, fo. 22r–v); *The military scribe* ... Tuesday 26 March to 2 April 1644, no. 6 (London, 1644), p. 43.

Prince Rupert's forces in England, which Ormond was to pay for.[28] The council deliberated for five days over this; then on 29 February they finally endorsed his plan to raise forces for the Isles and agreed to provide him, by 1 May 1644, with 2,000 muskets, 2,400 hundredweight of powder with match and 200 barrels of oatmeal – providing there was a safe port, such as Carlingford in County Louth or Greencastle in County Down, to receive them.

From the confederate perspective, the decision to finance Antrim's expedition to Scotland formed an important dimension of the wider struggle to draw the Scots out of Ulster. However, in a further effort to please the king they also agreed to provide the arms and munitions requested for Prince Rupert on condition that Ormond accepted as 'payment' the non-delivery of 2,800 cattle due to the crown under the terms of the cessation. Concerning the 10,000 men for England the council was less cooperative. Since they stood to gain little by sending ten regiments to England at a time when troops were desperately needed at home, they refused to commit themselves until they had heard how negotiations between their commissioners and the king (over the redress of their religious, tenurial and political grievances) were progressing at Oxford.[29] A rather dispirited Antrim therefore reported to Ormond that 'I have obtained part of my desires, and part is delayed, though not denied; but delays are equally dangerous to the king.'[30] Antrim and O'Neill, to judge from the letters sent to court, nevertheless remained confident that the council would finally agree to send the troops to England.[31]

Since Antrim had been primed 'to improve his own interest' amongst the confederates 'if the Irish would not come to such terms as his majesty could descend to', he lingered on in Kilkenny rather than following O'Neill to meet Ormond in Dublin.[32] At this point the earl decided that, in order to win any real influence (or to have 'any credit') over confederate policy making, he should both take the confederate oath of association and become a member

---

[28] O'Neill's notes on Antrim's audience with the supreme council, 1644 (Bodl., Carte MSS 13, fo. 168, and MSS 63, fo. 291). See also Antrim to Ormond, 25 February 1644 (*ibid.*, MSS 9, fo. 330); Carte, *Ormond*, VI, 42; Hazlett, 'A history of the military forces', pp. 309–14.

[29] Gilbert, *Ir. confed.*, III, 113; Carte, *Ormond*, VI, 43–5; O'Neill's notes on Antrim's audience with the supreme council, 1644 (Bodl., Carte MSS 13, fo. 168, and MSS 63, fo. 291); Stevenson, *Scottish Covenanters*, pp. 168–9; Cregan, 'Daniel O'Neill', pp. 399–401.

[30] Antrim to Ormond, 2 March [1644] (Gilbert, *Ir. confed.*, III, 114).

[31] Carte, *Ormond*, VI, 56; Digby to Antrim, 14 March 1644 (*Cal. SP Ire., 1633–47*, pp. 392–3/PRO, SP 63/260/120). The earl even tried (unsuccessfully) to press-gang the army being prepared against Monro's forces and to send it instead to England, *Desid. cur. Hib.*, p. 245.

[32] PRONI D2977/5/1/2.

of the supreme council.³³ Though the king had promised 'to protect him from any inconveniency that should be offered to him or his family, by taking the Oath of Association with those in the late Irish rebellion',³⁴ by officially and publicly siding with the confederates before a formal peace treaty – rather than a mere ceasefire – had been concluded with the king, the earl offered a great hostage to fortune. Clanricard realized at once the dangers involved in 'entering into their association in so high a degree, and carrying such with him, as may perhaps stand charged with the foulest actions committed here'.³⁵

In the short term, however, it suited his personal interests: on the one hand, he was now in a position whereby he could manipulate both the royalists and the confederates to his own ends and thereby, hopefully, drive Monro's army from East Ulster and revive the anti-Campbell crusade in the Western Isles.³⁶ On the other hand, he was able to establish a set of contacts within the Catholic party on which he could fall back in the event that Charles lost the war against parliament. Antrim's eagerness to 'hedge his bets' in this manner was to be the pattern for the future.

However, in the meantime, as a member of the Catholic executive, the earl actively promoted the king's cause and did his utmost to sow dissension amongst those supreme councillors who were opposed to intervention in the British war-effort. His 'divide and rule' tactics quickly bore fruit and within a short period of time he had not only managed to split the supreme council into two clearly opposed factions but also to stir up so much trouble that Daniel O'Neill was convinced that 'it is not in the power of either Catholic clergy, or pope's nuncio, Spanish or French, to make any party against the king'.³⁷ While his zeal for the king's service (''tis so much that it hurts') was placed uppermost, Antrim obviously also enjoyed his new political status and used it to his own advantage wherever possible: 'he hath received late letters of high expressions of affection and trust both from the king and queen,

---

³³ *Ibid.*; Carte, *Ormond*, VI, 71–3.
³⁴ Hill, *MacDonnells*, p. 306.
³⁵ Clanricard to Ormond, 25 March 1644 (Carte, *Ormond*, VI, 72). Certainly, at the Restoration, this is exactly what happened. The earl's enemies repeatedly cited the fact that he had both taken the oath of association in 1644 and sat on the supreme council before the peace treaties of 1646 and 1649 as evidence of his complicity with the 'rebels', petition of adventurers and soldiers to the king, [August, 1663] (Bodl., Carte MSS 44, fos. 376–7); Hill, *MacDonnells*, p. 313; Lowe, 'The earl of Antrim', p. 196.
³⁶ Stevenson, *Scottish Covenanters*, pp. 170–1. But, as Ormond observed, 'I doubt he [also] minds other business' – no doubt a reference to Antrim's efforts to secure a commission for 'the government of Coleraine and Londonderry', Ormond to Radcliffe, 11 March 1644 (Carte, *Ormond*, VI, 59). Also see *ibid.*, 34–5, 79–82.
³⁷ O'Neill to Digby, 2 March 1644 (Carte, *Ormond*, VI, 43, 45).

which he shows to all men of considerable condition, and upon my word, my lord, that, with his ways, gains him no small opinion amongst the people, he being of their council and association'.[38] His popularity at large was mirrored by the influence he enjoyed within the supreme council. For instance, no sooner had he been elected to the executive than it was rumoured that he had persuaded them to 'offer £4,000 by the month to the queen' if she came to Ireland to give birth to her baby.[39]

Antrim had little to lose and everything to gain by raising and sending Irish troops to fight in Scotland and in England. But the position was exactly the reverse for the king since mobilizing Catholic Irish aid would inevitably cause problems. The ever-astute earl of Clanricard was quick to recognize the dangers and feared that it 'may somewhat reflect upon the king of England, and lessen his party in that kingdom; there being those that will make use of the least shadows to put a prejudice upon his government and proceedings'.[40] Predictably, Charles's enemies did indeed seize on news of the invasion plans as yet further evidence of an insidious plot by the papists (led by the queen) to engulf and destroy the king's loyal, Protestant subjects.[41] The parliamentary press, for instance, vigilantly monitored, and then broadcast to the nation, Antrim's movements. Late in January 1644, *The kingdomes weekly intelligencer* announced that he had been sent to Ireland to raise '10,000 popish and natural Irish rebels' to fight for the royalist cause.[42] *A perfect diurnall* then followed this up with a more detailed, misleading, account of his commission:

that the king had given a commission to the new created marquis of Antrim, that notorious popish and professed rebel, to be general and commander-in-chief over all his Catholic good subjects in the province of Ulster, and all the provinces adjacent, and with such forces as he should raise, to use all possible means to suppress all the British and Scottish Protestants that submitted not to the late hellish cessation.[43]

---

[38] O'Neill to Digby, 2 March 1644 (*ibid.*, 46). Also see Gilbert, *Ir. confed.*, III, 139–40.
[39] Trevor to Ormond, 9 March 1644 (Carte, *Ormond*, VI, 57). Also see *ibid.*, 69–70. If the queen agreed to move to Ireland the French promised to give them 72,000 crowns towards the Irish war-effort, Gilbert, *Contemp. hist. 1641– 52*, IV, 81.
[40] Clanricard to Ormond, 25 March 1644 (Carte, *Ormond*, VI, 72).
[41] *Mercurius Britanicus* ... From Monday 18 to Monday 25 March 1644, no. 28 (London, 1644), p. 219; *The spie, communicating intelligence from Oxford* ... From Tuesday 5 to 13 February 1644, no. 12 (London, 1644), p. 96; *The kingdomes weekly intelligencer* ... From Wednesday 10 to Tuesday 16 April 1644, no. 50 (London, 1644), p. 405.
[42] *The kingdomes weekly intelligencer* ... From Tuesday 30 January to Wednesday 7 February 1644, no. 42 (London, 1644), p. 322.
[43] *A perfect diurnall* ... From Monday 22 to Monday 29 April 1644, no. 39 (London, 1644), p. 311.

The weekly account, *The Scottish dove* and *The kingdomes weekly intelligencer* all ran similar stories condemning with varying degrees of accuracy the activities of the popish earl.[44]

More serious for Antrim, however, was the resentment and jealousy which his enterprise had generated in Ireland and at court. The earl of Clanricard for instance was particularly affronted that he had been passed over in favour of Antrim.[45] British royalists were equally distressed by their master's willingness to support 'popish undertakers'.[46] Digby was not alone in fearing a Gaelic revival in Ireland with the earl acting (as his grandfather, Hugh O'Neill, had done) as the focal point:

> Antrim's friends and dependents of Ulster should, upon the pretense of serving the king under his command, carry along designs of reestablishing themselves in their ancient territories of their ancient septs ... and that when they had got a power together, under colour of serving his majesty's interest, they should apply it to serve their own ... This is so dangerous a point, especially with all those who having been of those great and powerful families, have now nothing left.[47]

Therefore, contrary to parliamentary propaganda, the court's attitude towards Irish intervention was distinctly hostile and, as a result, the negotiators sent by the general assembly to discuss their grievances with the king received a frosty reception upon their arrival in Oxford (March 1644).[48] Though Antrim was no longer at court he was nevertheless accused of being sympathetic to their demands because his brother was one of the negotiators and he himself was 'a person likely to encourage the agents to demand in that kind [religion]'.[49] Ironically, however, the earl's immediate success in

---

[44] *The weekly account. Truly and faithfully communicating the choisest and most remarkable intelligence* ... From Wednesday 10 to Wednesday 17 April 1644, no. 33 (London, 1644); *The Scottish dove* ... From Friday 26 April to Friday 3 May 1644, no. 29 (London, 1644), p. 228; *The kingdomes weekly intelligencer* ... From Thursday 25 to 30 April 1644, no. 52 (London, 1644), p. 421; *Gazette [de Naples]*, no. 40, p. 252.

[45] Gilbert, *Ir. confed.*, III, 139–40; *Clanricarde letter-book*, pp. 42, 59, 80–1; Carte, *Ormond*, VI, 63–4.

[46] Nicholas to Ormond, 4 March 1644 (Bodl., Carte MSS 63, fo. 325). See also Radcliffe to Ormond, 17 January 1644 (*ibid.*, MSS 8, fo. 528); Carte, *Ormond*, VI, 125, 166–7; Lowe, 'Charles I and the confederation', pp. 2–4.

[47] Digby to Ormond, 29 March 1644 (Carte, *Ormond*, VI, 80–1).

[48] *The kingdomes weekly intelligencer* ... From Wednesday 10 to Tuesday 16 April 1644, no. 50 (London, 1644), p. 405; *The spie, communicating intelligence from Oxford* ... From Tuesday 5 to 13 February 1644, no. 12 (London, 1644), p. 96; duchess of Buckingham to Ormond, 17 June 1644 (Bodl., Carte MSS 11, fo. 221).

[49] Digby to Ormond, 14 March 1644 (Carte, *Ormond*, VI, 63). Also see Bellings to Ormond, 19 December 1643 (Bodl., Carte MSS 8, fo. 163); Carte, *Ormond*, VI, 43–5, 57. This was nonsense: at this point the earl's devotion to Catholicism was, as even Digby was forced to admit, 'quite overborne by the interest of his majesty's honour and power', Digby to Ormond, 14 March 1644 (*ibid.*, 62).

persuading the confederates to send 2,000 troops to Scotland only served to undermine further any bargaining power enjoyed by the agents in Oxford.[50] Why, it was asked, should Charles alienate his Protestant followers further by making formal concessions to the Catholic party when he could evidently secure Irish aid without doing so?

For the time being, however, despite their envy, the majority of Charles's courtiers and Ireland's Catholic grandees were prepared, for the good of the royalist cause, to assist Antrim. Towards the middle of March a number of prominent noblemen – including Lords Taaffe, Dillon, Clanricard and Castlehaven – held a council of war at Loughreagh (in County Galway).[51] At this meeting the earl secured the support of a host of prominent military commanders – Owen Roe O'Neill, Thomas Preston, Roger Moore, Sir Piers Crosby, Colonel Plunkett, Sir James Dillon and James MacDonnell – who between them were capable of raising 12,000 men, the majority of which could be fully armed.[52]

In fact the cordial ambience was quickly soured by a squabble between Antrim and Castlehaven over who was the supreme commander of the confederate armies.[53] Nevertheless, the earl continued his troop-raising progress along the west coast of Ireland: on 24 March he left Loughreagh for Galway town and from there he moved on to Counties Mayo, Sligo and Roscommon before journeying into the north in search of volunteers for the king's army and support for the confederate cause.[54] By the middle of April he had finished recruiting and prepared to leave County Roscommon amid rumours that he, 'with a great army, is marching towards Monro, with the relicks of our army. God be there; else, if they be defeated, it will be very ill for Scotland.'[55] The Protestant garrison in Londonderry, whose supplies were exhausted and morale was low, was particularly alarmed by this turn of events: 'we receive daily intelligence that two great armies of the rebels are preparing to fall upon us of the North; one to be led by the new created marquis of Antrim, the other by the earl of Castlehaven'.[56]

Though Antrim had succeeded in raising a formidable army he failed to win over Monro and other key commanders (such as Sir Robert Stewart in

---

50 Gilbert, *Ir. confed.*, III, 137–8; Elkin, 'The interactions between the Irish rebellion and the English civil wars', pp. 162–5.
51 Carte, *Ormond*, VI, 63–4; *Comment. Rinucc.*, I, 457.
52 Gilbert, *Contemp. hist. 1641–52*, I, 651–2.
53 Carte, *Ormond*, VI, 71–3. For further details, see pp. 140–2, 149 below.
54 Carte, *Ormond*, VI, 71–3; *Clanricarde letter-book*, p. 68.
55 Baillie to Spang, 12 April 1644 (Laing, *Letters*, II, 164). Also see James Galbraithe to Owen O'Neill, 19 April 1644 (Bodl., Carte MSS 10, fo. 300).
56 Major and citizens of Londonderry to the committee of estates, 28 March 1644 (SRO, PA 7/23/2/20).

Londonderry) to the royalist cause.[57] Early in April, Captain John Gordon – 'least [a] MacDonnell should give offense' – was dispatched to discuss the major-general's defection from parliament.[58] When Monro refused to countenance it, hoping rather to 'catch him [Antrim] the third time to vindicate myself from aspersion of the wicked', Antrim tried intimidation.[59] According to a London newspaper, he 'sent express to General Monro commander of the Scots regiments, to be gone out of Ulster or else he will compel him. To which the valiant general, having received the supplies ... from Holland, returned this answer – that he would see him and take his leave [in battle] before he did go.'[60] Thus nothing came of the earl's efforts to neutralize the parliamentary enemy in East Ulster, and towards the end of April he hurried to County Westmeath 'to be near those men for Scotland'.[61]

But who exactly were 'those men for Scotland'? The rank and file were almost exclusively native Irishmen 'of Ulster, [and] some of the Old Irish in other parts of the kingdom'.[62] Many were Antrim's 'own dependents, the residents of his land and Clandeboy' who had been forced into exile by Monro and were (according to Daniel O'Neill) 'hardy and stout for any service'. A further 800 (at least) were displaced Highlanders under the command of Alasdair MacColla.[63] Much more is known about the officers selected to command the force; an extant muster roll for the army lists the names of seventy-three officers who appear to have originated largely in Counties Antrim or Londonderry. The bulk of these names (fifty-six) were native Irish: MacAllesters, MacCormacks, MacDonnells, MacDermots, MacHenrys, MacQuillans, O'Cahans, O'Haras and O'Neills, as one might expect, predominated.[64] These men were supplemented by 'discontented

---

[57] Antrim to O'Neill, 14 April 1644 (Bodl., Carte MSS 10, fo. 209); Antrim to Ormond, 23 April 1644 (*ibid.*, fo. 344r–v); *Clanricarde letter-book*, p. 71.

[58] O'Neill to Ormond, 23 April 1644 (Carte, *Ormond*, VI, 97).

[59] Monro to [the committee of the estates of Scotland], 23 February 1644 (HMC *rep. 13*, pp. 172–3).

[60] *The weekly account. Truly and faithfully communicating the choisest and most remarkable intelligence ... From Wednesday 10 to Wednesday 17 April 1644*, no. 33 (London, 1644).

[61] Taaffe to Ormond, 13 April 1644 (Gilbert, *Ir. confed.*, III, 139–40). Also see Antrim to O'Neill, 14 April 1644 (Bodl., Carte MSS 10, fo. 209); Antrim to Ormond, 27 April 1644 (*ibid.*, fo. 435).

[62] Clanricard to Ormond, 25 March 1644 (Carte, *Ormond*, VI, 71). Also see O'Neill to Ormond, 21 June 1644 (Bodl., Carte MSS 11, fo. 256).

[63] *Comment. Rinucc.*, I, 456; Clarendon, *Rebellion*, III, 516. Ormond had refused to employ MacColla, Ormond to Alexander MacDonald, 2 August 1643 (Bodl., Carte MSS 6, fo. 154); Carte, *Ormond*, VI, 71–3.

[64] Gilbert, *Ir. confed.*, IV, 54–6; Ó Danachair, 'Montrose's Irish regiments', pp. 62–6; Cowan, *Montrose*, pp. 153–4.

officers' – particularly from Ulster and the Pale – who had been unable to find employment in the confederate armies.[65] But by the beginning of April the earl had still not found a suitable commander for his expeditionary force. Ideally he wanted the continental veteran Hugh Dubh O'Neill to lead his army but, since he was unable to secure O'Neill's release from Londonderry, he nominated his kinsman Alasdair MacColla as his major-general.[66] Ultimately it made better sense to have a kinsman, who was familiar to Antrim's Irish and Scottish followers, lead the expedition. Moreover, MacColla was already a veteran soldier with experience of warfare in both Ireland and Scotland, where he had made prolonged raids into the Isles until his defeat at the hands of Argyll in May 1644.[67]

Nothing is known about how Antrim's army was trained for the wars in Scotland, but their subsequent performance suggests that they included a fair number of seasoned veterans, who had learnt the ways of modern warfare (presumably from Owen Roe O'Neill or other continental officers) over the course of the previous two and a half years. Others may well have gained additional military experience by fighting in the Thirty Years' War or in Spanish Flanders. Either way, the force was blessed with remarkable stamina, courage and endurance.[68] Even Edward Hyde, never one to praise Irish Catholics needlessly, later asserted that Antrim's levies were 'very good, and with very good officers; all so hardy, that neither the ill fare nor the ill lodging in the Highlands gave them any discouragement'.[69] Moreover, the fact that Antrim's men were nearly all musketeers indicates that they were well versed in the most up-to-date European methods of warfare, where firearms dominated over bows and pikes.[70]

Antrim's army was, however, poorly disciplined. While Alasdair Mac-Colla's 800 Highlanders were in County Galway, Clanricard vowed either to destroy them or to send them into another county on account of the damage

---

[65] Clanricard to Ormond, 25 March 1644 (Carte, *Ormond*, VI, 71). Also see Stevenson, *Alasdair MacColla*, pp. 106–7.
[66] Antrim to O'Neill, [c. 1 April] 1644 (Bodl., Carte MSS 10, fo. 95); Carte, *Ormond*, VI, 96–8; Blair, *Life*, ed. M'Crie, p. 173; P. B. Ó Mórdha, 'The battle of Clones, 1643', *Clogher Record*, 4, no. 3 (1962), p. 153; Hill, 'Notices of the Clan Ian Vor', pp. 309–10; Stevenson, *Scottish Covenanters*, pp. 171–2. For details on Hugh Dubh's military career, see David Hayton and G. O'Brien (eds.), *J. G. Simms. War and politics in Ireland 1649–1730* (London, 1986), pp. 21–9. David Stevenson, *Alasdair MacColla*, p. 105, suggests that from the outset Antrim intended using MacColla.
[67] Stevenson, *Alasdair MacColla*, p. 93.
[68] Ó Danachair, 'Montrose's Irish regiments', pp. 62, 66–7; Stevenson, *Alasdair MacColla*, pp. 106–7; James Michael Hill, *Celtic warfare 1595–1763* (Edinburgh, 1986), chapter 4.
[69] Clarendon, *Life*, II, 80.
[70] Gilbert, *Ir. confed.*, IV, 139.

they were doing, while in County Roscommon, Lord Taaffe claimed that 1,500 of Antrim's recruits had 'destroyed all my tenants'.[71] They seemed to have wreaked havoc far and wide: early in May it was reported that 'some of those northern men that say they belong to my lord of Antrim do wander as far as Cashel [County Tipperary] and are now there, others are in the County of Sligo, most part in the County of Longford and Westmeath'.[72] As time passed, the number of complaints escalated. The supreme council lamented to Ormond that the inhabitants of Meath, Westmeath, Longford, King's and Queen's Counties 'do suffer by those Ulstermen who are designed for the service of the Isles and such (who are many in number) that join themselves unto them and do eat upon the country'. The council even feared that the local population 'may use force to expel them, and that unless the counties be eased it will be utterly disabled to contribute assistance to any service'.[73] The earl was distressed by these complaints; but in the absence of any vessels to ship his men to Scotland, or of a regular supply of provisions for them, he could do nothing (except, of course, disband them).[74]

What angered him above all was the persistent refusal of the supreme council to appoint him commander of *all* of their forces. Since taking the confederate oath, Antrim had nurtured hopes that the restrictions which had been attached to his command, namely that the council retained ultimate control over the army, which Antrim was forbidden to take out of the country unless he was ordered to do so by the executive, and that he could have no jurisdiction over Castlehaven's force of 6,000 foot, would be lifted.[75] Daniel O'Neill outlined the dilemma to Ormond:

> Here are symptoms of great distraction in this most irregular commonwealth. They [the supreme council] gave my lord of Antrim an absolute command of all their forces; unto my Lord Castlehaven they gave another, independent of any but themselves. The one desires the benefit of his commission, which the council will not give him; the other endeavours to preserve his possession.

Worse still, O'Neill feared that 'This folly is grown to such a high, that if it be not prevented by your lordship, evidently the country will be destroyed. The supreme council passionately maintain Castlehaven; the other [Antrim] clearly can draw the army from him and them.'[76]

[71] Clanricard to Ormond, 25 March 1644 (Carte, *Ormond*, VI, 73); Taaffe to Ormond, 15 April 1644 (Gilbert, *Ir. confed.*, III, 140).
[72] Bellings to Ormond, 6 May 1644 (Bodl., Carte MSS 10, fo. 531).
[73] Supreme council to Ormond, 18 May 1644 (*ibid.*, fo. 686).
[74] Antrim to Ormond, 12 May 1644 (*ibid.*, fo. 612); supreme council to Ormond, 30 May 1644 (*ibid.*, MSS 11, fo. 67r–v); Carte, *Ormond*, VI, 121–2.
[75] Propositions sent to Antrim and his reply, [*c*. 25 March] 1644 (Bodl., Carte MSS 10, fo. 80r–v); *Desid. cur. Hib.*, pp. 241–50; order by the supreme council, 1 April 1644 (Bodl., Carte MSS 10, fo. 88).
[76] O'Neill to Ormond, 24 May 1644 (Carte, *Ormond*, VI, 134–5).

Despite O'Neill's attempts to soothe Antrim's hurt pride, the earl was unable to contain his temper for long and, towards the end of May, the supreme council bore the full brunt of his rage as he threatened to invade Ulster with the army he had levied for service in Scotland. 'Unless he might be satisfied of his pretensions', the supreme council related to Ormond,

> he would desert the employment into the Isles, and for his part his men should not go. Now my lord his pretensions being to command this army into Ulster which by instructions under his own signature, whereunto his commission [is] express worded ... we may not condescend thereunto, so as we fear the bad event of that resolution, wherein his lordship has persisted these two days, and much the more by his carriage towards us. We find him full of haughtiness, and desire to be at distance with us.[77]

Antrim's temper tantrum and his threat to take the war in Ulster into his own hands obviously worried the supreme council, who feared that he would, simply out of spite, torpedo both the Scottish expedition and Castlehaven's campaign. They attributed 'this unsettledness in his resolution, concerning so weighty a matter ... both in his private fortune and particular undertakings to his majesty' to the earl's 'own inclination, his youth and want of experience in managing affairs of this nature'. As a precautionary measure they arrested two of his friends (Roger Moore and Philip MacMulmore O'Reilley) – 'men of their own disposition turbulent and much taken ... with the condition of troublesome times' – whom they believed had been misadvising him, and they publicly gave Castlehaven 'full and absolute power and authority' over the Army of Ulster. They also begged Ormond to placate the earl.[78]

This request placed the lord lieutenant in an awkward position. Until this point, thanks largely to Daniel O'Neill's skills as a diplomat and to his high regard for the duchess of Buckingham, relations between Ormond and Antrim had been remarkably amicable and the latter (according to Digby) went on 'cheerfully, without mutiny and discontent'.[79] For his part, Ormond had pressurized his clients within the supreme council – especially Dr Gerald Fennell and Secretary Richard Bellings – to meet all of the earl's demands and to prepare for the Scottish expedition with all haste.[80] But Ormond at once recognized the importance of settling the dispute with Castlehaven as amicably as possible, since

> the contention that is betwixt two great men for the chief command ... is said to be risen to that height, and the factions divided so equally, as to threaten the frustrating

---

[77] Supreme council to Ormond, 30 May 1644 (Bodl., Carte MSS 11, fo. 67r–v).
[78] *Ibid.* Also see Gilbert, *Ir. confed.*, III, 170–1; Carte, *Ormond*, VI, 133–5; proclamation by the supreme council, 20 June 1644 (Hunt., HA MSS 15001).
[79] Digby to Ormond, 29 March 1644 (Carte, *Ormond*, VI, 78–82). Also see duchess of Buckingham to Ormond, 8 May 1644 (Bodl., Carte MSS 10, fo. 559); Antrim to Ormond, 10 March 1644 (*ibid.*, MSS 9, fo. 481); Carte, *Ormond*, VI, 9.
[80] Gilbert, *Ir. confed.*, III, 160–1.

of their designs against the Scots, the loss of very great and irrecoverable preparations, and the embroiling of them in unseasonable and destructive quarrels amongst themselves.[81]

Therefore, in an attempt to salvage matters, he berated the volatile earl, hoping that the outburst 'proceeded rather from some present passion or resentment, than from any settled resolution' and that it was now forgotten.[82] To sweeten his rebuff, however, the lord lieutenant demonstrated his confidence in Antrim by handing over to him full control of the shipping which was being prepared for the expedition in Wexford and Waterford.[83]

Time was clearly of the essence if the Scottish expedition was to enjoy any chance of success. By the end of April circumstances in Scotland seemed uniquely favourable for Irish intervention, for although Montrose had been unable to recruit allies, Huntly seized Aberdeen and thus drew the covenanting army northwards, while Antrim's kinsmen in the Isles declared themselves ready to join him, being 'disgusted with the present government of their country'.[84] 'Now or never is the time to complete the distraction of that fatal kingdom' observed Ormond 'and to return to their bosom their own mischief.'[85]

Back in Ireland, even though the earl had fulfilled his part of the bargain by the end of April, the invasion of Scotland was still beset by logistical difficulties.[86] First, the confederates had failed to provide Antrim with his full quota of meal, arms and munitions.[87] Finding 40,000 pounds of biscuit (which was sufficient for two pounds of biscuit per day per soldier for ten days) had proved especially difficult, and so Ormond had to agree to supply the outstanding meal together with match and powder, a number of spades, shovels

---

[81] Ormond to Digby, 9 July 1644 (Carte, *Ormond*, VI, 154–5). O'Neill urged that Ormond should take over 'the command and conduct of the Irish forces against the Scots' (*ibid.*, 154).
[82] Ormond to Antrim, 1 June 1644 (*ibid.*, 139).
[83] Ormond to Archer, 1 June 1644 (Bodl., Carte MSS 11, fo. 82).
[84] O'Neill to Ormond, 23 April 1644 (Carte, *Ormond*, VI, 97). Also see Carte, *Ormond*, VI, 97; Gilbert, *Ir. confed.*, III, 160–1; Ormond to Fennell and Bellings, 28 April 1644 (Bodl., Carte MSS 10, fo. 447).
[85] Ormond to O'Neill, 22 April 1644 (Carte, *Ormond*, VI, 91). Also see Cowan, *Montrose*, pp. 147–8.
[86] Carte, *Ormond*, VI, 106; Digby to Ormond, 4 May 1644 (Bodl., Carte MSS 10, fos. 521–2).
[87] The confederates had managed to come up with 1,200 muskets (instead of 2,000), 2,500 hundredweight of powder 'without match', and 100 barrels of oatmeal (instead of 200). For further details, see Bellings to Ormond, 14 May 1644 (Bodl., Carte MSS 10, fo. 629); Archer to Ormond, 19 May 1644 (*ibid.*, fo. 690r–v; Bellings to Ormond, 26 March 1644 (*ibid.*, fo. 26); supreme council to Ormond, 17 April 1644 (*ibid.*, fo. 419); Ormond to Bellings, 19 June 1644 (*ibid.*, 11, fo. 238); Bellings to Ormond, 6 May 1644 (*ibid.*, 10, fos. 530–1); Gilbert, *Ir. confed.*, III, 157–8; Carte, *Ormond*, VI, 152–3; Hill, *MacDonnells*, p. 269.

The 'War of the Three Kingdoms' 143

and pickaxes.[88] Secondly, suitable shipping to transport the troops to Scotland was hard to find. The king was unable to send vessels from England due to the parliamentary blockade of Liverpool, and so this responsibility also fell entirely on Ormond's shoulders.[89] At last, towards the middle of April, two well-armed Flemish frigates, the *Angel Gabriel* of 350 tons and the *Christopher of Surdame* of 450 tons, together with an Irish vessel, the *Jacob of Ross*, armed with twelve guns, were commissioned to transport Antrim's army.[90] To protect the transport ships Ormond also recruited 'some pirate friends of mine' (Antonio Nicholas Vanderkipp and his frigate) to accompany them.[91] However, the captains of the frigates, who were also privateers sailing under confederate letters of marque, were quite understandably worried about how and when they would receive payment for their services and so a few more precious weeks were wasted while Ormond scratched around for the necessary collateral.[92] Eventually, Patrick Archer, a leading merchant from Kilkenny, agreed to provide the financial backing needed, though Ormond, his brother (Richard Butler) and his factor (Patrick Comerford) were all obliged to enter into bonds with Archer to cover all costs.[93] Only towards the end of May was the lord lieutenant able to reassure Antrim that 'The ships are certainly ready, and taken on for three months.'[94]

Even then, there was dispute and much confusion over the ports at which the troops, arms and provisions should be loaded.[95] Although Ormond refused to hand over one of the few ports in Ulster in his possession ('which will be odious to the English') as the confederates had demanded, he finally agreed that Antrim's troops and the necessary provisions could be mustered

---

[88] *Ormonde MSS*, I, 82–3.
[89] *Cal. SP Dom., 1644*, pp. 317–18.
[90] Milo Power to Ormond, 18 April 1644 (Bodl., Carte MSS 10, fos. 289–91); Gilbert, *Ir. confed.*, V, 225.
[91] Ormond to Antrim, 17 May 1644 (Carte, *Ormond*, VI, 122). Also see *ibid.*, 134.
[92] For further details on the privateering community, see Jane H. Ohlmeyer, 'Irish privateers during the civil war, 1642–50', *The Mariner's Mirror*, 76, no. 2 (May, 1990), pp. 119–30; idem, '"The Dunkirk of Ireland": Wexford privateers during the 1640s', *Journal of the Wexford Historical Society*, 12 (1988–9), pp. 23–49.
[93] Ormond to Comerford, 22 April 1644 (Bodl., Carte MSS 10, fo. 315); Milo Power to Ormond, 18 April 1644 (*ibid.*, fos. 289–91); Ormond to Archer, 27 April 1644 (*ibid.*, fo. 393v); Ormond to Power, [28] April 1644 (*ibid.*, fo. 447); Ormond to Archer, 2 May 1644 (*ibid.*, fos. 393v–4); Bellings to Ormond, 6 May 1644 (*ibid.*, fos. 530–1). If Archer had refused to provide collateral Ormond was prepared to mortgage his own and his brother's house in order to raise sufficient funds for the shipping, Ormond to Richard Butler, 22 April 1644 (*ibid.*, fo. 311). For details on Archer, see Cregan, 'Some members of the confederation of Kilkenny', pp. 36–8.
[94] Ormond to Antrim, 17 May 1644 (Carte, *Ormond*, VI, 122). Also see Archer to Ormond, 8 May 1644 (Bodl., Carte MSS 10, fo. 557).
[95] Archer to Ormond, 12 May 1644 (Bodl., Carte MSS 10, fo. 610); Antrim to Ormond, 12 May 1644 (*ibid.*, fo. 612).

at Carlingford.[96] In the event, the presence of parliamentary vessels along the east coast of Ireland and in Dublin harbour itself convinced Ormond that the expeditionary force should now assemble at one of the harbours held by the confederates along the south-east or west coasts.[97] The port of Ballyhack in County Wexford was quickly selected. It was the perfect choice. Conveniently situated between the large privateering ports of Wexford and Waterford, where even parliamentary vessels feared to patrol, it also enjoyed easy access to the deep yet fairly sheltered waters of the Passage.[98] In an attempt to keep the place and day (6 June) of embarkation secret from enemy shipping, all vessels in confederate harbours were allowed to set sail only with the council's express command, while Ormond monitored Dublin shipping equally carefully.[99]

At long last, Antrim – who had 'these three months maintained by my credit with my friends at least 2,000 men, which in these times [is] no small charge' – was instructed to march his men to Ballyhack.[100] To minimize the destruction which the passage of 2,000 restless soldiers was likely to cause, the supreme council appointed a committee 'to set down what way they shall march to the waterside and where they shall lodge each night, without being dispersed into the country, and from what places provision shall be brought into them'. The earl was, however, warned that if his men wandered into the 'unwasted parts of the country' the local inhabitants 'will lay about them most unmercifully'.[101]

The troops were finally embarked on 24 June (nearly three weeks after the date originally set for their departure) but remained windbound. A week later, as Antrim recounted to Ormond, they tried again: 'After the ships went to sea they were driven back by a violent storm, and after one day's stay they went yesterday to sea and I am confident they will not return any more into any harbour till they land unless they be beaten by shipping stronger than

[96] Ormond to O'Neill, 22 April 1644 (Carte, *Ormond*, VI, 92). Also see *ibid.*, 60–1; Ormond to Digby, [*c*. mid-March] 1644 (Bodl., Carte MSS 13, fo. 134).
[97] Carte, *Ormond*, VI, 106; Ormond to Archer, 10 May 1644 (Bodl., Carte MSS 10, fo. 593); Ormond to Archer, 13 May 1644 (*ibid.*, fo. 623); Ormond to Bellings, 14 May 1644 (*ibid.*, fos. 633r–v); Tirlogh O'Neale to Daniel O'Neill, [20] May 1644 (*ibid.*, fo. 698). Also see Michael L. Baumber, 'The navy and the civil war in Ireland, 1643–1646', *The Mariner's Mirror*, 75, no. 3 (Aug. 1989), p. 260.
[98] Ormond to Archer, 10 May 1644 (Bodl., Carte MSS 10, fo. 597); Archer to Ormond, 12 May 1644 (*ibid.*, fo. 608); Archer to Ormond, 15 May 1644 (*ibid.*, fos. 646v–7); Carte, *Ormond*, VI, 133–5.
[99] Supreme council to Ormond, 29 May 1644 (Bodl., Carte MSS 11, fo. 56).
[100] Antrim to Ormond, 16 May 1644 (Carte, *Ormond*, VII, 121). Also see *ibid.*, 133–5.
[101] Bellings to Ormond, 24 May 1644 (Bodl., Carte MSS 10, fo. 781). Also see Antrim to Ormond, 27 May 1644 (*ibid.*, MSS 11, fo. 20).

themselves.'[102] Some 1,600 fully armed soldiers under the command of Alasdair MacColla were thus dispatched, while the earl reluctantly disbanded a further 800 troops due to lack of arms and provisions.[103]

After leaving Ballyhack the small flotilla sailed up the west coast of Ireland towards its destination, the Dunkirk frigates taking some prizes along the way (including a passenger vessel carrying a number of Presbyterian ministers '[that] came out of Scotland to promote the covenant and sow sedition here [in Ireland]').[104] Early in July the expeditionary force arrived safely on Ardnamurchan where they captured and garrisoned two of Argyll's castles. At this point Alasdair MacColla, who had intended marching the troops to the Isle of Skye and handing over his command to Sir Donald MacDonald of Sleat, learnt of Sir Donald's sudden death and of his son's refusal to command the force. Alasdair's immediate reaction was to order a retreat to Ireland, but he was prevented from doing so by the capture of his transport vessels by parliamentary warships. He therefore pressed on instead to Inverlochy – 'burning, killing, pillaging and spoiling all the way' – where he was joined by the captain of Clanranald and the earls of Sutherland and Seaforth.[105] Their combined forces finally met up with Montrose (created a marquis on 6 May) in Atholl late in August 1644.[106]

The London newspapers offered their own interpretations of the invasion. *The weekly account, The Scottish dove* and *A perfect diurnall*, for instance, reported that 2,500 Irish soldiers – with six heavily armed warships at their disposal – had just landed in Scotland 'intending to cut the throats of the

---

[102] Antrim to Ormond, 1 July 1644 (Bodl., Carte MSS 11, fo. 322). Also see *Comment. Rinucc.*, I, 457–8.
[103] Apparently some of the 800 were subsequently rallied so that, by the middle of July, between 2,000 and 3,000 troops had been dispatched to serve in the Isles. NLS, Adv. MS 34.6.11, pp. 452–3; Carte, *Ormond*, VI, 150, 164–5, 179; Sir James Ware's diary of occurrences (City Library, Dublin, MS 169, p. 239); Balfour, *Historical works*, III, 215; Bagwell, *Stuarts*, II, 62; Stevenson, *Scottish Covenanters*, pp. 172–3.
[104] Ormond to Nicholas, 22 July 1644 (Carte, *Ormond*, VI, 179). Also see *ibid.*, 164–5, 179–80; HMC, *Supplementary report*, p. 77; Stevenson, *Alasdair MacColla*, pp. 108–9; *Comment. Rinucc.*, I, 458.
[105] Alexander McDonnell to Ormond, 13 August 1644 (Bodl., Carte MSS 12, fo. 82).
[106] NLS, Adv. MS 26.2.7, fos. 44v–7; Carte, *Ormond*, VI, 209; HMC, *Supplementary report*, p. 78; Murdock and Simpson (eds.), *Memoirs of James, marquis of Montrose*, pp. 54, 79; Leith (ed.), *Memoirs of Scottish catholics*, I, 280, 287–92; Cowan, *Montrose*, pp. 154–8; Stevenson, *Scottish Covenanters*, pp. 173–4; idem, *Alasdair MacColla*, pp. 109–18, 120–1; McKerral, *Kintyre*, pp. 42–8; Alexander MacBain and John Kennedy (eds.), *Reliquiae Celticae. Texts, papers and studies in Gaelic literature and philology* ... (2 vols., Inverness 1892–4), II, 177–9.

146   *Civil War and Restoration in the three Stuart kingdoms*

Protestants of that kingdom, as they have already in Ireland'.[107] In a similarly biased editorial, *The true informer* further suggested that the force had in fact been destined for England: 'The marquis of Antrim, who hath gained that title of honour since his rebellion in Ireland, is come out of Ireland into the north of Scotland. His design (as is reported) was for Liverpool in Lancashire, but divers of the earl of Warwick's ships' forced him to Scotland.[108]

Perhaps significantly, the weeklies failed either to perceive or to discuss the implications of the invasion for British politics. But the Edinburgh parliament was in no doubt about the danger: it immediately adjourned and sent an army of 6,000 covenanters, led by Argyll, against 'these idolatrous butchers'.[109] This force, Baillie reported 'no doubt will handle them ... and let Antrim know, though he once brake prison yet if he is caught again, he is not like to have such kind usage'.[110] The Irish brigade's role in the string of royalist victories ('those wonderful acts', as Hyde called them) at Tippermuir (1 September), Aberdeen (13 September), Inverlochy (2 February 1645), Auldearn (9 May), Alford (2 July) and Kilsyth (15 August) was to prove Baillie's confidence wholly misplaced.[111]

In the short term the invasion also impinged significantly on English affairs. Argyll's pursuit of Montrose immediately reduced the pressure on the king and thus gave a breathing space to the English royalist cause, which was in a shambles after Marston Moor (July 1644).[112] Moreover, Montrose's continued victories in the north resulted in the removal of regiment after regiment of the covenanting army from English soil and also prevented a second Scottish army of invasion from crossing the border. Ultimately, of course, the

---

[107] *The weekly account containing special and remarkable* passages ... no. 49 (London, 1644), p. 240; *The Scottish dove* ... From Friday 2 to Friday 9 August [1644], no. 43 (London, 1644), p. 344. *A perfect diurnall* ... From Monday 12 to Monday 19 August 1644, no. 55 (London, 1644), p. 440, estimated that 3,000 Irish troops had landed.

[108] *The true informer* ... From Saturday 3 to Saturday 10 August 1644 (London, 1644), p. 305. Again, Antrim's title was incorrectly given.

[109] 'For Glasgow', 7 August [1644] (Laing, *Letters*, II, 214). Also see Leith (ed.), *Memoirs of Scottish catholics*, I, 289–90; Stevenson, *Alasdair MacColla*, pp. 123–4. Between 16 July 1644 and February 1645 Argyll spent roughly £1,200 preparing his forces against these 'Irish rebels' (Inverary castle, Argyll muniments, bundle 7/165).

[110] Baillie to Spang, 10 August 1644 (Laing, *Letters*, II, 217). Also see *The parliamentary scout* ... From Thursday 8 to 15 August 1644 (London, 1644), p. 482.

[111] Clarendon, *Life*, II, 80–1. Also see Carte, *Ormond*, VI, 225–6; Ó Danachair, 'Montrose's Irish regiments', pp. 61–2; Stevenson, *Scottish Covenanters*, pp. 174–7; Hill, *Celtic warfare*, pp. 48–60. See pp. 153, 160 below.

[112] Duchess of Buckingham to Ormond, 17 June 1644 (Bodl., Carte MSS 11, fo. 221); dispatch from London, 7/17 September and 20/30 September 1644 (Bibl. Apost. Vat., Barberini Latini MSS 8673, fos. 139r–v and 147r–v); Carte, *Ormond*, VI, 221.

victories of Antrim's Irish brigade, which was the only concrete aid provided by the Catholic confederates for the king's British war-effort, did not prevent Charles's defeat in the first Civil War; but they did throw Scottish affairs into chaos for a year and thereby reduced to a bare minimum covenanting aid for the English parliament's war-effort.[113] Moreover, they offered the king, as the duchess of Buckingham astutely observed, 'most hopes to bring him with honour out of his misfortunes'.[114]

In Ireland, however, the success of the expeditionary force brought the Catholic party little immediate military reward. Though 1,400 of Monro's soldiers and Argyll's regiment, which had been garrisoned on the Antrim estates, retreated across the North Channel to protect their homes, a sizable force remained in Ulster.[115] And the dispute between Antrim and Castlehaven over who was supreme commander meant that, instead of a well-organized two-pronged attack against the Scots, the confederate Ulster offensive over the summer of 1644 was uncoordinated and ineffective.[116] Moreover, the need to put into the field simultaneously these two armies, together with four provincial ones, dramatically increased the competition for men and resources and strained to the limit the uneasy alliance between the Old Irish and Old English within the Catholic party. Finally, although the upheavals in Scotland prevented the Scots, who from this point on were very poorly supplied, from taking the offensive, this limited feat was only achieved through Antrim's enormously costly expedition, which the confederates had to fund almost single-handed.[117] The largest known expense was the hire of the shipping, a total of well over £2,500.[118] But arms, ammunition and provisions were also costly; twenty barrels of powder alone had cost £154-14-4. How much more was spent on the remaining powder and the 1,200 muskets, all of which had been imported from the continent, remains a mystery. Presumably it was, as was claimed at the time, equivalent to 'a small

---

[113] Stevenson, *Scottish Covenanters*, pp. 178–9; Lowe, 'The earl of Antrim', p. 197; *The Scottish dove ... From Friday 16 to Friday 23 August 1644*, no. 45 (London, 1644), p. 354.
[114] Duchess of Buckingham to Ormond, 20 August 1644 (Gilbert, *Ir. confed.*, III, 257).
[115] Perceval-Maxwell, 'Ireland and Scotland', p. 206.
[116] Casway, *Owen Roe O'Neill*, pp. 102–14.
[117] Stevenson, *Scottish Covenanters*, pp. 179–80.
[118] £2,006 of this was owed to Archer and the remainder to Vanderkipp and Stafford, Gilbert, *Ir. confed.*, V, 225; Milo Power to Ormond, 18 April 1644 (Bodl., Carte MSS 10, fos. 289–91); Antrim to Ormond, 23 April 1644 (*ibid.*, fo. 344r–v); Archer to Ormond, 8 May 1644 (*ibid.*, fo. 555); bond to Archer, 8 May 1644 (*ibid.*, fo. 477); Antrim to Ormond, 6 September 1644 (*ibid.*, 12, fo. 297); Ormond to Captain Stafford, 7 November 1644 (*ibid.*, fo. 579); Archer to Ormond, 17 July 1644 (*ibid.*, 11, fo. 471); Ormond to Andrew Moore, 17 October 1644 (NLI, Ormonde MSS 2310, fo. 551).

fortune'.[119] Moreover, the supreme council had to placate the disgruntled population which had borne the burden of quartering and feeding more than 2,000 hungry, restless men for over three months.

These expenses, combined with the fact that it was the autumn before news of the Irish brigade's victories reached Kilkenny, meant that Antrim's requests over the summer of 1644 for further provisions and arms were not well received.[120] Furthermore, in an attempt to reduce the overall cost of the expedition, it was also decided that the frigates (which, unbeknown to the supreme council, had already been captured by the enemy) should be recalled from Scotland.[121] The earl, equally ignorant of the ships' fate, bitterly opposed this decision and begged that the ships should be allowed to remain in the Isles for at least another month.[122] Antrim even suggested to Ormond that the vessels should be used as privateers in order to cover the hiring costs: 'I cannot but acquaint your lordship that there will be this next month more occasion for the ships than in all this time past, by reason of the herring fishing where many boats will be employed which may be easily taken by those ships.'[123] Ormond was convinced, and urged the supreme council not only to agree to Antrim's request but also to bear the cost (since crown funds earmarked for shipping had already been exhausted).[124] He argued that 'if those ships be now recalled we conceive that such inconveniences will fall upon the king's party in Scotland, that perhaps it had been better those men had not been sent at all'.[125]

Antrim's relationship with the Catholic confederates in the months after his force sailed was thus ambiguous. The supreme council, aware that his first loyalty was to the king, felt ill at ease with him and where possible excluded him from policy making.[126] The duchess of Buckingham, who had recently arrived in Ireland, explained his predicament to Ormond as follows: 'My Lord is believed here so much the king's creature as I was told by good hands that was the reason they would not trust him.'[127]

Yet Antrim enjoyed a popular following among the members of the fourth

---

[119] Bellings to Ormond, 26 August 1644 (Bodl., Carte MSS 12, fo. 194); Bellings to Ormond, 4 June 1644 (*ibid.*, 11, fo. 111).
[120] Carte, *Ormond*, VI, 209.
[121] Ormond to Bellings. 20 July 1644 (Bodl., Carte MSS 11, fo. 526); Ormond to Archer, 3 August 1644 (*ibid.*, 12, fo. 16); Gilbert, *Ir. confed.*, III, 256–7, 268.
[122] Gilbert, *Ir. confed.*, III, 257–8.
[123] Antrim to Ormond, 20 August 1644 (*ibid.*, 255). Also see *ibid.*, 248–9.
[124] *Ibid.*, 259–60; Archer to Ormond, 25 September 1644 (Bodl., Carte MSS 12, fo. 368).
[125] Ormond to Plunkett, 23 August 1644 (Gilbert, *Ir. confed.*, III, 259). Also see Ormond to [Plunkett], 23 August 1644 (Bodl., Carte MSS 12, fo. 177).
[126] Gilbert, *Ir. confed.*, III, 268; *Comment. Rinucc.*, I, 464, 475.
[127] Duchess of Buckingham to Ormond, 20 August 1644 (Gilbert, *Ir. confed.*, III, 258).

general assembly which convened at Kilkenny (between 20 July and 31 August) to discuss the terms of the peace treaty which had been referred back to Ormond after the breakdown of talks with the king at Oxford. Antrim was elected to serve, along with his brother, both on the supreme council and as one of the thirteen commissioners to negotiate a peace with the royalists; he was also appointed 'a commissioner to regulate the affairs of the nation, and putting the judiciaries [sic] in order and finding subsistence for the army'.[128] Towards the end of August the earl, taking advantage of his following within the general assembly, revived his vendetta against Castlehaven. He complained of the limitations placed on his commission and claimed that the supreme council had in fact violated the order of the previous assembly by circumscribing his powers. Then the earl, according to Bellings, 'laid down his commission, thinking it would be restored to him without those clogs and restrictions which accompanied it'. Much to the disgust of Antrim's enemies, a body within the assembly rose in his support, criticizing the supreme council and charging it with neglect; but the terms of his commission were not altered as he wished and the patent was not renewed.[129]

As far as Antrim was concerned this was the final affront and, unable to play one side off against the other any longer, he left Kilkenny for Dublin, where fresh talks ('the main business') between the king and the confederates were about to begin.[130] The cessation of arms which had been concluded for one year the previous September had temporarily united the Irish royalists and the Catholic party, but it was now about to expire. Since the confederate delegation which had been sent to negotiate directly with Charles in Oxford had failed to secure redress of any of their grievances, it was now necessary to begin discussions afresh. In June 1644 Charles had authorized Ormond to initiate the talks and, towards the end of August, had agreed to a further cessation of arms.[131] The confederates, the majority of whom genuinely wanted to heal the breach with the crown, to which they never ceased to profess their loyalty, readily agreed. Their position was, however, ambiguous for they were intent on preserving any gains – political, tenurial and religious – which the insurrection had brought them. 'Above all they wanted an

---

[128] Hill, *MacDonnells*, p. 314. Also see *A true copie of two letters brought by Mr Peters ...* (London, 1642), and *A declaration made by the rebels in Ireland ...* (Waterford 1644; reprinted London, [19 November] 1644), pp. 5–7; Plunkett to Ormond, 11 August 1644 (Gilbert, *Ir. confed.*, III, 252).

[129] *Desid. cur. Hib.*, pp. 250–1.

[130] John Walshe to Ormond, 30 August 1644 (Gilbert, *Ir. confed.*, III, 268). Also see Elkin, 'The interactions between the Irish rebellion and the English civil wars', p. 188; *Comment. Rinucc.*, I, 486, 523.

[131] Commission of the delegates of the supreme council, 31 August 1644 (Bodl., Carte MSS 12, fo. 230r–v).

independent parliament so that they could deal with the crown on the same terms as the English parliament.'[132]

Throughout the autumn of 1644 Antrim wholeheartedly supported Ormond's peace initiatives and, despite rumours to the contrary, the two most powerful figures in Stuart Ireland worked together harmoniously.[133] For his part, the lord lieutenant urged the earl to use his political influence at Kilkenny to secure terms advantageous to the king. He was advised

> to make use of your power and interest in this assembly now at Kilkenny, to bring them into that moderation, and humble submission to his majesty, as befits the duty of good subjects, and is most like to bring this kingdom into a happy and lasting peace; for I am confident this was a great part of your business into the kingdom, and I believe a principal reason that induced you to join yourself to their party.[134]

For his part Antrim, who genuinely wanted a more permanent peace settlement, even if this meant that the confederates did not achieve all of their religious and political aims, promised Ormond 'to use all my endeavours for the settlement of this kingdom in which I find much difficulty and cunning, but I hope your lordship's wisdom will find remedies to bring it under one governor which will be a huge happiness to all that has relation and interest in it'.[135]

The earl not only promoted the interests of 'Ormond's faction' within the council against those of Castlehaven; but he also tried to undermine the influence of the more extreme clerical commissioners, who were determined not to make peace with the king without key religious concessions.[136] No peace treaty was in fact signed until 1646, although in November 1644 the two sides agreed to an extension of the ceasefire until 10 January 1645. However, Antrim's stand, according to his wife, 'lost [him] credit with the most of the bishops and supreme council. If it were not for the king's service and good of this kingdom, he had little reason to stay amongst them.'[137]

Throughout the peace negotiations Antrim was preoccupied by the need to reinforce his brigade in Scotland, for he quickly realized that their continued success there (they took Aberdeen by storm on 13 September 1644) not

---

[132] Lowe, 'Charles I and the confederation', p. 2. Also see Perceval-Maxwell, 'Ireland and Scotland', p. 207; *idem*, 'Ireland and the monarchy', pp. 294–5.
[133] Hill, *MacDonnells*, p. 269; Carte, *Ormond*, VI, 152–3.
[134] Ormond to Antrim, 22 July 1644 (Carte, *Ormond*, VI, 179–80). Also see *Cal. SP Dom.*, *1644*, pp. 317–18 – this letter was then printed in *A full relation of the late expedition of ... Monroe ...* (London, 27 August 1644), pp. 13–14.
[135] Antrim to Ormond, 24 August 1644 (Bodl., Carte MSS 12, fo. 181).
[136] Carte, *Ormond*, VI, 315; Gilbert, *Ir. confed.*, III, 249–50; Antrim to Ormond, 24 August 1644 (Bodl., Carte MSS 12, fo. 181); *Cal. SP Ire., 1633–47*, p. 395.
[137] Duchess of Buckingham to Ormond, 23 August 1644 (Gilbert, *Ir. confed.*, III, 260).

only increased his own chances of ousting Argyll from the Western Isles but, more importantly, of regaining his Ulster estates, which would in turn relieve his pressing financial burdens. In principle, the supreme council favoured sending supplies, but in practice they were

> jealous that the honour and thanks of any service, that was or may be done there, shall be rather attributed to a particular person [Antrim] than to this nation; at whose cost only they conceive all that expedition from hence was effected, and they will hardly be drawn to be at further charges upon the same terms.[138]

Ormond generously responded with a reminder that Antrim had originally conceived the whole strategy and that 'if he attribute to himself more than belongs to his part, his vanity cannot be reason for sober men to leave the pursuit of a design of such huge advantage'.[139]

But it was not enough. And so, since the confederates had refused to aid him, and his English master's hands were tied, he decided to approach the great continental, Catholic powers of France and Spain 'for arms and munition in that service'.[140] Before seeking foreign aid, however, the earl first had to secure the king's permission and so, in November 1644, he and the duchess left Dublin for Wexford in search of shipping for England.[141] Towards the end of the month they managed to hire a frigate for the extortionate sum of £200 and left for England shortly afterwards, arriving safely in Exeter early in December, despite being chased by a parliamentary warship.[142] From there they joined the king in Oxford once again.

---

[138] Fennell to Ormond, 2 November 1644 (Carte, *Ormond*, VI, 212). Also see *Cal. SP Ire., 1633–47*, p. 396.
[139] Ormond to Fennell, 2 November 1644 (Carte, *Ormond*, VI, 213).
[140] Ormond to Digby, 19 October 1644 (*ibid.*, 209). He was not 'banished' from the council as claimed in Gilbert, *Contemp. hist. 1641–52*, I, 89.
[141] Gilbert, *Ir. confed.*, IV, 57–8.
[142] *Ibid.*, 58.

6

The 'War of the Five Kingdoms' (January 1645–June 1646)

Antrim and his wife arrived in Oxford early in January 1645. *The London post*, speculating on what had brought them back to England, concluded that they had come either to 'acquaint some evil councillors here with their new designs, or to provide monies for the continuing of the war in Ireland, or to give, or to receive instructions'.[1] While this was certainly the case, Antrim was also eager to bask in the royal favour which the successful outcome of the 'Scottish business' had brought him and to claim his marquisate which, according to one covenanter, was 'the reward of misdeserving'.[2] He now enjoyed an equal social footing with Ireland's most influential peer, the marquis of Ormond (who was created a duke only in 1661) and one of Antrim's kinsmen claimed 'that Ormond envied Antrim the success of the expedition and his favour with the king, formerly great, but now very considerable'.[3]

For the time being, however, preserving cordial relations with Ormond was to Antrim's advantage since the responsibility for maintaining the Irish presence in Scotland was left entirely in the lord lieutenant's hands. Early in January 1645, before Antrim's arrival at court, messengers had been sent from Oxford to Dublin pestering Ormond to send further supplies for Scotland.[4] Ormond took prompt action: the following month he began to lobby the supreme council for a renewed offensive in Scotland and, anticipating speedy compliance with his demands, he promised Montrose, the master of Reay and the earl of Seaforth, that 'no time shall be lost or pains spared to

---

[1] *The London post* ... 13 December 1644, no. 17 (London, 1644), p. 5. See also *The true informer* ... From Saturday 21 to Saturday 28 December 1644, no. 59 (London, 1644), p. 441.
[2] Baillie to Spang, 12 April 1644 (Laing, *Letters*, II, 164). Also see *Clarendon SP*, I, 255; PRONI, T473/1, pp. 43–5. More practically, he was granted an annual fee of £40 out of the customs of the port of Coleraine, *ibid.*, p. 44. Antrim received his first payment from the Coleraine customs in February 1663, see order of Ormond, 10 January 1663 (Bodl., Carte MSS 165, fo. 65v). Also see p. 131 above.
[3] Quoting James MacDonnell, *Comment. Rinucc.*, I, 464.
[4] Carte, *Ormond*, III, 157–8; *Clarendon SP*, I, 255.

procure and send your lordship from hence armed men and ammunition'.⁵ The supreme council, however, was less enthusiastic. 'The sending of two thousand fighting men last summer to that service' Ormond was reminded 'hath taught us the charge and difficulties interposed [sic] in such enterprises.'⁶

But despite these grumblings it was fast becoming apparent that Antrim's Irish brigade was enjoying great victories. Daniel O'Neill, referring to the battle of Inverlochy (2 February), reported that 'within this three weeks MacDonnell gave an overthrow [to the] earl of Argyll [and] killed fourteen or fifteen hundred men'. The report continued that the rest of Argyll's army was captured and that he himself had only narrowly escaped by fleeing to Edinburgh.⁷ The continuing successes in Scotland, together with renewed hopes of regaining Ulster soon, eroded the confederates' reserve. On 14 March the supreme council agreed to send 1,000 armed men with one month's provisions, match and powder for service in Scotland, but on three conditions: Ormond must supply the shipping, hand over the port of Carlingford (in Ulster) to the confederates and declare against the Scots in Ulster.⁸ Unfortunately, the lord lieutenant was unable to meet any of these demands. The presence of parliamentary warships outside Dublin frustrated his attempts to secure the necessary transport vessels; he flatly refused to deliver Carlingford into Catholic hands, and he declined to declare war on the Scots in Ulster since this would have increased his dependence on the confederates.⁹ As a result, reinforcements were never sent. By early May a rather disconsolate Ormond reported to the king that he should not 'expect any considerable succour from hence, either into England or Scotland'.¹⁰

---

⁵ Ormond to Montrose, 10 February 1645 (Carte, *Ormond*, VI, 247). Also see Ormond to Reay, 10 February 1645 (Bodl., Carte MSS 14, fo. 53); Ormond to Seaforth, 10 February 1645 (*ibid.*, fo. 55); Ormond to Mountgarret, 1 February 1645 (*ibid.*, fos. 14–15); remembrances [by Ormond] for Sir Edmund Butler, 3 February 1645 (*ibid.*, 63, fo. 311); Carte, *Ormond*, VI, 251.
⁶ Mountgarret to Ormond 13 February 1645 (Bodl., Carte MSS 14, fo. 80).
⁷ [Mathew] to Ormond, 24 February 1645 (*ibid.*, fo. 121). Also see Captain Audley Mervyn to Ormond, 1 February 1645 (*ibid.*, fos. 2–3); Carte, *Ormond*, VI, 250.
⁸ Supreme council to Ormond, 14 March 1645 (Bodl., Carte MSS 14, fo. 258v).
⁹ Duchess of Buckingham to Ormond, 24 March 1645; Ormond to Muskerry, Fennell, 21 March and 2 April 1645 (*ibid.*, fos. 283, 279; Carte, *Ormond*, VI, 275); Mountgarret to Ormond, 13 February 1645 (Bodl., Carte MSS 14, fo. 80). On a more personal level the duchess of Buckingham, who like Alexander acted as a watchdog for her husband's interests, was absolutely disgusted with Ormond's refusal to compromise. The lord lieutenant – obviously fearing that the duchess, or for that matter Antrim himself, would pursue the matter further with Charles I – confessed to Clanricard that he hoped to be 'restored to her favour' as soon as possible, see Ormond to Clanricard, 30 May 1645 (Carte, *Ormond*, VI, 296).
¹⁰ Ormond to Charles I, 8 May 1645 (Carte, *Ormond*, VI, 282).

Back in Oxford, however, the need to maintain the offensive against the covenanting armies in general (and against the marquis of Argyll in particular) no doubt weighed heavily on Antrim's mind and formed the basis of his discussions with the king. He was now determined to procure continental arms, munitions and shipping for his men.[11] The previous November, while he was still in Wexford, he had offered the Spanish envoy in Ireland '6,000 [men] from the Isles of Scotland and Ireland which are all his [Antrim's]'. The envoy, François Foissotte, had duly notified Philip IV of the offer (even though he had feared that nothing would come of it) since the earl's wife 'being a confident of the queen of England, and so much a friend of France and enemy of Spain, would not let him do it if it were not for the extreme shortage they have of money'. More seriously, he argued that Antrim's first condition would be for an advance, 'and then he will find problems which will prevent him from seeing through the affair'.[12] Nevertheless, according to Foissotte's own account an agreement was finally struck early in 1645 with Alexander MacDonnell (who acted on his brother's behalf) for the 'levy of a tercio of 1,200 men for the Low Countries ... [in return] they ask for nothing more than some arms [and] munitions of war'.[13]

To ensure that the deal was honoured Antrim asked for the king's permission to travel to Flanders. Charles supported his plan with enthusiasm, which was hardly surprising considering that the failure of the peace negotiations held between the king and parliament at Uxbridge (29 January – 22 February 1645) made a continuation of hostilities inevitable. From Charles I's perspective, Montrose's Scottish army had to maintain its offensive and therefore needed to be constantly supplied with ordnance and troops.

The marquis left Oxford and arrived in the Spanish Netherlands late in the spring of 1645, presumably armed with appropriate letters of introduction from Charles I.[14] He secured an audience with the papal representative in

[11] *Ibid.*, 209; instructions for Arthur Trevor, 21 June 1644 (Bodl., Carte MSS 11, fo. 266); *Cal. SP Dom., 1644–5*, p. 507. He claimed that he had already approached the pope for money, *Comment. Rinnucc.*, I, 456.

[12] Foissotte to Melo, 25 November/5 December 1644 (AGS, Eo. 2525, unfol.). A reply, advising Foissotte against the levy, was only sent from Madrid late in February 1645, see consulta of the junta on Irish levies, 29 January/8 February 1645 (*ibid.*, 2523, unfol.); Contreras to Foissotte, 19 February/1 March 1645 (*ibid.*, 2525, unfol.).

[13] *Relación de los servicios de D. Francisco Foissotte en Borgoña, Flandes, Inglaterra, Francia, y en ocho años y medio que assistío en Irlanda en negocios del Real servicio de V. Magestad* (Biblioteca Nacional, Madrid, MS 2367, fos. 9r–9v). For a summary of these, see AGS, Secretarias Provinciales 2499, unfol. I am grateful to Geoffrey Parker for bringing this reference to my attention.

[14] The exact date of his arrival is unknown. He had, however, visited the papal internuncio in Brussels some time before 28 April which suggests he arrived in the middle of April, Cathaldus Giblin (ed.), 'Catalogue of material of Irish interest in the collection of

Brussels, Internuncio Bichi, towards the end of April 'for the purpose of protesting his attachment to the Holy See'. Bichi praised his 'zeal for the Catholic cause', and his disapproval of Ormond's policies, and encouraged him to continue his labours. However, in his subsequent dispatch back to Rome the internuncio reported that the marquis's true loyalties lay elsewhere. 'Antrim', he wrote, 'is not inclined to join with the Irish confederates, as he wishes to be in good grace with the king of England.'[15] The marquis was also well received and handsomely entertained by the Spanish court in Brussels and especially by Don Manuel de Moura y Cortereal, marquis of Castel Rodrigo, governor-general of the Spanish Netherlands.[16] Castel Rodrigo was obviously impressed by Antrim and later, in a letter to Philip IV, described him as an 'Irish gentleman and one of the most rich and important of that kingdom of Ireland'. To complete his depiction of someone presumably hitherto unknown in Spanish court circles, the governor-general added that he was 'married to the widow of Buckingham'.[17]

Official negotiations with Castel Rodrigo began almost at once.[18] In return for Spanish military and naval support, Antrim was prepared to do almost anything. In the contract signed with Castel Rodrigo on 6 May 1645 he was offered 'two ships each of 160 tons, armed, gunned, and furnished with everything necessary' which were to be supplied 'on account'. For his part Antrim promised to recruit, from amongst his Irish and Scottish dependants, '2,000 men, of which he is to be the colonel'.[19] On 22 May 1645 in a ciphered letter to Madrid, Castel Rodrigo informed Philip IV of the offer of two regiments of 'well-seasoned veterans'.[20] Less than two months later the

---

Nunziatura di Fiandra, Vatican archives', *Collect. Hib.*, 1 (1958), p. 66; Foissotte to Cárdenas, 22 May/1 June 1645 (AGS Eo. 2566, unfol.).

[15] Bichi to secretariat of state, 26 April/6 May 1645, Bichi to Cardinal Panzirolo, 28 September/8 October 1645 (Giblin (ed.), 'Catalogue of material of Irish interest', pp. 66, 74–5).

[16] Leopold William to La Torre, 10/20 January 1648 (AGR, SEG 239, fo. 56).

[17] Castel Rodrigo to Philip IV, 22 May/1 June 1645 (*ibid.*, 233, fo. 184v). Also see *Wild Geese*, p. 366.

[18] Unfortunately, the particulars of their understanding are somewhat obscure since the conditions upon which they agreed, though often mentioned in various missives and reports, appear to have been lost, Castel Rodrigo to Philip IV, 22 May/1 June 1645 (AGR, SEG 233, fo. 184v) and consulta of the council of state, 16/26 July 1645 (AGS, Eo. 2523, unfol.), both refer to 'conditions' which are no longer 'enclosed'. Philip IV to Castel Rodrigo, 17/27 July 1645 (AHN, Eo. Libro 97, unfol.) suggests that the original conditions were deposited among the papers of the secretary of war ('en la secretaría de guerra'); but I was unable to find them.

[19] 'Registre aux ordres' 4/14 September (AGR, SEG 45, fo. 65r–v). Also see *Wild Geese*, p. 368.

[20] Minute of the letter from Castel Rodrigo to Philip IV, 22 May/1 June 1645 (AGR, SEG 233, fo. 184v). Also see *Wild Geese*, p. 366; Bichi to secretariat of state, 29 April/6 May 1645 (Giblin (ed.), 'Catalogue of material of Irish interest', p. 66).

Spanish council of state appears to have accepted the offer without any qualms, probably because of its eagerness to augment the hard-pressed Army of Flanders. The king was more cautious and, obviously unaware that Antrim's men would all be Catholic, in a holograph annotation to the consulta and in his subsequent reply to Brussels, he cautioned against recruiting any possible 'fifth column', or even worse, heretics, into the Army of Flanders.[21] 'The Scots are new in my service but have served the Crown of France for a long time' warned the king, and added 'moreover they are of a different religion.'[22] Apart from this word of warning, however, he left the matter entirely to his governor-general's discretion.[23]

Others, however, questioned both Antrim's sincerity and his ability to provide the Spanish crown with soldiers. An anonymous author 'well known to the court' believed that the marquis lay 'under suspicion of dealings with England, because he allows himself to be much influenced by his wife the duchess of Buckingham, an Englishwoman'.[24] Another anonymous correspondent caustically predicted that the troops would never arrive: 'In return for this great gift he is to procure us a few men this summer, which I must tell you freely I esteem very little considering the delays and difficulties which may occur in their coming hither.' The author patronizingly concluded his letter by adding that this generous gesture by the administration in Brussels at least indicated 'how on this side we are not wanting to contribute to his [Charles I's] prosperity'.[25]

But Castel Rodrigo was so eager to attract well-trained Catholic troops to Flanders that he remained unperturbed by the carping of his compatriots.[26] In fact, anticipating the king's approval for the enterprise, he had already set in motion the paperwork involved in any seventeenth-century troop levy long before he received Philip IV's guarded approval early in the autumn of 1645. A commission was issued to the marquis on 22 May to act as colonel of his embryonic regiment, together with blank commissions for fifteen officers – a

---

[21] All the mercenary components of the Army of Flanders were Catholic, Parker, *The Army of Flanders*, p. 29.
[22] Philip IV to Castel Rodrigo, 17/27 July 1645 (AGR, SEG 233, fo. 242).
[23] Consulta of the council of state, 16/26 July (AGS, Eo. 2523, unfol.). Also see *Wild Geese*, pp. 367–8.
[24] 'La relación del estado del Reyno de Irlanda desde Deziembre de 1644', enclosed in a letter to Philip IV from 'a person in Spain', 11/21 June 1645 (AHN, Eo. Libro 975, unfol.).
[25] Letter of intelligence from the continent, 10/20 May 1645 (*Cal. SP Dom., 1644–5*, p. 507).
[26] Copy of the recommendations of the committee dealing with Irish levies, 22 January 1644/1 February 1645 (AGS, Eo. 2523, unfol.); recommendations of the committee of state, 2/12 June 1645 (*ibid.*, 2525, unfol.).

The 'War of the Five Kingdoms' 157

sergeant-major and fourteen captains.[27] The 2,000 new recruits for Flanders were to be divided into fifteen companies of roughly 130 soldiers each and they were to receive the same treatment, privileges and pay as Spanish soldiers.[28] In return, the regiment was required to 'obey, comply with and execute the orders which are given to them by paper or by mouth with regard to the service of his Majesty [Philip IV]'.[29] Towards the end of June 1645 a licence was also issued to Antrim's illegitimate half-brother Maurice, releasing him for one year from service in Patrick Daniel's regiment (then garrisoned at Nieuport) with full retention of his pay, 'to help in the recruiting to be done by the marquis of Antrim and to bring these soldiers to these states [Flanders]'.[30]

An arms dealer from Dunkirk, Martin Clausen Van der Ripen, made arrangements in November for the actual transport of the new regiment from Ireland and Scotland to Flanders. But he only agreed on the following conditions: first, that the voyage should take place during the winter of 1645–6; second, that fifteen days should be allowed for the crossing, and if it took longer a daily supplement would be charged; third, that if the embarkation had to take place in Scotland, 'where there is more risk', Van der Ripen should receive a higher fee; and, finally, that the shipper should be paid 20 florins for each man landed in Flanders, half of which was to be paid in advance (20,000 florins/£1,540), and the remainder in two instalments, after the 'merchandise' had been safely disembarked on Flemish soil.[31]

Word quickly filtered back to England that Antrim's mission had been an amazing success. An anonymous source reported from Brussels on 20 May that he was 'negotiating here something for his Majesty's service, which is

---

[27] 'Registre aux ordres', 4/14 September 1645 (AGR, SEG 45, fo. 65). Interestingly, in the spring of 1645 Castel Rodrigo had been given 25,000 florins/£1,923 specifically for a levy of Irish troops for Flanders, see consulta of the junta of state, 2/12 June 1645 (AGS, Eo. 2525, unfol.); *ibid.*, 22 May/1 June 1645 (AGR, SEG 45, fos. 28–9). In *Wild Geese*, p. 366, Jennings states that the blank commission was for the major of the Irish regiment: in fact, it was for the sergeant-major.
[28] For further details on recruiting for the Army of Flanders, see Parker, *The Army of Flanders*, pp. 35–48 and 158–61; the rates of pay for Irish officers and soldiers in the Army of Flanders are discussed in *Wild Geese*, pp. 25–6.
[29] 'Registre aux ordres', 22 May/1 June 1645 (AGR, SEG 45, fo. 28).
[30] *Ibid.*, 20/30 June 1645 (*ibid.*, fo. 46). See also *Wild Geese*, p. 367; Hill, *MacDonnells*, p. 223, stated that Maurice was 'hanged in Coleraine in 1643' which does not appear to have been the case. Mauricio MacDonel (as he is referred to in the Spanish sources) is mentioned again in 'Registre aux ordres', 7/17 February 1647 (AGR, SEG 46 bis, fo. 68) as a member of Daniel's regiment.
[31] 'Registre aux ordres', 26 November/6 December 1645 (AGR, SEG 45, fos. 116–17). There was also provision for what would happen if Antrim's soldiers forced Van der Ripen's ships into an enemy harbour; or if any of the vessels were captured by the enemy.

now concluded, and in which he hath been very fortunate, considering our extreme wants here'. The writer continued that the marquis 'has carried himself discreetly, and gained much upon our ministers', adding that the Spanish authorities 'have promised in writing to give him instantly two brave frigates of twenty pieces of artillery each, and well provided, with which he intends to depart away for Scotland, and will carry along with him a great quantity of arms, to arm men there, and so have a considerable army for reducing those rebels'.[32] The marquis's power, status and standing could only have been enhanced in the eyes of his numerous patrons and contemporaries — particularly Charles I in England, Henrietta Maria in Paris and the confederates. He had suddenly become an asset of great potential value to both the royalists and the Irish Catholics, because in addition to serving as troop and munition carriers for all three kingdoms, his frigates could (as Ormond had observed) 'annoy the rebels of Scotland, hinder the relieving of their army here, and secure intelligence'.[33] Moreover, the Dunkirkers were precious additions to the confederate armada of privateers which protected the Irish coasts and victualled the Irish armies with remarkable efficiency.[34]

By agreeing to serve as a military contractor to the Spanish administration in Flanders (and later by offering troops to the French) Antrim transformed the 'War of the Three Kingdoms' into a 'War of Five Kingdoms', and from this point on he was able to exploit to his personal advantage the wars raging on the continent between the two great Catholic powers. For the Spanish Habsburgs were not only deeply involved in a protracted and bitter struggle in the Netherlands, which became particularly acute in 1645 as the French amplified their assault on Dunkirk, but were also totally committed to the Imperial cause in Germany. The Spanish Empire clearly did not have sufficient troops to man its already overextended armies, and therefore it is hardly surprising that officials in both Brussels and Madrid eagerly sought Catholic mercenary soldiers from Ireland.[35] Moreover, Irish mercenaries

---

[32] Letter of intelligence from the continent, 10/20 May 1645 (*Cal. SP Dom.*, *1644–5*, p. 507). The identity of this anonymous correspondent with royalist sympathies is unclear: presumably he was either an official, or someone with close connections, at the court in Brussels. The fact that the dispatch is now found amoung the State Papers Domestic suggests that it was intercepted by parliamentary agents before it reached Oxford.

[33] Ormond to Digby, 4 February 1645 (Carte, *Ormond*, VI, 244).

[34] For details, see Ohlmeyer, 'Irish privateers', pp. 121–7; Dan Bryan, 'The Irish admiralty, 1642–3', *An Cosantóir*, 7 (June 1947), pp. 285–7.

[35] Furthermore, the revolts in the Iberian peninsula meant that new recruits tended to be sent first to Spain itself and that cannon fodder for Flanders was in particular demand, see Philip IV to Owen Roe O'Neill, 2/12 March 1645 (AGS, Eo. 2525 unfol.); consulta of the committee on Irish levies, 30 January/8 February 1645 (*ibid.*, 2523 unfol.).

were reputed to be 'men inured to war and accustomed to hardship'.[36] According to one Spanish official, 'The Irish are foreign Catholics, neighbours affected to Spain and brave soldiers – a combination which will not easily be found in any other nation.'[37] While even the staunchly Protestant William III of Orange acknowledged the tenacity of the Irish soldier: 'There lives not a people more hardy ... neither is there any will endure the miseries of warre ... so naturally, and with such facility and courage that they do.' He added that 'the Irish are soldiers the first day of their birth'.[38] Moreover, the Spaniards realized that if they failed to take up Irish troops from contractors such as Antrim there was always the chance that the mercenary units would be offered to their great rival, France, which was no less eager than Spain to recruit soldiers to fight in Germany, Italy, the Netherlands, Catalonia and Portugal.[39]

Antrim managed to procure Spanish aid at a time when royalist fortunes were at their lowest ebb in England. Though the king's northern army had been routed at Marston Moor (July 1644), royalist resistance was tenacious and the numerically superior parliamentary armies were unable to follow up this victory. The royalists' success at Newbury (27 October 1644) emphasized the parliamentary failure and engendered recriminations and heart searching in London. The result was the Self-Denying Ordinance, which required members of both Houses of Parliament to resign their military commands and led in turn to the creation of the New Model Army, which gave parliament the edge over the king's army at the battle of Naseby on 14 June 1645. The defeat at Naseby was so complete that it 'relapsed his majesty's affairs into a doubtful condition' and was promptly followed by the surrender of eighteen royalist garrisons, including Leicester (21 June), Carlisle (2 July), Pontefract (21 July) and Scarborough (22 July).[40] By the spring of 1646 'the noose of New Model regiments around Oxford was being drawn tighter' as parliament sensed an outright victory which excluded any need for a

---

[36] Leopold William to Philip IV, 11/21 February 1653 (*Wild Geese*, p. 390).
[37] Consulta of the council of state, 20/30 March 1647 (AGS, Eo. 2068 unfol.).
[38] Quoted by John P. Prendergast, *The Cromwellian settlement of Ireland* (revised edn, London, 1870; 3rd edn, Dublin, 1922), pp. 86–7.
[39] Louis XIV intended to recruit sufficient numbers of Irishmen to maintain two regiments in French service, mémoire from Louis XIV to Bellièvre, 20/30 March 1647 (AMAE, Correspondance politique, Angleterre, Côte 50, fos. 70–1v).
[40] Digby to Ormond, 19 June 1645 (Carte, *Ormond*, VI, 301). John P. Kenyon, *The civil wars in England* (New York, 1988), pp. 147–8, assesses the implications of these calamities.

negotiated settlement.⁴¹ For a time, continued royalist victories in Scotland – Alford (2 July) and Kilsyth (15 August) – partly compensated for the débâcle at Naseby, and after Kilsyth it was even hoped that Montrose and his army would march into England.⁴² But on 13 September these hopes were dashed with the rout of Montrose's royalist army, which included a portion of the Irish brigade, at Philiphaugh.⁴³

Military disaster in Britain increased Charles I's desire and need for immediate and substantial support from Ireland. 'It hath pleased God by many successless misfortunes to reduce my affairs of late from a very prosperous condition to so low an ebb as to be a perfect trial of all men's integrities to me', the king informed Ormond, 'and I do principly rely upon you for utmost assistance in my present hazards.'⁴⁴ The safe and speedy dispatch of Antrim's frigates to the British Isles, together with their precious cargo of munitions, was thus now more important to the royalist war-effort than ever before.

Antrim had been promised the required munitions in May, but he still had not received them when he left Spanish Flanders for France some time late in July.⁴⁵ From Flanders he travelled directly to Henrietta Maria, at St Germain outside Paris, to deliver the 'letters from his Majesty' which he had been given at Oxford the previous spring.⁴⁶ Parliamentary news reporters speculated on the nature of his mission. For instance, on 4 August it was reported in the *Perfect occurrences of parliament* that: 'From France we hear that the earl of Antrim hath been received by the Queen with a great deal of respect and favour, that he brought letters to her, of the prosperous success of her good subjects the Irish Catholics, there against the Protestants, and what hope there is of routing them out of Ireland.' This parliamentary correspondent was also convinced (no doubt correctly) that Antrim and the queen were formulating fresh schemes and plots against parliament: 'something was desired of the queen for the encouragement of their proceedings, and divers

---

⁴¹ Mark A. Kishlansky, *The rise of the New Model Army* (Cambridge, 1979), p. 76.
⁴² Carte, *Ormond*, VI, 313; Byron to Ormond, 16 August 1645 (Bodl., Carte MSS 15, fo. 442).
⁴³ Ormond later hinted that Antrim and MacColla were responsible for the disaster which he claimed was caused 'through the treachery of some seeming friends'. Ormond's caustic comment was justified to the extent that MacColla and a substantial portion of his Irish brigade had retreated to the Western Isles shortly after the battle of Kilsyth and thus saved themselves from extermination, see Ormond to Montrose, 9 April 1646 (Bodl., Carte MSS 17, fo. 106).
⁴⁴ Charles I to Ormond, 31 July 1645 (Carte, *Ormond*, VI, 305).
⁴⁵ Antrim received permission to pass from Dunkirk to France on 22 May, 'Registre aux ordres', 22 May/1 June 1645 (AGR, SEG 45, fo. 29v).
⁴⁶ 'A narrative of the marquis's deportment ... ', undated [*c.* 1663] (PRONI, D2977/5/1/2). This version is significantly different from the one published in Hill, *MacDonnells*, pp. 270–5.

others passages, which brought great joy to the papists and priests about her majesty, but such their joying is but sad for us'.[47]

The marquis remained with the queen and her exiled court throughout August and into early September, meeting also with the newly appointed papal nuncio to Ireland, Giovanni Battista Rinuccini, archbishop of Fermo, who had been delayed in France due to lack of shipping for his entourage. According to Antrim's own account of this meeting, the nuncio 'desired to borrow those frigates to transport him, with which the marquis of Antrim acquainted the queen, and was commanded by her not to lend them, or have any hand in bringing him over'. Henrietta Maria did add the significant proviso, however, that once Rinuccini had arrived in Ireland 'there might be a necessity for the king's service of being civil and complying with him'.[48] That is to say, Antrim was to refuse to transport the nuncio, despite being offered £1,000 to do so, but he was given a *carte blanche* by the queen to cooperate with the nuncio should the need ever arise at some later date. After spending about six weeks in France attending on the queen, Antrim returned to Dunkirk to take charge of his frigates.[49]

Parliamentary journalists once again monitored the marquis's movements closely, and late in October headlines in *Mercurius civicus* reported that Antrim had returned to Dunkirk but misleadingly suggested that he was there to take to Ireland 'four and twenty thousand pound sent from the Pope to the Marquis of Antrim to bring over Irish rebels'.[50] In fact his mission was both more complex and more deadly; to collect the two frigates weighing 160 tons and armed with sixteen guns, which had cost Castel Rodrigo (rather than the pope) 44,445 florins – roughly £3,420 – plus '1500 arms with ammunition'.[51] The negotiations involved in purchasing and outfitting the Dunkirkers were already underway when he arrived: one of the ships had been

---

[47] *Perfect occurrences of parliament and chief collections of letters from the armie* ... From Friday 1 to Friday 8 August 1645, Week 32 (London, 1645), p. 6. Also see *Perfect passages of each days proceedings* ... From Wednesday 30 July to Wednesday 6 August 1645, no. 41 (London, 1645), pp. 321–2.
[48] 'A narrative of the marquis's deportment ... ', undated [*c.* 1663] (PRONI, D2977/5/1/2).
[49] Hill, *MacDonnells*, p. 272. It seems, however, that at some point, possibly in 1647, Antrim sold Rinuccini one of his frigates (the *San Pedro*), Leopold William to Torre, 28 August/7 September 1648 (AGS, Eo. 3019, unfol.); *Comment. Rinucc.*, I, 709, 732, II, 1–8; Aiazza, *Embassy*, pp. 77–8.
[50] *Mercurius civicus* ... From Thursday 23 to Thursday 30 October 1645, no. 127 (London, 1645), pp. 1117–18.
[51] Gilbert, *Contemp. hist. 1641–52*, I, 89, the anonymous author of the *Aphorismical discovery* valued Antrim's frigates at a conservative £1,500. He also stated that Antrim acquired the frigates in 1644 which is incorrect, see 'A narrative of the marquis's deportment ... ', undated [*c.* 1663] (PRONI, D2977/5/1/2); *Egmont MSS*, I, 295.

bought by the Brussels government from Jacques Le Goveurneur, a military contractor, and the other from Dunkirk 'arms-dealers and merchants'.[52] Antrim was not even required to provide any collateral for the frigates he received 'in view of his high quality and the zeal he has for the service of his majesty [Philip IV]'.[53]

One of these frigates was called the *San Pedro* and the other very probably was the ship later known as the *Mary of Antrim*.[54] Certainly the former, and very probably the latter, were manned in part by crews provided by the king of Spain.[55] The virtues of the Dunkirk frigate were well known: fast and powerful, according to an Irish agent in Flanders, they were 'accustomed to go whithersoever they will, caring nothing from anybody';[56] while one distinguished modern naval historian described them 'as combining something of the agility of the Mediterranean oared craft with the fighting power of the Northern broadside ship'.[57] Thus Antrim had procured two of the most sophisticated and formidable warships of the day for the royalist cause.

---

[52] Copy of the relación sent by secretary Miguel Routtarte to the marquis of Monasterio, 30 November/10 December 1647 (AGS, Eo. 2576, unfol.); 'Registre aux ordres', 4/14 September (AGR, SEG 45, fo. 65r–v). In *Wild Geese*, p. 368, Jennings states that Jacques Vandeval made his original agreement with the marquis of Lede on 9/19 September, but this should in fact be 19/29 September. On 10/20 October 1645 a letter of exchange for 1,000 escudos (£200) was sent to Alonso de Urribarri for the 'preparation of some ships' delivered to 'Antrain [sic]'; and on 2/12 November 1645 Urribarri and Le Goveurneur were finally paid in full for providing Antrim with two frigates (AGS, CMC 3A época, Legajo 2871, Cuentas of Thomas López de Ulloa, 1642–5, 'Datta de lo pagado extraordinariamente a differentes personas', pliego 60).

[53] Leopold William to La Torre, 10/20 January 1648 (AGR, SEG 239, fo. 56). For further details on Le Goveurneur and Urribarri, see Robert Stradling, *The armada of Flanders: Spanish maritime policy and the European war 1568–1668* (Cambridge, 1992), pp. 69, 120, 122, 156, 171, 180, 183–6, 193, 200, 224.

[54] Ohlmeyer, '"The Dunkirk of Ireland"', p. 31; Massari, 'My Irish campaign', *The Catholic Bulletin*, 6 (1916), p. 155; John C. Appleby, 'An Irish letter of marque, 1648', *Ir. Sword*, 15, no. 61 (Winter 1983), pp. 218–21; examination of Undermerch [sic], 5 February 1649 (PRO, HCA 13/250, part I).

[55] Copy of the relación sent by Miguel Routtarte to the marquis of Monasterio, 30 November/10 December 1647 (AGS, Eo. 2526, unfol.).

[56] Hugh Bourke to Luke Wadding, 23 February/5 March 1642 (*Franciscan MSS*, p. 123).

[57] R. C. Anderson, 'The ancestry of the eighteenth-century frigate', *The Mariner's Mirror*, 27, no. 2 (1941), p. 158. For a more technical definition, see Gregory Robinson, 'The seventeenth century frigate', *The Mariner's Mirror*, 15, no. 2 (1929), pp. 271–81. More recently a Flemish historian noted that 'as a class of ship the frigate was brought into service at sea by the Dunkirkers. It rode low in the water and could be distinguished by the number of cannon with which it was equipped', R. Baetens, 'The organization and effects of Flemish privateering in the seventeenth century', *Acta Historiae Neerlandicae*, 9 (1977), p. 57.

Due to the French blockade, the marquis's departure from Dunkirk proved difficult and he later complained to Hyde that he had 'more trouble in getting out his frigates than in procuring them'.[58] Rather than sailing directly to Scotland as originally planned, Antrim led his armada in November 1645 instead to Falmouth in Cornwall 'to wait on his now Majesty [i.e. Charles, prince of Wales], who having employment for arms, did make use of the said arms, with store of ammunition, and eight or ten pieces of cannon, and soon after did also make use of both the frigates'.[59] In his autobiography, Hyde, who was at Falmouth when Antrim's frigates arrived, observed that

> most of the arms and ammunition were employed with his [Antrim's] consent, for the supply of the troops and garrisons in Cornwall; and the prince made use of one of his frigates to transport his person into Scilly, and from thence to Jersey; without which convenience his highness had been exposed to great difficulties, and could hardly have escaped the hands of his enemies.[60]

Thus by his timely arrival at Falmouth Antrim had saved the prince of Wales from capture, and provided supplies, which were subsequently stored in Pendennis Castle, for the beleaguered royalist garrisons in Cornwall. He thus further ingratiated himself with the royal family and their hard-pressed lieutenants.[61]

There was still an outstanding obligation to the king of Spain, it is true, but on his return to Ireland in December 1645 Antrim apparently made no effort to secure confederate approval for a new levy of troops. Instead he immersed himself in the factional jostling over a proposed peace treaty between the confederates and the king which had been engineered by Edward Somerset, earl of Glamorgan. Glamorgan, a Catholic, had arrived in Ireland the previous June with instructions from an increasingly isolated and desperate Charles I to conclude a peace among the Irish factions and to persuade the supreme council, in return for religious concessions, to provide Irish troops for royalist service. A secret treaty was agreed on 25 August whereby the confederates, in return for guarantees of complete tolerance for Catholics and other significant religious concessions, agreed to supply Charles I with

---

[58] Antrim to Clarendon, 19 November 1645 (*Clarendon SP*, I, 287).
[59] Hill, *MacDonnells*, p. 272. Antrim's change of itinerary may have been at the queen's insistence; or due to Montrose's rout at Philiphaugh (13 September).
[60] Clarendon, *Life*, II, 82.
[61] *Clarendon SP*, I, 303. Clause 173 of the Act of Explanation (1665) referred to this: 'besides assisting him [Charles II] with arms and ammunition when he was in the west, [Antrim] furnished him with ships to make his escape into foreign parts', *Statutes at large passed in the parliaments held in Ireland (1310–1761)* (8 vols., Dublin, 1765), III, 101.

10,000 troops: but the deal was ultimately frustrated by the arrival of the papal nuncio, Rinuccini.[62]

Rinuccini reached Kilkenny on 12 November armed with an unequivocal papal mandate 'to restore and re-establish the public exercise of the Catholic religion in the island of Ireland'. He swiftly rejected the Glamorgan treaty on the grounds that he was unsatisfied with the provisions made for the Catholic religion and because he feared that Glamorgan had insufficient powers to implement them.[63] However, he was also aware of Sir Kenelm Digby's mission to Rome on behalf of Henrietta Maria, which resulted on 20 November 1645 in a treaty, known as the 'Roman treaty', between the pope and Digby. This was far more favourable to Catholicism than the Glamorgan treaty since it allowed freedom of worship for the Catholic church, the abolition of the penal laws, the establishment of a free and independent parliament and freedom for Catholics to hold high-ranking civil and military positions. In return for these concessions the confederates were to send an army of 12,000 foot, financed by a papal subsidy of 100,000 crowns, into England. Hardly surprisingly, Rinuccini wanted the Roman treaty to be accepted in Ireland and so negotiations with the royalists began again. A further treaty was finally concluded between Rinuccini and Glamorgan on 20 December, but shortly afterwards Ormond discovered the extent to which Glamorgan had acquiesced to the nuncio's demands and on 26 January 1646 had him arrested.[64]

Ormond's intervention threw Kilkenny politics into disarray and further divided the confederates who, instead of concentrating on winning the war, were side-tracked by 'malicious intrigues, pettifogging debates and missed opportunities'.[65] Simply stated there were two principal factions within the confederation throughout the 1640s. The first was made up of members of Old English families, many of whom were Ormond's clients ('Ormondists'). They dominated the supreme councils and, as the 1640s progressed, were eager to conclude a peace with Charles I even if the future safety of the Catholic religion were compromised by such a treaty. They included men such as Lord Mountgarret (who was Ormond's maternal great uncle), president of the first six supreme councils; Mountgarret's son-in-law, Richard

---

[62] John Lowe, 'The Glamorgan mission to Ireland 1645–6', *Studia Hib.*, 4 (1964), pp. 161–6; S. R. Gardiner, 'Charles I and the earl of Glamorgan', *EHR*, 2, no. 8 (Oct. 1887), pp. 695–708.
[63] Patrick J. Corish, 'Ormond, Rinuccini and the confederates, 1645–9', in *NHI*, p. 317, and idem, 'The origins of catholic nationalism', in *A history of Irish catholicism*, III, part 3 (Dublin, 1968), pp. 38–9.
[64] Patrick J. Corish, 'Ireland's first papal nuncio', *Irish Ecclesiastical Record*, 5th series, 81 (Jan.–June, 1954), pp. 177–9.
[65] Lowe, 'The negotiations of Charles I and the confederation of Kilkenny', p. 689.

Bellings, secretary of the council; and Viscount Muskerry, Ormond's senior brother-in-law, a supreme councillor. The lawyer Patrick Darcy, described by the Spanish agent as the most important person in the council, was also 'one of Ormond's creatures'.[66]

The second faction consisted of members of Gaelic families (predominantly from Ulster), of Generals Owen Roe O'Neill and Thomas Preston, and of clerics who were intent on securing freedom for the Catholic religion as the inevitable price of any compromise with the royalists.[67] Rinuccini was the natural leader of this Old Irish faction, which promptly rallied around him upon his arrival in Ireland. For his part the nuncio quickly realized that the principal weakness of the Catholic party was its inability to comprehend that the king was using them as pawns in an effort to stave off defeat in England, making promises right and left that he never intended to keep. As a result he regarded the 'Ormondists' as a 'fifth column' and furthered, where possible, the interests of the Old Irish faction.[68]

The polarization of the confederate cause put Antrim in an awkward position. While he was sympathetic to the Old Irish faction, he had up to this point furthered Ormond's interests. For the time being, however, he was anxious to negotiate a suitable compromise between the Catholic party and the king and therefore enthusiastically supported Glamorgan and his peace treaty. The terms of this treaty certainly suited his personal interests: on the one hand, it offered considerable concessions for the Catholic cause and more importantly, as far as Antrim was concerned, stated that the next lord lieutenant was to be a Catholic; on the other, it promised considerable aid – in the form of 10,000 troops, arms and ammunition – for the royalist cause in England.[69] Antrim's support for Glamorgan was admirably reflected in the fact that, together with Clanricard and others, he put up £20,000 as the earl's bail late in January 1646.[70] By supporting Glamorgan so vigorously, and thereby obliquely condemning the actions of the lord lieutenant, the marquis

---

[66] Foissotte to Melo, 25 November/5 December 1644 (AGS, Eo. 2525 unfol.). [Nicholas French], *The historical works of the right reverend Nicholas French, bishop of Ferns … containing the unkinde desertor of loyall men and true frinds* (2 vols., Dublin, 1846), II, 154; Gilbert, *Ir. confed.*, IV, 147; Massari, 'My Irish campaign', *The Catholic Bulletin*, 6 (1916), p. 396.
[67] Torre to Philip IV, 20/30 April 1647 (AGS, Eo. 2523 unfol.); Foissotte to Rosas, 14/24 October 1644 (AGS, GA 1570 unfol.)
[68] For a perceptive account of Rinuccini's policies in Ireland, see S. O'Riordan, 'Rinuccini in Galway 1647–1649', *Journal of the Galway Archaeological and Historical Society*, 23, nos. 1 and 2 (1948), pp. 19–51.
[69] Lowe, 'The Glamorgan mission to Ireland', pp. 166–7.
[70] *Several letters of great consequence intercepted by Colonel Milton … concerning Irish forces to be brought into England …* (London, 17 February 1645[-6]), p. 6; *Desid. cur. Hib.*, p. 313.

superficially at least joined ranks with Rinuccini and the supreme council, which had also been badgering Ormond for Glamorgan's release.[71]

Whether this gesture is evidence that Antrim genuinely sympathized with Glamorgan's plight, or merely that he was using the earl to further his own political career, is unclear. Certainly, the nature of Glamorgan's mission was very similar to the one Antrim had been commissioned to undertake in 1644 and, interestingly, some contemporaries saw many parallels between the two noblemen. Thus, in an 'Account of the war and rebellion in Ireland since the year 1641', which has been ascribed to Nicholas Plunkett, the author suggested that Antrim and Glamorgan were alike 'in their deportment' and added that they had both been manipulated by the nuncio and his followers, who 'made use of these noblemen's weaknesses and vanity'. The author also noted that during this period they behaved like 'a pair of stalking horses to gain their villainous ends under pretence of zeal to God and their king'.[72] Finally, he suggested that Antrim's devotion to the nuncio's faction was exclusively based on self-interest and political ambition: 'Here you may see how the marquis of Antrim too gave his helping hand to the destruction, he being married to the widow of Buckingham ... [who] vainly dreams of making himself viceroy by preventing Ormond from being employed in the same place as formerly.'[73]

More convincing evidence that Antrim's support of Glamorgan, and indirectly of the nuncio and the Old Irish party, did indeed reflect a decisive change in his political outlook is found in an unusual, and particularly revealing, letter which he wrote to his wife on 10 January 1646. It began reassuringly enough.

I will follow your advice concerning the nuncio. The earl of Ormond was ever false, and now it will be discovered. We must think only of Ireland unless there be a peace. I am beholding to the king for his good opinion, but I will rely on myself and not on him or any about him, they were ever base and so they will ever be. It is impossible Montrose or I can keep the Scots from coming into England in the condition wherein the king now stands, therefore let him think of nothing but a peace upon any terms, and be sure to make our peace with the parliament as other of the king's friends have. I believe you will be sacrificed, and so will my name and men in [Scotland].[74]

---

[71] Lowe, 'The Glamorgan mission to Ireland', p. 184; *The weekly account containing special and remarkable passages* ... From Wednesday 14 to Tuesday 20 January 1646, no. 4 (London, 1646), suggested that, save for the nuncio's influence over the marquis, there would have been a reconciliation between Antrim and Ormond.
[72] NLI, MS 345, p. 942.
[73] *Ibid*.
[74] Antrim to [duchess of Buckingham], 10 January 1646 (*Cal. SP Dom.*, 1645–7, pp. 301–2/PRO, SP 16/513, fos. 7–8v). This highly compromising letter is particularly important since it offers an unusual insight into the mind and personality of a man who

In a lengthy postscript he enquired about his old friend Hamilton, instructed his wife to take all necessary steps to ensure that they were 'not forgot in the peace', and requested that 'my letters should not come through Ormond's hands ... because Ormond and I be not upon good terms'. Finally, he apologized for not sending her money, begged her to 'be cheerful, though I grieve for us both' and declared his deep affection for her: 'I am only [yours], or God forsake me, your own, Randel.'[75]

This letter shows Antrim as a hard-headed political realist, very much in control of his own affairs, who was intent on protecting his family and his MacDonnell inheritance no matter what the cost. The winter and spring of 1645–6 represented a turning point in his career because external developments – the destabilization of Irish politics caused jointly by the arrival of Rinuccini in Ireland and by the defeat of the royalist forces in England and Scotland – reinforced Antrim's personal disillusionment with Ormond and convinced him that the only means of satisfying his political and territorial ambitions was to abandon (however reluctantly) the cause of Charles I. At the same time, Antrim's success as a diplomat and military entrepreneur in Europe gave him the confidence to abandon the principles upon which his life had heretoforeto been founded and to recognize that he could no longer be loyal both to the Protestant crown and the Catholic religion. In short his actions were shaped by events in all three Stuart kingdoms as well as by the Habsburg–Bourbon struggle on the continent.

In order to be 'his own man', however, Antrim needed money and since his only real assets were the frigates which he had procured in Flanders, he now focused his attention on setting them up as privateers.[76] He obtained letters of marque from the confederate high court of admiralty, and probably from the king as well, which authorized them to 'hinder at sea' the enemies of Charles I and of the Catholic cause in Ireland.[77] A contemporary noted that he stationed his frigates in Wexford 'where he appointed some of the best sort in that art captains of those frigates which, with two others of Owen O'Neill's,

---

rarely committed his thoughts, emotions and ambitions to paper. No doubt this is merely one of several letters 'Randel' (as he signed himself) wrote to his wife; unfortunately the rest have perished. This one only survived because it was intercepted by parliament.

[75] *Ibid.*

[76] During his lengthy sojourns in Waterford and Wexford in 1644 Antrim had not only made useful contacts with other privateers but had also seen at first hand just how lucrative the trade could be. For a more general account of these privateering communities, see Ohlmeyer, 'Irish privateers'.

[77] *Cal. SP Dom., 1645–7*, 302; *Clarendon SP*, I, 287. For examples of letters of marque, see Gilbert, *Ir. confed.*, II, 96–7; *A declaration of the commons assembled in parliament ...* pp. 46–7; Appleby, 'An Irish letter of marque', pp. 218–21.

did scour the coasts and brought in many rich prizes, to the advantage of the confederates, if well managed'.[78] Antrim's personal armada was not exclusively based in Wexford, however, and his frigates were often anchored in the other privateering ports scattered along Ireland's coastline, particularly Waterford.

Both Wexford and Waterford were ideal havens for freebooters. The Atlantic ocean and the Irish sea meet along the lengthy County Wexford coastline, which bristles with off-shore islands (the most important being the Saltees); furthermore, during the seventeenth century the port of Wexford was the nearest safe harbour in Ireland to England, Wales and mainland Europe. Waterford was valued as a safe harbour because of its location thirty miles inland on a river estuary which was able to provide much-needed shelter against the winter storms and gales for even the larger privateering men-of-war.[79]

In addition to privateering, Antrim's frigates were earmarked for supplying and reinforcing his army in Scotland, which had been isolated after Montrose's defeat at Philiphaugh. But in order to do this the marquis first had to secure confederate support. In a proposal which he submitted to the supreme council early in 1646 he chastised them because his brigade, which had cost the confederates so much to send, had been in Scotland for 'a year and three quarters ... and have received no manner of relief or assistance in all that time from this kingdom, nor any correspondence kept from hence with them'. He drew the council's attention to the possible consequences of their negligence: 'they will, if so continually neglected, forget any tie that the nation may imagine to have on them; and consequently not only so many able, experienced soldiers lost, but also become probably serviceable against us, if not looked on with more from hence, than hitherto they have been'. In an attempt to remedy the situation Antrim suggested that he should raise 'two thousand men sometime inhabitants in the County of Antrim' and place them under the command of his brother, Alexander. He also assured the council that those 'Islanders and Highland Scots ... having greater affection to the Irish than they have to the other inhabitants of Scotland' who had failed to join

---

[78] Gilbert, *Contemp. hist. 1641–52*, I, 89–90. See pp. 194–5 below for details on the captains of the frigates and their prizes.
[79] Nicholas Furlong, 'Life in Wexford port 1600–1800', and John de Courcy Ireland, 'County Wexford in maritime history' in Kevin Whelan (ed.), *Wexford: history and society. Interdisciplinary essays on the history of an Irish county* (Dublin, 1987), pp. 150 and 490; Julian Walton, 'The merchant community of Waterford in the sixteenth and seventeenth centuries' in P. Butel and L. M. Cullen (eds.), *Cities and merchants. French and Irish perspectives on urban development, 1500–1900* (Dublin, 1986), p. 183; Massari, 'My Irish campaign', *The Catholic Bulletin*, 6 (1916), p. 396.

Montrose's army would be encouraged to join the war by the presence of further forces from Ireland under a MacDonnell commander.[80]

Almost immediately Antrim's suggestions were presented to the sixth general assembly, which had initially been convened to discuss a resumption of the war following Glamorgan's arrest. They were embraced with enthusiastic approval. On 28 February, the assembly ordered that Antrim 'shall have and receive ... the sum of three thousand pounds sterling, for the raising, arming and transporting of the said two thousand [troops], and furnishing them with ammunition, shipping, victuals and all other necessaries'. The assembly insisted, however, that Antrim should give 'very good and sufficient security' for the money he was to receive and that Rinuccini, who strongly supported Irish intervention in Scotland, should be asked 'for the loan of the three thousand pounds'.[81] But the nuncio was either unwilling or unable to lend the assembly the money and therefore the supreme council was ordered 'to cause the said three thousand pounds to be brought in, and by Saturday next'. By 10 March the necessary capital, which was to be paid directly to the marquis, had been raised 'by way of loan on security of able merchants within our quarters'. Ultimately, then, it was the confederates, not the marquis, who provided the necessary funds, offering as collateral 'the accruing profits of the excise in the cities of Waterford, Kilkenny and Limerick and in the towns of Galway, Wexford and Clonmell Ross'.[82] As it happened Antrim's proposed offensive coincided with attempts by Montrose and the king to rally the royalist war-effort in Scotland; but, on this occasion, he refused to throw his weight behind them. Instead, together with MacColla, he was determined to wage his own personal war against Argyll.

The marquis was, however, prepared to ship to Wales some soldiers whom Glamorgan had received permission to levy in Ireland for the king. On 3 April, Glamorgan reported to Ormond, from Waterford, that 'my Lord of Antrim's frigates are come', that five other well armed men-of-war were available at Waterford to ship his troops and that only the fall of Chester (3 February) to parliament was delaying the embarkation of the three

---

[80] 'Reasons propounded by the marquis of Antrim ... ', undated [c. February, 1646] (PRONI, D2977/5/1/1); Hill, *MacDonnells*, pp. 446–7, misleadingly suggested that these documents date from 1645.

[81] Order by the general assembly, 28 February 1646 (PRONI, D2977/5/1/1). Also see Stevenson, *Alasdair MacColla*, p. 224.

[82] Order of the general assembly, 2 March and order of the supreme council, 10 March 1646 (PRONI, D2977/5/1/1). The extent to which Ormond was involved in the organization of Antrim's expedition is unclear. The lord lieutenant did appear, however reluctantly, to support the design and in a letter to the supreme council recommended that supplies be sent to Scotland at once, see Ormond to Muskerry, 28 March 1646 (Bodl., Carte MSS 17, fo. 21).

regiments.[83] And then, while both Antrim and Glamorgan were frantically trying to export cannon fodder to Britain, Lord Digby also arrived with orders to mobilize Irish aid for the royalists holding out in the isles of Scilly and informed Ormond that he had written to Antrim requesting the services of his frigates.[84] The lord lieutenant's reply noted sarcastically that 'I fear your lordship will find it a harder task to persuade my lord of Antrim out of his frigates, the rather that my lord of Glamorgan is gone before you to Waterford, whose oratory he will perhaps more listen to, as more suitable to his capacity, than anything you can descend unto.'[85] Digby, however, would not have received Ormond's warning before he travelled to Waterford to broach the matter in person with the marquis. The outcome of the encounter was as Ormond has foreseen; Antrim refused to lend his frigates. Disgusted, Digby reported to Ormond 'that we discover clearly in him a desire rather to hinder than further anything that shall be propounded, as advantageous to Ireland; especially under any kind of relation to your excellence, or indeed to the supreme council, it being hard to tell against which of the two he discovers the greater animosity'.[86]

As it happened, any plan Antrim may have had for transporting Glamorgan's troops fell through when, on 8 April, the supreme council ordered that the 3,000 men destined for England were now required to besiege Bunratty castle in County Clare, which had recently been captured by a parliamentary expeditionary force.[87] Yet despite this, the marquis still refused to lend Digby his frigates. For their part the council was clearly infuriated by Antrim's uncooperativeness and claimed that because 'my Lord of Antrim would by no means lend his frigates, being absolutely averse to the whole design' it would cost the council in excess of £1,000 to provide alternative shipping.[88]

Antrim's reluctance to ship Digby's levy might be ascribed merely to jealousy and personal rivalry between two courtiers. But in fact he also desperately needed the frigates to ship his own levy to Scotland since 'the Cantyre [Kintyre] people' who had been contracted to transport Antrim's troops from Grenagh Castle in County Cork to the Western Isles had failed to arrive, which delayed the departure of his two regiments 'and forced all my men to scatter'.[89] This already unpromising situation was further exacerbated early in March when the French resident in Ireland – Dumolin – fired

[83] Glamorgan to Ormond, 3 April 1646 (Gilbert, *Ir. confed.*, V, 319).
[84] Carte, *Ormond*, VI, 363.
[85] Ormond to Digby, 5 April 1646 (*ibid.*, 365).
[86] Digby to Ormond, 7 April 1646 (*ibid.*, 369).
[87] Supreme council to Ormond, 8 May 1646 (Bodl., Carte MSS 17, fo. 94 r–v).
[88] Fennell to Ormond, 14 April 1646 (Gilbert, *Ir. confed.*, V, 329).
[89] 'A narrative of the marquis's deportment...', undated [c.1663] (PRONI, D2977/5/1/2). Also see Hill, *MacDonnells*, pp. 297–8.

his own broadside against the expedition. Dumolin had caught wind of Antrim's outstanding obligation to levy two regiments of Irish infantry for Flanders and on 7 March 1646 he wrote an agitated (and rather garbled) letter which highlights the interrelationship of France, the Spanish Netherlands, Scotland and Ireland during these years. He begged the lord lieutenant to do everything possible to prevent Antrim from sending his Irish troops to Scotland, because he feared that they were ultimately destined for Flanders:

> In a word ... I say that my lord marquis of Antrim cannot carry twelve hundred men over to Flanders, as he hath declared himself to the said Assembly, except he gets here the two thousand, for the enemies in Scotland will grant him none for that purpose except he furnish [them] with others, being not in case to lessen their strength. These reasons and many [more] I have will persuade all the world that the said marquis intends to send those men to Flanders.[90]

Dumolin also broached the matter with the supreme council, and with apparent success for he later reported to Cardinal Mazarin that 'the Spanish are waiting for Antrim's [levy], which is being held up because of the opposition which I made'.[91] By the end of March, Dumolin's lobbying – plus a timely gift of '3,000 pistoles' (roughly £750) to the Catholic cause – appeared to have paid off and he gleefully reported to Mazarin that 'the permission to raise 2,000 men here for Scotland has been stopped'.[92]

What was the truth of the matter: were these soldiers raised (as Antrim stated) as reinforcements for the remains of Montrose's decimated army; or were they (as Dumolin claimed so confidently) really destined, via a port in Scotland, for Flanders? The surviving evidence is too fragmentary to allow a clear answer but there was certainly something to Dumolin's story, because towards the middle of June an anonymous French source claimed that a portion of Antrim's levy had landed in Flanders. This is confirmed by the records of the paymaster of the Army of Flanders (Contaduría Mayor de Cuentas) which indicate that twenty-four Irish soldiers reported for service at Dunkirk late in July, while in August, about 250 further new recruits, who 'have just come from Ireland', received payment for the services they had already rendered. Almost certainly, some (at least) of these men were from Antrim's levy, because Castel Rodrigo was prepared to 'do business' again

---

[90] Dumolin to Ormond, 7 March 1646 (Gilbert, *Ir. confed.*, V, 265). Also see Dumolin to Brienne, 4/14 July 1646 (BL, Harl. MSS 4551, fos. 226–7).
[91] Dumolin to Mazarin, 14/24 March 1646 (Gilbert, *Ir. confed.*, V, 275). Also see Dumolin's protest against the transport of Irish soldiers to Scotland, 4/14 March 1646 (Bodl., Carte MSS 16, fos. 582v–3).
[92] Dumolin to Mazarin, 22 March/1 April, (Gilbert, *Ir. confed.*, V, 315). Also see *ibid.*, VI, 50, and VII, 322–3.

with the marquis in the autumn of 1646 (see p. 179 below): had he defaulted totally on the earlier levy, this would have been highly unlikely.[93]

Despite Dumolin's efforts, however, Antrim persevered with the levy for Scotland and in April 1646 implored Ormond to intervene with the supreme council on his behalf.[94] It is hardly surprising that the lord lieutenant's response was cool and unhelpful and at this point, according to Antrim, 'such of the supreme council as were always opposed to my ways' – 'the Ormondists' – placed an embargo on the levy.[95] An obstructive circular was issued on 26 May to the mayor of Waterford, and presumably to the mayors of the other Irish ports under confederate control, instructing them 'to keep their men for any foreign employment, accordingly they enjoin the mayor not to allow any vessel to leave his harbour carrying any soldiers to serve beyond the seas without the writers' special license and command'.[96] The council followed up the embargo by ordering the captain of the fort at the Passage where Antrim's own ships were anchored 'to take the sails from my ships [and] to stop my voyage'.[97]

In desperation, the marquis therefore cut the ships' cables and, although 'his men dispersed', he put to sea with 'such of his friends as willingly followed him'.[98] Antrim and 'his friends' (between 500 and 800 infantry) thereupon sailed to the Western Isles and arrived at Campbeltown in Kintyre in late May or early June 1646.[99] His fellow clansmen had been eagerly awaiting the arrival of this 'youthful lord that shall aid his people in their

---

[93] For further details, see McNeill, *Tanner letters*, p. 223; 'Registre aux ordres', 24 October/4 November and 25 October/5 November 1646 (AGR, SEG 46, fos. 154v–5, 172v–3). Since Antrim did not accompany these soldiers, they probably formed the skeleton of a new regiment, commanded by one John Morphy, mentioned in the cuentas of Thomas López de Ulloa, 1646–8, 23 July/2 August 1646 and 17/27 August 1646 (AGS, CMC 3A época, Legajo 937, 'Datta de lo pagado a la infantería yrlandesa e inglesa', pliegos 2, 3 and 4).
[94] Antrim to Ormond, 17 April 1646 (Bodl., Carte MSS 17, fo. 169); Gilbert, *Ir. confed.*, V, 334. In a letter to Hyde, the marquis averred his desire to be reconciled with Ormond, *Clarendon SP*, I, 312.
[95] Hill, *MacDonnells*, p. 298. Also see Ormond to Antrim, 22 April 1646 (Bodl., Carte MSS 17, fo. 204).
[96] Supreme council to mayor of Waterford, 26 May 1646 (PRONI, D2977/5/1/1). See also Hill, *MacDonnells*, p. 274. The following week, Ormond was informed of the council's decision, see Bellings to Ormond, 2 June 1646 (Bodl., Carte MSS 17, fo. 439v).
[97] Hill, *MacDonnells*, p. 298.
[98] *Ibid.* See also 'A narrative of the marquis's deportment ... ', undated [c. 1663] (PRONI, D2977/5/1/2).
[99] *Comment. Rinucc.*, II, 163; HMC *rep. 11*, app. 6, p. 111; Stevenson, *Alasdair MacColla*, p. 225; Gilbert, *Ir. confed.*, V, 351, and VI, 51. Antrim later (misleadingly) claimed that he 'went to Scotland in April 1646', 'A narrative of the marquis's deportment ... ', undated [c. 1663] (PRONI, D2977/5/1/2); while DNB, 'Randal MacDonnell', suggests that he arrived in Scotland in July 1646: this was clearly not the case.

need' and had prayed that God would indeed protect 'The two frigates of Moy Linny's chief and all their appointed crew safe from terror of wind and sea that no weakness may distress our hearts.'[100] The anonymous author of the *Aphorismical discovery* recorded the rapturous reception that the marquis and his invasion force received: 'his lordship and his freight was welcome, to his Irish party ... though thitherunto [they] went bravely forward[,] this relief did highly encourage them, so that within a short time there were 3,000 men'.[101]

Whether Antrim actually commanded an army of 3,000 at this point is unclear. *The moderate intelligencer* suggested late in June that he had 'three ships and nine galleys, with near 2,000 Irish'[102] at his disposal, while Montrose's chaplain George Wishart misleadingly asserted that Antrim arrived 'without men or arms'.[103] Undoubtedly numbers were bolstered when the remains of Montrose's army joined with the marquis's force.[104] Safe in Scotland at last, Antrim could be forgiven for believing, like the anonymous kinsman who composed this verse welcoming him to the Isles, that now 'Every rogue will get what he deserves, every traitor will be snuffed out. We will not have to bear the yoke, and the spiteful ones will not get their wishes. Those of the twisted mouths [i.e. the Campbells] will be under our heels and Clan Donald will be on top as is the custom of the progeny.'[105]

---

[100] R. Flower (ed.), 'An Irish-Gaelic poem on the Montrose wars', *Scottish Gaelic Studies*, 1 (1926), pp. 117–18.
[101] Gilbert, *Contemp. hist. 1641–52*, I, 89.
[102] *Moderate intelligencer* ... From Thursday 18 to Thursday 25 June 1646, no. 68 (London, 1646), p. 511.
[103] Murdock and Simpson (eds.), *Memoirs of James marquis of Montrose*, p. 184. Also see Henry Cary (ed.), *Memorials of the great civil war 1642–52* (2 vols., London, 1842), I, 40; Stevenson, *Alasdair MacColla*, p. 225.
[104] MacBain and Kennedy (eds.), *Reliquiae Celticae*, II, 203.
[105] Quoted in Allan I. Macinnes, 'Scottish Gaeldom, 1638–51: the vernacular response to the convenanting dynamic', in John Dwyer, Roger A. Mason and Alexander Murdoch (eds.), *New perspectives on the politics and culture of early modern Scotland* (Edinburgh, 1982), p. 78.

7

Gaelic warlord and Irish politician (June 1646 – August 1647)

WAR IN SCOTLAND, IRELAND AND FLANDERS

Even before Antrim disembarked his troops the political situation in all three Stuart kingdoms was transformed when Charles I handed himself over to the Scots, near Newark in Nottinghamshire, on 5 May 1646. Almost immediately, the king sent orders that all men in arms in Scotland in his name should disband their forces. This unexpected change put Antrim in an impossible situation and forced him to declare publicly where his true loyalties lay: with the king, or with his personal interests in Kintyre. Initially, Antrim – perhaps misled by the enthusiasm that attended his arrival in Scotland – chose the latter; and certainly his clansmen in the Western Isles at first supported his decision, for at this point the bard of Clanranald recorded that 'A good many of the gentry of the Hebrides flocked to the earl of Antrim, such as the Clan Maclean and the Clanranald, intending to set an army on foot again on behalf of the king.'[1]

However, after at least three direct orders from the king – on 15 and 19 June and on 29 July – commanding him to lay down his arms, the marquis finally agreed to commit no further act of hostility 'as far as it may stand with the preservation of me and mine'.[2] And with evident relief *The moderate intelligencer* further reported that 'it's certified that the earl of Antrim is willing to return to Ireland'.[3] The king, in an attempt to pacify the Scots, also

---

[1] MacBain and Kennedy (eds.), *Reliquiae Celticae*, II, 203. Also see Charles I to the committee of Scotland, 19 June 1646 (Buckminster, Tollemache MSS 3750, fo. 15v).

[2] Antrim to Charles I, 13 July 1646 (SRO, GD 406/1/1993). Also see Charles I to the committee of Scotland, 19 June 1646 (Buckminster, Tollemache MSS 3750, fos. 15v–16); *Desid. cur. Hib.*, p. 305; Hill, *MacDonnells*, p. 273; R. Scrope and T. Monkhouse (eds.), *State papers collected by Edward, earl of Clarendon, commencing 1621* (3 vols., Oxford, 1767–86), II, 237, 242; HMC *rep. 11*, app. 6, p. 112. Interestingly, the king sent a copy of his order of 29 July to Argyll, see Inverary castle, Argyll muniments, bundle 8.

[3] *Moderate intelligencer* ... From Thursday 9 to Thursday 16 July 1646, no. 71 (London, 1646), p. 547.

instructed the marquis to return immediately the parliamentary frigate and four other vessels belonging to Glasgow merchants which one of Antrim's privateers had captured after depositing him in Kintyre.[4] Over this, however, the marquis remained evasive. In his reply he informed Charles I that it 'is a misfortune to me, that it lies not now in my power to obey ... by reason I had transmitted them into Ireland within [a] few days after they had been taken, where I understand they are disposed amongst those who were interested with me in the adventure'.[5]

The following month Antrim, who was furious that Argyll had executed 'a prisoner, being a gentleman of my name' in defiance of the ceasefire, had second thoughts about capitulating to the Scottish parliament at all. In a letter to the king dated 4 August he threatened 'to violate my engagement to your Majesty' on the grounds that 'I can hardly any longer keep those whose fortunes and security depended upon your Majesty's grace and fortune, seeing the remnant of Argyll's forces are drawn to a head not far from hence.'[6] Finally on 15 August, having taken 'the advise of my friends ... in whose hands and power I am at this time', he flatly refused to surrender.[7]

The precise size of Antrim's army during the autumn of 1646 remains elusive. One parliamentary newspaper reported that it consisted of 12,000 men 'a greater army than ever the rebels had in that kingdom since the beginning of these wars';[8] *The Scottish dove* estimated the force at a more modest 6,000 troops'[9] while *The moderate intelligencer* hedged its bets by merely claiming that Antrim's army was 'very numerous' and 'well appointed'.[10] But whatever the actual number, it was clearly insufficient to risk a descent upon Newcastle in order to free the king, as the parliamentary propagandists had predicted, and so Antrim and his army adopted a defensive stance and entrenched itself in Argyll's lands. Throughout August and September Sir James Lesley, the future Lord Lindores and a privy councillor, attempted to mediate a truce between the marquis and the covenanters. His efforts were, however, to little avail. 'Antrim and Kilketto [reported *The*

---

[4] Charles I to Antrim, 29 June and 31 July 1646 (Buckminster, Tollemache MSS 3750, fos. 16v–17, 23).
[5] Antrim to Charles I, 13 July 1646 (SRO, GD 406/1/1993). Also see Gilbert, *Ir. confed.*, VI, 250–1; *Egmont MSS*, I, 295.
[6] Antrim to Charles I, 4 August 1646 (SRO, GD 406/1/2005). Also see HMC *rep. 11*, app. 6, p. 113; Hill, *MacDonnells*, p. 273; *Diplomatic correspondence*, I, 225.
[7] Antrim to Charles I, 15 August 1646 (SRO, GD 406/1/2010).
[8] *Perfect occurrences of both houses of parliament* ... The 37th week ending the 11 September 1646 (London, 1646).
[9] *The Scottish dove* ... From Wednesday 23 September to Thursday 1 October 1646, no. 153 (London, 1646), p. 52.
[10] *Moderate intelligencer* ... From Thursday 3 to Thursday (*sic*) 9 September 1646, no. 79 (London, 1646), p. 635.

moderate intelligencer] ... will by no means obey His Majesty's letters as to laying down arms; they say he is not free in writing and hope in a few months to be able with an army to restore him to his crown again.'[11]

Antrim's decision to remain in arms in the Western Isles was fired both by his desire to keep the traditional Clan Donald heartland under his command and by the hope that his continued presence there would free his lands in County Antrim from the Scottish army of occupation. For his part, however, Argyll was equally determined to retrieve his estates in Kintyre which had been virtually annexed by Antrim and MacColla between 1644 and 1647. Like Antrim he was also deprived of his rents but, worse still, he had a Catholic army of occupation living off his lands and promoting the Roman faith. 'The sword of the rebels', the Argyll synod complained, 'has bereft us of our friends, spoiled us of our goods and burnt our dwellings.'[12] In an effort to free his property from the MacDonnells, Argyll returned briefly to Ulster in mid-April to induce Monro and the Scots army to return to fight in Scotland.[13] He failed.

Antrim's continued recalcitrance in Kintyre alarmed the royalists as well as the Scottish covenanters. The king's English supporters feared that it would undermine Charles's bargaining power with parliament, while in Scotland as early as mid-June Lord Loudoun had advised that Antrim and Alasdair MacColla should be ordered back to Ireland since their presence in Kintyre 'may be prejudicial to the King's cause and a hindrance to peace, which all men are looking for'.[14] In Paris it was rumoured that Charles I had made Antrim commander-in-chief of his forces in Scotland, and one prominent royalist was worried that this clandestine arrangement would divide the king's supporters even further: 'for my own part, I do fear that the marquis of Antrim's going to Scotland will be the occasion of some dissension amongst the king's party'.[15] The covenanters, for their part, were terrified that Antrim would serve as a rallying point for the renewal of the king's war effort. Robert Baillie noted with some consternation in June that Antrim and Montrose had refused to lay down their arms and that if 'the king escape to them, it will be a woeful case'.[16]

The covenanters' worst fears were almost realized during the late summer and autumn of 1646 when Antrim mooted 'a design to raise ... 30,000 men

[11] *Ibid.*, From Thursday 6 to Thursday (*sic*) 13 August 1646, no. 75 (London, 1646), p. 609; *ibid.*, ... From Thursday 3 to Thursday 9 September 1646, no. 79 (London, 1646), p. 636.
[12] Cited in Cowan, *Montrose*, p. 253.
[13] Stevenson, *Scottish Covenanters*, pp. 211–14.
[14] Loudoun to Charles I, 15 June 1646 (HMC *rep. 11*, app. 6, p. 111). Also see *Cal. SP Ven., 1643–7*, p. 285.
[15] Leyburn to Clanricard, 18/28 August 1646 (Gilbert, *Ir. confed.*, VI, 105).
[16] Baillie to Spang, 26 June 1646 (Laing, *Letters*, II, 377).

... to reduce Scotland this winter ... and from hence to march into England ... Their quarrel', royalists at the exiled court in France later reported to the king, 'is to be to free your majesty from imprisonment.'[17] And Antrim had indeed secured promises from the leading clans – MacDonald, MacLean, MacRanald, MacLeod (of Harris), MacDougal (of Dunnollie), McNeill (of Carskey) and some MacAllesters (of Loup) together with the lesser Highland clans of Gregor, Grant and Farquharson, and the personal armies of Lords Seaforth, Airlie, Nithsdale, Reay and Huntly – that an army of 23,400 men should be raised on the king's behalf.[18] The outstanding quota of men was to be supplied from Ireland. Montrose's right hand man Ludovic Lindsay, earl of Crawford, was sent to Ireland to discuss the matter with the nuncio, who readily agreed to send the men providing 'they may be satisfied in the effect of my Lord Glamorgan's articles touching the Roman religion'.[19] Crawford then travelled on to Paris to secure approval from the royal family for the venture: the young prince of Wales responded warmly to the enterprise in October and asked Antrim to keep his men ready for action.[20] Early in September, *The kingdomes weekly intelligencer* caught wind of the plan and warned its readers that it would not be long before 'those malignants' descended upon Newcastle to release the king.[21]

Antrim's military endeavours in Scotland were thus no longer merely an embarrassment, but rather a serious threat to any chance of securing a British peace. Finally Charles I himself offered a way to break the deadlock. After being reminded by the Scottish commissioners that he 'had promised they should be free of the enemy in Scotland, and yet they were in and like to do great mischief', the king suggested that 'one of Antrim's gentlemen may come unto me and see in what condition I am, and to receive my express command, and I will undertake that they will lay down arms'.[22] The Scottish privy council was loathe to grant safe conduct to one of Antrim's own men, presumably on the assumption that this would give the perfidious king an

---

[17] Jermyn and Culpepper to Charles I, 9/19 October 1646 (Scrope and Monkhouse (eds.), *State papers*, II, 271).
[18] *Ibid.*; Cowan, *Montrose*, p. 253; Hill, *MacDonnells*, pp. 273–4; Alexander F. Mitchell and James Christie (eds.), *The records of the commissioners of the general assemblies of the church of Scotland holden in Edinburgh in the years 1646 and 1647* (Scottish History Society, vol. XI, Edinburgh, 1892), p. 68.
[19] Jermyn and Culpepper to Charles I, 9/19 October 1646 (Scrope and Monkhouse (eds.), *State papers*, II, 271). Also see Crawford to Charles I, 15 August 1646 (SRO, GD 406/1/2009); *Comment. Rinucc.*, II, 753.
[20] *Clarendon SP*, I, 340; Scrope and Monkhouse (eds.), *State papers*, II, 271.
[21] *The kingdomes weekly intelligencer* ... From Tuesday 1 to Tuesday 8 September 1646, no. 164 (London, 1646), pp. 226, 229, 232.
[22] *Moderate intelligencer* ... From Thursday 17 to Thursday 24 September 1646, no. 81 (London, 1646), p. 641.

opportunity to encourage the marquis; but on 13 October they finally agreed that Charles I should send a messenger, who was 'not forfeited or excommunicated', to treat with Antrim and so to solve 'our troubles'.[23]

Sir James Lesley was therefore once again sent to Kintyre. On this occasion, according to his own account at the Restoration, Lesley was instructed by the king to

> show Antrim that as he trusted my verbal promise to protect him from any inconvenience that should be offered to him or his family, by the taking the oath of association with those in the late Irish rebellion, which begot that interest with them to afford us that party from Ireland to Montrose ... so by that token we do expect that he will disband those people under his command, and trust to our word for the lands of Kintyre, which shall be given to him so soon as the marquis of Argyll is forfeited.

Now at last, in accordance with Charles's wishes, the marquis ordered his army to disband, his compliance purchased by an express verbal undertaking that, as soon as Argyll's estates in Kintyre could be forfeited, he would receive all those lands that he claimed belonged to the MacDonnells.[24]

However, although they obeyed the king's command to be at peace with the covenanters and sent home the troops from other clans, Alasdair MacColla and Antrim nevertheless remained in Kintyre with their own men and continued to ravage Argyll's territory.[25] During the autumn of 1646 it was reported that Antrim's somewhat diminished force took 'diverse forts and sconses about Forlane, quite close to Eyll and [made] much spoil upon Lorne', terrorizing the fishing boats which frequented the waters around the Western Isles.[26] In November *The moderate intelligencer*, which seemed to see the black side of everything, assured its readers that 'There is a ship come

---

[23] Scottish privy council to Charles I, 13 October 1646 (SRO, GD 406/1/2034). Also see Charles I to committee of estates, 3 October 1646, and to the parliament of Scotland, 30 October 1646 (Buckminster, Tollemache MSS 3750, fos. 34v and 38v). I am grateful to Dr John Adamson for bringing these references in the Tollemache MSS my attention.

[24] Hill, *MacDonnells*, p. 306. Also see Scottish privy council to Charles I, 13 October 1646 (HMC *rep. 11*, app. 6, p. 113); Stevenson, *Alasdair MacColla*, p. 231, suggests that Antrim and MacColla had agreed to divide Clan Mor lands between them: Antrim's portion would be Kintyre, and MacColla's Islay. Presumably, under different circumstances (as the Scottish parliament feared), Charles I would have encouraged Antrim's continued resistance. Sir James Lesley certainly suggested this as the Restoration: 'he [Lesley] did hear, in the year 1646, his late royal majesty often express as great and as high a sense of the marquis of Antrim's loyalty and sufferings, as ever he [Lesley] ... heard his majesty speak of any subject', Hill, *MacDonnells*, pp. 306–7. It seems that the king both knew and approved of Crawford's efforts to secure Irish aid for Antrim's cause, Crawford to Charles I, 15 August 1646 (SRO, GD 406/1/2009); *Comment. Rinucc.*, II, 753.

[25] MacBain and Kennedy (eds.), *Reliquiae Celticae*, II, 203.

[26] *Papers from the Scots quarter, containing some passages concerning the king, the*

from Hamburg with arms to the Islands where Antrim and Kilketto are.' The editor also lamented Antrim's failure to lay down his arms and claimed that this 'was not fair play'.[27] In a last desperate attempt to rid Scotland of the marquis's army, commissioners were dispatched from Edinburgh to persuade Antrim and MacColla to be gone from Scotland, but they met with little success; although some stragglers from Montrose's army did surrender, Antrim's brigade – reinforced by arms and munitions from the continent and by eighty barrels of powder and two field pieces received from the nuncio – remained in the Western Isles.[28]

During these months Antrim continued to hope that his fortunes would mend. His confidence was reflected by his eagerness to levy troops for Flanders again. Due to the unsettled nature of affairs in the Western Isles he was unable to travel to Brussels in person again and so, during the late summer of 1646, his wife, who was then resident in Flanders, struck a deal on his behalf and offered Castel Rodrigo 1,200 armed troops. What the duchess asked in return is unclear – although the French agent in Ireland, Dumolin, claimed she demanded an annual pension of 10,000 escudos (roughly £1,900).[29] To ensure that Antrim fulfilled his side of the bargain Castel Rodrigo urged Foissotte 'to attend the marquis of Antrim so that we do not lose the fruit of what has been arranged and accorded'.[30]

Whatever the terms, the contract for the levy was drawn up in October, and vessels to ship a force of 1,200 troops from 'the port of Kintyre in Scotland' to Ostend were hired at once. The conditions of this agreement were significantly different from the contract of November 1645. To begin with the rates

estates of Scotland ... (London, 14 October 1646), pp. 4–5. Also see *A perfect diurnall* ... From Monday 12 to Monday 19 October 1646, no. 168 (London, 1646), p. 1345; *Moderate intelligencer* ... From Thursday 5 to Thursday 12 November 1646, no. 88 (London, 1646), p. 735.

[27] *Moderate intelligencer* ... From Thursday 19 to Thursday 26 November 1646, no. 90 (London, 1646), p. 763. The fact that a ship from Hamburg was harboured off the Passage the following spring adds substance to the *Moderate intelligencer*'s claims, see Jacques Talbot to Du Bosc, December 1647 (AMAE, Correspondence politique, Angleterre, Côte 55, fo. 412r–v).

[28] *Moderate intelligencer* ... From Thursday 26 November to Thursday 3 December 1646, no. 91 (London, 1646), p. 780, and from Thursday 10 to Thursday 17 December 1646, no. 93 (London, 1646), p. 799. On arms from Ireland, see Scrope and Monkhouse (eds.), *State papers*, II, 253.

[29] Gilbert, *Ir. confed.*, VI, 51. The duchess appears to have been poverty stricken during her stay in Flanders. Madame Preston in a letter to her husband noted that the duchess of Buckingham wanted to borrow '3,000 mil fran [sic]' (*Cal. SP Ire.*, 1633–47, p. 603). She remained in Flanders until October 1647 when Rinuccini paid for her passage back to Ireland, Dumolin to Brienne, 5/15 October 1647 (BL, Harl. MSS 4551, fo. 266v), and *Comment. Rinucc.*, II, 757–8.

[30] *Relación de los servicios de D. Franciso Foissotte* ... (Biblioteca Nacional, Madrid, MS 2367, fo. 10v).

charged by the shipper (Jacques Le Goveurneur) were exceedingly high: he demanded 30 florins (£2.30) for every man reaching Ostend (10 florins more per man than Van der Ripen's price) and he required half of this – some 18,000 florins/£1,385 – in cash and in advance. He further stipulated that if the journey from Kintyre to Flanders took more than fifteen days, a daily surcharge of 100 florins/£7.70 per boat would be payable to cover the cost of feeding at least 1,200 mouths.[31] Yet the remarkable speed with which the negotiations were concluded and the efficiency with which the transportation was arranged once again clearly illustrates how desperately trained soldiers were required in Flanders.[32]

Castel Rodrigo's confidence in Antrim's ability to raise seasoned soldiers for Spanish service also reflects the advantageous position that Spain enjoyed in Ireland after the summer of 1646. There were a number of reasons for this. First, Pope Innocent X clearly favoured Spain; and therefore the papal nuncio in Ireland, in accordance with his master's wishes, was also obliged to favour the Spanish cause there. Bellings feared that the pope 'might have disposed the Irish to have an absolute dependence upon the Catholic king [Philip IV]'.[33] Second, Spanish influence over the nuncio and his party was greatly enhanced by the fact that their envoys (Diego de la Torre and François Foissotte) had been carefully cultivating their own party among the Old Irish and the clerics; Generals Owen Roe O'Neill and Thomas Preston, the archbishops of Cashel and Tuam and of Down, the bishops of Ferns and Clogher were all Spanish pensioners, as was Antrim.[34] One French traveller,

---

[31] 'Registre aux ordres', 26 October/5 November 1646 (AGR, SEG 46, fos. 172v–3). On 25 October 1646, the day after the initial agreement with Le Goveurneur was concluded, a warrant was issued paying him the 18,000 florins, which had been requested as an advance payment, see *ibid.*, 25 October/4 November 1646 (*ibid.*, fos. 154v–5). Also see p. 157 above.

[32] Consulta of council of state, 1/11 May 1647 (AGS, Eo. 2523, unfol.). The most illuminating indication of how urgently Antrim's recruits were needed was the bizarre strategem considered by the Flanders Treasury in order to pay the 36,000 florins/£2,270 needed for shipping at a time when the Spanish crown was virtually bankrupt. The Pagaduría General, the military Treasury in the Netherlands, had been unable to pay Jacques Le Goveurneur his 18,000 florin advance and was therefore forced to ask García de Yllán, a Portuguese banker based in Antwerp and victualler of the Army of Flanders, to pay Le Goveurneur on their behalf 'with the right to reimburse himself with the first money from Spain to arrive in January 1647 ... and if there is no money in January 1647, then from the first arrival of money after that', see 'Registre aux ordres', 25 October/5 November 1646 (AGR, SEG 46, fos. 172v–3). For further details on these Portuguese bankers, and on García de Yllán in particular, see James C. Boyajian, *Portuguese bankers at the court of Spain 1626–1650* (New Brunswick, 1983), pp. 35, 152, 157, 177.

[33] *Desid. cur. Hib.*, p. 267. Also see *Cal. SP Dom., 1645–7*, p. 52.

[34] Foissotte to Rosas, 14/24 October 1644 (AGS, GA 1570 unfol.); La Torre to Philip IV, 20/30 April 1647 (AGS, Eo.2523 unfol.).

Monsieur de la Boullaye le Gouz, who visited Ireland in 1644 noted how successful the Spanish envoys had been in rallying popular support. The Irish, he recorded in his journal, 'love the Spaniards as their brothers, the French as their friends'.[35] This was particularly true in the privateering and merchant communities of southern Ireland. After Wexford fell to the confederation in September 1642 the lords justices reported to London that 'the rebels have set up Spanish colours on their walls in defiance of the king and kingdom of England', while a popular chant heard in the streets of Wexford during the early 1640s was 'God bless the king of Spain; For but for him we should all be slain.'[36] The extent of Spanish influence over the town of Waterford and the proficiency with which the Irish clerics in the city spoke Spanish also distressed the French envoy.[37] Finally, throughout the summer and autumn of 1646 the Spanish envoys had wholeheartedly supported the Old Irish party, which under Rinuccini's leadership had gone from strength to strength.[38]

To begin with, on 5 June 1646, at the battle of Benburb, Owen Roe O'Neill and his Catholic army of 5,000 at last routed the Scottish army under Monro. This was the military highlight of the Irish Civil Wars for the confederates because it meant that Monro's forces (now reduced to *c.* 3,500) were no longer a threat. But as far as Antrim was concerned this text-book victory meant little, for it had failed to draw away the remaining Scottish soldiers from his estates. In fact, Benburb merely served to prolong the war in Ireland, for instead of capitalizing on his victory and ridding Ulster of the Scottish and parliamentary garrisons, O'Neill marched south to Kilkenny to suborn those who favoured a peace with the king and thus 'helped to strengthen the nuncio's intransigence and to upset the arrangements which had been proceeding for a peace'.[39]

The declaration of the 'Ormond peace' between the Irish royalists and the confederates (July – August 1646) therefore threw events in Ireland back into the melting pot and further divided an already fragmented nation into 'a woeful spectacle, cantonized into severall sundry factions, drawing all divers

---

[35] Croker (ed.), *The tour*, p. 43.
[36] Lords justices to the commissioners for Irish affairs, 1 September 1642 (*Ormonde MSS*, II, 185–6). By 1647 it was reported that Spain had established a court of admiralty in Wexford, Dumolin to Brienne, 28 January/7 February 1648 (BL, Harl. MSS 4551, fo. 247).
[37] Dumolin to Mazarin, 8/18 May 1646 (Gilbert, *Ir. confed.*, V, 340). Also see p. 342.
[38] La Torre's secret accounts reveal that he did indeed subsidize the nuncio's cause with modest payments throughout the autumn of 1646, see accounts of La Torre (AGS, TMC, Legajo 4A/2635, unfol.).
[39] Gerald A. Hayes-McCoy, *Irish battles. A military history of Ireland* (Belfast, 1989), p. 197. Also see Casway, *Owen Roe O'Neill*, p. 139, and Stevenson, *Scottish Covenanters*, pp. 233–5.

waies, and driveing on several interests'.⁴⁰ The ranks of the Irish confederates were irremediably split between the Old English, who would have been satisfied with tacit toleration and the freedom to worship quietly while remaining loyal subjects to the crown, and the Old Irish (led by Rinuccini), who were loath to settle with the king without first securing formal freedom of worship for the Catholic religion.

The crisis reached a climax early in August when Rinuccini and the clerical faction at Kilkenny declared the 'Ormond peace' unacceptable and convened a legatine synod at Waterford which proclaimed that confederate Catholics adhering to the peace had broken the oath of association.⁴¹ On 1 September the Waterford synod went further and excommunicated all who favoured the 'Ormond peace', and on 18 September Rinuccini arrived at Kilkenny to dictate the terms for an acceptable agreement and ordered the arrest of the 'Ormondists' within the council, including Lord Muskerry, Lord Mountgarret, Sir Piers Crosby, Sir Lucas Dillon and Richard Bellings. Dumolin, who was busy fortifying his house in Kilkenny, reported the ensuing chaos to Ormond and added that it was rumoured that Antrim would be recalled to act as a mediator.⁴² On 26 September a new supreme council – free from Ormond's influence – was nominated. According to the account ascribed to Nicholas Plunkett, Rinuccini 'compose[d] a council of his own bigoted creatures, himself the President ... [or] Generalissimo'.⁴³ Antrim's brother, Alexander, was one of the 'bigoted creatures' nominated by the nuncio to sit on the supreme council, and Antrim, who was still in Scotland, thus gained a voice within the new regime.⁴⁴

Meanwhile the confederate armies marched on Dublin.⁴⁵ Possession of the capital would have placed the confederates in a superior position to the parliamentarians, who were their only real opponents by the winter of 1646; but although their armies reached Lucan, Dublin was not taken because of poor weather and because O'Neill and Preston quarrelled violently, ending in the latter entering into secret negotiations with Ormond. As a result the siege of Dublin was abandoned and a great opportunity was lost. The confederates then fell back on their usual remedy to a crisis by calling a general assembly, which frittered away three months in recriminations and reconciliations.

---

⁴⁰ *A letter from Sir Lewis Dyve to the lord marquis of Newcastle* ... (The Hague, 10/20 July 1650), p. 5.
⁴¹ Carte, *Ormond*, III, 253.
⁴² Dumolin to Ormond, 14 September 1646 (Bodl., Carte MSS 28, fo. 509).
⁴³ NLI, MS 345, p. 55.
⁴⁴ It is even possible that the marquis himself returned briefly to Ireland during September – as Hill, *MacDonnells*, pp. 273–4, asserts – in order to pay homage to Rinuccini and to provide for a MacDonnell presence in the new regime.
⁴⁵ Carte, *Ormond*, III, 247–52; Casway, *Owen Roe O'Neill*, pp. 141, 149–52.

But at least calling another general assembly brought the marquis of Antrim back to Ireland. He left MacColla and his men in Kintyre and arrived in Ireland on 7 January 1647. He was warmly received by Rinuccini who according to Clanricard sent his personal coach to Ross to welcome him, while 'a great number of the Irish nobility, splendidly arrayed on horseback, met him'.[46] Hardly surprisingly, Rinuccini was eager to secure the marquis's support for his coup d'état and in one letter described him as 'a most considerable and faithful child of ours, upon whom this congregation doth look as a principal protector of the Roman Catholic faith'. Certainly, during his absence in Scotland, the nuncio – using the Franciscan Father Hegarty – had remained in constant communication with his 'faithful child' and had kept him abreast of the latest developments in Ireland.[47]

Antrim reached Kilkenny on 10 January, just as the seventh general assembly convened to discuss the rejection or ratification of the 'Ormond peace'.[48] 'The morning of that day', noted C. P. Meehan in his nineteenth-century history of the Catholic confederates, 'saw the confederate representatives assisting at High Mass in the cathedral'.[49] Rinuccini sat on the left of the altar, with eleven bishops seated close to him, and behind the bishops sat the temporal peers, who undoubtedly included Antrim for, according to his enemies at the Restoration, the marquis 'sat in public assemblies, and in great solemnity through Kilkenny Street bore up one end of the canopy over the head of the said nuncio'.[50]

Later the same day, in Kilkenny castle – Ormond's family residence – Antrim proposed to the general assembly that the confederates should send yet more reinforcements to Scotland where they would join up with the forces which Montrose and Crawford hoped to raise in the king's name.[51] The assembly received his proposal warmly. After reminiscing about 'the great benefit accrued unto the king by a small party heretofore employed from

---

[46] *Comment. Rinucc.*, II, 752; Carte, *Ormond*, VI, 490.
[47] Rinuccini to Antrim, 28 August 1646 (Scrope and Monkhouse (eds.), *State papers*, II, 253). Also see Hill, *MacDonnells*, p. 331. For details on Hegarty, see p. 94 above, and Giblin, *The Irish Franciscan mission*, p. 187.
[48] Charles Lambert to Ormond, 10 and 12 January 1647 (Bodl., Carte MSS 20, fo. 103); Carte, *Ormond*, VI, 489, 490, 491.
[49] C. P. Meehan, *The Confederation of Kilkenny* (Dublin, 1860), pp. 204–5. Meehan incorrectly suggested that no serious business was discussed on the first day. In fact Meehan failed even to allude to Antrim's proposed expedition in his account.
[50] Petition of adventurers and soldiers to king, [August, 1663] (Bodl., Carte MSS 44, fos. 376–7).
[51] Henrietta Maria to Montrose, 26 January/5 February 1647 (SRO, GD 220/3/99); Sir James MacDonnell to the prince of Wales, 18 May 1647 (Christ Church, Oxford, Brown correspondence, 'M–P', unfol.)

hence into Scotland' and, mindful of the advantages of making Scotland 'the seat of war', it agreed to Antrim's design and ordered that an expedition should be dispatched to Scotland as quickly as possible.[52] Antrim smugly reported this victory in his own account of the day's proceedings, noting that he had received 'permission to raise five thousand [men] and [was] given £7,000'.[53] The burden of paying this was to be divided between the cities and corporation towns of Leinster, Munster and Connaught; while the task of provisioning Antrim's force was also divided between the counties occupied by the confederate armies in the three provinces. County Wexford, for instance, was responsible for providing the marquis with 300 barrels of corn by the end of May.[54]

Antrim's success on 10 January horrified Ormond and his supporters, who had fervently hoped that the general assembly would have discussed and approved the 'Ormond peace' instead of being side-tracked by Antrim's schemes. The following day, when the peace was debated, Clanricard even felt it necessary to reassure the lord lieutenant that despite Antrim 'and all opposers' he himself would remain loyal.[55] Two days later Ormond was informed that Antrim met with most of the other Irish leaders in Kilkenny where, it was claimed, 'they will contrive and design all the mischief that possibly they may against your Excellency and your party'.[56] The prediction was borne out on 2 February when, no doubt thanks in part to Antrim's considerable influence over the rank and file members of the general assembly, the 'Ormond peace' was rejected.[57]

Antrim, no doubt revelling in the shift of events in his favour, now sent a Scottish Protestant messenger called James Boyd, one of his chief tenants from County Antrim, to France 'for new commissions' from the queen and the prince of Wales.[58] It was hoped that the fresh invasion from Ireland

---

[52] Order of the general assembly, 10 January 1647 (St Peter's College, Wexford, Hore MSS F, p. 239).
[53] 'A narrative of the marquis's deportment ... ', undated [c. 1663] (PRONI, D2977/5/1/2). Also see Carte, *Ormond*, VI, 493. In fact the marquis had only been awarded £5,000 for his mission.
[54] Order by the general assembly, 23 March 1647 (St Peter's College, Wexford, Hore MSS F, p. 240, E, p. 1897); *Cal. SP Ire.*, *1633–47*, p. 666.
[55] Clanricard to Ormond, 11 January 1647 (Carte, *Ormond*, VI, 493).
[56] Charles Lambert to Ormond, 12 January 1647 (Bodl., Carte MSS 20, fo. 117).
[57] Hill, *MacDonnells*, pp. 331–2; Meehan, *Confederation*, pp. 206–7; *Moderate intelligencer ... From Thursday 11 to Thursday 18 February 1647*, no. 102 (London, 1647), p. 913. The adventurers were thus quite right to claim (when they opposed Antrim's restoration) that he was totally opposed to peace with Ormond.
[58] 'A narrative of the marquis's deportment ... ', undated [c. 1663] (PRONI, D2977/5/1/2). Boyd shuttled back and forth between Ireland and France on Antrim's behalf until May 1648, *Comment. Rinucc.*, III, 386–7.

would form part of the plan, mooted by Montrose and Crawford, to win Scotland for the king using Irish resources and men. Sure enough in February (presumably after Boyd's arrival), Oliver Fitzwilliam wrote from Paris to the supreme council, on behalf of 'our English court', urging them 'to keep in mind your great supplies for the marquis of Antrim, by which you will keep Ireland from ever being the seat of war'.[59] While, on the eve of his departure for Ireland the following month, a royalist agent was instructed by the prince of Wales to encourage the Irish 'to send such sufficient succors to the earl of Antrim in Scotland, as may continue a footing there, and so confirm the king's party in that kingdom'.[60] Meanwhile the marquis was doing his utmost to ensure that his new troops were levied. On 18 February, he mortgaged one of his warships, the *Mary of Antrim*, to James Dillon and Michael Tooting, Wexford merchants, as collateral for 'certain sums of money'.[61]

As always, however, Antrim had more than one iron in the fire. Early in 1647, even as he was making every effort to rekindle the war in Scotland and to raise troops for Flanders, he made it clear to the French agent in Ireland that he would be prepared, providing the price was right, to send his mercenaries to France instead.[62] In the event the French considered it futile to recruit Antrim as a *créature* on the grounds that he was too closely allied to the 'Spanish faction'.[63] So the marquis continued his efforts to raise sufficient troops, at the supreme council's expense, both to fulfil his obligation to Castel Rodrigo and to bolster the MacDonnell presence in the Western Isles.[64] The French ambassador in Edinburgh, who monitored all troop movements closely, perversely hoped that Antrim's forces would indeed launch a new offensive in Scotland, since 'France would thereby also derive some advantage, for it would give the marquis of Antrim an opportunity of occupying here the thousand men that he is raising in Ireland to send to Spain.'[65] But Montereul need not have worried, for the following week he discovered that (fortunately for France) Antrim's plan had misfired. 'As regards the thousand men the marquis of Antrim was to send to Spain [Montereul reported], I have

---

[59] Fitzwilliam to the supreme council, 9 and 25 February 1647 (Gilbert, *Ir. confed.*, VI, 180, 182).
[60] George Leyburn, *The Memoirs of George Leyburn ... chaplain to Henrietta Maria ... being a journal of his agency for Prince Charles in Ireland ...* (London, 1722), p. 8.
[61] Petition of James Dillon to Ormond, *c.* 21 April 1649 (Bodl., Carte MSS 155, fos. 71–2v).
[62] Dumolin to Brienne, 7 February 1647 NS (BL, Harl. MSS 4551, fo. 247).
[63] Brienne to Grignon, 22 April/2 May, 29 April/7 May, 13/23 May, 15/25 July 1648 (BN, Fonds Français 15,996, fos. 339v, 349v, 367v, 424v). *Cal. SP Ven.*, 1643–7, p. 308, suggested that both France and Spain were competing for these men.
[64] This is also what Dumolin believed, Dumolin to Brienne, (BL, Harl. MSS 4551, fos. 252–3).
[65] Montereul to Cardinal Mazarin, 2/12 March 1647 (*Diplomatic correspondence*, II, 41).

seen letters in which it is stated that a ship from Spain had arrived in order to take a part of them, but that it had returned without having a single man.'[66]

Despite Antrim's failure to rendezvous with the Spanish troopship he continued to try to muster forces in Ireland. But the failure of the corporate towns in the province of Leinster to contribute £2,000 out of the £5,000 voted by the general assembly jeopardized the entire expedition. In an attempt to circumvent this, the supreme council ordered one of its members (Nicholas French, bishop of Ferns) to advance £800 from the tenths of prizes collected by Wexford, Ross and Enniscorthy. Other bishops were likewise instructed to contribute £600 out of the tithes of their dioceses, and the oustanding £600 was to be paid by the town of Kilkenny. The cash was to be forwarded as quickly as possible to Nicholas FitzHarris, a Ross merchant, or any other agent nominated by the marquis.[67] In addition to this £5,000, the council at the end of March voted the marquis £300 towards supplies for Scotland from the tenths of prizes due to the council.[68]

Even so, and despite the enthusiastic support of Rinuccini and his clerics, progress with the levies remained painfully slow.[69] The marquis blamed Owen Roe's intervention for the delays, and O'Neill was indeed terrified that a new Scottish enterprise would undermine his position in Ulster; 'I suppose all the nation knew how little kindness was between Owen Roe and me' the marquis later complained, 'who often fouled ... my undertakings ... for the king's service'.[70] Even Clanricard regretted (in a letter to Antrim) the consequences of the confederates' inability to mobilize their resources quickly:

There is none can have a more deep apprehension and sad impression than myself of the king's condition in England; and that falls more heavily upon me by the consideration of our misfortunes here that have continued in such a lasting division that we have not attended the sending of those expected supplies that might probably have prevented much of the inconveniences that have since happened, to the hazard of monarchy, religion and all other interests of our own.[71]

---

[66] *Idem* to *idem*, 9/19 March 1647 (*ibid.*, II, 50).
[67] *Cal. SP Ire., 1633–47*, p. 723.
[68] *Ibid.*; order by the supreme council, 1647 (St Peter's College, Wexford, Hore MSS F, p. 240).
[69] The corn still had not been delivered by June and therefore the council issued another order requesting the immediate delivery of '300 barrels of wheat, oatmeal and rye' to the marquis, see order by the supreme council, 7 June 1647 (St Peter's College, Wexford, Hore MSS F, p. 236).
[70] Hill, *MacDonnells*, p. 301.
[71] Clanricard to Antrim, 31 March 1647 (*Clanricarde letter-book*, p. 383). It is possible that Dumolin had a hand in the delays since he believed that these troops also were ultimately destined for service in Flanders, Gilbert, *Ir. confed.*, VII, 321–3.

Preparations to send the two regiments of Irish soldiers to Scotland continued until the summer of 1647. The necessary arms and ammunition for the venture (according to Montereul) arrived in Ireland towards the end of April, when:

> It is reported from the west of Scotland that a Dutch ship carrying ammunition to the marquis of Antrim, having been obliged by bad weather to take shelter in the Lewis islands, the captain, contrary to what he expected, was well received by the earl of Seaforth's people, and obtained permission to continue his voyage as soon as the weather permits.[72]

However, as late as July powder, match and lead were still being gathered from the various provinces.[73]

These incessant delays forced the marquis to abandon all hope of sending a portion of this new levy to Flanders via Kintyre, as had been promised in the autumn of 1646. Instead, MacColla's veterans were now offered. MacColla requested permission from the government in Edinburgh to leave Scotland 'with his men' provided they were allowed to go to Spain. The Scottish parliament, eager to be rid of them and fearing a fresh invasion from Ireland, intended to give his request serious consideration until Argyll intervened and vindictively asserted (much to Montereul's delight) that he 'would effectively deprive him of the means of leaving the country and of taking men with him'.[74]

Argyll was true to his word and did indeed ensure that MacColla's regiment was never shipped to Spain. On 24 May, Leslie's army entered Kintyre and, in a series of encounters, routed MacColla's main force, still awaiting reinforcements from Ireland. Thus in one fell swoop Antrim lost not only his foothold in Kintyre but also, it would seem, a large part of the force he had hoped to transport to the territories of Philip IV. 'The defeat of MacDonald', Montereul reported to Mazarin, '[has] removed from me every reason to fear that Spain may obtain forces from this kingdom.'[75] But not all of the brigade was lost. Shortly after the covenanter offensive began in earnest Alasdair retreated to Ireland with the rump of the force he had brought over in 1644,

---

[72] Montereul to Cardinal Mazarin, 20/30 April 1647 (*Diplomatic correspondence*, II, 117).
[73] *Cal. SP Ire., 1633–47*, p. 734.
[74] Montereul to Cardinal Mazarin, 11/21 May 1647 (*Diplomatic correspondence*, II, 140). Also see Stevenson, *Alasdair MacColla*, p. 230. The ambassador also hoped, however, that it would be possible to divert these troops – whom Antrim 'was intending for service in Spain' – to France, see Montereul to Brienne, 12/22 March and 5/15 June 1647 (Bodl., Carte MSS 83, fos. 148v–50v, 179v–81). Also see 'History of events, 1635–62' (NLS, MS 2263, fos. 195v–6).
[75] Montereul to Mazarin 15/25 June 1647 (*Diplomatic correspondence*, II, 167–8). Also see David Stevenson, 'The massacre at Dunaverty, 1647', *Scottish Studies*, 19 (1975), pp. 30–6.

188   *Civil War and Restoration in the three Stuart kingdoms*

and early in June 1647 it was reported in Dublin that 'all, or most of the force, late in Scotland with Colketto [*sic*], are for certain landed in Ulster'. They came in fifteen vessels, which they 'ran upon the sands near Dundrum'. From County Down the brigade, which was estimated to number 800 men, marched to Charlemount.[76] MacColla was subsequently followed (according to an anonymous chronicler of the MacDonnells) by 'all the Irish that lay' in Daniel laird of Clanranald's lands, under Angus, laird of Glengarry's command.[77]

Antrim, jealous of Owen Roe O'Neill and perhaps anxious to spread his influence around, was reluctant to allow these veterans to serve in Ulster and so it was decided that MacColla's brigade should join the Army of Munster and that Glengarry's men should be seconded to fight in the Army of Leinster.[78] But the marquis's Scottish venture was over: after three years, his forces had been driven out and, from this point on, his fortunes largely depended on the volatile situation in Ireland.

ANTRIM AND THE SUPREME COUNCIL

Antrim experienced considerable problems in levying troops for Scotland which is surprising given the political power which he wielded during the first half of 1647. From January onwards he had played a key role in the general assembly by leading the opposition to any peace with Ormond.[79] On 17 March his position was formalized when the general assembly selected him to the new supreme council which, unlike the others, was dominated by supporters of the nuncio.[80]

---

[76] John Rushworth, *Historical collections of private passages of state* ... (7 vols., London, 1659–1701; later edns 8 vols., 1680–1701, 1721), part IV, I, p. 561. Also see *Moderate intelligencer* ... *From Thursday 10 to Thursday 17 June 1647*, no. 118 (London, 1647), p. 1127; Stevenson, *Alasdair MacColla*, pp. 234–41, 245; *idem*, 'The massacre at Dunaverty', p. 30; McKerral, *Kintyre*, pp. 49–66.

[77] 'History of the MacDonalds' (PRONI, D358, p. 9). Also see Robert Menteith, *The history of the troubles of Great Britain, containing a particular account of the most remarkable passages in Scotland* ([London], 1739), p. 254. Sir Charles Coote reported back to London that a large number of soldiers 'suspected to be Highlanders driven out of Scotland by the state's forces there' in 'certain frigates' en route to Connaught were picking off enemy shipping in Derry harbour. Already these vessels had 'taken above thirty small barques belonging to this kingdom and to Scotland freighted with provisions and other commodities' with disastrous consequences for the parliamentary garrison there, see Coote to the committee at Derby House, 11 June 1647 (Bodl., Carte MSS 67, fo. 133r–v).

[78] Stevenson, *Alasdair MacColla*, pp. 247–8; Gilbert, *Contemp. hist. 1641–52*, I, 153.

[79] See p. 184 above.

[80] 'The names of the supreme council chosen by the late assembly at Kilkenny, 1647' (Bodl., Carte MSS 21, fo. 571v). The positioning of this document in the Carte papers among other

Antrim's eagerness to serve as a member of the supreme council marked a new phase in his political career and illustrates his willingness to be formally associated with the Irish Catholic – as opposed to the royalist – cause. For while he had been intimately involved with the confederates since the autumn of 1643, when he took the oath of association, he had only served on the council briefly in 1644 and with Charles I's express approval.[81] The supreme council was at once an executive, legislative and judicial body with supreme authority in all matters civil and military. The army generals and provincial administrators were to obey its decrees and keep it abreast of national developments; and if they failed to do so the council had the authority to punish them, since it had the right to determine all matters capital, criminal and civil (unless the general assembly decided otherwise).[82]

Since Rinuccini had, on 11 January, resigned as president of the confederate government formed at Waterford the previous September (in order according to Meehan 'to conciliate and unite all parties'), a new president of the supreme council was needed. Circumstantial evidence of three sorts strongly suggests that from the moment he joined the council Antrim served as president. First, contemporaries specifically referred to him as 'the president of the council'. For example, George Leyburn noted that he had sat 'in a chair not far from my Lord of Antrim their Lord President' during his visit to Kilkenny in April 1647.[83] While Patrick Barnewall, in the summer of 1647, assured the king of Spain that Antrim 'is President of the Council'.[84] Second, at the Restoration, it was claimed that, after Antrim had successfully frustrated the 'Ormond peace', he was 'made president of the confederate council, and signed all orders and was of all committees'.[85] Third, these assertions are corroborated by the fact that Antrim's signature does indeed appear on all

---

documents dating from November 1647 misleadingly suggests that it refers to the supreme council chosen by the eighth general assembly (12 November – 24 December 1647). However, internal evidence – naming Owen Roe O'Neill who was present for the seventh, but not the eighth general assembly, as a member for Ulster – suggests that this document refers to April 1647.

[81] See pp. 134–5 above for details. Alexander, by contrast, was a familiar face at the supreme council and had served on it continuously since July 1644.

[82] Gilbert, *Ir. confed.*, VI, 212.

[83] Leyburn, *Memoirs of George Leyburn*, p. 12.

[84] Barnewall to Philip IV, undated (because it was presented in person) AGS, Eo. 2525, unfol.). Also see consulta of the council of state, 20/30 July 1647 (*ibid.*, 2523, unfol.; there is also an undated copy of this consulta in Eo. 2525 unfol.). In a memorial presented by Monasterio, undated [*c.* late 1647] (*ibid.*, 3019, unfol.), Antrim was described as 'president of the council of war of Ireland'. He was also regarded by the French as president of the supreme council, see Dumolin to Brienne, 30 April/10 May 1647 (BL, Harl. MSS 4551, fo. 249v).

[85] Hill, *MacDonnells*, p. 332.

surviving orders and legislation from the council during the first half of 1647. Moreover, his was always the first signature, an honour usually reserved for the president.[86]

The assembly's choice of Antrim as their leader was based on solid foundations. Socially, he was the most senior member of the supreme council, rivalled only by Lord Muskerry who, as Ormond's brother-in-law, had unacceptable 'Ormondist' sympathies. Moreover, he was relatively experienced in the workings of the confederation and enjoyed a popular following within the general assembly, where it was felt that he was the only suitable person to head the government.[87] Inadvertently Ormond paid tribute to this when he informed Clanricard that personally he would not care what happened to Glamorgan and Antrim 'if there were not a natural propension in this people to love their cozeners'![88]

On ideological grounds the marquis was also sound. Despite his royalist record, he was evidently a staunch Catholic with no 'Ormondist' sympathies. Antrim soon proved his devotion to Catholicism again by taking the revised oath of association early in March. He thereby swore that he would never lay down arms until full religious toleration for the Catholic religion was granted, until the Catholic clergy should secure all their pre-Reformation privileges, immunities and jurisdictions, and until the clergy should be restored to their benefices as they were before the rebellion. It was a hollow promise on Antrim's part, as subsequent events were to show; but, in the short term, it demonstrated where his loyalties lay.

The marquis also enjoyed a good working relationship with the most powerful man in Catholic Ireland, the papal nuncio, who appeared to like the marquis personally. For instance, he had sent his coach to meet him upon his arrival in Ireland the previous January, and later that spring he provided the duchess of Buckingham with the funds to bring her back to Ireland from Flanders.[89] Antrim and the nuncio also shared a desire to continue the war in Scotland (though for very different reasons), and even an interest in privateering.[90] It seems that their frigates hunted together regularly while Antrim

---

[86] For numerous examples, see orders of the supreme council, 4–8 April 1647 (*Cal. SP Ire., 1633–47*, pp. 605–6); and orders of the supreme council, 4 April–12 May 1647 (PRO, SP 63/263/98; *ibid.*, 63/264/12/19/56, pp. 130, 148, 167–8).

[87] Dumolin to Brienne, 30 April/10 May 1647 (BL, Harl. MSS 4551, fo. 249v); *ibid.*, 14/24 May, 1647 (*ibid.*, fo. 258v). For a list of members see T. de Burgo, *Hibernia dominicana siue historia provinciae Hiberniae ordinis praedictorum* ... (n.p., 1762), pp. 884–5. I am grateful to Father Donal Cregan for bringing this reference to my attention.

[88] Ormond to Clanricard, 8 January 1647 (Carte, *Ormond*, VI, 489).

[89] See p. 183 and n. 29 above.

[90] Upon his arrival in Ireland the nuncio had claimed that he had 'four frigates to join with the rest of that nation', NLI, MS 345, p. 53. Details on only two of his warships have been located, see Ohlmeyer, '"The Dunkirk of Ireland"', pp. 34–5, 37.

readily put his own men-of-war at Rinuccini's disposal.[91] In addition, the nuncio and his followers controlled the privateering ports of Wexford, Ross, Duncannon, Waterford, Limerick and Galway, which served as a further factor to bind Antrim firmly to his party.[92]

Finally, Antrim had been carefully cultivating his own power base among the Old Irish community outside Ulster and by 1647 had built up a sizable following throughout the country. Thanks to his sisters' marriages he already enjoyed strong connections in Counties Meath, Louth, Sligo and Kerry. He now reinforced his connections in Leinster by securing the support of the Kavanaghs of County Carlow and the O'Byrnes of County Wicklow. The timely marriages of two of the most eligible MacDonnell men (Sir James MacDonnell, his second cousin, and Alasdair MacColla's son Daniel) to two daughters of Sir Daniel O'Brien of Duagh, County Clare, who served on the eighth supreme council, added to his patronage network in Munster.[93] In addition, largely due to his privateering activities, he secured the support of prominent figures in Counties Waterford and Wexford. For instance, Hugh Rochford, a lawyer, recorder of Wexford and a member of the seventh supreme council, was one of his staunchest supporters, as was Dr Walter Enos, later president of the Irish College at Louvain, who spent most of the 1640s in Wexford, and Nicholas FitzHarris, a prominent merchant from Ross. The building up of centres of support outside Ulster during the later 1640s was no coincidence, but rather a political statement that the marquis now intended to throw in his lot with the Old Irish faction. He also looked to members of the clergy for support. Oliver Darcy, a Dominican and bishop of Dromore, was an Antrim client, as was Patrick Crelly, Cistercian abbot of Newry – described at the Restoration as 'the great intelligencer and confident of the said marquis and of the late usurper [Oliver Cromwell]'. He loyally

---

[91] Thomas Birch (ed.), *An inquiry into the share which Charles I had in the transactions of the earl of Glamorgan* (London, 1756), p. 243; *Comment. Rinucc.*, II, 381.

[92] After June 1647, when Dublin was handed over to the parliamentarians, Ormond commanded no major Irish port. Even after the truce with Lord Inchiquin, in May 1648, the lord lieutenant only had nominal control over the important Munster ports of Youghal, Cork and Kinsale, see John A. Murphy, 'The politics of the Munster protestants, 1641–49', *Journal of the Cork Historical and Archaeological Society*, 76, no. 223 (Jan.–June 1971), pp. 16–19; Liam Irwin, 'Politics, religion and economy: Cork in the seventeenth century', *ibid.*, 85, nos. 241–2 (Jan.–Dec. 1980), pp. 8–9; Ormond to Piers Butler, 22 August 1646 (Bodl., Carte MSS 18, fo. 320); Lambert to Ormond, 25 December 1646 (*ibid.*, 19, fo. 699v).

[93] Hector McDonnell, 'A noble pretension', *The Glynns*, 8 (1980), pp. 22–3.

served Antrim as his agent, mentor and friend throughout the 1640s and early 1650s.[94]

For all these reasons, from March until November 1647, when the eighth general assembly convened, the marquis was made responsible for the day-to-day administration of, and the tactics employed by, the confederate armies of Leinster, Munster and Ulster, for the smooth running of the confederate provincial assemblies, for the distribution of confederate material and financial resources, and for dealing with foreign princes.[95] At the meetings of the supreme council he allocated aid out of local excise duties to 'the poor Clares' of Wexford and Athlone and to the nuns of Ross; he awarded salaries, pensions and expenses to government officials; and he arbitrated in disputes over land and debts.[96] He oversaw the levy of fresh recruits for the Army of Leinster and the payment of compensation to supporters who had suffered at the hands of confederate troops.[97] He also acted as the principal liaison officer with the lord lieutenant, whose fortunes were now at their lowest ebb; and it was to Antrim that Ormond wrote, no doubt reluctantly, if he wanted any favours from the supreme council. Thus, late in April the lord lieutenant was worried about the treatment of two royalist officers imprisoned in Kilkenny castle and requested that Antrim should take care of the matter. He also asked that a package addressed to Sir George Hamilton, which had been intercepted by confederate forces, be forwarded to his sister, Lady Hamilton.[98] The following month, he complained that a party of royalist troops had been attacked and imprisoned by soldiers under Preston's command and asked Antrim to secure their release.[99]

During this period much of Antrim's energy was focused on how best to take Dublin. Having failed to capture the city by force, the confederates now tried diplomacy, but it was too late: Ormond had already resolved to surrender the capital, together with all other remaining royalist strongholds, to the

---

[94] Some observations of the adventurers and soldiers, [April], 1661 (Bodl., Carte MSS 44, fo. 330); *Cal. SP Ire., 1633–47*, p. 396; Gilbert, *Contemp. hist. 1641–52*, I, 103; Stevenson, *Alasdair MacColla*, pp. 87, 243. For further details on Crelly, see pp. 204–9, 212–14, 220–1, 223–5, 228–9, 232, 234–5, 253 below.

[95] For numerous examples, see orders of the supreme council, 4 April – 8 April 1647, *Cal. SP Ire., 1633–47*, pp. 605–6; orders of the supreme council, 4 April – 12 May 1647 (PRO, SP 63/263/98; *ibid.*, 63/264/12/19/56, pp. 130, 148, 167–8); supreme council to Philip IV, 21 April 1647 (AGS, Eo. 2523, unfol.); supreme council to Mazarin, 27 April 1647 (AMAE, Correspondence politique, Angleterre, Côte 55, fo. 170); *Comment. Rinucc.*, II, 620, 658, 664, 668, 693.

[96] *Cal. SP Ire., 1633–47*, pp. 659, 663, 665, 667, 715.

[97] *Ibid.*, pp. 675, 735.

[98] Ormond to Antrim, 21 April 1647 (Bodl., Carte MSS 20, fo. 631); *idem* to *idem*, 23 April 1647 (*ibid.*, fo. 643).

[99] Ormond to Antrim, 10 May 1647 (Bodl., Carte MSS 21, fo. 56).

English parliamentarians rather than hand it over to the 'papist rebels'. The rejection of the 'Ormond peace' by the general assembly in January 1647 merely served to strengthen his determination. Antrim did his best to persuade the lord lieutenant to break off his negotiations with parliament and to win his Catholic supporters over to the confederate camp.[100] On behalf of the general assembly he wrote to Lord Dunsany, Sir Nicholas White, Sir Henry Talbot and Sir Andrew Aylmer pleading for their support.[101] But he met with little success.

Nevertheless, by overtly joining Rinuccini's party Antrim had not completely broken with the Stuart cause. After all, Henrietta Maria had instructed the marquis, in the autumn of 1645, that if need arose he was to manipulate the nuncio in order to further the king's interests in Ireland.[102] And in May 1647 a message was sent to the prince of Wales by one of Antrim's closest supporters warning him that, contrary to rumours circulated 'by some malicious persons', the marquis 'with his kinsmen and confederates, is the only life of your business, both in Ireland and Scotland, if God forwards him as He is likely to do in so godly an expedition'.[103] In other words Antrim was anxious to keep open the paths of communication with the royalists but was only prepared to act or to commit his men or frigates to ventures which suited his own needs. Moreover, he drew the line at doing anything which nurtured friendship between Ormond and Rinuccini, for to have done so would have undermined his own position.

The marquis also refused to negotiate a fresh peace between Ormond and the confederates despite being urged to do so by the queen. In one last desperate attempt to heal the breach between the two sides Henrietta Maria had sent as a mediator her chaplain George Leyburn, using the pseudonym 'Winter Grant'. Upon his arrival in Ireland early in April 1647, Leyburn proposed that 'each government should continue their respective governments independent of each other' but that they should agree to join forces 'both at land and at sea' against parliament; and in return for this he assured the confederation that there would be freedom of worship for all Irish Catholics.[104] Ormond rejected Leyburn's proposals and repeated his threat 'that if there were necessity, he would rather give up the city and the places under his command to the English, than to the Irish rebels'.[105] Antrim, for his

[100] Supreme council to Ormond, 10 May 1647 (*ibid.*, fo. 42).
[101] Antrim to Dunsany, 28 March 1647 (*ibid.*, 27, fos. 13, 20); Antrim to White 28 March 1647 (*ibid.*, 20, fo. 556); Antrim to Talbot, 28 March 1647 (*ibid.*, fo. 558); Antrim to Aylmer, 28 March 1647 (*ibid.*, fo. 560). [102] See p. 161 above.
[103] Sir James McDonnell to the prince of Wales, 18 May 1647 (Christ Church, Oxford, Brown correspondence, 'M–P', unfol.).
[104] Leyburn, *Memoirs of George Leyburn*, p. 19; *Comment. Rinucc.*, II, 595.
[105] Leyburn, *Memoirs of George Leyburn*, pp. vii, 14.

194   *Civil War and Restoration in the three Stuart kingdoms*

part, was prepared to let Leyburn try to procure another ceasefire; but in the event the negotiations, which dragged on throughout May and June, ended in failure. Despite further pressure, particularly from the queen, to intervene in the proceedings and to urge the confederates to submit to Leyburn's proposals, Antrim remained elusive, and shortly after Leyburn's arrival in Ireland he accompanied the nuncio from Kilkenny to Wexford.[106]

Antrim's appointment as a member of the papal entourage at Wexford not only provided a plausible excuse for his absence from the negotiations but also enabled him to pay some attention to his privateering business. Despite the fact that the *Mary of Antrim* (commanded first by William O'Doran and then by Anthony Vandermarche) had been mortgaged in February 1647, the marquis continued to enjoy the profits from its prizes until early in 1648 when it was repossessed by his creditors. He also owned at least four other frigates (probably captured prizes which had been renamed). The *St Peter of Waterford*, commanded by Joseph Constant, was a vessel of between fifty and sixty tons, while the *Mary of the Isles* (initially commanded by Vandermarche and then by O'Doran) was armed with at least fourteen guns. The names of the two remaining frigates in Antrim's personal armada are as yet unknown, but one was armed with twenty-two pieces of ordnance ('one of the best frigates that the earl of Antrim hath') and the other with twenty-six guns.[107] It is even possible (though no specific details appear to have survived) that he owned other men-of-war.[108] As it was, apart from the Flemish merchant and entrepreneur Antonio Nicholas Vanderkipp, Antrim ran the largest, and possibly the most profitable, privateering business in Ireland during the later 1640s.

Unfortunately, calculating the exact number of prizes captured by his privateers during these years is, in the absence of quantitative sources, impossible. However, the extant literary and second-hand accounts suggest that his men-of-war were extremely successful and, together with those of Vanderkipp, Rinuccini and others, exacted a heavy toll from English, Scottish,

---

[106] 'A narrative of the marquis's deportment ...', undated [*c.* 1663] (PRONI, D2977/5/1/2); St Peter's College, Wexford, Hore MSS 22, p. 36.

[107] For further details on O'Doran, Vandermarche and Constant, and on the individual warships, see Ohlmeyer, '"The Dunkirk of Ireland"', pp. 31, 33, 36, 40; *A great victory at sea against the Irish rebels by Captaine Robert Dare commander of the English ...* (London, 9 February 1647[-8]), pp. 2–3; Jacques Talbot to Du Bosc, December 1647 (AMAE, Correspondance politique, Angleterre, Côte 55, fo 412).

[108] 'The earl of Antrim hath two frigates of sixteen guns apiece, and there are five or six frigates more at Wexford and Waterford, which are very busy on the sea, and have lately taken one of Parliament's frigates', Valentine Savage to [Sir Philip Percivall], 26 June 1646 (*Egmont MSS*, I, 295).

Dutch, French and Spanish shipping.[109] During 1645, together with Owen Roe O'Neill's frigates, Antrim's flotilla took 'many rich prizes'.[110] In June 1646 one of his frigates captured a parliamentary warship and four merchant vessels from Glasgow, allegedly worth £1,000, off the west coast of Scotland and took them to Wexford.[111] Later the same year two merchant ships coming from the Canaries, laden with wine and fruit, 'were set upon by two lusty frigates well manned that were Antrim's frigates ... these being light, and nimble, boarded the two merchant ships, and bound their men ... and manned the [captured] ships with Irish'.[112] However, as the frigates were returning to sell their quarry at Waterford they were intercepted by parliamentary men-of-war: the prizes were captured and sixty Irish sailors thrown overboard. Early in 1647 a ship which was presumably English, carrying wool from Laredo to Holland, was taken and sold as a 'good prize' in Ireland.[113] In June 1647 it was probably Antrim's frigates that captured in Derry harbour over thirty small Irish and Scottish vessels.[114] During 1648 the *St Peter* took at least two Dutch vessels carrying rye and the *Unitie of Yarmouth* as prizes; while the *Mary of the Isles* seized three more Dutch vessels also laden with grain.[115] There were undoubtedly many other prizes of which no record has survived.[116] Antrim also ensured that his 'tenths' (a tenth of the value of each prize, normally due to the confederates) were paid directly to the duchess of Buckingham, who during his long absences from Wexford and Waterford administered his privateering business.[117]

Antrim's frigates also served as troop carriers for the Spanish crown. In June 1647 he put his vessels (no doubt for a price) at the disposal of the

---

[109] Dumolin to Brienne, 30 October/9 November 1646 (BL, Harl. MSS 4551, fo. 235); memorial presented by Monasterio, [*c.* 1647] (AGS, Eo. 3019, unfol.); Ohlmeyer, '"The Dunkirk of Ireland"', pp. 30–41; *idem*, 'Irish privateers', pp. 126–8.
[110] Gilbert, *Contemp. hist. 1641–52*, I, 90.
[111] See p. 175 above; 'History of events, 1635–62' (NLS, MS 2263, fos. 192v–3). The merchantmen belonged to John Com[yng], Thomas Pedie, James Watson and Patrick Smith, Charles I to Antrim, 29 June and 31 July 1646 (Buckminster, Tollemache MSS 3750, fos. 16v–17, 23).
[112] *The Scottish dove ... From Wednesday 12 to Wednesday 19 August 1646*, no. 147 (London, 1646), p. 7.
[113] Barnewall to Philip IV, [July 1647] (AGS, Eo. 2525, unfol.).
[114] Sir Charles Coote to the committee at Derby House, 11 June 1647 (Bodl., Carte MSS 67, fo. 133).
[115] Ohlmeyer, '"The Dunkirk of Ireland"', pp. 33, 36, 40.
[116] For further details, see Ohlmeyer, 'Irish privateers', pp. 126–7.
[117] Duchess of Buckingham to Ormond, 25 March 1649 (Bodl., Carte MSS 24, fo. 247); Ormond to the duchess of Buckingham, 3 April 1649 (*ibid*., fo. 304). She was by no means unusual: for other examples, see Mary O'Dowd, 'Women and war in Ireland in the 1640s', in Margaret MacCurtain and Mary O'Dowd (eds.), *Women in early modern Ireland* (Dublin, 1991), pp. 91–109.

196   *Civil War and Restoration in the three Stuart kingdoms*

Spanish agents who were preparing to ship an Irish regiment raised by Patrick Barnewall to Spain. Towards the end of the month the troops were duly embarked onto one of Antrim's frigates, armed with twenty-six pieces of artillery, and another German vessel of 500 tons.[118] Despite 'the weather being the most favourable and suitable that one could desire', however, his sailors refused to make the voyage.[119] This mutiny – as French diplomatic sources reveal – was in fact the work of the French agents in Ireland who, unable to sabotage the levy before it was embarked, had at the last minute managed to stir up trouble among the crews of the two frigates. The ship from Hamburg was wrecked between the Passage and Ross and Antrim's crew, fearing a similar fate, abandoned their posts.[120]

Patrick Barnewall, furious and frustrated, knew nothing of this French involvement. Looking for a scapegoat he instead laid the blame for the mutiny entirely on Antrim's shoulders:

There can be no doubt that the marquis has thwarted this voyage because without the support of a person of such great authority the sea captains could not have conceived such a plan; nor, without his consent and approval, would the sailors have dared to disband, fearing the punishment and example they would deserve. And this will not be inflicted, nor would it be appropriate to try it because the marquis, with his [personal] authority, and as he is President of the Council, will always find means – and excuses – to exonerate them, or at least to protect them.[121]

Barnewell suggested that Antrim himself should be punished by having his frigates either embargoed when next in an Iberian port or repossessed on the grounds that 'the marquis was given them in Flanders on condition that they were to carry from his lands to the service of your Majesty 2,000 men; and since he did not comply ... , failing in his promise and obligation, it does not

---

[118] Jacques Talbot to Du Bosc, December 1647 (AMAE, Correspondance politique, Angleterre, Côte 55, fo. 412); Dumolin to Brienne, 30 April/10 May 1647 (BL, Harl. MSS 4551, fo. 253).

[119] Barnewall to Philip IV, undated (because it was presented in person) (AGS, Eo. 2525, unfol.). Also see consulta of the council of state, 20/30 July 1647 (*ibid.*, 2523, unfol.; there is also an undated copy of this consulta in *ibid.*, 2525, unfol.); *Cal. SP Ire., 1633–47*, p. 695. (*Wild Geese*, p. 601, incorrectly cites the date as 8 June.)

[120] Jacques Talbot to Du Bosc, December 1647 (AMAE, Correspondance politique, Angleterre, Côte 55, fo. 412r–v).

[121] Barnewall to Philip IV, undated (AGS, Eo. 2525, unfol.). Barnewall offered three reasons for Antrim's 'base and infamous conduct'. First, the marquis might have been influenced by 'activity by France' (viz. he had been bribed); second, he was well aware that he had not fulfilled the promises that he had made in Flanders in 1645 and 1646 and realized that his frigates 'would be detained there'; and, finally, he felt guilty about the ship carrying wool from Laredo to Holland on behalf of Philip IV's Portuguese bankers, which his frigates had captured and sold as a 'good prize' in Ireland (p. 195 above).

seem that the frigates belong to him'.[122] The Spanish council of state accepted these recommendations and ordered that the frigates be sequestered at the earliest opportunity.[123]

Just as Antrim had tried to make the most of the opportunities created by the 'War of the Five Kingdoms', by raising and shipping mercenaries and by privateering, he now became a victim of the Spanish–French struggle for cannon-fodder. For over the summer of 1647 France had slowly reemerged as the leading foreign force in Irish affairs and successfully undermined Spanish diplomacy there.[124] Relations between Spain and the Old Irish were soured late in 1646 by the capture by a frigate belonging to the nuncio of an English ship carrying Spanish treasure to pay the Army of Flanders. Initially Antrim was blamed for the incident, since the warship (the *San Pedro*) which had committed the violation was one of the frigates which he had been given in 1645 by Castel Rodrigo. In the dispute which followed Rinuccini and Antrim totally undermined their Spanish power base in Ireland.[125]

The break-up of the Old Irish–Spanish alliance coincided with the decline of Antrim's influence over Irish politics in the autumn of 1647.[126] The marquis's fall from grace, after considerably less than a year at the helm, can be partly explained by his own political ineptitude. On the one hand, he appears to have been a poor administrator, and the supreme council over which he presided was later criticized for having failed to carry out the instructions of the previous general assembly.[127] On the other, he was a selfish man, motivated by the desire to enjoy a prominent political position and by his patrimonial ambitions to regain control over the MacDonnell estates in East Ulster and the Western Isles. These personal considerations seriously distorted his effectiveness as leader of the confederation. In short, Antrim pursued policies, such as renewing the war in Scotland and undermining any alliance with the royalists, which did little to further the confederate cause. It was therefore inevitable that sooner or later even his most loyal supporters among the Old Irish faction would become disenchanted by his attempts to funnel whatever meagre resources the confederates had into

---

[122] *Ibid.*
[123] *Wild Geese*, p. 41; consulta of the council of state, 20/30 July 1647 (AGS, Eo. 2523, unfol.).
[124] La Torre to Philip IV, 8/18 February 1648 (AGS, Eo. 2566, unfol.) and Monnerie to Mazarin, 31 January/10 February 1648 (AMAE, Correspondence politique, Angleterre, Côte 57, fos. 55–62).
[125] In the lengthy and acrimonious enquiry which followed, however, it became clear that the *San Pedro* now belonged to Rinuccini; Antrim had sold it to him earlier in 1647. Aiazza, *Embassy*, pp. 406–7, 421, 424, 426–8, 442. Also see p. 161 above.
[126] *Comment. Rinucc.*, II, 664, 693.
[127] Gilbert, *Ir. confed.*, VI, 212.

abortive, myopic, self-interested ventures instead of concentrating on how best to defeat their enemies in Ireland.

But Antrim's political status was also weakened by a realignment of confederate factions during the late spring and summer of 1647. Although Rinuccini and the Old Irish had successfully undermined Ormond's influence over the confederates, they had failed to create a party capable of purging the 'Ormondists' altogether, and in order to rule at all they had been forced to dilute their ranks by admitting Ormondist sympathizers back into the supreme council. The result was virtual political deadlock. 'This kingdom' Ormond had informed Louis XIV 'is divided into so many several parties, scarce anyone adhering to another, and so little portion thereof is at present actually under the king my master's obedience.'[128] Since Antrim was firmly attached to the nuncio's party it was only natural that any resurgence by its opponents would undermine his own political position.

The factional divisions among the confederates were perpetuated and exacerbated by defeat on the battlefield. In June 1647, after lengthy talks, Ormond handed over Dublin to a parliamentary army of 1,400 foot and 600 horse under the command of Colonel Michael Jones, and the following month, after securing favourable financial terms for himself, withdrew first to England and later to France. Almost at once, the confederates launched a campaign against the parliamentarians, and Preston, after taking Carlow in May and Naas and Maynooth in July, decided to invest Trim before marching on Dublin itself. Jones marched to the relief of Trim and the two armies met at Dungans Hill on 8 August, where Preston's army of 6,000 men was virtually annihilated. The defeat was a particular disaster for Antrim, since the army included five regiments of soldiers loyal to him, and 'amongst those slain were 400 of Kilketto's men'.[129] Fortunately, MacColla and a regiment of his veterans escaped unscathed and joined the Army of Munster.[130] But the military fortunes of the confederates fared no better elsewhere. In September Inchiquin sacked Cashel and, on 13 November, at the battle of Knockanauss (County Cork) his army defeated the Army of Munster, under Lord Taaffe's command. Like Dungans Hill, this defeat was a personal disaster for Antrim, for Alasdair MacColla was killed along 'with most of his redshanks, of whom

---

[128] Ormond to Louis XIV, 19 May 1646 (Bodl., Carte MSS 20, fo. 127v).
[129] Gilbert, *Ir. confed.*, VII, 347. For a summary account of Michael Jones, see Alma Brooke-Tyrrell, 'Michael Jones, governor of Dublin', *Dublin Historical Record*, 24, no. 1 (Dec. 1970), pp. 159–71.
[130] *An exact and full relation of the great victory obtained against the rebels at Dungans-Hill in Ireland, August 8 1647. By the forces under the command of Colonel Michael Jones ...* (London, 19 August 1647), p. 10; Stevenson, *Alasdair MacColla*, p. 248.

... there was not above a fourth part that escaped'.[131] A few of Antrim's kin, including Colonel Randal MacDonnell, escaped death but were imprisoned by Inchiquin.[132] Thus within four months the confederates had lost two armies, and Antrim's personal forces in Leinster and Munster had been virtually eliminated. Moreover, the presence of a parliamentary army in Dublin and another in Munster (under the command of Lord Inchiquin) rendered Catholic military supremacy over Ireland unattainable. Confederate fortunes were at their lowest ebb and Antrim's brief and inglorious career as the Catholic figurehead was over.

These defeats in 1647 also brought to an end another phase of the Irish Civil War which began with the September 1643 'cessation of arms'. It had been characterized by tortuous negotiations in Dublin, Oxford and Kilkenny for peace between the royalists (represented by Ormond, Glamorgan and Leyburn) and the confederates, and culminated in a repudiated peace treaty and in the political fragmentation of the Catholic party (despite their victory at Benburb). Throughout this four-year period the confederates had been aware of the need to prevent the English parliament, their implacable enemy, from becoming so powerful that it could invade and destroy them. To achieve this, two options had been open to them: either they could aid Charles I with all their might, in return for religious, political and tenurial concessions, and hope for a royalist victory in Britain; or they could abandon the king altogether and make Catholic Ireland, with the aid of foreign powers, impregnable to invasion from England. By failing to decide between these viable but incompatible policies, the confederates failed to achieve their principal objective and thus safeguard their own survival.

The marquis of Antrim, too, had not managed to choose. Until the end of 1645 he clearly favoured the first option; the papal representative in Brussels, while praising his 'zeal for the Catholic cause', had noted that he was 'not inclined to join with the Irish confederates, as he wishes to be in good grace with the king of England'.[133] However, events in Britain – especially the king's defeat in the first English Civil War and the covenanting victory in Scotland – together with Antrim's success in attracting foreign support for his

---

[131] *A true relation of a great victory obtained by the forces under the command of Lord Inchiquin ... against the rebels* ... (London, 30 November 1647), p. 4; MacBain and Kennedy (eds.), *Reliquiae Celticae*, II, 205; Aiazza, *Embassy*, pp. 335–7; Cary (ed.), *Memorials*, I, 360–7; Stevenson, *Alasdair MacColla*, pp. 249–50.

[132] *A perfect narrative of the battell of Knocknones, within the county of Cork ... betwixt parliament's forces ... and the forces of the Irish rebells* ... (London, 1647), p. 10.

[133] Bichi to secretariat of state, 29 April/6 May 1645, Bichi to Cardinal Panzirolo, 29 September/8 October 1645 (Giblin, 'Catalogue of material of Irish interest', pp. 66, 74–5).

personal war in Scotland meant that in 1646 he turned his back on the king and thereafter supported the second option as the best means of achieving his own goals.

However, his continued support of Rinuccini's party, and his unwillingness to promote the royalist cause over his personal ambitions, combined with his failure to fulfil obligations to the Spanish crown (whether in terms of levying or of shipping troops), ensured that he lost the favour he had previously enjoyed not only among the Spanish faction in Ireland and the Spanish court in Brussels, but with Charles I and his queen. Moreover, his estates in Ulster were still occupied by Scottish troops, while Kintyre and Jura had been regained by Argyll. Antrim had thus failed to preserve his assets, whether measured in terms of men and land or political standing, and had gained nothing. Instead of manipulating international warfare and diplomacy to his own advantage, he had become yet another victim of them.

8

In search of new patrons (November 1647–August 1649)

ANTRIM AND HENRIETTA MARIA

The eighth confederate general assembly, which convened on 12 November 1647 at Kilkenny, was faced by 'a country not only divided but full of suspicion of treachery, [and] without a chief ruler capable of cutting the knot of difficulty'.[1] The confederates had three options open to them. The first was to continue the war, alone, against the English parliament. The second was to invite one of the European Catholic powers – Spain, France or the papacy – to become the 'protector' of Ireland in return for military and financial support. The third was to persuade Charles I or his son to continue, with confederate support, the royalist war effort from Ireland in return for certain concessions over religion, either in person or through a Catholic deputy who would rule Ireland on their behalf.[2] The military disasters of the late summer and autumn of 1647 – Dungans Hill and Knockanauss – forced the confederates to give serious consideration to all three possibilities.

The composition of the new assembly was very different from its predecessor, which had been dominated by the Old Irish faction. On this occasion, the majority of the nuncio's followers were unable to attend the assembly; for example only nine (including Antrim and his brother Alexander) out of a possible sixty-three representatives from Ulster were present. As a result the members from Leinster dominated the proceedings.[3] La Torre later complained to Philip IV that

> the deputies of this province of Leinster took the initiative in the assembly ... Almost all of them inclined towards France because they are clients of the ex-viceroy, the marquis of Ormond ... They were joined by some gentlemen from the provinces of Munster and Connaught who, because they tended the same way and were there from the beginning, began to discuss and decide certain issues without waiting for the views

---

[1] Rinuccini to Panzirolo, 26 September/6 October 1647 (Aiazza, *Embassy*, p. 326).
[2] Monnerie to [Brienne], 31 January/10 February 1648 (BL, Harl. MSS 4551, fos. 34v–5).
[3] La Torre to Philip IV, 8/18 February 1648 (AGS, Eo. 2526, unfol.).

of many other gentlemen ... who are known to be (and are) naturally affected to Spain.[4]

The composition of the new supreme council elected by the assembly naturally reflected the bias against the Old Irish faction. Many leading 'Ormondists' were once again returned to the council: Mountgarret and Bellings were chosen as members for Leinster; Muskerry and Fennell for Munster; Darcy, Dillon and Brown for Connaught. Only the members from Ulster, who included Antrim, Alexander and Heber MacMahon, Catholic bishop of Clogher, continued to represent the interests of the Old Irish faction.[5] Inchiquin, who was at this stage still technically a parliamentarian, was delighted that the factional balance within the council had once again shifted in Ormond's favour:

> At the last General Assembly there was [at] first a great contention between the two factions, but Muskerry prevailed. And [they] have followed good example in now moulding their council; Gerrald Fennell is now put in again with divers others whom they term moderate men, and Dermot O'Bryen and divers (whom they accompt violent) thrust out.[6]

Thus when the council began to debate future strategies the Old Irish were at a decided disadvantage. Initially the 'Ormondists' suggested a direct appeal to Charles I, but this proposal was abandoned when news arrived of the king's arrest by parliament at Carisbrooke castle.[7] Since any alliance with Charles himself was now out of the question, the assembly was forced to examine the other alternatives open to them. Rejecting outright the notion that they should simply surrender to parliament, the assembly debated whether to secure the support of the queen and prince of Wales, or to invite either Pope Innocent X, Louis XIV or Philip IV to become Ireland's saviour. Discussion of who should be made protector raged for thirty-six days. Ormond, in an account drawn up for Cardinal Mazarin, assumed that they would choose a foreign protector: 'It is impossible that Ireland can subsist [alone] but must immediately submit to England, and so considerably increase the power thereof; or else give herself to the pope or the king of Spain.'[8]

As the 1640s progressed the desire to become Ireland's 'protector' and to interfere in Irish politics became a marked objective of French and Spanish diplomacy for, as one foreign agent noted, 'whoever protects Ireland will

---

[4] Ibid.
[5] Gilbert, *Ir. confed.*, VI, 211–12; Monnerie to Mazarin, 31 January/10 February 1648 (AMAE, Correspondance politique, Angleterre, Côte 57, fos. 55–62).
[6] Inchiquin to Ormond, 19 January 1648 (Bodl., Carte MSS 22, fo. 5).
[7] Meehan, *Confederation*, p. 239; *Moderate intelligencer*... From Thursday 13 to Thursday 20 January 1648, no. 148 (London, 1648), p. 1496.
[8] An account of the political condition of the dominions of Great Britain drawn up for Mazarin by Ormond, 1647 (Bodl., Carte MSS 21, fo. 573).

control it'.⁹ Ideally, France wanted Charles I to rule Ireland; but failing that Mazarin wished Ireland to become a French satellite state (like Tuscany, Savoy and Lorraine), and his agents suggested to the general assembly that Louis XIV should 'not only become arbiter but absolute master of all the affairs of the confederates'.¹⁰ Philip IV of Spain, by contrast, while not opposed to Charles I, was a staunch supporter of the Old Irish faction and wanted Ireland to return to the Catholic fold. The Spanish agent Don Diego de La Torre therefore urged the special committee of twenty-four deputed by the assembly to debate the matter to choose Spain, since a French 'protector' would not only refuse to restore Catholicism but would leave the reins of power in the hands of Ormond and other 'heretics'.¹¹ So, superimposed on the already heated debate between the two opposing Irish factions of how best to provide for Ireland's future was a separate struggle between France and Spain to manipulate Irish affairs to their own advantage.

In the end the assembly rejected the arguments of both the French and the Spanish agents and decided instead to invite the prince of Wales either to come in person to Ireland as their 'protector' or to nominate a Catholic lord deputy.¹² Viscount Muskerry, Geoffrey Brown and the bishop of Clogher were appointed to visit the royal court, in exile in France, to solicit the queen's support for their venture.¹³ Clogher, however, refused to participate in the mission on the grounds that he was 'hated by the queen' and had no knowledge of French or English.¹⁴ Five days later Antrim was nominated in his place.¹⁵ On 24 December 1647 the assembly broke up.

By selecting Antrim as a member of the delegation the council presumably hoped that his royalist connections would stand the mission in good stead and also forestall any protests from the beleaguered Old Irish faction within

---

[9] La Torre to Philip IV, 20/30 April 1647 (AGS, Eo. 2523, unfol.).
[10] Foissotte to Philip IV, 8/18 May 1648 (*ibid.*, 2566, unfol.).
[11] La Torre's reasons for not allowing the French faction to control Ireland, [1648] (*ibid.*, unfol.). Also see La Torre to Philip IV, 8/18 February 1648 (*ibid.*, unfol.).
[12] If this failed Brown was instructed to solicit French aid, Brown's secret instructions from the supreme council, [February 1648] (*ibid.*, unfol.).
[13] Patrick J. Corish, 'Ormond, Rinuccini and the confederates', in NHI, p. 325; *Wild Geese*, pp. 378–9; La Torre to Philip IV, 8/18 February 1648 (AGS, Eo. 2566, unfol.). At the Restoration it was insisted that the confederates would only have asked 'aid and protection of some of those foreign princes' as a last resort, 'The defense of his majesty's catholic subjects of Ireland', [1661] (Bodl., Carte MSS 44, fo. 259).
[14] Account of what happened to the bishop of Clogher, 8/18 December 1647 (Aiazza, *Embassy*, p. 340).
[15] Jerrold I. Casway, 'The clandestine correspondence of Father Patrick Crelly, 1648–49', *Collect. Hib.*, 20 (1978), p. 8; Inchiquin to Ormond, 19 January 1648 (Bodl., Carte MSS 22, fo. 5); Carte, *Ormond*, III, 346; *Comment. Rinucc.*, II, 796, III, 1, 392.

the assembly.[16] For his part, the marquis (according to the French agent, Monnerie)

> was delighted to be named for this mission hoping that it would serve to replace him in the good opinion of their majesties, whose very humble servant he showed himself to be; and he repented having done what he had done, attributing it to necessity and to the impoverished situation in which he then found himself.[17]

Interestingly, Monnerie added that even at this stage Antrim 'is a very popular man and one who could be easily won over. He has scarcely any spirit; he is a courtier'.[18] Rinuccini also feared that the marquis might be bullied by the other delegates and so he insisted that Antrim's Cistercian agent, friend and mentor Patrick Crelly, abbot of Newry, 'accompany Antrim to temper his excessive good nature and to bring it about that he remain firm in the midst of the plots of the other two envoys who will always make an effort to trip him up'.[19] The marquis, for his part, promised the nuncio that he would not agree to anything in France without Crelly's advice; but he also warned that the prince of Wales would never consider coming to Ireland as long as Rinuccini was there.[20] In addition to acting as watch-dog for the Catholic interest in Paris, Antrim was instructed to collect money promised to the nuncio by the pope; and he was to agitate, via the nuncio in Paris, for a fresh alliance with Montrose so that a renewed offensive in Scotland could be launched.[21]

The preparations involved in dispatching the delegation began early in January 1648. Letters of introduction from the supreme council were drawn up on behalf of the delegates and the envoys were issued with their instructions.[22] 'The key point of the instructions', Patrick Corish has recently pointed out, 'was that in any agreement with the queen they were to secure the terms for the catholic religion already granted by Glamorgan, and also

---

[16] Cárdenas to Philip IV, 8/18 December 1648 (AGS, Eo. 2524, fo. 80).
[17] Monnerie to Mazarin, 31 January/10 February 1648 (AMAE, Correspondance politique, Angleterre, Côte 57, fos. 55–62).
[18] *Ibid.* The choice of the marquis as the Old Irish representative was not, however, universally welcomed: Owen Roe O'Neill, for instance, later complained to Philip IV that Antrim favoured France and should be excluded, O'Neill to Philip IV, 1/11 February 1648 (AGS, Eo. 2566, unfol.).
[19] *Comment. Rinucc.*, III, 381. Also see Aiazza, *Embassy*, p. 369.
[20] Cárdenas to Philip IV, 8/18 December 1648 (AGS, Eo. 2524, fo. 80); Aiazza, *Embassy*, p. 365.
[21] Aiazza, *Embassy*, pp. 397, 463, 368–9; Massari, 'My Irish campaign', *The Catholic Bulletin*, 10 (1920), p. 735; *Comment. Rinucc.*, IV, 106, 274.
[22] Supreme council to Mazarin, 18/28 January 1648 (AMAE, Correspondance politique, Angleterre, Côte 55, fo. 62); Gilbert, *Ir. confed.*, VI, 226–7; Aiazza, *Embassy*, p. 363; Carte, *Ormond*, III, 347–8, 350. A set of private instructions – signed by Taaffe and Preston – was issued to Muskerry and Brown.

In search of new patrons 205

that the viceroy should be a catholic, unless the pope waived this point'.[23] The general assembly had already agreed that the envoys were not to reach a final accord until they received papal approval, which Nicholas French and Nicholas Plunkett were sent to Rome to secure.

Antrim and Crelly left Waterford late in February, thanks to the good offices of the nuncio and the Spanish agent, who lent them the necessary money for the voyage.[24] The French agent interpreted Antrim's early exit as an attempt to ensure that Ireland was placed under Spanish – rather than French – protection, but it seems more likely that Antrim and Crelly hoped to beat the 'Ormondists' to St Germain so that they would have an opportunity of giving the queen their version of events before the others arrived.[25] It is also plausible to suppose that Antrim was, as Carte later suggested, 'full of hopes of being made the Roman Catholic lord lieutenant ... a dignity which his vanity had long made him desire, and which the nuncio had flattered him with hope of obtaining'.[26]

Antrim and the abbot made excellent progress and were in St Germain, near Paris, by early March, arriving shortly after Ormond himself. Muskerry and Brown, who had been delayed in Ireland due to poor weather and lack of funds, reached France only around the middle of the month;[27] but on arriving at the Stuart court-in-exile, they immediately joined up with Ormond, Muskerry's brother-in-law, and 'agreed to do everything Ormond told them'.[28]

Official negotiations with Henrietta Maria began at once (23 March/2 April NS), but since their directives forbade the confederate agents from making any agreement until instructions had been received from Rome, the audience produced no decisions.[29] Nevertheless, Henrietta Maria pondered

---

[23] Corish, 'Ormond, Rinuccini and the confederation', p. 325.
[24] Monnerie to Mazarin, 31 January/10 February 1648 (AMAE, Correspondance politique, Angleterre, Côte 57, fos. 52–3); Hill, *MacDonnells*, p. 274.
[25] Indeed Antrim later claimed that 'he himself approached the queen before the other envoys [had arrived] and obtained everything according to the confederates' wishes from her'. Ormond, Muskerry and Brown then persuaded her to change her mind, *Comment. Rinucc.*, III, 450.
[26] Carte, *Ormond*, III, 350, 393–4. Also see *Comment. Rinucc.*, III, 49.
[27] *Cal. SP Ven.*, *1647–52*, p. 50; Gilbert, *Ir. confed.*, VII, 37. To ensure that France should not be disadvantaged by their late departure, Monnerie agreed to lend them 1,200 pistoles (roughly £320) for the trip, Monnerie to Mazarin, 31 January/10 February 1648 (AMAE, Correspondence politique, Angleterre, Côte 57, fos. 52–3).
[28] Cárdenas to Philip IV, 8/18 December 1648 (AGS, Eo. 2524, fo. 80). Also see Brienne to Grignon, 29 April/9 May 1648 (BN, Fonds Français 15,966, fo. 394v); Brienne to Grignon, 6/16 May 1648 (*ibid.*, fo. 357v).
[29] Gilbert, *Ir. confed.*, VI, 228–31; Casway, 'The clandestine correspondence of Father Patrick Crelly', p. 8; *Comment. Rinucc.*, VI, 127; Carte, *Ormond*, III, 351.

their proposals and sought Ormond's advice on how they should be dealt with.[30] Just over a month later, on 30 April (10 May NS), the agents had a further meeting: Antrim acted as the chief confederate negotiator, while Ormond represented the queen. Ormond asked whether the confederates were willing to offer any concessions over religion and whether Antrim had the power 'to alter and to recede from what they have proposed, and to conclude thereupon'.[31] Antrim replied that 'we are not yet ready to propose any certainty in the matter concerning religion, being [bound] by our instructions, to be judged in that particular by his holiness'. He explained that agents had been sent to Rome 'from whom we expect to hear very speedily'; but he requested that the queen should make clear what compromise she would accept, so that the negotiations might continue.[32] Religion, as Ormond had no doubt anticipated, was once again the major stumbling block to any political settlement.[33] On 3 May the queen told the envoys that 'we shall speedily give power to some such as we think fit' and that this person – presumably Ormond himself – would be empowered to grant 'whatever may consist with justice and with his Majesty's interest and honour'.[34] The queen's address brought the talks to a seemingly harmonious end.[35]

From Antrim's perspective, however, the negotiations had been a defeat. On a personal level, his rival Ormond had dominated the proceedings while, more generally, he had failed to find practical help for the Old Irish cause. Unlike his fellow negotiators, Antrim had remained loyal to the Old Irish interest, and his steadfast devotion to the nuncio's faction was duly reported back to Ireland by Crelly: Brown and Muskerry had 'played the traitors', wrote the abbot, while Antrim conducted himself 'devotedly and honourably ... He continually sets himself in opposition to the queen of England, the prince, Ormond, Muskerry, Brown and the remaining Presbyterians.'[36]

---

[30] Carte, *Ormond*, III, 352.
[31] Ormond to Antrim, 30 April/10 May 1648 (Bodl., Carte MSS 22, fo. 76; *ibid.*, 65, fo. 417). Also see Carte, *Ormond*, III, 359.
[32] Antrim's answer, [30 April/10 May] 1648 (Bodl., Carte MSS 22, fo. 87; *ibid.*, 63, fo. 540).
[33] Muskerry and Brown to Bellings, 30 May/10 June 1648 (*ibid.*, 44, fo. 349v); Brienne to Grignon, 13/23 May 1648 (BN, Fonds Français 15,966, fo. 367v).
[34] Reply from the queen and the prince of Wales, 3/13 May 1648 (Gilbert, *Ir. confed.*, VI, 231).
[35] *Comment. Rinucc.*, III, 184, 367, 378, 383; Carte, *Ormond*, III, 360–1.
[36] Crelly to Rinuccini, 14/24 May 1648 (*Comment. Rinucc.*, III, 385). Also see Cárdenas to Philip IV, 8/18 December 1648 (AGS, Eo. 2524, fo. 80).

The breakdown of the negotiations had serious consequences. First, unknown to Antrim, Henrietta Maria, Jermyn, Ormond and Digby set in motion an ambitious plan, which was supported by the French, to use Ireland 'as the great and principal instrument to reduce Scotland and England'.[37] This involved Ormond's return to Ireland in order to unite the Irish confederate factions, to win over Owen Roe O'Neill and to join forces with the 'Baron [Inchiquin] and the Presbyterians in England, Scotland and Ireland', who (as Crelly informed Rinuccini early in May) 'all form against the present parliament and the Independents'.[38] Once the forces of Clanricard, Inchiquin, Taaffe, Preston and O'Neill had been amalgamated, their army was to take Dublin and then send an expeditionary force under the prince of Wales's command to invade England and Scotland.

For, despite losing the first Civil War in England, Charles I refused to acquiesce to parliament's demands; 'he would not abandon the episcopacy entirely, and he adamantly refused to sacrifice his command of the armed forces, his choice of ministers and his veto over legislation'.[39] He also rejected the *Heads of proposals* put forward by the army over the summer of 1647 and instead signed an 'Engagement' with the Scots (26 December) which did not encroach on his military and civil powers. In return for Scottish military assistance against the English parliament, the king agreed to sign the Solemn League and Covenant and to introduce Presbyterianism into England for a period of three years. In May 1648 the 'engagers' made a tentative alliance with the Irish royalists, led at this point by Inchiquin, and with those confederates who favoured an alliance with Ormond, pledging to support those Irish 'who are willing to submit to the king's authority' (without prejudice to the Protestant religion).[40]

According to the scheme hatched by Henrietta Maria and her advisers, France was to provide the necessary money for this combined assault and in return was promised possession of all major ports and forts in Ireland

---

[37] Paper I, presented by Crelly to parliamentary committee, December 1648 (AGS, Eo. 2524, fo. 81). Crelly's paper, translated into Spanish, was enclosed in Cárdenas's letter to Philip IV, 8/18 December 1648 (*ibid.*, fo. 80). Apparently no version of Crelly's proposals in English has survived. Crelly discovered the plot from various sources including Dr Tirrell, the confederate envoy in Paris and the count of Brienne, see Foissotte to Philip IV, 8/18 May 1648 (*ibid.*, 2566, unfol.); Grignon to Brienne, 1/11 May 1648 (BN, Fonds Français 15,966, fo. 347).
[38] Crelly to Rinuccini, 14/24 May 1648 (*Comment. Rinucc.*, III, 385).
[39] David L. Smith 'The impact on government', in Morrill (ed.), *The impact of the English civil war*, p. 42.
[40] 'A copy of an answer of the committee of estates in Scotland...', May 1648 (Bodl., Carte MSS 22, fo. 222). Also see David Stevenson, *Revolution and counter-revolution in Scotland 1644–1651* (London, 1977), pp. 94–7.

together with a supply of mercenaries to be raised by Muskerry.[41] Admittedly from May 1648, as the Civil Wars in France (known as the Fronde) gained momentum, it became increasingly difficult for the Bourbon Treasury to divert scarce resources into foreign ventures; nevertheless, the French secretary of state, Brienne, felt that at all costs Ireland should not fall under Spanish control, which would be worse in his eyes than if it became Protestant.[42] So Muskerry and Brown, who prepared to leave France for Ireland in mid-June, were deputed to arrange the Irish dimension of the plot.[43] Brienne for one hoped that they would 'sabotage the designs of the Spaniards and will succeed in convincing the Catholics [in Ireland] to support the king's party'.[44] To make the mission easier Louis XIV issued an edict which prevented Antrim from leaving St Malo until the admiralty officials there had received news of Muskerry's safe arrival in Ireland.[45] Stranded, the marquis went into hiding in France, under the pseudonym 'Francis Chapman', and remained there for a month.[46]

His exclusion from the exiled royalist court forced Antrim to initiate an alternative strategy to preserve his personal influence. Rather than simply turning to Spain for help, as the 'Ormondists' and the French expected him to do, he (together with Crelly) adopted a more sophisticated and ultimately more dangerous plan: soliciting aid for Ireland from the 'Independent' faction in the English parliament.[47] Since the creation of the New Model Army in February 1645, the dominance of the Presbyterian party — which was conservative in outlook, opposed to religious toleration and in favour of a negotiated peace with the king — had been slowly undermined; while the influence of the Independent party, more tolerant of religious issues, and supported by the army, steadily increased.[48] Matters became critical over the summer of 1647, and a dispute between the two parties over control of the

---

[41] Paper I, presented by Crelly to parliamentary committee, December 1648 (AGS, Eo. 2524, fo. 81); *Comment. Rinucc.*, III, 371, 378–9; Gilbert, *Contemp. hist. 1641–52*, I, 210–11.
[42] Brienne to [Grignon] 24 April/2 May 1648 (BN, Fonds Français 15,966, fo. 339v); Brienne to Grignon, 30 April/9 May 1648 (*ibid.*, fo. 394v)
[43] Carte, *Ormond*, III, 361–2.
[44] Brienne to Grignon, 29 July/8 August 1648 (BN, Fonds Français 15,997, fo. 452r–v).
[45] Order of Louis XIV to admiralty officials in St Malo, 25 June/5 July 1648 (AMAE, Correspondance politique, Angleterre, Côte 57, fo. 247).
[46] 'Francis Chapman' [= Antrim] to Mr Williams, 8 June 1648 (*Clarendon SP*, I, 426); Hill, *MacDonnells*, p. 259; *Comment. Rinucc.*, III, 450, 514.
[47] Brienne to Grignon, 15/25 June 1648 (BN, Fonds Français 15,999, fo. 247r–v. Early in May 1648, Crelly notified Rinuccini that a channel of communication with the Independent party in parliament had been opened, *Comment. Rinucc.*, III, 386–7, 395, IV, 274.
[48] Kishlansky, *New Model Army*, pp. 130, 180, 226, 285, 323–3.

London militia resulted in the army throwing their weight behind the Independents and occupying Westminster. It was more from these men that Antrim and the abbot intended to secure support in the hope that their policy of religious toleration and liberty of conscience would preserve the Catholic religion in Ireland.[49]

In addition to the improbable goal of uniting the resources, and forces, of the English Independents and the Old Irish and clerical followers of Rinuccini, Antrim – who never lost sight of his personal goals – intended to launch a fresh expedition, in conjunction with Montrose, who was also in France at this point, against Scotland. Since the autumn of 1646 Montrose had been wandering around Europe – he had visited Denmark, the Netherlands, France and the Empire – searching either for a job as a condottiere or for arms with which to launch a fresh offensive in Scotland. But in February 1648 he indicated his willingness to ally again with Antrim. His resolve to do so was strengthened by the fact that like Antrim he was shunned by the English court in France, whose hopes for a fresh offensive in Britain were pinned instead on Ormond.[50] As a result, some time in May 1648 (according to Crelly), 'Montrose and Antrim made an agreement according to your [Rinuccini's] directive which will result (I hope) in some good.'[51] For his part, the nuncio favoured this alliance because 'I have always believed that a diversion of the war into Scotland will be most useful to Ireland.'[52] However, Antrim needed money and munitions for the new campaign. Having burned his bridges with his Spanish benefactors, he hoped instead to take advantage of the war between Venice and the Ottoman Turks and dispatched Crelly to see the Venetian ambassador in Paris. According to the ambassador's report of their interview, Crelly

> told me that the Catholics there [in Ireland] have considered your serenity's need of men and their own need of money, and are disposed to listen to overtures, as they consider war against the Turk and against the heretic as equally important. They felt sure that as many could be supplied as the most serene republic would pay for.

In return Crelly asked for a cash advance and offered 'as a security the most important fortresses and ports of the kingdom'.[53] In the end nothing came of

---

[49] Elkin, 'The interactions between the Irish rebellion and the English civil wars', pp. 284–5; A.S.P. Woodhouse (ed.), *Puritanism and liberty. Being the army debates (1647–9) from the Clarke manuscripts with supplementary documents*, preface by Ivan Roots (London, 1938; 2nd edn, 1974), pp. 17–18.
[50] Cowan, *Montrose*, pp. 257–63.
[51] Crelly to Rinuccini, 1/11 May 1648 (*Comment. Rinucc.*, III, 383). Also see *ibid.*, II, 756, III, 387–8, IV, 274.
[52] Rinuccini to Panzirolo, 26 January/5 February 1648 (Aiazza, *Embassy*, p. 369).
[53] Gio. Battista Nani to Doge and senate, 11/21 April 1648 (*Cal. SP Ven., 1647–52*, p. 54).

Antrim's last-ditch attempt to act as a military entrepreneur in the continental wars, for his plans were overtaken by the outbreak of the second English Civil War.

ANTRIM AND ORMOND

As Antrim languished in France, the situation in Britain and Ireland was transformed. In March Pembroke castle declared for the king; the following month a combined force of royalists and Scots occupied Berwick; while in May a series of uncoordinated uprisings against parliamentary oppression (the 'revolt of the provinces') took place in Wales, East Anglia, Kent and Essex. Finally in July a poorly disciplined and inadequately armed Scottish army of about 9,000 (which was later bolstered by some 5,000 experienced Englishmen) under the command of Antrim's erstwhile friend, the duke of Hamilton, marched slowly south towards Lancashire in the king's name.

In Ireland the royalist war-effort crystallized with Inchiquin's declaration for the king (3 April) and with an alliance between Inchiquin and the confederates (20 May). However, seven days later Rinuccini tried to sabotage the royalist design to unite Ireland under Ormond's authority by excommunicating the supporters of the 'Inchiquin truce'.[54] On this occasion the supreme council was not intimidated by the nuncio and in retaliation appealed to Rome against the excommunication.[55] An already divided Catholic Ireland was thus more polarized than ever before, and the battle lines between the 'moderate', pro-Ormond party and the 'violent', pro-nuncio faction were formalized on 11 June when Owen Roe O'Neill and the Army of Ulster declared war on the supreme council.

So by June 1648 there were two *ad hoc* alliances among the Catholics. On the one hand, there stood the 'Ormondists' who were supported by the combined forces of the Army of Leinster and Lord Inchiquin. On the other, were the nuncio and his isolated caucus of clerics, together with the more radical members of the Old Irish community, who depended exclusively on Owen Roe O'Neill and the Army of Ulster for military assistance.[56] These internecine quarrels mystified foreign observers, who could not understand the myopia of the Irish:

---

[54] *Comment. Rinucc.*, III, 70–1, 73.
[55] Aiazza, *Embassy*, pp. 376–9, 380–1; Patrick J. Corish, 'Rinuccini's censure of May 22 1648', *Irish Theological Quarterly*, 18 (Oct. 1951), pp. 323–9; *idem*, 'Bishop Nicholas French and the second Ormond peace, 1648–9', *IHS*, 6, no. 22 (Sept. 1948), pp. 90–100; *idem*, 'The crisis in Ireland in 1648: the nuncio and the supreme council: conclusions', *Irish Theological Quarterly*, 22 (Jan. 1955), pp. 231–57, discusses the contemporary controversy over the excommunication. [56] William Paterson to [?], 22 June 1648 (SRO, GD 406/1/2413).

What really surprises the majority of those who contemplate the affairs of Ireland [the French ambassador in London reported back to Paris] is to see that people of the same nation and of the same religion – who are well aware that the resolution to exterminate them totally has already been taken – should differ so strongly in their private hostilities; that their zeal for religion, the preservation of their country and their own self interest are not sufficient to make them lay down – at least, for a short time – the passions which divide them one from the other.[57]

It was easy to take such a detached viewpoint of Irish politics in London; in Kilkenny or Dublin matters were less clear-cut. And it was into this quagmire of factional intrigue that Antrim sank when he finally arrived back in Ireland late in July 1648.[58] But the marquis never lost sight of personal goals. He was as determined as ever both to protect his own interests in Ulster and in Western Scotland and to prevent Ormond's return from France; for an Ireland united under the leadership of the lord lieutenant, which would inevitably exclude him from political power, was totally unacceptable.

In an attempt to derail Ormond's efforts to involve Ireland in the second English Civil War, Antrim threw in his lot with his former rival, Owen Roe O'Neill, suggesting that the Army of Ulster should seize Kilkenny, the seat of confederate government, and that a new supreme council, controlled by Rinuccini and the clerical party, should be established. According to one cleric: 'Antrim is wholly devoted to O'Neill and the Ulster army, and he will procure all his [forces] to side with him. He [Antrim] most earnestly desires that Owen O'Neill and the Ulster army should come without delay towards Kilkenny; and let them not doubt that all Leinster, nay, Ireland, will be at their dispose.'[59] But the element of surprise, which was crucial if the seizure of Kilkenny were to succeed, was lost when a number of incriminating letters were intercepted by the 'Ormondists' and one of the conspirators was arrested.[60] O'Neill, however, unaware of this disaster, marched his army into County Kilkenny where the troops wreaked havoc on Lord Mountgarret's estates until early August when they were forced by the combined forces of Preston and Inchiquin to retreat.[61] Antrim's proposed coup d'état had failed.

This setback to Antrim's plan to prevent Ormond from reestablishing his

[57] Bellièvre to Brienne, 3/13 November 1648 (AMAE, Correspondance politique, Angleterre, Côte 57, fos. 314–15).
[58] Unlike his brother Alexander, the marquis refused to have anything to do with the 'Ormondists', [Hogan (ed.)], *History of the warr*, p. 69; *Comment. Rinucc.*, III, 450, 514, 664.
[59] King to bishop of Clogher, [27 July 1648] (Gilbert, *Ir. confed.*, VII, 103–4); *Comment. Rinucc.*, III, 632.
[60] Casway, *Owen Roe O'Neill*, p. 219; *Comment. Rinucc.*, III, 633, 636; Gilbert, *Ir. confed.*, VII, 104. Plunkett described Father King, the arrested conspirator, as a 'favourite' of the bishop of Clogher and as 'an implacable firebrand and instigator of mischief', see NLI, MS 345, p. 941.
[61] Carte, *Ormond*, III, 381, 386; Casway, *Owen Roe O'Neill*, p. 221.

control in Ireland coincided with the resounding defeat of Hamilton's Scottish army at the battle of Preston (17 August 1648) and with the speedy suppression of sporadic royalist outbreaks in Wales and southern England. Charles I had lost the second Civil War and the victors were free to dictate the peace. But instead, 'Parliament launched a round of leisurely negotiations at Newport, lending a sympathetic ear to the king's demands.' This proved too much for the New Model Army to tolerate; now that it had won the war, it was determined to win the peace as well and to call Charles I 'that man of blood, to an account for that blood he had shed, and mischief he had done to his utmost against the Lord's cause and people in these poor nations'.[62] The army's decision to bring the king to trial was bitterly debated within the Independent party, which split into two bodies. The more radical faction supported the army's decision, while the moderates, who allied with the Presbyterian party, agitated for a compromise with the king.[63] Ironically, this development in England worked in Antrim's favour, for it offered a golden opportunity for the Old Irish/clerical faction, to which he still adhered, to exploit the factional deadlock at Westminster to its own advantage.

However, before proceeding further in his talks with the Independents (see pp. 208–9 above) Antrim wanted to secure papal approval for the proposed alliance, and towards the end of May 1648 he sent Patrick Crelly to Rome.[64] Crelly spent three weeks in Rome, and in an audience with Innocent X he implored the pope to recognize the legitimacy of the English parliament which, he claimed, would then grant toleration for the Catholic religion. Since his election to the papal throne in 1644 Innocent had been keen 'to exploit the struggle between the king and parliament with a view to restoring Catholicism not only as the national religion of Ireland but of England as well';[65] and so, while he refused to intervene directly, he referred Crelly to the nuncio in Paris and the Spanish ambassador in London.[66] By 22 August the abbot had arrived in Paris and immediately visited the nuncio there, who advised him that the best course of action would be for the 'Old Irish to negotiate a settlement with the faction of the Independents in England and that this was the pope's intention not only in Ireland but in all the dominions of this crown'.[67]

[62] Ian Gentles, 'The impact of the New Model Army', in Morrill (ed.), *The Impact of the English civil war*, p. 99, also see p. 44.
[63] David Underdown, *Pride's purge. Politics in the puritan revolution* (London, 1971; reprint, 1985), pp. 96–7; Austin Woolrych, *Soldiers and statesmen. The general council of the army and its debates 1647–8* (Oxford, 1987), pp. 332–6.
[64] Muskerry and Brown to Bellings, 30 May/10 June 1648 (Bodl., Carte MSS 44, fo. 349v); Gardiner, *Commonwealth and protectorate*, I, 81–2, (incorrectly) suggested that Antrim sent Crelly to Rome in 1647.
[65] Lowe, 'The negotiations between Charles I and the confederation', p. 367.
[66] *Clarendon SP*, II, 509–10.
[67] Cárdenas to Philip IV, 8/18 December 1648 (AGS, Eo. 2524, fo. 80). Also see

Shortly afterwards Crelly made his way to the royalist court, which was now in Louvain, and Francis Walsingham (Digby's private secretary) reported to Ormond the proceedings of an interview between the abbot and the queen. Crelly offered the queen three pieces of advice: first, that a 'person well thought of by the fierce party in Ireland' – presumably Crelly himself – should be sent there to convince the nuncio's faction to negotiate with Ormond; secondly, that she should intervene on behalf of a 'particular person for what is past' (this anonymous individual was almost certainly Antrim) and soothe relations between this individual and Ormond; thirdly, that Crelly should be nominated as an adviser to Ormond 'to deliver freely his opinion to you especially concerning the several most eminent persons that lead amongst the untractable party'. Walsingham, though suspicious of Crelly's motives, urged Ormond to accept these proposals at face value in an attempt to manipulate the nuncio's party to the king's best advantage.[68]

What is one to make of all this? Was Crelly genuinely trying to negotiate a settlement that was both favourable to the nuncio's party and advantageous to the interests of himself and Antrim? Or were his three proposals merely a skilful ploy to divert royalist attention away from his true purpose – concluding an alliance with the Independents in the English parliament? The most plausible verdict is that Crelly's diplomacy was a last-ditch attempt to secure royal recognition for the Catholic cause in Ireland and to undermine Ormond's position while at the same time promoting Antrim as Catholic Ireland's leader.[69]

In the event nothing came of these attempts at reconciliation, and, significantly, Crelly made no reference to the subject in the letters he wrote later that same week to Antrim, the nuncio, the duchess of Buckingham and the Catholic bishop of Clogher, which were all subsequently intercepted.[70] The

Casway, 'The clandestine correspondence of Father Patrick Crelly', p. 9. Confirmation of Crelly's account came from an English Jesuit who was staying with the French nuncio at the time and was instructed to assist Crelly in his mission by writing to all Jesuit priests in Britain.

[68] Walsingham to Ormond, 6/16 September 1648 (Casway, 'The clandestine correspondence of Father Patrick Crelly', pp. 16, 17).

[69] *Ibid.* Presumably Crelly was instructed, either by the confederate envoys in Rome or by Antrim or, more likely, by the duchess of Buckingham (from whom he had received at least two letters), to make a last attempt to secure the queen's favour for the 'fierce party'.

[70] It is unclear who actually intercepted these letters dated 6/16 September. Walsingham's letter to Ormond, also dated 6/16 September, included no direct reference to Crelly's missives. If they were enclosed with Walsingham's letter, they must have been intercepted the day Crelly wrote them; and Walsingham must have decyphered and dispatched them to Ormond immediately. More likely, they were captured by the supreme council – certainly the duchess of Buckingham complained, late in September, that this was the case – and presumably forwarded to Ormond, see deputy mayor of Wexford to supreme council, 21 September 1648 (Bodl., Carte MSS 44, fo. 349).

abbot, though frustrated by the poor communications with Ireland, nevertheless seemed pleased with the progress of the design. He extended the pope's good wishes to Antrim and added 'I suppose very shortly you shall see some badge of his thankfulness to you and her grace.' Claiming to have 'license from his holiness in the business you know', he begged the marquis both to refrain from making a treaty with Ormond, and to restrain Rinuccini, O'Neill and the bishop of Clogher from doing so.[71] In a similar letter he urged the nuncio to continue 'whatever discussions might have taken place with Montrose, [the] Independents and others'.[72]

The defeat of the Scots at Preston and the subsequent overthrow of the royalists in England had greatly increased the importance of Ormond's mission in Ireland, since any hope of continuing the royalist war-effort in the other two kingdoms now depended exclusively on the ability of the lord lieutenant to unite the divided factions in Ireland under the authority of the king (now a prisoner of the English parliament). Despite Antrim's various attempts to sabotage his mission, Ormond landed at Cork on 30 September with arms (paid for by the French) for 4,000 foot and 1,000 horse, and immediately joined forces with Inchiquin.[73] This not only jeopardized any chance Antrim may have had of rallying the Irish to the nuncio's cause but also crushed his hopes of being created viceroy of Ireland. To make matters worse the confederates had already convened a general assembly to negotiate a new peace with Ormond. In protest Antrim, despite attempts to win him over, together with the rest of the nuncio's followers, refused to take his seat or even to recognize the assembly, which he claimed had been unlawfully convened. In retaliation the assembly condemned the nuncio's followers and declared Owen Roe O'Neill a traitor.

The battle lines were now clearly drawn and during the autumn of 1648 Antrim, who was now living in Wexford, formulated yet another strategy designed to topple Ormond's party and restore the nuncio's faction to power.[74] His plan was simple. He proposed to call out his followers in Ulster, together with the Highland veterans serving under the command of his kinsman the laird of Glengarry in the Army of Leinster, and others sent from the Isles early in 1648 by the captain of Clanranald under Donald

---

[71] Crelly to Antrim, 6/16 September 1648 (Casway, 'The clandestine correspondence of Father Patrick Crelly', p. 14). The duchess of Buckingham and the bishop of Clogher received similar letters.
[72] Crelly to Rinuccini, [September 1648] (*ibid.*, p. 13).
[73] Paper I, presented by Crelly to parliamentary committee, December 1648 (AGS, Eo. 2524, fo. 81).
[74] He lived with Brian MacPhelim O'Byrne, Gilbert, *Contemp. hist. 1641–52*, II, 19.

MacDonald's command.⁷⁵ Early in October Rinuccini noted that Antrim 'has declared for us, and is now in Wexford with 2,000 Scotch-Irish, good Catholics and expects to be joined by others'.⁷⁶ These crack troops were to muster at Wexford and from there to march to County Wicklow where they would be joined by men raised by Brian O'Byrne (a favourite of Rinuccini) and Charles Kavanagh and equipped with 1,600 guns and ammunition which had been purchased in France.⁷⁷ This army was to rendezvous with Antrim at Arklow on 11 October and then march against Ormond.⁷⁸

The plan ran awry from the start. Colonel 'MacThomas' (Pierce Fitzgerald) – a former member of Rinuccini's party – caught wind of the proposed rising, and in an attempt to defuse it tried to dissuade Glengarry, who had just arrived in Wexford, from joining with the O'Byrnes and Kavanaghs on the grounds that they were 'strangers in the kingdom' and had no quarrel with Ormond. Glengarry, 'having already engaged with his kinsman the marquis of Antrim', refused to be persuaded, and so his 600 Highlanders joined with Charles Kavanagh's troops. But Fitzgerald tipped off forces loyal to Ormond, for when Glengarry marched from Wexford on 8 October 'with a party of six or seven hundred Scotch and five hundred Kavanaghs with forty or fifty horse towards the Kavanagh's and O'Byrne's country to put them all in arms', they were ambushed by two regiments of cavalry whereupon they fled into a nearby wood.⁷⁹ The cavalry was soon reinforced by Sir Thomas Esmond, major-general of the Army of Leinster, and his infantry, and their combined force 'hunted them out until night'.⁸⁰ The next morning '300 dead bodies were found in the wood besides eighty prisoners [including Glengarry and his uncle, the laird of Clanranald] wherein all the Scotch officers were either taken or killed'.⁸¹ Meanwhile, Antrim's frigates, carrying the arms and

---

75 *Comment. Rinucc.*, III, 514; MacBain and Kennedy (eds.), *Reliquiae Celticae*, II, 205–7; Stevenson, *Alasdair MacColla*, pp. 257–8; Casway, *Owen Roe O'Neill*, p. 217. He also tried to win Preston's support. Late in August it was mistakenly rumoured in Brussels that 'the differences between O'Neill and Preston have been composed by Antrim at the direction of Rinuccini', see news from Brussels and Bichi to Panzirolo, 28 September/8 October 1648 (Giblin, 'Catalogue of material of Irish interest', pp. 74–5).
76 Rinuccini to Panzirolo, 30 September/10 October 1648 (Aiazza, *Embassy*, p. 423).
77 Theobald Butler to Ormond, 10 October 1648 (Bodl., Carte MSS 22, fo. 335); La Torre to Philip IV, 13/23 June 1648 (AGS, Eo. 2566, unfol.); Birch (ed.), *An inquiry*, p. 221.
78 Theobald Butler to Ormond, 10 October 1648 (Bodl., Carte MSS 22, fo. 335); Aiazza, *Embassy*, p. 419. O'Neill's role in the rebellion is unclear and no reference is made to it in Casway, *Owen Roe O'Neill*.
79 Theobald Butler to Ormond, 10 October 1648 (Bodl., Carte MSS 22, fo. 335); MacBain and Kennedy (eds.), *Reliquiae Celticae*, II, 207.
80 NLI, MS 345, p. 944.
81 Theobald Butler to Ormond, 10 October 1648 (Bodl., Carte MSS 22, fo. 335). Also see

munitions for the rising, were captured and held at Wexford. ('His great armada is broken at present' the supreme council was informed on 9 October.) The marquis himself appears to have escaped, but his 'plot' was yet again quashed in its infancy.[82]

News of the abortive rising spread quickly. On 11 October Taaffe informed Ormond that 'the town of Wexford desired the council to remove my lord of Antrim and his duchess thence'. Antrim's whereabouts remained unknown – it was rumoured that he had fled either to Arklow castle or to Owen Roe O'Neill – but the duchess certainly remained uncomfortably at Wexford. Taaffe added 'I am sorry for the poor lady, though she be guilty of his late folly.'[83] Antrim's civilian accomplices in the rebellion – Hugh Rochford, who had served on the 'revolutionary' seventh supreme council as a member for Leinster, and other 'suspected persons' including Dr Walter Enos – were quickly rounded up, despite protests against their arrest by the duchess of Buckingham.[84] On 12 October Ormond persuaded the assembly to declare the nuncio and his adherents traitors, although they were given twenty days in which to change their minds and return to the fold.[85] Thus, ironically, the only person to benefit from Antrim's abortive rising, at least in the short term, was Ormond himself.[86]

One account of these events, ascribed to Nicholas Plunkett, condemned Antrim for using Glengarry and his Highlanders to satisfy his personal ambitions: 'pleasing only his maggot paled brains with a dream of being great, [Antrim] involved these innocent soldiers in his unjust contrivances, and they being strangers never examined the matter further than to advance one faction against another, concluding they were still to fight against their old enemies the parliament of England'. The author continued that because of

---

MacBain and Kennedy (eds.), *Reliquiae Celticae*, II, 207; Gilbert, *Contemp. hist. 1641–52*, II, 20; MacKenzie, *History of the MacDonalds*, pp. 333–4. The lairds of Clanranald and Glengarry were later ransomed by the duchess of Buckingham. Glengarry 'then went to Wexford; a ship was sent for him by the marquis of Antrim which conveyed him to ... Uist'. Preston later suggested that some of the prisoners captured after Antrim's rebellion (except Highlanders) should be exchanged for officers from the confederate party held by O'Neill, see Preston to supreme council, 26 October 1648 (Bodl., Carte MSS 44, fo. 349).

[82] Esmond to supreme council, 9 October 1648 (Bodl., Carte MSS 44, fo. 349); *idem* to *idem*, 18 October 1648 (*ibid*., fo. 349v). Hill, *MacDonnells*, pp. 333–4. The following week, Antrim's frigates were allowed to return to sea, see Esmond to supreme council, 19 October 1648 (Bodl., Carte MSS 44, fo. 349).

[83] Taaffe to Ormond, 11 October 1648 (Bodl., Carte MSS 22, fos. 347–8).

[84] Esmond to supreme council, 14 October 1648 (*ibid*., 44, fo. 349).

[85] Ormond to Jermyn, 12 October 1648 (*ibid*., 63, fo. 548); Casway, *Owen Roe O'Neill*, p. 233.

[86] Theobald Butler to Ormond, 10 October 1648 (Bodl., Carte MSS 22, fo. 335).

Antrim's desire to be made viceroy of Ireland he 'deceived those good and otherwise well meaning men ... and drove them headlong into their own ruin'.[87] This attack was not entirely justified since the marquis was in fact promoting the interests of Clan Donald as well as his own cause, and it was therefore only appropriate that he should be supported by his Scottish kinsmen and allies. Admittedly, Antrim's rebellion was motivated by his jealousy towards Ormond but, seen from his personal perspective, it was also his last chance to overthrow the lord lieutenant before peace negotiations with the confederates officially began. Had it been well organized – properly coordinated with the Army of Ulster – rather than an impulsive, isolated gesture of defiance against Ormond, the outcome might have been very different. For if Antrim had succeeded in humiliating Ormond on the battlefield, the desperation of the Stuart cause in England might have forced the queen to replace Ormond with a commander acceptable to the clerical party; namely Antrim himself. Alternatively, the general assembly might have been persuaded to abandon their talks with Ormond and return to the nuncio's fold.

ANTRIM AND THE INDEPENDENTS

Meanwhile, talks had begun between the parliamentarians in Dublin and the nuncio's party. Father Edmund O'Reilly, vicar-general of Dublin and later Catholic archbishop of Armagh, had served as the Catholic intermediary since the spring of 1648, while Henry Jones, Protestant bishop of Clogher (and brother of Colonel Michael Jones, the commander in Dublin) represented the parliamentary regime.[88] By August Owen Roe and Jones were reported to be in direct correspondence 'upon which it is believed Owen has released Sir Theophilus Jones [another brother] with who[m] Father Rely [O'Reilly] is gone to Dublin'.[89] After the abortive October rebellion Antrim and O'Neill, using Father O'Reilly and the bishop of Clogher as mediators, renewed these talks, and by mid-November they were 'in daily treaty' with Colonel Jones in Dublin.[90] Jones's willingness to parley was justified by the fact that he was desperately short of supplies and was therefore anxious to ensure that the Army of Ulster did not join forces with those of Ormond and

---

[87] NLI, MS 345, pp. 943, 946.
[88] Casway, *Owen Roe O'Neill*, p. 227; Carte, *Ormond*, III, 467; Gilbert, *Ir. confed.*, VII, 102–3. O'Reilly is often referred to in the documents as 'Rely'.
[89] Inchiquin to Ormond, 19 August 1648 (Bodl., Carte MSS 65, fo. 420). Also see *Comment. Rinucc.*, II, 691.
[90] Rinuccini to Panzirolo, 19/29 November 1648 (Aiazza, *Embassy*, p. 441). Also see Carte, *Ormond*, VI, 584–5; NLI, MS 345, p. 140; Irish news, 3/13 April 1649 (Bodl., Clarendon MSS 37, fo. 70r–v). Casway, *Owen Roe O'Neill*, pp. 232–3.

the Irish confederates in a combined assault on the capital.[91] At this point it was rumoured that O'Neill and his commanders had agreed, in writing, to make Antrim general of the Army of Ulster and that he would 'bring all the Irish and Scots of that province [Ulster] to a right understanding and perfect unity', and that the army (then in County Cavan) was daily awaiting the marquis's arrival.[92] Why O'Neill should have offered Antrim the command of 'his' army is unclear. Perhaps he believed that Antrim's presence would give the beleaguered Ulstermen fresh hope and prevent them from deserting to the confederates; or perhaps he was merely following instructions from Rinuccini (who was now a virtual prisoner in Galway).[93]

Whatever the reason, this new prospect of power lured the marquis out of hiding and on 6 November he wrote to Sir Richard Blake, chairman of the supreme council, requesting information on the progress of the treaty with Ormond but declining Blake's offer of a safe-conduct to Kilkenny.[94] Instead, he requested a passport for Ulster; his request, hardly surprisingly, was refused.[95]

Within three days of snubbing the council, however, Antrim was well on his way to Ulster under parliamentary aegis. *The moderate intelligencer* noted his trip in remarkably neutral terms: 'The lord marquis of Antrim has relinquished the marquis of Ormond and is empowered Generalissimo for the pope's interest in this kingdom, and to that purpose rode through our quarter by Maynooth, to Owen Roe (as is conceived) to claim his authority.'[96] The report denied, however, that Colonel Jones had had any contact with this Irish papist.

By the way he wrote a letter to Colonel Jones, desiring that a gentleman might be admitted to Dublin, with propositions tending to engage the northern party under the command of Owen Roe to the parliament's service, which (if this his request might be

---

[91] *Moderate intelligencer* ... From Thursday 23 to Thursday 30 December 1648, no. 193 (London, 1648), p. 2012; Michael Jones to Lenthall, 18 October 1648 (Bodl., Ballard MSS 53, fo. 54). Also, Jones's policy toward the Irish was based on the assumption that 'the Irish being a people to be bought, though to the betraying of their dearest friend', see Jones to House of Lords, 10 November 1647 (Bodl., Carte MSS 118, fo. 41r–v).

[92] Dillon to supreme council, 10 November 1648 (Bodl., Carte MSS 44, fo. 349v). Also see Gilbert, *Contemp. hist. 1641–52*, II, 19–20.

[93] [Hogan (ed.)], *History of the warr*, p. 60. Apart from noting that the army was both 'ill-provisioned' and 'discontented', no explanation of the decision to offer Antrim command of the army is given by Casway in his biography of the general, see Casway, *Owen Roe O'Neill*, p. 233.

[94] *Comment. Rinucc.*, III, 664.

[95] Antrim to Sir Richard Blake, 6 November 1648 (Bodl., Carte MSS 44, fo. 349v).

[96] *Moderate intelligencer* ... From Thursday 30 November to Thursday 7 December 1648, no. 194 (London, 1648), p. 2022.

granted) in his opinion it was reputed feasible, but his overture being denied, he made no further stay but marched on.[97]

Other accounts of Antrim's unmolested passage through the parliamentary-held areas paint a very different picture, however. Lord Castlehaven, for instance, informed Ormond that Jones and Antrim had met and reached an agreement:

> The meeting between my Lord of Antrim and Colonel Jones was at Killcock; from whence my lord, with friar Rely [O'Reilly] ... (the instrument in the agreement between Jones and O'Neill) were conveyed to Trim where my Lord expressed himself at large against your excellency and that he would join with the devil rather than with you.[98]

Ormond was less circumstantial, but clearly suspected a deal had been struck. He reported to the Stuart court-in-exile:

> My lord of Antrim (having raised an unsuccessful commotion, against not the king nor his old masters the supreme council, but has he says against me) is now gone to command the Ulster army; whereunto he is invited, as some believe, not so much for his conduct as for his quality, to give countenance by it to that declining faction. Jones has given him rope enough; for so his giving him passage and convoy through his quarters, which was refused by this assembly.[99]

Ormond went on to condemn Jones for his hypocritical actions and for supplying O'Neill with sixty barrels of powder in return for cattle.[100]

In late November 1648 Antrim arrived safely in O'Neill's camp in Ulster and, although he never seems to have taken up his military command,[101] he persuaded O'Neill and the leading officers of the northern army to declare their severance from the general assembly on the grounds that they disapproved of the negotiations with Ormond for peace.[102] According to Rinuccini, the 'Ormondists' were 'greatly in fear of O'Neill and the marquis of Antrim, and therefore make them large offers; but, on the other hand, the parliamentarians offer still more'.[103] So there were now three main factions in Ireland: the forces of the English parliament; the uneasy alliance of the Irish royalists (led by Ormond and Inchiquin) and the moderate confederates; and, in between and weaker than either, the clerical faction supported by Antrim

---

[97] Ibid. For a similar account see *A perfect diurnall* ... From Monday 4 to Monday 11 December 1648, no. 280 (London, 1648), p. 2251.
[98] Castlehaven to Ormond, 27 November 1648 (Bodl., Carte MSS 22, fo. 694). Also see Carte, *Ormond*, VI, 584–5, 585–6.
[99] Ormond to Digby, 21 November (Carte, *Ormond*, VI, 585–6).
[100] Ibid., 584–5.
[101] Because, according to the anonymous author of the *Aphorismical discovery*, 'a provincial assembly' voted against it, see Gilbert, *Contemp. hist. 1641–52*, II, 20.
[102] Antrim and others to Sir Richard Blake, 30 November 1648 (Bodl., Carte MSS 44, fo. 350); NLI, MS 345, pp. 943, 946; Giblin, 'Catalogue of material of Irish interest', p. 75.
[103] Rinuccini to Cardinal Panzirolo, 30 October/9 November 2648 (Aiazza, *Embassy*, p. 426).

and the Army of Ulster. In order to maintain their influence, the nuncio and his allies needed to turn the tenuous association with the parliamentary forces into something more permanent. This task was entrusted to Patrick Crelly, abbot of Newry.

Late in September Crelly, then in France (p. 212 above), made contact with the Spanish ambassador in London, Don Alonso de Cárdenas, and asked him to procure a passport and protection so that he could come to England. Before granting him a pass Cárdenas insisted on being informed of the details of his business, and it is only thanks to Cárdenas's subsequent dispatch to Madrid that the full extent of Antrim's design is known. Crelly had a dual mission: first, to warn the English parliament about French ambitions in Ireland; secondly, to press upon parliament the desperate position of the nuncio's party in Ireland, so that it might be persuaded to form a military alliance with the Army of Ulster. Cárdenas warned Crelly that it was rash to deal with parliament without first securing a safe-conduct since the 'Irish had been declared rebels and were hated with an extreme passion, especially the Old Irish to whom were attributed all the cruelties and atrocities committed against the English in Ireland at the beginning of this rebellion'. Furthermore, Crelly was a Roman Catholic priest who had been intimately and publicly involved in negotiations against parliament in France and Italy. However, once Cárdenas was satisfied that Crelly's mission was genuine and 'without risk' to Spain he agreed to secure a safe-conduct for him from 'a trustworthy Independent'. Crelly appears to have arrived in England in late October 1648.[104]

The abbot's presence in London 'as agent with the parliament for Antrim and O'Neill' was well known in Ireland by the time he met with a parliamentary delegation in late November.[105] This committee included 'five Independent commissioners: two peers and three commoners with authority from parliament to listen to Crelly'.[106] Presumably the peers were drawn from those most closely allied to the radical Independents at this time (the earls of Denbigh, Pembroke, Kent, Mulgrave and Nottingham and Lord Grey of Warke);[107] and of these the two involved in the talks with Crelly were

---

[104] Cárdenas to Philip IV, 8/18 December 1648 (AGS, Eo. 2524, fo. 80). Leading Independents – Henry Marten, Henry Nevill, Thomas and James Chaloner, Thomas Scott, Colonel Popham and Denis Bond – were all on Cárdenas's pay roll, see Cárdenas's secret accounts (*ibid.*, 2532, unfol.).

[105] Castlehaven to Ormond, 27 November 1648 (Bodl., Carte MSS 22, fo. 694). Also see Irish news, 3/13 April 1649 (Bodl., Clarendon MSS 38, fo. 70v).

[106] Cárdenas to Philip IV, 8/18 December 1648 (AGS, Eo. 2524, fo. 80).

[107] *Heads of a diarie* ... From 26 December 1648 to 2 January 1649, no. 5 (London, 1649), p. 39. I am grateful to Dr John Adamson for bringing this reference to my attention and for sharing his views on this matter with me.

probably the earl of Pembroke, who was also a Spanish client, and the earl of Denbigh, who was particularly active in negotiations with radical Independents.[108] Identifying the 'three commoners' is more problematic but circumstantial evidence points to Thomas Scot, Denis Bond and Edmund Ludlow. All three were Independents and later became members of the first republican council of state, while Scott and Bond served on the standing committee responsible for Irish affairs and were also Spanish clients.[109]

As he had advised Cárdenas, Crelly brought two matters to the commissioners' attention. He relayed the details of the 'horrendous design' hatched in Paris the previous spring and suggested that there was a faction in Paris lobbying for peace with Spain in order to allow France to intervene more decisively in the British Isles.[110] He also explained how desperate was the plight of the Old Irish party in Ireland and how necessary it was to preserve Ireland 'under English rule'.[111] Two days later Crelly met with the commissioners again. They had apparently chewed over the abbot's information and now requested his advice on how the royalist plot could be undermined. Crelly offered three suggestions. First, parliament should unite its forces with those of Owen Roe against Ormond's armies. Second, if parliament agreed to this, 'someone of authority' must be sent to Ireland to alert the parliamentary commanders of their decision and to warn Antrim and O'Neill, and their followers, so that a 'suspension of arms' could be arranged while the forces united. Third, now that the French had made peace with their enemies in the German war, there was some support for France to do the same with Spain 'in order to apply themselves with more force to the plans they have for these three kingdoms'. Therefore parliament should either 'make a league' with Philip IV or try to prevent a peace between France and Spain 'at least until you have arranged and established matters in the three kingdoms'.[112] Early in December Crelly had two further meetings with the

---

[108] Both later served on the first republican council of state, Edward Raymond Turner, *The privy council of England in the seventeenth and eighteenth centuries 1603–1784* (2 vols., Baltimore, 1927–8), I, 248; Underdown, *Pride's purge*, p. 205. On Pembroke see Cárdenas's secret accounts (AGS, Eo. 2532, unfol.).

[109] Turner, *Privy council*, I, 248–9, II, 186–7, 235–6; Cárdenas's secret accounts (AGS, Eo. 2532, unfol.). Another of Crelly's contacts was 'the secretary of state of parliament', see *Comment. Rinucc.*, V, 5. Presumably this was a reference to the secretary of the council of state who was initially Walter Frost and after 1652 John Thurloe. Frost and Thurloe were also both on Cárdenas's pay roll.

[110] Paper I, presented by Crelly to parliamentary committee, December 1648 (AGS, Eo. 2524, fo. 81). The peace of Westphalia, which ended French intervention in Germany, was signed in October 1648.   [111] Ibid.

[112] Paper II, presented by Crelly to parliamentary committee, December 1648 (*ibid.*, fo. 83); Crelly's memorial, 23 January/2 February 1650 (*ibid.*, 3020, unfol.). Philip IV instructed Cárdenas to use every means at his disposal to obstruct French interests in Ireland

Independent representatives, who were particularly worried about a possible union between France and Spain in favour of Charles I and against parliament. Cárdenas forwarded a summary of the negotiations to Philip IV and noted that nothing had been decided.[113]

As it happened, before any action could be taken affairs in London were thrown into chaos when on 2 December 7,000 frustrated troops marched on Westminster to pressure the Commons to purge those members who had both refused to accept their call for Charles I to be put on trial and voted to continue peace negotiations with the king.[114] Parliamentary attempts to outmanoeuvre the troops forced the officers to cross 'their political Rubicon' and on 6 December Colonel Thomas Pride excluded from parliament 231 members (largely Presbyterians) who had voted in favour of a treaty with the king; a further 86 withdrew in protest.[115] This was the beginning of the constitutional revolution of 1648–9 which culminated in the trial and execution of a 'divine right' king, the abolition of the monarchy and the House of Lords, and the creation of an executive body in the form of a council of state to run the republic.

Pride's purge, together with the news of the 'Rump's' decision to try the king (which reached Ireland on 28 December), must have caused Antrim to think very seriously about his remaining options. After all, parliament had already tried and executed the king's most intimate advisers from the 1630s, the earl of Strafford and Archbishop Laud; would the king himself be next?

Probably only Antrim's personal hatred of Ormond, whose authority was formally recognized by the confederates on 17 January 1649, prevented him from returning to the royalist camp at this stage. In the second 'Ormond peace', signed the same day, the lord lieutenant verbally agreed to 'give unto the Roman Catholics full assurance that they shall not be molested in the possession of the churches and church livings, or of the exercise of their respective jurisdictions as they now exercise the same' until the king heard their case in a free parliament.[116] All attainders against Catholics issued since 7 August 1641 were to be declared null and void, and there was to

---

and in the English parliament, Philip IV to Cárdenas, [18/28 March 1649] (*ibid.*, 2576, unfol.).

[113] Cárdenas to Philip IV, 8/18 December 1648 (*ibid.*, 2524, fo. 80).

[114] Gentles, 'The impact of the New Model Army', p. 99.

[115] *Ibid.* Also see Smith, 'Impact on government', pp. 45–6. Underdown, *Pride's purge*, makes no reference to Crelly's negotiations. Interestingly, Cárdenas believed that the purge was advantageous to the causes of Spain and the nuncio since the Presbyterians were 'pro-royalist and pro-French', see Cárdenas to Philip IV, 8/18 December 1648 (AGS, Eo. 2524, fo. 80).

[116] Articles of peace, 17 January 1649 (Gilbert, *Ir. confed.*, VII, 184–211).

be some provision for the security of Catholic property.[117] By the treaty, the confederate government was formally dissolved and twelve 'commissioners of trust' – one of whom was Alexander MacDonnell – were appointed to mediate between Ormond and the confederates.[118] But Antrim and his isolated caucus in Ulster continued to support the nuncio; even after Charles I's execution on 30 January 1649 by 'usurpers', 'anarchists' and 'subverters of the true religion' the marquis refused to approve the election of the 'commissioners of trust' and denounced the 'Ormond peace'.[119] According to the count of Berehaven, who had recently arrived from Spain to replace La Torre as Spanish envoy, Antrim and O'Neill 'declared that they would support the nuncio with their arms and army'.[120]

News of the second 'Ormond peace' increased parliamentary fears in London that Ireland would now become the hub of royalist activity, and this gave Crelly a decided advantage in his negotiations. The willingness of some Independents to listen to a popish priest may at first seem surprising, but there are two possible explanations. On the one hand, they may merely have wished to keep the factional pot boiling in Ireland and to prevent any truce from being made between Ormond and O'Neill.[121] On the other, it could be interpreted as a genuine reflection of Leveller influence, which reached its peak between the autumn of 1648 and the late spring of 1649, because some Levellers (and other radicals) questioned England's right to intervene in the affairs of Ireland and 'saw in the Catholic Irish their fellow men, whose claim to liberty was as valid as their own'.[122] Totally opposed to English imperialism, the Levellers advocated the creation of an independent Ireland which would enjoy the status of a benevolent neutral.[123] One Leveller

---

[117] Corish, 'Ormond, Rinuccini and the confederates', p. 334.
[118] Carte, *Ormond*, III, 408. Was Alexander, however, acting as his brother's mole? In the light of the prominent role Alexander played in arranging the junction of the confederate Armies of Leinster and Munster during the spring of 1649, this is unlikely; but Antrim, nevertheless, now had access to a sympathetic ear within the Ormond regime, see Alexander MacDonnell and others to Ormond, 3, 6, 7, 9, 10 February, 2, 4 March, and 12 May 1649 (Bodl., Carte MSS 23, fos. 404, 419, 428, 438, 448, 457, MSS 24, fos. 6, 34, 689).
[119] Antrim and others to Blake, 30 January 1649 (Bodl., Carte MSS 44, fo. 350); Ormond to the bishop of Clogher, 14 February 1649 (*ibid.*, fos. 480–2); news from Brussels, 22 March/1 April 1649 (Giblin, 'Catalogue of material of Irish interest', p. 75).
[120] Berehaven to [Philip IV], 18/28 May 1649 (AGS, Eo. 2524, fo. 26). Berehaven was the son of Donal O'Sullivan Beare and grew up at the court of Philip III, Micheline Walsh, '*Destruction by peace*'. *Hugh O'Neill after Kinsale* (Monaghan, 1986), p. 127.
[121] Elkin, 'The interactions between the Irish rebellion and the English civil wars', p. 259.
[122] H. N. Brailsford, *The Levellers and the English revolution*, ed. Christopher Hill (Manchester, 1976), pp. 496–518.
[123] *Ibid.*, pp. 501–4.

pamphlet, *Several proposals for peace and freedom by an agreement of the people* published in December 1648 even suggested that Irish men who had not been involved in the 1641 rebellion should be allowed to compound for their estates on the same terms as English royalists.[124]

Such ideals were discredited when the Leveller movement became enmeshed in the mutiny by part of the New Model Army in April 1649, but in the early months of the year radical ideology together with an army discontented on account of its unpaid wages formed a potentially explosive mixture which had to be handled with extreme care by parliament. Only fear can explain satisfactorily why the newly created council of state was prepared to continue negotiations with Crelly, O'Neill and Antrim throughout the spring of 1649.[125]

According to Edmund Ludlow, the council refused Crelly an audience 'to avoid any misconstruction of their actions, but appointed a committee to speak with him'.[126] One of the members was Ludlow himself.[127] The committee, which was suspicious of Crelly, asked him why the clerical faction had not approached the royalists for assistance. Crelly replied that 'the king had broken his word with them; ... he had made them many fair promises, yet when he could make better terms with any other party, he had been always ready to sacrifice them'. Crelly was also asked why he and his associates had not approached them sooner. 'He told us', Ludlow later noted, that it was 'because such men had been possessed of the power, who had sworn their extirpation; but that now it was believed to be the interest of those in authority to grant liberty of conscience.' Crelly added that if religious toleration were granted to the Irish Catholics 'they would be as zealous for a commonwealth as any other party.'[128]

What actions the committee decided to recommend are unknown since no reference to these protracted talks was apparently allowed to survive in the records of the parliament or council.[129] Parliamentary legislation during the

---

[124] Christopher Hill, 'Seventeenth century English radicals and Ireland', in Patrick J. Corish (ed.), *Radicals, rebels and establishments* (Historical Studies, vol. XV, Belfast, 1985), pp. 40–3.

[125] Brailsford, *Levellers*, pp. 496–518.

[126] Charles H. Firth (ed.), *Memoirs of Edmund Ludlow. Lieutenant-general of the horse in the army of the Commonwealth of England, 1625–72* (2 vols., Oxford, 1894), I, 228. Also see Gardiner, *Commonwealth and protectorate*, I, 93, who suggested that this interview took place in July.

[127] Firth (ed.), *Memoirs of Edmund Ludlow*, I, 228. The other members probably included Scott, Bond and Frost, see pp. 220–1 above.

[128] *Ibid.*, I, 229.

[129] Certainly no trace of the negotiations are to be found in the relevant volumes of Rushworth, *Historical collections, Journals of the House of Commons* (or *Lords*), *Cal. SP Dom.* or *Cal. SP Ire.* Even Cárdenas's dispatches to Philip IV are unhelpful. Cárdenas merely urged

spring of 1649 does, however, provide a clue. Early in February the idea was mooted that the government would extend toleration to Catholics who agreed to renounce their belief that loyalty to the pope took precedence over their loyalty to the state; and in the following month 'an order was made in parliament for admitting Roman Catholics to compound for their estates on easy terms'.[130] So although Crelly got no immediate response to his proposal, he received some promise of religious toleration and security of landholding for the future.

The English political climate, however, was changing rapidly. The parliamentary negotiators, who now apparently included Oliver Cromwell and Henry Ireton, had no real interest in making a compromise with Irish papists, for they had already begun to muster an army of conquest (now free from Leveller influences).[131] They used the negotiations with Crelly simply to buy time. Only Charles I's alliance with the Scots had prevented an army being sent to reduce the rebellious Irish in 1648; now in the spring of 1649, with Scotland temporarily subdued and royalist resistance in England totally crushed, parliament was at last ready to deal with the 'Irish problem'.[132] For as David Stevenson recently noted, Ireland simply 'had to be reconquered, as historically subordinate to England, as a potential strategic threat, and as the home of barbarous papists whose crimes must be punished, whose religion must be suppressed'.[133]

It was a point that was totally lost on Crelly, who continued to reside in the Spanish embassy under the pseudonym 'Mr Haley'. Instead, he felt that good progress was being made and believed that his talks about 'the entire Catholic faith' with 'great men' were 'general and serious' and would soon produce results.[134] His only worry at this point was the lack of communication from Ireland. In a letter to Antrim dated 6 March he assumed that the marquis, Owen Roe and Rinuccini 'agree with Parliament', but he added that he must

---

Philip IV to send money to the 'clerical party' in Ireland because this would then enable the Old Irish to unite with parliament against the Scots and the 'Ormondists': consulta of the council of state, 3/13 March 1649 (AGS, Eo. 2524, fo. 82).

[130] Carte, *Ormond*, III, 423–4. Also see Elkin, 'The interactions between the Irish rebellion and the English civil wars', pp. 288–91; Gardiner, *Commonwealth and protectorate*, I, 81.

[131] Gilbert, *Ir. confed.*, VII, 239; Jerrold I. Casway, 'George Monck and the controversial catholic truce of 1649', *Studia Hib.*, 16 (1976), p. 66.

[132] Norah Carlin, 'The Levellers and the conquest of Ireland in 1649', *Historical Journal*, 30, no. 2 (1987), pp. 273, 276–83.

[133] David Stevenson, 'Cromwell, Scotland and Ireland', in John S. Morrill (ed.), *Oliver Cromwell and the English revolution* (London, 1990), p. 50.

[134] Crelly to Rinuccini, 9 July 1649 (*Comment. Rinucc.*, IV, 281).

have 'timely notice' of what their intentions were, or else his cause would be lost.[135]

In fact it was lost already. Antrim and O'Neill were increasingly isolated, particularly after Rinuccini's departure for the continent on 25 February, and eventually, 'Being not able to subsist in opposition (as *The kingdomes weekly intelligencer* had predicted in December 1648), they were at last forced to 'unite themselves with the marquis of Ormond.'[136] In the spring of 1649 another cleric, Francis Nugent, a Capuchin and probably one of Antrim's kinsmen, was sent to France to discuss a reconciliation with the queen mother and Charles II; while Antrim and O'Neill opened negotiations directly with the Irish royalists.[137] On 28 February Antrim was granted a safe-conduct to go where he pleased in the territories which Ormond controlled,[138] and he travelled first to Kilkenny and then to Wexford where, early in March, he wrote to the lord lieutenant suggesting that the two should meet. Their parley was delayed by Ormond's departure from Kilkenny to Limerick; nevertheless, Antrim persisted. On 17 March he requested an audience either on Ormond's return to Kilkenny or at Carrick. No reply was received to this letter and so Antrim renewed his request on 25 March: 'finding no time by your lordship appointed to the bishop of Dromore for my going to wait upon you, I have sent my servant express to desire [from] your lordship [that] my safe conduct may be renewed, and as soon as you please to appoint me your time to kiss your hands'.[139] Shortly afterwards, despite being warned that

---

[135] Crelly to Antrim, 6 March 1649 (Casway, 'The clandestine correspondence of Father Patrick Crelly', pp. 18–19). Also see Aiazza, *Embassy*, p. 465. Unbeknown to Crelly the Spanish council of state, despite some pressure from leading ministers (including the marquis of Castel Rodrigo), instructed Cárdenas not to interfere further in Irish affairs on the grounds that if the troubles in France continued, the French would not be able to intervene in Ireland either. Subsequent events in Ireland were to vindicate Philip IV's decision; but Spain's lack of support undermined Crelly, see consulta of the council of state, 3/13 March and Philip IV to Cárdenas, 8/18 March 1649 (AGS, Eo. 2524, fo. 82, and 2579, unfol.).

[136] *The kingdomes weekly intelligencer* ... From Tuesday 12 to Tuesday 19 December 1648, no. 290 (London, 1648), p. 1192. See also Casway, 'George Monck and the controversial catholic truce', pp. 71–2. Antrim only told Crelly on 29 March that Owen Roe, who was 'without assistance from any quarter, will force those of that party to make a deal with Ormond on the best conditions that can be obtained', Cárdenas to Philip IV, [August] 1649 (AGS, Eo., 2524, fo. 33).

[137] Gardiner, *Commonwealth and protectorate*, I, 76; Cárdenas to Philip IV, [August] 1649 (AGS, Eo., 2524, fo. 33); Irish news, 3/13 April 1649 (Bodl., Clarendon MSS 37, fo. 69); Gilbert, *Contemp. hist. 1641–52*, I, xl.

[138] Gilbert, *Ir. confed.*, VII, 268; *The marquesse of Ormond's proclamation concerning the peace concluded with the Irish rebells* ... (London, 27 February 1649), p. 16.

[139] Antrim to Ormond, 25 March 1649 (Bodl. Carte MSS 24, fo. 246). See also *idem* to *idem*, 17 March 1649 (*ibid.*, fo. 168).

'for all his ... pretenses [Antrim] pursues his old ways', Ormond agreed to meet him.[140]

Ormond's grand strategy still envisaged an offensive against the parliamentary garrison in Dublin followed, once the capital was in royalist hands, by a campaign into England. But for his plan to succeed he needed to unite the various Irish factions under his leadership and to neutralize individual warlords such as Antrim who was still capable of mustering a personal army of 'three hundred of the northern men and hilanders' under Brian MacPhelim O'Byrne and a further 200 men under Charles Kavanagh.[141] According to Bellings's account, the two noblemen met at Kilkenny and Antrim promised 'to employ all his endeavours in procuring Brian MacPhelim and the Kavanaghs, who were of General O Neale's party, so that he [Ormond] might not have an enemy to the back of him while he sat at the siege of Dublin'.[142]

But Antrim did not keep his word. In a letter dated 29 March to Crelly, he claimed he would do everything possible to cripple Ormond's war-effort and to ensure that 'nothing decisive is done'.[143] This is no doubt why he tried to strike up a separate deal with Prince Rupert of the Rhine, who had arrived at Kinsale with the royalist fleet late in February 1649, with the intention of uniting the Irish privateering fleet with his own.[144] 'I pray you tell his excellency [Ormond]' Daniel O'Neill wrote on 29 March 'that lately there has passed two or three expresses between Prince Rupert and my lord of Antrim ... that Prince Rupert assures my lord of Antrim he shall be admiral of this kingdom under him as soon as the king comes.'[145] Though O'Neill condemned their 'foolish designs', this arrangement made perfect sense since Rupert was experiencing severe difficulties in finding enough sailors to man his fleet and had resorted to the press-gang.[146] Antrim, thanks to his privateering contacts, was not only in a position to provide him with the necessary manpower but also to put his own frigates, and those of his privateering accomplices, at Rupert's disposal. The London press quickly

---

[140] Edmund Butler to Ormond, 24 March 1649 (Bodl., Carte MSS 24, fo. 208). Also see Irish news, 3/13 April 1649 (Bodl., Clarendon MSS 37, fo. 69).
[141] Bellings to George Lane and Ormond, 30 March 1649 (Gilbert, *Ir. confed.*, VII, 277).
[142] *Ibid.*, 123.
[143] Cited in a letter from Cárdenas to Philip IV, [August] 1649 (AGS, Eo., 2524, fo. 33). Also see Rinuccini to Panzirolo, 19/29 November 1648 (Aiazza, *Embassy*, p. 441).
[144] Casway, *Owen Roe O'Neill*, p. 239; Gilbert, *Ir. confed.*, VII, 273.
[145] Daniel O'Neill to Lane, 29 March 1649 (Bodl., Carte MSS 24, fo. 304). Also see Carte, *Ormond*, III, 438–9.
[146] Michael L. Baumber, *General-at-sea. Robert Blake and the seventeenth-century revolution in naval warfare* (London, 1989), p. 75; Gardiner, *Commonwealth and protectorate*, I, 13–14, 87; Gilbert, *Ir. confed.*, VII, 273.

caught wind of this: 'Many of Prince Rupert's men have left him; and he hath scarce half men enough to man his ships ... Divers of the Irish mariners have declared that they will not sail under him, but desire that the earl of Antrim ... may be their admiral.'[147]

Considering how successful the Irish privateers were at this point – 'Every day brings in some intelligence or other of their piracies on the western seas' *The kingdomes weekly intelligencer* lamented in December 1648 – appointing Antrim vice-admiral of the fleet was a small price to pay for such powerful reinforcements.[148] For his part, Antrim hoped that this position would help him both to protect his privateering fleet from interference by an administration loyal to Ormond and to provide him with a much-needed source of revenue, since the royalist ascendancy over the confederates denied him, and his wife, the pensions they had formerly received from the Catholic administration. Moreover, Antrim's status as a 'traitor' to the royalist cause had given Andreas FitzPatrick, high sheriff of Queen's County, an opportunity to seize estates there belonging to the second duke of Buckingham, which had up to that point provided the couple with £500 per year.[149]

Ultimately Antrim's ambitions were frustrated by the parliamentary blockade of Kinsale over the summer of 1649.[150] And, to make matters worse, the news from London was depressing. Although a truce had been concluded on 8 May between O'Neill and the parliamentary commander in Ulster, George Monck, it was subsequently condemned by parliament and Monck was recalled.[151] Then, early in August, negotiations with Crelly were abandoned because the Independents did not wish 'to take upon themselves the conclusion of an agreement with the Old Irish (even though they wanted to) because they know the populace abhors them [the Irish] passionately'.[152]

---

[147] *Continued heads of perfect passages* ... From Friday 27 April to 4 May 1649, no. 3 (London, 1649), p. 17.

[148] *The kingdomes weekly intelligencer* ... From Tuesday 12 to Tuesday 19 December 1648, no. 290 (London, 1648), p. 1192; Ohlmeyer, 'Irish privateers', pp. 124–6.

[149] Petition of Colonel James MacDonnell to Ormond, c. September 1649 (Bodl., Carte MSS 155, fo. 85). The second duke of Buckingham – via Lord Byron – also requested that Ormond should secure 'such ease for the tenants, that his grace may hope for some benefit out of it ... Notwithstanding his mother's follies which no man [censures] more than he', see Byron to Ormond, 27 July/6 August (*Ormonde MSS*, I, 131).

[150] Baumber, *General-at-sea*, pp. 75–7; Gardiner, *Commonwealth and protectorate*, I, 87.

[151] The truce negotiations are discussed in Casway, 'George Monck and the controversial catholic truce'; *The true state of the transactions of Colonel George Monk with Owen-Mac-Art-O-Neal; as it was reported to the parliament by the counsel of state* ... (London, 15 August, 1649), pp. 3–5; Elkin, 'The interactions between the Irish rebellion and the English civil wars', pp. 287–90; Casway, *Owen Roe O'Neill*, p. 247.

[152] Cárdenas to Philip IV, [August] 1649 (AGS, Eo. 2524, fo. 33). Also see *Comment. Rinucc.*, IV, 282; Gardiner, *Commonwealth and protectorate*, I, 93–4.

Isolated and desperate, Antrim once again approached Ormond, who reluctantly agreed to 'employ his present and effectual endeavours in the king's service' and advanced him £100 'least he should not be able to put his good intentions into execution through want of means'.[153] But this half-hearted reconciliation was both too little and too late to save the royalist cause, for on 15 August 1649 a large parliamentarian army landed in Ireland under the personal command of Oliver Cromwell and thereby opened a new Pandora's box.

---

[153] Ormond to the commissioners of trust, 21 August 1649 (PROI, Carte Transcripts 25, p. 200).

9

Cromwellian conquest and occupation (August 1649 – May 1660)

COMPROMISE AND COLLABORATION (1649–51)

'Crumwell came over' Bishop Nicholas French later reminisced, 'and like a lightening passed through the land.'[1] The rout of the marquis of Ormond's army by the parliamentarians under Michael Jones at Rathmines on 2 August 1649 enabled Oliver Cromwell and his force of 12,000 veterans, armed with heavy artillery, to land unmolested near Dublin. Within three months the key royalist and confederate strongholds of Drogheda (11 September), Wexford (11 October), New Ross (19 October),and Carrickfergus (2 November) were in English hands. The capture of Kilkenny (27 March 1650), Clonmel (10 May), Carlow (24 July) and Charlemount (14 August), of Limerick (27 October 1651) and finally of Galway (12 April 1652) completed the Cromwellian conquest of Ireland. In just under three years the parliamentary army had succeeded in uniting Ireland under one ruler, something Ormond, the Scottish covenanters and the confederate armies had all failed to do.

But what did the military conquest of Ireland mean to the marquis of Antrim, who was based in Waterford during the 1649 offensive? The extermination of the 'flower of Ormond's army' at Drogheda affected him little[2] but the extirpation of the privateering fleet, which doubled as Ireland's navy, at Wexford – now described as 'the Dunkirk of Ireland, and a place only famous for being infamous' – was another matter.[3] On the eve of Wexford's fall (10 October 1649) 'a party of his Excellencies [Cromwell] foot, by the help of some vessels, took the Earl of Antrim's frigate with 14 guns'.[4] This was probably the *Mary of the Isles* and was the fourth of Antrim's warships to have been captured by the parliamentary navy in less than two years.

---

[1] Nicholas French, *The unkinde desertor of loyall men and true frinds* (1846 edn.), II, p. 13.
[2] Hayton and O'Brien (eds.), J. G. Simms, *War and politics*, p. 4.
[3] *The Irish monthly mercury*, Issue 1 (Cork; reprinted London, 1649), p. 3.
[4] *A history or brief chronicle of the chief matters of the Irish warres...* (London, 1650). Also see Denis Murphy, *Cromwell in Ireland. A history of Cromwell's Irish campaign* (Dublin, 1897), p. 160.

In February 1648 a formidable frigate ('one of the best frigates that the earl of Antrim hath') had been seized by parliamentary warships off the southwest coast of Ireland. Twenty-two guns, three barrels of gunpowder, 100 muskets, 200 'halberts', pikes and other weapons, twenty barrels of beef, forty barrels of beer and wine, plus 'good store of furniture ... and divers chests, trunks and boxes' were plundered from this vessel.[5] The *Mary of Antrim*, which had been mortgaged in February 1647 but was still referred to as Antrim's 'vice-admiral', was also taken prize by a parliamentary frigate, the *Tiger*, off Land's End in February 1649.[6] In July 1649 the *St Peter of Waterford* met a similar fate when it was captured by the *Phoenix* near Portland Bill after a chase lasting two days.[7] According to a London newspaper 'ten guns, fourteen oars and seventy-five men' were taken off the frigate, which was described as 'an excellent sayler'.[8] Thus the capture of the *Mary of the Isles* in Wexford harbour three months later spelt the end of Antrim's brief yet remarkably successful career as a privateer.

During the autumn of 1649, however, the marquis was apparently more worried about his wife than his privateering flotilla. Though the duchess had been granted permission to join her son and the exiled royal court in France towards the end of August, lack of funds forced her to remain in Waterford with her husband.[9] The marquis badgered Ormond for money 'by reason my good woman must be forced for security to move further and if the danger increases she must part this kingdom'.[10] But no money arrived and the duchess remained in Waterford, where her health took a dramatic turn for the worse in late October. This time Antrim pleaded with the lord lieutenant to send Dr Fennell at once to tend to his dying wife. In a desperate attempt to force Ormond to act immediately Antrim concluded his distraught letter: 'I beg this favour upon my knees ... and for her son's sake, which will be of much more force than any argument that can possible [*sic*] be alleged by your

---

[5] *A great victory at sea ...*, pp. 2–3, 6.
[6] See pp. 185, 194 above; James Peacock to Warwick, 6 February 1649 (Bodl., Tanner MSS 57/2, fo. 514); Appleby, 'An Irish letter of marque', pp. 218–21; examination of Antonio 'Undermerch', 5 February 1649 (PRO, HCA 13/250, part I), and *ibid.*, 34/4, fos. 76–7, 96–7. The frigate was allegedly en route to Newfoundland, *Continued heads of perfect passages ... From Friday 4 to Friday 11 May 1649*, no. 4 (London, 1649), p. 34.
[7] Sentence delivered on the *St Peter of Waterford*, 3 August 1649 (PRO, HCA 34/4/131–2).
[8] *Perfect occurrences of every daies journall in parliament ... From Friday 6 to Thursday 12 July 1649*, no. 131 (London, 1649), p. 1105.
[9] Gilbert, *Ir. confed.*, VII, 268; Robert Long to Ormond, 24 July/3 August 1649 (Bodl., Carte MSS 25, fo. 138). Antrim's permit was, however, only to be issued at Ormond's discretion.
[10] Antrim to Ormond, 1 October 1649 (Bodl., Carte MSS 25, fo. 640).

excellence's most humble servant.'[11] His efforts were to no avail. Shortly afterwards Katherine, duchess of Buckingham and marchioness of Antrim, died, perhaps from the plague that was raging through Ireland.[12] She was buried outside the walls of Waterford.[13]

With the death of the wife, whom he had loved and cherished deeply, Antrim's prospects looked bleaker than ever. Any claims he may have had to at least some of her extensive English estates and properties all passed now to her son, the second duke of Buckingham. He also lost an influential and powerful partner who was experienced in manipulating the networks of patronage on which his survival was so dependent. Finally, her death left him a childless widower – albeit aged only thirty-nine.

Politically speaking, Antrim was also now bereft, and so, in yet another remarkable volte-face, he clandestinely threw in his lot with the Cromwellians. Though the details are obscure, he appears to have been in fairly close contact with the invaders – especially with Henry Ireton, Cromwell's son-in-law – ever since their arrival in Ireland the previous summer.[14] He communicated with them through Patrick Crelly who, after the failure of his talks with the Independents in London, had followed Cromwell to Ireland in the knowledge that, even though negotiations for religious toleration for Catholics had foundered, 'Cromwell or anyone else who goes as general will carry an order and full powers to negotiate with the marquis of Antrim and O'Neill.'[15] Whether, as some suggested, Antrim was actively involved (using Hugh Rochford as his intermediary) in persuading the inhabitants of Wexford to surrender to Cromwell is unclear.[16] But he certainly demonstrated his willingness to serve the Cromwellians by securing the surrender of nearby New Ross (19 October 1649), and Ireton later reminded the English council of state of the 'singular service' Antrim had done the army 'since the first day

---

[11] Antrim to Ormond, 26 October 1649 (*ibid.*, 26, fo. 35).
[12] Antrim begged yet again for money so that he could 'perform the last office I owe unto a friend so dear unto me', Antrim to Ormond, 2 November 1649 (*Ormonde MSS*, I, 139).
[13] *Comment. Rinucc.*, IV, 362.
[14] Inchiquin to Ormond, 3 November 1649 (Bodl., Clarendon MSS 38, fo. 101); John Dongan to Ormond, 24 August 1649 (Bodl., Carte MSS 25, fo. 349); warrant by Ireton, 7 January 1650 (*ibid.*, 118, fo. 45v, and TCD, MS 844, fo. 96); Henry Jones to Antrim, 11 February 1650 (*ibid.*). Robert W. Ramsey, *Henry Ireton* (London, 1949), chapters 15 and 16, highlights the compromising, conciliatory nature of Ireton's rule in Ireland.
[15] Cárdenas to Philip IV, [August] 1649 (AGS, Eo. 2524, fo. 33). For further details on Crelly's talks see pp. 220–5 above.
[16] John Dongan to Ormond, 24 August 1649 (Bodl., Carte MSS 25, fo. 349); Robert Dunlop (ed.), *Ireland under the Commonwealth. Being a selection of documents relating to the government of Ireland, 1651–9* (2 vols., Manchester, 1913), I, 124; Murphy, *Cromwell in Ireland*, p. 145; Carte, *Ormond*, III, 489–90.

they came before Rosse'.[17] Without Antrim's intervention the town might not have been taken so soon, for according to royalist rumours en route to Ross Cromwell's army had threatened to mutiny 'for winter quarters', and only continued after being reassured that the town 'would be rendered upon summons'.[18]

There are several possible reasons for the marquis's decision to side with 'the enemy'. First, he believed that only Cromwellian support would enable him to retrieve his Ulster inheritance and protect the interests of Clan Donald. The situation in East Ulster was unusually complex during the later 1640s; the Scottish army remained in Counties Antrim and Down (despite being routed at Benburb in 1646) until the bulk of the force returned to fight for the king in Scotland late in 1648, then over the course of the next twelve months effective military control of the key strongholds in East Ulster passed to parliamentary forces. Second, it offered him an opportunity to regain some of the political power he had enjoyed during the later 1640s. Third, and equally important to Antrim, it provided a base from which to continue his personal feud against the lord lieutenant.

Ormond's future at this moment looked bleak indeed. His troops were dispirited and mutinous; the 'men of our side' he complained to Inchiquin 'have as much mind to destroy one the other, as either have to destroy the common enemy'.[19] Admittedly Ormond had managed to offset some of the disastrous losses suffered by his armies at the hands of the Cromwellians by persuading Owen Roe O'Neill and the Army of Ulster to join him; but O'Neill's death (6 November), less than three weeks after the treaty had been signed, created a power vacuum. Ormond was determined to keep O'Neill's veteran warriors in the royalist camp, but Antrim, who saw himself as O'Neill's heir apparent, as usual had an alternative strategy. After burying his wife, he hurried from Waterford to Clonmel where he assured the mayor of the town 'that all the Ulster men were ready to forsake ... [Ormond] and are discontented',[20] and directed the 'dispersing of printed papers amongst his majesty's garrisons for debauching the soldiers therein'.[21] He also disseminated the rumour, which he claimed that he had from a reliable parliamentary source, that Lord Inchiquin, commander-in-chief of the king's army in Ireland and lord president of Munster, had sold out to the Commonwealth

---

[17] The substance of the earl of Antrim's declaration, undated (Bodl., Carte MSS 28, fo. 366).
[18] Ormond to Castlehaven, 24 October 1649 (*ibid.*, 26, fo. 16). Ormond was furious and ordered an enquiry into why the town surrendered, Ormond to Castlehaven, 22 October 1649 (*ibid.*, fo. 15).
[19] Inchiquin to Ormond, 3 November 1649 (Bodl., Clarendon MSS 38, fo. 101).
[20] John Walshe to Ormond, 16 November 1649 (*ibid.*, 26, fo. 219).
[21] Petition of adventurers and soldiers to Charles II, [August, 1663] (Bodl., Carte MSS 44, fos. 376–7).

(England had been declared a 'Commonwealth' on 19 May 1649).²² Inchiquin denied the charge. But, as Gardiner noted, 'Whatever the truth may have been, the mere fact that the charge was made weakened the authority of Inchiquin, weak enough already.'²³

Ormond, at least, saw Antrim's efforts as highly effective. In a revealing letter to Charles II, he claimed that the royalist war-effort in Ireland was crippled by the 'natural distrust of the people and by the use thereof made by my lord marquis of Antrim, who hath not ceased ... to disturb the minds of the [people] and to render my Lord of Inchiquin and me suspected of them'. Ormond admitted that he had intended to arrest Antrim but 'he, suspecting my intention, pretended sickness'. In utter desperation the lord lieutenant even contemplated resigning his post: 'I should not esteem myself unhappy or much prejudiced by having no more to do with a people that can be wrought upon by so shallow an engine as my Lord Antrim' he complained to Charles II.²⁴

Ormond's despair was entirely justified for it was soon reported in royalist circles that the people were so fed up with the lord lieutenant that they wanted the papal nuncio Rinuccini to come back and take over the reins of power.²⁵ This rumour was no doubt occasioned by Crelly's return to Rome late in the autumn of 1649 to secure foreign assistance for Antrim's attempts to unseat Ormond.²⁶ Towards the end of January 1650 the abbot approached the Spanish ambassador there for assistance. After explaining (as best he could) the factional alignments in Ireland, and the influence of the French over the 'New Irish' (as he termed them) led by Ormond and Inchiquin, he begged that Spain intervene on behalf of the Old Irish, led by Antrim and supported by the Independents, in order to prevent a French takeover in Ireland.²⁷ In addition,

---

²² *Cal. SP Ire., 1660–2*, pp. 293–4.
²³ Gardiner, *Commonwealth and protectorate*, I, 138; Gilbert, *Contemp. hist. 1641–52*, III, 332–3. Inchiquin had been a parliamentarian from 1644 to 1648, which made Antrim's charge seem more plausible.
²⁴ Ormond to Charles II, 15 December 1649 (Bodl., Carte MSS 26, fos. 381–3v).
²⁵ A report on Irish affairs, 21/31 January 1650 (Bodl., Clarendon MSS 39, fo. 56).
²⁶ *Comment. Rinucc.*, IV, 283. By early January 1650 Crelly, described by one royalist source as 'a cunning fellow and a boldface', was living 'incognito among the O'Neilists at St. Isidors' in Rome, Robert Meynell to Cottington, 8/18 January 1650 (*Clarendon SP*, II, 509–10).
²⁷ Copy of a memorial given to the duke of Infantado by an Irish gentleman [Crelly], 23 January/2 February 1650 (AGS, Eo. 3020, unfol.); *Comment. Rinucc.*, IV, 536. Ignorant of Irish affairs, Infantado could only refer Crelly's request to Madrid where it appears to have been ignored, Infantado to Philip IV, 10/20 February 1650 (AGS, Eo. 3020, unfol.). Relations between the Spaniards and the Independents were at this point remarkably harmonious, see Loomie, 'Cárdenas and the Long Parliament', pp. 306–7; *idem*, 'London's Spanish chapel', p. 413.

Crelly continued to work for 'a right understanding ... between independence [sic] and Catholics'.²⁸ In other words, the abbot's negotiations also included Catholics in England who, in return for religious toleration, would offer their support to the new regime.²⁹

In all Crelly spent six months in Rome lobbying leading cardinals for aid and finally, thanks to Rinuccini's intervention, he secured another audience with the pope himself. The abbot set out to demonstrate that 'Cromwell was much disposed to a liberty of religion, if not formal toleration of popery, and would much incline the parliament thereto, and therefore that it was not safe to provoke either.'³⁰ The papacy accepted Crelly's analysis and much to the disgust of the royalists not only refused to assist Charles II but even sent an agent (Anthony Geoghegan) to take the matter up with the Irish clergy.³¹ Ultimately, nothing came of these talks, though the following year it was rumoured that, together with Antrim, Crelly had secured concessions for Irish Catholics of which the English parliament, the pope and Philip IV all approved.³² So in June 1650 Crelly jubilantly hurried back to England to attend to 'affairs of the Catholic faith and his own house'.³³

Meanwhile, in Ireland, Antrim sought to have himself elected by the Ulster provincial council, made up of two representatives from the nine counties and others from the important towns and cities, as Owen Roe's successor as commander of the Army of Ulster. There were four leading candidates: Hugh Dubh O'Neill, who was Owen Roe's nephew and major-general of the army;

---

²⁸ Anthony Geoghegan to Mr Haly [Crelly], 4 February 1652 (Bodl., Clarendon MSS 42, fo. 347). Crelly was not alone. For example a Catholic Englishman (William Metham) believed that 'cooperation with the protectorate was the right policy for catholics, and he went to Rome to act as an unofficial agent of the policy', Hugh Aveling, *Northern catholics* (London, 1966), p. 307.

²⁹ Carte, *Ormond*, III, 423–4.

³⁰ C. H. Firth, 'Thomas Scot's account of his actions as intelligencer during the Commonwealth', *EHR*, 12, no. 45 (Jan. 1897), p. 120.

³¹ *Ibid.*, p. 120; Loomie, 'London's Spanish chapel', p. 413.

³² Gilbert, *Contemp. hist. 1641–52*, III, xvi; *Comment. Rinucc.*, IV, 536, V, 210. Royalist spies in Rome also feared the conclusion of some sort of alliance, however unlikely, between the parliament and the pope, Father Thomas Babth[orpe] to Cottington, 21/31 July 1650 (Bodl., Clarendon MSS 40, fo. 75v). On Crelly's death in 1655 Geoghegan appears to have continued negotiations with the Independents in his place, P[eter] T[albot] to Ormond, 2/12 August 1656 (*ibid.*, 52, fo. 164).

³³ Copy of a memorial given to Infantado by an Irish gentleman, 23 January/2 February 1650 (AGS, Eo. 3020, unfol.). Also see Robert Meynell to Cottington and Hyde, 14/24 June 1650 (Bodl., Clarendon MSS 40, fo. 75v). Crelly also served as a papal agent in London, Gilbert, *Contemp. hist. 1641–52*, II, 138–9.

Antrim's Protestant cousin and former ally Daniel O'Neill; Heber Mac-Mahon, Catholic bishop of Clogher, who had been an intimate of Owen Roe; and Antrim himself. Since the election date was set for March 1650, the candidates and their factions spent most of January and February jockeying for support.[34] Little is known about Antrim's faction except that he was supported by Sir George Monro (a nephew of Major-General Robert Monro who in 1648 had embraced the royalist cause) together with those clerics who had followed Rinuccini.[35] The marquis must also have enjoyed a considerable following among the Ulster gentry since Ormond genuinely feared that they intended electing him, although he was a 'known instrument of Cromwell'. The lord lieutenant could only hope that Clogher's influence would prevent a person 'so unfit that cannot keep his own foolish council' from being chosen.[36]

Despite rumours that Antrim had in fact won the election, Ormond's hopes were realized; the politically astute but militarily inexperienced bishop of Clogher was appointed commander of the army on 18 March.[37] But it would seem that every effort was made to buy Antrim's continued support. The archbishop of Dublin (according to an Ormondist informer) suggested that 'if his lordship and his friends would give way to the election of bishop Mc-Mahon to be general, means should be used that Antrim should be made lord lieutenant in your excellency's place'.[38]

Rather than winning the marquis over to the royalist side, however, the failure to secure military command and thus political power pushed him even deeper into the Commonwealth camp. Immediately after the election, he made for Cromwellian quarters in County Meath where, apart from the odd visit to his Country Antrim estate, he appears to have remained with the main army for the remainder of 1650.[39] The bishop of Cork later asserted that Ireton's tent 'was his sanctuary' and that Antrim spent most of his time with

---

[34] Jerrold I. Casway, 'The Belturbet council and election of March 1650', *Clogher Record*, 12, no. 2 (1986), pp. 160–8; Cregan, 'An Irish cavalier ... 1642–51', pp. 128–9; Gilbert, *Contemp. hist. 1641–52*, II, 70, III, 212.
[35] Clanricard to Ormond, 15 February 1650 (Bodl., Carte MSS 26, fo. 408); Anthony Geoghegan to Mr Haly [Crelly], 4 February 1652 (*ibid.*, 42, fos. 345–6); *Comment. Rinucc.*, V, 5, 26; [Hogan (ed.)], *History of the warr*, pp. 113–15; Casway, 'The Belturbet council', pp. 163–4; Gardiner, *Commonwealth and protectorate*, I, 171; Stevenson, *Scottish Covenanters*, pp. 277–8.
[36] Ormond to Clanricard, 16 February 1650 (Bodl., Carte MSS 26, fo. 696).
[37] HMC *rep. 13*, p. 523.
[38] Humphrey Galbraith to Ormond, 26 March 1650 (Bodl., Carte MSS 27, fo. 203).
[39] He certainly returned to his estates in the autumn of 1650, *Cal. SP Ire.*, 1647–60, p. 380.

the general who, after Cromwell's departure for Britain at the end of May, became commander-in-chief of the parliamentary forces in Ireland.[40] While Antrim appears to have played no direct part in defeating the Army of Ulster under MacMahon at Scarrifhollis in County Donegal (21 June 1650), he was present at the siege of Carlow (July) and tried to persuade his former followers there to surrender peacefully.[41] Those who agreed to do so were sometimes rewarded with the return of their farms. For example, Captain William Stewart, 'coming in by capitulation with the earl of Glenarm [i.e. Antrim] under whom he served in this nation. He is by these articles to have his estates restored to him ... according to the said agreement made between him and the said earl.'[42]

During these months relations between Antrim and Ireton and his officers became increasingly friendly and intimate. So much so that in May 1650 the marquis revealed to them the late king's eagerness in the spring of 1641 to use Strafford's 'new Irish army' against his recalcitrant English parliament.[43] Antrim's confessions clearly delighted the Cromwellians, who then insisted that he formally swear to their authenticity, since they offered further justification for the recent decision to execute their late sovereign. Colonel Venables, commander of the parliamentary forces in Ulster, lost no time in informing the bishop of Cork of Charles I's involvement with Irish papists early in 1641. When the bishop suggested (or so he claimed at the Restoration) that the colonel was lying, Venables 'broke forth into a violent declaration against all cavaliers, blaming them that they should still continue obstinate [in] the discoursing of that which was so conspicuous to all [in]different persons in the world'.[44]

For his part, Antrim received several important favours from the new regime. In addition to restoring his followers to their property, Ireton promised Antrim that he should either be allowed to compound for his estates in Ulster or be awarded lands equivalent to them elsewhere in

---

[40] Examination of bishop of Cork, Cloyne and Ross, 1 February 1661 (*ibid.*, 1660–2, p. 208/PRO, SP 63/306/45 (fo. 87)).
[41] *Cal. SP Ire.*, 1663–5, pp. 214–17; some observations of adventurers and soldiers on the estate claimed by Antrim, [1661] (Bodl., Carte MSS 44, fos. 328–31); petition of adventurers and soldiers to Charles II, [August, 1663] (*ibid.*, fos. 376–7); Hill, *MacDonnells*, p. 336.
[42] George Monck to Captain Talbot, 29 August 1654 (PRONI, T473/1. p. 49).
[43] The details and significance of this 'Antrim plot' are discussed at length in Ohlmeyer, 'The "Antrim plot" of 1641', and on pp. 96–9 above.
[44] Examination of bishop of Cork, Cloyne and Ross, 1 February 1661 (*Cal. SP Ire.*, 1660–2, p. 208/PRO, SP 63/306/45 (fo. 87)).

Ireland.⁴⁵ Accordingly, the marquis received permission in August 1650 to put his case before the council of state in London and to 'go among his tenants to gather what money he could for the fitting of him for his journey and by virtue thereof he raised £1,000 amongst them'.⁴⁶ He was also given an amnesty from being arrested by his creditors for two months.⁴⁷ The marquis arrived at Chester on 3 December with his factors, Archibald Stewart and Daniel MacNaughten, whom he sent on to London to make the necessary arrangements for his sojourn there. Within six days Antrim had reached the earl of Newport's house in London 'but he was scarce lighted, when Stewart and [Mac]Naughten finding what entertainment he was like to receive sent him word that he should instantly return to Barnard [Barnet?] until he heard from them'.⁴⁸ He left at once but 'it being late, he took up his lodging at Highgate, where he was scarce settled when the constable of the town did beset the house with his guard and secured him until the next morning and then carried him before a justice of the peace'.⁴⁹ The council of state was immediately informed of Antrim's mission and of Ireton's support for his case but, though loath to offend Ireton, they felt obliged to instruct the local officers to send Antrim 'back from wither he came'. The 'Day's Proceedings' of the council of state for 10 December recorded that the marquis of Antrim had been 'denied his composition with Parliament' and that the appropriate officials in Ireland be notified accordingly. Forbidden even to set foot in London, the marquis returned to Dublin, arriving early in January 1651.⁵⁰

Depressed at being denied a hearing, the marquis visited Ireton in Kilkenny before returning to Ulster where he continued to promote the Cromwellian war-effort, and to hinder 'all levies and assistances' in the province on the king's behalf.⁵¹ His success in winning over the general population in Ulster –

---

⁴⁵ See for instance George Monck to Captain Talbot, 29 August 1654 (PRONI, T473/1, p. 49). A similar offer was made to Castlehaven: Ireton promised him that 'if I would retire and live in England, I should not only enjoy my estate, but remain in safety with esteem and favour of the parliament', *The earl of Castlehaven's review*, p. 172.
⁴⁶ The substance of the earl of Antrim's declaration, undated (Bodl., Carte MSS 28, fo. 366).
⁴⁷ The substance of the earl of Antrim's declaration, undated (*ibid.*, fo. 366); some observations of the adventurers and soldiers, [April] 1661 (*ibid.*, 44, fo. 330); Hill, *MacDonnells*, p. 278. For further details on Antrim's debts, see pp. 61–8 above.
⁴⁸ The substance of the earl of Antrim's declaration, undated (Bodl., Carte MSS 28, fo. 366). Newport was a court favourite during the 1630s and had served the king until his capture by parliament in 1646. He was tried but allowed to live in London, *DNB*, 'Newport'.
⁴⁹ The substance of the earl of Antrim's declaration, undated (Bodl., Carte MSS 28, fo. 366).
⁵⁰ *Cal. SP Dom., 1650*, pp. 463, 465, 567.
⁵¹ Petition of adventurers and soldiers to Ormond, [30 July 1663] (Bodl., Carte MSS 44, fo. 374). Whether or not he was allowed to reside on his estates is unclear.

'the marquis of Antrim having too great an influence upon the affections of most of that province' – was duly reported to Ormond, who had left for the continent the previous December.[52]

Equally valuable to the Commonwealth were Antrim's efforts to disrupt the Scottish royalists' war-effort. The 'third Civil War' had begun with Charles II's arrival in Scotland in June 1650 and the raising of a formidable royalist army under David Leslie. However, the following month Cromwell and a parliamentary army of 15,000 invaded Scotland and on 3 September routed Leslie's army at Dunbar, leading an increasingly desperate Charles II to counterattack the next year by marching into England. This shift in events greatly strengthened Antrim's position since the Republic now needed his support for an anti-Stuart coalition more than ever. Just as his 'secret weapon' during the Bishops' Wars and the 1640s had been the political geography of East Ulster and the Western Isles, and the influence he enjoyed on both sides of the North Channel, so too from the summer of 1650 he played upon the fear among his enemies that he was about to invade Scotland again.[53] For instance in July 1651 Ormond was informed of 'the malicious folly of Antrim, who is now as vainly, though more dishonestly, as in my Lord Strafford's time threatening Scotland with an invasion'.[54] But Antrim's threat was not 'vain': he had, after all, previously planned at least five separate invasions of the Isles under much less favourable circumstances, and one of them, in 1644–5, had succeeded beyond all expectation. Unfortunately, evidence detailing how the marquis intended to assemble men and ships in 1650–1 is entirely lacking, but presumably he proposed to call out his followers, kin and tenants as he had done so many times before.

Antrim's intrigues infuriated King Charles II, whose political survival now depended on Scottish support:

The disloyal proceedings and undertakings of the marquis of Antrim with the English rebels to secure the North of Ireland to them, and so disturb the north of Scotland on their behalf, are so open and notorious that you cannot but be well aware of him, and watchful (as we are here) to prevent any mischief he can attempt.

In order to distract him the king advised Clanricard (Ormond's successor as royalist commander in Ireland) 'to raise up such a disturbance to himself [Antrim] in the enjoyment of his possessions there (which were not given by

[52] Lane to Ormond, 6/16 March 1651 (*ibid.*, 29, fos. 320–2).
[53] G. M. Paul, D. H. Fleming and J. D. Ogilvie (eds.), *Diary of Sir Archibald Johnston of Wariston 1632–9, 1650–4, 1655–60* (3 vols., Scottish History Society, 1st series, vol. LXI, 2nd series, vol. XVIII, 3rd series, vol. XXXIV, Edinburgh, 1911–40), II, 13.
[54] Montgomery to Ormond, 26 June/6 July 1651 (Bodl., Carte MSS 29, fo. 590v). Also see 'Charges against Randal marquis of Antrim contained in the petition of adventurers and soldiers', *c.* December 1663 (PRONI, D2977/Book 8).

the Crown to this use) as may make him soon repent... of his bargain'.⁵⁵ In the event, however, the plan was abandoned when Charles II's army was routed at the battle of Worcester on 3 September 1651. The Cromwellian conquest of Scotland quickly followed this 'crowning mercy' and the 'War of the Three Kingdoms' was to all intents and purposes over.⁵⁶

SURVIVING THE STORM

Even before Worcester, as Clanricard tartly related to Ormond, Antrim's personal fortunes had begun to wane once more:

The marquis of Antrim hath long been quartered by the rebels in Lord Viscount Gallmoy's [sic] house not far from Kilkenny in a very obscure and unregarded condition and I believe his undertakings are so well understood by them that I apprehend little danger can proceed from him unless he can find a contrivement to appear for His Majesty, having gained the reputation of pulling down the side he is on.⁵⁷

Clearly Antrim's very success in rallying support for the parliamentary cause alarmed his new benefactors, who feared that he would in turn incite rebellion against the Commonwealth.⁵⁸ Therefore towards the end of March 1651 the council of state ordered that 'the earl of Antrim do within ten days after the sight of this repair to Dublin and there remain for the space of six months'.⁵⁹

The reluctance of the London government to use Irish Catholics to fight their battles, combined with peace on the Celtic Fringe, proved disastrous for Antrim. As long as Scotland and Ireland were submerged in warfare, the marquis was able to exploit his abilities as a military entrepreneur and troop-raiser in the hope that his traditional estates would be returned to him as his reward; but peace in all three kingdoms deprived him of his one surviving asset. Matters were made worse by the death in November 1651 of his Cromwellian benefactor Henry Ireton, which jeopardized Antrim's already uncertain position within the new regime.

---

⁵⁵ Charles II to Clanricard, 10 March 1651 (Bodl., Carte MSS 29, fos. 66–7).
⁵⁶ The war officially dragged on in Ireland until 27 April 1653 when Philip McHugh O'Reilly surrendered at Cloughoughter.
⁵⁷ Clanricard to Fanshaw, 27 August 1651 (*Ormonde MSS*, I, 194). 'His lordship lives "honourably" upon free quarter from one house to another and was lately at my Lord of Galmoys', Montgomery to Ormond, 26 June/6 July 1651 (Bodl., Carte MSS 29, fo. 590v). For a cursory account of Galmoy, see Sean O'Brien, 'The Butlers of Lower Grange, Viscounts Galmoy', *Old Kilkenny Review*, 16 (1964), p. 18.
⁵⁸ *Cal. SP Dom.*, 1651, p. 109.
⁵⁹ *Ibid.*, p. 105/PRO, SP 25/65/153.

From this point onward, however, references to the marquis of Antrim in the extant historical sources all but cease. For instance, nothing is known about him – where he was living, what he was doing or with whom – between May 1652 and April 1654; between July 1654 and July 1655; between October 1655 and January 1657; and between May 1657 and June 1658. In other words nearly sixty-five months, or the better part of seven years (1652–9), of Antrim's life remain unaccounted for.[60] The surviving extracts and contemporary references indicate that there was once a certain amount of information about him in the now lost Commonwealth records for Ireland.[61] Yet it probably did not amount to much; Antrim's political importance during the 1650s should not be overstated. There is little concrete evidence elsewhere to suggest that he was anything more than a 'Cromwellian pensioner' who focused all his energies and his meagre resources on trying to salvage what he could out of his mangled inheritance.

When Antrim first sold out to the new regime, in 1649–50, the Cromwellian land settlement – albeit firmly rooted in the 'Adventurers' Act' of 19 March 1642 and the 'Doubling Ordinance' of 14 July 1642 which allotted Irish forfeited lands to Protestant adventurers – was still by no means inevitable. Even though Antrim's estates had been declared forfeit by the English parliament in February 1642, and reserved for these property speculators, every effort was made by the English administration in Dublin 'to preserve him [Antrim], and to free him from being an excepted person for life and estate'. Thus early in January 1652 parliamentary commissioners requested that Antrim – 'not having been so active as most others have against the parliament, nor being a man of designing head, or guilty of the massacres' – might be 'left out of the exception for life and estate' and allowed to compound for his property.[62] Until a decision on this matter had been reached in England the commissioners ordered that he should live in Ulster in

---

[60] He did not, however, 'retire to England, where he lived till the Restoration', as stated in *Clan Donald*, II, 729–30.

[61] Petition of adventurers and soldiers, 23 December 1663 (PRONI, D2977/Book 8). A brief glance at the nineteenth-century listings of the Commonwealth records highlights the loss suffered in 1922, *Second report of the deputy keeper of the public records in Ireland* (Dublin, 1870), pp. 57–8; *Tenth report of the deputy keeper of the public records in Ireland* (Dublin, 1878), pp. 24–7; *Fourteenth report of the deputy keeper of the public records in Ireland* (Dublin, 1882), pp. 14–52; J. O'Hart (ed.), *Irish landed gentry when Cromwell came to Ireland* (Dublin, 1887), pp. 233–47.

[62] Commissioners in Dublin to lord lieutenant, 8 January 1652 (Dunlop (ed.), *Commonwealth*, I, 124–5).

a 'convenient place' (probably Glenarm) provided by Colonel Venables.[63] But, as in 1650, Antrim's application was rejected by the English council of state.

To make matters worse, in June 1653 lots were finally drawn for the adventurers' lands in Ireland and the barony of Dunluce was accordingly set aside for sixteen entrepreneurs, largely Londoners, who had advanced a total of £8,656 in return for 42,611 Irish acres of land.[64] In the months following the lottery the speculators either sold or exchanged their adventures. Sir John Clotworthy (later Lord Massareene), who had originally invested £2,254 and received 11,231 acres in the baronies of Massareene and Dunluce, doubled his territorial empire in County Antrim by buying up lots in the barony of Dunluce to the value of £3,187.[65]

Unfortunately for Antrim, the land settlement did not end there. In 1654 the remainder of his estate was surveyed (the 'Civil survey') in order to establish how much land was available for distribution to the Commonwealth's unpaid soldiers in lieu of wages.[66] As a result, over the course of the next two years over 65,000 acres of the Antrim estate were parcelled out to

---

[63] Commissioners in Dublin to Venables, 8 January 1652 (*ibid.*, 123); Antrim to the council of state, [*c.* January, 1652] (BL, Add. MSS 34,326, fos. 2–3).

[64] The adventurers who received their debentures in the barony of Dunluce were John Brockhoven, John Clotworthy, Samuel Cooper, Charles Doe, James Edwards, John Fischer, John Gray, John Harves, John Lucas, John Mosyer, Nathaniel Overton, William Peckett, William Robins, Maurice Thompson, Thomas Tipping and John Wood, *Cal. SP Ire., 1660–2*, pp. 648–9; Karl S. Bottigheimer, *English money and Irish land. The 'Adventurers' in the Cromwellian settlement of Ireland* (Oxford, 1971), pp. 200–13; *Cal. SP Ire., Adventurers 1642–59*, p. 354/PRO, SP 63/300/170 gives a similar list of adventurers but includes George Thompson and John Lucas. Also see Marsh's Library, Dublin, MS Z.2.1.5, p. 57.

[65] Bottigheimer, *English money and Irish land*, p. 201. Assignments to Clotworthy (between 10 November 1653 and 26 April 1654) by Richard Darnelly, William Firth, Thomas Andrews, Nicholas Williams, Bartholomew Fosson, *Cal. SP Ire., Adventurers 1642–59*, pp. 6, 7, 64, 119. Clotworthy also bought a residence from 'one Doc a goldsmith' which was never paid for, Broderick to Clarendon, 16 September 1663 (Bodl., Clarendon MSS 80, fos. 204–6). On Clotworthy, also see P. J. Duffy, 'The evolution of estate properties in South Ulster 1600–1900', in Smyth and Whelan (eds.), *Common ground*, p. 102.

[66] Thus in the survey of his lands in County Londonderry, Antrim was listed as 'the proprietor' of three parishes in the barony of Coleraine, *Civil survey*, III, pp. 155–7. Unfortunately, the County Antrim 'Civil survey' itself has not survived but the books of survey and distribution for the county have. Though drawn up during the Restoration period, they were probably based on the civil survey and may therefore serve as an alternative source to the missing volumes, *Civil survey*, X, pp. xv, 56–7, 60–1; Hill, *MacDonnells*, pp. 451–66; Geraldine Talon, 'Books of survey and distribution, County Westmeath: a comparative survey, with reference to their administrative context and chronological sequence', *Anal. Hib.*, 28 (1978), pp. 105–15.

over 800 Cromwellian soldiers.[67] Troops in seven separate companies were allotted 'debentures' in the baronies of Kilconway, Cary and Glenarm and in the Long Liberties. The average debenture was between nine and fifteen acres, with the officers receiving substantially more than the enlisted men. For example, Captain Richard Franklin received 1,476 acres while privates Henry Langdale and Abraham Thompson were each allotted just under two acres.[68]

The majority of Cromwell's troops were eager for cash and merely sold their debentures and went home so that, as with the adventurers' lots, there was an immediate redistribution.[69] Three categories of individuals purchased the new acres. First, several Cromwellian officers with debentures in the area added to their own holdings by acquiring those of their men. Secondly, local landowners, particularly Clotworthy and Dr Ralph King, MP for Coleraine and Derry in 1654, 1656 and 1659, bought up this cheap land so as to expand and consolidate their own estates. Finally, the original tenants of the marquis's estates, who were naturally anxious to return to their farms, also purchased debentures wherever they could.[70]

This rapid turnover of landholding makes it impossible to estimate accurately the number of adventurers and soldiers who actually settled on the Antrim estates during the later 1650s. Even at the Restoration the matter was hotly disputed. Antrim's enemies suggested that 900 persons had established themselves on the estate between 1656 and 1659, while the marquis argued that no more than five adventurers and one hundred soldiers had taken up residence.[71] The latter figure was confirmed by contemporary observers. One

---

[67] This figure varied between 65,000 and 72,688 acres (the latter included 23,224 acres in Glenarm), *Cal. SP Ire.*, 1663–5, pp. 338–40; *ibid.*, 1660–2, pp. 649–60.

[68] The officers in charge of the seven companies (all from Fleetwood's regiment) were Captains Barrington, Claypoole, Sterne, Franklin, Galland and Major Smith. Hill, *MacDonnells*, pp. 283–4, 339–42; King's Inn Library, Dublin, Prendergast papers 6, p. 681; Antrim's case, no date [late 1663] (Bodl., Carte MSS 44, fo. 332r–v); *Cal. SP Ire.*, 1660–2, pp. 648–60. Also see Duffy, 'The evolution of estate properties in South Ulster', pp. 102–3. For an English parallel, see H. J. Habakkuk, 'The parliamentary army and the crown lands', *The Welsh History Review*, 3, no. 4 (Dec. 1967), pp. 403–26.

[69] This appears to have been the case throughout Ireland. See, for example, Monica Brennan, 'The changing composition of Kilkenny landowners 1641–1700', in Nolan and Whelan (eds.), *Kilkenny*, p. 175.

[70] For an English parallel, see Ian Gentles, 'The purchasers of Northamptonshire crown lands 1649–1660', *Midland History*, 3, no. 3 (Spring 1976), pp. 207–11.

[71] Petition by adventurers and soldiers to Ormond, [c. August/?September] 1663 (PRONI, D2977/Book 8); *Cal. SP Ire.*, 1663–5, pp. 338–40; Hill, *MacDonnells*, pp. 466–7. The accuracy of Antrim's calculations is supported by the fact that this was precisely the case in County Kilkenny, see Brennan, 'The changing composition', pp. 176–80.

noted that the only adventurer 'of condition' was Clotworthy while 'the rest [were] without names, save some citizens of London, for whom he [Clotworthy] is an undertaker'.[72] The same source added that 'there were not six English tenants placed by those into the north unto whom it was assigned'.[73] While Antrim claimed at the Restoration that those few adventurers and soldiers who had actually settled did nothing to encourage further the English plantation or to improve their holdings. Only one even bothered to build a house of 'stone and timber', while others allowed the property on their lots to fall into disrepair. Antrim's house at Dunluce, which had been improved during the 1630s, was totally neglected.[74] Moreover, the adventurers and soldiers bled their holdings for a quick economic return on their investment, with the result that within a three-year period the adventurers whose lots fell in the barony of Dunluce were said to have 'received treble their adventure or debenture money'. Other settlers allegedly 'received more than seven fold'.[75]

Yet despite having his inheritance carved up, and well over 100,000 acres of it parcelled out to mercenary entrepreneurs, Antrim was able to maintain very close links with his estates throughout the Interregnum. This was largely thanks to the fact that over 200,000 acres (roughly two-thirds of his property) was apparently not doled out to adventurers and soldiers. Who actually 'owned' or, at least, controlled these acres is unclear; presumably they remained in government hands and continued to be farmed by Antrim's previous tenants. Perhaps some of them were set aside for those of Antrim's followers who agreed to submit to the Commonwealth. This would certainly explain why a considerable portion of the estate rental continued to find its way into the marquis's pocket. For instance, after 1652 he received a monthly allowance of £40 'out of the profits from his estate in Ulster'.[76] In May 1654, he was awarded £100 'out of the rents and profits that Archibald Stewart makes out of the said earl his estate in Ulster'.[77] In addition to these legitimate stipends, he was involved in endless schemes designed either to raise further revenue from the land or to reestablish his hold over it. In the barony of Cary, for example, he was somehow able to conceal from the authorities

---

[72] Broderick to Clarendon, 16 September 1663 (Bodl., Clarendon MSS 80, fo. 206).
[73] Ibid. fo. 205.
[74] Cal. SP Ire., 1663–5, pp. 338–40; Hill, MacDonnells, p. 451.
[75] Hill, MacDonnells, p. 340. Also see Antrim's case, no date [late 1663] (Bodl., Carte MSS 44, fo. 332r–v); Broderick to Clarendon, 16 September 1663 (Bodl., Clarendon MSS 80, fo. 206).
[76] E. MacLysaght (ed.), 'Commonwealth state accounts, 1650–56', Anal. Hib., 15 (1944), p. 245; commissioners in Dublin to commissioners in Belfast, 14 April 1652 (Dunlop (ed.), Commonwealth, I, 175); transcript of an undated order (King's Inn, Library, Dublin, Prendergast papers 3, p. 674).
[77] Hill, MacDonnells, p. 278; MacLysaght (ed.), 'Commonwealth state accounts', p. 247.

over 2,194 acres of land which were later 'discovered' by Dr Ralph King. He also collected over £200 worth of rents in the barony of Glenarm between 1658 and 1660.[78] Finally, he instructed his old tenants to purchase back land for him. Thus during the later 1650s John Shaw of Ballygally bought 'four town[land]s and a half' in the barony of Kilconway for £359-3-9 from Alderman Thomas Miller of Limerick and other property from Captain Samuel Porter, which he conveyed to Antrim in 1666 (when it was at last safe to do so). In addition to paying the principal, the marquis allowed Shaw, as his reward, the annual rental (of £11) from the lands for forty-one years.[79] Presumably Antrim made similar arrangements with the inhabitants of the barony of Glenarm who paid £2,000 to Major Smith and his men for their Glenarm holdings, with the former occupier of a farm of eighty acres in the barony of Cary who was able to reenter his holding on paying the soldier to whom it had been allotted the sum of £10, and with the tenant on a neighbouring farm who repurchased it from soldiers for a relatively small sum, explaining to them 'that as it had become overgrown with "whins" the land was of little value!'.[80]

A further factor which minimized disruption on the Antrim estate was the continuing residence of Archibald Stewart, overseeing the daily running of the property during the 1640s and watching over Antrim's interests during the 1650s. Despite the upheaval caused first by the rebellion and then by the covenanting army of occupation, Stewart had striven to protect the interests and economic welfare of Antrim's tenants.[81] Conditions were only really desperate between 1642 and 1644 when Antrim's four baronies were quartered with over 1,200 of Argyll's men, who had levied 'intolerable taxe[s] and sess [= cess] upon my lands', had quartered an insufferable number of soldiers on Antrim's property, had harassed the local population and had threatened to dispossess 4,000 of them.[82] Matters improved somewhat after

---

[78] Hill, *MacDonnells*, p. 286; Charles II to lords justices of Ireland, 10 October 1661 (Bodl., Carte MSS 42, fo. 404).
[79] PRONI, D2977/3A: Kilconway barony. Only this example appears to have survived among the Antrim papers; undoubtedly there were others.
[80] Ormond to James Hamilton, 27 October 1663 (Bodl., Carte MSS 49, fo. 238); *Cal. SP Ire.*, *1669–70*, p. 421; *ibid., Adventurers 1642–59*, pp. 6, 7, 64, 119, 165, 175; Hill, *MacDonnells*, pp. 451, 466–7.
[81] For further details, see pp. 107–14 above. For a recent discussion of the impact of the war on an English county, see Ann Hughes, 'Parliamentary tyranny? Indemnity proceedings and the impact of the civil war: a case study from Warwickshire', *Midland History*, 11 (1986), pp. 49–78.
[82] Stewart to Ormond, 23 February 1644 (Bodl., Carte MSS 9, fo. 312). Also see remonstrance from Stewart to Ormond, [23] February 1644 (*ibid.*, fo. 301r–v); remonstrance by Archibald Stewart to Sir William Stewart and others, 5 March 1644 (Hunt., HA MSS Box 8/15904); Furgol, *A regimental history*, p. 81.

1645 when most of Argyll's men were recalled across the North Channel to protect their own farms from the ravages of Antrim's brigade. With fewer men to feed and quarter, the marquis's tenants were able to focus their energies on repairing the damage.[83] Nevertheless, by 1650 Antrim's estates were in a 'sad condition ... by reason of the army'[84] and any efforts to improve them were no doubt further interrupted by the Cromwellian conquest of Ulster in 1649–50 and by the imposition of government taxes or 'cess' throughout the 1650s. Another local landowner, George Rawdon, complained in 1657 that 'we are unfairly cessed here. In Antrim and Down the cess is so severe that our tenants and their stocks leave us, yet the cess does not follow them. The cess here is more for a barony than elsewhere for a county.'[85] It was no exaggeration; over a four-month period in 1658 Antrim's four baronies (Kilconway, Dunluce, Cary and Glenarm) paid £682-1-8 – out of a total of £1,763 for the entire county – in 'cess' charges, while the barony of Dunluce alone paid nearly as much as the more prosperous barony of Belfast.[86]

A final factor which ensured continuity on the Antrim estates was the survival in place of many tenants, particularly Protestant ones, who had taken long leases for their farms from the marquis in 1637. Thus in 1651 it was reported to the council of state how the northern tip of County Antrim was 'planted and inhabited by the Scots and some Irish, very few English being among them',[87] while a decade later the tenants on the Antrim estate were essentially 'such Scotch and Irish whose fathers and grandfathers were undertenants to the old earl'.[88] Not only was there continuity of landholding at the tenant level but the Commonwealth also recognized as legally binding leases that Antrim had made with his Protestant tenants before the rebellion. Therefore in February 1655 Colonel Arthur Hill was awarded 'the quiet possession of those lands [that] formerly the earl of Antrim granted him' and the state refused to countenance Clotworthy's claim to them.[89] Two years

---

[83] The Antrim estates still had to finance, quarter and feed the Scottish soldiers who stayed on until the late 1640s; but the burden was less than during the earlier period, see for example orders by Monck, 13 December 1648 and 3 January 1649 (Hunt., HA MSS Box 8/15301 and Box 9/15307); Raymond Gillespie, 'Landed society and the interregnum in Ireland and Scotland', in Mitchison and Roebuck (eds.), *Economy and society*, pp. 39–41.
[84] Rawdon to Conway, 17 December 1650 (*Cal. SP Ire.*, 1647–60, p. 380).
[85] Rawdon to Conway, 11 July 1657 (*ibid.*, p. 641).
[86] *Ibid.*, p. 685.
[87] [?] to council of state, 1 August 1651 (St Patrick's College, Maynooth, O'Renehan MSS 2, fo. 257).
[88] Broderick to Ormond, 19 September 1663 (Bodl., Carte MSS 44, fos 624–5). Also see Broderick to Clarendon, 16 September 1663 (Bodl., Clarendon MSS 80, fos. 204–6).
[89] Order 1 February 1655 (NLI, MS 11,959, p. 389).

later, Antrim's former tenants refused to give up lands in the Long Liberties (which had been assigned to Captain John Galland and his troop) 'by virtue of a lease or leases from the earl of Antrim' and in this they received the support of the Dublin administration.[90] As the 1660 poll tax abstracts (the so-called '1659 census') of the 'tituladoes' (or individuals with local influence) illustrate, Antrim's leading Protestant tenants from the 1630s (the Shaws, Stewarts, Dunlops, Boyds and Kennedys) continued to influence local affairs and they were only occasionally supplemented by fresh settlers such as Galland.[91]

What then of Antrim's Catholic tenants? Only a third of the people counted in the poll tax were either 'Scottish or English' (and presumably Protestant), while almost two-thirds were 'Irish' or from the Western Isles and Highlands (and presumably Catholic).[92] It therefore seems clear that as the 1650s progressed increasing numbers of native Irishmen had returned 'home' to their old farms and dwellings.[93] No doubt some, like Captain William Stewart, simply followed their lord back to Ulster;[94] others may have been encouraged to return by their Protestant neighbours who needed the labour of Irish subtenants, 'being easier to get, and of more present profit than English'.[95] This was apparently true throughout Ireland. A study of the parish of Donaghmore in County Tyrone indicates that while there was 'a change of proprietors', the Cromwellian settlement 'had but little effect on the local population' since the Cromwellian settlers needed the native Irish to

---

[90] Captain John Galland to Henry Cromwell, 6 March 1657 (BL, Lansd. MSS 821, fo. 318).
[91] Séamus Pender (ed.), *A census of Ireland circa 1659, with supplementary material from the poll money ordinances (1660–1661)* (IMC, Dublin, 1939), pp. ix, 3–21, 139–40; R. C. Simington, 'A "census" of Ireland, c. 1659', *Anal. Hib.*, 12 (1943), pp. 177–8.
[92] The population of Antrim's three parishes in the Long Liberties of Coleraine, County Londonderry (Ballyrashean, Ballywillin and Ballaghran) have been included in these calculations. In County Antrim as a whole, 56 per cent of the population was Irish and presumably Catholic and 44 per cent Scottish or English and presumably Protestant. It is worth noting, as Pender did in the introduction to the *Census*, that in order to avoid possible transplantation many evaded the census and therefore the figures should be regarded as a conservative estimate, *Census Ire. 1659*, pp. ix, 3–21, 139–40. Also see William J. Smyth, 'Society and settlement in seventeenth century Ireland: the evidence of the "1659 census"', in William J. Smyth and Kevin Whelan (eds.), *Common Ground. Essays on the historical geography of Ireland presented to T. Jones Hughes* (Cork, 1988), pp. 55–6, 58.
[93] Major Brian Smith to Henry Cromwell, 9 June 1658 (BL, Lansd. MSS 823, fo. 60).
[94] George Monck to Captain Talbot, 29 August 1654 (PRONI, T473/1, p. 49).
[95] Fleetwood to Thurloe, 4 July 1655 (Thomas Birch (ed.), *A collection of state papers of John Thurloe, esq.; secretary, first to the council of state, and afterward to the two Protectors Oliver and Richard Cromwell* (7 vols., London, 1742), III, 612.

hew their wood and draw their water. Similarly, in the baronies of upper and lower Ormond in County Tipperary, there was 'no general clearance' of native Catholics.[96] A recent study of County Kilkenny indicates that less than a third of the old Catholic elite actually moved to Connaught and many of the rest remained in control of their lands, while in the city of Kilkenny Commonwealth officials had no alternative but to allow Catholic merchants to trade as usual.[97]

The English government did draw the line at allowing Catholic proprietors in Ireland to resume formal control over their pre-war estates, but nevertheless in 1654 Antrim tried again, with the full backing of the Cromwellian regime in Ireland, to compound for his inheritance. On this occasion he was provided with £30 'for and towards the defraying the charge of his journey' to London and with a letter of recommendation from Charles Fleetwood, Henry Ireton's replacement as commander-in-chief.[98]

> I think [he] is as much an object of pity as any of this nation, and I should be glad [if] something were done for his future subsistence; but, because of his relations, and some about him, I should not desire he might come often to my lord, though I know no man deserves so much mercy to be showed him as he does, of this nation.

While he sympathized with Antrim's plight, however, Fleetwood did not trust him: 'the truth is, these people are an abominable false, cunning and perfidious people; and the best of them to be pitied, but not to be trusted'.[99] The council of state shared Fleetwood's basic mistrust of Irish Catholics, and in June 1654 refused Antrim permission to 'represent his condition' since his petition would be denied in any case.[100]

Though the administration in Dublin might be unable to restore the marquis to his estate, it could still reward him financially for his loyalty to the regime. Right up to his death in November 1651, Ireton had been 'very

---

[96] T. E. Ó Doibhlin, 'The Cromwellian settlement and its aftermath', *Seanchas Ardmhacha*, 4 (1961), pp. 190, 193, 197; D. F. Gleeson, *The last lords of Ormond. A history of the 'countrie of the three O'Kennedys' during the seventeenth century* (London, 1938), p. 104 and chapters 7 and 10. For other examples, see T. Bartlett, 'The O'Haras of Annaghmore 1600–1800: survival and revival', *Ir. Econ. & Soc. Hist.*, 9 (1982), pp. 34–52; H. Gallwey, *The Wall family in Ireland 1170–1970* (Naas, County Kildare, 1970), pp. 71–3, 93; Ivar O'Brien, *O'Brien of Thomond. The O'Briens in Irish history 1500–1865* (Chichester, 1986), p. 89.
[97] Smyth, 'Territorial, social and settlement hierarchies', pp. 154–5, 158; Neely, *Kilkenny*, pp. 98–100.
[98] Hill, *MacDonnells*, p. 278; MacLysaght (ed.), 'Commonwealth state accounts', p. 249; extract from the books of the Irish privy council, 1651–4 (BL, Eg. MSS 212, fo. 25).
[99] Fleetwood to Thurloe, 2 June 1654 (Birch (ed.), *Thurloe state papers*, II, 343).
[100] *Cal. SP Dom., 1654*, pp. 202–3.

sensible of the hard condition of the Lord Antrim who not only submitted to him, but so far endeavoured to serve him, as had gained him some esteem and place in his Lordship's opinion, and some tenderness and care of his future well-being' and had awarded him an annual pension of £500 which was later increased to £800.[101] This substantial regular income was supplemented throughout the 1650s by occasional, additional contributions towards everyday expenses.[102] For example, in December 1651 Antrim received, out of Customs and Excise duties, £500 which Ireton had promised him.[103] As the 1658 'civil list' clearly demonstrates, Antrim received a larger allowance than any other Irish pensioner (Lord and Lady Mayo were his closest competitors, with a combined stipend of only £134). In fact he was paid nearly as much as Lord Deputy Henry Cromwell, whose official annual salary was only £1,000, and considerably more than the average civil servant, who received between £20 and £30 per annum.[104] However, compared with his pre-1641 annual income of around £20,000, this was pitiful. In addition, he was deprived of the bulk of his rents and thereby lost, between 1641 and 1660, at least £150,000 together with some of his most precious household goods which were confiscated and sold by the Commonwealth.[105]

Antrim's situation during the 1650s was somewhat alleviated by the fact that he now had access to the assets of his second wife – Rose O'Neill – whom he married some time in 1652 or 1653. Rose was the daughter of Sir Henry O'Neill, chief of the O'Neills of Clandeboy, who had died in 1638, and Martha Stafford, daughter of the English administrator Sir Francis Stafford. While she was not in the same social league as the duchess of Buckingham, she

---

[101] Commissioners in Dublin to lord lieutenant, 8 January 1652 (Dunlop (ed.), *Commonwealth*, I, 124–5).
[102] Hill, *MacDonnells*, p. 278; *Cal. SP Ire., 1663–5*, p. 215; MacLysaght (ed.), 'Commonwealth state accounts', pp. 245, 317, 318; order 6 January 1657 (King's Inn Library, Dublin, Prendergast papers 2, p. 679); BL, Eg. MSS 212, fos. 8v, 66. At the Restoration Antrim claimed that his pension was £500, later reduced to £300 under Henry Cromwell, see *Cal. SP Ire., 1660–2*, p. 542.
[103] Hill, *MacDonnells*, p. 278; *Cal. SP Ire., 1663–5*, p. 215; MacLysaght (ed.), 'Commonwealth state accounts', pp. 245, 317, 318; order 6 January 1657 (King's Inn Library, Dublin, Prendergast papers 2, p. 679); BL, Eg. MSS 212, fos. 8v, 66.
[104] The civil list for Ireland for 1658 (BL, Add. MSS 19, 833, fo. 27v).
[105] PRO, SP23/237/25, fos. 62–9. It would seem that Antrim's losses were even greater than those suffered by his contemporaries. For instance the earl of Thomond calculated that between 1641 and 1646 the war deprived him of £45,412. Of this the bulk (£35,000) was due to his inability to collect his rents, but he also lost cattle and sheep to the tune of £5,000 and £3,200 worth of plate and household goods; finally, it had cost him £2,000 to support a garrison on his estate for three months, see Hogan (ed.), *Letters and papers*, pp. 200–3.

was both a Protestant and the heiress to her father's estates in the barony of Toome in County Antrim which were reputed to have brought in an annual rental of £1,600 throughout the 1650s.[106] By their union Antrim also acquired Rose's marriage portion of 699 acres in the barony of Toome.[107] Like the Antrim estate, Lady O'Neill's property had been damaged in 1641, and for the remainder of the war she had been obliged to support Scottish soldiers, who destroyed her orchards and 'fishings'.[108]

Though he gained property in County Antrim, despite being judged an 'innocent papist' in March 1655, the marquis does not appear to have been granted any of the lands in Connaught or Clare reserved by the 'Act of satisfaction' (September 1653) for transplanted Irish families.[109] However, in 1655–6 Rose was allotted 26,664 Irish acres of good-quality land, 'with convenient accommodation', in Connaught (8,888 acres in County Galway and the remaining 17,776 in County Mayo).[110] The state agreed to provide her with 'some convenient seat that is undisposed of and that doth belong unto the Commonwealth', although there is no evidence to suggest that she ever left Ulster.[111] Where the couple actually resided remains unclear; Rose's address in 1656 was given as 'Dunluce', while the marquis was living in a small village (Eden) near Carrickfergus in 1657, and in Belfast when the 1660 poll tax was taken.[112] Interestingly, Sir William Petty's map of the barony of

---

[106] Hill, *MacDonnells*, pp. 246–51, 338; E. MacLysaght, *Irish families, their names, arms and origins* (Dublin, 1957), pp. 119–20; Gillespie, *Colonial Ulster*, pp. 104, 111, 140–1, 150–1; Cunningham and Gillespie, 'The East Ulster bardic family', p. 109; Ó Cuív (ed.), 'Some Irish items relating to the MacDonnells of Antrim', p. 147.

[107] PROI, Lodge MSS 11, fo. 19.

[108] Unlike Antrim she received (in 1646) compensation for the damage done by the soldiers, see *Cal. SP Ire., 1633–47*, pp. 417, 448.

[109] J. O'Hart, *Irish landed gentry when Cromwell came to Ireland* (Dublin, 1887), p. 305.

[110] In addition Antrim's brother Alexander was granted a further 7,000 acres in County Galway, R. C. Simington (ed.), *The transplantation to Connaught 1654–58* (IMC, Shannon, 1970), pp. 172, 206, 214, 123, 175; order 30 July 1655 (NLI, MS 839, fo. 20).

[111] Order of 7 September 1655 (NLI, MS 11,961, p. 208). Significantly, Antrim's name is not mentioned in the list of transplanted Irish Catholics 1655–9, *Ormonde MSS*, II, 114; O'Hart, *Irish landed gentry*, pp. 247, 328, 359.

[112] Simington (ed.), *Transplantation to Connaught*, pp. 172, 206, 214; PRONI, D597/1, p. 8; Pender (ed.), *Census Ire. 1659*, p. 8; Robert W. Ramsey, *Henry Cromwell* (London, 1933), p. 183. It is possible that they lived at Ballymagarry (near Dunluce) and also spent time at Rose's house at Edenduffcarrick (also known as Shane's castle). Antrim was later joined by his younger brother, Alexander (who had spent nearly three years in a London jail), *Cal. SP Dom., 1651–2*, pp. 146, 165, 182, 401; *ibid., 1653–4*, p. 82; *Cal. SP Ire., 1669–70*, p. 421. By 1652 his mother, Lady Ellis, appears to have returned to her castle in Ballycastle, Hickson, *Ireland*, I, 279.

Glenarm, drawn in c. 1654, described the impressive family castle at Glenarm as the 'earl of Antrim's house' and so that perhaps served as his principal residence for most of the 1650s.[113]

Clearly, then, Antrim did not spend the Interregnum 'in great misery' as he claimed at the Restoration, for his average annual income throughout the 1650s probably totalled at least £2,000, as indeed some later claimed.[114] Unfortunately, however, even an income of £2,000 was slight in comparison with the marquis's outstanding debts from the 1630s still amounting to roughly £42,000 plus interest.[115] Only state intervention ensured that he was not arrested (as his rival Argyll was) by his creditors when he visited England in 1650 and 1654.[116] Admittedly Antrim and his brother made some effort to pacify the creditors – thus in November 1656 Alexander agreed to pay off £1,000 (plus £300 in interest) owed by his brother since July 1638 to a London merchant, Humphrey Adby.[117] But an already unsatisfactory situation was exacerbated in 1656 when the barony of Cary, which had been mortgaged as collateral for Antrim's debts in 1637, was allotted to some of Fleetwood's unpaid troops. The majority of Antrim's creditors thereby lost any guarantee that the money owed to them would ever be repaid.[118] By the spring of 1657 matters had become so desperate that Antrim begged Henry Cromwell (made lord deputy in November 1656) for help. 'I am reduced to such a condition that I cannot forbear to make my complaint to your lordship and to beg that you will commiserate and relieve me from the continual persecution of my creditors who are now so violent that they do daily employ bailiffs and soldiers to arrest me.' Their constant harassment, Antrim claimed, 'has kept me for a long time in the nature of a prisoner that I dare not

---

[113] Downe Survey maps for the parishes in County Antrim, PRONI, D597/1, p. 8. This would also explain why he was occasionally referred to as the 'earl of Glenarm', see p. 237 above.
[114] Hill, *MacDonnells*, p. 338. Also see Antrim's petition to Charles II, [April, 1661] (Bodl., Carte MSS 44, fo. 326); *Cal. SP Ire.*, 1663–5, pp. 214–17; some observations of adventurers and soldiers on the estate claimed by Antrim, [1661] (Bodl., Carte MSS 44, fos. 328–31); petition of adventurers and soldiers to Charles II, [August, 1663] (*ibid.*, fos. 376–7).
[115] In 1656 the earl of Crawford owed £24,000 plus £1,000 in interest to his creditors, NLS, Yester papers, MS 7032, fo. 89.
[116] *Cal. SP Ire.*, 1660–2, p. 70. Argyll's debts were due to military expenses and damage caused by the MacDonnells, John Willcock, *The great marquess. The life and times of Argyll* (Edinburgh and London, 1903), pp. 295–7.
[117] PRONI, D2977/3A: Kilconway barony. In July 1638 Antrim had borrowed £1,000 from Robert Ramsey, on Ramsey's death it passed to Robert and Henry Thompson who then assigned it to Adby, for further details see Ohlmeyer, 'A seventeenth century survivor', p. 444.
[118] Petition of Archibald Stewart to Ormond [1663?] (Bodl., Carte MSS 33, fo. 275); *Cal. SP Ire.*, 1660–2, p. 70.

look out of my door and they threaten withal to force the house and carry me to prison'. Finally he implored Cromwell to

> find some certain means to secure my person or to satisfy my debts which is a grace I hear his Highness has been pleased to grant the nobility of Scotland ... and until your lordship has seriously considered of this ... I beseech you to grant a positive order to all soldiers to forbear to execute any writ against [me] ... which will be a means to give some little ease from these perpetual alarms and will be a new addition to all your favours.[119]

As it was the Cromwellians did pay off a significant number of Antrim's debts. For example, Sir David Cunningham, an important Ayrshire landowner and London merchant, who was owed £1,000, was allowed to set the rents first of Wallingford House and later of the duchess's houses on the Strand, against the debt, and Henry Dawson, a London skinner who was owed £950, was briefly allowed the rents of York House in a similar arrangement.[120] Others received direct compensation. In April 1650 the council of state agreed to pay in full the £5,566 plus interest owed by Antrim to Arthur Hill since 1639 'out of the sequestrations of the estates in Ireland'.[121] Hill was paid £6,000 the following September.[122] Similar payments of between £60 and £5,000 were also made to at least eight of Antrim's other creditors – Edward Basse, Humphrey Bradbourne, Abraham Corsellis, Henry Dawson, James Duart, Ralph Grinder, Adam and John Lawrence – from the sale of the king's goods during the 1650s.[123]

One is left wondering why, as the 1650s progressed, the Cromwellians should have continued to support and protect Antrim. There are several possible explanations. First, though it may not have seemed like it at the time, in the long term Antrim's heavy debts actually worked in his favour, for his creditors harangued the Commonwealth, as they were later to badger the Restoration government, to help them secure repayment.[124] Second, Antrim was also protected by friends and benefactors from the 1630s, such as Sir Robert Pye, who were now favoured servants of the Commonwealth and therefore in a position to help him (just as other Cromwellians, such as John Rushworth, helped English Catholics).[125] His other friends and patrons in

---

[119] Antrim to Henry Cromwell, 11 April 1657 (Ramsey, *Henry Cromwell*, p. 183).
[120] For further details on Cunningham and Dawson, see Ohlmeyer, 'A seventeenth century survivor', pp. 431–2.
[121] *Cal. SP Dom., 1650*, pp. 100–1.
[122] PRO, SP 28/350/7, fo. 31.
[123] Ohlmeyer, 'A seventeenth century survivor', pp. 427–39.
[124] *Cal. SP Dom., 1650*, pp. 100–1.
[125] Peter Roebuck, 'The Constables of Everingham. The fortunes of a catholic royalist family during the civil war and interregnum', *Recusant History*, 9 (1967), pp. 77–9, 84; Aveling,

London during the 1650s included the duke of Lennox, the eighth earl of Rutland (the duchess of Buckingham's cousin), Lord Conway and his English agent John Traylman.

By far the most important and influential of Antrim's contacts at the Cromwellian court, however, was Abbot Patrick Crelly who, according to the Spanish ambassador, Cárdenas, was 'a well informed person with excellent contacts with several members of parliament in our [Spain's] confidence ... The said abbot enjoyed the entire confidence of secretary of state John Thurloe, who was most trusted by Oliver Cromwell.'[126] In addition to the government's chief minister, Crelly cultivated some leading Independents. For example, between 1649 and 1653 he supplied Thomas Scot (who was the Commonwealth intelligencer and also a regicide) with information about the royalists' activities in Ireland and their fund-raising activities in France, Spain, Italy, and 'the general affairs of Vienna'.[127] No doubt in return for accurate intelligence Scot, who served on the council of state and on numerous *ad hoc* committees dealing with Irish affairs, was willing to watch over the interests of Crelly and therefore of his erstwhile benefactor, the marquis of Antrim.

Antrim also enjoyed good relations with leading Cromwellians in East Ulster and was related to Colonels Robert Stewart and Arthur Hill. Hill had not only been responsible for supplying Cromwell's army during the 1649 offensive but was an important local official during the later 1650s (representing Belfast in the parliament in 1654) and was responsible for paying the marquis his allowance from his old estates.[128] Colonel Stewart, married to

---

Northern catholics, p. 305; P. G. Holiday, 'Land sales and repurchases in Yorkshire after the civil wars, 1650–1670', *Northern History*, 5 (1970), pp. 73–80. Whether the second duke of Buckingham, who married General Fairfax's daughter in 1657 and moved into York House, was also prepared to help him is debatable. Interestingly, Pye also protected Clanricard, see p. 285 below.

[126] Cárdenas's secret accounts, 1638–55 (AGS, Eo. 2532, unfol.). Between April 1651 and his death in August 1655 Crelly was the recipient of a healthy (600 escudos) annual Spanish pension; the embassy also paid his expense account – he spent £249-15-0 on 'various banquets, lunches, dinners and presents made to certain members of parliament and other of his friends in the said parliament' between 1651 and 1653. In royalist circles it was claimed that Crelly was Cárdenas's 'oracle', P[eter] T[albot] to Charles II, 6/16 October 1655 (Bodl., Clarendon MSS 50, fo. 156v). Firth, 'Thomas Scot's account', p. 119; Loomie, 'London's Spanish chapel', p. 413. It was later rumoured that Crelly converted to Protestantism and married, *Comment. Rinucc.*, V, 210.

[127] Firth, 'Thomas Scot's account', pp. 116–26. Also see Turner, *Privy Council*, I, 249, 348, 353, 358, II, 186–7, 223, 235–6, 239; Underdown, *Pride's purge*, pp. 126, 138, 182. Crelly also supplied the Vatican with intelligence from London, Gilbert, *Contemp. hist. 1641–52*, II, 138–9.

[128] Hill, *MacDonnells*, pp. 352–3; Birch (ed.), *Thurloe state papers*, II, 445–6; Firth, 'Thomas Scot's account', p. 118; MacLysaght (ed.), 'Commonwealth state accounts', p. 318.

one of Antrim's distant O'Neill cousins, for his part helped Lady Ellis MacDonnell recover her jointure and served as a useful contact with the Cromwellian administration.[129] George Rawdon was another powerful ally. Rawdon, his wife's uncle and factor to Lord Conway, was a favourite of Henry Cromwell and MP for Down, Antrim and Armagh in 1659 in the Westminster parliament.[130] Furthermore, many of Antrim's tenants from the 1630s (such as Alexander and Robert Colvill, Thomas Boyd of Lisrahan, Alexander MacCauley of Ballycastle, and Thomas Boyd of Ballyhuderland) were also prominent Cromwellian sympathizers or officials, which could only have worked in his favour.[131]

Having friends (or creditors) in high places, however, while extremely useful, is not enough by itself to explain Antrim's survival during the 1650s. Other, less personal, factors were also crucial. The Commonwealth protected Antrim because what it needed above all was stability, and this could only be achieved through a policy of persuasion rather than compulsion, by cooperation rather than coercion. This was particularly true in the years following the 'revolution' of 1649 when the English army was mutinous, Scotland and Ireland were hostile, and England's constitutional position was precarious. Bulstrode Whitelocke, a member of the ruling council of state, summarized the dilemma the Commonwealth faced in July 1649: 'This was a year of great perplexity and danger as to the public affairs in the cause of the Parliament... [for] if the Parliament had lost but one battle, all who were engaged with them had been in great danger of ruin, as to their lives and fortunes.'[132]

Indeed, the need for a 'deal' between rulers and ruled was explicitly stated by many leading Commonwealth apologists, such as Anthony Ascham and Marchamont Nedham, editor of the influential Republican newspaper *Mercurius politicus*. All of them urged political cooperation from the subjects of the late King Charles in return for 'protection' from the new regime, for, as Ascham indelicately put it, 'He who spits against the wind, spits in his own face.'[133] These (and other) apologists desperately sought to legitimize and bolster up the Republic, whose power it is easy to overestimate. This

---

[129] Hill, *MacDonnells*, pp. 352–3.
[130] *Cal. SP Ire., 1647–60*, pp. 380, 658.
[131] Transcripts of inquisitions, Counties Antrim and Down, 1657 (RCB, MS Libr. 26, p. 1).
[132] Bulstrode Whitelocke, *Memorials of English affairs from the beginning of the reign of Charles I to the happy restoration of King Charles II* (4 vols., Oxford, 1853), III, 78.
[133] Quoted in Hardacre, *The royalists*, p. 85. For further details, see Quentin Skinner, 'Conquest and consent: Thomas Hobbes and the engagement controversy', in G. E. Aylmer (ed.), *The Interregnum. The quest for settlement 1646–1660* (London, 1970), pp. 79–98; idem, 'Presidential address: collective mentalities in mid-seventeenth century England: IV. cross

was particularly true in Ireland where there had never been a substantial 'parliamentary party'. In any case, the Cromwellian mission was to defeat the supporters of Charles II, not to extirpate the native Irish. Consequently, the Commonwealth pursued a strategy of buying off 'considerable' royalist supporters (both Catholic and Protestant) as a 'ready way for shortening the war' wherever possible.[134] The same was true in Scotland, where Cromwell tried to conquer 'with words rather than bloodshed'. In fact, according to David Stevenson, 'Cromwell was turning away from ambitions of radical change to concentrate on more immediate problems of maintaining stability and winning support for a regime which was deeply unpopular throughout Britain, back peddling on some of the policies which alienated powerful interests.'[135]

The volatile nature of politics on the Celtic Fringe increased the state's dependence on local power-brokers like Antrim. Throughout the 1650s reports of royalist invasions and uprisings were rife in both England and Scotland and Henry Cromwell's Scottish counterpart, Lord Broghill, was aware of 'a close correspondence between the royal party in Scotland and that in Ireland'.[136] For instance, in 1655 it was rumoured that 'both the Scottish and Irish are in great expectations of some sudden change in England, which may encourage their attempts here' and that Inchiquin and Ormond ('or some of that gang') were planning an invasion of Ireland.[137] The following year, intelligence that the Irish regiments serving in Flanders were about to invade Ireland led Henry Cromwell to round up any priests and other 'considerable, active and dangerous persons'.[138] As it happened the only serious royalist rising erupted in Scotland in 1654 and was quickly controlled by Cromwell's veterans and Broghill's skilful management of the Highland chiefs. But had Glencairn's rebellion succeeded, no doubt the

---

currents: neutrals, trimmers and others', *R. Hist. Soc. Trans.*, 39 (1989), pp. 6–7. Needham himself changed sides four times: in 1642 he joined the parliament, in 1647 he became a royalist, in 1650 he turned to the Commonwealth and in 1660 he embraced the royalist cause again.

[134] Account of the state of Ireland [by Henry Jones, *c*. 1651] (CUL, Add. 4352, fos. 67–9v). Also see Elkin, 'The interactions between the Irish rebellion and the English civil wars', pp. 299, 303–4, 321.
[135] Stevenson, 'Cromwell, Scotland and Ireland', p. 170. Also see pp. 154, 161, 164–5, 169.
[136] Thurloe to Henry Cromwell, 8 January 1656 (Birch (ed.), *Thurloe state papers*, IV, 403). Also see *ibid.*, IV, 446, 483; Gillespie, 'Landed society', p. 38. Broghill served as lord president of the council of Scotland between 1656 and 1657, for further details on Broghill, see p. 286 below.
[137] Fleetwood to Thurloe, 6 March 1655 (Birch (ed.), *Thurloe state papers*, II, 196).
[138] Henry Cromwell to Thurloe, 30 January 1656 (*ibid.*, IV, 483). See also *ibid.*, 446, 509, 607, V, 348–9, 349–50, 443, 477–8, VI, 378, 539–40.

Commonwealth would have been obliged to rely upon Antrim's services in Scotland again, just as they had to call upon those of his Scottish counterparts.[139]

Matters were not much better in England itself. Competition between the army and the politicians for control at Westminster destabilized English affairs; in April 1653 Cromwell expelled the Rump Parliament which was replaced by an equally unpopular nominated assembly (Barebone's Parliament). The establishment of the Protectorate in December 1653, headed by Cromwell, brought a measure of stability; however, this was interrupted by the outbreak in March 1655 of a royalist rising (known as 'Penruddock's Rising') and the rule of the major-generals between the summer of 1655 and January 1657. Domestic unrest was made even worse by the outbreak of the first Anglo-Dutch war which was followed in October 1655 by a lengthy and costly war with Spain. A fragile regime such as this simply could not afford to alienate its potential supporters.

This was especially true when one remembers that there was never sufficient government personnel to administer peripheral areas, and so the Commonwealth, and later the Protectorate too, was forced to use, however reluctantly, members of the local community to act as its officers and watchdogs.[140] This was also true in Cromwellian Scotland, where 'It was impossible to find administrators who were loyal, efficient and politically reliable. Those who immediately offered their loyalty had to be appointed to the most crucial positions of authority, even if an impartial choice would not have put them there.'[141] The development of 'localism', as a self-protecting response to the social and economic upheaval caused by the Irish Civil Wars, further increased the dependence of central government on local, traditional power-brokers.

The 'difficult' geography of Ulster exacerbated the security problem even further. The physical terrain of the province was particularly hostile – for as Henry Jones noted 'bogs, woods and mountains hath ever found us most work' – and internal communications were further hampered by the absence

---

[139] Sir James MacDonald, for instance, was also a Cromwellian pensioner and informant: the civil list for Scotland (*ibid.*, VI, 527); Fleetwood to Thurloe, 6 March 1655 (*ibid.*, III, 196); Broghill to Thurloe, 22 April 1656 (*ibid.*, 725–7); *idem* to *idem*, 13 May 1656 (*ibid.*, V, 18). For details on Glencairn's rising, see F. D. Dow, *Cromwellian Scotland 1651–1660* (Edinburgh, 1979), chapters 4 and 5.

[140] For instance in East Ulster only Antrim could effectively control his fractious Catholic kinsmen, see Major Brian Smith to Henry Cromwell, 9 June 1658 (BL, Lansd. MSS 823, fo. 60).

[141] Lesley M. Smith, 'Scotland and Cromwell: a study in early modern government' (unpublished DPhil thesis, University of Oxford, 1979), p. 246.

of decent roads.¹⁴² East Ulster's geographic isolation, and its strategic proximity to Scotland, thus constituted a permanent potential threat to the newly founded Republic, as it had to the Stuarts – unless it could secure the support of individuals like Antrim. Without them, the Celtic Fringe could fast become ungovernable, as it had been for much of the fifteenth and sixteenth centuries. In return for effective policing of the periphery, putting a few hundred pounds a year from state funds into Antrim's pocket could seem like the bargain of the decade.

The sudden death of Oliver Cromwell in September 1658, the subsequent collapse of republican government under his son Richard, followed by the restoration of the Stuart monarchy in the spring of 1660 overturned this comfortable *modus vivendi*. The marquis of Antrim was merely one of many ex-Cromwellian collaborators who was forced to find a fresh niche in the new regime. Therefore, in the hope of being received at Charles II's court, he secured on 10 May 1660 a letter of recommendation from Arthur Annesley to Ormond.

This gentleman, Mr Dalmahoy, husband to the late duchess of Buckingham having resolved to kiss his majesty's hands and being unacquainted at court. Being much his servant and sensible of his merit I cannot let him pass without a line or two to your lordship that by being known to you he may have the free admittance to his majesty's presence.¹⁴³

The marquis arrived in London shortly after Charles II made his formal entry into the city, on 29 May. The king, according to Hyde, 'had been very few days in London ... when he was informed that the marquis of Antrim was upon his way from Ireland towards the court'. But he was never given the opportunity of presenting himself to Charles. Upon his arrival in the capital Antrim was 'by the king's special order committed to the Tower; nor could any petition from him, or entreaty of his friends, of which he had some very powerful [ones], prevail with his majesty to admit him into his presence'.¹⁴⁴ It must have seemed that at last the marquis's luck had run out.

[142] Account of the state of Ireland, [by Henry Jones, *c.* 1651] (CUL, Add. 4352, fo. 67).
[143] Annesley to Ormond, 10 May 1660 (NLI, Ormonde MSS 2324, fo. 205).
[144] Clarendon, *Life*, II, 76. Also see *Comment. Rinucc.*, V, 418; extract of news from England, 13/23 July 1660 (BN, Fonds Français 20,674, fo. 209).

10

Antrim after the Restoration (1660–1683)

Once in the Tower of London the marquis of Antrim was accused of having committed twelve 'crimes' during the 1640s and 1650s. To begin with, his enemies (largely adventurers and soldiers from County Antrim) claimed that he had been involved in plotting the Irish rebellion of October 1641, that he had then been a spy for the 'rebels' and that he had supplied them with money, ammunition and intelligence of royalist manoeuvres. Most of his other 'crimes' revolved around his relationship with the Catholic confederates. His opponents asserted that he had entered the 'Roman Catholic Confederacy' before the peace of 1649, had signed the oath of association, had been commissioned as a lieutenant-general of the confederate army, had sat on the supreme councils before the peace treaties of 1646 and 1649 made it lawful to do so, had constantly adhered to the papal nuncio's party, had stirred up a rebellion against Ormond and had consistently opposed the 1649 'Ormond peace'. Antrim's remaining 'crimes' concerned his behaviour during the Interregnum. According to his enemies, he was after January 1649 in 'constant correspondence' with the parliamentarians and directed the 'dispersing of printed papers amongst his majesty's garrisons for debauching the soldiers therein'. In May 1650, they claimed, he had joined the Cromwellians rather than submit to Ormond, had accused Charles I of having tried to stir up rebellion in Ulster in the spring of 1641 and had done his utmost to turn Ulster against the king between 1649 and 1651. In addition, he had received yearly stipends and pensions first from Henry Ireton and later from his successors, and, finally, had been 'employed by the said Ireton in preparing forces and boats to be transported into Scotland against his majesty's interest there'.[1]

As the preceding chapters have shown, these charges were almost all

---

[1] Petition of adventurers and soldiers, [26 July] 1663 (*Cal. SP Ire.*, 1663–5, pp. 214–17); petition of adventurers and soldiers to king, [August, 1663] (Bodl., Carte MSS 44, fos. 376–7); some observations of adventurers and soldiers on the estate claimed by Antrim, [1661] (*ibid.*,

entirely correct. With the exception of the first two, Antrim was guilty of each of them. It therefore comes as little surprise to learn that the MacDonnell family historian considered 'the years 1660 to 1665, as 'perhaps the most anxious and distracting in Antrim's eventful life'.² How did he survive?

From July 1660 until May 1661 the marquis languished in the Tower of London 'under strict restraint' and, so he later claimed, 'in a condition worse than death'.³ The main charge investigated at this time was 'aspersing the memory of the late king in reference to the scandal raised against him of being author of the Irish rebellion'.⁴ Early in 1661 the English privy council wrote to the Irish lords justices requesting that all material relating to Antrim's statements to the Cromwellians in 1650 should be sent at once to London.⁵ Accordingly, in February 1661 Henry Jones, bishop of Clogher, Michael Boyle, bishop of Cork, the earl of Orrery (formerly Lord Broghill), Henry Owen and Valentine Savage, men who had all either heard Antrim's assertions of May 1650 in person or had seen transcripts of them, were questioned by officials in Dublin and their testimonies were then forwarded to London.⁶

However, in May 1661 Antrim's case was referred back to the Irish council. After bail of £20,000 had been agreed the marquis was released from the Tower and ordered to appear before the lords justices in Ireland within six weeks.⁷ His months in jail had left 'his fleece dry and himself broken'; but he

---

fos. 328–31); petition of adventurers and soldiers, c. December 1663 (PRONI, D2977/Book 8). Also see Firth (ed.), *Memoirs of Edmund Ludlow*, II, 289, 342.
² Hill, *MacDonnells*, p. 290.
³ Antrim's petition to Charles II, [April, 1661] (Bodl., Carte MSS 44, fo. 326). Also see *Cal. SP Ire.*, 1663–5, p. 216; David Laing (ed.), *A diary of public transactions and other occurrences chiefly in Scotland. From January 1650 to June 1667 by John Nicholl* (Bannatyne Club, vol. LII, Edinburgh, 1836), p. 295.
⁴ Ormond to Clarendon, 27 October 1663 (Bodl., Carte MSS 143, fo. 201). Though not technically accused of revealing details of the 'Antrim plot' of 1641 (to his Cromwellian accomplices in May 1650), this is what was investigated, for details, see Ohlmeyer, 'The "Antrim plot" of 1641' and pp. 96–9, 237 above.
⁵ Ormond and lords justices to Bennet, 31 July 1663 (Bodl. Carte MSS 44, fos. 370–3).
⁶ *Cal. SP Ire.*, 1660–2, pp. 207–9, 217. Richard Baxter later claimed that at the Restoration Antrim 'was forced to produce in the ... house of commons, a letter of the king's [Charles I], by which he gave him order for his taking up arms; which being read in the House, did put them into a silence', M. Sylvester (ed.), *Reliquiae Baxterianae, or ... Baxter's narrative of the most memorable passages of his life and times* (London, 1696), part III at p. 83; and Richard Baxter, *A vindication of the royal martyr King Charles I from the Irish massacre in the year 1641 ...* (3rd edn, London, 1704), pp. 2–3. But this seems unfounded.
⁷ Warrant to Sir John Robinson, lieutenant of the Tower authorizing Antrim's bail, 29 March 1661 (BL, Eg. MSS 3349 (Danby papers), fo. 22r–v). Henry Viscount Moore, Thomas Viscount Dillon of Costelloe and Theobald Viscount Taaffe provided security to the tune of £20,000, *Cal. SP Ire.*, 1660–2, p. 325. The recognizance was cancelled fourteen months later in August 1662, petition of the Lady Antrim, 29 June 1662 (Bodl., Carte MSS 44, fo. 353);

had little time to recover for upon his arrival in Dublin early in June he was rearrested and committed 'to the custody of the black rod with a guard' while investigations into his 'crimes' continued.[8] At this point Antrim must have seriously wondered whether he was to suffer the same fate as his great rival, Argyll, who had also hurried to London in July 1660 to welcome the restored king only to be imprisoned in the Tower. He remained there until December when he was dispatched to Edinburgh for trial. On 25 May 1661 he was found guilty of treason and executed.[9] It can have been little consolation to learn that 'God was very gracious to him in clearing him from the most heynous crimes and articles of his charge and in giving him strength to die with much Christian courage'.[10]

No doubt shaken by Argyll's sudden fall, Antrim was careful (in a letter to Ormond) to deny that he had accused Charles I of fomenting the 1641 rebellion:

I have been accused of laying an assertion on the late king concerning the Irish rebellion. I may have been apt enough to do things indiscreet but to commit an action so abominable as the relating of a falsehood against so gracious a prince is baseness so horrid and so far from my intentions, that it never entered into my thoughts.[11]

As we now know, in this instance he was telling the truth. However, in July, during his examination in Ireland, Antrim also denied his role in the 'Antrim plot' and stated categorically that 'he never had any message or direction from his late majesty to ... raise any forces within this kingdome to any such purpose or intent as to keep in awe the parliament'. He also denied that Bourke, Digby or Hamerton had brought him instructions 'about the keeping up the 8,000 men that were raised by the late earl of Strafford ... nor about employing them in any service'. Moreover, while he admitted having been in Ireton's camp, he denied having discussed the matter with Clogher, Owen and Reynolds in May 1650.[12] In a second examination in May 1662 he further asserted that he was only acquainted with Ireton 'in

---

minutes of the meeting of the privy council, 29 June 1662 (*ibid.*, fo. 355); *Cal. SP Ire., 1663–5*, p. 212.

[8] Petition from Antrim to Charles II, [before 19 December] 1660 (*Cal. SP Ire., 1660–2*, p. 493). His health was certainly adversely affected by his imprisonment, medical certificate for Antrim, 29 December 1660 (*ibid.*, p. 494). Also see 'Brief occurrences touching Ireland begun 25 March 1661 [–29 October 1666] (Bodl., Carte MSS 64, fo. 470v); Ormond and council to Bennet, 31 July 1663 (*ibid.*, 44, fos. 370–3); Antrim to Ormond, 24 April 1661 (*ibid.*, fo. 334); *Cal. SP Ire., 1660–2*, pp. 195, 207–9, 217, 363–4, 384–5, 542.

[9] Hutton, *Charles II*, pp. 171–2; Willcock, *Great marquess*, pp. 303–20.

[10] Loudoun to Lorne, 6 June 1661 (Inverary castle, Argyll Muniments, bundle 100).

[11] Antrim to Ormond, 24 April 1661 (Bodl., Carte MSS 44, fo. 334).

[12] Examination of Antrim, 23 July 1661 (*Cal. SP Ire., 1660–2*, pp. 384–5/PRO, SP 63/307/159, fos. 265–6).

relation to his own subsistence' and that he had never written to Ireton, Cromwell or Michael Jones.[13]

All of this, as we have seen, was totally false. However, aware that his political and economic survival were at stake, Antrim probably had no alternative but to renege on all his earlier statements to the Cromwellians about his plan to raise an Irish army at the behest of Charles I for use in England in 1641 and to deny any close relationship with the Cromwellian leaders. With Argyll's fate before his eyes, he can have had no illusions about the consequences to him, his dynasty and his estates should he be proved guilty of betraying Charles I. To save them, he lied.

Fortunately for Antrim the lies worked and he was formally cleared of having implicated Charles I in the Ulster rebellion; late in October 1662 Ormond informed Charles II that 'what he is committed for in England, when it came to be examined here, was not found to be of weight to bring him to trial'.[14] However, Ormond and the Irish privy council drew the line at restoring him to his Ulster inheritance, which would have involved inserting a special clause concerning him in the 'bill of explanation' which was then being debated and drawn up by the Irish parliament.[15] The bill was a sequel to the act of settlement (July 1662) designed to resolve the conflicting claims concerning land acquired during the 1650s. It was administered by seven commissioners appointed to hear the claims of those who believed that they had lost their estates unfairly and to decide whether a claimant's behaviour during the 1641 rebellion and its aftermath made him worthy of restoration. However, difficulties in executing the decrees of the 'court of claims' (as this body was known) quickly arose and further legislation to cover the intricacies of the land settlement – the bill of explanation – became necessary.[16]

The refusal of the Dublin administration to include Antrim in this bill left him in a difficult position and forced him to apply instead for a hearing before the court of claims.[17] This, however, panicked those who had acquired Antrim's lands. Led by Lord Massereene (formerly Sir John Clotworthy), they called for a further investigation into his behaviour during the 1640s in the hope that new evidence would be found which would disqualify him from being declared an 'innocent papist' by the commissioners and thereby

---

[13] Examination of Antrim, 8 May 1662 (*Cal. SP Ire.*, 1660–2, p. 542/PRO, SP 63/310/38, fos. 111–12).
[14] Ormond to Charles II, 20 October 1662 (Bodl., Clarendon MSS 78, fo. 39).
[15] *Cal. SP Ire.*, 1660–2, p. 643; *ibid.*, 1663–5, pp. 216, 279–80.
[16] Karl S. Bottigheimer, 'The restoration land settlement in Ireland: a structural view', *IHS*, 18, no. 69 (Mar. 1972), pp. 9–10.
[17] *Cal. SP Ire.*, 1660–2, p. 695; *ibid.*, 1663–5, p. 29.

recovering his former lands from them.[18] In February 1663, to appease the petitioners, Charles II referred their complaints to an English *ad hoc* committee made up of Lords Clarendon, Albemarle, Northumberland, St Albans and Holles 'or any three of them'; but they also ruled in Antrim's favour and urged him to apply for a trial before the court of claims.[19] According to the committee's report, his actions were all 'warranted by his instructions and the trust reposed in him' by the late king and the queen mother.[20] In a letter dated 10 July 1663, Charles II declared the marquis 'innocent of any malice or rebellious purpose towards the crown' and ordered Ormond to assist him to recover his estates by making known the king's wishes to the commissioners of the court of claims.[21]

This royal bombshell threw the Irish council into a quandary. For, as Ormond complained to Clarendon, 'I know not what kind of letter the king can write, or what we here can do upon any letter for my lord of Antrim. You know the king, as well as me, is bound by the act of settlement'.[22] The council therefore decided to ignore the king's request and refused to forward his letter of recommendation to the commissioners.[23] But as soon as Antrim learned of their decision he procured a copy of the same royal letter (although now dated 11 August) which Lady Antrim made haste to deliver directly to the commissioners just before his case was heard on 20 August 1663.

The hearing itself was a dramatic affair. It began with a reading of the king's letter, which declared the marquis an 'innocent papist', to the court. At this point one of the commissioners, Sir Richard Rainsford, declared the letter to be 'evidence without exception' and suggested that Antrim be declared innocent without the prosecution being heard at all.[24] However, Sir Edward Dering, whose summary minutes of the proceedings have survived, insisted that the case be heard since it contained 'new evidence'. In all, over twenty witnesses for the prosecution took the stand, and numerous letters, orders and other documentation (some in Antrim's own hand) supporting their

---

[18] *Ibid.*, 1660–2, pp. 648–60; *ibid.*, 1663–5, pp. 44, 216; Ormond and council to Bennet, 31 July 1663 (Bodl., Carte MSS 44, fos. 370–3); petition of adventurers and soldiers to Ormond, [30 July 1663] (*ibid.*, fo. 374).

[19] *Cal. SP Ire.*, 1663–5, pp. 29–30, 216; *ibid.*, 1669–70, p. 453; Hill, *MacDonnells*, pp. 293–4.

[20] Charles II's instructions to the commissioners for executing the declaration and act of settlement, 11 August 1663 (*Cal. SP Ire.*, 1663–5, p. 216).

[21] Charles II to Ormond, 10 July 1663 (*ibid.*, pp. 207–9). Also see Hill, *MacDonnells*, pp. 467–8.

[22] Ormond to Clarendon, 17 July 1663 (Bodl., Carte MSS 143, fo. 147).

[23] *Ibid.* See also Ormond to Clarendon, 22 July 1663 (Bodl., Carte MSS 44, fo. 398r–v); *Ormonde MSS*, III, 62; *Cal. SP Ire.*, 1663–5, pp. 211–14; Broderick to Clarendon, 16 September 1663 (Bodl., Clarendon MSS 80, fos. 204–6); Ormond to Clarendon, 27 October 1663 (Bodl., Carte MSS 143, fos. 200–1).

[24] State of Antrim's case, [late August ?] 1663 (*Cal. SP Ire.*, 1663–5, p. 217).

testimonials and exposing 'to the world the history of his life during that time' were produced in court.[25] Although the evidence clearly showed that the marquis was not entitled to be restored in accordance with the regulations laid down in the act of settlement, the commissioners declared him by four votes to three to be an 'innocent papist' and decreed that he be restored forthwith to his property.[26] The following day, after eight months of hearings during which various Irish Catholics had received back some 850,000 acres of land, the court of claims adjourned.[27]

Hardly surprisingly, the public reaction to the verdict was mixed. According to one commissioner, when the judges found in Antrim's favour:

a great[er] shout of joy followed in the court than was ever heard since the opening of the commission. My lord's agent never desired any injunction to the sheriff for possession ... Many of the poor men [Antrim's tenants] coming from the north to this town in expectation of this jubilee, the rest in the country making bonfires and feasts throughout the four baronies.[28]

Any tenants disloyal to the marquis were now promptly evicted and so, before long, all but a few pockets of land in the Long Liberties of Coleraine and in the barony of Kilconway were once more under the control of Antrim's factor Archibald Stewart.[29]

The jubilation was naturally not shared by the adventurers and soldiers who had acquired farms on the Antrim estate during the 1650s. On the contrary, they immediately expressed their displeasure.[30] Opposition crystallized on 13 November at a fair in Dunluce where Tristram Beresford, a local landowner who had been a Cromwellian supporter and had bought up debentures in Antrim's baronies, attempted to collect 'the customs of the fair' which should have gone to the marquis.[31] When Antrim's agent intervened

---

[25] Ormond to Bennet, 26 August 1663 (Bodl., Carte MSS 143, fo. 172); *Murder will out: or the king's letter, justifying the marques of Antrim, and declaring that what he did in the Irish rebellions was by direction from his royal father and mother and for service of the Crown ...* (London, 1663), p. 4.
[26] Sir Richard Rainsford, Sir Thomas Beverly, Sir Allen Broderick and Mr Winston Churchill voted in Antrim's favour while Sir Edward Smith urged the case to be referred to Ormond as Patrick Sarsfield's case had been. For further details, see *Cal. SP Ire., 1663–5*, pp. 216–20; Hill, *MacDonnells*, pp. 430–44; Edward Smith to Clarendon, 17 October 1663 (Bodl., Clarendon MSS 80, fos. 233–4); petition of adventurers and soldiers to Charles II, [August, 1663] (*ibid.*, 44, fos. 376–7); act of settlement commissioners to sheriff of Antrim, 26 August 1663 (PRONI, D2977/Hambros bank box).
[27] Bottigheimer, 'Restoration land settlement', p. 18.
[28] Broderick to Clarendon, 16 September 1663 (Bodl., Clarendon MSS 80, fo. 205).
[29] Archibald Stewart to Antrim, 13 July 1664 (PRONI, D2977/Book 8).
[30] Petition of adventurers and soldiers to Charles II, [August, 1663] (Bodl., Carte MSS 44, fos. 376–7).
[31] *Cal. SP Ire., 1633–47*, p. 65; *ibid., 1660–2*, pp. 649, 676.

'William Cox, a disbanded soldier ... picked up the club he had in his hand and offered to beat him, whereupon the constable of Dunluce called for assistance in His Majesty's name to see the peace kept'. Shortly afterwards Beresford's men were disarmed and the 'affray was presently appeased' without violence or bloodshed.[32] While some rioted at Dunluce others refused to surrender their holdings; all called for a retrial on the grounds that the king's letter had intimidated a number of key witnesses such as Henry Jones, bishop of Clogher, who had refused to give evidence.[33] Anti-Antrim leagues were quickly organized and shortly after the trial it was reported from Dublin that 'my Lord Massereene from hence and my Lord Anglesey in England raised a strange alarum as if a total revolt of the English would ensue my Lord Antrim's adjudication'.[34]

The publication of a pamphlet entitled *Murder will out* towards the end of August 1663 drew public attention to their grievances.[35] After giving a detailed account of Antrim's trial and reproducing the king's letter in his favour, the anonymous author of the pamphlet concluded:

There never was so great a rebel, that had so much favour from so good a king. And it is very evident to me ... that the consequence of these things will be very bad; and if God of his extraordinary mercy do not prevent it, war, and (if possible) greater judgments, cannot be far from us, where vice is patronized, and Antrim, a rebel upon record, and so lately and clearly proved one, should have no other colour for his actions but the king's own letter, which takes all imputations from Antrim, and lays them totally upon his *own* father.[36]

Attempts were immediately made in all three kingdoms to suppress the pamphlet and to hush up the entire affair, but it was not long before it was

---

[32] Account of what happened at Dunluce fair on 2/11/63, 13 November 1663 (PRONI, T473/1, pp. 51–2). Also see instructions for Mr George Hull, 2 November 1663. (*ibid.*, D2977/Book 8); [Antrim] to [Mr George Hull], *c.* November 1663 (*ibid.*).

[33] *Cal. SP Ire., 1663–5*, pp. 282–3; 'H. P[arnell]' to Lady Massereene, 6 May 1665 (PRONI, D562/37); Antrim to Anglesey, 18 November 1665 (Bodl., Clarendon MSS 83, fos. 309–10); petition of adventurers and soldiers to Charles II, [August, 1663] (Bodl., Carte MSS 44, fos. 376–7).

[34] Broderick to Clarendon, 16 September 1663 (Bodl., Clarendon MSS 80, fo. 204). Massereene, who had the most to lose, 'took very much to heart [Antrim's restoration] and spoke very high in the face of the court, who were not at all daunted', Robert Lye [sic] to Williamson, 23 August 1663 (*Cal. SP Ire., 1663–5*, p. 222).

[35] *Murder will out* is partly printed, and discussed, in Hill, *MacDonnells*, pp. 317–21. A fragment is also in *Cal. SP Ire., 1669–70*, pp. 470–1, and a hand-written copy in Bodl., Rawlinson C. 841, fos. 27–32. The pamphlet was reprinted in Edinburgh in 1689 and London in 1698.

[36] *Murder will out*, p. 5.

being discussed throughout the three Stuart kingdoms.[37] In September 1663 it was reported from London that 'The cry here is so loud against that and other late proceedings of the court of claims',[38] while Samuel Pepys recorded in his diary how the 'king hath done himself all imaginable wrong in that business of my Lord Antrim in Ireland'.[39] The affair was deemed important enough to merit lengthy reports in the ambassadorial dispatches of the day.[40]

Gossip, rumour and rioting were merely some of the consequences of Antrim's restoration. The affair also had serious political repercussions in Ireland because it further aggravated an already paranoid Irish House of Commons, dominated by the Protestant interest, which was horrified by the number of Catholics declared innocent by the court of claims. In February 1663 the Commons 'threw out the Explanatory Act and voted a series of resolutions designed not only to narrow the definition of "innocent" Catholics but to submit land claims to the verdicts of (Protestant) juries instead of to the royal commissioners'.[41] Feeling that his authority was being undermined and determined to bring the Commons to heel, the king ordered Ormond to pressure them to retract their votes and even threaten to use force if necessary. A potentially explosive situation was, however, defused by Ormond's discovery of a minor conspiracy by a small number of Protestant extremists to take Dublin castle; as a result on 21 March the commons rescinded their votes against the commissioners. However, the court's decision in August 1663 to restore Antrim threw matters back into the melting pot and almost immediately Ormond asked for permission to dissolve the Irish parliament since 'there will now be greater reason to apprehend their ill temper'.[42]

The situation was indeed serious, for the entire future of the restoration land settlement in Ireland was threatened by 'His Majesty restoring some few innocent papists to their estates'.[43] Sir Daniel O'Neill was not alone in wondering 'how far what is done in his [Antrim's] favour will disfavour your

---

[37] Bennet to Ormond, 17 October 1663 (Bodl., Carte MSS 118, fo. 18); Ormond to Bennet, 27 October 1663 (*ibid.*, 143, fo. 205).

[38] Anglesey to Ormond, 1 September 1663 (*Ormonde MSS*, III, 82).

[39] Robert Latham and William Matthews (eds.), *The diary of Samuel Pepys. A new and complete transcription* (11 vols., Berkeley and Los Angeles, 1983), V, 57.

[40] Count of Comminges to Louis XIV, 23 June/3 July 1664 (BN, Fonds Français 10,712, fo. 200v); count of Comminges to M. de Lionne, 24 October/3 November 1644 (*ibid.*, fo. 233); Giblin (ed.), 'Catalogue of material of Irish interest', pp. 104, 116.

[41] Hutton, *Charles II*, p. 200.

[42] Ormond to Bennet, 26 August 1663 (Bodl., Carte MSS 143, fo. 172). Also see Bottigheimer, 'Restoration land settlement', pp. 11–15.

[43] [Bennet to Ormond], [*c*. Autumn 1663] (*Cal. SP Ire.*, *1663–5*, p. 29/PRO, SP 63/313/46, fo. 98). Also see Ormond to Bennet, 26 August 1663 (Bodl., Carte MSS 143, fos. 172–4).

act';[44] while Ormond, who had to face 'all the clamour that can be raised by undone men', despaired 'of any settlement by this or any other act'.[45] Moreover, if his Protestant enemies succeeded in making an example of Antrim, it would leave the other decrees made by the commissioners open to litigation. For if the king agreed to a retrial (albeit using the same witnesses and evidence), he would be obliged to do the same for a

> great number of the decrees, [which] will take up more time than can be spared, and will render the settlement of Ireland so dilatory and difficult, as those now living ... shall ever see the end thereof, which is perhaps the aim of the opposers of the decrees, who shall in the interim enjoy the profits of great quantities of lands.[46]

Nevertheless, in October the king did reverse the commissioners' verdict, claiming that Antrim had committed 'greater crimes than his majesty conceived him guilty of'. Towards the middle of November, another *ad hoc* committee was appointed in London to review the case for the third time.[47] As a result of this inquiry the controversy between Antrim and his opponents dragged on for a further two years.

In order to defend himself and promote his case, Antrim was forced to divide his time between London and Dublin while the *status quo* on the Antrim estates was maintained by Archibald Stewart.[48] But the marquis's tenacity was eventually rewarded. He was ultimately pardoned 'of all crimes and offences whatsoever whether the same were committed in England, Ireland [or] Scotland ... and without any exception or limitation whatsoever', and in December 1665, by the act of explanation, Antrim was restored for the second time to his property in East Ulster.[49] Clause 173 of the act

---

[44] O'Neill to Ormond, 25 July 1663 (Bodl., Carte MSS 32, fo. 732).
[45] Ormond to Clarendon, 1 October 1663 (*ibid.*, 47, fo. 65). Also see Ormond to Clarendon, 17 July 1663 (*ibid.*, 44, fo. 398, and 143, fos. 147–8); *Cal. SP Ire., 1669–70*, pp. 464–5; *Cal. SP Dom., 1663–4*, pp. 313–14. As soon as Tyrconnel heard of the verdict in Antrim's favour he begged for similar treatment, as did Lady Clanricard, *Ormonde MSS*, III, 82, and Lady Clanricard to Ormond, 18 May 1665 (Bodl., Carte MSS 215, fo. 201).
[46] An anonymous memorandum relating to Antrim's case [*c.* late 1663] (Buckminster, Tollemache MSS 5236).
[47] Bennet to Ormond, 27 October 1663 (Bodl., Carte MSS 118, fo. 18); Charles II to Ormond and council, late 1663 (*ibid.*, 44, fo. 392); Bennet to Orrery, 27 October 1663 (*ibid.*, 118, fo. 18); Ormond[?] to Clarendon, 17 October 1663 (*ibid.*, MSS 143, fo. 216); *Ormonde MSS*, III, 96–7, 102; *Cal. SP Ire., 1663–5*, pp. 279–80.
[48] In Dublin he lived on Bridge Street, where his neighbours were Sir Hercules Longford and Sir Winston Churchill, a commissioner of the court of claims, Sir John T. Gilbert, *A history of Dublin* (3 vols., Dublin 1854–9; reprint, Dublin, 1978), I, 332.
[49] Memorandum on behalf of Antrim, [*c.* 1664], *Cal. SP Ire., 1669–70*, pp. 520–1. Also see King's Inn Library, Dublin, Prendergast papers 5, fos. 310–16; *Ormonde MSS*, III, 185; Hill, *MacDonnells*, pp. 292, 326–43.

specified that 'the commissioners for execution of this act shall forthwith, and without staying for any previous reprizall, set out, restore, and allot unto the said marquess of Antrim ... the honors, manors, castles, messuages, lands, tenements ... possessed [by him] on the two and twentieth of October one thousand six hundred and forty one'.[50] Those adventurers and soldiers who had actually settled on his estate were compensated with land elsewhere.[51]

'There the evidence, and the puzzle, rests', Charles II's most recent biographer noted, adding that, 'Few episodes reveal so well the tortuous politics of the Restoration court, and the difficulty of charting them now.'[52] But what lay behind this extraordinary sequence of contradictory events? In the first place how did Antrim, who was after all 'guilty' of virtually every charge brought against him between 1660 and 1665, manage to get restored? Secondly, how was the marquis, poverty-stricken and a social pariah, able to secure both the king's support for his cause and a favourable trial before the commissioners of the court of claims? And finally, why, after going to such lengths to have the marquis restored in July 1663, did Charles II suddenly change his mind and reverse the commissioner's verdict two months later, only to change his mind for a second time in 1665? A careful examination of the voluminous documentation, both official and personal, which deals with Antrim's trials and tribulations between 1660 and 1665, indicates that his survival would not have been possible without the support of his family, his creditors, his patrons and his friends from the 1630s; his own ability to manipulate skilfully the corrupt and inefficient Caroline bureaucracy; and the disorganization and the ineptitude of his enemies.[53]

To begin with, Antrim's Irish and Scottish kinsmen on the one hand pestered the great men involved in his case in both London and Dublin, and on the other, provided him with some of the cash he so desperately needed to organize his legal defence.[54] Their generosity was more than matched by that of his second wife, Rose O'Neill, who mortgaged her own property, although

---

[50] Clauses 172–80 of the act relate to Antrim, Rose and Alexander (who were all restored), *Statutes at large*, III, 100–6; Charles II's patent for Antrim's restoration, 20 July 1666 (PRONI, D2977); *Cal. SP Ire.*, 1666–9, pp. 179, 564.
[51] *Cal. SP Ire.*, 1666–9, p. 52; petition of Massereene to Charles II, [c. 16 December] 1679 (NLI, MS 11,296) and PRONI, D562/10.
[52] Hutton, *Charles II*, p. 208.
[53] The Carte and Clarendon papers contain a mine of information, as do the State Papers for the 1660s.
[54] See, for example, bond by Antrim, Aneas MacDonnell, Sir James MacDonnell and Donald MacDonald to William Clerk, 25 August 1663 (SRO, GD 201/1/78).

it was already charged 'with Lady O'Neill's jointure and... encumbered with debts and engagements', to cover Antrim's legal expenses.[55] In addition, she acted as a courier between London and Dublin and bombarded the king, his secretaries, the privy council, Ormond and the lords justices with petitions and letters demanding either money or her husband's release.[56] She followed up her written offensives with verbal harangues. Her targets complained frequently about Lady Antrim's 'importunity' during these years.[57]

Lady Antrim's terrier-like qualities were almost equalled by those of her husband's creditors, who were still owned roughly £40,000, plus interest, from the late 1630s.[58] In addition to molesting Antrim physically while he was in London (he was, for instance, unable in May 1663 to deliver a letter to Whitehall 'by reason of the violence of my creditors'),[59] they regularly petitioned the king for his restoration so that he would be able to pay his debts 'which will be a preservation to many families of this city [of London]'.[60] In an attempt to pacify them, Charles's letter of 10 July 1663 specified that Antrim's estate should be liable for 'the payment of his just debts', while the act of explanation (December 1665) included a clause which also guaranteed this.[61] Antrim's longstanding debts were working to his advantage in two ways. On the one hand, the marquis benefited from the pressure exerted on the king on his behalf by a vocal, determined and influential caucus; on the other, he was able to argue that, if he were not restored, his lands (and anyone living on them) would become liable for his debts together with those of the first earl, his mother's jointure and other allowances charged to the estate.[62]

---

[55] Lords justices to Nicholas, 22 June 1661 (*Cal. SP Ire., 1660–2*, pp. 363–4/PRO, SP 63/307/115 (fos. 202–3)). Also see *Cal. SP Ire., 1669–70*, p. 460; *ibid., 1660–2*, p. 50; Lady Antrim's petition, [1664] (PRONI D2977/Book 8).

[56] Broderick to Clarendon, 16 September 1663 (Bodl., Clarendon MSS 80, fos. 204–6); Ormond to Clarendon, 22 July 1663 (Bodl., Carte MSS 44, fo. 398r–v); Ormond to St Albans, 3 August 1663 (*ibid.*, fo. 390); *Cal. SP Ire., 1660–2*, pp. 50, 323, 348, 363–4.

[57] For example, see Broderick to Clarendon, 16 September 1663 (Bodl., Clarendon MSS 80, fos. 204–6); Broderick to Ormond, 2 October 1663 (Bodl., Carte MSS 33, fo. 166).

[58] Some of Antrim's creditors had been paid off by the Commonwealth, see pp. 251–2 above.

[59] Antrim to Joseph Williamson, 29 May 1663 (*Cal. SP Ire., 1669–70*, p. 456/PRO, SP 63/345/153 (fo. 222)).

[60] Petition from Antrim's creditors to Charles II, [*c.* July 1663] (*Cal. SP Ire., 1663–5*, p. 342). Also see *ibid., 1660–2*, pp. 70–1; Hill, *MacDonnells*, pp. 324–5.

[61] *Cal. SP Ire., 1660–2*, p. 697; *ibid., 1663–5*, pp. 207–9; Hill, *MacDonnells*, pp. 467–8; *Statutes at large*, III, 102.

[62] Antrim's case, no date [late 1663] (PRONI, D2977/Book 8).

The queen mother and members of her court were a third pressure group instrumental in securing Antrim's restoration. Initially, the entire court had distanced itself from the disgraced marquis, but suddenly in the summer of 1662 Henrietta Maria took up his cause. She wrote numerous letters to Ormond pleading for Antrim's restoration.[63] She even prevailed upon her son to write similar letters pressing for the reinstatement of 'so ancient a family to its possessions'.[64] As Hutton has noted it would be misleading to see Charles II 'as a man of remarkable natural clemency and breadth of vision ... The king was using his prerogative of mercy to strengthen his position in Ireland.'[65] As it was, he had already restored his favourite Catholic servants; Taaffe was created earl of Carlingford, Clancarty was restored to his estates 'without waiting for compensation to the settlers', while Patrick Sarsfield was also only judged innocent because the king's letter was read in his favour.[66] The queen mother obviously persuaded her son to do the same for her former favourite, and it was she who railroaded through the controversial letter (10 July 1663) from the king ordering Ormond to arrange a hearing for Antrim before the court of claims. When Ormond refused to do so it was again Henrietta Maria who insisted that a second letter (11 August) be sent directly to the commissioners.[67] 'The queen mother' the marquis noted at the end of July 'upon advice out of Ireland has moved the king that my late letter relating to my restoration may be renewed and immediately directed to the commissioners of the court of claims.'[68]

Antrim's 'few (though very powerful) friends' (as Clarendon dubbed them) followed her lead and importuned the king on his behalf at every opportunity.[69] His wife's uncle, Sir Daniel O'Neill, now a groom of the bedchamber and an intimate of Charles II whom Antrim had supported during the 1630s, and who continued to receive an annual allowance of £400 from him, urged Ormond to restore him because of 'the Queen mother's concernment and the

---

[63] Henrietta Maria to Ormond, 8/18 June 1662 (Bodl., Carte MSS 44, fo. 351r–v); Henrietta Maria to Ormond, 9 October 1662 (*ibid.*, MSS 214, fo. 369); Henrietta Maria to Ormond, 22 March 1663 (*ibid.*, 44, fo. 361); St Albans to Ormond, 18 July 1663 (*ibid.*, fo. 366); Henrietta Maria to Ormond, 11 July 1665 (*ibid.*, 215, fo. 207).
[64] Charles II to Ormond, 8 December 1662 (*Cal. SP Ire., 1660–2*, p. 643/PRO, SP 63/312/pp. 5–6).
[65] Hutton, *Charles II*, p. 174.
[66] Ibid.
[67] *Cal. SP Ire., 1663–5*, p. 207; *ibid., 1669–70*, pp. 456, 463.
[68] Antrim to Williamson, 30 July 1663 (*ibid., 1663–5*, p. 207/PRO, SP 63/314/62, fo. 80). Also see *Cal. SP Ire., 1669–70*, p. 456.
[69] Clarendon to Ormond, 1 August 1663 (Bodl., Carte MSS 33, fo. 15). Also see Bennet to Ormond, 3 September 1663 (*ibid.*, 46, fos. 76–81).

king's intentions'.[70] Other influential patrons at court included Henry Jermyn, first earl of St Albans, who at Henrietta Maria's insistence also badgered those involved in the Antrim case for a decision in his favour;[71] and as a member both of the committee for Irish affairs and of the *ad hoc* committee appointed by the privy council to examine Antrim's case in February 1663, St Albans was in a position to press Antrim's suit to maximum effect.[72] The same was true of another benefactor, Denzil Lord Holles, who was appointed to the same *ad hoc* committee.[73] While Roger Boyle, earl of Orrery and lord president of Munster, assured Secretary Bennet in June 1664 that 'I have provided that my lord of Antrim shall be restored to every foot of his estates.'[74]

The question remains why the queen mother and her predominantly Catholic court suddenly took pity on the marquis mid-way through his ordeal. No doubt a sense of loyalty to the late duchess of Buckingham influenced Henrietta Maria. Perhaps, too, she hoped that if she helped Antrim he would not parade her and her late husband's clandestine negotiations with Irish Catholics before a predominantly Protestant populace. Samuel Pepys went so far as to suggest that the marquis, in return for her support, had agreed to settle his estate 'upon a daughter of the queen-mother's (by my Lord Germin [Jermyn], I suppose) in marriage'.[75] This was not true, but the fact remains that – for whatever reason – St Albans was 'very ready, for his profit, to engage himself in any undertaking where he had credit, in which he neither considered the justice of the suit, or the honour of the person with whom he desired to prevail'.[76] And he was indeed awarded the annual quit rents

---

[70] O'Neill to Ormond, 25 July 1663 (*ibid.*, 32, fo. 732). Also see Antrim's case, no date [late 1663] (PRONI, D2977/Book 8); Donal F. Cregan, 'An Irish cavalier: Daniel O'Neill in exile and restoration 1651–1664', *Studia Hib.*, 5 (1965), pp. 43, 63–70; P. Power, 'A Waterford tomb and its Ulster tenant', *UJA*, 1st series, 2, no. 1 (Oct. 1895), pp. 42–6; and W. O. Cavenagh, 'Colonel Daniel O'Neill, circa 1612–1664', *RSAI Jn.*, 5th series, 18, (1908), pp. 362–7.

[71] Hamilton to Ormond, 17 January 1663 (Bodl., Carte MSS 32, fo. 247v); Hamilton to Ormond, 10 February 1663 (*ibid.*, fo. 275r–v); St Albans to Hamilton, 4 March 1663 (*ibid.*, 44, fo. 359); St Albans to Ormond, 18 July 1663 (*ibid.*, fo. 366); Ormond to James Hamilton, 27 October 1663 (*ibid.*, MSS 49, fo. 238).

[72] *Cal. SP Ire.*, 1663–5, pp. 29–30; St Albans to Ormond, 13 December 1663 (Bodl., Carte MSS 33, fo. 259).

[73] *Cal. SP Ire.*, 1663–5, pp. 29–30; Holles to Antrim, 27 August/7 September 1663 (PRONI, D2977/Book 8).

[74] Orrery to Bennet, 6 June 1664 (*Cal. SP Ire.*, 1663–5, p. 407).

[75] Latham and Matthews (eds.), *The diary of Samuel Pepys*, V, 58.

[76] Richard Ollard (ed.), *Clarendon's four portraits. George Digby, John Berkeley, Henry Jermyn, Henry Bennet* ... (London, 1989), p. 125. Lord Henry Jermyn, allegedly the queen's lover, was created earl of St Albans in 1660.

charged on the Antrim estate.⁷⁷ As for Orrery, it seems that his brother-in-law, Colonel Gilbert Talbot, had persuaded him to secure Antrim's restoration; according to Orrery, 'Talbot and his friends had been very industrious and useful to the said marquis to procure him his estate' and in return the marquis had promised Talbot a thirty-one-year lease to lands on his estate worth £300 per annum.⁷⁸

In addition, greed also ensured that important royal administrators were on Antrim's side during the 1660s: Secretary of State Sir Henry Bennet (later first earl of Arlington and another favourite of Henrietta Maria) who, according to Clarendon, 'loves money immoderately, and would get it by all means imaginable'; Secretary Morris, through whose hands all of Ormond's letters to the king passed; and Joseph Williamson (Bennet's secretary). All were promised financial reward by Antrim in return for information, for the speedy processing of petitions and letters, and for securing the king's signature on letters which Antrim had drafted.⁷⁹ Since Antrim was unable to pay them fully at the time it was in their future interests to see him restored and he frequently promised 'that if ever I be again established in my fortune, I shall endeavour a return answerable to the trouble you take in assisting my restoration, and providing for my distressed condition'.⁸⁰ Clearly Antrim was able to exploit the fact that Charles II's English government during the early years of the Restoration was 'fluid and pluralist'; and, as a member of the queen's party, he was able to take advantage of internal government politics to further his own cause.⁸¹

Finally the weakness of his opponents also facilitated Antrim's restoration. While his enemies were extremely vocal they were nevertheless disorganized, disunited and unprepared. Even Ormond had to admit that 'my lord of

---

⁷⁷ After 1665 Antrim paid St Albans £777-13-10 in quit rents, PROI, Lodge MS 11, fo. 19; *Cal. SP Ire., 1663–5*, pp. 687–8; *ibid., 1666–9*, pp. 59, 67–8; *ibid., 1669–70*, pp. 250, 588.
⁷⁸ Orrery's memorandum, 2 December 1669 (*Cal. SP Ire., 1669–70*, p. 40/PRO, SP 63/326/67 (fo. 133r–v)).
⁷⁹ Ollard (ed.), *Clarendon's four portraits*, pp. 42–8, 134; *Cal. SP Ire., 1663–5*, p. 207; *ibid.*, pp. 464–5. Bennet later claimed that he was a 'purely passive' participant, Bennet to Ormond, 3 September 1663 (Bodl., Carte MSS 46, fos. 76–81). The marquis either drafted, or had a close hand in drafting, the king's letter in his favour dated 10 July 1663 since the draft is endorsed 'Mr Williamson. Pray let this be the draft', see Charles II to Ormond, 10 July 1663 (*Cal. SP Ire., 1663–5*, pp. 207–9); Hill, *MacDonnells*, pp. 467–8. It was mistakenly rumoured that Clarendon (the chancellor) had drawn up the king's letter in Antrim's favour, see O'Neill to Ormond, 25 July 1663 (Bodl., Carte MSS 32, fo. 732); Ormond to Clarendon, 8 August 1663 (*ibid.*, 143, fo. 157).
⁸⁰ Antrim to Joseph Williamson, 22 April 1663 (*Cal. SP Ire., 1669–70*, p. 452/PRO, SP 63/345/145 (fo. 210r–v)).
⁸¹ Hutton, *Charles II*, p. 194.

Antrim hath gained much by the negligence of his opponents'.[82] Their incompetence was typified by the fact that they forgot to present a copy of the decree issued by the court of claims when Antrim's case was reexamined in November 1663. Moreover, unlike the marquis, the soldiers and adventurers had few powerful patrons at court, while those who would normally have sympathized with their plight were, in the light of the royal family's evident support for the marquis, unwilling to articulate it. Even Arthur Annesley, earl of Anglesey, who had initially taken up their cause with enthusiasm, changed sides when his daughter Elizabeth, married Antrim's younger brother and sole heir Alexander in 1665.[83]

Although the adventurers and soldiers found Ormond and the lords justices in Dublin sympathetic to their cause, even they were reluctant to cross swords consistently with the king, the queen mother and their own English benefactors. Ormond, for his part, would have been personally delighted to see Antrim receive the punishment he felt that his behaviour deserved, but he was unwilling publicly to condemn him, and this greatly undermined the opposition's case.[84] Ormond was also hamstrung by the fact that he had been instrumental in securing the restoration of other Catholics whose record was as dubious as Antrim's. For example, neither Lord Galmoy, a known Cromwellian sympathizer with whom Antrim had associated during the early 1650s, nor the earl of Clancarty (formerly Lord Muskerry) who had been a leading confederate, nor Lord Dungan who according to one of the commissioners of the court of claims 'subscribed every roll with the marquis, and one more notorious, the renunciation of the peace which the marquis never subscribed', would not have been restored without Ormond's support.[85] The same was true of Lord Moutgarret (Ormond's uncle) and Richard Butler of Kilcash (his brother).[86] Antrim therefore had precedents to appeal to, while the lord lieutenant, who had favoured others in a similar predicament, was unable justly to single out Antrim for particular persecution.

---

[82] Ormond to Anglesey, 21 November 1663 (*Ormond MSS*, III, 106).
[83] Southwell to Ormond, 12 October 1665 (Bodl., Carte MSS 34, fo. 431). From then on Anglesey monitored the marquis's affairs very closely, no doubt to prevent his daughter's inheritance from being squandered. See, for instance, Antrim to Anglesey, 18 November 1665 (Bodl., Clarendon MSS 83, fos. 309–10); Anglesey to Antrim, 4 January 1668 (*ibid.*, 87, fo. 1r–v).
[84] Ormond to St Albans, 3 August 1663 (Bodl., Carte MSS 44, fo. 390); Ormond to James Hamilton, 27 October 1663 (*ibid.*, 49, fo. 238); *Ormond MSS*, III, 91; *Cal. SP Ire.*, *1663–5*, p. 252.
[85] Broderick to Ormond, 19 September 1663 (Bodl., Carte MSS 44, fo. 625).
[86] Hill, *MacDonnells*, pp. 467–8; *Cal. SP Ire.*, *1663–5*, pp. 144, 216–20; O'Brien, 'The Butlers of Lower Grange', p. 18; J. G. Simms, 'The Restoration, 1660–85', in *NHI*, p. 427; Bottigheimer, 'Restoration land settlement', p. 20.

Thanks to this extraordinary combination of factors, each the product of his remarkable and complex career – together with a large measure of good luck – Randal MacDonnell, first marquis of Antrim, was officially restored to his estates in 1665 and with that his dramatic political career came to an end. Henceforth, he distanced himself from international and even national affairs.[87] He divided his time between Dunluce, which was described by one visitor as 'a noble building, the palace is perched on a high rock, which is lashed on every side by the sea', his summer residence at Ballymagarry and his wife's estate near Randalstown. He passed his time hunting, gaming, arranging suitable matches for his family and friends, interfering in county politics and socializing with other local grandees in Belfast, Lisburn and Newry.[88] He is only glimpsed in public affairs when his skills as a military entrepreneur were once more required; at the outbreak of war first against the Dutch (1665) and then against the French (1666), when he helped mobilize the local militia, or in organizing Ulster's internal defence against local (including many MacDonnell) 'tories' and Scottish 'subversives' during the later 1660s and 1670s.[89]

Yet the marquis continued to maintain close links with his Scottish kin. In fact in 1663 he made one final attempt to regain his Scottish patrimony and petitioned for the restoration of the 'lordship of Kintyre and the lands of Cardadle [sic] which is now fallen into the king's hands, by Argyll's forfeiture, paying the king £10,000 sterling, which is near the full value of it, or so much towards Argyll's debts unto his creditors as the rest of the estate is liable to'. Though he claimed, quite correctly, that the 'late king gave the now marquis of Antrim a grant of the said lands, which is ready to be produced, for his services in the last troubles of Scotland', the request was apparently

---

[87] This determination to keep a low profile was not shared by other members of Antrim's immediate family. For instance Alexander, his brother and heir, married the sister of a leading Catholic, English peer, the duke of Norfolk. While other kinsmen carved out careers for themselves in the Royal Navy, for further details, see Hector MacDonnell, 'Irishmen in the Stuart navy 1660–90', *Ir. Sword*, 16, no. 63 (1985), pp. 87–104.

[88] Plunkett to Baldeschi, 13/23 February 1671 (Hanly (ed.), *Letters*, p. 167). Also see *Cal. SP Ire., 1666–9*, pp. 15, 105, 124, 267; D. A. Chart (ed.), 'Account book of the Rev. Andrew Rowan, rector of Dunaghy, Co. Antrim, c. 1672–1680', *UJA*, 3rd series, 5 (1942), pp. 68–9; Lady Antrim to Rawdon, 13 November 1683 (Hunt., HA MSS 15,231); Lady Antrim to Rawdon, 17 November 1683 (*ibid*., 15,232); Lady Antrim to Rawdon, 21 November 1683 (*ibid*., 15,233).

[89] *Cal. SP Ire., 1666–9*, pp. 252–3, 267, 608–9; *ibid*., 1669–70, p. 271; certificate for arms, 6 January 1677 (PRONI, D2977/Hambros bank box); duke of York to Antrim, 22 March 1681 (*ibid*.); Alexander MacDonnell to Clanricard, 14 June 1679 (Bodl., Carte MSS 221, fos. 409–10); Ormond to Rawdon, 28 June 1679 (*ibid*., fo. 415). I am grateful to Phil Kilroy for bringing these references from Carte to my attention.

denied.[90] Despite this Antrim continued to enjoy 'a great following in those islands' and continued to care for the inhabitants' spiritual welfare.[91] For instance in 1670 'at his own expense [he] sent three priests to these Isles in Lent to hear confessions and give Holy Communion'.[92] However, the marquis refused to support Archbishop Oliver Plunkett's plan to send fresh missionaries to the Scottish Isles. Plunkett later reported to Rome that

This gentleman is very powerful in these isles, but he is just like Monsignor Alberici, a wise man, but slow to act and full of scruples. I remember that servants could not be found for Monsignor Alberici in the whole of Italy – the Florentine was a charlatan, the Milanese a stupid fellow, the Marchesan mulish, the Neapolitan light-fingered, the Roman gloomy. In the same way the marquis is hard to please. I proposed more than twenty priests to him, but he found something to say against every one of them, and against Ronan Maginn, a worthy man, he finds the difficulty that he seemed too bold and presumptuous and proud.[93]

As a result Plunkett's missionary offensive in the Isles came to nothing.

Plunkett's account of the three days he spent with Antrim in 1671 provides a last revealing snapshot of the marquis. He remained 'a good Catholic' and continued to be 'very influential'.[94] Yet he was determined not to meddle in or to be drawn into sensitive issues; thus he urged Plunkett not to send priests to the Isles in case this interfered with the talks regarding a possible union between England and Scotland which 'is opposed by the islanders'.[95]

Antrim's decision to confine himself to local affairs was no doubt prompted by his eagerness to preserve what he had and, even more, by the pressing need to pay for his extravagant past. For despite being regarded as the third richest man in Ireland (after Cork and Ormond) Antrim was (as Plunkett indelicately put it), 'up to his eyes in debt'.[96] After 1665, in addition to servicing and paying off debts contracted up to thirty years before, he was also burdened with repaying money he had borrowed to cover his legal

---

[90] PRONI, T473/1, p. 58. See pp. 89, 130–1, 178 above for Charles I's promises that once Argyll's estates were forfeited Antrim could have possession of those lands which had formerly belonged to the MacDonalds.
[91] Plunkett to Baldeschi, 14/24 January 1671 (Hanly (ed.), *Letters*, pp. 156–7).
[92] Plunkett to Baldeschi, 13/23 February 1671 (*ibid.*, p. 167).
[93] *Ibid.*
[94] Plunkett to Baldeschi, 22 October/1 November 1670 (*ibid.*, p. 144).
[95] Plunkett to Baldeschi, 14/24 January 1671 (*ibid.*, p. 156). Also see Levack, *Formation*, pp. 10–11.
[96] Plunkett to [Airoldi], 17/27 September 1671 (Hanly (ed.), *Letters*, p. 247). Lady Antrim was considered to be the third richest lady in Ireland, nobility's subsidy, 1669 (London University Library, MS 30, fos. 24–6). I am grateful to Dr Raymond Gillespie for bringing this reference to my attention. According to Sir George Rawdon, Lady Antrim was 'very rich', Rawdon to Conway, 14 February 1683 (*Cal. SP Dom., Jan.–June 1683*, p. 56/PRO, SP 63/343, no. 94).

expenses after the Restoration.⁹⁷ His income between 1660 and 1665 had been negligible (a weekly allowance of £10 from the baronies of Dunluce and Kilconway and a small stipend from Rose's estate) and he had resorted once again to borrowing.⁹⁸ In all he appears to have contracted heavy loans totalling nearly £20,000 during the 1660s, mostly from acquaintances in London, from his family and from his tenants in County Antrim. Thus the earl of St Albans lent him at least £300, the Scottish entrepreneur William Ross lent him roughly £4,000, Sir Daniel Bellingham lent him £720, while his mother-in-law, Lady Martha O'Neill, advanced him £2,000, as did Sir Charles White of Leixlip, County Kildare. His Scottish kinsmen (Aneas MacDonald, Sir James MacDonald of Sleat and Donald MacDonald) guaranteed other debts; and his Irish tenants lent him well over £3,000.⁹⁹ As security for these and his earlier debts he either offered rentals from his property or granted his creditors land at a peppercorn rent.¹⁰⁰ Thus in March 1666, Antrim's sister Sarah was given a lease of a half townland in the barony of Dunluce for nine years at a rent of 6d 'if demanded' in lieu of the £2,000 she had lent him in 1637; while the following year, in return for a loan, Uriagh Babington was granted a very favourable lease in the Long Liberties.¹⁰¹ As in the 1630s, he also mortgaged property; in 1667 Rose's estate was mortgaged to an important local magnate and high sheriff of the county in 1670, Sir Robert Colvill, for £1,200, while in 1675 866 acres in the barony of Glenarm were mortgaged to cover debts totalling just under £2,000.¹⁰² By the later 1670s the marquis was so desperate for cash that he used his brother's marriage portion (to Annesley's daughter) of £3,000 to pay off his debt to William Ross,¹⁰³ and charged his tenants hefty entry fines and a low rent.¹⁰⁴

Despite these valiant efforts to pay off his debts, the marquis was involved

---

97 Petition of Lady Antrim, 29 June 1662 (Bodl., Carte MSS 44, fo. 353); minutes of the meeting of the privy council, 29 June 1662 (*ibid.*, fo. 355); Antrim to Anglesey, 18 November 1665 (Bodl., Clarendon MSS 83, fos. 309–10).
98 *Cal. SP Ire.*, 1660–2, pp. 296, 348, 363–4, 382, 384, 390; *ibid.*, 1663–5, p. 115.
99 Indenture, 11 October 1676 (PRONI, D2977/Hambros bank box; NLS, MS 3784, fos. 32–5, and SRO, GD 201/1/78). Robert Arton of Libert, Martin Garnon of Ballow together with Randal Buithill, Robert Boyd and Hugh Dunlop – from Glenarm – all lent him money, for further details, see Ohlmeyer, 'Seventeenth century survivor', pp. 426–50.
100 Ohlmeyer, 'Seventeenth century survivor', pp. 426–50.
101 PRONI, D2977/3A/3/6A/1.
102 *Ibid.*, D774, D896/30, D2977/3A/'Dunluce barony, 1700s and 1800s'.
103 *Ibid.*, D2977/1.
104 He raised in this way at least £4,250 (over sixteen years), *ibid.*, D2977.

in endless lawsuits with frustrated, unpaid creditors.[105] James Chapman, owed £700 since the late 1630s, sued him in 1677, as did Sir John Barlow of Pembroke in Wales who was owed £800 from 1638.[106] Such desperate problems called for desperate remedies and so, in the end, in 1682 he mortgaged his entire estate for thirty-one years so that his financial obligations to roughly 220 individuals – some incurred nearly fifty years before – could be honoured.[107] The following year Richard Dobbs, in his survey of County Antrim, described the marquis's estate as 'much altered, impaired, mangled, and engaged in debts, mortgages, grants and otherwise'.[108] Antrim had, it seemed, successfully seen off his political opponents only to succumb to his creditors. In this, however, he was not alone. Argyll had also died deeply in debt, while Antrim's great rival in Ireland, Ormond, passed on a debt of £150,000 to his grandson and this was 'ultimately to lead to the breakup of the Ormond estates'.[109]

Shortly after he had thus settled his affairs, his wife noted that 'his limbs are weak but I think his constitution strong being he has overcome several strange fits since winter and I hope will yet continue'.[110] She was wrong: within six months Randal MacDonnell, second earl and first marquis of Antrim died 'at his dwelling near Dunluce'.[111] He was seventy-four years old. Since he had not produced an heir, the marquisate died out and his younger brother Alexander succeeded him as the third earl.[112] Antrim's body lay in state from 3 February until 14 March 1683 when he was finally buried, after

---

[105] Chancery decree books 1669–85 (PROI, Decrees pronounced by High Court of Chancery, 1.A.49.129, fos. 3, 12–14, 41); Ormond to Arran, 1 September 1683 (Bodl., Carte MSS 40, fo. 118); St Albans to Arran, 14 September 1683 (*ibid.*, fo. 124); Ormond's report to Charles II, 11 November 1683 (*ibid.*, fo. 122).
[106] Ohlmeyer, 'Seventeenth century survivor', pp. 429, 449.
[107] This left his brother and heir powerless since he was unable to make leases without the permission of the trustees appointed by the marquis to administer the estate. Copy of a deed between Antrim and others, 18 February 1682 (NLI, Domville papers MS 9387); third earl of Antrim to Donald McDonald of Muddart, 12 December 1683 and 8 December 1684 (NLS, MS 3784, fo. 46); Donald McDonald of Muddart to the captain of Clanranald, 13 December 1684 (SRO, GD 201/4/28).
[108] Hill, *MacDonnells*, p. 377.
[109] Neely, 'The Ormond Butlers of County Kilkenny', pp. 116, 120–1, 123.
[110] Lady Antrim to Rawdon, 25 August 1682 (Hunt., HA MSS 15, 230).
[111] Rawdon to Conway, 14 February 1683 (*Cal. SP Dom., Jan.–June 1683*, p. 56/PRO, SP, 63/343, no. 94).
[112] Apart from a cursory discussion in Hill, *MacDonnells*, and Hector McDonnell, 'Jacobitism and the third and fourth earls of Antrim', *The Glynns*, 13 (1985), pp. 50–4, Alexander's career has not received the scholarly attention it deserves. Interestingly, had Alexander also failed to produce legitimate issue, the title and estate were settled on the sons of Sir James MacDonnell and failing that they were to pass to the Scottish MacDonalds, see copy of a deed between Antrim and others, 18 February 1682 (NLI, Domville papers MS 9387).

'a great funeral', alongside many of his ancestors in the family vault at the Franciscan friary of Bonamargy near Ballycastle.[113] And there he rests.

[113] Rawdon to Conway, 14 February 1683 (*Cal. SP Dom., Jan–June 1683*, p. 56/PRO, SP 63/343, no. 94); Hill, *MacDonnells*, pp. 346–7; F. J. Bigger, *The ancient Franciscan friary of Bun-Na-Margie, Ballycastle, on the north coast of Antrim* ... (Belfast, 1898). p. 36.

CONCLUSION: A SEVENTEENTH-CENTURY SURVIVOR

> Randalle, invincible for country, Charles, and God,
> Thyself a golden warrior, thou residest within the lead
> Whose fidelity in the adverse fortunes of war,
> Neither rebels nor gibbets could bend.[1]

This bold inscription on Antrim's coffin pays tribute above all to the simple fact of his survival, which was perhaps the greatest triumph of his political career, especially when one remembers that this was an achievement denied to his enemy Strafford (executed in 1641), his patron Laud (executed in 1645), his master Charles I (executed in 1649), his friend Hamilton (executed in 1649), his ally Montrose (executed in 1650) and his arch-rival Argyll, chief of Clan Campbell (executed in 1661).

It is true that Antrim had not won great political acclaim or power, except for a very brief spell during the later 1640s, or profited by the Civil Wars, as many had; but on the other hand, unlike many others, he had lost relatively little. Above all he had preserved what to him was worth preserving. First and foremost, after a twenty-three-year struggle (1642–65), he had regained his Irish property intact – 'thirty miles of territory and vast estates with several castles' – and was able to pass it on to his appointed successor.[2] Secondly, and closely related to this, he had preserved his power and influence in both Ireland and Western Scotland, despite failing to unite his dual Celtic inheritance under his leadership. Thirdly, the marquis remained a devout – 'very zealous' – Catholic in an age of 'confessional absolutism' when a timely conversion to Protestantism might have solved many of his problems.[3] Moreover, he was able to preserve the old faith on his own estates and in the Isles.[4]

---

[1] Quoted in Hill, *MacDonnells*, p. 347.
[2] Plunkett to [Airoldi], 17/27 September 1671 (Hanly (ed.), *Letters*, p. 247).
[3] John Bossy, *The English catholic community 1570–1850* (London, 1976), pp. 78–80, 102, 217. He never joined the many Catholics in all three kingdoms, including his kinsmen the Savages, who did renounce their faith, Brother Albert, 'The Savages (now Nugents) of the Ards', *Upper Ards Historical Society Journal*, 3 (1979), p. 22. For other examples, see B. G. Blackwood, *The Lancashire gentry and the great rebellion 1640–1660* (Manchester, 1970), p. 120; Gallwey, *The Wall family in Ireland*, pp. 93–4.
[4] As a result the north-east corner of County Antrim has remained predominantly

Seen from the standpoint of his own personal agenda, therefore, the marquis may be deemed remarkably successful. Yet his extraordinary career as a Caroline loyalist, Catholic confederate, Cromwellian collaborator and Restoration pragmatist has long since caused him to be the victim of vilification by historians. Undoubtedly, there was an unsavoury, greedy, myopic side to Antrim's character, and, equally, he was prepared both to abandon his friends and benefactors if he saw no other alternative, and to twist ruthlessly every opportunity and opening to his own advantage. However, there was also a very positive (and often overlooked) dimension to his character. Thus he was as loyal and devoted to both of his wives as they were to him, and, as we have seen, he genuinely cared for his tenants and for his immediate and extended family on both sides of the North Channel. Furthermore, as his entrepreneurial operations during the Civil Wars vividly demonstrate, he was enterprising, resourceful and determined; while his various trips to the continent during the 1640s highlight his abilities and energy as a diplomat. He was also blessed with a dynamic, charming and affable personality which, except with a select handful of powerful individuals, made him extremely likeable. In short, while he was not without faults he also possessed qualities overlooked or misrepresented by contemporaries such as Strafford or Ormond as well as by subsequent historians. Without them he could never have survived.

Moreover, a reexamination of Antrim's political career calls into question the adverse judgment of his principal critics at a more serious level. For instance, his record in Scotland (1644–6) admirably demonstrates that Lord Deputy Wentworth had underestimated his ability to raise an army during the first Bishops' War, while Ormond's authority as lord lieutenant in Ireland between 1648 and 1649 (and, again briefly, in 1663) was dangerously undermined by his failure to control the recalcitrant marquis.[5]

Just as a study of Antrim's career forces historians to see the crisis of the mid-seventeenth century as an equilateral triangle of conflict involving all three of the Stuart kingdoms, so too it demonstrates that Irish, like British, history 'need not be, and should not be, insular history'.[6] For events on the continent, especially in France and Spain, helped to shape the course of the Irish Civil Wars.

Forging and maintaining close ties with Catholic Europe was one of the real triumphs of Irish foreign policy during these years and it was largely the

Catholic until today, J. R. B. McMinn, 'The social and political structure of North Antrim in 1869', *The Glynns*, 10 (1982), p. 11.
[5] For details, see chapter 3 above.
[6] John H. Elliott, 'National and comparative history' (Inaugural lecture, University of Oxford, 1991), p. 14.

work of individual diplomats and entrepreneurs such as Antrim. But there were other successes which have been obscured by the internecine quarrels within the Catholic party and the Cromwellian conquest and occupation of Ireland after 1649. The confederate agent in Holland, Oliver French, paid his own tribute to the confederate diplomatic achievement. In 1641, he wrote, 'we were naked men, destitute of arms, ammunition and experienced commanders' yet within seven years 'with God's assistance we have provided ourselves of arms and ammunition and called home our experienced commanders ... from foreign services, and furnished ourselves with a considerable number of frigates and ships of war ... and thereby annoyed our enemies, both by sea and by land'.[7]

Absence of evidence makes it impossible to quantify French's generalizations. Certainly Irish soldiers in continental service began trickling home shortly after the outbreak of the rebellion in 1641, and the trickle soon turned into a flood until 1645 when there was only one regiment left in French service (there had been seven in 1641), while between 1641 and 1643 there were not sufficient Irish soldiers left in Flanders even to muster a regiment and by 1645 there was only one Irish regiment serving in Spain.[8] Where possible these veterans brought home with them their own weapons. In addition, piecemeal shipments of arms and munitions arrived in Ireland from the summer of 1642 and while there was never a surplus of ordnance in the country the confederate armies appear to have been reasonably well armed and supplied throughout the war.

Moreover, these channels of communication and supply were kept open – as French stated – by the remarkably successful and effective armada of privateers which doubled as the Irish navy. Antrim, with at least four Dunkirk frigates, together with Anthonio Nicholas Vanderkipp, from Flanders, ran the largest, best coordinated and most successful privateering operation in Ireland. In addition, numerous Irish merchants either owned or had shares in individual warships, as did the continental corsairs (especially from Flanders and France) who established themselves in Ireland during the 1640s.[9] At its peak the privateering fleet comprised between fifty and sixty frigates, half of which were 'foreign', and according to one reasonably reliable contemporary observer, 'these privateers took over a six year period, from the parliamentary ships of all three kingdoms, 1,900 vessels, and 1,500 captives ... and this does not include those ships which had been sunk in various naval

---

[7] Oliver French to the States General of the United Provinces, 5/15 May 1648 (Gilbert, *Ir. confed.* VI, 233–4).
[8] Carles, 'Troupes Irlandaises', p. 195; Gouhier, 'Mercenaires Irlandais', pp. 59–60; *Wild Geese*, pp. 8–13; and Philip IV to O'Neill, 20 February/2 March 1645 (AGS, Eo. 2525, unfol.).
[9] Ohlmeyer, 'Irish privateers', pp. 121–8; *idem*, '"The Dunkirk of Ireland"', p. 25–49.

encounters'.[10] A parliamentary newspaper in 1643 paid its own tribute to the 'great number of the Irish rebels ships, commanded by Dunkirkers, and with whom their frigates are employed do infest our coasts, and take divers small vessels, and derive their commission from the Free States of Ireland'.[11]

Nor was confederate success limited to logistics and naval affairs. This was the first (and only) time before 1922 when Ireland had its own fully fledged foreign policy, sent envoys – including the marquis of Antrim – abroad and received accredited diplomats at its 'sovereign seat of government', Kilkenny. Irish diplomacy also won the Catholic cause international acclaim; again, according to Oliver French, 'this defensive warr being approved of by most of the states and potentates of Christendom'.[12] Moreover, the presence of high-powered foreign dignitaries in Kilkenny gave the confederates an important moral boost and made them feel part of the international community.

Diplomatic ties were strengthened by human ones, as the exodus of 'wild geese' from Ireland during the later 1640s clearly highlights. Throughout the mid-seventeenth century individual military contractors traded mercenaries to France and Spain in return for financial or military assistance. In 1635 and 1647 Antrim tried to export men to France, while in 1645 and 1646 he committed himself to sending cannon-fodder to Flanders.[13] Again he was not alone. Sir Piers Crosby, descended from the bardic family of O'More with an extensive power base in County Kerry, commanded in 1627 one of the Irish regiments sent to La Rochelle. Then in 1629–30 he offered to raise men for service in Nova Scotia, in 1631 for Germany, in 1632 for the West Indies, in 1634 for Flanders, in 1635 for France, in 1639 for Scotland and in 1645 for Spain.[14] In 1647 the earl of Glamorgan, following in Antrim's footsteps, declared his willingness to send '4,000 of his vassals from Wales for service in these kingdoms ... [and] resolved to come and propose the same thing at the court of Spain'. However, on this occasion the Spanish agent in Ireland declined the offer 'because his [Glamorgan's] proposals possessed many outward signs of interest but no solid basis. It was intended solely to extract concessions from the royal grandeur of Your Majesty [Philip IV], which is something never lacking in persons of such illustrious blood as the said marquis.'[15] The same year Ormond, who as owner of an enormous estate and

[10] *Comment. Rinucc.*, I, 519–20. This estimate may be slightly inflated, see Ohlmeyer, 'Irish privateers', p. 126, but not by much.
[11] *The parliament scout ... From Tuesday 20 to Tuesday 27 June 1643* (London, 1643), p. 3.
[12] Oliver French to the States General of the United Provinces, 5/15 May 1648 (Gilbert, *Ir. confed.*, VI, 233–4).
[13] See pp. 28, 53, 154–7, 179–80, 209–10 above.
[14] Clarke, 'Sir Piers Crosby', p. 147; Carles, 'Troupes Irlandaises', pp. 194–6.
[15] *Relación de los servicios de D. Francisco Foissotte ...* (Biblioteca Nacional, Madrid, MS 2367, fos. 15v–16).

as head of one of the most important families in Ireland was capable (according to a Spanish observer) of raising between 4,000 and 6,000 men,[16] requested permission from the English parliament to send 5,000 infantry and 500 horse to France; while late the following year he proposed sending a further two regiments into foreign service in return for financial aid.[17] In 1649 he offered Spain 4,000 foot and hoped to raise between £3,000 and £4,000 in this manner. As the decade progressed other individuals muscled in on the opportunities created by military 'enterprising'. For instance, Patrick Barnewall, Colonel James Preston, Viscount Muskerry, Richard White, Christopher Mayo and Christopher O'Brien were all prepared to levy regiments of soldiers for continental service on a cash-on-delivery basis.[18] As a result, by the early 1650s there were twelve Irish regiments serving in Spain and Flanders and a further eight regiments in France.

The activities of these entrepreneurs raise in an acute form the question of patriotism during the 1640s and 1650s. Recently the journal *History Today* featured a series of articles, entitled 'A patriot for whom', which examined the theme of betrayal in history. A number of case studies of individuals were printed, ranging from Ancient Greece to the twentieth century, which illuminated the conflicting pressures and loyalties which threaten the concept of patriotism. For instance, devotion to the Catholic faith prompted Sir William Stanley and Captain Rowland York, two leading Elizabethan officers of the English expeditionary force sent to the Netherlands in 1586, to defect to the king of Spain and thus to betray both their commanding officer, the earl of Leicester, and their queen. While Marshall Schomberg, before dying at the battle of the Boyne in 1690 in command of William of Orange's invasionary force, had previously taken up commands in the separate armies of six different states: Lutheran Sweden, Anglican Britain, Calvinist Brandenburg and Holland and Catholic France and Portugal. Nevertheless, Schomberg managed to remain loyal both to his various employers and to his Calvinist beliefs.[19]

What then of Antrim: for whom was he a patriot? Was his 'fidelity' really such that 'neither rebels nor gibbets' could bend it up (p. 278 above)? Between 1638 and 1645, he indeed seems to have served the Stuart cause with unswerving loyalty both in Scotland and Ireland. However, over the winter of

[16] La Torre to Philip IV, 26 April/6 May 1647 (AGS, Eo. 2523).
[17] Ormond to Du Talon, 23 April 1647 (Bodl., Carte MSS 20, fo. 639); Ormond to Digby 12 October 1648 (*ibid.*, 63, fo. 550).
[18] Also see Prendergast, *Cromwellian settlement*, pp. 87–8; John A. Murphy, *Justin MacCarthy, Lord Mountcashel, commander of the first Irish brigade in France* (Cork, 1959), pp. 1–2.
[19] See, for instance, Simon L. Adams, 'Stanley, York and Elizabeth's catholics', *History Today*, 37, no. 7 (July 1987), pp. 46–50.

1645–6 and again in 1648 he openly, overtly and deliberately defied orders given to him by the royal family. Moreover, throughout the later 1640s, through hatred of the marquis of Ormond, he not only tried to sabotage royalist schemes to win the war in Ireland and Britain for the king, but he also joined forces first with the papal nuncio and then with the English parliament, both avowed enemies of Charles I. Little wonder that he quickly 'gained the reputation of pulling down the side he is on';[20] or, in the words of another contemporary, behaved like a spider who went about 'making poison out of everything', alienating and infecting 'the greater part of the kingdom'.[21]

Because Antrim failed to serve his sovereign as a 'loyal' subject should, he was tarred a 'traitor'; while his willingness to collaborate with the king's enemies conveyed the image of a 'chief for sale'.[22] However, concepts such as 'treachery' and patriotism' meant little in the early modern Gaelic world where a man's first loyalty was to his family and kinsmen, then to his religion and only finally to his sovereign and country. Although since the Reformation the MacDonnells, like many others in Gaelic Ireland and Scotland, had been forced to compromise and negotiate in order to survive at all, sooner or later a choice between the old faith and the new became inevitable. But, as Nicholas Canny recently noted, the necessity of choosing 'between accepting the state religion and taking a stand in the interests of the Counter-Reformation' came to different Irish leaders at different times.[23] For Antrim's grandfather, Hugh O'Neill, it had been the Nine Years' War, for many members of the Old English and Gaelic Irish it had been 1641–2; and so by holding out until 1646 Antrim had in fact remained 'loyal' to the crown longer than the majority of his Catholic compatriots.

Antrim, however, was not alone in doing whatever was necessary in order to protect his personal, patriarchal interests. Many other Irish Catholics could also be, and often were, branded 'collaborators' or 'traitors'. To begin with, in return for his support, Antrim's nephew, Lord Dunsany, was given permission 'to continue in possession of Dunsany which he holds from the Commonwealth'.[24] Another nephew, Sir Henry O'Neill of Killelagh, 're-covered an income of 4,000 scudi per annum' at the Restoration despite having compromised with the Cromwellians when he compounded for his estates in 1655.[25] The same was true of the earl of Westmeath (yet another

[20] Clanricard to Fanshaw, 27 August 1651 (*Ormonde MSS*, I, 194).
[21] *A letter from Sir Lewis Dyve* ... p. 40.   [22] O Riordan, *The Gaelic mind*, p. 20.
[23] Nicholas P. Canny, 'Early modern Ireland, c. 1500–1700', in Roy F. Foster (ed.), *The Oxford illustrated history of Ireland*, (Oxford, 1991), pp. 118–19. Also see O Riordan, *The Gaelic mind*, chapters 3 and 4.
[24] Order, 9 March 1653 (BL, Eg. MSS 1762, fo. 73v); Hill, *MacDonnells*, p. 250; order, 9 March 1654 (King's Inn Library, Dublin, Prendergast papers 1, p. 56).
[25] *Cal. SP Ire.*, 1647–60, p. 569.

nephew) who, together with 'most of the considerable gentry of Leinster', was also forced to compromise his loyalty to the king in order to survive.[26]

Elsewhere, the confederate Sir Robert Talbot, who was involved in 'the treacherous surrender of the castle of Athlone into the enemy' in 1651, was nevertheless restored under the Act of Explanation.[27] Likewise Nicholas, first Viscount Netterville, an ardent confederate, and his son Sir John, who initially 'trimmed between the English and Irish parties', eventually made their peace with Cromwell. As his reward, Sir John retired to England where he was allowed to enjoy part of the rental from his wife's estate and to live in London.[28] During the 1650s Edward Butler, second Viscount Galmoy, a favourite of the Commonwealth, continued to reside in County Kilkenny; yet he was restored to his estates by Charles II.[29] Another Butler, Piers, first Viscount Ikerrin, had been an active supporter of the nuncio during the Civil War but he too made a deal. In 1656 Oliver Cromwell, conscious that 'Lord Viscount Ikerrin hath been of late time serviceable to suppress the Tories', ordered that he be allowed 'some portion of his estate [in County Tipperary] ... [and] some competent pension or money out of the revenue'. His grandson was later restored to these lands.[30] Dr Gerald Fenell, another active confederate this time with royalist sympathies, was allowed to practise his profession during the 1650s and was, with Ormond's help, restored to his property after 1660.[31] Connor O'Brien, later Baron Moyarta and Viscount O'Brien, had been a supporter of the Irish rebellion yet in 1659 he was living on his hereditary lands in County Clare and all of his estates were restored to him after 1660.[32] A willingness to collaborate, together with the geographical remoteness of County Sligo, also explains why the O'Haras of Annaghmore were able to maintain their position in the county throughout the mid-seventeenth century.[33] The same was true of the Maguires of Tempo, County Fermanagh: during the 1650s Brian Maguire 'managed to retain his estate entire and even added to it.'[34]

Even staunch Catholic royalists such as Clanricard, who had taken over

[26] Fleetwood to Thurloe, 20 June 1655 (Birch (ed.), *Thurloe state papers*, III, 566).
[27] Muskerry to Ormond, 25 August 1651 (*Ormonde MSS*, I, 188).
[28] *DNB*, 'Netterville'.
[29] See pp. 240, 272 above and Brennan, 'The changing composition', p. 165.
[30] J. P. Prendergast, 'The Butlers, Lords Ikerrin, before the court of transplantation at Athlone AD 1656 ... ', *Butler Society Journal*, 3 (1987), pp. 72–3.
[31] Patrick L. Logan, 'Gerald Fennell – doctor and politician (?–1665)', *Irish Ecclesiastical Record*, 5th series, 93 (Jan.–June 1960), pp. 84–92.
[32] Donal F. Cregan, 'The confederation of Kilkenny: its organization, personnel and history' (unpublished PhD thesis, National University of Ireland, 1947), p. 417.
[33] Bartlett, 'The O'Haras of Annaghmore', p. 52.
[34] W. A. Maguire, 'The estate of Cú Chonnacht Maguire of Tempo: a case history from the Williamite land settlement', *IHS*, 27, no. 106 (Nov. 1990), p. 135.

command of the king's Irish war-effort after Ormond's departure for France in December 1650, were eventually forced to compromise. The anonymous author of the *Aphorismical discovery* accused Clanricard of selling out to the Cromwellians when he handed over Galway in June 1652: 'Clanricard's act was really the betraying of a whole nation, a whole kingdom.'[35] Perhaps this is too harsh; another leading royalist acknowledged the fact that Clanricard had been courted 'by Sultan Cromwell himself (as looking upon his lordship for the person likeliest now to give him the greatest opposition, and to contribute most to the preservation of what was left)'; he maintained that Clanricard remained 'loyal' to the king.[36] But this, too, is debatable. On the one hand, Clanricard rejected overtures from the parliamentary governor of Kilkenny in January 1651; but, on the other, after his surrender to the Commonwealth the following year he hurried to his English estate in Kent – 'where his lady is this twelve-month' – rather than joining the royalist court on the continent.[37] Moreover, in 1652 he was content for Cromwellian officials to pressure, on his behalf, the corporation of Galway for £1,000 which was owed him,[38] while in 1658, the year after his death, his wife was able to sell her late husband's estate in Herefordshire and to petition for her own jointure.[39] The fact that Clanricard was a step-brother of the late parliamentary champion, the earl of Essex, and was protected by influential men such as Sir Robert Pye and the earl of Northumberland undoubtedly helped; but it is also undeniable that, like Antrim, he had collaborated with the 'enemy'.

Even ardent royalists who did not compromise directly with the Commonwealth allowed a family member to hedge their bets for them. The best-known example was of Lady Ormond, wife of the lord lieutenant who after 1652 was involved in protracted negotiations with the Cromwellians regarding the fate of her husband's extensive estates in Counties Kilkenny and Tipperary. And with some success; in March 1653 she was assigned Dunmore House and lands worth £2,000 per annum.[40]

Irish Protestants also changed sides, some with alarming regularity.

---

[35] Gilbert, *Contemp. hist. 1641–52*, III, 123. [36] *A letter from Sir Lewis Dyve* ..., p. 42.
[37] Gilbert, *Contemp. hist. 1641–52*, III, 125. [38] BL, Eg. MSS 1762, fo. 54r–v.
[39] Instructions from Lady Clanricard and St Albans to the earl of Northumberland and Sir Robert Pye, 11 December 1658 (SCL, EM 1317); petition from Lady Clanricard, 8 June 1658 (BL, Lansd. MSS 823, fo. 55).
[40] Dunlop (ed.), *Commonwealth*, II, 313. I am grateful to Dr John Hughes for bringing this reference to my attention. She held nearly 18,000 acres of the family property in County Kilkenny; while three years later Lord Deputy Henry Cromwell allowed her a loan of £200 which was to be repaid from the income arising from this property (NLI, Ormonde MSS 5491, fos. 15, 59).

Consider the example of Murrough O'Brien, sixth baron of Inchiquin, who was motivated during the 1640s almost exclusively by 'tribal' ambitions and was prepared to offer his services to whoever was in a position to protect the Protestant ascendancy in Munster. The king's refusal to appoint him president of Munster on the death of St Leger forced him into the parliamentary camp in July 1644, just as parliament's lack of recognition for his military successes in Munster combined with their suspicions about his true loyalties led him to espouse the royalist cause again in 1648.[41] Another Munsterman Roger Boyle, Lord Broghill (and later earl of Orrery), who had initially served the royalists, joined the parliamentarians in 1647; however, after the execution of Charles I in 1649, he seriously contemplated returning to the royalist fold and only Cromwell's personal intervention prevented him from doing so. Yet in 1660 Broghill played a key role in the restoration of Charles II and secured Ireland for him; in return he was elevated to the earldom of Orrery and created lord president of Munster.[42]

Ulster Protestants were equally resilient survivors. Sir John Clotworthy, a prominent County Antrim landowner related by marriage to the parliamentary leader John Pym, was determined to protect the Presbyterian settlement in Ulster and took an important part in bringing Strafford and later Laud to trial. He remained active at Westminster until he was imprisoned in England between December 1648 and 1651 on charges of stirring up war between the parliament and the army and of embezzling supplies for the parliamentary army in Ireland. Eventually, like so many others, he also made a bargain with the Cromwellians and spent much of the 1650s on his Ulster estates; but at the Restoration he played a prominent role in representing the Protestant interest in Ireland to the king, and in November 1660 was created Viscount Massereene.[43] Similarly, Colonel Mark Trevor, originally a Welsh royalist whose family had settled in County Down, had embraced the Cromwellian cause and with the help of the regicide, John Jones, acquired extensive estates in Counties Down, Louth and Kildare. Thanks to Ormond's patronage, these lands were confirmed to him at the Restoration.[44] George Rawdon, Arthur Hill, Hugh Viscount Montgomery of the Ards and many others were also prepared to deal with both sides in order to survive.[45]

---

[41] Karl S. Bottigheimer, 'Civil war in Ireland: the reality in Munster', *Emory University Quarterly*, 22, no. 1 (Spring 1966), p. 48. Ironically he later embraced Catholicism in spite of the fact that this prevented him from being nominated lord president of Munster again.
[42] *DNB*, 'Roger Boyle'; Bottigheimer, 'Restoration land settlement', p. 4.
[43] *DNB*, 'Clotworthy'.
[44] H. C. O'Sullivan, 'The Trevors of Rosetrevor: a British colonial family in seventeenth century Ireland' (unpublished M Litt thesis, Trinity College, Dublin, 1985), chapter 6.
[45] Bottigheimer, 'Restoration land settlement', pp. 3–4.

Henry Cromwell attributed this willingness to compromise to Ireland's 'colonial' status: 'Tis true we are but a kind of colony the inhabitants of which places are commonly more compliant with their present governors, more flexible to changes, more dexterous in the practice of flattery than other men.' He concluded that this quality ('a genius') in the Irish was due to the fact that they were more used to the 'little tyrannies of county governors ... than those ... who reside [near] the seat of empire'.[46] This may well have been the case, but more realistically they were (in the words of Karl Bottigheimer) 'desperate men struggling to retain the estates which they, or their near ancestors, had so recently established in the sea of Irishry now tempest-tossed'.[47] Clearly, then, amid this sea of Cromwellian 'collaborators' and 'traitors', Antrim hardly stood out.

But how typical was Antrim's survival in a British context? The tolerant attitude adopted by the Cromwellians to the Catholic religion facilitated an atmosphere of conciliation and cooperation in both Scotland and England. In September 1650 all penalties on recusancy were repealed, and by and large Catholics were treated more favourably under the Protectorate than under any previous government; while Cromwell was unable to grant them toleration, he was not one to interfere with the liberty of men's consciences.[48] As one pamphleteer complained in 1656, there were no longer laws 'against any man's being and doing almost what he himself will in matters of religion'.[49]

Hardly surprisingly, many British Catholics made haste to take advantage of this leniency and, like Antrim, accept the republican regime. In Scotland by the mid-1650s General George Monck succeeded in winning the support of the Highland chiefs who, in return for certain privileges, agreed to support the new regime.[50] For example, Antrim's Catholic kinsman Angus, laird of Glengarry, who had fought for the Irish confederates during the later 1640s

---

[46] Henry Cromwell to Fauconbridge, 28 April 1658 (Birch (ed.), *Thurloe state papers*, VIII, 101).
[47] Bottigheimer, 'Restoration land settlement', p. 3.
[48] It was rumoured that Cromwell 'will give liberty of conscience even to Catholics', M. V. Hay (ed.), *The Blairs papers, 1603–60*, (London and Edinburgh, 1929), 48–9. Hyde attributed this to Crelly ('who hath always held good intelligence with Cromwell'), Hyde to Mr Taylor, 13/23 August 1652 (Bodl., Clarendon MSS 43, fos. 259–60). On the survival of English Catholics see Roebuck, 'The Constables of Everingham', pp. 75–85; Aveling, *Northern catholics*, pp. 305–9; B. G. Blackwood, 'Plebian catholics in the 1640s and 1650s', *Recusant History*, 18, (1986), pp. 45–9.
[49] Quoted in Hardacre, *The royalists*, p. 92.
[50] Macinnes, 'The impact of the civil wars', pp. 60–1; F. D. Dow, *Cromwellian Scotland 1651–1660* (Edinburgh, 1979), pp. 132–3; Allan I. Macinnes, 'Catholic recusancy and the penal laws, 1603–1707', *Records of the Scottish Church History Society*, 23 (1987), p. 53; Stewart, 'Peoples of the Clan Ranald', pp. 139–40.

and then raised men in the Isles for Glencairn, made his peace with the Protector in June 1655 after his castle was burned. Yet he was still raised to the peerage, as Lord MacDonnell and Aros, at the Restoration.[51] Likewise, the Catholic royalist James Ogilvie, captured and imprisoned by Cromwell in 1651, was eventually allowed to live quietly on his estates.[52] In England, according to one recent scholar, many Catholics were ready 'to do a deal with whoever came out on top in the civil wars, in order to improve the position of their own religion'.[53] One of the best known was Sir Kenelm Digby, a cosmopolitan Catholic royalist who, after returning to England in 1654, remained 'in close intercourse with Cromwell' and acted as his agent in France and Spain. Despite this, Digby was well received at the Restoration and continued to hold office as Henrietta Maria's chancellor.[54] Henry Arundell, third Lord Arundell of Wardour, and Henry Howard, sixth duke of Norfolk – both staunch Catholics – also reached an accommodation with both the Cromwellian and the Restoration regimes.[55] The same was true of John Paulet, fifth marquis of Winchester (and Clanricard's brother-in-law), known as the 'great loyalist', who was taken prisoner after the storm of Basing House in October 1645 but managed to reach a compromise with both regimes. Most celebrated of all, the devoutly Catholic (and royalist) marquis of Worcester – who, during the 1640s, as Lord Glamorgan, had first negotiated with and later joined forces with the Irish confederates – solicited Cromwellian employment in 1656, modestly boasting: 'I am able to do his highness more service than any one subject of his three nations'. At the Restoration he nevertheless recovered his extensive estates in Wales virtually intact.[56]

What really singled the marquis of Antrim out, and made him a more remarkable and influential figure, was thus not his ability to change his loyalties, which was what most political figures were obliged to do; nor his complex career, which, by and large, was moulded by immediate pressures or needs; nor yet his faith, for other Irish and British Catholics managed to survive and prosper amid all the wars and revolutions. It was the milieu in which he operated. For although none of the other 'trimmers' whose careers

[51] See pp. 188, 214–16 above. Duncan MacLean, 'Catholicism in the Highlands and Isles, 1560–1680', *Innes Review*, 3, no. 1 (Spring 1952), p. 12.
[52] *DNB*, 'James Ogilvy'. [53] Aylmer, 'Neutrals, trimmers and others', p. 20.
[54] *Ibid.*; *DNB*, 'Kenelm Digby'.
[55] *DNB*, 'Henry Arundell'; *ibid.*, 'Henry Howard'.
[56] Birch (ed.), *Thurloe state papers*, V, 713. Worcester returned to England in 1652, was imprisoned in the Tower until 1654 when he was released 'probably through Cromwell's influence'. His wife was awarded a tenth of his estate and he was granted a weekly pension of £6, *DNB*, 'Edward Somerset'.

have been recounted above changed their political colours as often as Antrim, so none of them exercised their power in such a fickle and remote area of the Stuart monarchies.

Though the Restoration may well have signalled the end of the Gaelic world as Antrim had known it, and marked a hardening of attitudes towards Irish Catholics, it did not alter the political geography of Antrim's world.[57] The continuities and constants were the same in the 1660s as they had been in the 1630s; Antrim's extensive empire, still united by the sea rather than the land, remained as close to Western Scotland and as remote from the seats of Stuart power; the 'MacDonnell archipelago' continued to be cemented primarily by clan and religious loyalties and ties of kinship. As long as this state of affairs lasted, the presence of Antrim and men like him would always be essential on Britain's Celtic Fringe. Hence even in the 1660s, according to Clarendon, 'the surest way to preserve that kingdom' – that is, to achieve a lasting settlement in Ireland – was by restoring handpicked Catholics, both Old English and native Irish, to their lands.[58] One of the commissioners of the court of claims went further and argued that the new land settlement would only succeed, and discontent among the Catholic population abate, if Antrim were restored in the north, Clanricard in the west and Clancarty in the south: 'Each of which beside their proper dependents have very considerable neighbours that have given good proof of their loyalty.'[59]

In its early years, the course of Charles II's government was just as unpredictable and turbulent as that of his father. There were republican risings in England, a covenanter rebellion in Scotland and a Cromwellian plot to seize Dublin in Ireland. In the absence of an army to coerce the population, without the support of local power-brokers in peripheral areas, the king was practically helpless. Thus Charles II, like Oliver Cromwell and Charles I before him, found it so hard to rule 'the dark corners' of the land that, for all his misgivings and scruples, he too needed Antrim. And if the histories of England, Scotland and Ireland are to be henceforth explained in their British contexts, as Professor Russell and others have so convincingly argued; and if the triple Stuart monarchy is to be set successfully in its European context, as Professors Elliott, Koenigsberger and Israel have pleaded; then historians ignore men from the periphery at their peril.

[57] Nicholas P. Canny, 'Identity formation in Ireland: the emergence of the Anglo-Irish', in Canny and Pagden (eds.), *Colonial identity*, pp. 200–2.
[58] Clarendon to Ormond, 18 July 1663 (Bodl., Carte MS 32, fo. 719).
[59] Winston Churchill to Bennet, 7 October 1663 (*Cal. SP Ire., 1663–5*, p. 248).

BIBLIOGRAPHY

ANTRIM'S ARCHIVES

Writing a convincing biography of a cosmopolitan, Catholic statesman, courtier, landlord, entrepreneur, collaborator and survivor, and placing him in his Irish, British and continental contexts, is handicapped by the absence of 'a body of "master" records'.[1] The 'Antrim archive' presently housed in the Public Record Office of Northern Ireland consists of 200 boxes containing grants, warrants, maps, land surveys and leases relating almost exclusively to the Antrim estate; roughly forty-three of these contain seventeenth-century material.[2] But although the Antrim papers are extensive and seminal for any study of his Irish property, they unfortunately contain virtually no personal correspondence. Instead one is forced to rely on letters written to or by the marquis which have been preserved among the papers of his contemporaries. In all, over 200 of his own letters have been located and used in this study; but, sadly, the majority of them are terse, allusive and uninformative. Only a handful (largely to his great friend, the marquis of Hamilton, and to his first wife, Katherine Villiers, duchess of Buckingham) can be considered either intimate or revealing.[3]

Writing an authoritative history of Antrim, or indeed of any seventeenth-century Irish grandee during this period, is further complicated by the loss of the records of the Irish government and of the confederation of Kilkenny, which were mostly destroyed by fire in either 1711 or 1922.[4] However, this is partly compensated for by the survival

---

[1] Geoffrey R. Elton, *The practice of history* (London, 1967), p. 93.

[2] Recently historians have emphasized the importance of estate records as historical sources. See, for instance, Nicholas P. Canny, 'Migration and opportunity. Britain, Ireland and the New World', *Ir. Econ. & Soc. Hist.*, 12 (1985), p. 10, and Whyte and Whyte, 'Some aspects of rural society', p. 33.

[3] A considerable number of Antrim's letters are printed in Knowler, *Letters*; Carte, *Ormond*; Gilbert, *Ir. confed.*; *Comment. Rinucc.*; *Cal. SP Ire.*; and in various contemporary newspapers and pamphlets. The remainder are located among the unpublished papers of the earl of Strafford (Sheffield City Library), the duke of Ormond (Bodleian Library, Oxford), the marquis of Hamilton (Scottish Record Office, Edinburgh) and the state papers (Public Record Office, London).

[4] This can be partly compensated for by a careful scrutiny of the transcripts of documents now lost made by contemporary, and later, antiquarians and historians, such as the earl of Clarendon, Edmund Borlase, Thomas Carte, Sir John T. Gilbert, J. P. Prendergast, P. H. Hore, C. H. Firth and S. R. Gardiner.

of a substantial amount of material relating to Antrim among the administrative records of the English and Scottish governments. The papers of the English High Court of Admiralty, for example, detail the fortunes of his privateering frigates, while the archive of the parliamentary committee of compounding sheds light on his English interests, and the records of the Scottish privy council report his activities in the Western Isles.

The destruction of so much material in 1711 and 1922 nevertheless makes it necessary to search more widely for documentation. First, other third-party sources, especially those compiled by or for the English government, are particularly rich. These include the papers of government ministers and politicians – royalist and Cromwellian alike – in Dublin and London; influential figures such as Lords Strafford, Ormond, Hamilton and Clarendon or Charles Fleetwood, Henry Ireton and Henry Cromwell all had to deal with Antrim and recorded his words and deeds. Various accounts by prominent Irishmen – including Richard Bellings and the earls of Castleheaven and Clanricard – have also survived.[5] These collections not only contain much pertinent information, but also illuminate the nature of the marquis's relationship with leading political figures in all three Stuart kingdoms.

Secondly, the archives of the continental countries involved in Irish affairs appear to be remarkably complete. The papers of governments in Paris,[6] Madrid[7] and Brussels[8] contain a wealth of tantalizing information: the dispatches, memos, reports and correspondence of their agents in Ireland – namely Foissotte and La Torre for the

---

[5] A number of histories by anonymous authors also discuss Antrim's antics, see especially *An aphorismical discovery of treasonable faction* reprinted in Gilbert, *Contemp. hist. 1641–52*; [Hogan (ed.)], *History of the warr*; 'An account of the war and rebellion in Ireland since the year 1641' and 'A light to the blind', NLI MS 345 and NLI MS 476.

[6] A considerable amount of Irish material from the Parisian archives is available in print. For the Bibliothèque Nationale, see the *NLI Report of the trustees 1949–50* (Dublin, 1950) and *1950–1* (Dublin, 1951) which contain an excellent French summary. Occasional letters from the BN are printed in Gilbert, *Ir. confed.*, III, 33, and M. A. Chervel, *Letters du Cardinal Mazarin* (Paris, 1872). As for the Ministère des Affaires Etrangères, a substantial number of letters from the French agents are reproduced in full in Gilbert, *Ir. confed*. Gilbert was given transcripts of these letters by Baschet and so they are presumably the same as those in the Baschet transcripts in the PRO, London (for a listing of Baschet see *Thirty-ninth annual report of the deputy keeper of the public records, appendix*, pp. 573–826). Also see J. J. Jusserand (ed.), *Recueil des instructions donnés aux ambassadeurs et ministres de France*, I: *1648–1665* (4 vols., Paris, 1929). There are also many references to Ireland in *Diplomatic correspondence*.

[7] There is no adequate listing to the Irish material in the Spanish government archive at Simancas. A useful introductory guide is John J. Silke, 'Spanish intervention in Ireland 1601–2', *Studia Hib.*, 3 (1963), pp. 179–90. Also see M. van Durme, *Les Archives générales de Simancas et l'histoire de la Bélgique (ixe-xixe – siècles)*, part II, *1508–1795* (Brussels, 1966).

[8] For further details on Irish material in the Archives Générales du Royaume, Brussels, see *Wild Geese*. J. Cuvelier and J. Lefèvre (eds.), *Correspondence de la cour d'Espagne sur les affaires des Pays Bas*, vol. III, *1633–1647* (Brussels, 1930), although not complete contains numerous references to Irish affairs.

Habsburgs and Dumolin, Monnerie and Talon for France – and of their ambassadors in London and Edinburgh, particularly the Spanish ambassador Cárdenas, together with discussions at the respective courts of the appropriate action to be taken. The papal archives – particularly the papers of Pope Urban VIII's nephew and 'cardinal protector of Ireland', Cardinal Barberini – are also rich in information.[9] Equally rewarding are the personal papers of the papal nuncio to Ireland after 1645, Giovanni Battista Rinuccini,[10] and an account left by his second-in-command, Dionysius Massari, the dean of Fermo.[11] These are international in perspective and help place Irish affairs in a wider setting.

Though diplomatic papers such as these have obvious biases and limitations, they are – especially in the absence of so many other sources – tremendously important for any study of mid-seventeenth-century Ireland. Largely thanks to them, Antrim's career as a troop raiser is particularly well documented; for details of his offers to raise Irish mercenaries to serve in Flanders, the logistics of transporting two regiments to the continent and the payments he received, are all noted in the correspondence between the Spanish envoys in Ireland and their masters in Madrid and Brussels, in the reports of the Spanish council of state, in the register of orders kept by the administration in Brussels, and in the accounts of various Spanish paymasters. In addition the numerous diplomatic dispatches of the day provide fascinating details, otherwise lost, on his activities as a member of the supreme council, and later, as its president; on his military campaigns in Ireland and Scotland; and on his relationship with the English parliamentarians after 1648.

Thirdly, the work of contemporary Scottish and Irish poets (such as Fear Flatha Ó Gnímh of County Antrim, Niall MacVurich, hereditary bard and historian of Clanranald, or John MacDonald, bard of Keppoch) helps to unravel the Celtic dimension to Antrim's character and reveals the viewpoint of his Gaelic kinsmen.[12] As one recent scholar has noted: 'Bardic poetry was ... imbued with fundamental elements of the Gaelic mentality, particularly those associated with the aristocracy. The poetry is in this way a fascinating and worthwhile source material in which to explore some of the

---

[9] For a general introduction to the Roman archives see Patrick J. Corish, 'Irish history and the papal archives', *Irish Theological Quarterly*, 21 (1954), pp. 375–81. For Irish material in the Archivio della Sacra Congregazione di Propaganda Fide, see B. Millett, 'The archives of the congregation de propaganda fide', *Irish Catholic Historical Committee* (1956), pp. 20–7, and *idem*, 'Catalogue of Irish material in 14 volumes of Scritture originali rieferite nelle congregazioni generali in Propaganda archives', *Collect. Hib.*, 10–12 (1967–9). For the Bibliotheca Apostolica Vaticana, see Giblin (ed.), 'Vatican Library: MSS Barberini Latini'; and *idem*, 'Catalogue of material of Irish interest'.

[10] *Comment. Rinucc.* For an English summary, see Michael J. Hynes, *The mission of Rinuccini, 1645–9* (Louvain, 1932). An invaluable series of Rinuccini's letters to two cardinal secretaries of state in Rome, 1645–9, are reproduced in Aiazza, *Embassy*.

[11] Massari, 'My Irish campaign', *The Catholic Bulletin*, 6 (1916), pp. 28–35, 82–8, 153–9, 217–22, 302–8, 367–73, 445–9, 502–5, 563–5, 618–20, 655–8; 7 (1917), pp. 111–14, 179–82, 246–9, 295–6; 8 (1918), pp. 140–2, 195–7, 247–9, 300–3, 396–8, 439–40, 478–80, 535–6, 538–40; 9 (1919), pp. 66–8, 116–17, 200–1, 310–11, 488–90, 535–40, 603–4, 649–52; 10 (1920), pp. 735–44.

[12] Ó Cuív (ed.), 'Some Irish items relating to the MacDonnells of Antrim'; *idem*, 'A poem on the second earl of Antrim', pp. 302–5; Cunningham and Gillespie, 'The East Ulster bardic family', pp. 106–14; Colm Ó Baoill, 'Some Irish harpers in Scotland', *Transactions of the*

perceptions of power, authority and the constraints on these'.[13] Finally, the extensive contemporary pamphlet collections – above all the Thorpe, Lough Fea, Thomason and Bradshaw tracts – and the broadsheets and newsletters printed by the thousand during the mid-seventeenth century not only reproduce documentation otherwise lost (especially letters intercepted by the parliamentarians) but offer a clear indication of how Antrim in particular and Irish papists in general were perceived by their English and Scottish counterparts.[14]

Unfortunately these gems are currently scattered among some thirty-six archives and libraries in Ireland, England, Scotland, Spain, France, Belgium, Italy and the United States. Mercifully, with the notable exception of material from the Archives du Ministère des Affaires Etrangères in Paris, they are almost all easily accessible to Irish historians on microfilm in the National Library of Ireland in Dublin and are conveniently and extensively listed in the exceptional compilation by R. J. Hayes, *Manuscript sources of Irish civilization* (11 vols., Boston, 1965).

MANUSCRIPT SOURCES

IRISH ARCHIVES

BELFAST

Public Record Office of Northern Ireland

D207/14/3, 207/15/1/4–7, 207/16/1–6/17 – Foster/Massereene papers
D265 – Leases and grants of the first three earls of Antrim, 1610–96
D282/1–3 – Leases with the second and third earls of Antrim, 1637–85
D301/1 – Mortgage with the marquis and his brother, 1685
D358 – MS of the MacDonnells, c. 1699
D556/10 – Lease, 1637

Gaelic Society of Inverness, 47 (1971–2), pp. 146–71; W. J. Watson, 'The MacDonald bardic poetry', *Transactions of the Gaelic Society of Inverness*, 36 (1931–3), pp. 138–58; MacKenzie, *Orain Iain Luim*; Keith N. MacDonald, *MacDonald bards from medieval times* (Edinburgh, 1900); A. J. MacDonald and A. M. MacDonald (eds.), *The MacDonald collection of Gaelic poetry* (Inverness, 1911); MacBain and Kennedy (eds.), *Reliquiae Celticae*, especially II, pp. 138ff; Macinnes, 'Scottish gaeldom', pp. 65–84.

[13] O Riordan, *The Gaelic mind*, p. 2.
[14] The biases of the various newspapers and the accuracy with which events were reported is discussed in A. N. B. Cotton, 'London newsbooks in the civil war: their attitudes and sources of information' (unpublished DPhil thesis, Oxford University, 1971) and Walter D. Love, 'Civil war in Ireland: appearances in three centuries of historical writing', *Emory University Quarterly*, 22, no. 1 (Spring 1966), pp. 58–64, 69.

D562/2/8/10/17/19/21/31–8/105–6 – Clotworthy and Massereene letters
D597/1/1–20 and /2/1–64 – Petty's Downe Survey maps for parishers in County Antrim, c. 1654
D695 – Waring manuscripts
D774 – Conveyance of lands, 1667. Copy in D896/30
D929 – Adair papers
D1375/3/40/1, 1375/8 boxes 1–2 – papers in the McGildowny collection relating to Antrim's estates
D1739/3/1A–B – Clotworthy house papers
D1759 – Extracts and transcripts from the Presbyterian church registers, muster roll (1618) and notes on the plantation of Ulster
D1835/38/55A–56 – O'Hara family papers
D1854/1/18 – Annesley family papers
D1928 – Brownlow family papers
D2171 – Estate papers relating to the second earl of Antrim, 1656–69
D2977 – Antrim papers. In addition to the catalogued material, there are c. 200 uncataloged boxes of documents relating to the Antrim estates; but only c. 43 actually contain material from the seventeenth century

T185 – Magennis family papers
T307/B – Hearth money rolls for Co. Antrim, 1669
T370/A – Books of survey and distribution for Co. Antrim, 1661
T372 – Copies of the crown and quit rent rolls, 1692
T473 – Antrim manuscripts
T549/1A/2A/3 – Leases of the first and second earl of Antrim
T588 – Notes concerning the Magennis family of Iveagh, 1614–1744
T694 – Rent roll of part of the Antrim estate, 1641
T811/3 – 'A report of the voluntary works done by servitors and other gentlemen of qualitie ... within the counties of Down, Antryme and Monahan', 1611
T808 – Groves manuscripts
T904 – Map, survey and valuation of Antrim's estate (by Archibald Stewart), 1734
T997 – Leases of the third earl of Antrim
T1703 – Map, survey and valuation of the barony of Cary (by Archibald Stewart), 1734
T2313/1/11–19 – Petty's Downe Survey maps for baronies in County Antrim, c. 1654–6
T2325/1 – Map, survey and valuation of the barony of Dunluce (by Archibald Stewart), 1734
T2352/2 – Maps and survey of the barony of Dunluce (by John O'Hara), 1782
T2490/13 – Letters patent for second earl of Antrim, 1637
T3726/2 – Muster roll for Co. Antrim, 1642

DUBLIN

City Library (Pearse St)

MS 169 – Sir James Ware's diary of occurrences
MS 254 – The memoirs of George Leyburn, 1647

King's Inn Library

J. P. Prendergast's papers – 14 volumes of transcripts from the Commonwealth records formerly in the PROI and the Carte papers

Marsh's Library

MS Z.2.1.5 – An account of the adventurers in Ireland during the 1650s

National Library of Ireland

MS 7–12 – Collectanea de rebus Hibernicis
MS 345 – Plunkett MSS: Account of the war and rebellion in Ireland since the year 1641
MS 476 – 'A light to the blind'
MS 758 – Copies of documents relating to government finance and administration in Ireland, 1650–6
MS 816 – Warrants from the commissioners of claims, 1661–6
MS 839 – Proceedings of the council of Ireland, 1653–9
MS 856–7 – Transcripts by J. T. Gilbert
MS 2307–35 – Letters and papers of Ormond relating to Ireland, 1640–65
MS 2481–6 – Undated letters to Ormond
MS 2494 – Undated petitions to Ormond
MS 2511–13 – Transcripts of petititons to Ormond, 1663–4, 1666
MS 8044 – Papers relating to revenue in Ireland, 1665, 1668, 1674–84
MS 9387 – Domville papers relating to the case of MacDonnell versus the earl of Antrim, 1681–1722
MS 9696 – Original documents about Wexford
MS 11,296 – Petititon from Lord Massereene, 1681
MS 11,959–61 – Transcripts from the Commonwealth records formerly in the PROI

GENEALOGICAL OFFICE
MS 93, 156, 160 – Pedigrees of the MacDonnells of Antrim
MS 172 – Pedigree of the MacDonalds and MacDonnells, *c.* 1317–1817

Public Record Office of Ireland

1.A.49.125 – Inquisitions, 1634–6
1.A.49.128 – Calendar of chancery proceedings, 1633
1.A.49.129 – Chancery decree books, 1669–85
1.A.53.55/56 – Lodge's extracts from the Cromwellian chancery rolls
MS 2448 – Petitions to Wentworth, 1638
MS 4974 – Caulfield MSS, extracts from the Commonwealth records formerly in PROI
Carte Transcripts vols. 1–29
Ferguson MSS IX, X, XII, XX – Extracts from Exchequer records formerly in PROI

Representative Church Body

MS Libr. 20 – Seymour's transcripts
MS Libr. 26 – Transcripts of inquisitions in Counties Antrim and Down, 1657

Royal Society of Antiquaries

7.B.6 – Transcript of the letter-book of the supreme council, 1642–5

Trinity College

MS 615 – Journal of the Irish House of Lords, 16 March 1639[-40] – 2 May 1646
MS 809–41 – Depositions taken in the 1640s and 1650s
MS 844 – A miscellaneous collection of letters and papers, 1647–53
MS 866 – Miscellaneous material
MS 1059 – Old rental of the estates of the [third?] earl of Antrim, [1690?]

MAYNOOTH

St Patrick's College

O'Renehan MSS – Bagwell's transcripts from the Commonwealth records formerly in PROI

WEXFORD

St Peter's College

Hore MSS E, F, 22, 33, 60

ENGLISH ARCHIVES

BUCKMINSTER PARK (near Grantham)

Estate Office

Tollemache MSS 3750, 4096, 4131, 4558, 4559, 4666, 5236 – The Lauderdale papers include a number of miscellaneous items relating to Antrim and Ireland, 1646–65

CAMBRIDGE

University Library

MS Add. 727 – Includes transcripts of letters from Charles I to Ormond
MS Add. 4246 – Collection of 247 letters and other papers relating to the Irish rebellion
MS Add. 4352 – Miscellaneous material
MS Add. 4353 – An account of the Irish rebellion, 1641
Mm.1.45–6 – Baker MSS

HUNTINGDON

Cambridgeshire Record Office

BUSH COLLECTION OF CROMWELL FAMILY PAPERS
Accession 731/11–14, 18, 20, 66–77, 144–7, 179 – Papers relating to Henry Cromwell in Ireland

Bibliography

LONDON
British Library
ADDITIONAL MSS
4155–9 – Thurloe papers
4165 – Copies of letters from the council at Dublin to Fleetwood, 1655
4763 – Miscellaneous papers on Irish affairs
4769 A/B – Letters from commissioners from Irish affairs, 1645–8
4771 – Minutes of the committee for Irish affairs, 1642–6
4794 – Milles collection (vol. XLI): letters from James I and his council to the government in Ireland, 1603–23
11,312 – Entry book of royal warrants addressed to Ormond, 1662–7
12,184–6 – Sir Robert Brown's dispatches, 1641–51
15,856 – Copies of official documents, 1634–58
15,857–8 – Brown's correspondence, 1624–1712
18,914 – Indenture between Antrim and the trustees of the second duke of Buckingham, 1635
19,833 – The civil list for Ireland, 1654
19,845 – Register of orders, 1655–9
21,125 – Proposals about lands in County Londonderry, 1638
21,500 – Letters of Thomas Carte
22,546 – Naval papers, 1643–77
25,277 – Miscellaneous material
28,937, fo. 140 – Copies of letters to Antrim from earl of Nithsdale and others, 1643
29,587 – Miscellaneous political papers
34,326, fos. 2–3 – Petition from Antrim to parliament
37,823 – The Nicholas papers
40,860 – Arthur, earl of Anglesey's diary, 1671–5
41,864 – Middleton papers
43,724 – Letters to Henry Cromwell from Thurloe and Fleetwood, 1654–9
46,926–9 – Egmont MSS

EGERTON MSS
80 – A collection of letters chiefly written by Richard earl of Cork, 1610–43
212 – Extracts from the books of the Irish privy council, 1649–60
789 – Abstracts of the decrees of the court of claims, 1662–3
917 – Miscellaneous papers, 1623–1728
1048 – Miscellaneous papers, 1642–9
1761–2 – Transcripts of orders by parliamentary commissioners, 1651–5
1779 – Copy of orders by the commissioners of Ireland, 1651–4
2533–6 – Letters from the lords justices in Ireland, 1641 and Ormond, 1652–9
2541–2 – Miscellaneous historical papers of Sir Edward Nicholas
2619 – Correspondence of Henrietta Maria, 1642–5
3349 – Danby papers

HARLEIAN MSS
430 – Register of petititons to Strafford, 1637–8
1579 – Letters from Ormond and Charles II in favour of Antrim, 1663
2099 – First earl of Antrim's patent
2138, fos. 111–16 – Survey of part of Antrim's lands, 1641
4551 – Brienne collection of diplomatic dispatches

6807 – Miscellaneous material
6988 – Letters from Charles I, 1625–48
7056 – Extracts from Ormond's history
7379 – Royal letters, 1643–5

LANSDOWNE MSS
821–3 – Collection of letters by various persons to Henry Cromwell, 1655–8

SLOANE MSS
1008 – A collection of letters and papers formerly belonging to Edmund Borlase
3838 – 'A short view of the state of Ireland ... ' c. 1652

STOWE MSS
82 – Borlase's history of the Irish rebellion

House of Lords Record Office

Main papers 30/10/1641, 16/12/1641, 4/2/1642, 18/6/1642, 7/10/1642, 18/5/1643, 7/6/1643, 8/5/1643, 10/6/1643, 27/10/1643, 28/6/1643, 15/3/1647, [1648]

Lambeth Palace

MS 943 – Letters from Conway to Laud, 1640

London University Library

MS 30 – Miscellaneous material, 1626–1739
MS 43 – Miscellaneous material, 1669–70

Public Records Office (Chancery Lane)

C 231/5 – Chancery office docquet book, 1629–43
C 231/6 – Chancery office docquet book, 1643–69

CP 25/2/bundle 482/16 Ch. I/Mic
E 190/1336/3 – Chester port book, 1639
E 190/1336/12 – Chester port book, 1640–1
E 351/440 – Pipe office, declared accounts, forfeitures, 16/10/43–16/6/53
E 405/285 – Pells, declaration book, 1636–44

HCA 13/60 – Examinations, 1645–7
HCA 13/62 – Examinations, 1649–50
HCA 13/244–51 – Examinations on commission, 1641–50
HCA 30/854 – Miscellanea, 1596–1662
HCA 30/869 – Miscellanea, 1638–55
HCA 34/1–2 – Sentences in prize courts, 1643–53
HCA 34/4 – Sentences in prize courts, 1649–52

LC 3/1 – Index to royal household of Charles I, 1641[-4?]
LC 4/185 – Index to recognizance rolls, 1625–54
LC 4/217 – Index to recognizance books, 1637–48
LC 5/134 – Entry books of warrants for lord chamberlain of household 1634–41

MPF 35 – 'A generall description of Ulster' by Richard Bartlett, 1602–3
MPF 88 – Map of north-east Ulster and western Scotland, [c. 1580]

PRO 31/3/68 – Baschet transcripts, 1634–5
PRO 31/3/69 – Baschet transcripts, 1636
PRO 31/3/71 – Baschet transcripts, 1637–8
PRO 31/3/77 – Baschet transcripts, May–Dec. 1645
PRO 31/3/87–8 – Baschet transcripts, Mar. – Oct. 1648
PRO 31/8/198 – Transcripts of Digby MSS, 1605–95

SP 16/316–27, 334–6, 344, 355, 365, 378, 393–8, 403, 428, 442, 467, 486, 488–502, 513, 540 – State papers, domestic, Charles I, 1635–46
SP 18/9, fos. 223–5 – Account of Irish prizes taken to Ostend and Dunkirk, 1649–50
SP 19/140/18 – Proceedings of the committee for advance of money
SP 23/71–2, 79, 81, 86, 89, 96–7, 114, 125, 128, 131, 135, 245–7, 237, 251–2, 256–7 – Papers of the committee for compounding with delinquents, 1643–59
SP 25/14, 32, 64–6, 70, 75, 96 – Records of the council of state, 1650–4
SP 28/350/7, 9 – Commonwealth exchequer papers: financial papers relating to Ireland, 1648–57
SP 29/16, 28, 78, 82, 379 – State papers, domestic, 1660–76
SP 44/13, 18, 23, 28 – State papers, domestic, Charlels II, entry books
SP 63/242, 244–5, 249, 260–5, 267–9, 271–4, 276–9, 288, 290–4, 300, 304–23, 326, 329, 338, 342–3, 345–8 – State papers, Ireland, 1626–83
SP 77 – State papers, Flanders
SP 78/111 – State papers, France, 1641–9
SP 94/42 – State papers, Spain 1640–9
SP 105/16 – Gerbier's entry book, 1639–40

Public Records Office (Kew)

AO1/1377/142 – Hanaper account, 1654–5
AO11/18 – Miscellaneous early seventeenth-century Irish financial material

Westminster City Archives

Rate Books, St Martin in the Fields
F357 – Receipts (overseer's accounts), 1630–1
F359 – Receipts (overseer's accounts), 1632–3
F360 – Receipts (overseer's accounts), 1633–4
F363 – Receipts (overseer's accounts), 1636–7
F364 – Receipts (overseer's accounts), 1637–8
F365 – Receipts (overseer's accounts), 1638–9
F366 – Receipts (overseer's accounts), 1639–40

OXFORD

Bodleian Library

CARTE MSS

1–51, 60, 63–70, 118, 142–5, 199, 214–15, 220–1 – Letters and papers of Ormond, 1633–87
80 – Wharton papers
83–4 – Letters and papers of the French ambassador, 1644–7
156–7, 160–1 – Registers of Irish petitions, 1649–50
159, 164–5 – Registers of army orders
225 – Papers designed to vindicate Charles I in the matter of the Irish rebellion, 1641

RAWLINSON MSS

A 14 – Proposals concerning the division and leasing of confiscated land, 1654
A 22 – Instructions for an expedition from Carrickfergus to the islands of Mull and Skye, 1654
A 54 – List of Irish conspirators, 1657
B 482 – The case of the Roman Catholics in Ireland
B 507 – Letters and papers relating to the Irish rebellion, 1641–6
C 841 – Letter giving an account of Antrim's trial, 1663
D 742 – Eighteenth-century letter discussing the blank commissions given to Antrim by Charles I

OTHER COLLECTIONS

Ballard MSS 53 – Sir Edmund Walker's papers
Clarendon MSS 7–87, 98 – State papers of the earl of Clarendon, 1635–67
Eng. Hist. MSS C37 – Copies of some of Ormond's official letters, 1639–79
Eng. Misc. C208 – Accounts of the household of the duchess of Buckingham, 1629–34
Fairfax MSS 32 – Correspondence, 1641–8
Nalson MSS Dep.C154, 163–5, 172, 174
Tanner MSS 57/2, 58/2, 59/1B, 60/2, 61, 62/1, 62/2

Christ Church Library

Sir Robert Brown's correspondence

SHEFFIELD

City Library

EM 1281, 1284/b, 1317–18, 1368, 1486, 1354/3 – Elmhirst collection (Pye deposit)
Wentworth Woodhouse Muniments 3–12, 14–22, 24, 34, 40 (Strafford papers)

SCOTTISH ARCHIVES

EDINBURGH

National Library of Scotland

MS 79, 81 – Morton papers, 1620–48
MS 577 – Watson collection

MS 2263 – Salt and coal: events, 1635–62
MS 3139 – Cunningham of Robertland correspondence, 1636–97
MS 3368 – Scottish historical letters and documents, 1608–1745
MS 3784, fos. 29–47 – Nineteenth-century copies of papers belonging to the first three earls of Antrim
MS 7032 – Yester papers, 1612–49
MS Ch. 2473 – Bond, 1644

ADVOCATES MSS
Adv. MSS 26.2.7 – Papers relating to the MacDonald family
Adv. MSS 34.6.11 – A history of the Gordon family
Adv. MSS 35.5.3 – Letters (copies) to the fifth earl of Argyll, c. 1642

WODROW MSS
Wod. Fo. 65–6 – Miscellaneous church and state papers, 1639–50

Scottish Record Office

GD 14/19 – Campbell of Stonefield papers
GD 16 – Airlie MSS
GD 34 – Hay of Hayston papers
GD 39 – Glencairn muniments
GD 44 – Huntly MSS
GD 52 – Forbes MSS
GD 112 – Breadalbane MSS
GD 201 – Clanranald papers
GD 220 – Montrose MSS
GD 406/1 – Hamilton MSS
GD 406/M1 – Miscellaneous Hamilton MSS
GD 406/M9 – Miscellaneous Hamilton MSS

PA 7/23 – Supplementary warrants and parliamentary papers, 1642–7

RH 1/2/452–3 – Guthrie castle papers, 1637–62
RH 15/91/33 – Papers relating to the plantation of Ulster, 1611–17

West Register House:

Film RH 4/124 – Edmonstone of Duntreath muniments
National Register of Archives listing (NRA 1209) of the Argyll muniments

INVERARY

Inverary castle

Bundle 3: Legal papers
Privy council to King (copy), 15 January 1635
Bundle 6: Miscellaneous legal papers 1640–5
Discharge by Major William Campbell ... to the marquis of Argyll, 12 April 1642

Bundle 7: Miscellaneous legal papers 1630, 1643–5
Account made by Argyll of his expenditure in 1644 against the Irish rebels and against the MacDonnells, 3 March 1649
Account of money due to Argyll for the expedition against the Irish rebels in 1644
Bundle 8: Miscellaneous legal papers 1630, 1643–5
Copy of instructions by Charles I to Argyll, 29 July 1646
Bundle 53: Miscellaneous correspondence
Account made by Argyll of his expedition in 1644 against the Irish rebels and the MacDonalds, 3 March 1649
Bundle 100: Personal correspondence
Letter from Lord Loudoun to Lord Lorne, 6 June 1661
Bundle 801:
1661 – Copy of legal suit by Aeneas, Lord MacDonald and other MacDonalds, against Argyll for losses sustained by the MacDonalds in 1640, 1645 and 1654
Bundle 823: Miscellaneous royal commissioners to members of House of Argyll, 1634–1911
Commimssion to pursue Archibald als Gillespick McDonell and others for the murder of John Donaldson, Glengarry, Co. Antrim

CONTINENTAL AND NORTH AMERICAN ARCHIVES

BELGIUM – BRUSSELS

Archives Générales du Royaume

SECRÉTAIRERIE D'ETAT ET DE GUERRE
42–7 – 'Registres aux ordres', 1642–50
232–44 – Correspondence of Castle Rodrigo and Archduke Leopold William with Philip IV, 1644–9

CONSEIL PRIVÉ ESPAGNOL
1573–4 – Letters on military matters between Spain and Flanders, 1629–48

FRANCE – PARIS

Archives Nationales (consulted on microfilm in the NLI)

FONDS GUERRE
AI Côtes 53–8, 61–3, 66, 70–9, 91, 93, 99, 102 – details on Irish regiments raised for service France, 1639–7

Bibliothèque Nationale

FONDS FRANÇAIS
9691, 10, 712, 15,994, 15,996–16,002, 17,979, 20,674 – Correspondence of French ambassadors in England and Scotland, 1645–64

Bibliography

Ministère des Affaires Etrangères

CORRESPONDANCE POLITIQUE, ANGLETERRE
Côtes 48–60 – Letters from various people (including Dumolin and Talon) relating to events in Ireland, 1646–7

ITALY – ROME (consulted on microfilm in the NLI)

Archivio della Sacra Congregazione di Propaganda Fide

SCRITTURE ORIGINALI RIFERITE NELLE CONGREGAZIONI GENERALI
Vols. 14, 102, 105–6, 129, 134, 138 – Letters, reports and other documents relating to Irish affairs, 1632–55

Bibliotheca Apostolica Vaticana

BARBERINI LATINI MSS
3603, 3631, 4729, 5253, 6485, 6768, 6827, 8222–3, 8238, 8642, 8649, 8651, 8653, 8655, 8671, 8672, 8673, – Letters to Cardinal Barberini concerning Irish affairs and despatches from London, 1638–62

NUNZIATURA DI FIANDRA
Vols. 27, 32–3, 45 – Letters relating to Irish and English affairs, 1645–9

SPAIN – MADRID

Archivo Histórico Nacional

SECCIÓN DE ESTADO
Libros 264, 372, 715, 961, 964, 966, 975, 978–9 – Miscellaneous documents relating to Ireland and to Irishmen in Spain, 1636–49

Legajo 1411 – Correspondence of Castel Rodrigo with Philip IV, 1646–7

Biblioteca Nacional

MS 2367 – *Relación de los servicios de D. Francisco Foissotte en Borgoña, Flandes, Inglaterra, Francia, y en ocho años y medio que assistió en Irlanda en negocios del Real servicio de V. Magestad*

SPAIN - SIMANCAS

Archivo General

CONTADURÍA MAYOR DE CUENTAS
Legajos 3A/937, 956, 993, 1049, 1851, 2871 – Accounts of T. López de Ulloa, 1642–51
Legajos 3A/1762, 1856 – Accounts of H. de Benero, 1651–6
Legajos 3A/3141 – Accounts of D. Enríquez de Castro, 1653–4

GUERRA ANTIGUA
Legajos 1566–70, 1572, 1597–9, 1601–2, 1608, 1615 – Documents concerning Irish troops in, and for, the armies of Spain, 1645–6

SECRETARÍA DE ESTADO

Flandes y Holanda
Legajos 2061, 2064–6, 2068, 2071–3, 2098, 2163–5, 2251, 2254, 2256 – Troop musters for Irish regiments in Flanders and letters on raising Irish troops for Flanders, 1644–53

Inglaterra
Legajos 2521–2526, 2565–6, 2576 – Reports and letters from Foissotte, Torre, Biraven, Cárdenas and the relevant consultas of the Spanish council of state, 1636–48

SECRETARIAS PROVINCIALES
Legajo 2499 – A summary of Foissotte's petition (see Madrid, Biblioteca Nacional, MS 2367)

Roma
Legajos 3016–21 – Despatches relating to Ireland from the Spanish ambassador in Rome, 1647–50

TRIBUNAL MAYOR DE CUENTAS
Legajo 4A/2635 – Secret accounts of Diego de La Torre, 1645–9

THE UNITED STATES OF AMERICA – SAN MARINO, CALIFORNIA

Huntington Library

ELLESMERE COLLECTION
EL 7060 – An indictment against Strafford

HASTINGS MSS
HA box 7–10 – Irish papers, 1640–60
HA 14,987 – 'A particular of ye walled citties ... ', 1643
HA 15,001 – Proclamation of the supreme council, 1644
HA 15,229–34 – Letters from Rose O'Neill, 1666–84

PAMPHLETS AND NEWSPAPERS (WITH LOCATION)

All published in London unless stated.

Another extract of more letters sent out of Ireland, informing the condition of the kingdom as it now stands (1643) CUL, HIB.7.643.3

Articles of impeachment against George Lord Digby ... (28 February 1642) CUL, HIB.7.642.12

A briefe relation of some affaires and transactions civill and military, both forraigne and domestique ... no. 17 (BL, Burney 34A/35A)

Certaine informations from severall parts of the Kingdome ..., nos. 22 (BL, E55(4)), 25 (BL, E59(21))

A collection of certain horrid murders in several counties of Ireland committed since the 23 of October 1641 ... (1679) NLI, Thorpe VI

A continuation of certain speciall and remarkable passages from both houses of parliament ... no. 13 (BL, E121(11))

A continuation of the diurnal occurrences and proceedings of the English army against the rebels in Ireland ... *from 1 April, to this present 1642* (1642) BL, E143(23)

A continuation of the diurnall passages in Ireland ... *being sent from the Lord Antrim* ... *to* ... *Rutland, dated February 25, 1641* (1641[-2]) BL, E137(28)

A continuation of the tryumphant and courgious [sic] proceedings of the protestant army in Ireland ... (1 April 1642) BL, E141(21)

A continuation of very good newes from Ireland ... (1642) NLI, Lough Fea V

Continued heads of perfect passages in parliament and proceedings of the councell of state and the army ... nos., 3 (BL, E529(30)), 4 (BL, E530(4))

A copie of certaine letters; which manifest the designe of the late plot discovered ... (10 February 1643) BL, E81(16)

A copie of a letter from the Lord Intrim [sic] in Ireland to the right honorable earle of Rutland, bearing date the 25 date of February anno dom. 1642 [sic] ... (1642) BL, E138(7)

The court mercurie relating for newes, the most remarkable passages of the king's army as also some newes from forraine parts communicated to both houses of parliament for truth from divers parts of this kingdom, nos. 6 (BL, E6(3)), 10 (BL, Burney 14A)

The daily proceedings of his majesty's fleet on the narrow seas, from 17 October to 15 November ... (18 November 1642) BL, E127(25)

A declaration of the commons assembled in parliament; concerning the rise and progresse of the grand rebellion in Ireland ... *with some letters and papers of great consequences of the earl of Antrim's* ... (25 July 1643) CUL, HIB.7.643.29

A declalration by the Irish armie in Ulster: sent to the parliament in a letter from William Basil ... (1650) NLI, Thorpe V

A declaration of the lords and commons in parliament ... (1641[-2]) NLI, Thorpe I

A declaration of the lords of his majesty's privie-councell in Scotland; and commissioners for conserving the articles of the treaty ... *together with a treacherous and damnable plot of the Irish, English and Scottish papists* ... (27 June 1643) BL, E56(9)

A declaration made by the rebels in Ireland ... (Waterford, 1644; reprinted London [19 November] 1644) BL, E17(14)

A declaration of the proceedings of the new moddel'd army in the kingdome of Scotland, against the Irish army, under the command of Generall Kilketto ... (22 February 1646[-7]) BL, E378(11)
A declaration sent to the king of France and Spayne, from the catholiques or rebells in Ireland ... (Paris, [14]/24 April 1642; reprinted London, 1642) BL, E145(7)
The demands of the rebels in Ireland unto the state and councell of Dublin, 3 February 1641[-2] (1641[-2]) NLI, Thorpe I
A diary, or an exact journall faithfully communicating the most remarkable proceedings in both houses of parliament ... no. 42 (BL, E271(17))
The earl of Glamorgan's negotiations and colourable commitment in Ireland demonstrated ... (17 March 1645) RIA, Box 41 (45)
The English and Scottish protestants happy tryumph over the rebels in Ireland ... (4 June 1642) BL, E149(24)
Estat general des affaires ... Gazette, nos. 34, 40, 68, 89 (Bodl., Antig.d.F)
An exact and full relation of the great victory obtained against the rebels at Dungans-Hill in Ireland, August 8 1647. By the forces under the command of Colonel Michael Jones ... (19 August 1647) NLI, Thorpe IV
An exact relation of all such occurrences as have happened in the severall counties of Donegal, Londonderry, Tyrone and Fermanagh in the North of Ireland ... *by Lieutenant Collonell Audeley Mervyn, the 4 of June 1642* (1642) BL, E149(34)
An exact and true relation of the late plots which were contrived and hatched in Ireland ... (1641) BL, E173(30)
A full relation, not only of our good successe in generall, but how, and in what manner God hath fought his own cause (1642) BL, E145(14)
A full relation of the late expedition of ... *Monroe* ... *with their severall marches and skirmishes with the bloody Irish rebels* ... *and a letter from the Lord Digby* ... *sent to the duchess of Buckingham* ... (27 August 1644) CUL, HIB.7.644.16
Full satisfaction concerning the affaires of Ireland; as they relate to the marquesse of Ormond's transactions, with the Lord of Inchiquin ... (1648) BL, E536(14).
A geographical description of the kingdom of Ireland (1642) BL, E149(11)
Gazette [de Naples], no. 40
Good and bad newes from Ireland: in a letter of credit from Youghall, not forged, as most of the pamphlets lately published. The particulars are these. The good newes ... *the bad newes* ... (14 March 1641[-2]) BL, E138(18)
Good newes from Ireland. Being a true and exact relation of two great victories ... *sent in a letter from Captain Courtney at Dublin to M. Snow* ... (21 November 1642) BL, E127(33)
A great victory at sea against the Irish rebels by Captaine Robert Dare commander of the English, where were taken the earl of Antrim his great ship ... (9 February 1647[-8]) NLI, Lough Fea X
Heads of a diarie, no. 5 (1649)
A history or brief chronicle of the chief matters of the Irish warres ... (1650) NLI, Thorpe V
The Irish monthly mercury. Issue 1 (Cork; reprinted London, 1649) NLI, Lough Fea XII
The kingdomes faithfull and impartiall scout ..., no. 11 (BL, E529(11))
The kingdomes weekly intelligencer. Sent abroad to prevent misinformation ..., nos. 21 (BL, Burney 16A), 24 (BL, E55(8)), 25 (BL, E59(11)), 26 (BL, E 59(22)), 38 (BL, E81(13)), 42 (BL, E31(21)), 50 (BL, E42(28)), 52 (BL, Burney 18A), 62 (BL, E54(9)), 84 (BL, E21 (11)), 164 (BL, Burney 22A), 290 (BL, E476(39)), 316 (BL, E560(16))

The last newes from the North. Shewing . . . their full intentions to march speedily against Montrose, Killetto, Antrim, with the rest of that barbarous crew . . . (19 February 1646[-7]) BL, E377(14)

The last speeches and confession of the Lord Maguire: the Irish generall, that was hanged at Tyburne, and drawn, and quartered on Thursday last, the 20 February 1644 (24 February 1644[-5]) BL, E270(19)

Late and lamentable news from Ireland, wherein are truly related, the rebellious, and cruel proceedings of the papists there . . . (1641) BL, E179(13)

A letter from the atturney of Ireland concerning the taking of the towne of Wexford by storme, on 11 of October last . . . (1649) NLI, Lough Fea XII

A letter from the lord lieutenant of Ireland, to the honorable William Lenthall . . . giving an account of the proceedings of the army there under his lordship's command . . . (1649) NLI, Lough Fea XII

Letters from the marquis of Argyle . . . intercepted by Sir Richard Willys (Oxford, 1645) BL, E278(25)

A letter from Sir Lewis Dyve to the lord marquis of Newcastle giving his lordship an account . . . of the king's affaires in Ireland . . . (The Hague, 10/20 July 1650) NLI, Thorpe V

A letter of great consequence; sent by the honorable Robert Lord Monro . . . to the committee for Irish affairs of his taking the earl of Antrim, about whom was found divers papers which discovered a dangerous plot . . . (8 July 1643) CUL, HIB.7.643.17)

A letter written from Sir William Parsons, one of the lords justices of Ireland, to Sir Robert Pye . . . (1642) BL, E142(20)

The London post: faithfully communicating his intelligence of the proceedings, and many other memorable passages, certified by letters and advertisements . . . nos. 2 (BL, E6(28)), 17 (BL, E22(21)), 26 (BL, E271(9))

The marquesse of Ormond's proclamation concerning the peace concluded with the Irish rebells . . . (27 February 1649) NLI, Thorpe IV

Mercurius aulicus. Communicating the intelligence and affaires of the court, to the rest of the kingdome . . . ([Oxford], 1645) BL, E302(14)

Mercurius Britanicus. Communicating the affaires of great Britaine: For better information of the people . . . , nos. 28 (BL, E39(5)), 78 (BL, Burney 20A)

Mercurius civicus. London's intelligencer or truth impartially related thence to the whole kingdome to prevent misinformation . . . , nos. 9, 34, 63 (BL, E4(28)), 127 (BL, Burney 22A)

Mercurius Diutinus, or Collector of the affaires of great Britaine and martiall proceedings in Europe . . . , no. 11 (BL, Burney 14A)

Mercurius Hibernicus: or, a discourse of the late insurrection in Ireland . . . (Bristol, 1644) BL, E52(17)

Mercurius Hibernicus, or the Irish mercurie . . . , (14 February 1645) BL, E269(16)

Mercurius militaris or the armies scout communicating from all parts of England, Scotland and Ireland, all martiall enterprises, designs and successes . . . , no. 3 (BL, E469(10))

Mercurius politicus . . . no. 13 (BL, Burney 34A),

Mercurius verdicus or, true informations of speciall and remarkable passages . . . , no. 22 (BL, E302(10))

A message from both houses of parliament sent to the king and queen's majesties touching certain letters lately intercepted . . . (1642[-3]) NLI, Thorpe II

The military scribe publishing his true war-like relations to the people ..., no. 6 (BL, E40(10))
The moderate: impartially communicating martial affaires to the kingdom of England ..., no. 52 (BL, E 564(1))
The moderate intelligencer: impartially communicating martiall affaires to the kingdomes of England ..., nos. 58 (BL, Burney 23A), 68 (BL, Burney 23A), 71 (BL, Burney 23A), 75 (BL, Burney 21A), 76 (BL, Burney 23A), 79 (BL, Burney 23A), 80 (BL, Burney 23A), 81 (BL, Burney 23A), 88 (BL, Burney 23A), 90 (BL, Burney 23A), 102 (BL, Burney 29A), 103 (BL, Burney 29A), 104 (BL, Burney 29A), 118 (BL, Burney 29A), 119 (BL, Burney 29A), 140 (BL, Burney 29A), 148 (BL, Burney 29A), 161 (BL, Burney 29A), 182 (BL, Burney 29A), 189 (BL, E470(1)), 193 (BL, E474(3)), 194 (BL, Burney 29A), 196 (BL, E477(14)), 204 (BL, E543(3)), 212 (BL, E550(19)), 221 (BL, Burney 33A), 229 (BL, Burney 33A), 233 (BL, Burney 33A)
Montrose redivivus, or the portraicture of James late marquis of Montrose ... ([July], 1652) BL, E1309 (1)
More good newes from Ireland, in two letters from Dublin ... (16 May 1642) CUL, HIB.7.642.65
A more perfect and particular relation of the late great victorie in Scotland obtained over Montrose and the rebels, by forces under the command of ... *David Lesley* (25 September 1645) RIA, Box 40 (44)
Murder will out: or the king's letter, justifying the marques of Antrim, and declaring that what he did in the Irish rebellion, was by direction from his royal father and mother, and for service of the Crown ... (1663) NLI, Thorpe V (reprinted Edinburgh, 1689, and London 1698) NLS, 1.24, and NLI, Thorpe IV
A new declaration of the last affairs in Ireland shewing the great overthrow given the Irish rebels ... (2 May 1642) BL, E146(9)
New treason plotted in France ...; *likewise a letter sent from the councell of Scotland, to the house of commons, June 20 concerning the earl of Antrim's answer and answer to the Scots concerning the said of earl of Antrim* (1642) BL, E153(19)
Newes from Dunkirke. Being a speciall relation of certaine passages there. Wherein is discovered the intentions and agitations of divers of this kingdom ... ([10 November 1642]) BL, E126(43)
No pamphlet but a detestation against all such pamphlets as are printed concerning the Irish rebellion, plainely [sic] demonstrating the falsehood of them ... (1642) BL, E134(3)
Occurences from Ireland, no. 3 (BL, E146(8))
O'Neale and Colonel Brunslow, chiefe of the rebels in Ireland ... *as also a description of the taking of a ship upon the coasts of Barbary bound with letters of commendations to the king of Spaine* ... (1642[-3]) BL, E138(31)
An ordinance and declaration of the lords and commons ... (20 October 1642) BL, E123(22)
Papers concerning the debates of the parliament of Scotland, about sending to the kings majesty; and how Colkittoth, is with his army within 30 miles of Edinburgh ... (18 February 1646[-7]) BL, E377(8)
Papers from the Scots quarter, containing some passages concerning the king, the estates of Scotland, the garrisons, the armies, and the proceedings for the settling of the kingdomes in peace (14 October 1646) BL, Burney 25A
The parliament scout: communicating his intelligence to the kingdome ..., no. 1 (BL, E56(7))

A perfect account of the daily inteligence [sic] *from the army in England, Scotland and Ireland* ... nos. 10 (BL, Burney 37A), 16 (BL, Burney 37A)
A perfect diurnall of some passages in parliament, and from other parts of this kingdome ..., nos. 2 (BL, Burney 16A), 27 (BL, E252(18)), 29 (BL, Burney 18A), 39 (BL, E252(30)), 50 (BL, E254(2)), 55 (BL, E254 (20)), 68 (BL, Burney 37A), 81 (BL, Burney 38A), 82 (BL, Burney 20A), 90 (BL, E260(18)), 168 (BL, Burney 25A), 181 (BL, Burney 26A), 184 (Bl, Burney 26A), 199 (BL, Burney 26A), 280 (BL, E526(40)), 297 (BL, E529(9)), 313 (BL, Burney 33A)
A perfect narrative of the battell of Knocknones, within the county of Cork and province of Munster on Saturday the thirteenth of November betwixt parliament's forces under the command of Lord Inchiquin ... ; *and the forces of the Irish rebells under Lord Taaff* ... (1647) NLI, Thorpe IV
A perfect and particular relation of the severall marches and proceedings of the armie in Ireland: from the taking of Drogheda to ... *the taking of Wexford* ... (1649) NLI, Thorpe V
Perfect occurrences of both houses of parliament ... The 37th week (1646) BL, Burney 25A
Perfect occurrences of every daies journall in parliament ... nos. 111 (BL, E527(21)), 122 (BL, E529(32)), 130 (BL, Burney 33A), 131 (BL, Burney 33A), 145 (BL, Burney 33A)
Perfect occurrences of parliament and chief collections of letters from the armie ..., nos. 7 (BL, E322(32)), 12 (BL, Burney 20A), 16 (BL, Burney 24A), 18 (BL, Burney 24A), 25 (BL, E252(43)), 32 (BL, Burney 21A), 33 (BL, Burney 17A), 37 (BL, Burney 25A), 38 (BL, Burney 22A)
Perfect passages of each days proceedings in parliament ... nos. 2 (BL Burney 36A), 28 (BL, E260(32)), 29 (BL, E 260(36)), 41 (BL, E262(38))
The perfect weekly account concerning speciall and remarkable passages from both houses of parliament ... (BL, E536(10))
The petition of the committees for Ireland ... (Oxford, 1642) NLI, Thorpe II
A plot discovered in Ireland ... *also a greate defeate to the rebels coming into Scotland by the earle of Argile* (1644) NLI, Lough Fea VII
The protestants wonderment, or, a strange and unheard of oraison put up by the papists, found in the pocket of Captain James Rauley, a rebell in Ireland ... (1642) BL, E136(13)
A relation of the particulars of the reduction of the greatest part of the province of Munster in Ireland ... (1649) no. 14 (BL, Burney 33A)
A relation of the present state and condition of Ireland ... (1641[-2]) NLI, Thorpe I
A relation of the sundry occurrences in Ireland, from the fleet of ships set out by the adventurers ... (1642) NLI, Lough Fea III
A remonstrance of the barbarous cruelties and bloody murders committed by the Irish rebels ... (12 June 1644) BL, E50(31)
A remonstrance of the right honourable James earl of Castleheaven and Lord Audley concerning his imprisonment in Dublin and escape from thence (Waterford, 1643) BL, E95(14)
A renowned victory obtained against the rebels on the first day of June, neere Burros, the duke of Buckingham's castle, by the valour of these noble and valiant commanders; ... *wherein is manifested how the Lord Don-luce tooke the Lord Dunsany prisoner* ... (9 June 1642) BL, E150(8)
The Scottish dove ... *brings intelligence from the armies of both kingdomes, and relates other passages observable, for information and instruction* ..., nos. 29 (BL, E45(5)), 43 (BL, E3(3)), 45 (BL, E7 (45)), 147 (BL, Burney 25A) 153 (BL, Burney 25A)

Several letters of great consequence intercepted by Colonel Milton . . . concerning Irish forces to be brought into England . . . (17 February 1645[-6]) BL, E322(32)
Severall proceedings in parliament . . . , nos. 21 (BL, Burney 34A/35A), 23 (BL, Burney 34A/35A), 40 (BL, Burney 34A/35A), 78 (BL, Burney 37A)
A short view of the life and death of George Villiers duke of Buckingham . . . (1642) RIA, Box 26 (30)
Sir Benjamin Rudyerd his speech made in answer to the Spanish and French ambassadors request for our souldiers at their disbanding (28 August 1641) BL, E199(E)
Speciall passages and certain informations from severall places, collected for the use of all that desire to bee truely informed, nos. 6 (BL, E118(10)), 7 (BL, E118(45)), 39 (BL, E101(39))
The spie, communicating intelligence from Oxford . . . nos. 3 (BL, Burney 14A), 12 (BL, Burney 14A)
State of the papist and protestant properties in the kingdom of Ireland, in the year 1641 . . . and how disposed in 1653 . . . and how disposed in 1662 (1689) NLI, Thorpe VII
The taking of Wexford. A letter from an eminent officer in the army, under the command of the Lord Lieutenant of Ireland . . . (1649) NLI, Lough Fea XII
A true copie of two letters brought by Mr Peters, this October 11 from my Lord Forbes . . . (1642) NLI, Thorpe III
A true and exact relation of divers principall actions of a late expedition, undertaken in the North of Ireland . . . (13 July 1642) CUL, HIB.7.642.1(11)
A true and exact relation of the most sad condition of Ireland . . . ([17 November] 1643) BL, E76(4)
A true extract of severall letters . . . relating the most remarkable passages of the English and Scotch armie in the province of Ulster . . . (1643) BL, E60(16)
The true informer: containing a perfect collection of the proceedings in parliament, and true information from the armies . . . nos. 4 (BL, Burney 21A), 42 (BL, E4(32)), 59 (BL, E22(14))
True intelligence from Dublin, April 3, touching those important passages . . . (1642) BL, E124(24)
A true and perfect diurnall: of the most remarkable passages in Ireland from 2 April to this present (3 May 1642) BL, E145(19)
A true relation of a great victory obtained by the forces under the command of the Lord Inchiquine . . . against the rebels under the command of Lord Taaff . . . (30 November 1647) NLI, Thorpe IV
A true relation of the last great battell, fought in Ireland: betwixt the Scots and the Irish . . . (1642) BL, E126(7)
A true relation of the present state of Ireland in a letter from one master Peters in Dublin . . . (9 February 1642[-3]) CUL, HIB.7.642.1(9)
A true relation of the proceedings of the Scots and English forces in the North of Ireland . . . (8 June 1642) BL, E149(2)
A true relation of the proceedings of the Scottish armie now in Ireland by three letters . . . the third sent by the earl of Antrim to General Major Monroe . . . (1642) NLI, Lough Fea V
A true relation of the taking of Mountjoy in the county of Tyrone by Colonel Clotworthy . . . as also what was done by the remainder of his regiment at Antrim . . . (1642) BL, E149(12)
The true state of the transactions of Colonel George Monk with Owen-Mac-Art-O-Neal: as it was reported to the parliament by the council of state . . . (15 August 1649) NLI, Thorpe V

The truest intelligence from the province of Munster . . . and the surprisall of many more of them . . . at sea . . . (1642) NLI, Lough Fea IV
The truest and most reall relation of the apprehension of three most notorious rebels in Ireland brought to the parliament in England . . . (1642) BL, E151(13)
A very particular relation of the great progresse and happy proceedings of the army of the Commonwealth of England toward the reducing of Ireland . . . (1649) NLI, Lough Fea XII
The weekly account containing special and remarkable passages from both houses of parliament; and collections of severall advertisements . . . nos. 4 (BL, Burney 24A), 16 (BL, E78(29)), 49 (BL, E4(23))
The weekly account. Truly and faithfully communicating the choisest and most remarkable intelligence from all parts of the kingdome . . . nos. 30 (BL, E294(8)), 33 (BL, Burney 18A), 40 (BL, Burney 39A), 41 (BL, Burney 39A)
The whole triall of Connor Lord Maguire, with the perfect copies of the indictment, and all the evidences against him . . . ([4 March] 1644[-5]) BL, E271(10)
Worse and worse newes from Ireland . . . (1641) NLI, Thorpe I

PRINTED SOURCES

Adair, Patrick, *True narrative of the rise and progress of the Presbyterian church in Ireland (1628–70)*, ed. W. D. Killen (Belfast, 1866)
Aiazza, Giuseppe, *The embassy in Ireland of Monsignor G. B. Rinuccini, archbishop of Fermo, in the years 1645–1649* . . . , translated by Annie Hutton (Dublin, 1873)
[Anonymous], 'Commonwealth records', *Archiv. Hib.*, 6 (1917), pp. 175–202, and 7 (1918–21), pp. 20–66
Balfour, Sir James, *The historical works of Sir James Balfour* (3 vols., Edinburgh, 1824)
Baxter, Richard, *A vindication of the royal martyr King Charles I from the Irish massacre in the year 1641* . . . (3rd edn, London, 1704)
Berwick, Edward (ed.), *The Rawdon papers, consisting of letters on various subjects* . . . (London, 1819)
Birch, Thomas (ed.), *A collection of the state papers of John Thurloe, esq.; secretary, first to the council of state, and afterward to the two Protectors Oliver and Richard Cromwell* (7 vols., London, 1742)
Blair, Robert, *The Life of Mr Robert Blair, minister of St. Andrews, containing his autobiography, 1593–1636, with supplement* . . . ed. T. M'Crie (Wodrow Society, Edinburgh, 1848)
Boyd, Hugh Alexander (ed.), 'Dean William Henry's topographical description of the coast of County Antrim and North Down c. 1740', *The Glynns*, 2 (1974), pp. 7–14
Brereton, Sir William, *Travels in Holland, the United provinces, England, Scotland and Ireland, 1634–1635*, ed. Edward Haskins (Chetham Society, vol. I, [London], 1844)
Burgo, T. de, *Hibernia dominicana siue historia provinciae Hiberniae ordinis praedictorum* . . . (n. p., 1762)
Burnet, Gilbert, *Memoirs of the lives and actions of James and William, dukes of Hamilton* . . . (London, 1677)
Calendar of the Clarendon state papers preserved in the Bodleian Library, ed. O. Ogle, W. H. Bliss and W. D. Macray (3 vols., Oxford, 1869–76), vol. IV, ed. F. J. Routledge (Oxford, 1932)

Calendar of the proceedings of the committee for advance of money, 1642–56, ed. Mary Anne Everett Green (3 vols., London, 1888)
Calendar of the proceedings of the committee for compounding, 1643–1660, ed. Mary Anne Everett Green (5 vols., London, 1889–92)
Calendar of state papers, domestic series
  1635–6 (London, 1866)
  1636–7 (London, 1867)
  1637 (London, 1868)
  1637–8 (London, 1869)
  1639 (London, 1873)
  1639–40 (London, 1877)
  1640 (London, 1880)
  1640–1 (London, 1882)
  1641–3 (London, 1887)
  1644 (London, 1888)
  1644–5 (London, 1890)
  1645–7 (London, 1891)
  1648–9 (London, 1893)
  Addenda 1625–49 (London, 1897)
  1649–50 (London, 1875)
  1650 (London, 1876)
  1651 (London, 1877)
  1654 (London, 1880)
  1655 (London, 1881)
  1655–6 (London, 1882)
  1656–7 (London, 1883)
  1657–8 (London, 1884)
  1658–9 (London, 1885)
  1659–60 (London, 1886)
  1660–1 (London, 1860)
Calendar of state papers and manuscripts, relating to English affairs, existing in the archives and collections of Venice
  1636–9 (London, 1923)
  1640–2 (London, 1924)
  1642–3 (London, 1925)
  1643–7 (London, 1926)
  1647–52 (London, 1927)
  1653–4 (London, 1929)
  1655–6 (London, 1930)
  1657–9 (London, 1931)
  1659–61 (London, 1931)
Calendar of state papers relating to Ireland
  1608–10 (London, 1874)
  1611–14 (London, 1877)
  1615–25 (London, 1880)
  1625–32 (London, 1900)
  1633–47 (London, 1901)
  Adventurers 1642–59 (London, 1903)
  1647–60 (London, 1903)
  1660–2 (London, 1905)

1663–5 (London, 1907)
1666–9 (London, 1908)
1669–70, with Addenda, 1625–70 (London, 1910)
Campbell, Herbert (ed.), *The Argyll sasines* (2 vols., Edinburgh, 1933–4)
Carte, Thomas, *A collection of original letters and papers concerning affairs ... found among the duke of Ormonde's papers* (2 vols., London, 1739)
[Castlehaven, James Touchet, earl of], *The earl of Castlehaven's review: or his memoirs ...* (London, 1684; reprint, New York, 1974)
Casway, Jerrold I., 'The clandestine correspondence of Father Patrick Crelly 1648–49', *Collect. Hib.*, 20 (1978), pp. 7–20
'Unpublished letters and papers of Owen Roe O'Neill', *Anal. Hib.*, 29 (1980), pp. 222–48
Chart, D. A. (ed.), 'Account book of the Rev. Andrew Rowan, rector of Dunaghy, Co. Antrim, c.1672–1680', *UJA*, 3rd series, 5 (1942), pp. 67–76
Chervel, M. A., *Lettres du Cardinal Mazarin* (Paris, 1872)
Clarendon, Edward Hyde, earl of, *The life of Edward, earl of Clarendon. Being a continuation of the history of the great rebellion from the restoration to his banishment in 1667* (3 vols., Oxford, 1827)
The history of the rebellion and civil wars in England, ed. W. D. Macray (6 vols., Oxford, 1888)
Clanricarde, Ulick de Burgh, marquis of, *The memoirs of Ulick, marquis of Clanricarde ... lord-lieutenant of Ireland and commander in chief of the forces of King Charles ... during the rebellion* (Dublin, 1757)
Courthope, E. J. (ed.), *The journal of Thomas Cunningham of Campvere, 1640–54* (Scottish History Society, 3rd series, vol. XI, Edinburgh, 1928)
Cox, Richard, *Hibernia Anglicana, or the history of Ireland from the conquest thereof by the English to this present time* (2nd edn, 2 vols., London, 1692)
Croker, Crofton T. (ed.), *The tour of the French traveller M. de Boullaye le Gouz in Ireland*, A.D. 1644 (London, 1837)
Cuvelier, J., and Lefèvre, J. (eds), *Correspondance de la cour d'Espagne sur les affaires des Pays Bas*, vol. III, 1633–1647 (Brussels, 1930), vol. IV, 1647–1665 (Brussels, 1933)
Dalrymple, David, *Memorials and letters relating to the history of Britain in the reign of Charles I* (Glasgow, 1766)
Dunlop, Robert (ed.), *Ireland under the Commonwealth: being a selection of documents relating to the government of Ireland, 1651–9* (2 vols., Manchester, 1913)
Eachard, Lawrence, *An exact description of Ireland ...* (London, 1691)
The earl of Castlehaven's review; or his memoirs ... (London, 1684; reprinted New York, 1974)
Falkiner, Litton C., *Illustrations of Irish history and topography mainly in the seventeenth century* (London, 1904)
Firth, Charles H. (ed.), *Memoirs of Edmund Ludlow. Lieutenant-general of the horse in the army of the Commonwealth of England, 1625–72* (2 vols., Oxford, 1894)
Scotland and the Commonwealth: letters and papers relating to the military government of Scotland from August 1651 to December 1653 (Scottish History Society, vol. XVIII, Edinburgh, 1895)
Scotland and the protectorate: letters and papers relating to the military government of Scotland from January 1654 to June 1659 (Scottish History Society, vol. XXXI, Edinburgh, 1899)

Firth, C. H., and Rait, R. S. (eds.), *Acts and ordinances of the Interregnum, 1642–1660* (3 vols., London, 1911)
Flower, R. (ed.), 'An Irish-Gaelic poem on the Montrose wars', *Scottish Gaelic Studies*, 1 (1926), pp. 113–18
Fotheringham, J. G. (ed.), *The diplomatic correspondence of Jean de Montereul and the Brothers Bellièvre, French ambassadors in England and Scotland, 1645–8* (2 vols., Scottish History Society, vols. XXIX and XXX, Edinburgh, 1898)
Fourteenth report of the deputy keeper of the public records in Ireland (Dublin, 1882)
French, Nicholas, *A narrative of the earl of Clarendon's settlement and sale of Ireland* ... (Louvain, 1668; reprinted in [Nicholas French], *The historical works of ... Nicholas French* ..., ed. S. H. Bindon (2 vols., Dublin, 1846))
  The unkinde desertor of loyall men and true frinds (1676; reprinted in [Nicholas French], *The historical works of ... Nicholas French* ..., ed. S. H. Bindon (2 vols., Dublin, 1846))
[French, Nicholas], *The historical works of the right reverend Nicholas French, bishop of Ferns ... containing the unkinde desertor of loyall men and true frinds*, ed. S. H. Bindon (2 vols., Dublin, 1846)
Gardiner, S. R. (ed.), *The Hamilton papers: being selections from original letters in the possession of his Grace the duke of Hamilton and Brandon, relating to the years 1638–1650* (Camden Society, London, 1880)
Giblin, Cathaldus (ed.), 'The "Acta" of the Propaganda archives and the Scottish mission, 1623–1670', *Innes Review*, 5, no. 1 (Spring 1954), pp. 39–76
  'Vatican Library: MSS Barberini Latini. A guide to the material of Irish interest on microfilm in the National Library, Dublin', *Archiv. Hib.*, 18 (1955), pp. 67–144
  'Catalogue of material of Irish interest in the collection Nunziatura di Fiandra, Vatican archives', *Collect. Hib.*, 1 (1958), pp. 7–125
  The Irish Franciscan mission to Scotland, 1619–1646. Documents from Roman archives (Dublin, 1964)
Gilbert, J. T. (ed.), *A contemporary history of affairs in Ireland*, from A.D. 1641 to 1652 ... (3 vols., Irish Archaeological Society, Dublin, 1879)
  History of the Irish confederation and the war in Ireland, 1641–3 ... (7 vols., Dublin 1882–91)
Gillespie, Raymond (ed.), *Settlement and survival on an Ulster estate. The Brownlow leasebook 1667–1711* (Belfast, 1988)
Goblet, Y. M. (ed.), *Index of parishes and townlands of Ireland from seventeenth century maps in Sir William Petty's manuscript barony maps (c. 1655–9)* (IMC, Dublin, 1932)
Green, Mary Anne Everett (ed.), *Letters of Queen Henrietta Maria* (London, 1857)
Hanly, John (ed.), *The letters of Saint Oliver Plunkett, 1625–81, archbishop of Armagh and primate of all Ireland* (Dublin, 1979)
The Harleian miscellany, or, a collection of scarce, curious and entertaining pamphlets and tracts ... (12 vols., London, 1808–11)
Hay, M. V. (ed.), *The Blairs papers, 1603–60* (London and Edinburgh, 1929)
Hennig, John, 'Irish soldiers in the Thirty Years' War', *RSAI Jn.*, 82 (1952), pp. 28–38
Hickson, Mary, *Ireland in the seventeenth century* (2 vols., London, 1884)
Hill, George (ed.), *The Montgomery manuscripts (1603–1706): Compiled from the family papers by William Montgomery of Rosemont Esquire* (Belfast, 1869)
Historical Manuscripts Commission
  Second report (London, 1874)
  Fourth report, part I (London, 1874)
  Fifth report (London, 1876)

Bibliography 315

Seventh report, part I (London, 1879)
Eighth report, part I (London, 1881)
Tenth report, app., part V (London, 1885)
Eleventh report, app., part IV (London, 1887)
Twelfth report, app., parts II (London, 1888), V (London, 1889)
Fourteenth report, app., part VII, vol. I (London, 1895), vol. II (London, 1899)
Fifteenth report, app., part VII (London, 1898)
Report on the manuscripts of Lord Montagu of Beaulieu (London, 1900)
Report on the manuscripts of the duke of Ormonde, NS (8 vols., London, 1902–20)
Report on the manuscripts of the earl of Egmont, vol. I, part I (London, 1905)
Report on the Franciscan manuscripts preserved at the convent, Merchants' Quay, Dublin (Dublin, 1906)
Supplementary report on the manuscripts of his grace the duke of Hamilton (London, 1932)
Report on the manuscripts of the Right Honourable Viscount De L'Isle, V.C., preserved at Penshurst Palace, Kent (London, 1966)
Calendar of the manuscripts of the most honourable the marquess of Salisbury ... preserved at Hatfield House, Hertfordshire, part XXI (1609–12) (London, 1970)
Hogan, Edmund (ed.), *The description of Ireland, and the state thereof as it is at this present in anno 1598* (Dublin, 1878)
[Hogan, Edmund (ed.)], *The history of the warr in Ireland from 1641 to 1653 by a British officer of the regiment of Sir John Clotworthy* (Dublin, 1873)
Hogan, J. (ed.), *Letters and papers relating to the Irish rebellion between 1642–46* (IMC, Dublin, 1935)
Irvine, Jimmy, 'Richard Dobb's notes for his description of County Antrim, written in 1683', *The Glynns*, 7 (1979), pp. 35–49
Jansson, Maija (ed.), *Two diaries of the Long Parliament* (New York, 1984)
Jennings, Brendan (ed.), *Wild Geese in Spanish Flanders, 1582–1700. Documents relating chiefly to Irish regiments from the Archives Générales du Royaume, Brussels, and other sources* (IMC, Dublin, 1964)
Louvain papers 1606–1827 (IMC, Dublin, 1968)
Journals of the House of Commons of the kingdom of Ireland ... (1613–1791) (28 vols., Dublin, 1753–91)
Journals of the House of Lords [of Ireland] (1634–1800) (8 vols., Dublin, 1779–1800)
Jusserand, J. J. (ed.), *Recueil des instructions donneés aux ambassadeurs et ministres de France* (4 vols., Paris, 1929)
Kenyon, John P. (ed.), *The Stuart constitution 1603–1688. Documents and commentary* (2nd edn, Cambridge, 1986)
Knowler, William (ed.), *The earl of Strafforde's letters and despatches with an essay towards his life by Sir George Radcliffe ...* (2 vols., London, 1739)
Laing, David (ed.), *A diary of public transactions and other occurrences chiefly in Scotland. From January 1650 to June 1667 by John Nicholl* (Bannatyne Club, vol. LII, Edinburgh, 1836)
The letters and journals of Robert Baillie, principal of the University of Glasgow, 1637–1662 (3 vols., Bannatyne Club, vol. LXXIII, 3 parts, Edinburgh, 1841–2)
Larcom, T. A. (ed.), *The Down survey by Dr. William Petty 1655–1556* (Dublin, 1851)

Latham, Robert, and Matthews, William (eds.), *The diary of Samuel Pepys. A new and complete transcription* (11 vols., Berkeley and Los Angeles, 1983)
Leith, William Forbes (ed.), *Memoirs of Scottish catholics during the seventeenth and eighteenth centuries* (2 vols., London, 1909)
Lenihan, Maurice, 'The fee-book of a physician of the seventeenth century', *RSAI Jn.*, 9 (1867), pp. 10–33, 139–76, 239–48
Leyburn, George, *The memoirs of George Leyburn ... chaplain to Henrietta Maria ... being a journal of his agency for Prince Charles to Ireland* ... (London, 1722)
[Lodge, John, (ed.),] *Desiderata curiosa Hibernica, or a select collection of state papers* (2 vols., Dublin, 1732)
Lowe, John (ed.), *Letter-book of the earl of Clanricarde 1643–47* (IMC, Dublin, 1983)
Lowry, T. K. (ed.), *The Hamilton manuscripts: containing some account of territories of Upper Clandeboye, Great Ardes, Dufferin in the county of Down, by Sir William Hamilton, afterward Viscount Clandeboye* (Belfast, 1867)
MacBain, Alexander, and Kennedy, John (eds.), *Reliquiae Celticae. Texts, papers and studies in Gaelic literature and philology* ... (2 vols., Inverness, 1892–4)
MacDonald, A. J., and MacDonald, A. M. (eds.), *The MacDonald collection of Gaelic poetry* (Inverness, 1911)
MacDonald, Archibald (ed.), 'A fragment of an Irish MSS: history of the MacDonalds of Antrim', *Transactions of the Gaelic Society of Inverness*, 37 (1934–6)
MacFarlane, Alan (ed.), *The diary of Ralph Josselin 1616–1683* (Oxford, 1976)
MacKenzie, Annie, M. (ed.), *Orain Iain Luim. Songs of John MacDonald, bard of Keppoch* (Scottish Gaelic Texts Society, Edinburgh, 1964)
MacLysaght, E. (ed.), 'Commonwealth state accounts 1650–56', *Anal. Hib.*, 15 (1944), pp. 229–321
McNeill, Charles, 'Report of the manuscripts in the Bodleian Library, Oxford', *Anal. Hib.*, 1 (1930), pp. 1–178
  'Copies of Down Survey maps in private keeping', *Anal. Hib.*, 8 (1938), pp. 419–27
  The Tanner letters. Documents of Irish affairs in the sixteenth and seventeenth centuries extracted from the Thomas Tanner collection in the Bodleian Library Oxford (IMC, Dublin, 1943)
MacPhail, J. R. N. (ed.), *Highland papers* (4 vols., Scottish History Society, 2nd series, vols., V, XII and XX, and 3rd series, vol. XXII, Edinburgh, 1914–34)
MacTavish, D. C. (ed.), *Minutes of the synod of Argyll, 1639–61* (2 vols., Scottish History Society, 3rd series, vols., XXXVII and XXXVIII, Edinburgh, 1943–4)
Massari, Dionysius, 'My Irish campaign', *The Catholic Bulletin*, 6 (1916), pp. 28–35, 82–8, 153–9, 217–22, 302–8, 367–73, 445–9, 502–5, 563–5, 618–20, 655–8; 7 (1917), pp. 111–14, 179–82, 246–9, 295–6; 8 (1918), pp. 140–2, 195–7, 247–9, 300–3, 396–8, 439–40, 478–80, 535–6, 538–40; 9 (1919), pp. 66–8, 116–17, 200–1, 310–11, 488–90, 535–40, 603–4, 649–52; 10 (1920), pp. 735–44
Maxwell, Constantia, *Irish history from contemporary sources (1509–1610)* (London, 1923)
Menteith, Robert, *The history of the troubles of Great Britain, containing a particular account of the most remarkable passages in Scotland* ([London], 1739)
Millet, B., 'Catalogue of Irish material in 14 volumes of Scritture originali riferite nell congregazioni generali in Propaganda archives', *Collect. Hib.*, 10–12 (1967–9)
The miscellany of the Irish Archaeological Society (Irish Archaeological Society, vol. 1, Dublin, 1846)

Bibliography 317

Mitchell, Alexander F., and Christie, James (eds.), *The records of the commissioners of the general assemblies of the church of Scotland holden in Edinburgh in the years 1646 and 1647* (Scottish History Society, vol. XI, Edinburgh, 1892)

Moody, T. W., and Simms J. G. (eds.), *The bishopric of Derry and the Irish society of London, 1602–1705*, I, *1602–70* (IMC, Dublin, 1968)

Moran, Patrick Francis (ed.), *Spicilegium Ossoriense: being a collection of original letters and papers illustrative of the history of the Irish church* ... (3 vols., Dublin, 1874–84)

Mountmorres, H. R. Morres, Lord, *The history of the principal transactions of the Irish Parliament (1634–66)* (2 vols., London, 1792; reprint, Shannon, 1971)

Murdock, A. S., and Simpson, H. M. F. (eds.), *The memoirs of James, marquis of Montrose, 1639–50, written by his chaplain, George (later Bishop) Wishart* (London, 1893)

Nalson, John, *An impartial collection of the great affairs of state from the beginning of the Scotch rebellion* ... (2 vols., London, 1682–3)

Napier, Mark, *Memorials of Montrose and his times* (2 vols., Maitland Club, Edinburgh, 1848 and 1850)

Memoirs of the marquis of Montrose (2 vols., Edinburgh, 1856)

NLI Report of the trustees 1949–50 (Dublin, 1950)

NLI Report of the trustees 1950–51 (Dublin, 1951)

Nott, H. E. (ed.), *The deposition books of Bristol*, vol. I: *1643–47* (Bristol Record Society Publications, vol. XIII, Bristol, 1935)

Ó Cuív, Brian, 'A poem on the second earl of Antrim', *Scottish Gaelic Studies*, 13, no. 2 (1981), pp. 302–5

O'Ferrall, Richard, and O'Connell, Robert, *Commentarius Rinuccinianus, de sedis apostolicae legatione ad foederatos Hiberniae catholicios per annos 1645–9*, ed. Rev. Stanislaus Kavanagh (6 vols., IMC, Dublin, 1932–49)

O'Hart, J. (ed.), *Irish landed gentry when Cromwell came to Ireland* (Dublin, 1887)

O'Meagher, J. Casimir (ed.), 'Diary of Dr Jones, scout-master general to the army of the Commonwealth ... ', *RSAI Jn.*, 5th series, 3 (1893), pp. 44–54

Ollard, Richard (ed.), *Clarendon's four portraits. George Digby, John Berkeley, Henry Jermyn, Henry Bennet* ... (London, 1989)

Paul, G. M., Fleming, D. H., and Ogilvie, J. D. (eds.), *Diary of Sir Archibald Wariston 1632–9, 1650–4, 1655–60* (3 vols., Scottish History Society, 1st series, vol. LXI, 2nd series, vol. XVIII, 3rd series, vol. XXXIV, Edinburgh, 1911–40)

Peacock, Mable (ed.), *An index of the names of those royalists whose estates were confiscated during the civil war* (London, 1879)

Pender, Séamus (ed.), *A census of Ireland circa 1659, with supplementary material from the poll money ordinances (1660–1661)* (IMC, Dublin, 1939)

Penn, Granville (ed.), *Memorials of the professional life and times of Sir William Penn* ... (2 vols., London, 1833)

Powell, J. R. and Timings, E. K. (eds.), *Documents relating to the civil war 1642–48* (Navy Records Society, vol. CV, London, 1963)

Register of the privy council of Scotland, 2nd series, II
    1630–2 (Edinburgh, 1902)
    1633–5 (Edinburgh, 1904)
    1638–43 (Edinburgh, 1906)

Rushworth, John, *Historical collections of private passages of state* ... (7 vols., London, 1659–1701, later edns 8 vols., 1680–1701, 1721)

Scott, W., and Bliss, J. (eds.), *The works of ... William Laud ... Archbishop of Canterbury* (7 vols., Oxford, 1847–60)
Scrope, R., and Monkhouse, T. (eds.), *State papers collected by Edward, earl of Clarendon, commencing 1621* (3 vols., Oxford, 1767–86)
Second report of the deputy keeper of the public records in Ireland (Dublin, 1870)
Simington, R. C. (ed.), *The civil survey, A.D. 1654–56* (10 vols., IMC, Dublin, 1931–61)
  The transplantation to Connaught 1654–58 (IMC, Shannon, 1970)
Sinclair, G., (ed.), *Letters from Archibald, earl of Argyll to John duke of Lauderdale* (Bannatyne Club, vol. XXXIII, Edinburgh, 1829)
Spalding, John, *The history of the troubles and memorable transactions in Scotland from the year 1642 to 1645* (2 vols., Aberdeen, 1792)
Statutes at large passed in the parliaments held in Ireland (1310–1761) (8 vols., Dublin, 1765)
Sylvester, M. (ed.), *Reliquiae Baxterianae, or ... Baxter's narrative of the most memorable passages of his life and times* (London, 1696)
Tenth report of the deputy keeper of the public records in Ireland (Dublin, 1878)
Thirty-ninth annual report of the deputy keeper of the public records (London, 1878)
Turner, Sir James, *Memoirs of his own life and times (1632–70)*, ed. T. Thomson (Bannatyne Club, vol. XXVIII, Edinburgh, 1829)
Van Durme, M., *Les Archives générales de Simancas et l'histoire de la Belgique (ixe–xixe-siècles)*, part II, *1508–1795* (Brussels, 1966)
Whitelocke, Bulstrode, *Memorials of English affairs from the beginning of the reign of Charles I to the happy restoration of King Charles II* (4 vols., Oxford, 1853)
Wood, Marguerite (ed.), *Extracts from the records of the burgh of Edinburgh 1642–1655* (Edinburgh, 1938)
Woodhouse, A. S. P. (ed.), *Puritanism and liberty. Being the army debates (1647–9) from the Clarke manuscripts with supplementary documents*, preface by Ivan Roots (London, 1938; 2nd edn, 1974)
Young, R. M. (ed.), *Historical notices of old Belfast and its vicinity* (Belfast, 1896)
  The town book of the corporation of Belfast 1613–1816 (Belfast, 1896)
  'A diary of the proceedings of the Leinster army, under governor Jones ... ', *UJA*, 2nd series, 3, no. 3 (Apr. 1897), pp. 153–61

SECONDARY WORKS

Adams, Simon, L., 'Stanley, York and Elizabeth's catholics', *History Today*, 37, no. 7 (July 1987), pp. 46–50
Adamson, J. S. A., 'The peerage in politics 1645–49' (unpublished PhD thesis, University of Cambridge, 1986)
  'The baronial context of the English civil war', *R. Hist. Soc. Trans.*, 5th ser., 40 (1990), pp. 93–120
Agnew, Andrew, *The Agnews of Lochnaw. A history of the hereditary sheriffs of Galloway 1330–1747* ... (Edinburgh, 1864)
Aikin, L., *Memoirs of the court of Charles the first* (2 vols., London, 1833)
Albert, Brother, 'The Savages (now Nugents) of the Ards', *Upper Ards Historical Society Journal*, 3 (1979), p. 22
Albion, Gordon, *Charles I and the court of Rome* (London, 1935)
Alcalá-Zamora y Queipo de Llano, J., *España, Flandes y el mar del norte 1618–1639* (Barcelona, 1975)

Bibliography 319

Alexander, Michael Van Cleave, *Charles I's lord treasurer. Sir Richard Weston, earl of Portland (1577–1635)* (London, 1975)
Anderson, A. C., *The story of the presbyterian church in Ireland* (Belfast, 1965)
Anderson, R. C., 'The royalists at sea in 1648', *The Mariner's Mirror*, 9, no. 2 (1923), pp. 34–46
  'The royalists at sea in 1649', *The Mariner's Mirror*, 14, no. 4 (1928), pp. 320–38
  'The royalists at sea in 1650', *The Mariner's Mirror*, 17, no. 2 (1931), pp. 135–68
  'The ancestry of the eighteenth century frigate', *The Mariner's Mirror*, 27, no. 2 (1941), pp. 158–65
Andrews, J. H., *Plantation acres. An historical study of the Irish land surveyor and his maps* (Ulster Historical Foundation, Omagh, 1985)
Andrews, K. R., Canny, N. P., and Hair, P. E. H. (eds.), *The westward enterprise. English activities in Ireland, the Atlantic and America 1480–1650* (Liverpool, 1978)
Anson, P. F., *Underground catholicism in Scotland 1622–1878* (Montrose, 1970)
Antrim, Lady Angela, *The Antrim MacDonnells* (Belfast, 1977)
[Anonymous], 'Gleanings in family history from the Antrim coast', *UJA*, 1st series, 8 (1860), pp. 196–210
  'High sheriffs of the county of Antrim', *UJA*, 2nd series, 11 (1905), pp. 78–83
  Historical collections relative to the town of Belfast: from the earliest period to the union with Great Britain (Belfast, 1817)
  'Metropolitan visitation of the diocese of Derry, A.D. 1397', *UJA*, 1st series, 1 (1853), pp. 184–97
  'Owen Roe O'Neill', *UJA*, 1st series, 4 (1856), pp. 25–39
Appleby, John C., 'An Irish letter of marque, 1648', *Ir. Sword*, 15, no. 61 (Winter 1983), pp. 218–21
Appleby, John C., and O'Dowd, Mary, 'The Irish admiralty: its organization and development, c. 1570–1640', *IHS*, 24, no. 95 (May 1985), pp. 299–326
Aston, Trevor (ed.), *Crisis in Europe 1560–1660* (London, 1970)
Atkinson, E. D., 'The Magennises of Clanconnell', *UJA*, 2nd series, 1, (1895), pp. 30–2
  An Ulster parish: being a history of Donaghcloney (Dublin, 1898)
  Dromore. An Ulster diocese (Dundalk, 1925)
Aveling, Hugh, *Northern catholics* (London, 1966)
Aylmer, G. E., *The king's servants. The civil service of Charles I, 1625–1642* (London, 1961; later edn, London, 1974)
  'Presidential address: collective mentalities in mid-seventeenth century England: II. royalist attitudes', *R. Hist. Soc. Trans.*, 37 (1987), pp. 1–30
  'Presidential address: collective mentalities in mid-seventeenth century England: IV. cross currents: neutrals, trimmers and others', *R. Hist. Soc. Trans.*, 39 (1989), pp. 1–22
Aylmer, G. E. (ed.), *The Interregnum. The quest for settlement 1646–1660* (London, 1970)
Baetens, R., 'The organization and effects of Flemish privateering in the seventeenth century', *Acta Historiae Neerlandicae*, 9 (1977), pp. 48–75
Bagwell, Richard, *Ireland under the Stuarts* (3 vols., London, 1909–16; reprint, 1963)
Barkley, J. M., 'Some Scottish bishops and ministers in the Irish Church 1605–1635', in D. Shaw (ed.), *Reformation and revolution. Essays presented to the very Reverend Principal Emeritus Hugh Watt* (Edinburgh, 1967), pp. 141–59

Barnard, T. C., 'Planters and policies in Cromwellian Ireland', *Past and Present*, 61 (1973), pp. 31–68
  Cromwellian Ireland. English government and reform in Ireland 1649–1660 (Oxford, 1975)
  'Sir William Petty, his Irish estates and Irish population', *Ir. Econ. & Soc. Hist.*, 6 (1979), pp. 64–7
  'Sir William Petty, Irish landowner', in Hugh Lloyd-Jones, Valerie Pearl and Blair Worden (eds.), *History and imagination. Essays in honour of H. R. Trevor-Roper* (London, 1981), pp. 201–18
  'Crises of identity among Irish protestants 1641–1685', *Past and Present*, 127 (1990), pp. 39–83
Bartlett, Thomas, 'The O'Haras of Annaghmore 1600–1800: survival and revival', *Ir. Econ. & Soc. Hist.*, 9 (1982), pp. 34–52
Baumber, Michael L., 'The navy and the civil war in Ireland, 1641–1643', *The Mariner's Mirror*, 57, no. 4 (Oct. 1971), pp. 385–98
  General-at-sea. Robert Blake and the seventeenth-century revolution in naval warfare (London, 1989)
  'The navy and the civil war in Ireland, 1643–1646', *The Mariner's Mirror*, 75, no. 3 (Aug. 1989), pp. 255–68
Beckett, J. C., *A short history of Ireland* (London, 1952)
  The making of modern Ireland 1603–1923 (London, 1966)
  'The Irish viceroyalty in the restoration period', *R. Hist. Soc. Trans.*, 5th series, 20 (1970), pp. 53–73
  Confrontations in Irish history (Totowa, 1972)
  The Anglo-Irish tradition (Belfast, 1976)
  The cavalier duke. A life of James Butler first duke of Ormond, 1610–88 (Belfast, 1990)
Begley, J. C., *The diocese of Limerick in the sixteenth and seventeenth centuries* (reprint, Dublin, 1958)
Bigby, D. A., *Anglo-French relations, 1641–9* (London, 1933)
Bigger, F. J., *The ancient Franciscan friary of Bun-Na-Margie, Ballycastle, on the north coast of Antrim* ... (Belfast, 1898)
  'The Bally Castle, County Antrim', *UJA*, 2nd series, 8, no. 1 (Jan. 1902), pp. 7–9
  'Some historical notes about Dunluce and its builders', *UJA*, 2nd series, 11, no. 4 (Oct. 1905), pp. 154–62, and 12, no. 1 (Jan. 1906), pp. 22–35
Birch, Thomas (ed.), *An inquiry into the share which Charles I had in the transactions of the earl of Glamorgan* (London, 1756)
  The court and times of Charles the first ... (2 vols., London, 1848)
Black, Ronald, 'Colla Ciotach', *Transactions of the Gaelic Society of Inverness*, 48 (1972–4), pp. 201–43
Blackwood, B. G., *The Lancashire gentry and the great rebellion, 1640–1660* (Manchester, 1970)
  'Plebian catholics in the 1640s and 1650s', *Recusant History*, 18 (1986), pp. 42–58
Blair, S. Alexander, 'Presbyterianism in Glenarm', *The Glynns*, 9 (1981), pp. 37–51
Bond, B., and Roy, I. (eds.), *War and society. A yearbook of military history*, I, (London, 1975)
Bone, Quentin, *Henrietta Maria* (Urbana, 1972)
Borrowes, Erasmus D., 'Tennekille castle, Portarlington, and glimpses of the Mac-Donnells', *UJA*, 1st series, 2, (1954), pp. 34–43
Bossy, John, *The English catholic community 1570–1850* (London, 1976)

Bottigheimer, Karl S., 'Civil war in Ireland: the reality in Munster', *Emory University Quarterly*, 22, no. 1 (Spring 1966), pp. 46–56
  'English money and Irish land. The "Adventurers" in the Cromwellian settlement of Ireland', *Journal of British Studies*, 7 (1967), pp. 12–27
  English money and Irish land. The 'Adventurers' in the Cromwellian settlement of Ireland (Oxford, 1971)
  'The restoration land settlement in Ireland: a structural view', *IHS*, 18, no. 69 (Mar. 1972), pp. 1–21
Boyajian, James C., *Portugese bankers at the court of Spain 1626–1650* (New Brunswick, 1983)
Boyd, Andrew, 'Rinuccini and civil war in Ireland, 1644–9', *History Today*, 41 (Feb. 1991), pp. 42–8
Brady, C., O'Dowd, M., and Walker, B. (eds.), *Ulster an illustrated history* (London, 1989)
Brady, Ciaran, 'Sixteenth century Ulster and the failure of Tudor reform', in C. Brady, M. O'Dowd and B. Walker (eds.), *Ulster an illustrated history* (London, 1989), pp. 77–103
Brady, Ciaran (ed.), *Worsted in the game. Losers in Irish history* (Dublin, 1989)
Brady, Ciaran, and Gillespie, Raymond (eds.), *Natives and newcomers. Essays on the making of Irish colonial society 1534–1641* (Dublin, 1986)
Brailsford, H. N., *The Levellers and the English revolution*, ed. Christopher Hill (Manchester, 1976)
Brennan, Monica, 'The changing composition of Kilkenny landowners 1641–1700', in William Nolan and Kevin Whelan (eds.), *Kilkenny: history and society. Interdisciplinary essays on the history of an Irish county.* (Dublin, 1990), pp. 161–96
Brooke-Tyrrell, Alma, 'Michael Jones, governor of Dublin', *Dublin Historical Record*, 24, no. 1 (Dec. 1970), pp. 159–71
Brown, Keith, 'Aristocratic finances and the origins of the Scottish revolution', *EHR*, 104, no. 410 (Jan. 1989), pp. 46–87
  'Noble indebtedness in Scotland between the reformation and the revolution', *Historical Research*, 62, no. 149 (Oct. 1989), pp. 260–75
  'Courtiers and cavaliers. Service, anglicisation and loyalty amongst the royalist nobility', in John S. Morrill (ed.), *The Scottish national covenant in its British context 1638–51* (Edinburgh, 1990), pp. 155–92
Brunskill, H. O., 'The battle of Rathmines, 2 August 1649', *Dublin Historical Record*, 2 (1939–40), pp. 18–29
Bryan, Dan, 'The Irish admiralty, 1642–3', *An Cosantóir*, 7 (1947), pp. 285–7
Butel, P., and L. M. Cullen (eds.), *Cities and merchants. French and Irish perspectives on urban development, 1500–1900* (Dublin, 1986)
Camblin, G., *Towns in Ulster* (Belfast, 1951)
Campbell, John Lorne, 'Some notes and comments on "the Irish Franciscan mission to Scotland" by the Rev. Cathaldus Giblin. O. F. M.', *Innes Review*, 4, no. 1 (Spring 1953), pp. 42–8
Canny, Nicholas P., 'Hugh O'Neill, earl of Tyrone, and the changing face of gaelic Ulster', *Studia Hib.*, 9 (1970), pp. 7–35
  The Elizabethan conquest of Ireland. A pattern established 1565–76 (New York, 1976)
  'Dominant minorities: English settlers in Ireland and Virginia, 1550–1650', in A. C.

Hepburn (ed.), *Minorities in History* (Historical Studies, vol. XII, Belfast, 1978), pp. 17–44
'The formation of the Irish mind: religion, politics and Gaelic Irish literature, 1580–1750', *Past and Present*, 95 (May 1982), pp. 91–116
The upstart earl. A study of the social and mental world of Richard Boyle, first earl of Cork, 1566–1643 (Cambridge, 1982)
'Migration and opportunity. Britain, Ireland and the New World', *Ir. Econ & Soc. Hist.*, 12 (1985), pp. 7–32
Kingdom and colony. Ireland in the Atlantic world 1560–1800 (Baltimore, 1988)
'In defence of the constitution? The nature of the Irish revolt in the seventeenth century', in *Culture et pratiques politiques en France et en Irlande XVIe-XVIIIe siècle* (Paris, 1991), pp. 22–40
Canny, Nicholas, and Pagden, Anthony (eds.), *Colonial identity in the Atlantic world 1500–1800* (Princeton, 1987)
Carles, Pierre, 'Troupes Irlandaises au service de la France, 1635–1815', *Etudes Irlandaises*, new series, 8 (Dec. 1983), pp. 193–212
Carlin, Norah, 'The Levellers and the conquest of Ireland in 1649', *Historical Journal*, 30, no. 2 (1987), pp. 269–88
Carlisle, Nicholas, *An inquiry into the place and quality of the gentlemen of his majesty's most honourable privy chamber* (London, 1829)
Carroll, J. S., 'Cromwell's plantation measure', *Decies, Old Waterford Society*, no. 3 (Oct. 1976), p. 25
Carte, Thomas, *The Irish massacre set in a clear light wherein Mr Baxter's account ... are fully considered* (London, 1714)
History of the life of James, first duke of Ormonde (2nd edn, 6 vols., Oxford, 1951)
Cary, Henry (ed.), *Memorials of the great civil war 1642–52* (2 vols., London, 1842)
Casway, Jerrold I., 'Owen Roe O'Neill's return to Ireland in 1642: the diplomatic background', *Studia Hib.*, 9 (1969), pp. 48–64
'George Monck and the controversial catholic truce of 1649', *Studia Hib.*, 16 (1976), pp. 54–72
Owen Roe O'Neill and the struggle for catholic Ireland (Philadelphia, 1984)
'Two Phelim O'Neills', *Seanchas Ardmhacha*, 11, no. 2 (1985), pp. 331–41
'The Belturbet council and election of March 1650', *Clogher Record*, 22, no. 2 (1986), pp. 159–70
Cavenagh, W. O., 'Colonel Daniel O'Neill, circa 1612–1664', *RSAI Jn.*, 5th series, 18 (1908), pp. 362–7
Chancellor, E. B., *The private palaces of London, past and present* (London, 1908)
Clarke, Aidan, 'The earl of Antrim and the first Bishops' War', *Ir. Sword*, 6, no. 23 (1963), pp. 108–15
The Old English in Ireland 1625–1642 (Cornell, 1966)
The Graces, 1625–41 (Irish Historical Series, vol. VIII, Dundalk, 1968)
'Ireland and the general crisis', *Past and Present*, 58 (1970), pp. 86–94
'The colonization of Ulster and the rebellion of 1641, 1603–1660', in T. W. Moody and F. X. Martin (eds.), *The course of Irish history* (Cork, 1978), pp. 189–203
'The genesis of the Ulster rising', in Peter Roebuck (ed.), *Plantation to partition. Essays in Ulster history in honour of J. L. McCracken* (Belfast, 1981), pp. 29–45
'The plantations of Ulster', in Liam de Paor (ed.), *Milestones in Irish History* (Cork and Dublin, 1986), pp. 62–71
'The 1641 depositions', in P. Fox (ed.), *Treasures of the library, Trinity College Dublin* (Dublin, 1986)

'Sir Piers Crosby, 1590–1646: Wentworth's "tawney ribbon"', *IHS*, 26, no. 102 (Nov. 1988), pp. 142–60
Cliffe, T. J., *The Yorkshire gentry from the reformation to the civil war* (London, 1969)
'The royalist composition papers and the landed income of gentry: a rejoinder', *Northern History*, 14 (1978), pp. 164–8
Clifton, R., 'Fear of catholics in the English revolution 1640–60', *Past and Present*, 52 (1971), pp. 23–56
Collinson, Patrick, *The Elizabethan puritan movement* (London, 1967)
Coonan, T. L., *The Irish catholic confederacy and the puritan revolution* (Dublin, 1954)
Corish, Patrick J., 'Bishop Nicholas French and the second Ormond peace, 1648–9', *IHS*, 6, no. 22 (Sept. 1948), pp. 83–100
'Rinuccini's censure of May 22 1648', *Irish Theological Quarterly*, 18 (Oct. 1951), pp. 322–37
'Two contemporary historians of the confederation of Kilkenny: John Lynch and Richard O'Ferrall', *IHS*, 8, no. 31 (Mar. 1953), pp. 217–36
'John Callaghan and the controversy among the Irish in Paris', *Irish Theological Quarterly*, 21 (Jan. 1954), pp. 32–50
'Ireland's first papal nuncio', *Irish Ecclesiastical Record*, 5th series, 81 (Jan.–June 1954), pp. 172–83
'Irish history and the papal archives', *Irish Theological Quarterly*, 21 (1954), pp. 375–81
'The crisis in Ireland in 1648; the nuncio and the supreme council: conclusions', *Irish Theological Quarterly*, 22 (Jan. 1955), pp. 231–57
'The origins of catholic nationalism' in *A history of Irish catholicism*, III, part 3 (Dublin, 1968), pp. 1–64
Corish, Patrick J. (ed.), *Radicals, rebels and establishments* (Historical Studies, vol. XV, Belfast, 1985)
Cosgrove, Art, and McCartney, Donal (eds.), *Studies in Irish history presented to R. Dudley Edwards* (Dublin, 1979)
Cotton, A. N. B., 'London newsbooks in the civil war: their attitudes and sources of information' (unpublished D Phil thesis, Oxford University, 1971)
Cowan, Edward J., *Montrose for covenant and king* (London, 1977)
'Clanship, kinship and the Campbell acquisition of Islay', *SHR*, 63, no. 166 (Oct. 1979), pp. 132–57
'The Angus Campbells and the origin of the Campbell–Ogilvie feud', *Scottish Studies*, 25 (1981), pp. 25–38
Crawford, W. H., 'The origins of the linen industry in North Armagh and the Lagan Valley', *Ulster Folklife*, 7 (1971), pp. 42–52
'Landlord–tenant relations in Ulster 1609–1802', *Ir. Econ. & Soc. Hist.*, 2 (1975), pp. 5–21
Cregan, Donal F., 'Daniel O'Neill, a royalist agent in Ireland, 1644–50', *IHS*, 2, no. 8 (Sept. 1941), pp. 398–414
'Some members of the confederation of Kilkenny', in S. O. O'Brien (ed.), *Measgra i gCuimhne Mhichic Uí Chleririgh* (Dublin, 1944), pp. 34–44
'The confederation of Kilkenny: its organization, personnel and history' (unpublished PhD thesis, National University of Ireland, 1947)
'An Irish cavalier: Daniel O'Neill', *Studia Hib.*, 3 (1963), pp. 60–100

'An Irish cavalier: Daniel O'Neill in the civil wars 1642–51', *Studia Hib.*, 4 (1965), pp. 104–33
'An Irish cavalier: Daniel O'Neill in exile and restoration 1651–1664', *Studia Hib.*, 5 (1965), pp. 42–76
'The confederation of Kilkenny', in Brian Farrell (ed.), *The Irish parliamentary tradition* (Dublin, 1973), pp. 102–14
Cullen, L. M., *Anglo-Irish trade 1660–1800* (Manchester, 1968)
An economic history of Ireland since 1660 (London, 1972)
Cullen, L. M., and Furet, F. (eds.), *Ireland and France, seventeenth–twentieth centuries. Towards a comparative study of rural history* (Paris, 1980)
Cullen, L. M., and Smout, T. C. (eds.), *Comparative aspects of Scottish and Irish economic and social history, 1600–1906* (Edinburgh, 1977)
Cunningham, Bernadette, 'Native culture and political change in Ireland, 1580–1640' in Ciaran Brady and Raymond Gillespie (eds.), *Natives and newcomers. Essays on the making of Irish colonial society 1534–1641* (Dublin, 1986), pp. 148–70
Cunningham, Bernadette, and Gillespie, Raymond, 'The East Ulster bardic family of Ó Gnímh', *Egise*, 20 (1984), pp. 106–14
'An Ulster settler and his Irish manuscripts' *Egise*, 21 (1986), pp. 27–36
'The purposes of patronage: Brian Maguire of Knockninny and his manuscripts', *Clogher Record*, 13, no. 1 (1988), pp. 38–49
Curry, J., *An historical and critical review of the civil wars in Ireland from the reign of Queen Elizabeth to the settlement under King William* ... (Dublin, 1810)
Curtis, Edmund, 'The MacQuillan or Mandeville lords of the Route', *RIA Proc.*, section C, 44 (1937–8), pp. 99–113
Cust, Richard, and Hughes, Ann (eds.), *Conflict in early Stuart England. Studies in religion and politics 1603–1642* (London, 1989)
Dallat, Cahal, 'Place names in the parish of Culfeightrin', *The Glynns*, 9 (1981)
Dalton, Charles, *Life and times of Sir Edward Cecil, Viscount Wimbledon* ... (2 vols., London, 1885)
Dawson, Jane E. A., 'Two kingdoms or three?: Ireland in Anglo-Scottish relations in the middle of the sixteenth century', in Roger Mason (ed.), *Scotland and England 1286–1815* (Edinburgh, 1987), pp. 113–38
de Courcy Ireland, John, *Ireland and the Irish in maritime history* (Dublin, 1986)
Devine, T. M., and Dickson, David (eds.), *Ireland and Scotland 1600–1850. Parallels and contrasts in economic and social development* (Edinburgh, 1983)
Dickson, David, 'Property and social structure in eighteenth century south Munster', in L. M. Cullen and F. Furet (eds.), *Ireland and France, seventeenth–twentieth centuries. Towards a comparative study of rural history* (Paris, 1980), pp. 129–38
Dickson, John M., 'The Colville family in Ulster', *UJA*, 2nd series, 5, no. 3 (May 1899), pp. 139–45
'The Agnews in County Antrim', *UJA*, 2nd series, 7, no. 4 (Oct. 1901), pp. 166–71
Dictionary of national biography, ed. Sir Leslie Stephen and Sir Sydney Lee (66 vols., London, 1885–1901; reprinted with corrections, 22 vols., London, 1908–9)
Dodgshon, R. A., *Land and society in early Scotland* (Oxford, 1981)
Donald, Peter, 'The king – and the Scottish troubles 1637–1641' (PhD thesis, Cambridge University, 1988)
An uncounselled king. Charles I and the Scottish Troubles 1637–1641 (Cambridge, 1990)
Dow, F. D., *Cromwellian Scotland 1651–1660* (Edinburgh, 1979)

Dow, John, 'The political ideal of the English commonwealth', *EHR*, 6, no. 22 (April 1891), pp. 306–30
Duffy, P. J., 'The evolution of estate properties in South Ulster 1600–1900', in William J. Smyth and Kevin Whelan (eds.), *Common ground. Essays on the historical geography of Ireland presented to T. Jones Hughes* (Cork 1988), pp. 84–109
Duggan, Lucy, 'The Irish brigade with Montrose', *Irish Ecclesiastical Record*, 5th series, 89 (Jan.–June 1958), pp. 171–84, 246–58
Dunlop, Robert, 'The forged commission of 1641', *EHR*, 2, no. 7 (July 1887), pp. 527–33
Dunne, T. J., 'The Gaelic response to conquest and colonization: the evidence of the poetry', *Studia Hib.*, 20 (1980), pp. 7–30
Dwyer, John, Mason, Roger A., and Murdoch, Alexander (eds.), *New perspectives on the politics and culture of early modern Scotland* (Edinburgh, 1982)
Elkin, Robert E., 'The interactions between the Irish rebellion and the English civil wars' (unpublished PhD thesis, University of Illinois at Urbana-Champaign, 1961)
Elliott, John H., *The revolt of the Catalans. A study in the decline of Spain 1598–1640* (Cambridge, 1963)
'The year of the three ambassadors', in Hugh Lloyd-Jones, Valerie Pearl and Blair Worden (eds.), *History and imagination. Essays in honour of H. R. Trevor-Roper* (London, 1981), pp. 165–81
The Count-Duke of Olivares. The statesman in an age of decline (New Haven and London, 1986)
'National and comparative history' (Inaugural lecture, University of Oxford, 1991)
Ellis, Steven, ' "Not mere English". The British perspective, 1400–1650', *History Today*, 38, no. 12 (Dec. 1988), pp. 41–8
Elton, Geoffrey, R., *The practice of history* (London, 1967)
Esson, D. M. R., *The curse of Cromwell. A history of the ironside conquest of Ireland 1649–1653* (Totowa, 1971)
Eustace, Timothy (ed.), *Statesmen and politicians of the Stuart age* (London, 1985)
Everitt, Alan, *The community of Kent and the Great Rebellion, 1640–1660* (Leicester, 1966)
Farrell, Brian (ed.), *The Irish parliamentary tradition* (Dublin, 1973)
Fenlon, Jane, 'Some houses in England owned by the dukes of Ormonde and their families', *Butler Society Journal*, 3 (1987), pp. 58–60
Firth, C. H., 'Thomas Scot's account of his actions as intelligencer during the Commonwealth', *EHR*, 12, no. 45 (Jan. 1897), pp. 116–26
Cromwell's army. A history of the English soldier during the civil wars, the commonwealth and protectorate (4th edn, London, 1962)
Firth, C. H., and Davies, G., *The regimental history of Cromwell's army* (2 vols., Oxford, 1940)
Fissel, Mark Charles (ed.), *War and government in Britain 1598–1650* (Manchester, 1991)
FitzPatrick, Brendan, *Seventeenth-century Ireland. The war of religions* (Dublin, 1988)
Fitzpatrick, T., *Waterford during the civil war (1641–1653)* (Waterford, 1912)
FitzPatrick, Thomas, 'The wars of 1641 in County Down: the deposition of High

Sheriff Peter Hill (1645)', *UJA*, 2nd series, 10, no. 2 (Apr. 1904), pp. 73–90, continued in 11, no. 1 (Jan. 1905), pp. 14–17, 11, no. 2 (Apr. 1905), pp. 58–64, 12, no. 1 (Jan. 1906), pp. 2–10, and 12, no. 2 (Apr. 1906), pp. 62–77

'The Ulster civil war, 1641. "The king's commission" in the County Fermanagh', *UJA*, 2nd series, 13, no. 3 (Aug. 1907), pp. 133–42, continued in 13, no. 4 (Nov. 1907), pp. 155–9

FitzSimon, R. D., 'Irish swordsmen in Imperial service in the Thirty Years' War' in *Ir. Sword*, 9 (1969), pp. 22–31

Fletcher, Anthony, *A county community in peace and war. Sussex 1600–1660* (London, 1975)

Flinn, Michael (ed.), *Scottish population history: from the seventeenth century to the 1930s* (Cambridge, 1977)

Forster, Roy F. (ed.), *The Oxford illustrated history of Ireland* (Oxford, 1991)

Frey, J., 'A catalogue of the eighteenth and early nineteenth century estate maps in the Antrim estate office, Glenarm, Co. Antrim', *The Glynns*, 16 (1953), pp. 93–103

Furgol, Edward M., *A regimental history of the covenanting armies 1639–1651* (Edinburgh, 1990)

Gallwey, H., *The Wall family in Ireland 1170–1970* (Naas, County Kildare, 1970)

Gardiner, Samuel R., *History of England from the accession of James I to the outbreak of the civil war, 1603–1642* (10 vols., London, 1863–81; new edn, 10 vols., 1883–4)

'Charles I and the earl of Glamorgan', *EHR*, 2, no. 8 (Oct. 1887), pp. 687–708

History of the great civil war, 1642–1649 (new edn, 4 vols., London, 1893; reprint, 1987)

History of the commonwealth and protectorate 1649–56 (new edn, 4 vols., London, 1903; reprint, 1988)

Gentles, Ian, 'The purchasers of Northamptonshire crown lands 1649–1660', *Midland History*, 3, no. 3 (Spring 1976), pp. 206–32

'The impact of the New Model Army', in John S. Morrill (ed.), *The impact of the English civil war* (London, 1991), pp. 86–102

Giblin, Cathaldus, 'St. Oliver Plunkett, Francis MacDonnell O.F.M. and the mission to the Hebrides', *Collect. Hib.*, 17 (1974–5), pp. 69–102

'Francis MacDonnell O.F.M., son of the first earl of Antrim (d. 1636)', *Seanchas Ardmhacha*, 8, no. 1 (1976–7), pp. 44–54

Gilbert, Sir John T., *A history of Dublin* (3 vols., 1854–9; reprint, Dublin, 1978)

Gillespie, Raymond, 'East Ulster in the early seventeenth century: a colonial economy and society', *Ir. Econ. & Soc. Hist.*, 10 (1983), pp. 92–4

'Harvest crises in early seventeenth century Ireland', *Ir. Econ. & Soc. Hist.*, 11 (1984), pp. 5–18

Colonial Ulster. The settlement of East Ulster 1600–1641 (Cork, 1985)

'Mayo and the rising of 1641', *Cathair na Mart*, 5 (1985), pp. 38–44

'The end of an era: Ulster and the outbreak of the 1641 rising', in Ciaran Brady and Raymond Gillespie (eds.), *Natives and newcomers. Essays on the making of Irish colonial society 1534–1641* (Dublin, 1986), pp. 191–213

'Migration and opportunity: a comment', *Ir. Econ. & Soc. Hist.*, 13 (1986), pp. 90–5

Conspiracy. Ulster plots and plotters in 1615 (Belfast, 1987)

'The trials of Bishop Spottiswood 1620–40', *Clogher Record*, 12, no. 3 (1987), pp. 320–33

'Landed society and the interregnum in Ireland and Scotland', in Rosalind Mitchison and Peter Roebuck (eds.), *Economy and society in Scotland and Ireland, 1500–1939* (Edinburgh, 1988), pp. 38–47

'Meal and money: the harvest crisis of 1621–4 and the Irish economy', in M. E. Crawford (ed.), *Famine. The Irish experience, 900–1900* (Edinburgh, 1989), pp. 75–95
Gillespie, Raymond, and Moran, Gerald (ed.), *'A various country'. Essays in Mayo history 1500–1900* (Westport, Mayo, 1987)
Gillespie, Raymond, and O'Sullivan, Harold (eds.), *The Borderlands. Essays on the history of the Ulster–Leinster border* (Belfast, 1989)
Gillies, William, 'Some aspects of Campbell history', *Transactions of the Gaelic Society of Inverness*, 50 (1976–8), pp. 256–95
Gillingham, John, 'Images of Ireland 1170–1600: the origins of English imperialism', *History Today*, 37 (Feb. 1987), pp. 6–22
Gleeson, D. F., *The last lords of Ormond. A history of the 'countrie of the three O'Kennedys' during the seventeenth century* (London, 1938)
  'Sources for local history in the period 1200–1700', *Journal of the Cork Historical and Archaeological Society*, 46 (1941), pp. 123–9
Glin, Knight of, *Irish furniture* (Dublin, 1978)
Gogarty, Thomas, 'The Ulster roll of goal delivery, 1615', *Archiv. Hib.*, 6 (1917), pp. 83–93
Goldstrom, J. M., and Clarkson, L. A. (eds.), *Irish population, economy and society. Essays in honour of the late K. H. Connell* (Oxford, 1981)
Gough, Hugh, and Dickson, David (eds.), *Ireland and the French revolution* (Dublin, 1990)
Gouhier, Pierre, 'Mercenaires Irlandais au service de la France (1635–1664)', *Ir. Sword*, 7 (1965), pp. 58–75
Gowen, Margaret, 'Seventeenth-century artillery forts in Ulster', *Clogher Record*, 10, no. 2 (1980), pp. 239–57
Groenveld, Simon, *Verlopend getij. De Nederlandse Republiek en de Engelse Burgeroorlog 1640–1646* (Dieren, 1984)
  'The English civil wars as a cause of the first Anglo-Dutch war, 1640–1652', *Historical Journal*, 30, no. 3 (1987), pp. 541–66
Habakkuk, H. J., 'The parliamentary army and the crown lands', *The Welsh History Review*, 3, no. 4 (Dec. 1967), pp. 403–26
Hamilton, Elizabeth, *Henrietta Maria* (London, 1976)
Hardacre, Paul H., *The royalists during the puritan revolution* (London, 1956)
  'Patronage and purchase in the Irish standing army, under Thomas Wentworth, earl of Strafford, 1632–1640', *Journal of the Society for Army Historical Research*, 67, no. 270 (Summer 1989), pp. 94–104
Hardiman, J., *The history of the town and country of the town of Galway from the earliest period to the present time ...* (reprint, Galway, 1926)
Hastings, M., *Montrose. The king's champion* (London, 1977)
Hayes-McCoy, Gerald A., *Scots mercenary forces in Ireland (1565–1603) ...* (Dublin, 1937)
  'The army of Ulster, 1593–1601', *Ir. Sword*, 1, no. 2 (1950–1), pp. 105–17
  'Gaelic society in Ireland', *Historical Studies*, 1 (1958), pp. 45–61
  'The making of an O'Neill: a view of the ceremony at Tullaghoge, Co. Tyrone', *UJA*, 3rd series, 33 (1970), pp. 23–42
  Irish battles. A military history of Ireland (Belfast, 1989)
Hayton, David, and O'Brien, G. (eds.), *J. G. Simms. War and politics in Ireland, 1649–1730* (London, 1986)

Hazlett, Hugh, 'The financing of the British armies in Ireland, 1641–9', *IHS*, 1, no. 1 (Mar. 1938), pp. 21–41

'A history of the military forces operating in Ireland, 1641–9' (unpublished PhD thesis, Queen's University, Belfast, 1938)

'The recruitment and organization of the Scottish army in Ulster, 1642–9', in H. A. Cronne, T. W. Moody and D. B. Quinn (eds.), *Essays in British and Irish history in honour of James Eadie Todd* (London, 1949), pp. 107–33

Healey, T. M., *Stolen waters. A page in the conquest of Ulster* (London, 1913)

Henry, Gráinne, ' "Wild Geese" in Spanish Flanders: the first generation 1586–1610', *Ir. Sword*, 17, no. 68 (1989), pp. 189–201

'The emerging identity of an Irish military group in the Spanish Netherlands', in R. V. Comerford, Mary Cullen, Jacqueline Hill and Colm Lennon (eds.), *Religion, conflict and coexistence in Ireland. Essays presented to Monsignor Patrick J. Corish* (Dublin, 1990), pp. 53–77

Hexter, J. H., *The reign of King Pym* (Cambridge, Mass., 1941; reprint, 1975)

Hibbard, Caroline M., 'The contribution of 1639: court and country catholicism', *Recusant History*, 16 (May 1982), pp. 42– 60

Charles I and the popish plot (Chapel Hill, 1983)

'Episcopal warriors in the British wars of religion', in Mark Charles Fissel (ed.), *War and government in Britain, 1598–1650* (Manchester, 1991), pp. 164–92

'The role of a queen consort. The household and court of Henrietta Maria 1625–1642', in Ronald G. Asch and Adolf M. Birke (eds.), *Princes, patronage, and the nobility* (Oxford, 1991), pp. 393–414

Hill, George, 'Chiefs of the Antrim MacDonnells prior to Sorley Boy', *UJA*, 1st series, 7 (1859), pp. 247–59

'Gleanings in family history from the Antrim coast', *UJA*, 1st series, 8 (1860), pp. 127–44

'The MacQuillins of the Route', *UJA*, 1st series, 9 (1861), pp. 57–70

'Notices of the Clan Ian Vor or Clan-Donnell Scots, especially of the branch settled in Ireland', *UJA*, 1st series, 9 (1861), pp. 301–17

'Shane O'Neill's expedition against the Antrim Scots, 1565', *UJA*, 1st series, 9 (1861), pp. 122–42

The Stewarts of Ballintoy: with notices of other families of the district in the seventeenth century (Coleraine, 1865; reprint, Ballycastle, 1976)

An historical account of the MacDonnells of Antrim: including notices of some other septs, Irish and Scottish (Belfast, 1873; reprint, Ballycastle, 1978)

An historical account of the plantation in Ulster at the commencement of the seventeenth century: 1608–1620 (Belfast, 1877; reprint, Shannon, 1980)

'The Londoner's plantation in the counties of Coleraine and Derry', *UJA*, 2nd series, 8, no. 2 (Apr. 1902), pp. 69–72

Hill, Jacqueline, R., 'Popery and protestantism, civil and religious liberty. The undisputed lessons of Irish history', *Past and Present*, no. 118 (Feb. 1988), pp. 96–129

Hill, James Michael, *Celtic warfare 1595–1763* (Edinburgh, 1986)

Hirst, Derek, *Authority and conflict. England 1603–1658* (London, 1986)

Hobsbawn, E., and Ranger, T. (eds.), *The invention of tradition* (Cambridge, 1983)

Holiday, P. G., 'Land sales and repurchases in Yorkshire after the civil wars, 1650–1670', *Northern History*, 5 (1970), pp. 67–92

Hore, P. H., *History of the town and county of Wexford* (6 vols., London, 1900–11)

Houston, R. A., and Whyte, I. D. (eds.), *Scottish society 1500–1800* (Cambridge, 1989)

Huband Smith, J., 'Letters patent of James MacDonnell, lord of the castle and manor of Tenekilly, in the barony of Portnehinch, and Queen's County', *UJA*, 1st series, 2 (1854), pp. 121–5

Hughes, Ann, 'Parliamentary tyranny? Indemnity proceedings and the impact of the civil war: a case study from Warwickshire', *Midland History*, 11 (1986), pp. 49–78

Hume, R. A., 'Origin and characteristics of the population in the counties of Antrim and Down with notices by M. N. and R. P. Klllinchy', *UJA*, 1st series, 1 (1853), pp. 9–26, 120–9, 246–54

Hutton, Ronald, *The Restoration. A political and religious history of England and Wales 1658–1667* (Oxford, 1985)
  Charles II. King of England, Scotland and Ireland (Oxford, 1989)
  The British republic 1649–1660 (London, 1990)

Huxley, Gervas, *Endymion Porter* (London, 1959)

Hynes, Michael J., *The mission of Rinuccini, 1645–49* (Louvain, 1932)
  'The Irish republic in the seventeenth century', *The Catholic Historical Review*, 23, no. 3 (Oct. 1937), pp. 293–311

Irwin, Liam, 'Politics, religion and economy: Cork in the seventeenth century', *Journal of the Cork Historical and Archaeological Society*, 85, nos. 241–2 (Jan.–Dec. 1980), pp. 7–25

Israel, Jonathan I, *The Dutch Republic and the Hispanic world 1606–1661* (Oxford, 1982)

Israel, Jonathan I. (ed.), *The Anglo-Dutch moment* (Cambridge, 1991)

Jackson, Donald, *Intermarriage in Ireland 1550–1650* (Montreal, 1970)

Jago, Charles, 'The influence of debt on the relations between crown and aristocracy in seventeenth century Castile', *Econ. Hist. Rev.*, 2nd series, 26, no. 2 (May 1973), pp. 218–36
  'The "crisis of the aristocracy" in seventeenth century Castile', *Past and Present*, 84 (1979), pp. 60–90

Kearney, Hugh F., 'Mercantilism and Ireland 1620–40', in T. Desmond Williams (ed.), *Historical Studies*, I (London, 1958), pp. 59–67
  Strafford in Ireland 1633–41. A study in absolutism (Manchester, 1959; 2nd edn, Cambridge, 1989)
  The British Isles. A history of four nations (Cambridge, 1989)
  'Strafford in Ireland, 1633–40', *History Today*, 39, no. 7 (July 1989), pp. 20–5

Kelly, Richard J., 'Dr O'Queely, Archbishop of Tuam. A great statesman and prelate', *Irish Ecclesiastical Record*, 17 (1905), pp. 247–53

Kenyon, John P., *The civil wars in England* (New York, 1988)

Kepler, Jon S., 'Fiscal aspects of the English carrying trade during the Thirty Years' War', *Econ. Hist. Rev.*, 2nd series, 25, no. 2 (May 1972), pp. 261–83
  The exchange of christendom. The international entrepôt of Dover 1622–1651 (Leicester, 1976)

Kerridge, Eric, 'The movement of rent 1540–1640', in E. M. Carus-Wilson (ed.), *Essays in economic history*, II (London, 1963), pp. 208–16

Kishlansky, Mark, A., *The rise of the New Model Army* (Cambridge, 1979)

Koenigsberger, H. G., *Politicians and virtuosi. Essays in early modern history* (London, 1986)

Lamont, W. D., 'Alexander of Islay, son of Angus Mor', *SHR*, 60, no. 170 (Oct. 1981), pp. 160–8

Lawlor, A. T., *Irish maritime survey* (Dublin, 1945)

Lee, Maurice, 'Charles I and the end of conciliar government in Scotland', *Albion*, 12 (1980), pp. 315–36
  The road to revolution. Scotland under Charles I, 1625–37 (Urbana and Chicago, 1985)
  Great Britain's Solomon. James VI and I in his three kingdoms (Urbana and Chicago, 1990)
Levack, Brian, *The formation of the British state: England, Scotland and the union 1603–1707* (Oxford, 1987)
Leyburn, James G., *The Scotch Irish: a social history* (Chapel Hill, 1962)
Lindley, Keith, 'The lay catholics of England in the reign of Charles I', *Journal of Ecclesiastical History*, 22, no. 3 (July 1971), pp. 199–220
  'The impact of the 1641 rebellion upon England and Wales 1641–5', *IHS*, 18, no. 70 (Sept. 1972), pp. 143–76
Lockyer, Roger, *Buckingham. The life and political career of George Villiers, first duke of Buckingham 1592–1628* (London, 1981)
Loeber, Rolf, 'English and Irish sources for the history of Dutch economic activity in Ireland 1600–89', *Ir. Econ. & Soc. Hist.*, 8 (1981), pp. 70–85
Logan, Patrick, L., 'Gerald Fenell – doctor and politician (?–1665)', *Irish Ecclesiastical Record*, 5th series, 93 (Jan.–June 1960), pp. 84–92
Loomie, Albert, J., 'Alonso de Cárdenas and the Long Parliament, 1640–1648', *EHR*, 97, no. 383 (Apr. 1982), pp. 289–307
  'The Spanish faction at the court of Charles I, 1630–8', *BIHR*, 59, no. 139 (May 1986), pp. 37–49
  'London's Spanish chapel before and after the civil war', in *Recusant History*, 18 (1987), pp. 402–17
Loomie, Albert, J. (ed.), *Ceremonies of Charles I. The note books of John Finet master of ceremonies, 1628–1641* (New York, 1987)
Love, Walter, D., 'Civil war in Ireland: appearances in three centuries of historical writing', *Emory University Quarterly*, 22, no. 1 (Spring 1966), pp. 57–72
Lowe, John, 'Some aspects of the wars in Ireland, 1641–1649', *Ir. Sword*, 4, no. 15 (Winter 1959), pp. 81–7
  'The earl of Antrim and Irish aid to Montrose in 1644', *Ir. Sword*, 4, no. 16 (Summer 1960), pp. 191–8
  'The negotiations between Charles I and the confederation of Kilkenny, 1642–9' (unpublished PhD thesis, University of London, 1960)
  Charles I and the confederation of Kilkenny, 1643–9', *IHS*, 14, no. 53 (Mar. 1964), pp. 1–19
  'The Glamorgan mission to Ireland 1645–6', in *Studia Hib.*, 4 (1964), pp. 155–96
Lynch, K. M., *Roger Boyle, first earl of Orrery* (Knoxville, 1965)
Lynn, Chris, and McDonnell, Hector, 'Glenarm friary and the Bissets' (privately printed, Glenarm, 1987)
McCarthy, William P., 'The royalist collapse in Munster 1650–1652', *Ir. Sword*, 6, no. 24 (Summer, 1964), pp. 171–9
McCarthy-Morrogh, Michael, *The Munster plantation. English migration to southern Ireland 1583–1641* (Oxford, 1986)
McCaughan, Michael, and Appleby, John (eds.), *The Irish sea. Aspects of maritime history* (Belfast and Cultra, 1989)
MacCurtain, Margaret, 'Rural society in post-Cromwellian Ireland', in Art Cosgrove and Donal McCartney (eds.), *Studies in Irish history presented to R. Dudley Edwards* (Dublin, 1979)

MacCurtain, Margaret and O'Dowd, Mary (eds.), *Women in early modern Ireland* (Dublin, 1991)
MacDonald, Angus J., and MacDonald, Archibald, *The Clan Donald* (3 vols., Inverness, 1896–1904)
MacDonald, D. J., *Clan Donald* (Loanhead, 1978)
MacDonald, Keith, N., *MacDonald bards from medieval times* (Edinburgh, 1900)
McDonnell, Hector, 'A noble pretension', *The Glynns*, 8 (1980), pp. 20–33
  'Irishmen in the Stuart navy 1660–90', *Ir. Sword*, 16, no. 63 (1985), pp. 87–104
  'Jacobitism and the third and fourth earls of Antrim', *The Glynns*, 13 (1985), pp. 50–4
  'The MacDonnells of Antrim in exile, 1615–1720 (unpublished monograph)
McDonnell, John, *The Ulster civil war of 1641 and its consequences; with the history of the Irish brigade under Montrose in 1644–46* (Dublin, 1879)
McGuire, James I., 'Why was Ormond dismissed in 1669?', *IHS*, 8, no. 71 (Mar. 1973), pp. 295–312
Macinnes, Allan I, 'Scottish Gaeldom, 1638–51: the vernacular response to the covenanting dynamic', in John Dwyer, Roger A. Mason and Alexander Murdoch (eds.), *New perspectives on the politics and culture of early modern Scotland* (Edinburgh, 1982), pp. 59–94
  'Repression and conciliation: the highland dimension 1660–1688', *SHR*, 65, no. 180 (Oct. 1986), pp. 167–95
  'Catholic recusancy and the penal laws, 1603–1707', *Records of the Scottish Church History Society*, 23 (1987), pp. 27–63
  'The impact of the civil wars and interregnum: political disruption and social changes within Scottish Gaeldom', in Rosalind Mitchison and Peter Roebuck (eds.), *Economy and society in Scotland and Ireland 1500–1939* (Edinburgh, 1988)
  Charles I and the making of the covenanting movement 1625–1641 (Edinburgh, 1991)
MacKenzie, Alexander, *History of the MacDonalds and lords of the Isles with genealogies of the principal families of the name* (Inverness, 1881)
McKerral, Andrew, *Kintyre in the seventeenth century* (Edinburgh, 1948)
  'West highland mercenaries in Ireland', *The Kintyre Antiquarian and Natural History Society Magazine*, 9 (June 1981), pp 5–15
McLaughlin, Mark G., *The Wild Geese. The Irish brigades of France and Spain* (London, 1980)
MacLean, Duncan, 'Catholicism in the Highlands and Isles, 1560–1680', *Innes Review*, 3, no. 1 (Spring 1952), pp. 5–13
MacLean, Hector, 'The MacDonnells of Antrim', *Transactions of the Gaelic Society of Inverness*, 17 (1890–1), pp. 85–101
MacLysaght, E., *Irish families, their names, arms and origins* (Dublin, 1957)
McMinn, J. R. B., 'The social and political structure of North Antrim in 1869', *The Glynns*, 10 (1982), pp. 11–22
MacSwiney, V. E. P., 'Notes on some Irish regiments in the service of Spain and Naples...', *RIA Proc.*, section C, 37, (1924–7), pp. 158–74
Maguire, W. A., 'The lands of the Maguires of Tempo in the seventeenth century', *Clogher Record*, 12, no. 3 (1987), pp. 305–19
  'The estate of Cú Chonnacht Maguire of Tempo: a case history from the Williamite land settlement', *IHS*, 27, no. 106 (Nov. 1990), pp. 130–44

Maguire, W. A. (ed.), *Kings in conflict. The revolutionary war in Ireland and its aftermath 1689–1750* (Belfast, 1990)
Malcolm, Joyce Lee, 'All the king's men: the impact of the crown's Irish soldiers on the English civil war', *IHS*, 21, no. 83 (Mar. 1979), pp. 239–64
Malo, Henri, *Les Corsaires dunkerquois et Jean Bart*, I, *Des origines à 1662* (Paris, 1912)
Manning, Brian, 'The aristocracy and the downfall of Charles I', in Brian Manning (ed.), *Politics, religion and the English civil war* (London, 1973), pp. 37–79
Manning, Brian (ed.), *Politics, religion and the English civil war* (London, 1973)
Marshall, John J., 'Sir Phelim O'Neill 1604–1652[-3]', *UJA*, 2nd series, 10, no. 4 (Oct. 1904), pp. 145–50
Marshall, Rosalind K., *The days of duchess Anne. Life in the household of the duchess of Hamilton 1656–1716* (London, 1973)
Henrietta Maria. The intrepid queen (London, 1990)
Martin, Angus, *Kintyre. The hidden past* (Edinburgh, 1984)
Mason, Roger (ed.), *Scotland and England 1286–1815* (Edinburgh, 1987)
Mayes, G. R., 'The early Stuarts and the Irish peerage', *EHR*, 73, no. 287 (Apr. 1958), pp. 227–51
Meehan, C. P., *The confederation of Kilkenny* (Dublin, 1860)
Meredith, R., 'A Derbyshire family in the seventeenth century: the Eyres of Hassop and their forfeited estates', *Recusant History*, 8 (1965), pp. 12–66
Millet, B., 'The archives of the congregation de propaganda fide', *Irish Catholic Historical Committee* (1956), pp. 20–7
Mitchison, Rosalind, and Roebuck, Peter (eds.), *Economy and society in Scotland and Ireland, 1500–1939* (Edinburgh, 1988)
Moody, T. W., 'The treatment of the native population under the scheme for plantation in Ulster', *IHS*, 1, no. 1 (Mar. 1938), pp. 59–63
The Londonderry plantation 1609–1641. The city of London and the plantation in Ulster (Belfast, 1939)
Moody, T. W. (ed.), *Nationality and the pursuit of national independence* (Historical Studies, vol. XI, Belfast, 1978)
Moody, T. W., and Martin, F. X. (eds.), *The course of Irish history* (Cork, 1978)
Moody, T. W., Martin, F. X., and Byrne, F. J. (eds.), *A new history of Ireland*, III, *Early modern Ireland 1534–1691* (Oxford, 1978)
A new history of Ireland, IX, *Maps, genealogies, lists* (Oxford, 1984)
Moore, T. (ed.), *A history of the first presbyterian church, Belfast, 1644–1983* (Holywood, 1983)
Morgan, Hiram, 'The end of Gaelic Ulster: a thematic interpretation of events between 1534 and 1610', *IHS*, 26, no. 101 (May 1988), pp. 8–32
Morgan, V., 'A case study of population change over two centuries: Blaris, Lisburn 1661–1848', *Ir. Econ. & Soc. Hist.*, 3 (1976), pp. 5–16
Morrill, John S., 'The Northern gentry and the great rebellion', *Midland History*, 15 (1979), pp. 66–87
Seventeenth century Britain 1603–1641 (Folkestone, 1980)
'The religious context of the English civil war', *R. Hist. Soc. Trans.*, 5th series, 34 (1984), pp. 155–78
Morrill, John S. (ed.), *Reactions to the English civil war 1642–1649* (London, 1982)
Oliver Cromwell and the English revolution (London, 1990)
The Scottish national covenant in its British context 1638–51 (Edinburgh, 1990)
The impact of the English civil war (London, 1991)

Morrissey, Thomas, *James Archer of Kilkenny* ... (Dublin, 1979)
Morrison, D., *The Morrison manuscript tradition of the Western Isles* (Stornoway, 1975)
Murphy, Denis, *Cromwell in Ireland. A history of Cromwell's Irish campaign* (Dublin, 1897)
Murphy, John A., *Justin MacCarthy, Lord Mountcashel, commander of the first Irish brigade in France* (Cork, 1959)
    'The politics of the Munster protestants, 1641–49', *Journal of the Cork Historical and Archaeological Society*, 76, no. 223 (Jan.–June 1971), pp. 1–20
Napier, Mark, *Montrose and the covenanters* ... (2 vols., London, 1838)
Neely, William, *Kilkenny. An urban history 1391–1843* (Belfast, 1989)
    'The Ormond Butlers of County Kilkenny 1515–1715' in William Nolan and Kevin Whelan (eds.), *Kilkenny: history and society. Interdisciplinary essays on the history of an Irish county* (Dublin, 1990), pp. 107–26
Newman, P. R., 'Catholic royalist activists in the north 1642–46', *Recusant History*, 14 (1977), pp. 26–38
    'Catholic royalists of Northern England, 1642–5', *Northern History*, 15 (1979), pp. 88–95
    'Roman Catholic royalists: papist commanders under Charles I and Charles II, 1642–60', *Recusant History*, 15 (1981)
Nicholls, Kenneth, *Gaelic and gaelicised Ireland in the middle ages* (Dublin, 1972)
Nolan, William, and Whelan, Kevin (eds.), *Kilkenny: history and society. Interdisciplinary essays on the history of an Irish county* (Dublin, 1990)
O Baoill, Colm, 'Some Irish harpers in Scotland', *Transactions of the Gaelic Society of Inverness*, 47 (1971–2), pp. 143–71
O'Brien, George (ed.), *The economic history of Ireland in the seventeenth century* (London, 1919)
O'Brien, Ivar, *O'Brien of Thomond. The O'Brien's in Irish history 1500–1865* (Chichester, 1986)
O'Brien, Sean, 'The Butlers of Lower Grange, Viscounts Galmoy', *Old Kilkenny Review*, 16 (1964), pp. 16–23
O'Cahan, T. S., *Owen Roe O'Neill* (London, 1968)
Ó Cuív, Brian (ed.), 'Some Irish items relating to the MacDonnells of Antrim', *Celtica*, 16 (1984), pp. 139–56
Ó Danachair, Caóimhin, 'Montrose's Irish regiments', *Ir. Sword*, 4, no. 14 (1959), pp. 61–7
Ó Doibhlin, T. E., 'The Cromwellian settlement and its aftermath', *Seanchas Ardmhacha*, 4 (1961), pp. 177–211
O'Dowd, Mary, 'Land inheritance in early modern county Sligo', *Ir. Econ. & Soc. Hist.*, 10 (1983), pp. 5–18
    'Gaelic economy and society', in Ciaran Brady and Raymond Gillespie (eds.), *Natives and newcomers. Essays on the making of Irish colonial society 1534–1641* (Dublin, 1986), pp. 120–47
    'Land and lordship in sixteenth and seventeenth century Ireland', in Rosalind Mitchison and Peter Roebuck (eds.), *Economy and society in Scotland and Ireland, 1500–1939* (Edinburgh, 1988), pp. 17–26
Ó Fiach, Tomás, 'The O'Neills of the Fews...', *Seanchas Ardmhacha*, 7, no. 2 (1974), pp. 263–315; 8, no. 2 (1977), pp. 386–413
    The Irish colleges in France (Dublin, 1990)
O'Hart, J., *Irish landed gentry when Cromwell came to Ireland* (Dublin, 1887)

O'Malley, Liam, 'Patrick Darcy, Galway lawyer and politician, 1598–1668', in Diarmuid Ó Cearbhaill (ed.), *Galway. Town and gown 1484–1984* (Dublin, 1984)

Ó Mórdha, P. B., 'The battle of Clones, 1643', *Clogher Record*, 4, no. 3 (1962), pp. 148–54

Ó Mórdha, Séamus P., 'Hugh O'Reilly (1581?–1653), a reforming primate', *Breifne*, 4, no. 13 (1970), pp. 345–69

'Heber MacMahon, soldier bishop of the confederation of Kilkenny', in Joseph Duffy (ed.), *Clogher record album. A diocesan history* (Monaghan, 1975), pp. 41–62

O Riordan, Michelle, *The Gaelic mind and the collapse of the Gaelic world* (Cork, 1990)

O'Riordan, S., 'Rinuccini in Galway 1647–1649', *Jornal of the Galway Archaeological and Historical Society*, 23, nos. 1 and 2 (1948), pp. 19–51

O'Sullivan, H. C., 'The Trevors of Rosetrevor: a British colonial family in the seventeenth century' (unpublished M Litt thesis, Trinity College, Dublin, 1985)

Ohlmeyer, Jane H., '"The Dunkirk of Ireland": Wexford privateers during the 1640s', *Journal of the Wexford Historical Society*, 12 (1988–9), pp. 23–49

'Irish privateers during the civil war, 1642–50', *The Mariner's Mirror*, 76, no. 2 (May 1990), pp. 119–33

'A seventeenth century survivor: the political career of Randal MacDonnell, first marquis and second earl of Antrim (1609–83)' (PhD thesis, Trinity College, Dublin, 1990)

'The "Antrim plot" of 1641 – a myth?', *Historical Journal* (1993, forthcoming)

Orme, R. A., 'Youghal, County Cork – growth, decay, resurgence', *Irish Geography*, 5 (1966), pp. 121–49

Parker, Geoffrey, *The Army of Flanders and the Spanish Road 1567–1659. The logistics of Spanish victory and defeat in the Low Countries' wars* (Cambridge, 1972; 3rd edn, 1990)

The Thirty Years' War (London, 1984)

The Military Revolution. Military innovation and the rise of the west, 1500–1800 (Cambridge, 1988; 2nd edn, 1989)

Parry, Graham, *Hollar's England – a mid-seventeenth century view* (Salisbury, 1980)

Pegge, Samuel, *Curialia or an historical account of some branches of the royal household* (5 parts, London, 1791–1806)

Curialia miscellanea; or anecdotes of old times (London, 1818)

Pender, Séamus (ed.), *Essays and studies presented to Prof. Tadhg Ua Donnchadha* (Cork, 1947)

Pennington, Donald, 'The war and the people', in John S. Morrill (ed.), *Reactions to the English civil war 1642–1649* (London, 1982), pp. 115–22

Perceval-Maxwell, Michael, *Scottish migration to Ulster in the reign of James I* (London, 1973)

'Strafford, the Ulster Scots and the covenanters', *IHS*, 18, no. 72 (Sept. 1973), pp. 524–51

'The Ulster Rising of 1641, and the depositions', *IHS*, 21, no. 82 (Sept. 1978), pp. 144–67

'Protestant faction, the impeachment of Strafford and the origins of the Irish civil war', *Canadian Journal of History*, 17 (1982), pp. 235–55

'Charles I and the Irish conspiracy in 1641', (unpublished paper presented at a conference in Urbana-Champaign, April 1990)

'Ireland and Scotland 1638–1648', in John S. Morrill (ed.), *Scottish national covenant in its British context 1638–51* (Edinburgh, 1990), pp. 193–211
'Ireland and the monarchy in the early Stuart multiple kingdom', *Historical Journal*, 34, no. 2 (1991), pp. 279–95
Perry, Nicholas, 'The infantry of the confederate Leinster army 1642–47', *Ir. Sword*, 15, no. 61 (Winter 1983), pp. 231–41
Petrie, Sir Charles, 'Ireland in Spanish and French strategy 1558–1815', *Ir. Sword*, 6, no. 24 (Summer 1964), pp. 154–65
Phillips, C. B., 'The royalist composition papers and the landed income of the gentry: a note of warning from Cumbria', *Northern History*, 13 (1977), pp. 161–74
'The royalist north: the Cumberland and Westmorland gentry, 1642–1660', *Northern History*, 14 (1978), pp. 169–92
Pinkerton, William, 'Saint Patrick's purgatory, part IV', *UJA*, 1st series, 5 (1857), pp. 61–81
'Proceedings of the Scottish and English forces in the north of Ireland, A.D. 1642', *UJA*, 1st series, 8 (1860), pp. 77–87
'Unpublished poems relating to Ulster in 1642–43', *UJA*, 1st series, 8 (1860), pp. 153–71
Pocock, J. G. A., 'British history: a plea for a new subject', *Journal of Modern History*, 47, no. 4 (Dec. 1975), pp. 601–28
'The limits and divisions of British history: in search of an unknown subject', *American Historical Review*, 87, no. 2 (Apr. 1982), pp. 311–36
Powell, J. R., *The navy in the English civil war* (London 1962)
Power, P., 'A Waterford tomb and its Ulster tenant', *UJA*, 1st series, 2, no. 1 (Oct. 1895), pp. 42–6
Prendergast, J. P., 'Records of the Kilkenny confederate assembly, AD 1642–1650', *RSAI Jn.*, 1 (1849–51), pp. 420–7
The Cromwellian settlement of Ireland (revised edn, London, 1870; 3rd edn, Dublin, 1922)
'The Butlers, Lords Ikerrin, before the court of transplantation at Athlone, AD 1656 ... ', *Butler Society Journal*, 3 (1987), pp. 72–6
Quinn, D. B., 'Ireland and sixteenth century European expansion', in T. Desmond Williams (ed.), *Historical Studies*, (London, 1958), pp. 20–32
Ramsey, Robert W., *Henry Cromwell* (London, 1933)
Henry Ireton (London, 1949)
Ranger, Terence, 'Richard Boyle and the making of an Irish fortune, 1588–1614', *IHS*, 10, no. 39 (Mar. 1957), pp. 257–97
'Strafford: a revaluation', in T. Aston (ed.), *Crisis in Europe 1560–1660. Essays from 'Past and Present'* (London, 1965), pp. 271–93
Reeve, L. J., *Charles I and the road to personal rule* (Cambridge, 1989)
Reid, J. S., *History of the presbyterian church in Ireland*, ed. W. D. Killen (3 vols., Belfast, 1867)
Reid, Stuart, *The campaign of Montrose. A military history of the civil war in Scotland 1639 to 1646* (Edinburgh, 1990)
Robinson, Gregory, 'The seventeenth century frigate', *The Mariner's Mirror*, 15, no. 3 (1929), pp. 271–81
Robinson, Philip S., 'Vernacular housing in Ulster in the seventeenth century', *Ulster Folklife*, 35 (1979), pp. 1–28

The plantation of Ulster. British settlement in an Irish landscape, 1600–1670 (Dublin, 1984)
Roebuck, Peter, 'The Constables of Everingham. The fortunes of a catholic royalist family during the civil war and interregnum', *Recusant History*, 9 (1967), pp. 35–88
'The making of an Ulster great estate: the Chichesters, barons of Belfast and viscounts of Carrickfergus, 1599–1648', *RIA Proc.*, section C, 72 (1979), pp. 1–25
'The economic situation and functions of substantial landowners 1600–1815: Ulster and lowland Scotland compared', in Rosalind Mitchison and Peter Roebuck (eds.), *Economy and society in Scotland and Ireland, 1500–1939* (Edinburgh, 1988), pp. 81–92
Roebuck, Peter (ed.), *Plantation to partition. Essays in Ulster history in honour of J. L. McCracken* (Belfast, 1981)
Roots, Ivan (ed.), *'Into another mould'. Aspects of the Interregnum* (London, 1981)
Roy, Ian, 'The libraries of Edward, second Viscount Conway and others: an inventory and valuation of 1643', *BIHR*, 41, no. 103 (May 1968), pp. 35–46
'England turned Germany? The aftermath of the civil war in its European context', *R. Hist. Soc. Trans.*, 5th series, 28 (1978), pp. 122–42
'Les puissances européenes et la chute de Charles I', *Revue d'Histoire Diplomatique*, 92 (1978), pp. 92–109
Rubinstein, Hilary, L., *Captain luckless. The life of James first duke of Hamilton* (Edinburgh, 1975)
Russell, C. W., and Prendergast, J. P., *Account of the Carte collection of historical papers* (London, 1871)
Russell, Conrad, 'The theory of treason in the trial of Strafford', *EHR*, 80, no. 314 (Jan. 1965), pp. 30–50
'Why did Charles I call the Long Parliament?', *History*, 69 (1984), pp. 375–83
'The British problem and the English civil war', *History*, 72, no. 236 (1987), pp. 395–415
'The British background to the Irish rebellion of 1641', *Historical Research*, 61, no. 145 (June 1988), pp. 166–82
'The first army plot of 1641', *R. Hist. Soc. Trans.*, 5th series, 37 (1988), pp. 85–106
The causes of the English Civil War (Oxford, 1990)
Unrevolutionary England, 1603–42 (London, 1990)
The fall of the British monarchies 1637–1642 (Oxford, 1991)
'The Scottish party in English parliaments 1640–1642 or the myth of the English revolution' (Inaugural lecture, Department of History, King's College, London, 1991)
Ryan, Conor, 'Religion and state in seventeenth century Ireland, *Archiv. Hib.*, 33 (1975), pp. 122–32
Sampson, George Vaughan, *Statistical survey of County Londonderry* (Dublin, 1802)
Savage-Armstrong, G. F. (ed.), *The ancient and noble family of the Savages of the Ards. With sketches of English and American branches of the house of Savage compiled from historical documents and family papers* (London, 1888)
A genealogical history of the Savage family in Ulster. Being a revision and enlargment of certain chapters of 'The Savages of the Ards' compiled by members of the family from historical documents and family papers (London, 1906)
Schlegel, Donald, M., 'The MacDonnells of Tyrone and Armagh. A genealogical study', *Seanchas Ardmhacha*, 10, no. 1 (1980–1), pp. 193–219

Senior, Clive, *A nation of pirates. English piracy in its heyday* (Newton Abbot, 1976)
Sharpe, Kevin, *Criticism and compliment. The politics of literature in the England of Charles I* (Cambridge, 1987)
Shaw, Frances J., 'Land ownership in the Western Isles in the seventeenth century', *SHR*, 56, no. 161 (Apr. 1977), pp. 34–48
  The Northern and Western Isles of Scotland (Edinburgh, 1980)
Sheppard, Edgar, *The old royal palace of Whitehall* (London, 1902)
Silke, John J., 'Spanish intervention in Ireland 1601–2', *Studia Hib.*, 3 (1963), pp. 179–90
  Ireland and Europe, 1559–1607 (Dundalk, 1966)
Simington, R. C., 'A "census" of Ireland c. 1659', *Anal. Hib.*, 12 (1943), pp. 177–8
Sims, J. G., *The Williamite confiscation in Ireland 1690–1703* (London, 1956)
  'Seventeenth century Ireland (1603–1702)', *IHS*, 15, no. 60 (Sept. 1967), pp. 366–76
  Jacobite Ireland 1685–1691 (London, 1969)
Skinner, Quentin, 'Conquest and consent: Thomas Hobbes and the engagement controversy', in G. E. Aylmer (ed.), *The Interregnum. The quest for settlement 1646–1660* (London, 1970), pp. 79–98
Smith, David L., 'The impact on government', in John S. Morrill (ed.), *The impact of the English civil war* (London, 1991), chapter 2
Smith, Lesley M., 'Scotland and Cromwell: a study in early modern government' (unpublished DPhil thesis, University of Oxford, 1979)
Smuts, Malcolm, *Court culture and the origins of a royalist tradition in early Stuart England* (Philadelphia, 1987)
Smyth, William J., 'Territorial, social and settlement hierarchies in seventeenth century Kilkenny' in William Nolan and Kevin Whelan (eds.), *Kilkenny: History and society. Interdisciplinary essays on the history of an Irish county* (Dublin, 1990), pp. 127–60
  'Society and settlement in seventeenth century Ireland: the evidence of the "1659 census"' in William J. Smyth and Kevin Whelan (eds.), *Common Ground. Essays on the historical geography of Ireland presented to T. Jones Hughes* (Cork, 1988), pp. 55–83
Smyth, William J., and Whelan, Kevin (eds.), *Common ground. Essays on the historical geography of Ireland presented to T. Jones Hughes* (Cork, 1988)
Sparks, May, 'Archbishop Rinuccini, papal nuncio', *Old Kilkenny Review, Journal of the Kilkenny Archaeological Society*, 7 (1954), pp. 35–9
Starkey, David (ed.), *The English court from the Wars of the Roses to the civil war* (London, 1987)
Stevenson, David, 'The financing of the cause of the covenants, 1638–51', *SHR*, 51, no. 152 (Oct. 1972), pp. 89–123
  The Scottish revolution, 1637–1644. The triumph of the covenanters (Newton Abbot, 1973)
  'The massacre at Dunaverty, 1647', *Scottish Studies*, 19 (1975), pp. 27–37
  Revolution and counter-revolution in Scotland 1644–1651 (London, 1977)
  'The desertion of the Irish by Coll Keitach's sons, 1642', *IHS*, 21, no. 81 (Mar. 1978), pp. 75–84
  'The Irish Franciscan mission to Scotland and the Irish rebellion of 1641', *Innes Review*, 30 (1979), pp. 54–61
  Alasdair MacColla and the Highland problem in the seventeenth century (Edinburgh, 1980)

Scottish Covenanters and Irish Confederates: Scottish–Irish relations in the mid-seventeenth century (Belfast, 1981)
'The century of the Three Kingdoms', *History Today*, 35, no. 3 (Mar. 1985), pp. 28–33
The covenanters. The national covenant and Scotland (The Saltire Society, Edinburgh, 1988)
'Cromwell, Scotland and Ireland', in John S. Morrill (ed.), *Oliver Cromwell and the English revolution* (London, 1990), chapter 6
Stevenson, David and Wendy (ed.), *Scottish texts and calendars. An analytical guide to serial publications* (Royal Historical Society. Guides and Handbooks, XIV; Scottish History Society, 4th series, vol. XXIII, Edinburgh, 1987)
Stewart, J. A., 'Peoples of the Clan Ranald: a traditional Gaelic kindred in decline 1644–1851' (unpublished PhD thesis, University of Edinburgh, 1982)
Stone, Lawrence, *The crisis of the aristocracy 1558–1641* (Oxford, 1965)
Family and fortune. Studies in aristocratic finance in the sixteenth and seventeenth centuries (Oxford, 1973)
The family, sex and marriage in England 1500–1800 (London, 1977)
Stradling, Robert, 'The Spanish dunkirkers, 1621–48: a record of plunder and destruction', *Tijdschrift voor geschiedenis*, 93 (1980), pp. 541–58
The armada of Flanders: Spanish maritime policy and the European war 1568–1668 (Cambridge, 1992)
Sumner, A. B., 'The political career of Lord George Digby until the end of the first civil war' (unpublished PhD thesis, University of Cambridge, 1985)
Swords, Liam (ed.), *The Irish French connection, 1578–1978* (Paris, 1978)
Talon, Geraldine, 'Books of survey and distribution, County Westmeath: a comparative survey, with reference to their administrative context and chronological sequence', *Anal. Hib.*, 28 (1978), pp. 105–15
Thomas, D. H., and Case, L. M., *The new guide to the diplomatic archives of western Europe* (Pennsylvania, 1975)
Thornton, Peter, *Seventeenth century decoration in England, France and Holland* (Yale, 1978)
Thompson, R. S., *The Atlantic archipelago. A political history of the British Isles* (New York, 1986)
Townsend, Dorothea, *George Digby, second earl of Bristol* (London, 1924)
Tranter, Nigel, *The Queen's Scotland. Argyll and Bute* (London, 1977)
Trevor-Roper, Hugh, 'The invention of tradition: the Highland tradition of Scotland', in E. Hobsbawn and T. Ranger (eds.), *The invention of tradition* (Cambridge, 1983), pp. 15–41
Archbishop Laud 1573–1645 (London, 1940; 3rd edn, London, 1988)
Catholics, anglicans and puritans. Seventeenth century essays (Chicago, 1988)
Turner, Edward Raymond, *The privy council of England in the seventeenth and eighteenth centuries 1603–1784* (2 vols., Baltimore, 1927–8)
The cabinet council of England in the seventeenth and eighteenth centuries 1622–1784 (2 vols., Baltimore, 1930–2)
Ulster dialects: an introductory symposium (Cultra, 1984)
Underdown, David, *Pride's purge. Politics in the puritan revolution* (London, 1971; reprint, 1985)
Victoria history of the counties of England, ed. W. Page, H. A. Doubleday, and others (Westminster, 1900–)

Walsh, Micheline, *The MacDonnells of Antrim on the continent* (O'Donnell lecture, Dublin, 1960)
'O'Neills in exile', *Seanchas Ardmhacha*, 8, no. 1 (1976–7), pp. 55–68
'Don Enrique Reynaldo MacDonnell, admiral of the Spanish navy 1753–1823', *The Glynns*, 2 (1983), pp. 47–58
'Destruction by peace'. Hugh O'Neill after Kinsale (Monaghan, 1986)
Walsh, P., 'Scots Clan Domhnaill in Ireland', *Irish Ecclesiastical Record*, 5th series, 48 (1936) pp. 23–42
Watson, W. J., 'The MacDonald bardic poetry', *Transactions of the Gaelic Society of Inverness*, 36 (1931–3), pp. 138–58
Weaver, Jack W. (ed.), *Selected proceedings of the Scotch–Irish heritage festival, II, at Winthrop College* (Baton Rouge, 1984)
Webb, A., *A compendium of Irish bibliography* (New York, 1970)
Webb, M., 'The clan of the MacQuillins of Antrim', *UJA*, 1st series, 8 (1860), pp. 251–68
Wedgwood, C. V., *Thomas Wentworth, first earl of Strafford 1593–1641. A revaluation* (London, 1935; revised edn, 1962)
The king's peace 1637–1641. The great rebellion (London, 1955)
Whelan, Kevin (ed.), *Wexford: history and society. Interdisciplinary essays on the history of an Irish county* (Dublin, 1987)
Whyte, I. D., *Agriculture and society in seventeenth century Scotland* (Edinburgh, 1979)
Whyte, I. D., and Whyte, K. A., 'Some aspects of the structure of rural society in seventeenth century lowland Scotland', in T. M. Devine and David Dickson (eds.), *Ireland and Scotland 1600–1850. Parallels and contrasts in economic and social development* (Edinburgh, 1983), pp. 32–45
Willcock, John, *The great marquess. The life and times of Argyll* (Edinburgh and London, 1903)
Williams, Ronald, *The lords of the Isles. The Clan Donald and the early kingdom of the Scots* (London, 1984)
Woolrych, Austin, *Soldiers and statesmen. The general council of the army and its debates 1647–8* (Oxford, 1987)
Wormald, Jenny (ed.), *Scotland revisited* (London, 1991)

INDEX

The following abbreviations are used:
abp	archbishop
bp	bishop
Co.	County
d.	died
LJ	lord justice
LL	lord lieutenant
LD	lord deputy
n	note
OFM	Franciscan
RC	Roman Catholic

Abercorn, earl of, *see* Hamilton, James
Aberdeen, 82, 142
Aberdeen, battle of (1644), 14, 146, 150
Aboyne, Lord, *see* Gordon, James
act of explanation (1665), 163n, 261, 265, 266, 268, 284
act of satisfaction (1653), 250
act of settlement (1662), 261, 262, 263
Adby, Humphrey, 251
adventurers act (1642), 241
Agnew, family, 40
Airlie, earl of, *see* Ogilvie, James
Albemarle, duke of, *see* Monck, George
Alford, battle of (1645), 14, 146, 160
Ancram, earl of, *see* Ker, Robert
Anglesey, earl of, *see* Annesley, Arthur
Anglo-Dutch wars, 256, 273
Anglo-Irish, *see* Old English
Anglo-Irish relations, 127
Annesley, Arthur (d. 1686), earl of Anglesey, 257, 264, 272, 275
Annesley, Elizabeth, 272, 275
Antrim, earls of, *see* MacDonnell, Alexander and Randal
Antrim, county, 7, 23–4, 33, 36, 38, 42, 52, 60, 66, 104, 105, 108, 109n, 111, 113, 114, 116, 138, 168, 176, 184, 233, 242, 246, 247n, 250, 258, 275, 276, 278n, 286, 292
'Antrim plot' (1641), *see under* Butler, James; Charles I; MacDonnell, Randal, marquis of Antrim
Antwerp, Spanish Netherlands, 180n
Aphorismical discovery, 111, 161, 173, 219, 285, 291n

Archer, Patrick, 143
Ardnamurchan, Scotland, 89, 145
Argyll, earls of, *see* Campbell, Archibald
Arklow, Co. Wicklow, 215, 216
Armagh, city, 114
armed forces of Dublin government, 289; 'new army', 94, 95, 97, 101, 237, 260–1
armed forces of English government, 102; *see also under* parliament
armed forces of Irish, *see* Gaelic society
Arran, island of, 85
Arundel, earls of, *see* Howard, family
Arundell, Henry, third Lord Arundell of Wardour, 288
Ascham, Anthony, 254
Athlone, Co. Westmeath, 192, 284
Athy, Queen's Co., 105
Auldearn, battle of (1645), 14, 146
Aylmer, Sir Andrew, 193

Babington, family, 86n
Babington, Uriah, 275
Bagwell, Richard, 3
Baillie, Dr Robert, 146, 176
Ballintoy, Co. Antrim, 108, 111, 113
Ballycastle, Co. Antrim, 25, 32, 33, 37, 65, 108, 109, 113, 250, 277
Ballygally, Co. Antrim, 25
Ballyhack, Co. Wexford, 144, 145
Ballymagarry, Co. Antrim, 250n, 273
Ballymoney, Co. Antrim, 250n, 273
Bann, River, 33, 41, 57, 108, 113
Barberini, Cardinal Antonio, 292
Barrington, Captain, 243n

Barry, John, 2n, 98
Basse, Edward, 252
Baxter, Richard, 259n
Beaumaris, Wales, 73
Belfast, Co. Antrim, 25, 110, 250, 253, 273
Belfast, barony, 246
Bellingham, Sir Daniel, 275
Bellings, Sir Richard (d. 1677), 141, 149, 165, 180, 182, 202, 227, 291; and Antrim, 2, 128–9, 141
Benburb, battle of (1646), 181, 199, 233
Bennet, Henry (d. 1685), earl of Arlington, 270–1
Berehaven, count of, *see* O'Sullivan Beare, Dermot
Beresford, Tristram, 263–4
Berwick-on-Tweed, England, 89, 92, 93; 210; treaty of (1639), 90, 93, 94
Beverly, Sir Thomas, land commissioner, 263n
Bichi, Cardinal, 154n, 155
Bishops' Wars, 13, 16, 239; first (1639), 77–94; second (1640), 94–5; *see also under* Charles I; covenanters; Hamilton, James; MacDonnell, Randal, marquis of Antrim; Wentworth, Thomas
Bisset, family, 18
Blake, Sir Richard, 218
Blount, Anne, Lady Newport, 54
Blount, Mountjoy, earl of Newport, 238
Bonamargy friary, Co. Antrim, 27, 47, 75, 277
Bond, Denis, 221, 244n
books of survey and distribution, 242n
Borlase, Sir John, 109n
Bottigheimer, Karl, 287
Bourke, Thomas, 96–7, 260
Boyd, family, 247
Boyd, James, 184, 185
Boyd, Robert, 275n
Boyd, Thomas of Ballyhuderland, 254
Boyd, Thomas of Lisrahan, 254
Boyle, Michael, bp of Cork, 236, 237, 259
Boyle, Richard (d. 1643), first earl of Cork, 4, 5, 74
Boyle, Richard (d. 1697), second earl of Cork, 274
Boyle, Roger (d. 1679), Lord Broghill, earl of Orrery, 255, 259, 270–1, 286
Boyle, Co. Roscommon, 116
Bradbourne, Humphrey, 252
Bramhall, John, bp of Derry, 57
Bramshill, Hampshire, 60–1, 62, 64, 65, 75, 76
Brereton, Sir William, 7
Brienne, count of, 144n, 207n, 208

Bristol, England, 132
Broderick, Sir Allen, land commissioner, 263n
Broghill, Lord, *see* Boyle, Roger
Brown (Browne), Geoffrey, 202, 203, 204n, 205, 206, 208
Brownlow, Sir William, 67, 111
Bruce, Sir Henry, 84n, 88n
Brussels, Spanish Netherlands, 77, 154n, 155, 156, 157, 158, 162, 179, 199, 200, 215n, 291, 292
Buckingham, duchess of, *see* Manners, Katherine
Buckingham, dukes of, *see* Villiers, George
Buithill, Randall, 275n
Bunratty, Co. Clare, 170
Burke, Anne, Lady Clanricard and countess of St Albans, 266n, 285
Burke, Honora, 29
Burke, Richard (d. 1635), fourth earl of Clanricard, 25, 29
Burke, Theobald, Viscount Mayo, 249
Burke, Ulick (d. 1657), fifth earl and first marquis of Clanricard, 1, 46, 53, 97n, 134, 135, 136, 137, 139, 153n, 165, 183, 184, 186, 190, 207, 239–40, 284–5, 288, 289, 291
Burke, Sir William, 46
Butler, Edward, Viscount Galmoy, 240, 272, 284
Butler, Elizabeth, countess of Ormond, 285
Butler, James (d. 1688), twelfth earl and first duke of Ormond, LL (1643–9 and 1662–9), 2, 53, 71n, 74, 105, 110n, 116n, 129n, 169, 170, 182, 183, 202, 205, 211, 213, 216, 219, 239, 257, 260, 261, 268, 272, 290n, 291
and Antrim: 'Antrim plot', 96, 97, 98, 99n; relationship with, 131, 132, 150, 152, 167, 184, 188, 192, 193, 206, 213, 216, 217, 218, 222, 226, 227, 229, 231–2, 233, 262, 269, 272, 279, 283; undermined by, 211, 213, 215, 216, 217, 219, 227, 233–4, 236, 258, 279, 283
assets and debts, 274, 276
defeat and exile (1649–60), 230, 239, 255, 285
and England: aid for royalist war-effort in, 153, 160
estates, 36, 281, 285
in Ireland: leader of Irish royalists, 119, 120, 127, 155, 191n, 199, 203, 206, 219, 221, 234, 285; influence in, 132, 281–2; 'Ormondists' in the confederation, 141, 150, 164, 165, 190,

Butler, James (cont.)
  in Ireland (cont.)
    198, 201, 202, 205, 208, 211, 214, 219, 225n; relationship with Irish confederates, 149, 151, 164, 166; restoration settlement, 261–2, 263n, 265–6, 269, 272, 284, 286; revival of the royalist war-effort in (1648–9), 207, 209, 210, 213, 214, 217–18, 219, 223, 228, 234; surrender of Dublin (1647), 191n, 192–3, 198
  military entrepreneur, 281–2
  Ormond peace (1646), 181–2, 183, 184, 188, 189, 193, 199, (1649), 214, 217, 219, 222, 223
  and Scotland: Scottish expedition (1644), 91, 132, 133, 140, 141, 142, 144, 148; aid for royalist war-effort in (1644–7), 152, 153, 169n, 172
  see also under Carte, Thomas; Irish royalists; Kilkenny, confederation of; MacDonnell, Randal, marquis of Antrim
Butler, Pierce, Viscount Ikerrin, 284
Butler, Richard (d. 1651), Viscount Mountgarret, 164, 182, 202, 211, 272
Butler, Richard of Kilcash, 143, 272
Byrne, see O'Byrne
Byron, John, Baron Byron (d. 1652), 228n

Campbell, family, 8, 12, 22–3, 43, 46, 51, 78, 90, 93, 110, 113, 173
Campbell, Archibald (d. 1638), seventh earl of Argyll, 22
Campbell, Archibald (d. 1661), Lord Lorne, eighth earl and first marquis of Argyll, 13, 22–3, 76, 114, 126, 139, 151, 178, 187, 273; and Bishops' Wars, 78, 79n, 80–1, 82, 83, 87, 88, 89, 90, 92, 93, 94; debts, 251, 273, 276; estates occupied by Antrim's brigade, 130, 145, 175, 176, 178, 246; forces occupy Antrim estates, 110, 113, 126, 136, 147, 151, 245–6; trial and execution, 260, 261, 273, 278; and war in Scotland (1645–7), 146, 153, 169, 175, 200
Campbell, Sir Duncan of Auchunbreck, 113
Campbell, James, Lord Kintyre, 22–3
Campbell, John, earl of Loudoun, 176
Campbell, Sir John of Calder, 22
Campbeltown, Scotland, 172
Canary Islands, 195
Canna, Scotland, 6
Canny, Nicholas, 4, 5, 283
Canterbury, abp of, see Laud, William
Cárdenas, Alonso de, Spanish ambassador in London, 220, 221n, 222, 224n, 225n, 226n, 253, 292

Carlingford, earl of, see Taaffe, Theobald
Carlingford, Co. Louth, 120, 133, 144, 153
Carlisle, England, 116, 159
Carlow, county, 191
Carlow, town, 116, 198, 230, 237
Carrickfergus (Knockfergus), Co. Antrim, 25, 82, 94, 101, 103, 108, 110, 115, 116, 121, 125, 128, 230, 250
Carrick-on-Suir, Co. Tipperary, 226
Carte, Thomas, 5n, 205, 290n; opinion of Antrim, 3n, 205
Cary, barony, 32, 33, 36, 38, 65, 108, 109n, 243, 244, 246, 251
Cashel, Co. Tipperary, 140, 198
Castel Rodrigo, marquis of, see Moura y Cortereal, Manuel de
Castile, Spain, 16, 67
Castlehaven, earl of, see Tuchet, James
Casway, Jerrold, 3
Catalonia, Spain, 16, 159
Catholic church, 107; bps, 150, 180, 183, 186; clergy, 165, 180, 181, 210, 235, 236, 255; counter-reformation, 283; see also under Kilkenny, confederation of; MacDonnell, Randal, marquis of Antrim; Rinuccini
Catholics, English, 235, 252, 273n, 278n, 287, 288
Catholics, Scottish, 78, 278n, 287, 288
Cavan, county, 218
Cavendish, William, marquis of Newcastle, 119, 130
Cecil, Sir Edward, Viscount Wimbledon, 66
'census' of 1659 (1660 poll tax returns), 247
'cess', see under taxation
'cessation of arms': 1643, 120, 127, 128, 133, 134, 135, 149, 199; 1644, 149; see also under Kilkenny, confederation of
Chapman, Francis (alias for Antrim), 208
Chapman, James, 276
Charlemount fort, Co. Armagh, 101, 111, 125, 188, 230
Charles I, king of England, Scotland and Ireland (d. 1649), 28, 31, 49–50, 51, 69, 73, 76, 112n, 115, 116, 117, 129, 148, 151, 153n, 158, 166, 199, 203, 219, 222, 252, 254, 259n, 262, 264, 289
  and Bishops' Wars: first (1639), 77–8, 79, 80–1, 82–3, 86–9, 90, 91, 92, 93n; second (1640), 94–5
  and British problem, 12, 13, 80, 98–9, 100–1, 119, 126
  imprisonment, trial and execution (1648), 202, 212, 222, 223, 278, 286
  Irish policy, 59–60, 71–2, 119–20

and Irish rebellion, 101–2, 259, 260–1
and negotiations with Irish confederates, 201–2, 208; 1643, 120, 127, 128, 133; 1644, 133, 134, 137, 149, 150; 1645, 153, 160, 163, 164, 165, 169; 1648, 207, 209–10, 213, 214
and negotiations with English parliament, 154, 177
plots with Antrim: 'Antrim plot' (1641), 96–9, 101, 102n, 125, 237, 258, 259, 260–1; 1642, 111, 125–6; 1643, 119, 123, 124, 125–6; 1644, 130–3, 134, 147, 148, 189, 273; 1645, 154; 1646–7, 176, 177–8, 184–5, 193
religious policy, 59–60, 207
royalist navy, 132, 167, 227
royalist war-effort, 127, 137, 146–7, 156, 157, 158, 159, 160, 161, 163, 165, 167, 169, 174, 176, 186, 201, 223, 283
surrenders to Scots (1646), 174, 176, 177
wife, *see* Henrietta Maria
see also under MacDonnell, Randal, marquis of Antrim; popish plots
Charles II, king of England, Scotland and Ireland (d. 1685), 226, 234, 261, 268, 269, 284, 289
Irish policy, 265, 267, 269, 284
and negotiations with Irish confederates (1648–9), 202, 203, 204, 207
prince of Wales, 163, 177, 184, 185, 206
relationship with Antrim, 239–40, 257, 262, 264, 265–6, 267, 269–70, 271, 272
Restoration, 257, 286; government of, 267, 270–1, 272
royal navy, 273n
royalist war-effort (1649–51), 229, 235, 239, 240, 255, 285
see also under Restoration
Chester, England, 73, 74n, 115n, 169, 238
Chichester, Arthur (d. 1675), first earl of Donegal, 64, 67, 70
Chichester, Sir Arthur (d. 1625), 21, 24
Church of Ireland, 69
Churchill, Sir Winston (d. 1668), land commissioner, 263n, 266n
civil survey, 33, 242
Clancarty, earl of, *see* MacCarthy, Donough
Clandeboy, 138
Clan Donald, *see* MacDonalds
Clan Ian Mor (Clan Donald South), *see* MacDonalds
Clanricard, earl and marquis of, *see* Burke, Richard and Ulick
Clare, county, 191, 250, 284
Clarendon, earl of, *see* Hyde, Edward

Clarke, Aidan, 86, 100, 117
Claypoole, Captain, 243n
clerical party, *see under* native Irish
Clogher, bp of, *see* MacMahon, Heber
Clonmel, Co. Waterford, 110, 169, 230, 233
Clotworthy, Sir John, Lord Massareene (d. 1665), 59, 78, 111, 112, 113, 286; adventurer, 242, 243, 244, 246; opposition to Antrim's restoration, 261, 264
Clough, Co. Antrim, 113
Coleraine, Co. Londonderry, 24, 56, 57, 95, 130, 134n, 152n, 242n, 243; Long Liberties of, 33, 56, 59n, 70, 73, 243, 247, 263, 275; town of, 33, 57, 73, 81, 101, 108, 111, 113, 115
Colonsay, Scotland, 93
collaborators, 233–4, 237, 238, 240, 249, 256n, 257, 272, 282–8; *see also under* MacDonnell, Randal, marquis of Antrim; patriotism
Colvill, Alexander, 254
Colvill, Sir Robert, 254, 275
Comerford, Patrick, 143
commission for defective titles, 54, 70
commissioners of trust, 223
Commonwealth and Protectorate, 115n, 234, 239, 240, 241, 242, 246, 252, 254, 268n, 284, 286
communications, 6–7, 33, 36, 86, 98, 205, 214, 225, 256–7, 280, 288–9
compounding, 224, 225, 237, 238, 241, 248, 291
Con, George, 54
confederation of Kilkenny, *see* Kilkenny, confederation of
Connaught, 248, 250; transplantation to, 247, 250
Constant, John, 194
Conway, Edward (d. 1631), Viscount Conway, 65n
Conway, Edward (d. 1683), Viscount Conway, 50, 67, 69, 112, 114, 116n, 253, 254
Cooper, Edmund, 66
Coote, Sir Charles (d. 1642), 79n, 67, 105
Coote, Sir Charles (d. 1661), earl of Mountrath, 188
Corish, Patrick, 204
Cork, bp of, *see* Boyle, Michael
Cork, earl of, *see* Boyle, Roger
Cork, city, 110, 191n, 214
Cork, county, 116, 170
Cornwall, 163
Corsellis, Abraham, 252
council of state (English), 221, 222, 224,

council of state (English) (*cont.*) 232, 238, 240, 242, 246, 248, 252, 253, 254

court of claims, 261, 262, 263, 264, 265, 267, 269, 272, 289; commissioners of the, 261, 262, 263, 265, 266, 267, 269, 289

court of wards, 54, 55n, 65n, 68, 70, 71, 72, 91

covenanters, Scottish, 13, 14, 77, 152, 289; aid to English parliament, 116, 124, 128, 147; and Bishops' Wars, 78, 79, 80, 81, 82, 88, 89, 90, 94, 95; and War of the Three Kingdoms, 119, 121, 123, 127, 128, 129, 130, 142, 146, 154, 175, 178, 187, 199, 230

covenants: national, 77, 78, 100; Solemn League and, 14, 123, 130, 145, 207

Crawford, earl of, *see* Lindsay, Ludovic

Crelly, Patrick (alias Mr Haley), Cistercian abbot of Newry, 191–2; negotiations with English parliament, 204–9, 212–14, 220–1, 223–5, 226n, 228–9, 232, 234–5, 253

Cromwell, Henry (d. 1674), LD (1657), LL (1658), 249, 251, 252, 254, 255, 287, 291

Cromwell, Oliver (d. 1658), LL (1649–53), 191, 225, 235, 236, 237, 239, 253, 255, 256, 257, 261, 284–8, 289; campaigns in Ireland, 229, 230–3, 238, 246; civil administration in Ireland, 241, 247, 248, 256, in Scotland, 256; religious views, 235, 287; *see also* Cromwellian land settlement

Cromwell, Richard, 257

Cromwell, Thomas, Viscount Lecale, 67

Cromwellian land settlement, 241–8, 261; adventurers and soldiers, 241, 242, 243, 244, 245, 251; continuity of landholding, 246–8; *see also* restoration land settlement

Crosby, Sir Piers, 3, 84, 137, 182, 281

Cunningham, Sir David, 252

Cunningham, Hugh, 114

Cushendall, Co. Antrim, 33

customs, *see under* taxation

Dalby, Matthew, 66

Dalmahoy, Mr (alias for Antrim), 257

Daniel, Colonel Patrick, 157

Darcy, Oliver, bp of Dromore (d. 1662), 191, 226

Darcy, Patrick (d. 1668), 36, 55, 66, 165, 202

Davies, Sir John, 6

Dawson, Henry, 252

debentures, 243, 263

debt, 25, 55, 67, 251, 268, 273, 276; *see also under* MacDonnell, Randal, marquis of Antrim

Delvin, Lord, *see* Nugent, Christopher

Denbigh, countess of, *see* Feilding, Susan

Denbigh, earl of, *see* Feilding, Basil

Denmark, 209

depositions, 108

Dering, Sir Edward, land commissioner, 262

Derry (Londonderry), 24, 57, 60, 101, 110, 116, 130, 134n, 137, 138, 139, 188n, 195, 243; bp of, *see* Bramhall, John

Desmond, earls of, *see* FitzGerald

Devereux, Robert (d. 1646), third earl of Essex, 285

Digby, George (d. 1677), Lord Digby, second earl of Bristol, 131, 132, 136, 141, 170, 207, 213

Digby, Sir Kenelm (d. 1665), 164, 288

Digby, Captain Thomas, 98, 106, 260

Dillon, James, 185

Dillon, Sir James, 137

Dillon, lord of Athlone, 84, 120, 137

Dillon, Sir Lucas, 182, 202

Dillon, Luke (d. 1629), viscount of Costelloe-Gallen, 46

Dillon, Thomas, viscount of Costelloe-Gallen, 259n

Dixon, Thomas, 114

Dobbs, Richard, 276

Donald, Peter, 12

Donegal, county, 25, 237

doubling ordinance (1642), 241

Douglas, family, 78

Down, county, 55, 57n, 81n, 114, 116, 121, 133, 188, 233, 246, 286

Down and Connor, bp of, *see* Magennis, Bonaventure

Drogheda, Co. Louth, 84, 230

Dromore, bp of, *see* Darcy, Oliver

Duart, James, 66, 252

Dublin, Ireland, 6, 14, 62, 67, 74n, 86, 87, 88, 90, 91, 94, 96, 97, 102, 103, 104, 105, 106, 110, 111, 115, 116, 122, 123, 124, 128, 133, 144, 149, 151, 152, 153, 182, 188, 191n, 192, 198, 199, 207, 211, 217, 218, 227, 230, 238, 240, 241, 248, 259, 260, 261, 264, 266, 267, 268, 272, 289, 291

Dublin, county, 73

Dublin castle, 101, 102, 103, 265

Dumbarton, Scotland, 82, 88, 94, 95

Dumfries, family, 78

Dumolin, Monsieur, French agent in Ireland, 170, 179, 182, 292; interferes with levies for Spain, 171–2, 186n

Dunbar, battle of (1650), 239

Duncannon, Co. Wexford, 191
Dundrum, Co. Down, 188
Dungan (Dongan), Lord, 272
Dungannon, Co. Tyrone, 116
Dungan's Hill, battle of (1647), 198, 201
Dunkirk, Spanish Netherlands, 16, 157, 158, 160n, 161, 162, 163, 171, 230
Dunkirk frigates, 143, 145, 162, 280–1; *see also under* MacDonnell, Randal, marquis of Antrim; privateering
Dunlop, family, 247
Dunlop, Hugh, 275n
Dunluce, barony, 25, 32, 33, 36, 37, 38, 39, 108, 113, 242, 244, 246
Dunluce, Co. Antrim, 14, 95, 106, 112, 113, 244, 250, 275, 276
Dunluce castle, 12n, 19, 25, 32, 52, 62, 73, 74–5, 96n, 98, 106, 108, 115, 273
Dunluce town, 25, 108, 263, 264
Dunsany, lord, *see* Plunkett
Dutch Republic, 138, 187, 195, 196n, 209, 281; Irish agent in, 280, 281

Eden, Co. Antrim, 250
Edenduffcarrick (Shane's castle), Co. Antrim, 250n
Edgehill, battle of (1642), 116
Edinburgh, Scotland, 14, 77, 78, 79, 95, 99n, 107, 122, 125, 146, 153, 179, 185, 187, 260, 292
Elizabeth I, queen of England and Ireland (d. 1603), 282
'engagement' (1647), 207
Elliott, John, 289
English attitudes towards the Irish, 24, 59–60, 248, 287, 293; *see also under* parliament
English Civil Wars: first (1642–7), 11, 14, 16, 100, 116, 147, 199, 207; second (1648), 210, 211, 212, 225; third (1650–1), 239–40
English royalists, 127, 129, 136, 176, 224, 234, 235, 255, 256, 288; in exile, 161, 205, 208, 209, 213, 219, 231, 253, 285
Enniscorthy, Co. Wexford, 186
Enniskillen, barons of, *see* Maguire
Enniskillen, Co. Fermanagh, 101, 116
Enos, Dr Walter, president of the Irish college at Louvain, 191, 216
Esmond, Sir Thomas, 215
Essex, earl of, *see* Devereux, Robert
Exeter, England, 151

Falmouth, England, 163

Farquharson, family, 177
Feilding, Basil, second earl of Denbigh, 220, 221
Feilding, Susan, countess of Denbigh, 50
Fennell, Dr Gerald, 141, 202, 231, 284
Fermanagh, county, 110, 284
Ferns, bp of, *see* French, Nicholas
Finch, Heneage, earl of Nottingham, 220
Firth, C. H., 290n
fisheries, 57, 70; *see also* Bann
FitzGerald, families: earls of Desmond, 43, 50, 53n, 66; earls of Kildare, 43, 53n, 74, 84
FitzGerald, Colonel Pierce, 215
FitzHarris, Nicholas, 186, 191
FitzPatrick, Andreas, 228
FitzPatrick, Brendan, 86, 101n
Fitzwilliam, Oliver, 185
Flanders, *see* Spanish Netherlands
Fleetwood, Charles (d. 1692), LD (1654), 243, 248, 251, 291
Fleming, Randal, twenty-first baron of Slane, 131
Fleming, William (d. 1641), nineteenth baron of Slane, 46, 71n, 99, 104
Foissotte, François, Spanish agent in Ireland, 154, 165, 179, 180, 291
Forth, Firth of, 88
Foyle, lough, 57
France, 16–17, 134, 135n, 154, 158, 159, 163, 181, 184, 189, 195, 196, 198, 203, 204, 205, 208, 209, 221, 222n, 226, 231, 253, 273, 279, 280, 281, 282, 285, 288; ambassadors and agents, 124, 125n, 179, 181, 185, 196, 203, 205, 211, 292, *see also* Dumolin, Monnerie, Montereul, Séneterre and Talon; and Antrim, offers to raise troops for, 28, 53, 185, visits (1625–7), 27–8, 53, (1645), 160–1, (1648), 203–4, 205, 208, 210; interest in Ireland, 197, 201, 202–3, 205, 207–8, 220, 222, 226n, 234; Irish soldiers serving in, 156, 280–2; military assistance of, to Ireland, 151, 201, 203n, 214, 215, to the English royalists, 207, 221, 222
Franciscan order, 47, 75, 94
Franklin, Captain Richard, 243
French, Nicholas (d. 1678), RC bp of Ferns, 180, 186, 205, 230
French, Oliver, confederate agent to Dutch Republic, 280, 281
Fronde, 208, 226n
Frost, Walter, 221n, 224n

Gaelic Irish, *see* native Irish
Gaelic society, 42, 69, 74–5, 83n, 96n, 128,

Gaelic society (*cont.*)
165, 283, 289; armed forces of, 83–5, 136, 227; inheritance, 19–21, 32; literature, 75, 292–3; social structure, 42, 83, 128, 255, 256: *see also* Kilkenny, confederation of; native Irish
Galland, Captain John, 243n, 247
Galloway, family, 78
Galloway, Scotland, 7
gallowglasses, 42–3
Galmoy, Viscount, *see* Butler, Edward
Galway, city, 110, 127, 137, 169, 191, 218, 230, 285
Galway, county, 137, 139, 250
Gardiner, S. R., 3, 10, 11, 234, 290n
Gee, Ralph, 96
Geoghegan, Anthony, 235
Germany, 16, 158, 159, 209, 281
Gilbert, Sir John, 3, 290n
Gillespie, Raymond, 100
Glamorgan, earl of, *see* Somerset, Edward
Glasgow, 175, 195
Glasse, John, 66
Glenarm, earl of (alias for MacDonnell, Randal, marquis of Antrim), 237, 251n
Glenarm, barony, 25, 32, 33, 36, 37, 38, 39, 40, 56, 109, 245, 246, 275
Glenarm, Co. Antrim, 6, 112, 113, 242, 243, 251
Glenarm castle, Co. Antrim, 25, 32
Glencairn's rising (1654), 255, 288
Glens, Co. Antrim, 18, 33, 113
Glynns, *see* Glens
Gordon, family, 46, 95
Gordon, George (d. 1649), second marquis of Huntly: and Bishops' Wars, 78, 83, 88; plots with Antrim, 119, 130, 177
Gordon, George, 46, 125, 142
Gordon, James (d. 1649), second Lord Aboyne, 119, 122n, 130
Gordon, Captain John, 138
Gordon, John, earl of Sutherland, 46, 125, 145
Gormanston, Viscount, *see* Preston, Nicholas
'graces', 96, 100
Graham, James (d. 1650), fifth earl and first marquis of Montrose, 3, 14, 19, 121, 173, 177, 179, 278; and royalist war-effort in Scotland, 1644–6, 130, 142, 146, 152, 154, 160, 163n, 166, 168, 169, 171, 178, 1646–8, 176, 183, 204, 209, 214
Grant, family, 177
Grant, Winter, *see* Leyburn, George
Greencastle, Co. Down, 120, 133
Gregor, family, 177
Grey, Henry, earl of Kent, 220
Grey, lord of Warke, 220
Grinder, Ralph, 252

Haley, Mr, *see* Crelly, Patrick
Hamburg, Germany, 179
Hamerton, William, 98, 260
Hamilton, family, 40, 46, 78
Hamilton, James (d. 1617), first earl of Abercorn, 26, 28
Hamilton, James (d. 1649), third marquis and first duke of Hamilton, 23n, 26, 27n, 51, 54, 97n, 104, 111n, 115, 124, 290, 291; and Bishops' Wars, 77, 78–9, 80, 82, 85, 88, 89, 94; and 'Londonderry business', 56–9, 60; relationship with Antrim, 62, 71, 80, 86, 90, 92, 167, 210, 278; and War of the Three Kingdoms, 119, 121, 210, 212
Harper, Robert, 66
Harriott, Alexander, 66
Heads of Proposals, 207
Hegarty, Father Patrick, OFM, superior of Bonamargy friary, 75, 94, 183
Henley, Robert, 76n
Henrietta Maria, queen of England (d. 1670), 28, 49–50, 69, 125, 135, 203, 288; alleged involvement in Irish rebellion, 102, 122; attempts to revive royalist war-effort (1648), 207; in exile, 158, 160, 161, 164, 184, 193, 194, 200, 202, 213, 226; negotiates with the Irish confederates, 204–6; relationship with Antrim, plots, 119, 120, 122, 123, 124, 135, 160, 163n, supports at Restoration, 262, 269–70, 271, 272
Herbert, Philip, earl of Pembroke, 31, 50, 220, 221
Herries, family, 78
Hibbard, Caroline, 27
Hill, Arthur, 54, 65n, 66, 112, 246, 252, 253, 286
Hill, George, MacDonnell family historian, 4, 61n, 116, 259
Hill, Sir Moses, 47, 54n
Hillman, Simon, 39
historiography: Antrim, 2–3; Irish rebellion, 100–1; three Stuart kingdoms, 10–12, 14–15, 279, 289
Holland, *see* Dutch Republic
Holles, Lord Denzil, 262, 270
Hore, P. H., 290n
House of Lords (Irish), 95, 96n, 104
Howard, family, earls of Arundel, 50
Howard, Henry, sixth duke of Norfolk, 273n, 288
Huntly, marquis of, *see* Gordon, George

Index

Hutton, Ronald, 11, 12, 269
Hyde, Edward (d. 1674), earl of Clarendon, 49, 62, 123, 139, 163, 172n, 257, 262, 269, 271, 289, 290n, 291; opinion of Antrim, 2, 163

Ikerrin, Viscount, *see* Butler, Pierce
Inchiquin, earl of, *see* O'Brien, Murrough
Independents, 207, 208, 209, 212, 220, 221, 234–5, 253; negotiations with Old Irish, 208n, 212, 213, 214, 221–2, 223, 228, 232
Innocent X, Pope (1644–55), 180, 202, 212, 235
'innocent papists', 250, 261, 262, 263, 265, 269
international relations, 14–17, 201; *see also under* Dutch Republic; France; Kilkenny, confederation of; Spain; Spanish Netherlands
Inverlochy, Scotland, 145, 153
Inverlochy, battle of (1644), 14, 146
Ireland, geography of, 6–8, 288–9; *see also under* communications; Ulster
Ireton, Henry (d. 1651), LD (1650), 225, 232, 236, 237, 238, 240, 248–9, 258, 260–1, 291
Irish rebellion (1641), 8, 13, 17, 96, 97n, 99, 100–1, 102, 104, 122, 123, 128, 134, 149, 178, 220, 224, 245, 258, 259, 260, 261, 280; *see also under* Charles I; MacDonnell, Randal, marquis of Antrim; 'O'More–Maguire' plot
Irish royalists, 116, 119, 124, 127, 128, 149, 181, 207, 219, 226, 233, 234; *see also under* Butler, James
Islay, Scotland, 85, 178
Isles, Lords of, 18
Israel, Jonathan, 289
Italy, 159, 220, 253
Iveagh, viscount, *see* Magennis, Arthur

James I and VI (d. 1625), king of Scotland, Ireland and England, 3n, 7, 21, 22, 26, 71–2; plantation of Ulster, 23–4, 59, 71
Jermyn, Henry, earl of St Albans, 207, 262, 270–1, 275
Jersey, 163
Jesuit order (Society of Jesus), 213n
Jigginstown House, Co. Kildare, 96n
Jones, Henry, bp of Clogher, 217, 256, 259, 260, 264
Jones, Colonel Michael (d. 1649), 198, 217, 218, 219, 230, 261

Jones, Sir Theophilus (d. 1685), 217
Jura, Scotland, 6, 8, 22–3, 93, 200

Kavanagh, family, 191, 215
Kavanagh, Charles, 215, 227
Kearney, Hugh, 4, 12n
Kennedy, family, 247
Kennedy, Walter, 66, 108n
Kent, earl of, *see* Grey, Henry
Keppoch, Scotland, 93, 119
Ker, Robert, earl of Ancram, 49n, 67
Kerr, Robert, earl of Lothian, 67
Kerry, county, 191, 281
Kettleby, Captain, 73
Kilconway, barony, 32, 33, 36, 38, 109, 243, 245, 246, 263, 275
Kildare, earls of, *see* FitzGerald
Kildare, county, 97, 104, 105n, 106, 111n, 275, 286
Kilkenny, city, 14, 110, 117, 125, 132, 133, 143, 148, 149, 150, 164, 169, 181, 182, 183, 184, 186, 189, 192, 194, 199, 201, 211, 218, 226, 230, 238, 240, 248, 281, 285
Kilkenny, county, 211, 248, 285
Kilkenny, confederation of, 117, 128, 137, 164, 189, 192, 290
  aid for royalist war-effort: in England, 132, 133; in Scotland (1644), 91, 129, 130, 132, 133, 137, 142, 147, 151, 153, (1645–7), 152, 153, 168–9, 172, 183–4, 185, 186, 187
  and Antrim: 2, 128–9, 140–1, 148, 151, 158, 170, 188–91, 214, 218, 258
  forces of: armies of, 114, 117, 127, 137, 139, 140, 147, 158, 181, 182, 184, 192, 230, 258, 287, Army of Leinster, 188, 192, 210, 214, 223, Army of Munster, 188, 198, 223, Army of Ulster, 141, 210, 211, 217, 218, 220, 233, 235, 237; navy of, 143, 158, 167, 191n, 227–8, 280–1
  ideas of: political, 117, 127, 149–50, 164, 165, 193, 205, 222–3; religious, 127, 136, 149, 150, 163–4, 165, 182, 190, 193, 201, 204, 206, 222–3
  negotiations with Charles I, Glamorgan, Henrietta Maria and Ormond: 1644, 136, 137, 149, 150, 192, 193, 199, 207–8; 1645–6, 163–5, 204, 288; 1647, 193–4; 1648, 205–6; cessation of arms (1643), 119, 120, 127, 128, 149, 258; Glamorgan treaty (1645), 164, 165, 177; Inchiquin Truce (1648), 210; Ormond peace treaty (1646), 134n, 150, 181–2, 183, 184, 193, 258;

Kilkenny, confederation of (*cont.*)
  negotiations (*cont.*)
    Ormond peace treaty (1649), 134n, 214, 217, 219, 222–3, 258
    negotiations with foreign powers, 171, 192, 199, 201, 202–4, 279–81; Irish agents in Europe, 162, 207n, 280
  organization of: factions in, 130, 132, 134, 147, 150, 163, 164, 181, 198, 199, 201, 202, 205, 207, 210, 214, 219, 223, 227, 280; general assemblies (1st, 1642), 117, (3rd, 1643), 128, 129, 136, (4th, 1644), 149, (6th, 1646), 169, (7th, 1647), 182, 183, 186, 188, 190, 192, 193, (8th, 1647), 192, 201, 202, 203, 205, (9th, 1648–9), 214, 216, 217; legatine synod (1646), 182; oath of association, 117, 133, 134, 140, 178, 182, 189, 190; supreme councils, 164, 189, (1642–4), 117, 129, 132, 134, 135, 140, 141, 144, 148, 149, 150, 151, (1645–6), 152, 153, 163, 166, 168, 169, 170, 171, 172, (1647), 182, 185, 186, 187, 189, 191, 192, 198, (1647–8), 202, 204, 210, 211, 213n, 216, 218, 219, 258, 292
  see also Butler, James; MacDonnell, Randal, marquis of Antrim; Rinuccini
Killcock, Co. Kildare, 219
Kilrush, Co. Kildare, battle of (1642), 105
Kilsyth, battle of (1645), 14, 146, 160
King, Paul, OFM (d. 1655), 211
King, Dr Ralph, 243, 245
King's County (Offaly), 105, 140
Kinsale, Co. Cork, 16, 21, 191n, 227, 228
Kintyre, Scotland, 6, 8, 14, 22–3, 79, 81, 83, 85, 88, 89, 90, 93n, 170, 172, 174, 175, 178, 179, 180, 183, 187, 200, 273
Knockanauss, battle of (1647), 198, 201
Koenigsberger, H. G., 14, 289

Laney, Co. Antrim, battle of (1642), 108
Langdale, Henry, 243
Laredo, Spain, 195, 196n
Larne, Co. Antrim, 33, 56, 108
La Torre, Diego de, Spanish agent in Ireland, 180, 181n, 201, 203, 223, 292
Laud, William (d. 1645), apb of Canterbury, 31, 58, 69, 77, 80, 87n, 222, 286; and Antrim, 32, 36, 50, 54, 68n, 72, 73n, 81, 278
Lawrence, Adam, 252
Lawrence, John, 252
Le Gouz, La Bouillaye, traveller in Ireland (1644), 181
Le Goveurneur, Jacques, 162, 180
Leicester, England, 159

Leicestershire, 30, 115
Leix (Laois), county, *see* Queen's County
Leixlip, Co. Kildare, 105n
Lennox, duchess of, *see* Villiers, Mary
Lennox, duke of, *see* Stewart, James
Lesley, Sir James, Lord Lindores, 175, 178
Leslie, Sir Alexander (d. 1661), first earl of Leven, 112, 116n, 179
Leslie, Lieutenant General David, 239
Levellers, 223–4
Leven, earl of, *see* Leslie, Alexander
Lewis, 187
Leyburn, George (alias Winter Grant), 189, 193–4, 199
Limerick, city, 110, 169, 191, 226, 230, 245
Limerick, county, 64
Lindores, lord, *see* Lesley, Sir James
Lindsay, Ludovic, earl of Crawford, 177, 178n, 183, 185, 251n
Lisburn, Co. Antrim, 101, 273
Lisnagarvey, Co. Antrim, 125
Liverpool, England, 73, 143, 146
localism, 256, 289
Lochhead fort, Kintyre, Scotland, 81
Loftus, Adam, Viscount Loftus of Ely (d. 1643), 96
London, city, 6, 14, 78, 88, 90, 95, 98, 102, 107, 112, 115, 116, 122, 188, 209, 211, 220, 222, 223, 232, 238, 240, 244, 250n, 252, 253, 257, 260, 265, 266, 267, 268, 275, 284, 291; Irish lands of, 56–9, 71, offers made for them, 57–9
Londonderry, county, 33, 56, 59, 60, 85, 108, 138, 242n, 247n
Londonderry, plantation, 24, 56, 69, 70, 71
Longford, county, 140
Longford, Sir Hercules, 266n
Long Liberties of Coleraine, *see under* Coleraine
lords justices (Irish), 99, 101n, 103, 104, 111n, 124n, 181, 259, 268, 272
Lorne, Lord, *see* Campbell, Archibald
Lothian, earl of, *see* Ker, Robert
Loudoun, earl of, *see* Campbell, John
Loughrea, Co. Galway, 116, 137
Louis XIV, king of France (d. 1715), 16, 159n, 198, 202, 203, 208
Louth, county, 116, 133, 191, 286
Louvain, Spanish Netherlands, 47, 191, 213
Low Countries, *see* Dutch Republic and Spanish Netherlands
Lucan, Co. Dublin, 182
Ludlow, Edmund (d. 1692), 221, 224

MacAllasters of Loup, 46, 177
MacAllester, family, 138
MacAuley, family, 40

Index

MacCarthy, Donough (d. 1665), Viscount Muskerry, earl of Clancarty, 97, 98, 165, 190, 202, 203, 204n, 205, 206, 208, 269, 272, 282, 289
MacCarthy More, Donal, 46
MacCauley, Alexander of Ballycastle, 254
MacColla, Alasdair, *see* MacDonald, Alasdair
McCollum, John Oge, 46
McCormack, family, 138
McCormack, Shane McVickar, 109n
MacDermot, family, 138
MacDonald (Clan Donald), family, 7–8, 12, 18, 21–3, 43, 46, 48, 79, 80, 93, 107, 173, 177, 276n
MacDonald, Alasdair (Colketto, Kilketto), 107, 108, 113, 116, 138, 139, 191; military campaigns of, in Ireland (1647), 188, 198–9, in Scotland (1644–7), 145, 153, 160n, 169, 175–6, 178, 179, 183, 187
MacDonald, Angus, laird of Glengarry, 188, 214, 215, 216, 287–8
MacDonald, Archibald, of Sanda, 87
MacDonald, Aneas, 275
MacDonald, Coll Ciotach MacGillespeck, 79, 93
MacDonald, Daniel, laird of Clanranald, 188, 214, 215, 216n
MacDonald, Donald, 275
MacDonald, Sir Donald of Sleat (d. 1644), 80, 82, 89, 92, 94, 130, 145
MacDonald, Sir James of Sleat, 256n, 275
MacDonald, John, bard of Keppoch, 119, 292
MacDonalds of Clanranald, 43, 79, 145, 174, 214, 292
MacDonalds of Dunyveg and the Glens, 43
MacDonalds of Glengarry, 43, 80
MacDonalds of Keppoch, 43
MacDonalds of Sanda, 79
MacDonalds of Sleat, 43
MacDonnell, Alexander (d. 1699), third earl of Antrim, 32–3, 65n, 67n, 103, 250n, 251, 272, 273n, 275; and Irish rebellion, 106, 107, 113, 114; and War of the Three Kingdoms, 120, 136, 149, 153n, 154, 168–9, 182, 201, 202, 211n, 223
MacDonnell, Sir Alexander of Moye (d. 1634), 19, 21, 46
MacDonnell, Anne, 46
MacDonnell, Catherine, 46
MacDonnell, Daniel (later Francis), OFM, 47
MacDonnell, Donnell Groome, 113
MacDonnell, Ellis, 46, 102, 103, 111

MacDonnell, James, 39, 105, 113, 137
MacDonnell, James MacColl, 107n, 108n
MacDonnell, Sir James of Dunluce (d. 1601), 19, 46, 107, 117, 191, 276n
MacDonnell, Katherine, countess of Antrim, *see* Manners, Katherine
MacDonnell, Mary, 46
MacDonnell, Captain Maurice, 32, 47–8, 84, 94, 157
MacDonnell, Randal, Lord Dunluce (1618–20), first earl of Antrim (1620–36), 18, 19–21, 22, 26–7, 32, 52, 96n
 Catholicism, 27, 71
 disputes, 32, 42, 72n
 estates of, 24–6; ability as a landlord, 24–6; grants of land to, 21, 23–4; tenants of, 25, 246; wealth of, 25, 268
 family: daughters, 46, 56; marriages of, 28–9, 32, 46–7; wife, *see* O'Neill, Ellis; younger sons of, 32, 47–8
 and plantation of Ulster, 23–6, 56, 59–60
MacDonnell, Randal, Lord Dunluce (1620–36), second earl (1636–45) and first marquis of Antrim (1645–83), alias Mr Chapman, Mr Dalmahoy, earl of Glenarm, 26–8
 appearance, 28, 74, 259
 career at court: Charles I, 28–32, 49–55, 74, 80, 98, 128, 129, 152, 154, 203, 279, 283; Charles II, 267, 269–71, 276, 279; marquisate, 131, 135, 152
 Catholicism, 8, 53–4, 60, 69–71, 74–5, 91–2, 106, 136, 155, 167, 183, 190, 199, 206, 209, 274, 278, 279, 280, 283, 289
 and confederation of Kilkenny, 119–20, 133–4, 163; general assemblies, 183–4, 186, 192–3, 201–2; military commands held from, 111, 128–9, 135, 137, 140–1, 149, 217–18, 219, 227, 235–6, 258; oath of association, 133, 134, 178, 190, 258; president of the supreme council, 189–90, 196, 199, 292; supreme council, 134, 188–9, 192–3, 202, 258, 292; war-effort, 192–3, 197–8
 contribution to royalist war-effort, 45–47, 150–1, 153, 159, 160, 163; attempts to mediate a settlement (1642–3), 110–12, 119–20; capture by Scots (1642), 112, 114–16, 117, (1643), 13, 121, 124–5, 128; involved in plots with Stuarts, 13, 122, 125–6, 'Antrim plot' (1641), 96–9, 101, 102n, 237, 258, 259–61
 Cromwellian collaborator and pensioner, 236–8, 240–1, 248–9, 250–1, 258;

MacDonnell, Randal (*cont.*)
Cromwellian collaborator and pensioner (*cont.*)
negotiations with Independents in London, 208, 212, 213, 214, 220–2, 223–6, 228–9, 234–5, 283; relationship with parliamentarians in Ireland, 218–19, 232–3, 236–7, 238–40, 248, 258, 260–1
English estates, 60–1, 291
family and dependants: among the Old English, 46–7; among the native Irish, 46–8, 74–5, 165, 292–3; British connections, 12–14; marriage, 28–9, 49, 232, 249–50; siblings, 46–8, 56, 113; supporters, 42–8, 50–5, 83–4, 106–7, 114, 129, 136, 138–9, 141, 142, 144, 154, 155, 166, 168–9, 172–3, 174–5, 191–2, 193, 214–15, 216, 217, 236–7, 239, 252–4, 256–7, 263, 267, 269–71, 273–5, 279, 283, 289
fate at the Restoration: charges brought against, 258–61, 266, 267; consequences of his restoration, 263–6; examinations conducted, 259–61, 262, 266, 270; imprisonment, 257–9, 260; opponents to his restoration, 258, 262, 264, 266, 271–2; reasons for his restoration, 267–73, 279; restoration land settlement, 261–7; trial before court of claims, 262–3, 264, 267, 269
finances: creditors, 61n, 62–3, 65–7, 68, 76, 96, 194, 238, 251–2, 254, 267, 268, 275–6; debts, 32, 61–8, 70–1, 73, 75–6, 249, 251–2, 268, 274–6; income, 63–4, 107, 111, 114, 129, 154, 179, 194–5, 204, 228, 244–5, 249, 250–1, 253, 274–5
and first Bishops' War (1639), 13, 78–93, 239, 279; animosity generated by Antrim's involvement in, 80–2, 86, 91–2; preparations for, 82–5; reasons for failure of, 86–92; significance of, 92–3
and France: negotiations with, 158, 185, 187n, 196n, 281; visits (1625–7), 27–8, 53, (1645), 160–1, (1648), 203, 205–6, 208, 210
historical reputation, 1–4, 279
historical sources concerning, 241, 262, 267, 290–3
Irish estates, 32–42, 55–6, 61, 64, 65, 70–1, 76, 81, 129, 279, 290; ability as a landlord, 36–42, 60, 271, 275–6; adventurers and soldiers, 242–4, 258, 263, 267, 272; attempts to recover, 114, 128n, 134, 151, 176, 181, 197, 200, 211, 217, 233, 240–1, 261–3, 266–7, 269, 273, 278; compounding for, 237, 238, 241–2, 248; Cromwellian land settlement, 241–8, 261; impact of war on, 76, 106–9, 113, 147, 245–6, 249n; 'Londonderry business', 56–60, 69, 70; quit rents charged on his, 270–1; restoration to his, 263, 266, 267, 273; tenants living on his, 37–42, 66, 76, 81, 104, 106–7, 110, 113–14, 184, 238, 239, 243, 245, 246–7, 254, 263, 267, 275, 279
and Irish rebellion of 1641: alleged involvement in, 102–4, 258; neutrality (1641–2), 103–6
letters, 86, 166–7, 290
lifestyle, 61–3, 73–5, 240, 251, 259, 260n, 273–4
military campaigns in Ireland: attempts to undermine Ormond's war-effort, 205, 211–12, 213, 214–17, 219, 227–8, 233–4, 258, 279, 283; defeat 198–9
military campaigns in Scotland: defeat (1647), 187–8, 200; 1644 expedition, 14, 91, 129–30, 132–3, 239, 279, army, 137–40, preparations, 137–8, 142–3, 147–8, shipping, 143–5, 148, success and significance, 145–7, 150–1, 153, 160; maintaining Scottish offensive (1645–7), 152–3, 154, 167–9, 172–9, 183–6, 279, 291, (1648), 204, 209; proposed expedition (1643), 119–20, 121, 122–3, 124, (1650–1), 239–40, 258; refusal to surrender (1646), 14, 174–8
military entrepreneur, 28, 53, 154, 155–7, 167, 179, 185, 197, 200, 209–10, 240, 255–6, 273, 279, 281, 292
negotiations with Spain: offer of troops for Spain, 185–6, 187; offer of troops for Spanish Netherlands, 154–8, 171–2, 179–80, 185, 187, 281, 292; relationship with Spanish administration, 180–1, 185, 197, 200, 209
personality, 1–3, 4n, 92, 141–2, 156, 158, 166–7, 170, 196n, 197, 204, 205, 216–17, 227, 236, 248, 274, 279; disputes, 68–71, 275–6, with Castlehaven, 137, 140–1, 147, 149; popularity, 135, 149, 182, 190, 196, 204, 234
privateering career, 167–8, 194–5, 197, 231, 280; frigates, 155, 158, 161–3, 167–8, 169–70, 172–3, 175, 190–1, 193, 194–5, 196, 197, 215–16, 227–8, 230, 280, 292, *Mary of Antrim*, 162, 185, 194, 231, *Mary of the Isles*, 194,

195, 230, 231, *San Pedro*, 161n, 162, 197, *St Peter of Waterford*, 194, 195, 231; prizes taken, 175, 194–5; troops shipped, 169–70, 172–3, 195–7, 200
political involvement and ambition, 95–6, 104, 188–94, 197–9, 211, 233, 273–4; to be lord lieutenant, 128n, 165, 166, 205, 213, 214, 217, 236
relationship with: Charles I and Henrietta Maria, 8, 28, 49–50, 103, 106, 112n, 117–18, 122, 131, 134–5, 152, 155, 157, 158, 174, 177–8, 193, 200, 203, 204, 208, 213, 226, 228, 262; Charles II, 239–40, 257; Irish confederates, 141–2, 148, 149, 151, 216, 218–19; Old Irish party, 188–92, 193, 197–200, 206, 211, 217–20, 258; Ormond, 132, 141, 150, 152, 166–7, 169–70, 188, 193, 206, 217, 226–7, 231, 261–2, 269, 272, 279, 283; Rinuccini, 183, 190–1, 193
Scottish patrimony, 8, 43, 46, 76, 93, 94, 167, 176, 178, 273; attempts to recover, 22–3, 48, 79–80, 89, 90, 130–1, 134, 151, 167, 169, 178, 197, 211, 217, 233, 273–4
see also Butler, James; Kilkenny, confederation of; Manners, Katherine; O'Neill, Rose; Rinuccini; Wentworth, Thomas
MacDonnell, Colonel Randal, 199
MacDonnell, Rose, 46
MacDonnell, Rose, marchioness of Antrim, *see* O'Neill, Rose
MacDonnell, Sarah, 46, 56, 275
MacDonnell, Sorley Boy (d. 1589), 19
MacDonnells of Antrim, 18–21, 43, 80, 84, 113, 138, 185, 283
MacDonnells of Tenekilly, 42
MacDougal of Dunnollie, 177
MacFies of Colonsay, 46
MacHenry, family, 84, 113, 138
MacHenry, James, 39
MacKay, John, Lord Reay, 152, 177
MacKenzie, George, earl of Seaforth, 130, 145, 152, 177, 187
Maclean, family, 174, 177
Macleods of Harris, 177
Macleods of Lewis, 46
MacMahon, family, 84
MacMahon, Heber (d. 1650), RC bp of Clogher, 180, 202, 203, 211n, 213, 214, 236, 237
MacMahon, Hugh, 55, 101
MacNaughten, family, 40, 66, 113
MacNaughten, Alexander, 113n

MacNaughten, Daniel of Benvarden, 40, 49n, 238
MacNeils of Gigha, 46
McNeills of Carskey, 177
MacQuillan, family, 19, 138
MacRanald, family, 177
MacVurich, Niall, bard of Clanranald, 292
Maddenstown, Co. Kildare, 97, 104, 105
Madrid, Spain, 103,155, 158, 220, 234n, 291, 292
Magee, Donnell, 109
Magennis, family, 67, 84
Magennis, Arthur, first Viscount Iveagh, 46, 54
Magennis, Arthur, second Viscount Iveagh (d. 1683), 54
Magennis, Bonaventure, RC bp of Down and Connor, 75
Maguire (MacGuire), family, 84, 284
Maguire, Brian, 284
Maguire, Conor (d. 1647), Lord Enniskillen, 74, 97, 98, 101
major-generals, rule of, 256
Manners, Francis, sixth earl of Rutland, 29
Manners, John, eighth earl of Rutland, 253
Manners, Katherine, duchess of Buckingham and countess of Antrim (d. 1649), 3, 5, 12, 13, 54, 62, 72n, 73, 75, 78, 96, 105, 111n, 115, 116, 120n, 121, 141, 147, 148, 150, 151, 152, 153n, 155, 166, 179n, 190, 195, 213, 214, 216, 231, 233, 257, 290; assets, income, 29–31, 64, 65n, 68, 114, 129, 232, debts, 61n, 179n; Catholicism, 30, 53–4; family, children, 29, 31, 50, 51n, 75, 228, 231, connections, 50–1, 52–3, 78n, 232, 249, 253, marriage, 29, 49, personality, 30–1; relationship with, Antrim, 31, 54, 131, 156, 231–2, 279, Charles I and Henrietta Maria, 31–2, 49–50, 128, 154, 270, Laud, 31, 50
Marston Moor, battle of (1644), 146, 159
Martin, Richard, 55
Mary of Antrim, 162, 185, 194, 231
Mary of the Isles, 194, 195, 230, 231
massacres, *see under* warfare
Massareene, lord, *see* Clotworthy, John
Massareene, barony, 242
Massari, Dionysius, dean of Fermo, 292
Maule, Sir Patrick of Panmure, 51
Maxwell, family, 50
Maxwell, Dr Robert, 102
Maxwell, Robert (d. 1646), first earl of Nithsdale, 51–2, 67, 78, 95; and Antrim, 120, 122n, 130, 177
Maynooth, Co. Kildare, 198, 218

Mayo, Christopher, 282
Mayo, viscount, see Burke, Theobald
Mayo, county, 137, 250
Mazarin, Jules (d. 1661), Cardinal, 171, 187, 202, 203
Meath, county, 56, 104, 140, 191, 236
Mellifont, Co. Louth, 125
mercenaries, 156n, 158–9, 185, 197, 208, 209, 281, 292
merchants, 181, 185, 186, 195, 248, 252, 280
military entrepreneurs, 80, 159, 162, 208, 209–10, 240, 281–2; see also under MacDonnell, Randal, marquis of Antrim
Miller, Alderman Thomas, 245
Monck, George (d. 1670), first duke of Albemarle, 228, 262, 287
Monnerie, Monsieur de la, French agent in Ireland, 204, 205n, 292
Monro, Sir George, 236
Monro, Major General Robert, 111, 112, 113, 114, 115, 120, 121, 124, 130, 133n, 134, 135, 138, 147, 176, 181, 236
Montereul, Jean de, French ambassador in Edinburgh, 185, 187
Montgomery, Hugh (d. 1663), third Viscount Montgomery of the Ards, 286
Montrose, marquis of, see Graham, James
Moore, Henry, Viscount, 259n
Moore, Dr John, 65n, 67n
Moore, Roger, 137, 141
Morphy, John, 172
Morrill, John, 11
Morris, Sir William, secretary of state, 271
mortgaging, 65–6, 143n, 185, 194, 231, 267, 275–6
Mountgarret, Viscount, see Butler, Richard
Mountjoy, Co. Tyrone, 25, 101
Mountrath, earl of, see Coote, Sir Charles (d. 1661)
Moura y Cortereal, Manuel de, marquis of Castel Rodrigo, governor-general of the Spanish Netherlands, 155, 156, 157n, 161, 171, 179, 180, 185, 197, 226n
Muddreman, Edward, 66
Mulgrave, earl of, see Sheffield, John
Murder will out, 264
Murray, Patrick, earl of Tullibardine, 54
Muskerry, viscount, see MacCarthy, Donough
mutiny, 196, 224, 233, 254

Naas, Co. Kildare, 198
Naseby, battle of (1645), 159, 160
native Irish, 8, 104, 107–8, 247, 248, 255, 283, 289; clerical party, 211, 212, 220, 224, 225n; Old Irish faction, 147, 165, 180, 181, 191, 197, 198, 201, 202, 203, 204n, 206, 209, 210, 212, 220, 221, 225n, 228, 234
Neagh, Lough, 57, 70
Nedham, Marchamont, 254, 255n
Netherlands, see Dutch Republic and Spanish Netherlands
Netterville, Sir John, 284
Netterville, Viscount Nicholas, 284
Newark, England, 174
Newburn, England, 95
Newcastle, marquis of, see Cavendish, William
'new army', see under armed forces of Dublin government
Newcastle-upon-Tyne, England, 95, 175, 177
Newbury, battle of (1644), 159
New Hall, Essex, 29, 60, 61
New Model Army, 159, 207, 208, 212, 224
Newport, earl of, see Blount, Mountjoy
Newport, lady, see Blount, Anne
Newport, England, 212
New Ross, Co. Wexford, see Ross
Newry, Co. Down, 101, 111, 273
newspapers, 112, 122–3, 135–6, 138, 145–6, 152, 160, 161, 173, 174, 175, 177, 178, 218, 224, 226, 228, 231, 254, 281, 290n, 293
Nicholas, Sir Edward, secretary of state, 103
Nieuport, Spanish Netherlands, 157
Nine Years' War (1594–1603), 283
Nithsdale, earl of, see Maxwell, Robert
Norfolk, duke of, see Howard, Henry
North Channel, 6, 13, 78, 79, 114, 147, 239, 246, 279
Northumberland, earl of, see Percy, Algernon
Nottingham, earl of, see Finch, Heneage
Nugent, family, 46
Nugent, Christopher (d. 1625), Viscount Delvin, 46
Nugent, Francis, Capuchin, 226
Nugent, Richard (d. 1642), first earl of Westmeath, 96
Nugent, Richard (d. 1684), second earl of Westmeath, 283

O'Brien, Conor, Viscount, 284
O'Brien, Christopher, 282
O'Brien, Sir Daniel of Duagh, 191
O'Brien, Donagh, fopurth earl of Thomond, 64, 249n
O'Brien, Murrough (d. 1674), Lord

Inchiquin, 191, 198, 202, 207, 210, 211, 214, 233–4, 255, 286
O'Bryen, Dermot, 202
O'Byrne, family, 191, 215
O'Byrne, Brian MacPhelim, 215, 227
O'Cahan, family, 40, 107, 138
O'Cahan, Brian Modder MacHenry, 113
O'Cahan, Donnell, 109
O'Cahan, Tirlough Oge, 107, 108
O'Connor, Donough of Sligo, 46
O'Donnell, family, 81
O'Doran, William, 194
Offaly, county, see King's County
Ogilvie, family, 95
Ogilvie, James, earl of Airlie, 119, 177, 288
Ó Gnímh (O'Gneeve; Agnew), family, 75
Ó Gnímh, Fear Flatha, 75, 292
O'Hara, Cahill, 41–2
O'Hara, family, 84, 113, 138
O'Hara, of Annaghmore, 284
Old English, 8, 46, 96, 101, 104, 147, 164–5, 283, 289
Old Irish, see native Irish
Old Irish party, see under native Irish
Oldstone, Co. Antrim, 37, 108, 109
O'Lurgan, family, 84
O'More, Rory (d. 1652), 97n, 101
'O'More–Maguire' plot (1641), 2n, 101, 102n
O'Neill, family, 19, 47–8, 81, 84, 113, 138, 254; on the continent, 47–8, 81
O'Neill, Sir Daniel (d. 1664), 55, 65, 84, 227, 236, 265, 269; Scottish expedition (1644), 132, 133, 134, 138, 140, 141, 153
O'Neill, Ellis (Alice), countess of Antrim (d. c. 1665), 18, 26, 32–3, 109, 113, 250n, 254, 268
O'Neill, Ellis, see MacDonnell, Ellis
O'Neill, Sir Henry of Edenduffcarrick (d. 1637), 67, 249
O'Neill, Sir Henry of Killelagh, 283
O'Neill, Hugh (d. 1616), third earl of Tyrone, 8, 16, 18, 21, 29, 47, 54, 81, 85, 136, 283
O'Neill, Hugh Dubh, 139, 235
O'Neill, Martha, see Stafford, Martha
O'Neill, Neal Oge of Killelagh, 46
O'Neill, Neill of Clandeboy, 46
O'Neill, Owen Roe (d. 1649), 3, 84, 117, 137, 139, 165, 167, 180, 181, 182, 186, 188, 195, 204n, 207, 210, 211, 214, 216, 217, 218, 219, 221, 223, 224, 225, 226, 227, 228, 232, 233, 235, 236
O'Neill, Sir Phelim of Kinard (d. 1652), 46, 55, 67, 74, 92, 98n, 101, 103, 107n, 111, 113, 120

O'Neill, Rose (d. 1695), marchioness of Antrim, 249, 254, 262, 268, 276, 279; assets, 249–50, 267, 273, 274n, 275
O'Neill, Tirlough Oge, 46, 111n
O'Neills, of Clandeboy, 19, 55
O'Neills, of Tyrone, 47
O'Reilley, Philip MacMulmore, 141
O'Reilly, Edmund, RC abp of Armagh, 217, 219
Orléans, duke of, 124
Ormond, earl of, see Butler, James
'Ormondists', see under Butler, James; Kilkenny, confederation of
Ormond peace: first (1646), 134n, 150, 181–2, 183, 184, 188, 189, 193, 199, 258; second (1649), 134n, 214, 217, 219, 222–3, 258
Orrery, earl of, see Boyle, Roger
O'Sheyll, family, 40
Ossory, Queen's Co., 113
Ostend, Spanish Netherlands, 179, 180
O'Sullivan Beare, Dermot (d. 1659), count of Berehaven, Spanish agent in Ireland, 223
Ottoman Turks, 209
Owen, Henry, 259, 260
Oxford, England, 95, 123, 129, 133, 136, 149, 151, 152, 154, 158n, 159, 160, 199

Pale, the, 46, 96, 103, 104, 116, 128, 139
pamphlets, see newspapers
papacy, 134, 154, 199, 201, 204, 205, 212, 213, 214, 225, 235, 253n; papal aid to Ireland, 161, 204; see also Innocent; Urban
Paris, France, 160, 176, 177, 185, 204, 205, 209, 211, 212, 221, 291
parliament (English), 150
  Barebones Parliament (July–December 1653), 256
  Long Parliament (1640–60), 95, 101, 102, 106, 110, 115, 116, 122, 124, 127, 128, 134, 138, 159, 166, 169, 201, 207, 208, 212, 213, 216, 222, 223, 224, 237, 241, 260, 282, 293; conquest of Ireland, 230–3, 240n, of Scotland, 239–40; navy, 143, 144, 145, 151, 153, 170, 175, 194–5, 228, 230–1; negotiations with Old Irish, 219, 220, 221, 224, 225, 228, 232, 235, 240, 283, 287; negotiations with royalists, 154, 166, 176, 193, 202, 212, 214; party in Ireland, 182, 192, 198, 199, 202, 217, 218, 219, 227, 228, 229, 255, 286; propaganda, 122–3, 135–6, 175, 254; tolerant attitude towards Catholics

parliament (English) (*cont.*)
  Long Parliament (*cont.*)
    adopted by, 247–8, 254–5, 287–8; war-effort in England, 147, 169, 170, 254
  Rump Parliament (1648–53), 222, 235, 253n, 256
  Short Parliament (April–May 1640), 95
  see also Independents; Presbyterian party
parliament (Irish): 1634–5, 96; 1640, 95; 1661–6, 261, 265
parliament (Scottish), 175, 178n
Parsons, Sir William (d. 1650), 66, 71, 103
Passage, the, 144, 179n, 196
patriotism, 6–10, 92, 103, 106, 117–18, 122, 136n, 148, 155, 156, 167, 174, 189, 190, 193, 199, 200, 206, 218n, 224–5, 228, 233, 240, 248, 282–3
Paulet, John, fifth marquis of Winchester, 288
Pembroke, earl of, *see* Herbert, Philip
Pembroke castle, 210
Pendennis castle, 163
Penruddock's rising (1655), 256
Pepys, Samuel, 265, 270
Perceval-Maxwell, Michael, 100, 101
Percy, Algernon, earl of Northumberland, 73, 87n, 262, 285
Petty, Sir William, 250; Downe Survey, 251n
Philip III, king of Spain (d. 1621), 15, 223n
Philip IV, king of Spain (d. 1665), 154, 155, 156, 157, 162, 163, 180, 181, 187, 196n, 201, 202, 203, 204n, 221, 222, 224n, 225n, 226n, 235, 281
Philiphaugh, battle of (1645), 160, 163n, 168
Pindar, Sir Paul, 66
piracy, 143
plague, 109, 232
plantations, *see under* Londonderry; Ulster
Plunkett or Plunket, family, 137
Plunkett, Edward of Castlecor (d. 1668), 46
Plunkett, Nicholas, alleged author of 'Account of the war and rebellion in Ireland since the year 1641', 166, 182, 211n, 216
Plunkett, Nicholas, 205
Plunkett, Oliver (d. 1679), sixth Baron Louth, 46
Plunkett, Oliver, RC apb of Armagh, 274
Plunkett, Patrick, ninth Baron Dunsany, 46, 66, 105, 283
Pocock, J.G.A., 10
Pontefract, England, 159
poor Clares, 192
popish plots, 13, 93, 102, 122–4, 125–6, 135, 237, 270; *see also under*

MacDonnell, Randal, marquis of Antrim
Porter, Endymion, 50, 54
Porter, Captain Samuel, 245
Portnaw, Co. Antrim, 108, 109n
Portpatrick, Scotland, 7
Portugal, 16, 159, 282
Portumna, Co. Galway, 116
Prendergast, J. P., 290
Presbyterian party (in the English parliament), 208, 212, 222
Presbyterians, 76, 145, 206, 286
Preston, James, 282
Preston, Nicholas, Viscount Gormanston, 99
Preston, Thomas (d. 1655), Viscount Tara, 117, 137, 165, 179n, 180, 182, 192, 198, 204n, 207, 211, 215n, 216n
Preston, battle of (1648), 212, 214
Pride, Colonel Thomas, 222
Pride's purge (1648), 222
privateering, 143, 144, 148, 167–8, 175, 181, 190–1, 194, 195, 197, 228, 230–1, 280–1
privy council, 268; English, 259, 270; Irish, 261, 262; Scottish, 22–3, 125, 177, 291
prizes, 145, 186, 194, 195, 231, 280–1
Purbeck, Viscount, *see* Villiers, John
Pye, Sir Robert, 50, 65n, 252, 285
Pym, John (d. 1643), 102, 186

Queen's County (Leix), 68, 105, 114, 140, 228

Rainsford, Sir Richard, land commissioner, 262, 263n
Ramsey, Robert, 251n
Randalstown, Co. Antrim, 273
Rathlin Island, 65, 76, 110, 113
Rathmines, battle of (1649), 230
Rawdon, Sir George, 246, 254, 286
Read, Colonel John, 84
Reay, Lord, *see* MacKay, John
rebellion of 1641, *see* Irish rebellion
refugees, 168; from Highlands to Ulster, 138; from Irish rebels, 106n; from Ulster to Scotland, 76
rents, 25, 37, 39, 40, 41, 57, 59n, 60, 63–4, 65, 76, 107, 111, 114, 176, 244, 245, 249, 250, 275
Restoration, 12, 68, 134n, 178, 183, 189, 191, 203n, 237, 242n, 243, 244, 245, 251, 252, 257, 259, 275, 283, 286, 288, 289
restoration land settlement, 261–7, 289; adventurers and soldiers, 258, 267, 272
Reynolds, Colonel John, 260

Rhum, Scotland, 6
Rich, Robert, earl of Warwick, 146
Rinuccini, Giovanni Battista (d. 1653), abp of Fermo, 235; and Irish politics, 164, 165, 198, 210, 211; leader of the Old Irish/clerical party, 181, 182, 188, 193, 198, 200, 201, 206, 209, 210, 215, 216, 220, 236; and offensive in Scotland, 169, 177, 179, 186, 191, 209; papal nuncio in Ireland, 17, 161, 164, 165, 166, 167, 179n, 180, 183, 189, 191, 194, 197, 205, 207, 208n, 213, 214, 218, 219, 220, 223, 225, 226, 283, 284, 292; relationship with Antrim, 179, 183, 186, 190–1, 200, 204, 205, 215; relationship with Irish confederates, 210, 216, 234
Ripon, treaty of (1640), 95
roads, *see* communications
Rochford, Hugh, 191, 216, 232
Rome, Italy, 102, 103, 112n, 155, 164, 205, 206, 212, 213n, 234, 235, 274
Roots, Ivan, 11
Roscommon, county, 137, 140
Ross, John, 66
Ross, William, 275
Ross, Co. Wexford, 110, 183, 186, 191, 192, 196, 230, 232–3
Route, the, 19, 33, 113
Rupert, Prince (d. 1682), duke of Cumberland, 133, 227–8
Rushworth, John, 252
Russell, Conrad, 10, 11, 80, 100, 102, 289
Rutland, eighth earl of, *see* Manners, John

St Albans, countess of, *see* Walsingham, Francis
St Germain, France, 160, 205
St Leger, Sir William (d. 1642), president of Munster, 68–9, 286
St Malo, France, 208
St Patrick's Purgatory, Co. Donegal, 27, 69, 71
St Peter of Waterford, 194, 195, 231
Saltee Islands, 168
San Pedro, 161n, 162, 197
Sarsfield, Patrick, 263n, 269
Savage, family, 19, 278n
Savage, Valentine, 259
Scarborough, England, 120n, 121, 159
Scarrifhollis, Co. Donegal, battle of (1650), 237
Scilly Isles, 163, 170
Scot, Thomas, 221, 224n, 253
Scotland, links with east Ulster, 6–8, 18–19, 43, 46, 48, 288–9; Scottish settlers in Ulster, 24–5

Scottish armies and forces, 129, 146, 154, 174, 176, 207, 210, 214, 225n, 239
Scottish army in Ireland, 110, 111–13, 119, 120, 121, 129, 130, 133, 134, 138, 147, 153, 176, 181, 233, 246n, 250
Scottish nobility, 252
Scottish royalists, 129, 288; and Bishops' Wars, 78, 79–80, 82, 87, 88, 89, 95; and War of the Three Kingdoms, 119, 121, 130
Seaforth, earl of, *see* MacKenzie, George
self-denying ordinance, 159
Séneterre, Henri de, French ambassador in London, 2n, 28, 64n
Seton of Winton, 78
Shaw, family, 40
Shaw, John of Ballygally, 245
Sheffield, John, earl of Mulgrave, 220
ships, 85, 132, 151, 161, 170; for levies to the continent, 157, 179–80, 186, 292; for Scottish expeditions, 140, 143, 144, 145, 147, 148
Sidney, Sir Henry (d. 1586), 72
Skye, Island of, 6, 90, 145
Slane, Baron, *see* Fleming, William
Sligo, county, 137, 140, 191, 284
Smerwick, Co. Kerry, 15
Smith, Sir Edward, land commissioner, 263n
Smith, Major, 243, 245
Solemn League and Covenant, *see under* covenant
Somerset, Edward (d. 1667), earl of Glamorgan, marquis of Worcester, 163, 166, 169–70, 190, 281, 288; negotiates with Irish confederates, 163–4, 165, 169–70, 177, 199, 204, 288
Spain, 84, 134, 142, 156, 158, 159, 186, 195, 197, 200, 208, 209, 221, 222, 226n, 234, 256, 279, 281, 288, 292; agents in Ireland, 154, 196, 203, 205, 223, 281, 292; aid for royalist war-effort, 155, 159, 281, 282; ambassador, in London, 212, 220, 225, 253, in Rome, 234; competing with France for troops, 159, 185n, 187n, 196, 197; Irish soldiers in, 255, 280, 282; pensioners, 180–1, 220–1, 253; recruiting troops for, 12, 154, 159, 179, 185, 187; relations with Ireland, 180, 181, 185, 197, 200, 201, 202, 205, 208; *see also* Cárdenas, Alonso de; Foissotte, François; La Torre, Diego de; Moura y Cortereal, Manuel de; O'Sullivan Beare, Dermot
Spanish Netherlands, 15–17, 48, 94, 103, 139, 155, 157, 158, 159, 171, 180, 190, 196, 280, 282; Antrim visits, 154–5, 158, 160; and Army of Flanders, 47–8, 117,

Spanish Netherlands (*cont.*)
156, 158n, 171, 180n, 197, recruiting troops for, 154, 155–7, 158, 171, 179, 185, 186n, 187, 196, 280–2, 292
Spottiswood, Henry, 84
Stafford, Sir Francis, 249
Stafford, Martha, Lady O'Neill, 249, 250, 267, 275
Stevenson, David, 11, 86, 225
Stewart, family, 40
Stewart, Archibald of Ballintoy, 23, 41, 49n, 57, 65n, 67n, 75n, 86n, 116; and Bishops' Wars, 79, 89; and War of the Three Kingdoms, 106, 107, 108, 114, 238, 244, 245, 263, 266
Stewart, James (d. 1655), fourth duke of Lennox and Richmond, 28, 50–1, 54, 66, 78, 253
Stewart, Colonel Robert, 253
Stewart, Sir Robert, 137–8
Stewart, Captain William, 237, 247
Strafford, earl of, *see* Wentworth, Thomas
Sutherland, earl of, *see* Gordon, John

Taaffe, Theobald (d. 1677), second Lord Taaffe and first earl of Carlingford, 137, 140, 198, 204n, 207, 216, 259n, 269
Talon, Monsieur, French agent in Ireland, 292
Talbot, Colonel Gilbert, 271
Talbot, Sir Henry, 193
Talbot, Richard (d. 1691), earl of Tyrconnell, 266n
Talbot, Sir Robert, 284
Tandragee, Co. Armagh, 101
taxation, 62, 70–1, 72n, 91; 'cess', 245, 246; customs, 30, 57, 58, 64, 65n, 152n, 249, 263
tenants, 58, 60, 82, 83, 140, 228n, 244; *see also under* MacDonnell, Randal, first earl and marquis of Antrim
Tenekilly, Queen's Co., 105
Thirty Years' War (1618–48), 16, 139, 158, 221
Thomond, earl of, *see* O'Brien, Donagh
Thompson, Abraham, 243
Thompson, Henry, 251n
Thompson, Robert, 251n
Thurloe, John (d. 1668), 221n, 253
Tipperary, county, 248, 284, 285
Tippermuir, battle of (1644), 14, 146
Tirrell (Tyrrell), Dr Edward, 207
Toome, barony, 250
Tooting, Michael, 185
tories, 273, 284
Torr Head, Co. Antrim, 6
Tower of London, 257, 258, 259, 288n

Traylman, John, 65n, 67n, 86n, 253, 260
Trevor, Colonel Mark, 286
Trim, Co. Meath, 219
Tuchet, James (d. 1684), third earl of Castlehaven, 97, 104, 106n, 115n, 137, 150, 219, 238n, 291; dispute with Antrim, 137, 140–1, 147, 149
Tullamore, King's Co., 105
Tullibardine, earl of, *see* Murray, Patrick
Tyrconnell, earl of, *see* Talbot, Richard
Tyrone, earl of, *see* O'Neill, Hugh
Tyrone, county, 113n, 247

Uist, Scotland, 6
Ulster: English efforts to control, 19, 23–6, 273, 288–9; geography of, 33, 36, 239, 256–7, 289; language, 7; proximity to Scotland, 7–8, 43, 46, 48, 239, 257, 289
Ulster plantation, 23–4, 58–60, 69, 70, 71, 100, 244; *see also* Londonderry plantation
Ulster rebellion, *see* Irish rebellion
United Provinces, *see* Dutch Republic
Urban VIII, Pope (1623–44), 292
Urribarri, Alonso de, 162n
Uxbridge, propositions of (1645), 154

Vanderkipp, Antonio Nicholas, 143, 194, 280
Vandermarche, Anthony, 194
Van der Ripen, Martin Clausen, 157
Vandeval, Jacques, 162n
Van Dyck, Anthony, 8, 62
Vane, Sir Henry, 101
Venables, Colonel Robert (d. 1687), 237, 242
Venice, Italy, 209
Villiers, George (d. 1628), first duke of Buckingham, 29, 31, 50, 51, 53, 62, 68, 155
Villiers, George (d. 1687), second duke of Buckingham, 29, 31n, 62, 65, 68, 228, 231, 232
Villiers, John, Viscount Purbeck, 66
Villiers, Mary, duchess of Lennox and Richmond, 29, 31n, 50, 51n

Wallingford House, London, 29, 49, 51, 252
Walsingham House, London, 29
Walsingham, Frances, countess of St Albans, 29
Walsingham, Francis, 213
warfare, 139; continental influences on Irish, 139; impact of, 93, 101, 104, 108, 109, 113–14, 139–40, 144, 145, 148, 176, 178, 211, 245–6, 249n, 250; massacres

committed during, 101, 108, 109, 110, 113n, 122, 123, 134, 220, 241
wardship, 71n, 131
Ware, Sir James (d. 1666), 73
War of the Three Kingdoms, 11, 116, 125, 158, 167, 240, 279
War of the Five Kingdoms, 17, 158, 167, 171, 197, 279
Warwick, earl of, *see* Rich, Robert
Waterford, city, 110, 128, 129, 142, 144, 167n, 168, 169, 170, 172, 181, 182, 189, 191, 194n, 195, 205, 230, 231, 232, 233
Waterford, county, 191
Wedgwood, C.V., 3, 10, 17
weekly newspapers, *see* newspapers
Wentworth, Thomas (d. 1641), earl of Strafford, LD (1633–40), LL (1640), 8, 50, 54–5, 61, 66, 68–72, 73, 75, 76n, 92, 237, 239, 260, 286, 290n, 291; and Antrim, opinion of, 1, 31–2, 47, 61, 67, 68, 72, 73, 81, 85n, 86, 87n, 91–2, 279, patron of, 32, 36, 41–2, 55, 62; and Bishops' Wars, 79, 82, 83, 84, 85, 87, 88, 89, 90; and 'Londonderry business', 56, 58, 59–60, 69, 71; 'new army', 94–5, 97; trial and execution, 95, 96, 100, 222, 278
Westmeath, earl of, *see* Nugent, Richard
Westmeath, county, 138, 140
Westminster, London, 209, 212, 222, 254, 256, 286

Wexford, city, 110, 142, 144, 151, 154, 167, 168, 181, 185, 186, 191, 192, 194, 195, 214, 215, 216, 226, 230, 231, 232
Wexford, county, 117, 184, 191
White, Sir Charles of Leixlip, 275
White, Sir Nicholas, 193
White, Richard, 282
Whitehall, London, 49, 268
Whitelocke, Bulstrode, 254
Wicklow, county, 191, 215
'wild geese', 281; *see also under* France; mercenaries; Spain; Spanish Netherlands
Williamson, Joseph, 271
Wimbledon, Viscount, *see* Cecil, Sir Edward, 66
Winchester, marquis of, *see* Paulet, John
Windebank, Sir Francis, secretary of state, 50
Wishart, George, 173
Wolstenhome, John, 66
Worcester, marquis of, *see* Somerset, Edward
Worcester, battle of (1651), 240

Yllán, García de, 180n
York, 88, 98, 115, 116, 117, 119, 120n, 121
York House, London, 29, 31, 49, 53, 62, 65, 252
Youghal, Co. Cork, 110, 191n

Cambridge Studies in Early Modern British History

Titles in the series

The Common Peace: Participation and the Criminal Law in Seventeenth-Century England*
CYNTHIA B. HERRUP

Politics, Society and Civil War in Warwickshire, 1620–1660
ANN HUGHES

London Crowds in the Reign of Charles II: Propaganda and Politics from the Restoration to the Exclusion Crisis*
TIM HARRIS

Criticism and Compliment: The Politics of Literature in the England of Charles I*
KEVIN SHARPE

Central Government and the Localities: Hampshire, 1649–1689
ANDREW COLEBY

John Skelton and the Politics of the 1520s
GREG WALKER

Algernon Sidney and the English Republic, 1623–1677
JONATHAN SCOTT

Thomas Starkey and the Commonwealth: Humanist Politics and Religion in the Reign of Henry VIII
THOMAS F. MAYER

The Blind Devotion of the People: Popular Religion and the English Reformation*
ROBERT WHITING

The Cavalier Parliament and the Reconstruction of the Old Regime, 1661–1667
PAUL SEAWARD

The Blessed Revolution: English Politics and the Coming of War, 1621–1624
THOMAS COGSWELL

Charles I and the Road to Personal Rule
L. J. REEVE

George Lawson's 'Politica' and the English Revolution
CONAL CONDREN

Puritans and Roundheads: The Harleys of Brampton Bryan and the Outbreak of the English Civil War
JACQUELINE EALES

An Uncounselled King: Charles I and the Scottish Troubles, 1637–1641
PETER DONALD

Cheap Print and Popular Piety, 1550–1640
TESSA WATT

The Pursuits of Stability: Social Relations in Elizabethan London
IAN W. ARCHER

Prosecution and Punishment: Petty Crime and the Law in London and Rural Middlesex c. 1660–1725
ROBERT B. SHOEMAKER

Algernon Sidney and the Restoration Crisis, 1677–1683
JONATHAN SCOTT

Exile and Kingdom: History and Apocalypse in the Puritan Migration to America
AVIHU ZAKAI

The Pillars of Priestcraft Shaken: The Church of England and its Enemies, 1660–1730
J. A. I. CHAMPION

Civil War and Restoration in the Three Stuart Kingdoms: The Career of Randal MacDonnell, Marquis of Antrim, 1609–1683
JANE H. OHLMEYER

Stewards, Lords and People: the Estate Steward and his World in Later Stuart England
D. R. HAINSWORTH

* Also published as a paperback

DATE DUE